THE POLITICAL ECONOMY OF PENSIONS

RICHARD LEE DEATON

In just over twenty years—in 2011—the "Baby Boom" generation will begin to retire. By then, the stark reality of the "greying" of the population in North America and Western Europe will have brought the inadequacies of the state and private pension systems home to all levels of society, and the pension crisis will be actual rather than impending.

In *The Political Economy of Pensions*, Richard Deaton explores the factors involved in this high-profile issue of public policy and shows the insufficiency of recent reform initiatives in Canada, the United States and Britain.

Four converging considerations explain the imminence of the pension crisis. First, while it is commonly assumed that 70 per cent of pre-retirement income will be sufficient for a one-earner couple to maintain its standard of living, few pensioners receive this amount, and polls show that those not yet retired expect or want full income replacement. Secondly, the proportion of elderly in the population will dramatically increase in coming decades; the number of employed workers for each retired person will fall from seven to three while the costs for elderly dependents rise. Thirdly, the majority of workers in all three countries have no coverage under employer-sponsored private pension schemes, the percentage of those covered has been dropping in recent years, and many of those who do have private pensions receive only partial or unindexed payments. Finally, the corporate sector and the state have been appropriating pension funds as a source of investment and social capital to meet their finance requirements.

The pension system now occupies a strategic economic position in advanced market economies. Consequently, the conflicting interests underlying the pension crisis could generate a heightened awareness of power and politics in capitalist countries and increase social tensions manifesting themselves through intergenerational, sectoral, political and industrial relations conflicts.

The Political Economy of Pensions identifies personal problems and structural issues which may have significance in terms of power, politics and social change in the future. This timely and provocative comparative inter-disciplinary study will be of interest to those involved in social policy, gerontology, economics, industrial relations, social work and others concerned with pensions and aging or with the social impact of public policies.

RICHARD LEE DEATON is assistant director of research, Canadian Union of Public Employees (CUPE), Ottawa. Formerly, he was senior policy analyst with the National Advisory Council on Aging (NACA) and assistant director of the Pensions Branch, Saskatchewan Labour.

The Political Economy of Pensions

Power, Politics and Social Change in Canada, Britain and the United States

Richard Lee Deaton

University of British Columbia Press
Vancouver 1989

©The University of British Columbia Press 1989
All rights reserved
Printed in Canada
ISBN 0-7748-0318-5

Canadian Cataloguing in Publication Data
Deaton, Richard Lee, 1946-
  The political economy of pensions

  Bibliography: p.
  Includes index.
  ISBN 0-7748-0318-5
  1. Pensions – Canada. 2. Pensions – Great Britain. 3. Pensions –
United States. 4. Aged – Canada – Economic conditions. 5. Aged – Great
Britain – Economic conditions. 6. Aged – United States – Economic
conditions. 7. Marxian economics. I. Title.
HD7129.D42 1989   331.25′2′0971   C89–091144–4

This book has been published with the help of a grant from the Social
Science Federation of Canada, using funds provided by the Social
Sciences and Humanities Research Council of Canada.

For my parents

Helen Sattler Deaton
and
Robert Brooks Deaton

and

my children

Emmanuelle
and Shoshanah

The life cycle is complete.

CONTENTS

TABLES

FIGURES

FOREWORD

"Pension mountain" is the term that has been coined to describe the projected increase in the number of pensioners and thus the cost of pensions resulting from population aging, but it could be applied equally to the mass of studies of pensions produced in Canada and elsewhere in recent years by commissions, task forces, councils, committees, interest groups and sundry others. The scope of these studies has varied from brief monographs on specific aspects of the subject to the massive ten-volume report of the Royal Commission on the Status of Pensions in Ontario published in 1980–81. The quality of the studies has varied from useless or, even worse, misleading to informative and in some cases insightful. The overall effect has been to create as much confusion as understanding. The impact on employment in printing and publishing has no doubt been positive, but it is less certain in regard to pensions.

It is therefore with real pleasure that I welcome an analysis that is both rigorous and based on comprehensive, painstaking research. Richard Deaton has made a significant advance in the study of "the political economy of pensions" in two major respects.

First, at the empirical level, he has mastered a wide range of primary and secondary material, reorganized it for his own purposes, and presented it in a closely reasoned and clearly expressed argument. The focus is on Canada, but an illuminating three-dimensional effect is created by placing the Canadian data in a comparative framework, presenting it consistently in the context of similar data from Great Britain and the United States. Information about other countries is also brought in from time to time when it is particularly helpful in providing depth of understanding. This analysis is a goldmine for students of pension policy and, to a considerable extent, students of public policy generally. Since the comparisons are comprehensive, much of what Deaton presents is already known to students of pensions. At the same time, there is also much that is new, as well as previously published material presented in new and provocative forms. To say that I am impressed with Deaton's research is an understatement.

This, however, is subsidiary to his main purpose. His second, more controversial but in his view all-important, contribution is to add to the development of Marxist theory. He views pensions as central to the analysis of socio-economic development under conditions of advanced capitalism, and pension funds (public and private) as a possibly decisive instrument in the transition to socialism. Proponents of critical social theory, therefore, will probably receive this book as a welcome addition to the growing volume of literature of their orientation, while those who do not share that view will find much to interest and challenge them in Deaton's well-argued presentation.

As one of the latter group, I am going to undertake the perhaps unconventional role for the author of a preface of serving as devil's advocate. I am mindful that it is easier to criticize than to construct and that no theory has yet been developed by humans that does not suffer from internal inadequacies and contraditions. I think, however, that it might help to stimulate the thinking of both proponents and opponents of critical social theory to set up a quasi-dialectic within the covers of the book itself.

I can applaud Deaton for his cogent analysis of "the immiseration and marginalization of the elderly," of the inadequacies of the public pension systems in the three countries studied, and of the inherent limitations of private pensions, an area in which the contribution of his research is particularly valuable. I find, however, that the framework into which the material is cast is often constrictive and sometimes leads to strained interpretations where a more modest approach would seem to explain the facts satsifactorily, even though it might leave one in an unreconstructed state of "economism and welfarism."

To take one important example, Deaton is at considerable pains to document the contemporary right-wing conventional wisdom about the rapidly approaching pension crisis occasioned by population aging. To the rightist this is an argument for cutting, or at least restraining, pension benefits. Deaton neatly shifts the focus so that the alleged pension crisis becomes a significant element in the growing crisis of capitalism, leading to social upheaval as pensioners are pitted against productive members of the labour force, the conflict between labour and capital becomes more bitter, and the fiscal crisis of the state is intensified.

There is a certain unreality in this argument, however, since it is based on long-term projections, and experience suggests that they are rarely even close to being accurate. A previous projection in Canada of looming disaster occasioned by escalating pension payouts turned out to be nothing short of laughable (Bryden, *Old Age Pensions and Policy-Making in Canada*, pp. 106–7) because of a simple logical error. There was a straightline projection of the demographic variable, while all other variables, including society's productive capacity, were assumed to remain constant. Exactly the same fallacy is inherent in some current projections of impending disaster from the emerging "pension mountain."

Deaton rounds out his argument in the last two chapters. Some people, however, may take exception to the interpretations he draws from his empirical evidence. In chapter 9, he develops fully the central theme running through the preceding analysis, viz., that the funds accumulated in private pension plans are becoming critical for capital accumulation in an advanced capitalist society and thus form part of "the nexus of corporate power." The evidence he presents shows that the role of such funds is growing in significance, but it does not necessarily support the centrality he attributes to them because he frequently refers to pension funds in the broader context of institutional investment and deals with the former as if they were all or most of the latter when they are not. Notwithstanding this, pension funds are now among the largest institutional investors.

This groundwork lays the foundation for his final argument in chapter 10. Since pension funds are becoming central to capital formation, they offer an instrument through which the state can replace capitalist control with progressive social change leading ultimately to the transition to socialism. Expansion of public pension plans would be the main means of doing so. Such expansion would not only increase benefits to levels where the elderly could live in dignity, but even more important in terms of the Marxist objective, it would involve full funding in order to transfer control over investment from the private to public sector.

There are several difficulties with this, but I will refer only to the one that disturbs me most. I have argued elsewhere that contributory pensions, in common with all contributory social security or social insurance programs, are a cleverly disguised device for shifting the cost burden to lower income people. In the case of pensions, this means making the working poor pay for the maintenance of the retired poor. Indeed, in Canada our system is so regressive because of the tax deductibility of pension contributions, that low-income people are actually taxed (forced to "contribute") to fatten the pensions of the well-to-do and rich. Is it fair to compound this injustice (as I would call it) by forcing wage-earners to contribute even more so as to provide investment funds for the state, admirable as the purpose of those funds might be?

The author is well aware of this problem and he discusses it in his usual incisive way with respect to both public and private pensions. At the same time, he offers only a sketchy remedy, proposing in broad terms a progressive contribution schedule for the public system and "nothing less than a revolution in the income tax system" for private pensions. Though I would regard these reforms as devoutly to be desired in themselves, the author offers no specifics on how they are to be harmonized with the principle of pensions bearing some identifiable relationship to contributions. Yet, only a contributory system will generate the investment funds that are essential to his overall strategy. With no relationship between contributions and benefits, "progressive contributions" are really just a disguised part of the general tax system or at most a special tax designated for public investment. Thus, they could (indeed, if honesty matters, should) be separated from pensions altogether, and we should abandon the regressive principle of contributory pensions. This consideration applies even more to general tax reform.

Having said all of this, I hasten to add that I am not so narrow-minded as to let my theoretical differences blind me to the great merit of this book. It makes a valuable contribution to Canadian scholarship in both policy analysis and critical theory.

University of Toronto   Kenneth Bryden
November 1988

ACKNOWLEDGMENTS

This book is the culmination of a professional, intellectual and personal journey. It is sometimes said that intellectual production is a lonely endeavour. Fortunately, I have been assisted throughout this odyssey by many co-operative and encouraging individuals and organizations.

To the Canadian Union of Public Employees (CUPE), its members and national officers I wish to acknowledge my gratitude. Having served CUPE between 1970 and 1980 in the capacity of Assistant Director of Research, responsible for employee benefit plans and social security, I was allowed a sabbatical leave with pay to study at the University of Warwick's Industrial Relations Research Unit to work on this project. That opportunity was most appreciated.

Dr. George S. Bain, Professor of Industrial Relations at the University of Warwick's School of Industrial and Business Studies and former Director of the Industrial Relations Research Unit, encouraged me to come to the University of Warwick for my sabbatical year. He generously extended to me the position of Visiting Fellow at the Industrial Relations Research Unit when I commenced my doctoral studies during the 1979–1980 academic year. His mentorship and the opportunity afforded me to immerse myself in work, study and reflection is a personal debt which I cannot hope to repay.

My thesis adviser, Professor Keith Sisson, Director of the Industrial Relations Research Unit at the University of Warwick, was encouraging and firm, without being unduly directive, throughout my endeavours. He gave generously of his time, advice and counsel. His assistance and efforts are genuinely appreciated.

During my stay in Britain I had the unique opportunity to make the acquaintance of a number of people in the trade union movement who were able to familiarize me with the inner workings of the British state and occupational pension systems. Mr. Bryn Davies, formerly Assistant Director of Social Insurance for the Trades Union Congress, Ms Sue Ward, then Assistant Director of Pensions and Social Services for the General and Municipal Workers' Union, and Mr. Jim Moher, Pensions Officer, Transport and General Workers' Union, all gave generously of their time and knowledge.

A number of government agencies, organizations and individuals were more than co-operative in assisting me by providing unpublished or confidential materials used in my research. Much of the raw empirical data contained in the chapters on the investment and capital accumulation function of the pension system and the formal structure of pension fund power were generated by Statistics Canada. In particular I would like to acknowledge my debt to Mr. Randal Geehan, formerly Chief, Financial Flows Section, and Mr. R. G. S. McLeod, Head, Financial Institutions Section, for providing me with unpublished data. Dr. O. M. Petrovici, management consultant, kindly furnished me with his unpublished studies which were prepared for the Toronto Stock Exchange and allowed me to refine certain methodological issues. Ms Judith Skuce of the federal Department of Finance, Corporate Finance Branch, helped generate the data with respect to the sources of corporate funds in Canada. Dr. Francis Green of the Kingston Polytechnic (London) kindly provided me with revised estimates of aggregate savings in the U.K. based on his earlier study. Mr. Ashley Blackman, consultant, gave freely of his considerable expertise in quantitative economics. What original contribution exists in this book is largely based on the information and assistance provided to me by these people.

A number of trust companies supplied me with confidential information concerning the pension fund assets under their administration. I would especially like to acknowledge the co-operation of Royal Trustco, Canada Permanent, and Montreal Trustco. The Toronto and London Stock Exchanges, as well as the Bank of Canada, supplied me with additional background information. The National Association of Pension Funds (Britain) and Stevenson, Kellogg, Ernst and Whinney (Toronto) kindly gave me permission to cite their respective surveys. Dr. Dennis Olsen, Department of Sociology, Carleton University, Ottawa, willingly supplied me with unpublished background material from his study on the state elite in Canada. None of these individuals or organizations, of course, is responsible for the use or interpretation which I have placed on the data.

Upon my return from Britain, I became Assistant Director, Pensions Branch, Saskatchewan Department of Labour between 1980 and 1982. Being involved in concrete policy and programme development work in the highly dynamic social security and pensions field allowed me to acquire first-hand insight into public policy formulation. This experience undoubtedly accounts, in large part, for the prescriptive social policy orientation and tone throughout the book. That was a learning experience requiring the transition from academic theory to bureaucratic practice. I was assisted in this metamorphosis by Mr. George Ford, formerly Executive Director, Pensions Branch, Saskatchewan Labour. Mr. Ford unwittingly served as critic and adviser with respect to many of the ideas and themes developed here. A superb research craftsman and a ruthless logician, he assisted me on more than one occasion.

After returning to the Canadian Union of Public Employees in 1983, I was responsible for handling litigation for workers in the nursing home sector. That experience impressed upon me that the elderly and nursing home workers are both victims of an ill-conceived social policy. Subsequently, as Senior Policy Analyst for the National Advisory Council on Aging (NACA) between 1987 and 1988, I learned that bureaucratic practice is not necessarily inspired by the need to formulate relevant or progressive public policy.

The completion of this project was perhaps hardest on and lonelier for my partner and family than for myself. This was more than true for Marie-Claire Pommez, my wife. She brought an unfailing spirit of adventure, enthusiasm and co-operation to our year in Britain. She was a constant source of encouragement, support and strength. It was humbling, and perhaps ironic, that at a time when I was working in the field of aging and pensions, I should be able to watch our newly born twin daughters crawling about on the floor and starting to grow up. Life-cycle, indeed. I hope that this study will contribute to a more secure old age for them. It was an exciting, and at times difficult, period for us all. It was our first experience as a family, and we are better for it. Marie-Claire realized how important this unique opportunity was for me to study and develop. Success, under unusual circumstances and in strange surroundings, was only possible because of her. It was Marie-Claire who understood that by Going Away we would be Coming Home.

An international study such as this must of necessity draw on a wide variety of disparate sources. Every effort has been made to put all statistical data on a consistent and comparable basis. An inevitable frustration is that government statistical information is at least two years out of date. The publication process compounds this problem. Rather than constantly rework a ream of transnational statistical data as this manuscript was being prepared, I have included some dated material if subsequent information revealed no significant change in trends. In order to minimize reporting and conversion difficulties, all monetary figures are presented in national currency units unless otherwise indicated.

My editor, Jane Fredeman of the University of British Columbia Press, was of invaluable assistance throughout the publication process helping to transform a thesis into a book. Ms Judy McGann and Mr. Kevin Murphy undertook the excellent graphic work which appears in this study.

All errors of fact, interpretation or conceptualization are solely those of the author.

1

Introduction: Towards a Political Economy of Pensions

Much of modern social science has been a frequently unacknowledged debate with the work of Marx.
C. Wright Mills

The concrete analysis of the concrete situation.
V. I. Lenin

The objective of this study is to contribute a critical analysis of pensions policy using the approach of Marxist political economy. The method adopted here is to identify and explore the linkages and interaction between those socio-economic structures and forces which will affect the development of social policy towards aging and pensions over the next thirty to fifty years in the advanced capitalist countries of Canada, Britain and the United States.

The public and private pension systems in these three countries are on the verge of a crisis which can be explained by four structurally determined considerations, or motor forces, which converge in the future: first, the inadequate level of retirement income of the elderly that results in their economic immiseration and social marginalization; second, the increasing proportion of the elderly in the population and the costs associated with supporting an aging population; third, the general and specific limitations of the employer-based occupational pension system; and fourth, the appropriation of the occupational and state pension systems by the corporate sector and the capitalist state as a source of investment and social capital to meet their finance requirements.

1

The aging of the population may be viewed as conceptually independent of the state and occupational pension systems. That is, it is an exogenous factor which affects pension arrangements. The other three factors are all intrinsic, or endogenously related to the employer-based occupational pension system.

The institutional power of the private pension system is related to its operation as financial intermediaries and institutional investors channelling investment to the private sector. They are organically linked to the broader finance sector by economic structure and capitalist ideology, and their power exhibits itself through formal and informal arrangements. Characterized by a high degree of concentration and centralization of capital, the private pension system increasingly facilitates the systemic fusion of the finance and industrial sectors of advanced capitalist economies and now occupies a position at the "commanding heights" of the economy because of its impact upon capital markets. The symbiotic relationship between the corporate sector and the private pension industry is the primary economic and political obstacle to reforming and expanding the state retirement income system in Canada, Britain and the United States.

The pension crisis transcends the traditional limitations of economism and welfarism by raising issues related to power, politics and social change, and it may result in both increased politicization and opportunities to put forward progressive alternative economic strategies. State and private pension arrangements as a matter of public policy are potentially explosive because they incorporate the key elements of political economy: power, capital accumulation, industrial relations, politics and social transformation. The pension issue is volatile because it represents the historical conjuncture where the interests of capital, labour and the state collide and simultaneously affect the interests of all key segments and institutions of society: the elderly, workers, unions, the industrial and finance sectors, and the state. The political economy of pensions identifies an important public policy issue which will have a profound long-term impact upon social policy, capital formation, profit levels, collective bargaining and the economic well-being of workers and the increasing proportion of the elderly.

The primary focus and emphasis in this book is on Canadian developments. British and American information is presented in order to compare and contrast the structures and forces examined in this study. Unlike the works of Helco and Rimlinger,[1] which are retrospective comparative analyses of social security history, this is a comparative prospective analysis. It is not intended to be an institutional or legislative history of state and private pension plans. These are outlined in Appendix A, which is a comparative chronology of retirement income arrangements and reform initiatives in these three countries. Nor is it intended as a primer on pension plan design. An overview of current state and occupational pension plan programme features is provided in Appendix B. Many excellent scholarly studies and technical texts on these subjects already exist. What is offered is an analysis of old information through a new paradigm[2] in order to obtain new insights into social reality and the public policy issues of aging and pensions. As Mills suggested, "social research of any kind is advanced by ideas; it is only disciplined by fact."[3]

HISTORICAL BACKGROUND AND POLICY CONTEXT

All three countries share a similar, though by no means identical, social security history which has developed from a common social and intellectual history and philosophy of social welfare. For example, the early craft unions in Canada and America based many of their activities on the functions performed by the British friendly and provident societies, and the early origins of occupational pension plans in Canada were modelled on developments in Britain.[4] Agitation for the introduction of a state pension system in Canada drew much "inspiration" from the United Kingdom,[5] where the non-contributory, means-tested old age pension was first introduced in 1908. Canada followed suit with its means-tested old age pension in 1927.

The trauma of the Great Depression and World War II led both Britain and the United States to move toward forms of the liberal welfare state as embodied in Roosevelt's New Deal reforms[6] and the Beveridge Report.[7] "Thus events in both the countries which have most influenced Canada were moving to the acceptance of social security legislation"[8] and served as a model for later Canadian initiatives. The United States introduced its earnings-related social security retirement system in 1935, while Britain waited until 1959 (the Boyd-Carpenter Plan). The Canada/Quebec Pension Plans were implemented in 1966.

"The most important single document in the history of the welfare state in Canada" is Marsh's *Report on Social Security of Can-*

ada, published in 1943.[9] Writing some twenty years after his report was issued, Marsh said that his proposals "were worked out quite independently, but the coupling of [the] Beveridge and Marsh reports led to some ill-informed allegations. The truth is that by 1941 there was *a common stock of ideas* and principles available to those who knew the literature."[10] One important factor generating this "common stock of ideas" was that Marsh had been a student of Sir William Beveridge at the London School of Economics. Furthermore, with respect to subsequent postwar social security programme initiatives, it is of some relevance that Beveridge in the U.K., Marsh in Canada, and Burns in the U.S. all served together on the same International Labour Organization (ILO) reconstruction committee in London during World War II.

In the evolution of the distinctive national social security traditions there are certain similar features of programme design, terminology, and the income tax regulations governing the state and employer-based occupational pension systems. The term "social security" was itself American, replacing the terms "social welfare" previously used in Canada and "social insurance" followed in Britain. Even today there is a close similarity between the Inland Revenue Code in the U.K., Revenue Canada's Interpretation Bulletin and the American Internal Revenue Service's regulations governing occupational pension plans.

Canada has long been linked to Britain and the United States by language, culture, politics and economic relations. Politically and economically, Canada was first a colony of Great Britain. In the mid-nineteenth century there was steep investment in infrastructure, such as railroads, by British investors. Political institutions, cultural background and trading patterns all served to establish an east-west Anglo-Canadian link.

Beginning in the 1920s, American transnational corporations penetrated Canada and expanded their influence. They brought with them their industrial relations practices, including occupational pension plan arrangements. American social welfare and social work practices influenced Canadian developments during the 1930s and 1940s.[11] In the post-World War II period the Canadian economy has become so influenced by American corporations that it is often characterized as being a dependent "branch plant" economy. Canadian economic affairs and culture are now dominated by the north-south relationship which affects all facets of life.

Retirement income arrangements in all three countries in recent years have been the subject of an intensive public policy review as a result of the similar problems found in their pension systems. In Canada the policy review was inaugurated when the Ontario Royal Commission on the Status of Pensions was created in April 1977. Since that time at least two dozen government, task force, Senate, Royal Commission and private research reports have been issued with recommendations for the reform of the Canada/Quebec Pension Plans (C/QPP) and the private pension system. The federal government sponsored a highly publicized multipartite National Pensions Conference on pension reform in March 1981. Pension reform was considered to be one of the federal Liberal government's highest ranking priorities in the social policy area. Consequently, bilateral discussions took place between the federal and provincial governments. A green paper and a report by the Parliamentary Task Force on Pension Reform were subsequently issued. The last Liberal government budget introduced a number of measures to reform the private pension system. The lack of political consensus and will, compounded by the sagging economy, resulted in an unfocused policy orientation.

The new Conservative government, elected in the fall of 1984, dealt with retirement issues in both the 1985 and 1986 budgets. A major package of remedial legislation was enacted in 1987 to reform occupational pension plans in the federal and Ontario jurisdictions, as were amendments to the CPP including increased contribution levels. Contribution limits for individual retirement savings vehicles were to be significantly increased in 1988.

The United States implemented the Employee Retirement Income Security Act 1974 (ERISA) after a lengthy period of congressional inquiry and public discussion. This was a massive omnibus piece of legislation, resulting for the first time in the uniform and systematic regulation of private sector pension plans in the U.S. Subsequently, in 1979 the Carter administration established the President's Commission on Pension Policy, which reported in February 1981 with major recommendations for the strengthening of the social security system and private pension plans. The Reagan administration implemented a number of the recommendations of the National Commission on Social Security Reform and introduced other controversial measures to "rescue" the social security system in 1983. Since that time no fewer than seven pieces of pension-related legislation have been passed.

In Britain in the postwar era there have been nine major reviews and overhauls of the state social security system. In addition, a considerable amount of legislation has been implemented to regulate occupational pension schemes. The most far-reaching reform measures were introduced in the Social Security Pensions Act 1975 (the Castle Plan). In the intervening years, the Occupational Pensions Board has introduced a number of major reports calling for changes. Just prior to its defeat in 1979, the Labour government issued a highly controversial white paper on the co-management of pension plans. The final report of the Wilson Committee to Review the Function of Financial Institutions (1980) was an in-depth inquiry into the impact of pension funds and other institutional investors on capital markets. The 1985 green paper on the reform of social security, with its original recommendation to eliminate the state earnings-related pension system (SERPS), and the subsequent white paper's proposal to introduce personal pensions are indicative of the Conservative government's concern with pension issues, which was manifested in the Social Security Act 1986 which scaled down state earnings-related pension benefits.

The Anglo-Canadian-American link has created an interactive demonstration effect, and these policy reviews have not gone unnoticed by their respective counterparts. In Canada, for example, the British system of "contracting-out," where an occupational scheme can opt out of the state plan under certain conditions, has received some interest and study. The U.S. President's Commission on Pension Policy's recommendation for mandated private pension plan coverage has received some support from the Canadian private pension industry. Individual retirement savings vehicles such as Registered Retirement Savings Plans (RRSPs) in Canada and Individual Retirement Accounts (IRAs) in the U.S. have served as a model for personal pensions (PPs) in Britain.

The public policy reviews in each of these countries have revealed a series of similar issues: the inadequate retirement income of the elderly, the economics of an aging population, the universal and particuliaristic limitations of employer-based pensions, the impact of private pension funds as institutional investors upon capital markets, and the use of pensions for economic development. These issues and their significance for power, politics and social change are the subject of this study.

ANALYTICAL FRAMEWORK

Marxist political economy[12] attempts to analyse the interaction of various social phenomena and relate them to a particular mode of production and social formation according to the principles of historical and dialectical materialism. As applied here to pensions and aging, this methodology attempts to integrate such diverse subjects as the sociology of aging, historical demography, social gerontology, the social history of aging, the economics of aging, and the formal aspects of social security and pension plan design, administration, and investment management.

In recent years virtually every institution and facet of capitalist society has been subjected to critical analysis: the state, income distribution, education, housing, health care, role-typing, industrial relations, racism, and so forth. Whither state social security retirement systems and employer-based occupational pension plans? Why have progressive social policy analysts not studied state and private pension arrangements from a critical perspective? And why have pensions been ignored in terms of radical economic analysis? A critique is as much concerned with the "silences" of a theory, that is, what is not said, as with what is articulated. The fact that the state and occupational pension systems have not been analysed, until very recently,[13] from the perspective of political economy rather than that of social history, ideology, social work, or social policy is peculiar, if not disturbing.[14] The "silences" are deafening.

A number of reasons account for the traditional lack of concern with respect to a critical economic analysis of the role, function and impact of the state and private pension systems. In the first instance, state and private pensions have traditionally been subsumed under the broad generic heading of "social welfare," which is imprecisely defined, cutting across such fields as health, welfare, education, retirement income and so forth. Further confusion results from the fact that "social welfare" programmes are often described in terms of their value to individuals and sometimes in terms of their social functions. Difficulty also arises from the absence of any standardized terminology: the terms "social security," "social services," "social welfare" and "social work" have no fixed meaning and are all too often used interchangeably and impre-

cisely. Since pensions have been treated under these broad head-
ings, they have not become a distinct, independent object of critical
study. Thus, one contemporary study of class and social policy, for
example, completely circumvents any analysis of "the very important question of pensions" because of "insufficient space."[15]
Another recent study on the political economy of the welfare state
relegates pensions to a footnote.[16]

A second reason why pensions have been ignored, perhaps
understandably so, is that the subject matter seems to be complex
and dull. This is compounded by an arcane and often obscurantist
technical jargon which is enough to deter even the best intentioned.
While social activists in recent years seem to have been able to
master the technical subject matter of law and medicine, that of
compound interest and present value seem to have escaped them.

A third reason is "juvenocentricism": that is, those who are being
trained in the various "helping professions" tend to be young. Being
old, and the problems associated with the elderly, are outside their
personal frame of reference. It is not uncommon for schools of social
work, for example, to cancel courses in the sociology of aging or
social gerontology as a result of a lack of interest on the part of young
students.

Fourth, social policy analysis has traditionally been concerned
with the level of benefits generated from the state and private pension systems and their adequacy, rather than with probing deeper
underlying issues. But the emphasis on benefit adequacy has
tended to obscure and limit analysis and understanding of the economic relationships associated with pensions. Put another way, this
preoccupation has limited economic analysis and is a reflection of a
deeper "economism."

A fifth and highly significant reason why state and private pension plans have not been subjected to serious analytical consideration is that they have been incorporated into broader based
ideology and social philosophy. Adequate pension benefits have
been equated with a "social right" to which all people are entitled
based on "human need." Such notions as "social right," "social
obligation," "human need" and "social justice" are moral considerations however, not analytical categories. Such idealistic and subjective moral considerations have resulted in analytic mystification.
To the extent that social welfare analysis has cloaked itself in such
subjectivism, it has not placed the study of pensions in established

analytical, economic categories. Ideology has therefore obscured reality.

Sixth and last, whether explicitly articulated or not, there has been an unintended convergence between liberal social welfare and traditional Marxist analyses which tend to view pensions (state and private), and social security expenditures more generally, as a "free good." That is, pensions are seen as a consumption good which have no cost associated with them. Merely to suggest that the distributional aspects of "many social problems are primarily issues involving conflicts of economic interests between . . . various social classes"[17] may describe everything, but it analyses nothing. The implicit assumption underlying many current analyses is that pensions are a "free good" because they are a "social right." Economic calculus is rarely applied to what are perceived as "rights." Such views are a form of subjectivism because pensions are no longer related to a particular mode of production, or social formation, and the economic relations governing them. It is because the "laws of economics" have been ignored that many commentators have implicitly viewed pensions as a "free good," requiring no further economic analysis with the tools of Marxist political economy.

The laws of economics govern the allocation of resources in all societies — capitalist as well as socialist. In Marx's words, some laws of economics have "universal validity [and] are so self-evident that there is scarcely need . . . for their special study"[18] and "no natural laws can be done away with. What can change, in changing historical circumstances, is the *form* in which these laws operate."[19] The neo-classical economic model, including the law of supply and demand and the allocative mechanism derived from budget constraints and production functions, is an integral part of classic Marxian political economy. As Sweezy has asserted, "the competitive supply-and-demand theory . . . forms an integral, if sometimes unrecognized, part of the labor theory [of value]."[20] Shedding subjective and idealistic notions allows economic analysis to proceed unfettered by ideological blinders. The study of pensions can thus be placed within the analytical categories of the labour theory of value, the reproduction of labour power and the circulation and accumulation of capital associated with the Marxian economic model.

Traditional analyses of the role and function of the state and private pension systems have, until recently, been primarily concerned with analysing the manifest functions of the pension system. By situating pensions within the Marxian framework of economics and its analytical categories, it is possible to identify the underlying or latent economic functions and relationships that the pension system fulfils under conditions of advanced capitalism. One of their economic functions is to augment the capital accumulation process. As a result of a complex interaction of factors, the latent capital accumulation function served by the pension system is now being transformed into a manifest function. Pensions are an integral part of the broader socio-economic system and their economic functions must be critically analysed as such.

If the recent critical literature is any example, two tendencies can be identified with respect to the study of the state social welfare system.[21] In one instance, those who analyse "social welfare" from the perspective of the legitimization and coercion functions of the state exclude the capital accumulation function from their framework. Alternatively, where the capital accumulation function is made central to the analysis, the coercion and ideological functions associated with the pension system are excluded. If the method of classic Marxist political economy has any relevance, it is to synthesize the different "levels" of a complex reality by integrating the social, cultural and economic dimensions of existence and laying bare the "laws of motion" without resorting to a crude determinism or global abstractions which obscure a complex social reality.

The methodology of Marxist political economy as applied to pensions and aging assumes a new relevance with respect to the public policy reviews recently concluded in Canada, Britain, and the United States. Using the method of political economy, one critical sociologist noted, "that does not incorporate the reworked and reanalysed accomplishments of the various social sciences in the last half century is a form of sectarian fundamentalism" because a "theoretical analysis of the social totality requires the integration of the various 'empirical' disciplines."[22] The political economy of pensions, like the social sciences more generally, "has a dialectical character and contains both repressive and liberative dimensions,"[23] therefore, only an integrated "social science approach . . . can offer new understanding of the aged, new solutions to their problems . . . and new definitions of their social role."[24] A balanced approach must incorporate a critical economic analysis of pension arrangements and the object for which pensions ostensibly exist: the elderly.

THE CONJUNCTURE: THE ELDERLY, AGING AND PENSIONS

"To be aware of the idea of social structure," Mills wrote, "is to be capable of tracing . . . linkages among a great variety of milieux."[25] It is within this context that the political economy of pensions must be studied for it represents the conjuncture, or intersection, between old age as a *personal* experience and the pension system as part of the broader socio-economic *structure*.

The pension issue cannot be separated from considerations related to the social and cultural history of aging and the broader social and economic position of the elderly in our society. To place the pension issue in its proper historical perspective requires that workers, social security administrators and social scientists confront what one social historian has called "the culture of aging." It has been succinctly argued that "old age is an age-old problem, and a distinct culture has surrounded it for centuries" because the "problems in dealing with old people go far deeper than the evils of capitalism . . . they lie deep in our cultural heritage."[26] Like racism and sexism, cultural attitudes towards the elderly and aging *predate* the advent of industrial capitalism. The attitudes carried over from pre-industrial formations, including those towards aging and the elderly, are a classic example of what Marx meant when he said that "the tradition of all the generations weighs like a nightmare on the brain of the living."[27]

The history of aging suggests that there are a series of universal problems and attitudes experienced by the elderly. These cultural manifestations often have a dynamic of their own, relatively independent of social structure. Cultural attitudes are not a mere mechanical "epiphenomenon"[28] or reflection, to use Marx's phrase, of the broader economic structure. As Engels forcefully stated, if the materialist conception of history is twisted so that

> the economic element is the only determining one, he transforms it into a meaningless, abstract and absurd phrase. . . . [The] various elements of the superstructure . . . also exercise their influence upon the course of the historical struggles and in many cases preponderate in determining their form. There is an interaction of all these elements.[29]

Within the context of the history of aging it is interesting to observe that "older workers have received little attention from labour historians, their fate lamented only in passing."[30] Much more is known about the history of women, childhood, ethnic groups and unions than the experience of older workers and how they perceive their reality. This lack of interest in the historical experience of the aged, and particularly elderly workers, is largely attributable to older people being used "to service the needs of larger and more powerful elements of the population."[31] Recent research in labour and social history for the United States and Canada has, unfortunately, completely ignored the working class experience with aging and the reality surrounding it.[32] The evidence which exists suggests that working class culture has had little veneration for the elderly.[33] As a result, "of all the silent groups yet uncovered by historians dealing with history 'from the bottom up,' the elderly as a group . . . remain the most inarticulate."[34]

The cultural dimension of the political economy of pensions exhibits itself in the form of agism and gerontophobia.[35] Agism, like sexism, is a prevailing and pervasive social attitude, and it is institutionalized and legitimized. Agism exists in employment, retirement practices, social stereotypes, legislation, income distribution, and the generally negative social attitudes towards the aged. One study concluded that while there have been some modest advances made against racism and sexism in recent years, the relative status of the elderly is declining and "age inequality appears to be getting substantially worse."[36]

The current inadequacies of the private and public pension systems are a reflection of the more general condition of the aged. The elderly in our society are deprived of status, authority and economic security. The aged lack adequate income, respect and purposefulness because of dominant negative social attitudes which are ascribed to aging and the elderly.[37] Most people still hold images and stereotypes of the elderly that existed earlier in the century because they do not consider the aged very active, alert, efficient, or contented.[38] There is a tremendous discrepancy between what old age is expected to be like and the actual experience of old people. At a social level, the inadequacies of the pension system exist because our youth-oriented society does not value the elderly as people.[39]

The socio-economic position of the elderly is not dissimilar to that of women and various national minority groups. Like them, the elderly are in general poor, vulnerable and victimized. This situation may be changing, however, since the elderly, and these other strata, are now becoming increasingly articulate, organized and vocal in defining their own interests and needs, as opposed to having them defined for them by other institutions with ulterior motives.[40]

There is a considerable difference between the retirement experience of an elderly slave and that of a patrician and that of an aged labourer and industrialist as de Beauvoir reminds us in her classic history of aging.[41] Both the elderly and women constitute a stratum within their respective social classes.[42] Recognizing the class basis for the difference in the aging experience, however, in no way negates the general proposition that there are certain universal problems and attitudes experienced by the elderly. The aging experience at the social and personal level is dialectical in character because it is both universal *and* historically specific. "Older people share with each other their chronological age, but factors more powerful than age," one study concluded, "determine the conditions of their later years."[43] Fundamentally, what are at issue are not just matters of economic analysis, or the income security programmes evolved by the capitalist welfare state, although these certainly are important, but society's *cultural* attitudes towards the elderly and how these affect public policy. Underlying the pension issue is the quality of life experienced by the current and future elderly. The elderly are increasingly developing their own life-style and asserting their right to self-esteem, dignity and, above all, independence. In this regard an expanded public pension system is a crucially necessary, but not sufficient, condition to improve their position. That will require major attitudinal and cultural changes in addition to substantial reform of the pension system.

Increasingly, there is a risk, because pensions are viewed as an economic problem, that the elderly will be defined as a "burden" and a "problem" themselves. The aging of the population in industrialized countries, especially in Canada and the United States, with all its economic and social implications, suggests that the elderly may be perceived as a "social problem" of the first magnitude.[44] Because "old age has become the object of a policy,"[45] if the elderly become a high profile "social problem" like the unemployed, unions, blacks and the Québécois, they may become the target of less benign welfare state policies.

It is "mechanical reductionism" of the worst type to simplify the process of aging and the experience of the elderly to the cash nexus as represented by pension arrangements. The aged are more than the stagnant form of the industrial reserve army,[46] and social security expenditures are considerly more complex than only being a form of variable capital or "social wage."[47] Limiting public policy reviews of pension arrangements solely to the issue of income adequacy perpetuates a narrow view of the problems associated with aging and reinforces the elderly's status as a dependent social category. Money alone will not resolve the problems associated with old age. Such a view is the best form of liberalism and the worst type of "economism." It is vulgar and simplistic because it ignores the totality of the social reality and the complex issues related to the elderly and aging.

The history of aging may contain within it the potential for progressive social change because "an adequate policy for old age . . . has to be much more than a policy for pensions. It has to be a policy which will help the elderly find a new way of life."[48] To question the quality and meaning of one's existence in old age is to begin to inquire about the purpose of one's entire life. The difficulties associated with old age are nothing but a continuation of what has gone before, because the injury a worker "has suffered during the course of his life is . . . radical. The reason that the retired man is rendered hopeless by want of meaning in his present is that the meaning of his existence has been stolen from him from the very beginning."[49] To be treated differently in old age therefore requires that a person be treated as a human being during his entire life. This being the case, "it is the whole system that is at issue and our claim cannot be otherwise than radical — change life itself."[50] A political economy of pensions which incorporates and is sensitive to the history of the aged and aging may become a liberative tool because it offers an analysis of the interrelationship between the individual and collective condition of the elderly and broader social institutions and structures.

2

The Condition of the Elderly: Immiseration and Marginalization

A man's aging and his decline always takes place inside some given society: it is intimately related to the character of that society and . . . the place that the individual in question occupies within it. In itself the economic factor cannot be isolated from the social, political and ideological superstructures that contain it.

Simone de Beauvoir

Aging is a socially defined process, individually experienced. The economic and social position of the elderly must accordingly be analysed in terms of both its universality and specificity. "Men make their own history, but they do not make it just as they please," Marx wrote, "but under circumstances directly encountered, given and transmitted from the past."[1] The current socio-economic position of the elderly in industrialized societies is a product of the historical process which preceded it, and it is central to the study of the political economy of pensions because the elderly are the object of pension policy.

Two themes are developed in this chapter. First, the economic position of a significant proportion of elderly throughout history has relegated them to a clearly identifiable lower stratum of society characterized by immiseraton and marginalization. There are both class-based and universal characteristics and problems associated with aging. While "one of the main functions of social class" in industrialized societies "has been to prepare a differential response to aging," the "elderly have encountered special problems, as a segment of the population, for centuries."[2] There is no mechanical relationship between the position held by the elderly and the mode of production. Like racism and sexism, the elderly's insecure economic position and the negative social values ascribed to aging predate the rise of industrial capitalism.[3] Both high and popular culture have continuously disdained old age and the elderly. There is an historical continuity between the past and present situation of the elderly.

Agism and gerontophobia are universal phenomena in Western society regardless of their specific institutionalized and legitimized forms. While Marx analysed the elderly as constituting the stagnant form, or Lazarus stratum, of the industrial reserve army along with the disabled, orphans and paupers, as a result of their peripheral attachment to the capitalist labour market,[4] in general the "old have consistently been treated unkindly in Western culture,"[5] both in pre-industrial and industrialized societies.[6] To attribute the current status of the elderly solely to the capitalist mode of production without recognizing the relatively independent cultural and social dimensions of aging is to engage in, to use Lukács's formulation, an "un- and anti-historical" analysis. "All history must be studied afresh," Engels recognized, because "the conditions of existence of the different formations of society must be individually examined before the attempt is made to deduce from them the . . . [cultural] notions corresponding to them."[7] For the elderly, unlike Engels's Manchester working class, there has never been an idyllic paradise lost. There has been no lost golden age for the elderly. They have always constituted and continue to be one of the poorest strata of society.

The second proposition put forward is that a significant proportion of elderly in the advanced capitalist countries of Canada, Britain and the United States is poor and socially dependent. The elderly's position in the modernization process has been the subject of considerable scholarly debate. The dominant "deterioration motif" has argued that "modernization has thus far tended to devalue old people and to reduce their status."[8] But the more recent liberal gerontological literature claims that "we must not suppose that the sufferings of some of the aged, and the miseries of the minority . . . are a proper indication of the condition of old people generally in . . . society"[9] because "a nationwide institutional approach . . . has helped to improve elderly people's overall financial situation."[10] Such assertions are an ideological reaffirmation of the liberal faith in the welfare state's incrementalism, but they are founded on statistical artifacts rather than social facts.

Aging occurs "within definite class relationships," Corrigan and Leonard have suggested; therefore, "we must first understand the structural determinants of working-class old age."[11] It is suggested here that the primary structural determinant is the economic position of the elderly. A corollary is that to the extent that the quality of life for the elderly has improved, it is a result of government intervention through the creation and expansion of the welfare state and the public pension system rather than through private sector initiatives.

HISTORICAL POSITION OF THE ELDERLY

The condition of the elderly has been characterized by their continuous impoverishment from at least the early nineteenth century to the present time. In British North America between 1815 and 1850 there is clear evidence that outdoor labourers, immigrants, women, and the very young, sick and old were impoverished, particularly in the winter.[12] In Hamilton, Ontario, for example, a rapidly industrializing centre in the early 1850s, the relationship between age and wealth corresponded roughly to the relationship between occupation and age. In the mid-1880s the City of Hamilton began to pay pensions to public employees,[13] who constituted the second largest occupational group over the age of 60. While the elderly represented only 6 per cent of the entire population of Hamilton, they accounted for 30 per cent of those who were poor.[14] During the 1889 Royal Commission hearings on the relations between capital and labour, an exchange between Chairman A. T. Freed and Hamilton MP Alex McKay offered an interesting insight into the extent of poverty among the elderly.

Q: Are those who are chronic applicants [for relief] such through illness, or physical disability, or mental disability or old age, or are they able-bodied people?

A: Of those that go by the term "chronic applicants" a large proportion are old women and men, and who apply on account of old age, poverty and so [on].[15]

Such information suggests that the elderly poor were a clearly identifiable dependent category during the period of early industrialization in Canada.

In Britain, Booth's 1891 estimates designated nearly 40 per cent of those aged 65 and over as paupers.[16] The 1893 Royal Commission on destitution and old age reported that it was shocked by the "deplorable fact that so large a proportion of the working classes are in old age in receipt of poor relief." In various other government studies between 1890 and 1906, 15 to 20 per cent of the elderly were labelled as paupers.[17] The Old Age Pension Act 1908, providing a non-contributory, means-tested benefit of 5 shillings a week, was recognized at that time as being 2 shillings per week below the subsistence minimum.[18]

Evidence to the Canadian House of Commons Special Committee on Old Age Pensions, convened between 1911 and 1913, gives a general impression of the extent of poverty among the elderly. The Salvation Army Commissioner for Canada testified that poverty among the aged was widespread not only in the large urban centres, but in smaller towns and villages as well.[19] The superintendent of Children's Aid Societies for Ontario reported that "there are thousands of worthy citizens . . . leading useful and respectable lives, who . . . live under the constant shadow of having to spend their declining years in penury and abject dependence on others." For the aged it was "a hopeless, heartless life."[20]

In the United States in 1910 at least 35 per cent of those over the age of 55 were below the elderly couple's family budget.[21] During the 1920s, at the height of American prosperity, it has been estimated that anywhere from 40 to 67 per cent of all older Americans could not support themselves.[22] It was during this period that one reformer could say that "old age, merely by that name, is a synonym for poverty."[23]

While there is no specific information regarding the economic position of the elderly in Canada during the 1920s, their situation can be inferred from that of the general population. According to the Economic Council of Canada, "most Canadians of the 1920's would be found to have been living below that [poverty] line."[24] Recent indepth studies of the working class in Montreal and Toronto confirm this conclusion. In Montreal in the early 1920s the average annual income for adult male workers in occupations which involved two-thirds of the city's labour force was 20 to 30 per cent below the federal Department of Labour's family budget.[25] The Toronto working class fared little better. Between 1902 and 1917 the real average annual earnings for workers employed in the building trades and manufacturing declined by roughly 33 per cent; the average annual earnings of blue-collar workers represented less than 64 per cent of what was required to support a family.[26] If times were difficult for the active labour force, there must have been extreme hardship among the elderly.

Most of the social surveys conducted in Britain during the 1920s and 1930s, for example, the studies by Rowntree and Trout, identified old age as one of the major causes of poverty. Rowntree's 1936 study found that it accounted for nearly 15 per cent of the incidence of all poverty.[27] But this figure obscures how many old people were in dire straits. Stevenson's review of social conditions in the twenties and thirties reported that the London survey found

that in the east end of London, as in the London area as a whole, poverty was still rife amongst the elderly. As the new survey observed, the pension for a single person was in itself insufficient to place them above the poverty line if they were living alone. The London survey found that in many cases the poverty of the elderly was associated with bad housing conditions. For many the Poor Law Institution with its stigma as the "workhouse" was the final destination when incapacity and lack of support from relatives prevented them from continuing on their own.[28]

The depression years undoubtedly compounded the economic difficulties associated with old age.

During the Great Depression, or the "Dirty Thirties" as they have become known in Canada, age, sickness and fecundity "were the hallmarks of hopelessness."[29] Between 1933 and 1936 about 12 per cent of the Canadian population received emergency relief, while another 5 per cent were dependent upon existing programmes such as charitable aid, mother's allowances and old age pensions. In the worst year of the Depression about 20 per cent of the total population were public dependents.[30] The non-contributory, means-tested old age pension, introduced in 1927 for those over the age of 70, was $20 a month.

Limited information prevents a detailed analysis of the elderly's economic situation during the depression years, however, many did speak and write of their own circumstances. One woman from Calgary wrote to the Prime Minister of Canada, R. B. Bennett, in 1935, saying, "Do please raise the Old Age Pension to at least thirty dollars per month. So many of your old friends . . . have really not enough to exist on." Another from Quebec pleaded, "I am a Poor Woman 70 years old and I have a sick husband and he is 71 and not able to work and we have no one to keep us . . . . Please send us a little money to get some coal and flour for one Winter." A woman in Saskatchewan wrote that "my husband was 64 May 22nd last I was 64 Nov. 5th 1 year older than you are worked hard all our lives. And surely a little comfort should be coming to us now."[31] When the elderly did break their collective silence, they revealed the terrible tragedy inflicted upon them. The Great Depression throughout the major industrialized countries not only created social chaos and human suffering, but also destroyed people's ability to save for retirement during their prime working years.

The end of World War II signalled an unparalleled period of prolonged prosperity in capitalist nations. However, "sheltering behind the myths of expansion and affluence," de Beauvoir observed, society "treats the old as outcasts."[32] In the immediate aftermath of the war, nearly 38 per cent of the elderly in Britain were in receipt of supplementary benefits. According to Rowntree's 1950 study, old people accounted for nearly 70 per cent of all those living in poverty.[33] By 1959 according to Titmuss, "it is possible to see two nations in old age."[34] In the heady postwar period between 1951 and 1965, according to the Economic Council of Canada, "the young benefited more from economic growth . . . than the middle-aged and elderly."[35] In 1951, 84 per cent and in 1961, 75 per cent of the elderly had an income of less than $2,000 a year. In 1961 their median income was $960, resulting in nearly 54 per cent of the aged being in receipt of an annual income of less than $1,000 a year.[36]

The 1960s heralded the rediscovery of poverty. The poor, including the elderly, became a major social policy concern for the liberal welfare state. In Britain, Townsend and Abel-Smith established on the basis of their 1960 study that approximately 18 per cent of households and 14 per cent of all people were living below the defined "national assistance" level. Nearly 35 per cent were living in households primarily dependent on pensions and another 23 per cent in households dependent on other state benefits. Townsend's massive 1968 survey of poverty in Britain (published ten years later) indicated, depending upon the criteria, that 34 to 63 per cent of all the elderly continued to live in poverty.[37] A 1960 U.S. Senate report stated that "at least one-half of the aged . . . cannot afford today decent housing, proper nutrition, adequate medical care—or necessary recreation."[38] The aged were clearly identified as being among "the invisible poor."[39] Subsequently, the elderly became a prime "target group" for the Johnson administration's "war on poverty." The 1966 report of the Senate Committee on Aging in Canada noted that "without question the most serious problem encountered . . . was the degree and extent of poverty which exists among older people."[40] A study of low incomes in Canada confirmed that in 1969 in excess of 50 per cent of all unattached individuals and 30 per cent of all families, or nearly 40 per cent of all those over the age of 65, were below Statistics Canada's low-income (poverty) cut-offs.[41] The economic position of the elderly may represent one of great social policy failures of the capitalist welfare state in the post- war period.

PUBLIC POLICY TOWARDS THE ELDERLY: IDEOLOGICAL PRINCIPLES

Poverty among the elderly is explained by the inadequacies of income security arrangements and a dominant ideology which has guided the formulation of public policy towards the aged. It is the interplay between ideology and institutional arrangements which explains the historical and contemporary impoverishment of the elderly.

The subsistence principle ("social minimum" or "poverty line") and individual "thrift" or "savings" have been central, if not always explicit, ideological principles which have guided the development of state income security arrangements for the elderly. Both notions are British in origin and have affected social security philosophy and institutional arrangements in Canada and, to a lesser extent, the United States. The focus here is on Canada since this aspect of social security history is less well known and documented than in Britain and the United States.

The subsistence principle was first enunciated in the British Poor Laws and subsequently incorporated into the 1942 Beveridge Report. Beveridge was quite clear that the responsibility of the welfare state was limited to the provision of a social minimum, while reaffirming the responsibility of the individual to engage in thrifty behaviour. He emphasized that "provision by compulsory insurance of a flat-rate . . . benefit up to subsistence level leaves untouched the freedom and responsibility of the individual citizen in making supplementary provisions for himself above that level."[42] "Nothing materially below the scales of benefit," he wrote, "can be justified on scientific grounds as adequate for human subsistence."[43] The "scientific grounds" used to justify the subsistence principle were Rowntree's 1937 minimum family budget and dietary requirements.[44] Those individuals who wished to rise above the social minimum would be required to undertake individual initiative and engage in thrifty savings behaviour.

From its inception, the state social security system in Canada was viewed as being only one of a number of sources of retirement income, and it was to provide only a minimum subsistence level, or floor benefit. Marsh stated that "the basic rate should be an amount sufficient for minimium maintenance . . . the rates which suggest themselves . . . [are] the minimum assistance standards."[45] The 1966 Senate Special Committee on Aging reiterated that what was necessary "is a floor of income security to maintain self-reliance."[46] When the Canada/Quebec Pension Plans became effective on 1 January 1966, the federal Minister of Health and Welfare, Judy LaMarsh, said that "the Canada Pension Plan . . . is designed to make available to all Canadians a satisfactory *minimum standard* of pensions . . . *the proper role of government is to provide a floor*."[47] Former federal Minister of Health and Welfare, Marc Lalonde, asserted in 1973 that the universal old age security (OAS) pension and the earnings-related Canada/Quebec Pension Plans "were geared to ensure adequacy," while occupational pension plans were "to provide whatever supplementatry margin of comfort was desired."[48] In practice, however, "adequacy" is equated with the "poverty line" cut-offs as defined by Statistics Canada.

The view that individuals should provide for their old age through personal savings has also played an important role in the development of welfare policies in capitalist nations in general, and the Anglo-American democracies in particular. The development of pension arrangements was marked by the Victorian expectation of individual thrift and responsibility. To engage in such desired social behaviour was viewed as a prerequisite for workers becoming part of the "respectable working-class," and so promoted a control function. The friendly societies of nineteenth-century Britain, which provided sickness, unemployment, death and superannuation benefits, were "traditionally the badge of the artisan."[49] For skilled workers and a scattering of lower middle-class occupations, the friendly society movement "made its impact upon the developing conception of independence and respectability."[50] But few workers saved for retirement because of limited financial resources and because the concept of retirement had not yet emerged. A friendly society member worked until he died. In the Calvinist tradition, the inability to save was viewed as a sign of personal failure, entitling one only to a subsistence existence provided by the state.

The 1889 Royal Commission on the Relations between Capital and Labour in Canada provides considerable evidence that certain sections of the working class had some opportunity for saving and home-ownership. It is equally evident, however, that workers did not engage in saving for retirement as such. One rare insight into aging and saving behaviour is found in an exchange between Alex McKay, Hamilton MP, and Mr. Freed, chairman of the Royal Commission.

Q: Do you know of many working people in Hamilton who are able to accumulate means for their support in old age?
A: I know of instances of people who have worked, and are now living comfortably without working.
Q: [Are] Any of these common labourers?
A: I think among the common labourers it is rare, though there are exceptional cases where men seem to accumulate property.[51]

Property accumulation, and the attendant "property mobility," were part of the working-class experience in the last half of the nineteenth century in North America.[52] More speculatively, it might be suggested that there was a substitution effect between retirement savings and investment in property and home-ownership. Investment in property was tangible, while saving for retirement required a long-time horizon based on a concept which had not yet evolved for the majority of workers.

The social pressures for individual saving for retirement were so great that at the turn of the century Canadian proponents of a non-contributory state pension were told that "a pension paid by the state would reward shiftlessness and profligacy" and "would thereby discourage thrift and initiative."[53] Subsequently, the Canadian Annuities Act of 1908, introducing the voluntary purchase of pensions from the government, was implemented as "a means of promoting thrift rather than . . . a type of social legislation or state aid."[54]

Associated with the development and expansion of the welfare state in advanced industrialized countries in the postwar period was a transformation in the conception of social welfare and the role of the state. The "residual" concept, based on the "protestant ethic," determined social policy up to the 1940s and placed reliance on private relief agencies and limited government intervention. In the aftermath of the Great Depression and World War II, it gave way to the "institutional" concept, which inaugurated active state intervention to protect the individual against the exigencies of unemployment, sickness, death, disability and old age as a universal right of citizenship.

Despite the major transformation in the role of the state and social welfare policy, the legacy of the "residual" approach to income security arrangements for the elderly has continued to influence Canadian public policy to the present day. The Carter Commission on Tax Reform in 1966 stated that

> it seems to be generally agreed that individuals should set aside a portion of their income in the working years to ensure an adequate command over goods and services in their retirement years. Such *private* provisions for retirement are thought to foster *self-reliance and reduce the need for the state to provide relief.*[55]

In 1973 the federal government concluded a major income security review by stating that "we believe . . . Canadians hold the value of independence or self-dependence. They expect to meet their own needs through their own efforts, and they expect others to do their best to do the same."[56] The historical legacy and ideology associated with the market ethos have thus served to legitimize limited government intervention in the social security field to provide only a minimum subsistence level of income replacement for the elderly. A representative of the Canadian private pension industry justified this situation by saying that "if we wipe out private pensions, we say goodbye to the traditional values of thrift and self-denial."[57] The current emphasis on individual retirement savings vehicles such as Registered Retirement Savings Plans (RRSPs) and the recent significant increase in contribution limits are indicative of the Conservative government's bias and its attempt to privatize retirement income arrangements.

The ability of individuals to undertake private savings in order to provide economic security against the universal risks of old age, disability, illness and so on is extremely limited. According to Statistics Canada, a worker at the average industrial wage only saved 4.2 per cent of his gross income for "security" (pensions, disability, life insurance, and so forth) in 1984. Kreps summarized the role of individual savings for retirement income by stating that

> the role . . . played by private savings would appear to be a very limited one for families whose incomes during [their] work life fall below the median. . . . Even when the marginal propensity to save is quite high . . . savings adequate to maintain the targeted level of consumption are not forthcoming.[58]

Only a collective pooling arrangement such as a social security system can effectively deal with this social reality.

But an overemphasis on the role of ideology—the subsistence principle and individual thrift—to explain the welfare state's limited income maintenance measures to improve the economic position of the elderly tends to obscure a much more fundamental set of structural and power relationships which are identified and elaborated upon in Chapters 6 to 9. Subsistence level retirement income from the state social security system effectively forces people to save for retirement by relying on the private pension system or to live in poverty. Controlling a portion of the labour force's discretionary savings for its own purposes ensures that the private pension industry will remain viable. The corresponding underdevelopment of the state pension system ensures the existence of the private pension industry and the continued immiseration of the elderly.

LEVEL OF RETIREMENT INCOME: ADEQUACY AND POVERTY

To put the economic position of the elderly, the underdevelopment of the state social security system and the limitations of the private pension system into analytical perspective requires that the concepts of adequate retirement income and poverty be identified and defined. Four criteria have been developed to assess the adequacy of retirement income:[59]
1. a level of retirement income which allows a person to subsist by providing no more than the barest necessities of life;
2. a level of income which keeps the elderly above the poverty line;
3. provision for a level of income which permits an individual to live at the same level as other pensioners; and
4. a level of income in the retirement period which allows people to maintain the standard of living to which they have become accustomed prior to retirement.

Adequate retirement income is usually defined in terms of total income from all sources, but such income is ordinarily restricted to that received from the state and occupational pension plans. Economists and social welfare administrators have tended to limit the definition of total income to these two sources rather than using the broader net wealth (or asset) concept, including services-in-kind, because of reporting, distributional, and measurement problems.

In recent years a consensus has emerged among economists, gerontologists, and social security and pension plan administrators that the appropriate level of retirement income is that which maintains a person's pre-retirement standard of living. As Schultz noted, "The trend seems to be toward developing public and private pension systems which will permit the retired population to . . . maintain a level of living which approximates that which they enjoyed during their working years."[60] This is referred to as the "continuity of income" approach. Discussion of this issue has centred on the level of pre-retirement income that is needed to prevent a sharp decline in living standards during retirement and the proportion of income that should come from public, private and individual sources. In his famous report on the Canadian railways' pension plans, Hall concluded that "a desirable principle would seem to be that the combined pension should enable the retired worker to maintain his living standard."[61] Tilove has argued that "it seems appropriate to consider continuance of [full] net income as a reasonable"[62] level for retirement income. A Toronto consulting actuary has defined the minimum retirement income standard as "that income which permits maintenance of an equivalent standard of living after retirement."[63]

The "full maintenance" or "continuity of living standard" definition of an adequate retirement income is in reality based on a "net income" approach; that is, net income in the retirement period must be compared with net income before retirement. Altered expenditure patterns and a lower rate of taxation will result in a couple or individual requiring less than the pre-retirement level of income. The relationship between the net retirement income equivalent to pre-retirement income is presented in Table 2.1. This evidence suggests that a one-earner couple at the average industrial wage (AIW) must receive a total income from all sources in retirement equivalent to 70 per cent of net pre-retirement income in order to maintain their standard of living.

TABLE 2.1

RETIREMENT INCOME EQUIVALENT TO PRE-RETIREMENT INCOME
FOR A ONE-EARNER COUPLE, ONTARIO, 1978

PRE-RETIREMENT INCOME (FINAL SALARY)	PERCENTAGE REQUIRED ON RETIREMENT
$10,000	73.1
20,000	61.2
30,000	52.0
40,000	48.3

Source: Roy Chittick, Vice-President, T-A Associates, *Pension Adequacy*. A Summary of a workshop presentation to the Canadian Pension Conference Annual Meeting, Toronto, 30 April and 1 May, 1979, p. 2.

To assess the economic status of the elderly requires a standard of income adequacy. Two such criteria exist. The total net income replacement standard was outlined above. The second criterion is the poverty line or low-income cut-off (LICO) approach ("social minimum") developed by various statistical or social welfare agencies. The poverty line concept measures both absolute and relative deprivation or what Rowntree called "primary" and "secondary" poverty.

"The exercise of drawing statistical poverty lines," the Economic Council of Canada has said, "while bound to be somewhat arbitrary, is necessary for good social planning."[64] In Canada a number of alternate poverty lines or LICOs have been constructed by social planners and policy analysts. The most common poverty lines are those developed by Statistics Canada, the Senate Committee on Poverty (the Croll Committee), the Canadian Council on Social Development (CCSD) and the Social Planning Council of Metro-Toronto. Six alternate low-income cut-offs or poverty lines, based on different expenditure patterns, family size, and size of community, are reported in Table 2.2.

Three different Statistics Canada low-income cut-offs are outlined. The LICO referred to here as Statistics Canada I is the most commonly used indicator of poverty in Canada. It is also the *lowest* of the poverty thresholds and therefore *underestimates* the incidence of poverty among the elderly. This low-income cut-off was originally based on 1978 Family Expenditure data and reflected the consumption patterns for different size family units and area of

TABLE 2.2

COMPARISON OF ALTERNATE POVERTY LINES, CANADA, 1986

POVERTY LINE	FAMILY SIZE	
	1	**2**
Statistics Canada		
I 1978 base by size of urban area[1]	$7,877-$10,651	$10,295-$14,053
II Weighted average[2]	9,635	12,635
III Major urban centres[3]	10,651	14,053
Canadian Council on Social		
Development	9,905	16,508
Senate Committee[4]	9,930	16,560
Social Planning Council of		
Metro-Toronto[5]	12,090	18,165

Notes: 1 Statistics Canada's low-income cut-offs differentiated by size of urban area and family size.
2 Statistics Canada's national weighted average low-income cut-offs based on a weighted average of urbanization categories. Note Statistics Canada, *Rebasing Low Income Cut-offs to 1978.* Technical Reference Paper (n.p.: Minister of Supply and Services Canada, September 1983).
3 For urban areas over 500,000 population. As of 1981, nearly 80 per cent of older adults lived in urban centres, with 40 per cent residing in centres of 500,000 or more population.
4 Updated for 1986 on the basis of 55 per cent of the average income for a four-person census family($46,206) based on Statistics Canada's *Survey of Consumer Finance,* times a factor of 0.43 for unattached individuals and a factor of 0.71 for a couple.
5 Social Planning Council of Metropolitan Toronto, *Guidelines for Family Budgeting, 1987* (Toronto: Social Planning Council of Metropolitan Toronto, December 1987).

residence. Families or individuals who spend 58.5 per cent of their income on food, shelter and clothing are deemed to be in "straitened circumstances."[65] In this instance, the LICO varies according to urban size and the number of people in the family unit. LICOs are adjusted annually for inflation.

Statistics Canada II, as it referred to here, is a weighted average low-income cut-off based on different urbanization categories—that is, adjusted for the size of community. The resulting single national LICO is thus weighted on the basis of community size. Statistics Canada III is the low-income cut-off for urban areas of over 500,000 population. Currently, nearly 80 per cent of all the elderly live in urban centres, with 40 per cent of seniors residing in centres of 500,000 or more people.

Three additional poverty thresholds are employed to measure the incidence of poverty among the elderly in Canada. The guidelines constructed by the Senate Committee on Poverty and the CCSD are both national poverty lines. They are based on average family income and are adjusted for the number of people in the family unit. The Social Planning Council of Metropolitan Toronto's poverty line threshold, however, is based on their budget guideline for the elderly in that city.

Each of these poverty lines or low-income cut-offs has different implications for the measurement of poverty among the elderly. What should be noted, however, is that each of the guidelines outlined in Table 2.2 generally results in a successively higher poverty line threshold. Specifically, the guidelines formulated by the CCSD, the Senate Committee on Poverty and the Social Planning Council of Metropolitan Toronto all have higher poverty thresholds for elderly couples than does the "official" Statistics Canada cut-off. Similarly, these agencies' poverty guidelines for single elderly people are generally higher than most of Statistics Canada's LICOs. In short, the "official" Statistics Canada low-income cut-offs are generally the lowest of the poverty thresholds and significantly underestimate the extent of poverty among the elderly. This situation has clear political and policy implications.

In the United States, an "official" poverty line and a Bureau of Labor Statistics intermediate family budget for the elderly have been established. In Britain the poverty level is generally defined as the supplementary benefits level. It must be emphasized that all these poverty line or low-income cut-off measures are set at the minimum subsistence level. The extent of poverty among the current elderly in Canada, Britain and the U.S. and the implications for public policy are examined in later sections.

WELFARE STATE SOCIAL SECURITY EXPENDITURES
ON THE ELDERLY

As a result of the relative underdevelopment of the state social security system and the limitations of the private pension system, the current retirement income system is not generating an adequate level of total income for the elderly. The key variables identified in the technical literature causally explaining the level of welfare state expenditures, in order of descending importance, include the age structure of the population and the proportion of elderly, the level and rate of economic development, the length of operation of the social security system, the level of per capita

TABLE 2.3

INTERNATIONAL COMPARISON OF STATE OLD AGE, INVALIDITY AND SURVIVORS' PENSIONS, 1977

COUNTRY	PENSION BENEFITS [1, 2]	TOTAL SOCIAL SECURITY EXPENDITURES [1]	GROSS DOMESTIC PRODUCT [1]	PENSIONS AS A % OF ALL SOCIAL SECURITY EXPENDITURES	PENSION BENEFITS AS A % OF GROSS DOMESTIC PRODUCT [2]
Sweden	58,029	104,368	350,921	55.6	16.5
Italy	24,578,704	35,416,000	172,987,900	69.4	14.2
Holland	35,210	69,862	262,410	50.4	13.4
Finland	15,895	23,759	127,065	66.9	12.5
U.K.	15,393	20,095	123,081	76.6	12.5
W. Germany	140,707	268,525	1,197,000	52.4	11.8
Denmark	32,149	64,948	278,325	49.5	11.6
Austria	91,051	159,180	792,500	57.2	11.5
Switzerland	15,599	22,157	145,790	70.4	10.7
France	183,682	421,289	1,875,200	43.6	9.8
U.S.A.	162,095	244,488	1,889,157	66.3	8.6
Belgium	218,614	672,659	2,838,200	32.5	7.7
Canada	7,909	27,368	193,085	28.9	4.1

Notes: 1 In millions of national currency units.
2 Old age, invalidity and survivors' pensions.

Source: Calculated from the International Labour Organization, *The Cost of Social Security, 1975–1977* (Geneva: ILO, 1981), pp. 95–106, 70–77, 110–15.

income, the level of unionization, the official ideology, the strength of the socialist movement, and the type of economic system.[66] The historical interaction of these factors has resulted in the considerable variation found in national social security systems.

Old age pensions are the welfare state's largest social security expenditure.[67] Retirement benefits (including invalidity and survivors' benefits) as a proportion of total social security expenditures and as a percentage of gross domestic product are presented in Table 2.3. In most industrialized countries state pension benefits account for 50 to 70 per cent of all social security expenditures and 10 to 17 per cent of GNP. Pension payments as a proportion of total social security expenditures are a function of the number of recipients, the level of benefits, the maturity of the pension system and the type of funding.

In general, there is a close relationship between the level of state old age pension benefits and the proportion of the elderly in the population. This relationship is outlined in Table 2.4 for selected countries. The technical literature indicates that there is a more robust statistical correlation based on time-series data[68] than exists using the cross-sectional information presented in Table 2.4. The latter is reported for the purpose of illustration.

TABLE 2.4

RELATIONSHIP[1] BETWEEN STATE OLD AGE BENEFITS[2] AND AGE COMPOSITION, SELECTED COUNTRIES, 1975-1977

COUNTRY	PERCENTAGE OF POPULATION AGE 65 AND OVER, 1975	STATE OLD AGE PENSION BENEFITS AS A PERCENTAGE OF GDP, 1977
Austria	15.1	11.5
Sweden	14.9	16.5
West Germany	14.3	11.8
Belgium	14.2	7.7
U.K.	13.6	12.5
France	13.3	9.8
Netherlands	10.7	13.4
U.S.	10.4	8.6
Canada	8.7	4.1

Note: 1 The relationship between state expenditures on old age pensions and the proportion of elderly in the population has a correlation coefficient (r) of 0.6, suggesting a moderate, but not necessarily causal, relationship.
2 Including old age, death and survivors' benefits.

Sources: Harry Weitz, *The Foreign Experience with Income Maintenance for the Elderly* (Hull: Canadian Government Publishing Centre, 1979), Table 2-1, p. 6 and the International Labour Organization, *The Cost of Social Security, 1975-77* (Geneva: ILO, 1981), pp. 70-77.

To determine the income replacement rate in the retirement period and to compare it with the adequacy standard requires that the level of total income generated from the state and private pension systems be assessed. The policy goal of most state social security systems is to provide an income replacement rate of 40 to 50 per cent of pre-retirement income.[69] The current International Labour Organization (ILO) Convention calls for a 45 per cent income replacement rate under state pension plans.[70]

Table 2.5 compares the income replacement rate provided for under state social security pension arrangements in selected Western European countries and North America. By international standards, the benefit levels provided by the British and Canadian public retirement systems are quite low. State retirement benefits for individuals in Canada and Britain rank in the bottom quartile of the countries surveyed, while the U.S. is near the median. For a couple, a similar pattern emerges.

TABLE 2.5

INCOME REPLACEMENT RATES FOR SOCIAL SECURITY RETIREMENT BENEFITS,
SELECTED COUNTRIES, 1980

| COUNTRY[1] | REPLACEMENT RATIO AS A PERCENTAGE OF FINAL YEAR'S EARNINGS[2] | |
	Individual	Couple
Italy	68%	69%
Austria	68	68
Sweden	68	83
France	66	75
West Germany	49	49
United States	44	66
Netherlands	44	63
Switzerland	37	55
Canada	34	49
United Kingdom	31	47
Denmark	29	52

Notes: 1 Countries are arranged in descending order based on the replacement rate for a single worker.
        2 For a male at the average industrial wage in manufacturing.

Source: Retabulated from Jonathan Aldrich, "The Earnings Replacement Rate of Old-Age Benefits in 12 Countries, 1969–1980," Social Security Bulletin 45, no. 11 (1982), Table 1, p. 5. Japan has been dropped from this ranking.

What is of significance is the *total combined* replacement rate generated from the state *and* private pension systems. Table 2.6

TABLE 2.6

TOTAL COMBINED INCOME REPLACEMENT RATES UNDER STATE AND PRIVATE PENSION ARRANGEMENTS.[1]
SELECTED COUNTRIES. MID-1980s

Country	INDIVIDUAL			ONE-EARNER COUPLE		
	Social Security[2]	Private Pensions[3]	Targeted Total[4]	Social Security[2]	Private Pensions[3]	Targeted Total[4]
West Germany	50%	12–22%	62–72%	50%	25%	75%
Sweden	59	6[5]	65	55–60	10	65–70
France	46	8[5]	54	50	20	70
Netherlands	38	7–11	45–49	40	30	70
U.K.	26	23	49	40	20	60
U.S.[6]	38	32	70	40	32	72
Canada[6]	38	32	70	51	19	70

Notes: 1 For a male in manufacturing at the average industrial wage.
2 Including flat-rate benefit and earnings-related pension where applicable.
3 For those in the countries surveyed, private pension plan coverage ranged from 45 to 80 per cent of the paid labour force. Because of the limitations of the private pension system, receipt of benefits will be low.
4 Targeted, but not necessarily received, level of retirement income.
5 At maturity the replacement income rate will double.
6 Included for comparative purposes.

Source: Adapted from Leif Haanes-Olsen, "Earnings Replacement Rate of Old-Age Benefits, 1965–75, Selected Countries, *Social Security Bulletin* 41 (January 1978), Table 1, p. 4, Table 2, p. 5 and p. 14; updated based on Max Horlick, "The Relationship between Public and Private Pension Schemes," *Social Security Bulletin* 50 (July 1987), Table 1, p. 22.

identifies the total combined income replacement rate for selected countries where complete information was available. A number of points should be noted. First, and most important, retirement income flowing from the public pension system accounts for 60 to 90 per cent of the total income replacement ratio in the case of individuals, depending on the country, and 55 to 85 per cent for retired couples. It is the state pension system which is the primary source of retirement income for the aged; only 50 to 60 per cent of the elderly in these countries receive income from an occupational pension plan. This situation is the result of the limitations of the private pension system which are dealt with in Chapter 4.

A second consideration is the difference in the level of income replacement rates between countries. Canada and Britain tend to provide below average levels of retirement income through the state social security system by international standards.[71] A third point is that the total income replacement ratio for individuals is in most instances below the 70 per cent income adequacy level cited earlier, while the situation for an elderly couple more nearly conforms to that standard. This situation in particular negatively affects elderly single women. The relative underdevelopment of the state social security retirement system and the limitations of the private pension system have resulted in the immiseration of the current elderly.

CURRENT POSITION OF THE ELDERLY

Here two separate but interrelated issues are analysed: first, the extent of poverty among the elderly; and second, the sources of retirement income. Old age compounds and accentuates the unequal distribution of income. Table 2.7 compares the distribution of income between and among the elderly and the general population. Income distribution is a measure of equity, power and control over financial resources. As reported, 25 per cent of the general population had an income below $15,000 a year in 1986; however, 75 per cent of all elderly persons had an income below that amount. Furthermore, while 48 per cent of the overall population received an annual income of $30,000 or more, only 6 per cent of all seniors were in this upper income group.

These data indicate that a disproportionate number of the elderly are concentrated among low-income recipients when compared with the population as a whole. While the income distribution of elderly couples more nearly conforms to that of the general popula-

TABLE 2.7

COMPARISON OF INCOME DISTRIBUTIONS BETWEEN GENERAL POPULATION
AND THE ELDERLY, CANADA, 1986

INCOME GROUP	GENERAL POPULATION, FAMILIES AND UNATTACHED INDIVIDUALS[1]	ELDERLY 65 AND OVER		
		Total[2]	Families[3]	Unattached Individuals
Under $10,000	13.9%	52.9%	3.0%	49.5%
$10,000–14,999	11.1	23.3	18.1	30.1
$15,000–19,999	9.8	8.7	23.8	8.4
$20,000–24,999	9.0	5.5	13.2	3.7
$25,000–29,999	8.4	3.5	10.5	3.1
$30,000 +	47.7	5.9	31.4	5.2

Notes: 1 All age groups.
        2 All elderly persons regardless of family status.
        3 Age of head 65 years and over.

Source: Statistics Canada, *Income Distributions by Size in Canada, 1986*
         (Ottawa: Minister of Supply and Services Canada, 1987), Table 35, p. 95;
         Table 49, p. 122; Table 5, p. 56, and Table 29, p. 90.

tion, unattached individuals—and women in particular—are especially disadvantaged. This information suggests that the elderly—as a social category or stratum—have limited access to, and less control over, economic resources than do other age groups in society.

The elderly's income is substantially below that of others in society. The information in Table 2.8 indicates that in the period between 1970 and 1986, the income of pensioners in Canada was on average about 50 per cent of that received by the actively employed labour force. Furthermore, in the order of one-third of the elderly have non-taxable returns as a result of their low income.

In the period since 1970, the elderly's income has been affected by the many changes in the expansion of the public pension system. The Old Age Security (OAS) pension became payable at age 65 in 1970 and the Guaranteed Income Supplement (GIS) was substantially increased four times (in 1971, 1972, 1979 and 1980). Both the OAS and the GIS have been indexed to the cost of living since 1972. In addition, the Canada/Quebec Pension Plans, as well as many occupational pension plans, have matured and are now paying full benefits.

Notwithstanding the expansion and improvement of income security arrangements for the elderly, the average income of pen-

TABLE 2.8

COMPARISON OF AVERAGE INCOME[1] OF PENSIONERS AND EMPLOYEES
BASED ON REVENUE CANADA TAX RETURNS,[2] SELECTED YEARS, 1970–1986

| YEAR | AVERAGE INCOME[1] | | PENSIONERS' INCOME AS A % OF AVERAGE INCOME OF EMPLOYEES |
	Pensioners	Employees	
1970	$ 2,929	$ 5,018	58%
1972	2,875	6,791	42
1974	3,556	8,614	41
1976	4,517	11,199	40
1978	5,591	12,963	43
1980	8,323	15,555	54
1982	10,732	19,346	56
1984	12,553	21,118	59
1986 (P)	13,210	22,543	59

Notes: 1 Total assessed income.
          2 Including all taxable and non-taxable returns. In the order of one-third of
             the elderly have non-taxable returns due to low income.

Source: Calculated from Revenue Canada, *Taxation Statistics* (Ottawa: Canadian
          Government Publishing Centre, various years), Summary Table 3. This is
          the most recent information available.

sioners was substantially below that recorded for employees in the
period between 1970 and 1986. A recent study reported by Statistics Canada concluded that while "The income of people aged 65
and over has improved relative to that of other Canadians since the
early 1970s . . . it remains well below levels of the rest of the population."[72] The elderly experience a significant decline in their absolute
income relative to the active labour force as a result of the loss of
their employment status.

The sharp decline in the economic position of the elderly relative
to the general population[73] is suggested by the significant proportion of seniors who currently live in poverty. Table 2.9 summarizes
the incidence of poverty in Canada among elderly couples, unattached individuals and total elderly persons based on the alternate
poverty thresholds and low-income cut-offs previously described.
The poverty rate among elderly couples ranged from nearly 7 per
cent (Statistics Canada) to 50 per cent (Social Planning Council of
Metropolitan Toronto) in 1986, while the incidence of poverty varied
from 36 per cent (Statistics Canada I) to 71 per cent (Social Planning
Council of Metropolitan Toronto). Significantly, however, nearly 20
per cent (Statistics Canada I) to 53 per cent (Social Planning Council
of Metropolitan Toronto) of *all* elderly persons in Canada, depending

TABLE 2.9

INCIDENCE OF POVERTY AMONG ELDERLY COUPLES, UNATTACHED INDIVIDUALS AND
TOTAL ELDERLY PERSONS, ALTERNATE POVERTY LINES, CANADA, 1986

| | PROPORTION OF ELDERLY[2] BELOW POVERTY THRESHOLD | | | |
| POVERTY LINE OR LOW-INCOME CUT-OFF[1] | Couples[3] | | Unattached Individuals | Total Elderly Persons |
	Spouse < 65	Spouse 65 +		
Statistics Canada				
I 1978 base by size of community	9.5%[4]	6.6%	36.3%	18.8%
II Weighted average	16.0	6.5[5]	43.2	21.0
III Major urban centres	23.0	14.6	59.6	31.6
Canadian Council on Social Development	35.0	35.9	51.7	39.2
Senate Committee	35.5	36.2	51.9	39.5
Social Planning Council of Metro-Toronto	42.0	49.5	70.5	52.9

Notes: 1 Note Table 2.2 for the absolute poverty lines or low-income cut-offs.
2 Census family definition.
3 Head age 65 and over. Couples account for 60 per cent of the elderly. Aged couples with the spouse age 65 and over are nearly 40 percent of all the elderly and account for two-thirds of elderly couples. Conversely, aged couples where the spouse is below age 65 are 20 per cent of all the elderly and represent one-third of elderly couples.
4 Irrespective of spouse's age.
5 Statistics Canada II in this instance is marginally below the Statistics Canada I definition because of the weighting factor.

Source: Unpublished 1986 Statistics Canada, *Survey of Consumer Finances* data, cited in Richard Deaton, *The Economic Position of the Current Elderly: Retirement Income as a Barrier to Independent Living*. A report prepared for the National Advisory Council on Aging (Ottawa: NACA, April 1988), Table 5, p. 18, and information supplied 12 July 1988. This is based on an analysis of micro-data files by Statistics Canada.

upon the low-income cut-off, currently live in, or on, the margin of poverty.

The drop in post-retirement income is most severe for middle-income earners, while poverty is particularly pronounced among single elderly women. According to the Task Force on Retirement Income Policy, "between *one-third* and *one-half* of those now of working age and with incomes in the middle ranges are likely to encounter *significant reductions* in their living standards in retirement."[74] A survey of Old Age Security and Canada Pension Plan recipients carried out by Health and Welfare Canada in 1981 and 1986 found that 40 per cent of all seniors felt that their income was "less" or "much less" than adequate. Furthermore, one-third of elderly respondents reported that their financial situation had deteriorated since retirement.[75] A *Maclean's*-Decima poll in late 1984 found that nearly 50 per cent of new retirees in the middle-income range felt that their financial situation had worsened in the retirement period.[76] In total, in the order of 49 per cent of all the elderly were in receipt of either the full or partial income-tested Guaranteed Income Supplement in 1987.

Women are among the poorest of the elderly and are one of the major victims of current retirement arrangements."Poverty in old age," according to the National Council of Welfare, "is largely a women's problem."[77] Poverty is more common among elderly women than men. In Canada one-quarter of families headed by women over 65 were low income, compared to only one-tenth of those headed by elderly men as of 1982. The economic position of unattached elderly women is particularly difficult: 60 per cent of unattached elderly women were poor as opposed to 49 per cent of single elderly men in 1982. Poverty among elderly women increases with age: nearly two-thirds of all unattached women aged 70 and over—that is, the very old, or frail old, and the widowed—were poor in 1981. The poverty gap between elderly men and women has widened in recent years.

This analysis indicates that a significant proportion of elderly remain poor in Canada. While the incidence of poverty has declined among certain segments of the elderly, a large proportion of *total* elderly persons continue to live on, around or below recognized poverty lines. The conclusion arrived at here is neither new nor startling. The National Council of Welfare, for example, concluded: "An astonishing number of this country's aged are poor," and "most are concentrated on the lower rungs of the income ladder."[78] Another recent study suggested that while the elderly are now the "wealthiest of the poor," the "income statistics clearly show that the economic status of the elderly is below the national average."[79] This suggests that inadequate retirement income is still a barrier to independent living for many seniors, despite the present attempt of the Gerontological Establishment to "package" the elderly as

WOOPIES—well-off older persons, or as the "wellderly." The facts, however, suggest a quite different social reality.

The economic position of the elderly and the extent of poverty among the aged in the United States have received considerable attention.[80] One study concluded that "trends in the economic status of the aged and nonaged over the period 1950–82 indicate numerous fluctuations rather than a consistent improvement in the income of either group in relation to the other."[81] Another study found that in the period between 1967 and 1984, "the relationship between age and median income was altered only slightly. In 1984, aged family units continued to have relatively low median income, especially compared with the incomes of those in middle age."[82]

The conventional wisdom promoted by the liberal gerontological literature in the United States suggests that the proportion of people aged 65 and over living in poverty has declined from 25 per cent in 1970 to 12 per cent in 1986.[83] This compares with 20 to 53 per cent of all the elderly in Canada in 1986 who are poor, depending upon the poverty threshold (Table 2.9). The seemingly impressive difference between the U.S. and Canada is more apparent than real and warrants further examination.

In the United States there are in reality *two* poverty guidelines. What is of importance is the absolute level at which these alternative poverty thresholds are set. The "official" poverty line in the U.S. in 1986 was $5,255 for unattached individuals 65 years and over and $6,630 for elderly couples.[84] Since the 1971 White House Conference on Aging, however,the Bureau of Labor Statistics (BLS) intermediate retired couples budget has been endorsed as the appropriate poverty line standard; for unattached individuals the level is 75 per cent of the couple's budget.[85] Adjusting the BLS intermediate budget for inflation results in a poverty guideline of $13,189 for an aged couple and $9,892 for an elderly unattached individual.[86] Thus, BLS intermediate budget in 1986 was nearly *double* the "official" poverty line in the U.S. Applying the more realistic BLS immediate budget standard to the income distributions of elderly couples and unattached individuals suggests that an estimated 35.6 per cent of all seniors lived in poverty in the United States in 1986. The proportion of elderly persons living in poverty in the United States, based on the BLS intermediate budget, therefore is nearly *three times greater* than indicated by the "official" poverty line.[87]

"The majority of the elderly in Britain," according to Age Concern, "are living below, on, or just over the poverty line."[88] Townsend's exhaustive survey of poverty in Britain in 1968 found that 34 per cent of the elderly were living below the supplementary level and 63 per cent of the aged were below 140 per cent of that standard.[89] The 1975 Family Expenditure Survey (FES) confirmed that in the order of 37 to 78 per cent of the elderly were living in or on the margin of poverty. Recent U.K. Department of Health and Social Security data indicate that 37 per cent of elderly persons still lived below or on the supplementary benefit level in 1983.[90] In addition, it is estimated that another 10 to 50 per cent of pensioners in the U.K. live in households which have an income below the supplementary level because they are not claiming benefits.[91] As Townsend put it, "The problem of poverty in old age is massive and [its] continuing cannot be doubted."[92] Another recent study concluded, "Pensioners are still the largest group in poverty. They are in poverty because the level of [the state flat-rate] pension, together with any earnings-related element . . . is not sufficient to lift them above the poverty level."[93]

The data in Table 2.10 indicate that on average well *over one-third* of the elderly in the advanced capitalist countries of Canada, Britain and the United States currently live in poverty. This is a perpetuation of their general historical position in society as is indicated by Table 2.11.

TABLE 2.10

COMPARISON OF THE PROPORTION OF TOTAL ELDERLY PERSONS LIVING IN POVERTY, U.S., CANADA AND U.K., 1983 AND 1986

COUNTRY	PERCENTAGE OF TOTAL ELDERLY PERSONS LIVING IN POVERTY
U.S.	35.6[1]
Canada	31.6–39.5[2]
U.K.	37.4–46.7[3]

Notes: 1 Based on the BLS intermediate budget for 1986.
2 The lower range figure is Statistics Canada's low-income cut-off for major urban centres in 1986. The upper range figure is the Senate Committee on Poverty's threshold for 1986.
3 The lower range figure is for those below or on the supplementary benefit (SB) level in 1983, while the upper range figure is for 110 per cent of the SB level.

Source: Text notes and tables.

TABLE 2.11

LONGITUDINAL COMPARISON OF THE PERCENTAGE OF ELDERLY LIVING IN POVERTY. U.K., CANADA AND U.S., 1850–1986

COUNTRY	1850s	1890–1910	1920s	1930s	1945–1950	1961	1969	1971	1975	1978	1983	1986
U.K.	—	15–39[1]	—	15[1]	38–70[1]	35[1]	34–63[4]	44	37–78[4]	—	37.4–46.7[5]	—
Canada	30[1]	—	(2)	20[3]	—	54	40	—	—	43	—	31.6–39.5[6]
U.S.	—	35	40–67	—	—	50	—	—	—	61[7]	—	35.6[7]

Notes: 1 Proportion of those living in poverty or designated as poor.
2 According to the Economic Council of Canada the majority of all people were living below the poverty line.
3 Percentage of total population on emergency relief.
4 Lower range figure refers to the proportion of elderly below the 1975 Supplementary Benefit (SB) level; the upper range figure is the percentage of elderly below 140 per cent of the supplementary benefit standard.
5 Total persons living on or below SB level at 110 per cent of the SB.
6 Major urban areas (Statistics Canada III) and Senate Committee poverty line.
7 Total persons living below the BLS intermediate budget.

Sources: See text sources and tables.

The reasons why a significant proportion of the current elderly are poor remain to be determined. An analysis of the composition of the elderly's income by source, outlined in Table 2.12, reveals the structural reasons for this situation. In the advanced industrialized countries of Britain, Canada and the United States, a similar pattern is emerging. In all these countries the state social security system is the primary source of retirement income, accounting for nearly 40 to 60 per cent of all income for the elderly. Of some interest is the fact that in a country such as Canada, the universal flat-rate pension

TABLE 2.12

COMPARISON OF PERCENTAGE COMPOSITION OF INCOME OF THE ELDERLY,[1]
U.K., CANADA AND U.S., 1984–1986

SOURCE OF INCOME	U.K[2]	CANADA[3]	U.S.[4]
State Social Security	59.2	51.9	39.0
Demogrant	[5]	34.4	[6]
Earnings-Related Pension	[5]	13.9	38.0
Other Gov't	3.5	3.6	1.0
Employment Earnings	6.4	9.8	16.0
Investment Income	14.1	21.2	28.0
Employer-Sponsored Pensions, Annuities	20.4	15.7	14.0
Other Income	0.0	1.4	2.0
Total Income	100.0	100.0	100.0
Average Income	$8,384[7]	$13,212	$11,126

Notes: 1 Unattached individuals and couples, total units aged 65 and over.
2 For 1985.
3 For 1986.
4 For 1984.
5 Prior to 1959 the old age pension was a flat-rate demogrant. It was only after that date that an earnings-related component was added. Official figures are not broken out. However, since the earnings-related plan will not reach maturity until the end of the century, most of the benefits generated would have to come from the old-age demogrant.
6 The American OASSI from its inception had a minimum floor benefit, but it was not intended as a demogrant. Since 1972 a new "special" minimum has been added. Only 11 per cent of all beneficiaries received the SSI minimum benefit as of May 1986.
7 Converted into Canadian currency based on the average annual 1985 exchange rate.

Sources: For Britain, calculated from Andrew Dawson and Graham Evans, "Pensioners' Incomes and Expenditures, 1970–85," *Employment Gazette* (May 1987), Table 5, p. 247; for Canada, Statistics Canada, unpublished 1986 Survey of Consumer Finances data; and for the U.S., Department of Health and Human Services, *Income of the Population 55 and Over, 1984* (Washington, D.C.: Government Printing Office, 1985), Table 46, p. 90.

(OAS) accounts for over two-thirds of all state pension benefits. In an earnings-related state pension system such as that in the U.S., the high proportion of income generated is a reflection of the social security system's maturity. The flat-rate Old Age Security pension in Canada, as a demogrant or universal benefit, results in a higher income replacement rate for those in the lower income categories and a lower ratio for those in the higher income groups. An earnings-related state pension system such as the Canada/Quebec Pension Plans or the U.S. social security retirement system yields a progressively higher replacement ratio for those in the upper income groups up to the earnings ceiling and tails off thereafter.

Investment income is now the second most important source of retirement income for the elderly in the U.S. and Canada. This is a result of the diminishing importance of employment earnings as a source of income for the elderly. The high ranking of investment earnings as a source of retirement income is deceptive, however, since what is of importance is the distribution and level of investment income, reflecting the marginal propensity to save based on "life chances." Receipt of investment income is directly related to socio-economic class. Furthermore, the amount of investment earnings accrued by the elderly over their life-cycle is modest: $6,468 in the United States, $4,800 in Canada and $1,180 (£666) in the U.K.[94] More importantly, however, the "average" amount of income from assets obscures the *distribution* of investment earnings among the elderly. In Canada, for example, despite the high level of aggregate savings,[95] 42 per cent of all seniors received *no* investment income whatsoever, and an additional 18 per cent of the elderly received less than $1,000 in investment earnings.[96] Fully *60 per cent of all seniors*, then, received *$1,000 or less* in investment income in 1986.

In the United States, nearly one-half of recent retiree couples and two-thirds of unattached elderly individuals had less than $1,200 a year in investment income as of 1982.[97] The U.S. President's Commission on Pension Policy concluded that "It appears from the available data that 'savings' is not now a strong leg of the three-legged stool of retirement income."[98] Thus, the ideology of individual responsibility for retirement savings is at considerable variance with the social reality. For the great majority of people, investment earnings and savings are an insignificant source of retirement income.

Income generated from occupational pension plans and annuities ranks as the third most common source of retirement income in the U.S. and Canada (and is comparable with earnings from employment in the U.S.) and is the second most common source in the U.K. The private pension system, however, is only responsible for generating 14 to 20 per cent of the elderly's total retirement income. The low proportion of the elderly's retirement income attributable to occupational pension plans is a result of the limitations of the private pension system. In these countries 50 to 60 per cent of the elderly received no income at all from the employer-sponsored occupational pension system.[99] In the mid-1980s, for those fortunate enough to be in receipt of income from an occupational pension plan, the amount of the average benefit was quite low: $5,972 in Canada, $4,280 in the U.S., and $3,014 (£1,612) in Britain.[100]

Table 2.13 identifies those sources of retirement income which differentiate the poor elderly from the non-poor elderly. A number of distinguishing features emerge. In the first instance, the public pension system (OAS/GIS and C/QPP) in Canada is the major source of income for the poor elderly, accounting for over 90 per cent of total

TABLE 2.13

PROPORTION OF INCOME BY SOURCE, POOR AND NON-POOR,[1]
TOTAL ELDERLY AGE 65 AND OVER, CANADA, 1986

SOURCES OF INCOME	TOTAL ELDERLY PERSONS[2]	
	Poor	Non-Poor
Total Public	90.9%	47.1%
OAS/GIS	73.8	29.6
CPP/QPP	11.4	14.2
Other Gov't	5.7	3.3
Total Private	9.0	52.8
Earnings	0.2	10.9
Investment Income	4.8	23.2
Private Pensions and Annuities	3.4	17.2
Other Income	0.6	1.5
Total[3]	100.0	100.0

Notes: 1 Those above and below the Statistics Canada I low-income cut-off (1978 base).
    2 All elderly persons regardless of family status.
    3 May not total 100 due to rounding.

Source: Unpublished Statistics Canada 1986 Survey of Consumer Finances data, cited in Richard Deaton, The Economic Position of the Current Elderly: Retirement Income as a Barrier to Independent Living. A report prepared for the National Advisory Council on Aging (Ottawa: NACA, April 1988), Table 7, p. 26.

income. This situation results from the low proportion of income flowing from the private pension system and the low level of investment earnings accumulated over the poor elderly's working life-time.

Conversely, the economic position of the non-poor aged is characterized by a balance in the mix of income from public and private sources and, in particular, the high proportion of income from occupational pensions and earnings from assets. In short, the poor elderly and middle-income earners are dependent upon the public—that is, the state—pension system.

While some commentators have stated that the traditional purpose of "social security is to fulfil what is in effect a residual function . . . or at the most filling the gaps in the . . . private sector,"[101] the evidence suggests the opposite conclusion. It is the state retirement system which is the primary source of income maintenance for the elderly, with income from the private pension system and individual savings playing a residual role. Given these circumstances, ameliorating the impoverishment of the current and future elderly will require an increased level of public expenditure through an expanded state social security retirement system.

THE CONDITION OF THE ELDERLY: IMPLICATIONS

A number of general implications can be drawn about the condition of the elderly. First, their precarious economic position compounds their isolation and segregation from the broader community as a result of the "culture of aging," where

the elderly have come to live increasingly in a separate world. Changes in housing patterns have acted to weaken ties across the generations. Changes in health standards have concentrated relatively more of the total burden of ill-health on the elderly. The elderly are separate too in their experience of mental as well as physical ill health. There are differences in living standards. . . . Changes in society have accentuated the differences in outlook and aspiration which arise from the natural course of aging.[102]

While a new and positive "culture of aging" emphasizing an independent life-style for the elderly has emerged in recent years, it is premised upon an adequate level of retirement income.

Second, a considerable proportion of old people have "drifted to the very bottom of the financial structure in society."[103] The distribution of income among them, whether in terms of wages, assets or retirement benefits, Talley and Burkhauser concluded, "has a greater variance than any other age group, indicating that differences in relative income position are greatest within the oldest group."[104] Under contemporary capitalism, the situation suggests that

> the most fundamental . . . problems experienced by older people are linked to the maldistribution of power, income, and wealth in society as well as to class, racial, and sexual stratifications that are perpetuated and legitimized through . . . market relations. These are not only reinforced, but exacerbated, during old age.[105]

While the new gerontological "joy literature" invokes Browning's optimistic passage—"Grow old along with me! The best is yet to be"—the current reality for a significant proportion of the elderly in these advanced capitalist societies is more easily captured by the pathos of the Beatles' lament: "Will you still need me, will you still feed me, when I'm 64?"

Third, the state social security system is the primary source of income for the elderly because limited income from occupational pension plans and personal savings play only a residual role, which suggests that the public pension system must be expanded to improve their economic position. In 1986 the minimum guaranteed retirement income floor in Canada from the combined Old Age Security and the Guaranteed Income Supplement was still nearly 20 per cent below the weighted average low-income cut-off for individuals and marginally below that poverty threshold for couples.[106]

However, the elderly's need for economic security may in the future conflict with the interests of the actively employed labour force and the corporate sector. The conflict arises from workers' desire to maintain their current consumption and the corporate sector's drive to reduce labour costs by minimizing expenditures such as those associated with social security contributions. This is elaborated upon in the next chapter. Furthermore, as is argued in Chapter 6, the corporate sector's control over and acquisition of investment capital through the private pension system would be curtailed if the state pension system was expanded.

Fourth, adequate retirement income is a necessary, but not sufficient, condition to improve the quality of life for the elderly. While they have historically been collectively inarticulate, their passivity may be coming to an end because "the aging population, with its increasing political power, will not tolerate indefinitely a life of poverty in retirement."[107] The Gray Panthers in the United States, the One Voice seniors' network in Canada, and various active pensioner organizations in the U.K. attest to their increased political activism.

Fifth, as one recent study concluded, even if the poverty line was raised to maintain the relationship between median incomes and the low-income cut-offs, "incomes would not rise fast enough to cause any substantial decline in the percentage of old people who are considered to be poor."[108] The continued poverty among the elderly is a major concern for public policy because "the number of people over 65 is growing and will continue to grow until well into the next century," creating "the prospect of major increases in the numbers of poverty-stricken old people."[109] Furthermore, if there is no fundamental change in the economic position of the elderly in the future, there will be more poor-aged as a result of the impending demographic transition.

3

The Demographic Transition and the Economics of Population Aging

When examining a given country from the standpoint of political economy, we begin with its population. . . . The sphere of economy with population . . . forms the basis and the object of the whole social process of production.
Karl Marx

Demography is fundamental to understanding the material conditions of a society and has sometimes played a decisive role in economic history. However, it has generally been ignored by contemporary Marxist political economy, despite Marx's concern with the subject.[1] Political economy's circumvention of demography and its implications is peculiar for a tradition which bases itself on a materialist analysis of a concrete situation, but its traditional aversion to the topic can be traced and largely understood as a reaction to the determinism associated with the Malthusian "trap" and its more modern neo-Malthusian variants. Recognizing the critical importance of demography, however, is not the same thing as suggesting that it is mechanically determinant. While demographic projections and trends sometimes have a futuristic quality about them, it remains true, as Sweezy reminds us, that "if population has been important in the past, it will be no less so in the future."[2]

The aging of the population in advanced industrialized societies such as Canada, Britain and the United States will have profound

48

ramifications with respect to the economics of aging, pension arrangements, social policy, politics and cultural attitudes towards the elderly.[3] The importance of population aging, in conjunction with the economic position of the elderly outlined in the previous chapter, is that there will be a new and significantly larger generation of poor elderly in the future unless there is major reform of retirement income arrangements, and the increasing number and proportion of the elderly in society will require an increased level of public expenditure to support them.

There are important macro-economic considerations associated with the aging of the population such as the type of funding and level of contributions necessary to finance the public pension system in the future. And the increased number of elderly will affect the level of taxation required of the actively employed labour force to support elderly dependents and the allocation and mix of social resources devoted to the aged. "If there is one source of welfare spending that is most powerful—a single proximate cause," Wilensky concluded in his exhaustive study of welfare state expenditures,"it is the proportion of old people in the population."[4] The economics of an aging population may also generate an age-based politics—that is, demographic politics—and a shift from the values of a youth-oriented society to those of a "mature" society.

HISTORICAL BACKGROUND: DEMOGRAPHY AND PENSION PROGRAMMING

The demographic transition is a necessary accompaniment of the modernization process (industrialization and urbanization) if society is to generate an economic surplus. The first demographic transition associated with the industrial revolution saw the transition from a high birth/death rate to a low birth/death rate pattern. The long-term trends and fluctuations with respect to the interrelationship between birth (fertility), death (mortality), longevity and net immigration rates determine population growth and age distribution. Declining birth rates combined with increased life expectancy in industrialized countries has meant that there has been a growth in both the number and the proportion of older people in the population. In the future there will be a relative decline in the labour force in relation to the older age cohort as a result of these trends.

The second and impending demographic transition is a matter of magnitude rather than of process. Demographic aging may be defined as

> either the process, that is the increase in the *proportion* of elderly persons, or the results of the process, that is the existence of a large proportion of elderly persons. The threshold of aging, namely the level beyond which a population can be described as old, may be situated at 7 or 8 per cent of inhabitants aged 65 or older.[5]

Since 1950 virtually all Western European countries as well as Canada and the United States have come to exceed this "threshold" and are often referred to as aging societies. Currently in North America and Western Europe, 10 to 15 per cent of the population is age 65 or over.[6] All projections point to increasing proportions and numbers of older persons in the future.

North American demographic patterns have tended in the past to follow European trends with some time lag. After World War II, however, the demographic histories of the two continents markedly diverged.[7] After World War II there was a "baby boom," followed by a "baby bust." While the baby boom in most Western European countries only lasted about five years, in North America it spanned the period from 1945 to 1960 and was accompanied by a *doubling* of the birth rate. The reasons for the difference between North American and European experience as well as for the resumption of the long-term decline in birth rates have been the subject of considerable scholarly speculation and controversy.[8]

The birth of the baby boom generation has had a considerable economic and cultural impact on North America and Western Europe. Some commentators have referred to the baby boom cohort as the "mega-generation," the "big generation" or simply the "tidal wave." Its impact has been critical on the education and health-care systems, labour and housing markets, and student politics as well as on sexual mores and tastes in music, hairstyles and dress.

The aging of the baby boom generation is as important as its birth. As this generation moves through and retires, their robust numbers, combined with increased longevity, will create a bulge in the older population, which will peak in North America between the years 2011 and 2031.

In pre- and early-industrialized societies, support of the elderly was primarily a family or individual responsibility. In advanced

industrialized countries, as a result of complex historical and institutional processes, financial responsibility for the non-working or
dependent elderly generally tends to fall on the state and the
actively employed labour force. The question then arises whether
society or the employed population will be able, or willing, to support the increased number and proportion of the elderly in the
future and provide them with an adequate level of retirement
income. The aging of the population therefore has serious social,
economic and political implications.

These implications were not lost on the architects of the American, British and Canadian social security systems. In the United
States, when the social security system was first being put into
place in 1935, Harry Hopkins, a member of the President's Committee on Economic Security, understood that "there are going to be
twice as many old people thirty years from now" and realized that
the "old age thing is a bad curve."[9] For political reasons the economics of an aging population were ignored, but some fifty years later
the tax-based U.S. social security system is in chronic fiscal difficulties. In Britain, according to Titmuss, "much of the . . . anxiety
about the effects of an 'aging' population can be traced back to the
Beveridge Report."[10] While history has shown that the white paper
upon which Beveridge based his population projections and similar
studies in Canada overstated the situation, it is apparent that the
the concerns were real. Marsh observed in 1943 that because "the
birth rate in Canada is declining steadily, it will not be difficult to see
that the problem of provision for old age will become one of increasing importance in future years."[11]

The implications of an aging society are of no less importance to
current social security programming. The U.S. President's Commission on Pension Policy, for example, pointedly concluded that

> as the population of the country matures severe strains will be
> placed on our already overburdened retirement income sys-
> tem. The inequities and inadequacies of the present retire-
> ment income system will become more critical as more people
> retire and the active work force to support them [relatively]
> shrinks.[12]

Similar policy conclusions have also been advanced for Canada in a
number of studies, and the issue was raised in the recent social
security review in Britain.[13]

DEMOGRAPHIC TRENDS: THE CASE OF CANADA

Throughout the course of this century, the proportion of the aged in Canada is expected to grow at an accelerated rate. In 1981, 9.7 per cent of the Canadian population was over the age of 65. This group will increase to 12 to 15 per cent of the population by the year 2011 when the baby boom generation begins to retire and will rise to nearly 17 to 25 per cent in 2031 when the shift in age composition will peak. These projections are outlined in Table 3.1. The proportion of elderly in the Canadian population over the next fifty years is therefore projected to increase by nearly 80 to 180 per cent.

While some commentators have suggested that population trends in Canada only lag behind those of Western Europe by twenty years,[14] it is interesting to note that in Sweden, viewed as the prototype of an aging society by some demographers, the proportion of the elderly in the population peaked at 16 per cent. This figure compares with mid-range projections for Canada of 20 to 24 per cent of the population being over the age of 65 in 2031. More recent Statistics Canada projections suggest, however, that in the order of 24 to 26 per cent of the population will be 65 or over by 2031, based on medium and low fertility rate assumptions respectively.[15] This change is reflected in the rising median age, which will increase from nearly 30 years in 1981 to 42 years in 2031, when the baby boom peaks. In this regard the Economic Council of Canada noted that "by the second decade of the coming century this country will experience the same high levels of aging as now exist in Europe; by 2031 it will surpass them."[16]

Within the aging population two trends are of particular interest.[17] In the first instance an increasing proportion of the elderly will be women as a result of their longer life expectancy. A striking feature of an aging population is the increasing numerical imbalance between males and females, particularly among the very old. In 1981 women represented 57 per cent of the aged; by the year 2001 they will account for over 60 per cent and will significantly increase their proportion thereafter. A second trend is the aging of the older population itself. The growth in numbers of those aged 75 and over will be even more dramatic than that of those 65 and over. The "very old" or "frail" elderly, as they are sometimes called, are one of the fastest growing age groups within the age 65-and-over cohort. Those 75 and older will increase from 37 per cent of the aged population in 1981 to a projected 50 to 55 per cent by 2041. By the year

TABLE 3.1

COMPARISON OF POPULATION PROJECTIONS,
PERCENTAGE OF POPULATION AGE 65 AND OVER,
CANADA, 1981–2051

YEAR	STATISTICS CANADA[1]		ECONOMIC COUNCIL OF CANADA[2]				ROMANIUC[3]				FOOT[4]
	P-I	P-III	P-01	P-05	P-06	P-10	P-I	P-II	P-V	PVI	
1981	9.4	9.4	9.4	9.5	9.5	9.6	9.4	9.3	9.3	9.2	9.7
1991	10.7	11.0	10.7	11.3	11.0	11.6	11.3	10.9	11.1	10.7	11.4
2001	11.2	11.9	11.5	12.7	12.0	13.2	13.1	12.4	12.7	12.1	12.3
2011	11.8	12.9	12.4	14.4	13.1	15.2	14.9	13.9	14.5	13.5	13.5
2021	13.6	16.4	15.4	19.1	16.2	20.0	19.2	17.4	18.6	17.0	16.6
2031	16.9	20.2	18.3	24.2	19.2	25.3	23.5	20.8	22.7	20.2	20.9
2041	n.a.	n.a.	17.5	25.2	18.6	26.6	23.3	20.3	22.6	19.8	20.8
2051	n.a.	n.a.	17.6	25.2	18.7	26.7	23.3	20.6	22.6	20.1	20.7

Notes: 1 Demographic assumptions as follows: P-I constant mortality, increase in fertility net replacement level of 2.1, high migration of 100,000 per year; P-III constant mortality, decline in fertility to 1.7, medium migration of 75,000 per year.

2 Demographic assumptions as follows:

P-01 Medium mortality, fertility, immigration

P-05 Medium mortality, low fertility, medium immigration

P-06 Low mortality, medium fertility, medium immigration

P-10 Low mortality, low fertility, medium immigration

3 Demographic assumptions as follows:

P-I   Mortality increasing to 76.7 years for males and 84.5 for females by 2000. Low fertility of 1.9, low migration of 60,000 per year.

P-II   Same mortality as in P-I, net replacement level of 2.13, low migration of 60,000 per year.

P-V   Same mortality as in P-I, low fertility of 1.9, high migration of 100,000 per year.

PVI   Same mortality as in P-I, net replacement level of 2.13, high migration of 100,000 per year.

4 Assumptions based on no change from current demographic trends.

Sources: Statistics Canada, *Population Projections for Canada and the Provinces, 1976–2000* (Ottawa: Minister of Trade, Industry and Commerce, February 1979), pp. 29, 121, 131, 215, 255, 466, and 468; Frank T. Denton, Christine H. Feaver, and Byron G. Spencer, *The Future Population and Labour Force of Canada: Projections to the Year 2051. A study prepared for the Economic Council of Canada* (Hull: Supply and Services Canada, 1980), p. 29 and Table 5–4, p. 32; A. Romaniuc, "Potentials for Population Growth in Canada," *A Population Policy for Canada?*, The Conservation Council of Ontario and The Family Planning Federation of Canada (Toronto: CCO and FPF, 1974), Table II, p. 15; and David K. Foot, *Canada's Population Outlook: Demographic Futures and Economic Challenges* (Ottawa: Canadian Institute for Economic Policy, 1982), Table 3–9, p. 106 and assumptions in Table 3–1, p. 86.

2001, women will account for two-thirds of those in this group. Similar patterns are emerging in the United States and Britain.

Demographers and economists divide the population for analytic purposes into dependent and non-dependent categories of people. The total dependent category is defined as youth (or young) dependents plus elderly (or aged) dependents. One of the characteristics associated with an aging population is the decreasing proportion of young and the increasing proportion of elderly. It is the compositional shift *within* the total dependent category, that is, between young and old dependents, and the costs associated with each that are crucial in terms of public expenditures on and income security programming for the elderly.

TABLE 3.2

HISTORICAL AND PROJECTED TOTAL, YOUTH AND ELDERLY DEPENDENT CATEGORIES AS A PERCENTAGE OF POPULATION, CANADA, 1901–2051

CENSUS YEAR	(1) YOUTH DEPENDENTS[2]	(2) ELDERLY DEPENDENTS[3]	(1 + 2) TOTAL DEPENDENT CATEGORY[4]
Historical			
1901	34.4	5.0	39.4
1911	32.9	4.7	37.6
1921	34.4	4.8	39.2
1931	31.6	5.6	37.2
1941	27.8	6.7	34.5
1951	30.3	7.8	38.1
1961	33.9	7.6	41.5
1971	29.6	8.1	37.7
1981	22.5	9.7	32.2
Projected[1]			
1991	21.4	11.4	32.8
2001	19.4	12.3	31.7
2011	17.4	13.5	30.9
2021	17.2	16.6	33.8
2031	16.4	20.9	37.2
2041	16.2	20.8	36.9
2051	16.4	20.7	37.1

Notes: 1 Based on no change from current demographic trends.
        2 Defined as those under 14 years of age.
        3 Defined as those over the age of 65.
        4 Those aged 0 to 14 plus those 65 and over divided by total population.

Source: David K. Foot, *Canada's Population Outlook: Demographic Futures and Economic Challenges* (Ottawa: Canadian Institute for Economic Policy, 1982), Table 1–2, p. 9, Table 3–9, p. 106, Table 4–1, p. 129.

The historical and projected trends with respect to the total youth and elderly dependent categories is presented in Table 3.2. A series of key trends become evident. The long-term total dependency category as a proportion of the population remained within a relatively stable range during the twentieth century until 1971. Historically, there has been a secular decline in the proportion of the young and a long-term increase in the percentage of the elderly, which has resulted in a fairly stable total dependency ratio. Until now, in other words, the increasing proportion of elderly in the population has generally been offset by the decreasing proportion of young.

Beginning in the early 1980s a number of significant trends reverse themselves with far-reaching consequences. Between 1981 and 2011 the decline in the proportion of young is greater than the increase in the proportion of elderly. This is reflected in the decline of the total dependency category as a result of the baby boom having swelled the size of the working-age population. After 2011, however, the total dependent category begins to increase. This reflects the greater increase in the number and proportion of elderly relative to the decline in the proportion of youth dependents because of continued low birth rates. Between 1981 and 2031, youth dependents will decline by 6.1 percentage points, whereas elderly dependents will increase by 11.2. The total numerical dependency proportion will therefore increase by some 5.0 percentage points, reflecting the compositional shift in the non-working (or dependent) population.

The relevant consideration with respect to demographic trends as they affect the economics and political demography of an aging population is the number of non-earners or dependents in the population who must be supported by the active labour force. Table 3.3 outlines the pension ratio and the inverse pension ratio. These proxies indicate, in somewhat different ways, the relationship between the increasing proportion of elderly and relatively declining labour force. The pension ratio is the elderly category as a percentage of the labour force; the inverse pension ratio is the number of labour force members per elderly person. From 1981 to 2031, the elderly as a proportion of the active labour force dramatically increases from 14.3 to 33.2 per cent. Thus the elderly category more than doubles in size in relation to the labour force supporting it. The significance of the increasing proportion of elderly in Canadian society is further illustrated by the fact that there are presently seven employed persons for each retired person; by the year 2031 there will be only three workers for each elderly dependent.

TABLE 3.3

HISTORICAL AND PROJECTED PENSION RATIO
AND INVERSE RATIO, CANADA, 1901–2051

CENSUS YEAR	PENSION RATIO[1]	INVERSE PENSION RATIO[2]
Historical		
1901	8.3	12.0
1911	7.5	13.4
1921	7.9	12.7
1931	8.8	11.3
1941	10.2	9.8
1951	12.5	8.0
1961	13.1	7.7
1971	13.0	7.7
1981	14.3	7.0
Projected		
1991	17.0	5.9
2001	18.1	5.5
2011	19.5	5.1
2021	25.9	3.9
2031	33.2	3.0
2041	32.9	3.0
2051	32.9	3.0

Notes: 1 Number of persons aged 65 years and over divided by the number of persons aged 15 to 64 years.
   2 Inverse of pension ratio, indicating the ratio of labour force members per elderly dependent.

Source: David K. Foot, *Canada's Population Outlook: Demographic Futures and Economic Challenges* (Ottawa: Canadian Institute for Economic Policy, 1982), Table 7–1, p. 219, Projection 1, current trends.

There will be an increasing "burden" on the employed population because

the relatively larger proportion of the elderly will lead to an increase in public expenditures, and hence to [an] . . . increased tax burden on . . . the reduced portion of those of working age.

This increasing tax burden on those of working age, especially in an aging population, is also predicted [because] . . . in general, this group bears the greatest share of the costs of and receives the least share of the benefits from public service.[18]

From a social policy perspective, it has been suggested that resources must be transferred from the young to the elderly if the increasing needs of the aged are to be met without increasing the tax burden on the employed.[19] Whether such a transfer can in fact be achieved is highly problematic because of the rigidity of the capitalist state's budget[20] and the resistance of vested interest groups to the reallocation of budgetary resources. This suggests that there will be "a substantial increase in the tax burden on the working population in the future."[21] These intergenerational and sectoral transfers are all the more politically volatile under a tax-based state social security system and during periods of stagflation and slow economic growth.

Higher direct taxation or payroll tax deductions (contributions) to finance the tax-based state pension system to support the elderly reduces the current consumption of the actively employed labour force and increases labour costs for the corporate sector. Therefore, the economic needs of the increasing proportion of elderly will conflict with the desire of the active labour force to preserve its standard of living and the cost minimization behaviour of the corporate sector. These opposing economic interests may generate increased tension and conflict in the future.

COMPARATIVE TRENDS: CANADA, U.S. AND BRITAIN

Many of the problems associated with population aging in advanced industrialized countries are similar. The following analysis briefly compares and contrasts the demographic trends which will affect the operation of the pension system in Canada, Britain and the United States.

Historically, North America has had a young age structure, while Western European countries have exhibited old population pyramids. Currently, Western Europe is in a stable state with 10 to 12 per cent of the population over the age of 65. This trend is expected to continue until roughly 1990 when the median age of the population will gradually begin to increase until 16 to 18 per cent of the population is over the age of 65.[22] In North America, in the early 1980s, 9 to 11 per cent of the population is elderly. This is rapidly and continuously increasing. By the year 2030, 20 to 25 per cent of all people will be over the age of 65 in North America.

TABLE 3.4

COMPARISON OF THE PERCENTAGE OF POPULATION OVER RETIREMENT AGE,[1]
CANADA, U.S. AND U.K., 1980–2041

YEAR	CANADA			United States[5]	U.K.[6]
	Statistics Canada[2]	ECC[3]	Foot[4]		
1980–81	9.7	9.5[7]	9.7[8]	11.3	17.5
1990–91	11.9	11.3	11.4	12.8	17.5
2000–01	13.9	12.7	12.3	13.1	16.4
2010–11	16.0	14.4	13.5	14.0	17.2[9] (18.6[10])
2020–21	20.9	19.1	16.6	17.9	n.a.
2030–31	26.6	24.2	20.9	22.6	n.a.
2040–41	n.a.	25.2	20.8	23.6	n.a.

Notes:
1 Retirement age is 65 in Canada and the U.S. In Britain, age 65 for males and 60 for females.
2 Statistics Canada Projection I, low fertility, current migration, based on 1983 data.
3 Economic Council of Canada, Projection 5, low fertility, medium immigration.
4 Projection 1, constraint current fertility.
5 U.S. Bureau of Census, Series III, low fertility, based on 1980 data.
6 Office of Population Censuses and Surveys, 1978 variant.
7 Series projected on basis of 1976 data.
8 Projected on basis of 1979 data.
9 Principal, or medium, fertility assumption.
10 Low fertility assumption.

Sources: For Canada, Statistics Canada, *Population Projections for Canada, Provinces and Territories, 1984 to 2006* (Ottawa: Minister of Supply and Services, 1985), Projection I, p. 338; Frank L. Denton, Christine H. Feaver, and Byron G. Spencer, *The Future Population and Labour Force of Canada: Projections to the Year 2051*, a study prepared for the Economic Council of Canada (Hull: Supply and Services Canada, 1980); and David K. Foot, *Canada's Population Outlook: Demographic Futures and Economic Challenges* (Ottawa: Canadian Institute for Economic Policy, 1982). For the U.S., U.S. Bureau of the Census, *Current Population Reports*, Series III. The data for the U.K. was calculated from the Central Statistical Organization, *Social Trends 10. 1980 Edition* (London: HMSO, 1980), Table 1.2, p. 64 and Table 1.8, p. 68.

Table 3.4 reports the proportion of the population in Canada, Britain and the U.S. over retirement age between 1980 and 2041. The demographic trends in Canada and the United States are substantially similar, while those in Britain diverge from this pattern.

Over the next 50 years in the United States and Canada those age 65 and over are projected to be well in excess of 20 per cent of the population. Based on current demographic trends, Canada is expected to have a somewhat larger elderly population than the U.S. in the future. Differences in demographic history account for these variations. Canadian fertility and birth rates have been higher than in the U.S., only converging in the late 1960s. After World War II both countries experienced a similar jump in fertility rates that peaked in the late 1950s. At the height of the baby boom, the Canadian fertility rate was 3.9, while that in the U.S. was 3.8. However, in the 1950s the number of births rose more sharply in Canada, where in the mid-1950s there were 28 births per 1,000, compared with a high of 25 in the United States.[23] Since that time the fertility rate has dropped dramatically in both countries.

Historically the marginally greater proportion of elderly in the United States in comparison with Canada, despite a higher birth and lower death rate in the latter, is attributable to the higher rate of immigration in Canada and the somewhat lower fertility rate assumption used for the U.S. in these projections.[24] This has resulted in a higher net rate of population increase in Canada, marginally reducing the proportion of elderly in the population. This may change in the future, however, if immigration begins to moderate.

In Britain nearly 18 per cent of the population was over retirement age in 1980. Britain therefore already has an elderly population which is 55 to 80 per cent greater than in Canada and the U.S. respectively. This large elderly cohort in Britain was the result of the large increase in births around 1920. Unlike Canada and the United States, which experienced one long period of high birth rates between 1945 and 1960, Britain in fact has gone through two distinct high birth rate periods: 1941 to 1947 and 1955 to 1964.[25] This discontinuity will be correspondingly mirrored by the number of elderly dependents some sixty-five years in the future. Those in the mini-baby boom (1941–1947) will represent nearly 17 to 19 per cent of the total population in the first decade of the next century. The first wave of the second, and larger, British baby boom will retire around 2000 and will probably represent an even larger proportion of the population, depending on the demographic assumptions used.[26]

There are a number of characteristics differentiating North American and British population structures in the short and long term. While Britain already has a higher proportion of elderly than Canada or the United States, in the long term the proportion of elderly in all of these countries will be roughly similar. Moreover, there is an important difference in the *rate of increase* in the number and proportion of elderly in these countries. The proportion of elderly in the U.K. has levelled off and will only incrementally increase by 6 per cent over the next thirty years (using the low fertility assumption), while in North America it will increase by nearly 25 to 65 per cent over the same time period. During the next fifty years, however, the population aged 65 and over will increase by nearly 100 to 175 per cent in the U.S. and Canada respectively based on recent projections. Also, at the peak of the demographic transition between 2020 and 2040 when the baby boom generation retires, the elderly population in Canada and the United States will probably exceed that of Britain, with the demographic pressures being the most pronounced in Canada.

The critical demographic future for Britain after 2010 is not known with any certainty. The U.K. statistical services have been reluctant to project that far. The second baby boom (1955–1964) is already in the labour force; however, the number of future workers to support it can only be tentatively projected because of the uncertainty surrounding the important, and sensitive, fertility rate assumption used in these forecasts. On the basis of the medium assumption used by the U.K. Office of Population Censuses and Survey's, a "baby boomlet" is forecast between 1980 and 2000. Since 1963 fertility rates in Britain have dropped precipitously as they have in all other industrialized countries;[27] the low fertility assumption, therefore, may be more realistic.

Table 3.5 presents two sets of data for Canada, Britain and the United States: the elderly as a proportion of the actively employed labour force (pension ratio) and the inverse pension ratio (labour force to elderly). In the United States and Canada the elderly as a proportion of the labour force continuously rises over the next half century peaking in 2030 at 33.2 per cent in Canada and 39 per cent in 2040 for the U.S. The trends in Britain are somewhat more moderate. Based on the more realistic low fertility projection, however, the elderly will be in the order of 30 per cent of the labour force.

TABLE 3.5

COMPARISON OF PENSION[1] AND INVERSE PENSION RATIOS,[2] CANADA, U.S. AND U.K., 1980–2041

YEAR	CANADA		UNITED STATES		U.K.	
	Pension Ratio	Inverse Ratio	Pension Ratio	Inverse Ratio	Pension Ratio	Inverse Ratio
1980–81	14.3	7.0	18.4	5.4	29.2	3.4
1990–91	17.0	5.9	20.0	5.0	29.2	3.4
2000–01	18.1	5.5	20.2	4.9	27.5[3](27.9[4])	3.6[3](3.6[4])
2010–11	19.5	5.1	21.2	4.7	27.9[3](29.6[4])	3.6[3](3.4[4])
2020–21	25.9	3.9	28.6	3.5	n.a.	n.a.
2030–31	33.2	3.0	37.6	2.7	n.a.	n.a.
2040–41	32.9	3.0	39.0	2.6	n.a.	n.a.

Notes: 1 Elderly dependents as a percentage of labour force. In Canada and the U.S. those over age 65; in Britain males over 65 and females over 60.
    2 Inverse of pension ratio.
    3 Principal, or medium, fertility assumption.
    4 Low fertility assumption.

Sources: David K. Foot, *Canada's Population Outlook: Demographic Futures and Economic Challenges* (Ottawa: Canadian Institute for Economic Policy, 1982), Table 7. 1, p. 219; for the U.S., Bureau of Census, *Current Population Reports*, Series P-25, No. 704, Series III, July 1977. Data for the U.K. was calculated from the Central Statistical Organization, *Social Trends 10, 1980 Edition* (London: HMSO, 1980), Table 1.2, p. 64 and Table 1.8, p. 68.

This roughly corresponds to the pension ratio around 1990, which had been affected by the earlier high 1920 birth rate and subsequent low fertility during the depression years. However, if low fertility is projected into the future, it may be expected that the proportion of the elderly in the total U.K. population, and the elderly in relation to the labour force, will increase after 2010 and will more nearly resemble the anticipated North American trends. This analysis suggests that demographic pressures will be relatively more acute in the U.S. and Canada and more moderate in the U.K.

While the general trend towards an aging society is evidenced in all these countries and will generate similar pressures, the specific forms of political resistance to supporting an increasingly aged population may be different in each case. This does not nullify, however, the general proposition that the economic interests of the elderly are at variance with those of the active labour force and business sector.

This situation is largely a consequence of the differences in the level of current contributions required to support the state social security retirement system in these countries. In Britain and the United States the state pension system is tax-based (payroll deductions), referred to technically as pay-as-you-go (PAYGO) financing, where each generation pays for the cohort which precedes it. The Canada Pension Plan (CPP) is on a PAYGO basis, while the Quebec Pension Plan (QPP) is partially funded. Pension systems based on PAYGO are highly sensitive to demographic changes; as the proportion of elderly increases, the level of contributions required to pay retirement benefits goes up. Therefore, intergenerational tensions and political resistance to increasing public expenditures and social security contributions to support the elderly might be greater in the United States and Canada, where there is a more dramatic *rate of increase* in the proportion of the elderly.

In the United States total contributions to the social security retirement system are 15.02 per cent (shared between the employee and employer) of eligible earnings in 1988. Further substantial increases will be necessary in the future to accommodate the aging population. The existence of the well publicized "cut-back" mentality, exemplified by California's "Proposition 13," and the periodically threatened reduction in social security benefits suggest that the upper limit of political tolerance may have already been reached.

The political dynamic in Britain may be expected to be compa-

rable to that in the U.S. Despite the fact that Britain's elderly dependent category is relatively stable, total contributions to National
Insurance for retirement benefits are 13.5 per cent of income to the
upper earnings limit (the 16 per cent contribution figure frequently
cited includes other benefits such as maternity and redundancy
payments). According to a study by the Organization for Economic
Co-operation and Development (OECD), the level of taxation in Britain is one of the highest in Western Europe.[28] In 1980 for a one-
earner family at the average production worker's salary level,
Britain ranked fourth of all Western European countries in terms of
income tax paid as a percentage of gross earnings; but it ranked
tenth out of sixteen OECD countries with respect to disposable
income as a percentage of gross earnings. Increasing the level of
public expenditures to provide an adequate retirement income on
behalf of the elderly would therefore require even higher levels of
direct taxation or payroll tax deductions than presently exist. "One
implication of the increasing ratio of elderly to . . . [those] working,"
Wroe noted, "is that if the standard of living of the elderly is growing
in line with earnings, an increasing proportion of each [active] worker's earnings is required to support them."[29] Britain may already be
at the upper limit of political tolerance and social resources, as
evidenced by the fact that the method of indexation for state retirement benefits has been adjusted from the higher earnings index to
the lower price index; in addition, the benefit formula under the
state earnings-related pension has recently been reduced.

In Canada political resistance to supporting an aging population
is likely to grow over the long term, but for quite different reasons.
Total contributions to the earnings-related Canada/Quebec Pension
Plans (C/QPP) are currently 4 per cent (shared between the
employee and the employer) as of 1988. *This is the lowest contribution level to a social security retirement system in any major
industrialized country.* In order to maintain *current* benefit levels,
the contribution rate will have to be increased to a minimum 7.6 per
cent by the year 2011. Additional contribution increases will be
required when the baby boom generation begins to retire after that
date. To double the income replacement rate to bring it up to comparable international standards would require an increase in total
contributions from 4 to an estimated 16 per cent. Unlike the U.S.
and Britain, where resistance to further social security contribution
increases may exist because contribution levels are already high, in
Canada there may be political resistance because they presently are

low and will require a series of continuous increases in the foreseeable future. Any increase from a low to a high level of state pension contributions represents a reduction in the standard of living for the active labour force and an increase in the corporate sector's labour costs. As a result of a massive government deficit, the Liberal government's June 1982 Budget limited the indexation of the tax-based Old Age Security pension to 6 per cent, half of the increase in the cost of living at that time. Subsequently, the Conservative government also attempted to limit the indexation of the OAS pension in 1985. The political manoeuvring is a further indication of the volatility of the trade-off between the economic needs of the elderly (expenditures) and an increased level of taxation (revenue) on the work force.

While the underlying dynamic in each of these national cases is somewhat different, the problems associated with the aging of the population are basically the same. Pensions policy and politics will be affected by the change in age composition and the cost of an aging population.

THE COST OF AN AGING POPULATION

An important factor in pensions policy and social policy towards the elderly is the cost associated with an aging population. It has been suggested by some that the dramatic increase in elderly dependents is of no major consequence since it will be offset by a declining youth dependency ratio, resulting in no significant net increase in total public expenditures. This conclusion has been put forward in various analyses, including the Croll Special Senate Committee on Retirement Age Policies. It argued that "despite certain pessimistic predictions that have been made about the projected aging of the Canadian population, the outlook for the future can be considered bright" because "the cost of supporting a growing older population should be offset by the savings from the reduced expenditures on a declining young dependent population."[30]

Such an optimistic conclusion is based on an incomplete analysis and a series of unwarranted technical and political assumptions. The questionable assumptions are the following: equating the absolute numerical dependency ratio with an expenditure dependency index, an implicit assumption that the costs associated with supporting an elderly dependent population are the same as for a young dependent, and a hidden technical assumption that public expenditure on young and elderly dependents is held constant in the future.

An analysis based solely on absolute numerical dependency ratios, as outlined in Table 3.2 above, is of limited value because it ignores the implications of the higher relative per capita cost, such as state retirement benefits and health care, of maintaining an elderly dependent associated with the increasing proportion of older people in the population. To gauge fully the economic implications of an aging society requires that the level of public expenditures associated with each dependent category (youth and elderly) be established since the future costs of these programmes can be anticipated to reflect their numbers in the population. Based on U.S. and Canadian studies it has been established that the per capita public expenditure for an elderly dependent is 2.5 to 3 times greater than for a young dependent; the available evidence for Britain suggests a similar conclusion.[31]

The future cost of each dependent category can be related to its changing proportion in the population by constructing what Foot has called an Expenditure Dependency Index.[32] This is a weighted dependency ratio where the weights reflect the per capita public expenditures of servicing the youth and elderly dependent categories. Table 3.6 reports the change in the total Expenditure Dependency Index, *with benefits held constant*, based on the increase in the proportion of the elderly in the population. Between 1981 and 2031, the Expenditure Dependency Index rises, depending on the assumption used, 49 to 65 per cent. What is most significant in terms of economic impact and social policy is that these total dependency expenditure levels are the highest recorded in modern times.

In assessing the implications of an aging society at the demographic peak in 2031, the Economic Council of Canada estimated that the cost of public expenditures on retirement income programmes alone will increase from the current 4 per cent of GNP to 12 to 17 per cent, depending on benefit levels and demographic assumptions.[33] "Since support costs are much greater for the old than the young," the ECC report notes, "total dependency costs are likely to continue to increase; they may even accelerate."[34]

The claim that the rising cost associated with an increasing proportion of the elderly in the population will be offset by the declining proportion of young dependents is also highly questionable because of a critical and usually unidentified underlying assumption in this formulation. The Expenditure Dependency Index analysis is based

TABLE 3.6

HISTORICAL AND PROJECTED EXPENDITURE DEPENDENCY RATIO,[1]
CANADA, 1901–2051

CENSUS YEAR	EXPENDITURE DEPENDENCY INDEX[2] (1979 = 1.0)	
	W = 2	W = 3
Historical		
1901	1.17	1.07
1911	1.08	0.98
1921	1.15	1.05
1931	1.08	1.00
1941	1.00	0.95
1951	1.18	1.13
1961	1.34	1.27
1971	1.17	1.13
1981	0.98	0.99
Projected[3]		
1991	1.05	1.08
2001	1.03	1.08
2011	1.02	1.09
2021	1.24	1.35
2031	1.47	1.64
2041	1.46	1.62
2051	1.46	1.63

Notes: 1 This is a weighted dependency ratio, where the weights reflect the relative costs of servicing the different age groups in the population.

2 W denotes the relative cost of servicing the elderly (those 65 and over) compared to the young (ages 0 to 17). Thus W = 2 denotes that the per capita cost for an elderly dependent is twice that of a young dependent and where W = 3 the cost of an elderly person is three times that of a young dependent. The estimate for W2 is based on a Canadian study by Linda McDonald, "Changing Population and the Impact on Government Age-Specific Expenditures," an unpublished study prepared for the Federal Treasury Board Secretariat, Ottawa, 1977. The value for W3 is based on an American study by R. Clark and J. Spengler, "Changing Demography and Dependency Costs: The Implications of New Dependency Ratios and Their Composition," Aging and Income: Programs and Prospects for the Elderly, ed. Barbara Herzog (New York: Human Science Press, 1978), pp. 55–89. It must be emphasized that W is held constant throughout the projection horizon. This means that expenditures are assumed to be held constant both retrospectively and in terms of future cost projections. This analysis also assumes that current institutional arrangements and their associated costs have been in place throughout Canadian history. This has the effect of inflating the historical Expenditure Dependency Index by imputing post facto costs to it. A higher base figure has the effect of arithmetically reducing or diminishing the rate of increase in the index over time. Furthermore, expenditures over time may not be fully comparable because the analysis

ignores the transition from an agrarian to an industrial economy. Comparisons of the Expenditure Dependency Index between different historical periods, with their varying institutional arrangements and costs, must therefore be viewed with considerable caution.

3   Based on a no change scenario with respect to fertility and mortality assumptions.

Source: David K. Foot, *Canada's Population Outlook: Demographic Futures and Economic Challenges* (Ottawa: Canadian Institute for Economic Policy, 1982), Tables 4–4 and 4–5, pp. 138–39, and pp. 136–37.

on the static *ceteris paribus* assumption that per capita public expenditures on young and old dependents are *constant* in the future in terms of their impact on cost projections.[35] This is an unrealistic assumption. In the first instance it is at variance with the economic needs of the elderly as established in Chapter 2. Second, in a fluid policy environment where it is anticipated, for example, that retirement income payments from the state pension system will increase, this static assumption underestimates the public expenditures associated with an aging population in the future.

Some rough orders of magnitude, based on existent empirical research, have established cost estimates associated with a rising elderly dependent category. For example, to improve the benefit formula under the Canada/Quebec Pension Plans, from the present 25 to 40 per cent of the average industrial wage, would result in an estimated 125 per cent increase in pension costs as a percentage of total output.[36] Hospital expenditures, as estimated by Statistics Canada, could rise by as much as 109 per cent (in constant dollars) by the year 2031, primarily as a result of the increasing number of older people.[37] In Britain the average cost of care and treatment of an elderly person currently is seven times that of a person of working age.[38] In the U.S., the Senate Special Committee on Aging estimated that the elderly's share of the federal budget will increase from 26 per cent in 1981 to 63 per cent by 2025.[39] The point is that the "constant expenditure" assumption incorporated into the Expenditure Dependency Index analysis, reflecting the compositional change in the total dependency ratio, is unrealistic. The weight of evidence suggests that the costs associated with an aging population will probably be considerably greater than anticipated. The cost of an aging population will accordingly have an impact on social policy and politics.

THE DEMOGRAPHICS OF POLITICS AND THE POLITICS OF AGING

The politics of aging will be a concomitant of the demographic transition. Age-based politics are likely to take at least two forms: first, a profound difference in intergenerational expectations; and, second, the political mobilization of the elderly into age-based organizations. This political dimension will have long-term implications for pensions and aging policy.

A series of comprehensive surveys in Canada, Britain and the United States between 1974 and 1986 have established that the current and future elderly have fundamentally different attitudes and expectations with respect to retirement income adequacy, pension arrangements, and the willingness to pay for improved benefits.[40] These different expectations may generate their own set of social tensions and political problems in the future, especially as they affect the large baby boom cohort.

A number of important intergenerational differences emerge. Significantly, 60 per cent of the elderly in the U.S. and 40 to 85 per cent of the aged in Canada perceive their current economic situation as *adequate*,[41] despite the reported incidence of poverty among the current elderly. However, recent survey information indicates that the elderly now rank the lack of money as their second most "serious problem."[42] Nearly 75 per cent of the baby boom generation, however, view the elderly's current level of retirement income as *inadequate* and have considerably greater expectations about what does constitute an "adequate" level.[43] This divergence of views is readily explained in terms of the different life-cycle experience of each age cohort. The current elderly, it can be argued, have internalized the trauma of the depression years and World War II and are marked by an "invisible scar"[44] that has served to diminish or limit their expectations, whereas the future elderly have had their expectations inflated by a generally buoyant and prosperous postwar economy.

This sharp intergenerational difference with respect to retirement income expectations is also reflected by the fact that more than 80 per cent of the baby boom generation in Canada and the U.S. expect to maintain their pre-retirement standard of living,[45] contrary to the reality experienced by the current elderly. In Canada 45 per cent of the baby boom cohort expect a total income replacement rate on retirement of 50 to 80 per cent; in Britain 60 per cent want a replacement rate of 75 per cent or more.[46] Furthermore, nearly 70 per cent of the baby boom generation in the U.S. and 50 per cent in Canada expect to receive income from the private pension system.[47] This hope is at variance with reality, which suggests that no more than 40 per cent of the elderly in those countries will receive retirement income from this source. It also ignores dependence on the state pension system as the primary source of retirement income. Over 90 per cent of the baby boom generation, however, are of the view that an "adequate" retirement income should be "guaranteed" as a right.

If the baby boom generation has considerably higher expectations of retirement income adequacy than does the current generation of elderly, are they willing to pay the necessary level of taxes or pension contributions? And are the younger generation who will have to support them prepared to accept this "dependency burden"? Apparently not. According to American survey data, only 48 per cent of those between age 18 and 39 are currently prepared to raise social security taxes.[48] In Britain, 53 per cent of people between age 16 and 34 are prepared to pay additional pension contributions, but only by 25 to 74p per week.[49] Survey data in Canada indicate that only 49 per cent of all people, 51 per cent of the baby boom cohort and 46 per cent of blue-collar workers are willing to pay increased contributions to the state pension plan. And only 30 per cent of these are prepared to pay as much as an additional 2 per cent towards the current low level of C/QPP contributions.[50] This information suggests that while the baby boom generation has "great expectations," they have a limited willingness to pay for them.

With respect to the generation aged 16 to 24—that is, those who will be required to support the baby boom cohort—recent Canadian surveys found them characterized by "defeated hopes," "security consciousness," and "social conservatism."[51] More than 80 per cent of this age group are of the view that people should rely more on "individual initiative" than on government and nearly 85 per cent agreed that the current budget deficit is "unfair."[52] Thus, the "dependency burden" associated with an aging population is at variance with their "security consciousness" and "individualism" because it would result in a reduction of their current consumption.

This difference in intergenerational expectations and attitudes and the ability of the pension system to satisfy those expectations may well be the "long fuse" to the "population bomb." The unwillingness of the future elderly and young to pay increased social security contributions may frustrate the baby boom generation's aspirations and create a new and larger generation of poor-old dependent on government tax-based "safety net" programmes.

The second manifestation of the politics of aging may witness the political mobilization of the elderly into age-based organizations.[53] From an historical perspective the political behaviour of the elderly may be understood in terms of Simmel's theory of conflict which postulates that suppression of conflict results in either apathy and withdrawal or alternative forms of strife will exhibit themselves.[54] The historical passivity of the elderly suggests the former mode of accommodation. But the rise of age-homogeneous groups and politics in recent years may be viewed as a response to the increasingly unstable structural position which the elderly experience in terms of their role, status and economic positions in advanced capitalist societies.[55]

In the United States, England and Canada between 1900 and 1930 there was only sporadic and unsustained activity by retired groups.[56] Political activity by the elderly to advance their own interests did not surface in any serious way until the 1930s. In the United States during the Depression two grass roots movements of the elderly appeared: Upton Sinclair's EPIC (End Poverty in California) programme and the Townsend Movement advocating that all people over age 60 receive a monthly pension of $200.[57] With Townsend claiming five million supporters and at least sixty sympathetic congressmen in 1935, "to defuse such public clamor, the federal government clearly had to enact some sort of program."[58] The result was the Social Security Act of 1935. In Britain, "the old were to become organized and articulate for the first time by the end of the thirties."[59] There was considerable Trades Union Congress and Labour Party agitation for better pensions during this period. The forerunner of the influential National Federation of Old Age Pensioners Associations was founded in Britain in 1938. Concerted political activity among the elderly in Canada during the 1930s was forestalled by the introduction of the flat-rate old age pension in 1927; however, the first provincial organization of old age pensioners was formed in 1932.[60]

The potential for organized political activity among the elderly has been recognized for some time, and it has often been viewed with considerable suspicion. During the 1950s, for example, there was a fear that the "failure to integrate [the] ever-growing numbers of older people in American society" would "heighten opportunities for political deviancy."[61] Within the context of Simmel's theory, it is probably more accurate to suggest that the emergence of age-based politics is an overt manifestation of suppressed conflict which is now surfacing as the elderly become a significantly larger proportion of the polity.

Age-based politics will require heightened generational consciousness and cohesion among the elderly in order for them to carry out successful political action. The extent to which the elderly have increasingly organized themselves in recent years is indicative of this situation. The politics of aging is rapidly becoming a reality. In the United States in 1984 the four major elderly and pensioners' organizations represented nearly 75 per cent of those over 65 and in Canada 30 per cent.[62] In Britain, however, the proportion is much lower. Organizations such as the American Association of Retired Persons and the Gray Panthers in the U.S., the National Federation of Old Age Pensioners Association in Britain and One Voice in Canada have all increasingly engaged in and oriented themselves toward political and lobbying activities. The Conservative government's attempt to de-index the old age pension in Canada in 1985 galvanized seniors' organizations and forced them into action. In addition, some associations, such as the Canadian Council of Retirees, the U.S. National Council of Senior Citizens and the British Pensioners and Trade Union Action Committee, have developed links to organized labour.

There is strength in numbers. The elderly will have political clout, both organizationally and electorally. In this regard so-called liberal, "pluralistic" democracies are particularly vulnerable to vested interest group politics. Politicians are increasingly aware of, and sensitive to, the elderly and the politics of aging. For example, William Davis, the former Conservative premier of Ontario, noted that "the retirement income issue will take hold, and become a fundamental element of the politics of this country over the next few years."[63] The "gray lobby" in the U.S. has been recognized as a political force since the mid-1960s. In the United States those 65 and over will represent 30 per cent of the voting age population by 2000; currently, in the order of two-thirds of the elderly participate in elections. In Canada, 86 per cent of seniors aged 75 and over vote.

While some suggest that an aging population will be a conservatizing political influence,[64] it may be argued that the elderly may be a force for progressive social change. Contrary to the conventional wisdom, there is no mechanical relationship between aging and conservatism.[65] While the elderly may be more "conservative" than the young at any moment in time, studies indicate that people become more "liberal" over their lifetime and that "the political orientations of older people are not peculiar . . . and are very much in the mainstream of . . . political opinion."[66] Other studies have established that the closer a political issue is to an individual, the more age has a significant effect upon the attitude towards that issue.[67] Therefore, age-related issues such as pensions policy will have broader and more immediate political repercussions as the population ages.

Another important consideration is that studies indicate that the political behaviour of those in the baby boom cohort, that is the future elderly, is highly volatile. This is compounded by a diminution of traditional party loyalties and an increase in "cross-over" voting patterns.[68] In the United States, for example, over one-third of baby boomers consider themselves to be political "independents."[69] This suggests that the electorate is increasingly issue oriented and interested in "ends" rather than "means."

The foregoing suggests that increasing proportion of elderly in the future, particularly in the U.S. and Canada, will become more politically conscious, cohesive and mobilized in response to issues which affect them personally, such as pension and aging related matters. This is not to say that the politics of aging will be without its class contradictions, as evidenced by the women's movement. The economic interests and expectations of the future elderly, an increasingly large, volatile and organized proportion of the population, however, may conflict with the "security consciousness" and "social conservatism" of that young age cohort required to support them under current retirement income arrangements, which suggests that heightened intergenerational tensions may become a reality as the demographic future unfolds.

AN AGING POPULATION: IMPLICATIONS

Population aging, accompanied by declining fertility, decreased mortality and greater longevity, has significant implications for the economics of aging, retirement income arrangements, politics and social policy towards the elderly. The economics of aging and the politics of demography in the advanced industrialized countries of the United States, Canada and Britain lead to three central conclusions. First, there is an economic cost associated with the increasing proportion of the elderly in the population because it costs 2.5 to

3 times more to support an elderly dependent than a young one. These costs may be significantly greater than expected. Second, there is a divergence of economic interests between the elderly, the active labour force and the business sector because increased public expenditures such as retirement income and health care costs for the aged, given existing institutional arrangements, result in reduced current consumption for the work force and increased labour costs for the corporate sector. Third, the aging of the population coupled with the immiseration of the elderly suggests that unless there is a major reform of retirement income arrangements, a new and larger generation of elderly poor will be created in the future because the state and private pension systems will have a larger group of elderly dependents to support in the future, particularly single women and the very old (those over 75).

The baby boom generation is already in the labour force. A state pension system ordinarily requires thirty to forty years to mature (unless there is a fast phase-in of benefits). Thus, the necessary social planning, particularly in the case of Canada, must be initiated in the near term in order to cope effectively with the long-term demographic situation which is inexorably unfolding. In Canada, doing so would require an increase in the income replacement rate under the state pension plan (C/QPPs) to avoid a larger generation of poor elderly being created in the future. In Britain the state earnings-related pension (SERPS) was originally designed to mature in 1998. Benefits are now to be reduced as of 2010, coinciding with the retirement of the baby boomers and thus depriving this large cohort of elderly of an important source of income. Any attempt to phase out or tax back the old age security (OAS) pension in Canada prior to or concurrent with the retirement of the baby boom generation would have a similar negative effect. In terms of formulating progressive public policy, social programming must be synchronized with the underlying demographic trends.

Demography as an element in the political economy of pensions will have an important effect on public policy and social security programming in the future. Demographic trends and their implications are now sufficiently predictable and critical that they can no longer be ignored. In the final analysis pensions policy is really nothing more than a concrete manifestation of the more universal problem of old age. Increasingly, however, one pressing problem has created a commonality of interest among the elderly—pensions.

4

The Universal Limitations of the Private Pension System

Rapid and unceasing change and the uncertainties of a working lifetime make individual planning for security essentially unrealistic. Economic security now depends on social or collective arrangements.

Robert Tilove

There are "private troubles and public issues."

C. Wright Mills

The previous chapters have established that a significant proportion of the elderly in Canada, Britain and the United States are poor and that because of population aging in the future there is the prospect of a larger generation of poor elderly. This chapter describes and analyses in some detail the universal limitations of the private pension system which explain its marginal role in the provision of retirement income. These limitations, along with the underdevelopment of the state retirement income system as outlined in Chapter 2, are the fundamental reasons for the elderly's current impoverishment.

During the course of the exhaustive public policy review of the retirement income system in Canada, any number of government studies concluded that the private pension system was a failure.[1] The federal Department of Health and Welfare, for example, stated that

the failure of the retirement income system lies largely with the private employer-sponsored pension system.
The major shortcomings of the retirement income system

are easy to summarize. Most basic is the lack of coverage by private pension plans, in conjunction with a lack of portability and of immediate vesting; few private pension plans index either pensions in pay or deferred pensions; and finally, few survivors have private pensions in their own right.

These observations suggest that large proportions of the aged will continue to receive little or no private pension income in the future.[2]

Monique Bégin, former federal Minister of Health and Welfare in Canada, pointedly noted that "the failure of the private pension plans has been the great disappointment in social programs in the 70's," because "private pensions are NOT doing the job Canadians expect them to do."[3]

In assessing the operation and social utility of the private pension system, the following evaluation criteria are commonly used: coverage, vesting (preservation), portability (transferability), inflation-proofing and income adequacy. The limitations of the private pension system are universal features common to the employer-sponsored occupational pension plans in Canada, Britain and the United States. These inadequacies are interactive and impact upon one another, limiting the efficiency and cost-effectiveness of the private pension system as a delivery mechanism for retirement income. Recent pension reform initiatives have done little to remedy this situation.

LIMITED OCCUPATIONAL PENSION PLAN COVERAGE

One of the critical factors explaining the inadequate level of retirement income generated from the employer-sponsored private pension system, necessitating reliance upon the state social security retirement system, including tax-based "safety net" programmes, is the limited and uneven distribution of occupational pension plan coverage. That only privileged groups within the labour force have been successful in achieving occupational pension coverage reflects the stratification of the capitalist labour market.[4]

Employer-based pension plan coverage varies significantly according to income, occupation, industry, sector of the economy, size of enterprise, geographic location, degree of unionization, labour force attachment and sex. Most commonly excluded are those earning below the average industrial wage, employees in small or labour

TABLE 4.1

INTRODUCTION OF STATE, PRIVATE AND PUBLIC SECTOR PENSION PLANS, U.K., U.S. AND CANADA

COUNTRY	STATE PLAN		PRIVATE SECTOR		PUBLIC SECTOR		
	Flat-Rate	Earnings-Related	Employer-Sponsored	Manufacturing	Federal/Central Gov't	State/Provincial	Municipal/Local Gov't
U.K.	1908 conditional, non-contributory Old Age Pension Act; 1925 Widows, Orphans and Old Age Contributory Act	1959 contributory, graduated scheme	1854 London and North Western Railway	1842 Gas and Light Coke Company	1834 Superannuation Act	Not applicable	1829 Metropolitan Police; 1922 Local Authorities
U.S.	Left to the discretion of the individual states; 1914 Arizona,[1] 1929 California relief for the needy elderly	1935 Old-age, survivors and disability insurance system (OASDI)	1759 Presbyterian Ministers' Fund; 1875 American (Railway) Express	1901 Carnegie Steel Co.	1920 Federal Civil Service Retirement System	1911 State of Massachusetts	1857 New York City Police

COUNTRY	STATE PLAN		PRIVATE SECTOR		PUBLIC SECTOR		
	Flat-Rate	Earnings-Related	Employer-Sponsored	Manufacturing	Federal/Central Gov't	State/Provincial	Municipal/Local Gov't
Canada	1927 non-contributory, means-tested Old Age Pensions Act; 1952 universal Old Age Security Act	1965 Canada/Quebec Pension Plans	1860 Bank of Montreal and 1874 Grand Trunk Railway of Canada; 1903 CPR	1908 International Harvester and Nova Scotia Colliery Workers	1870 Federal Superannuation Act	1876 Quebec Superannuation Aid Fund	1888 Hamilton, Ontario and 1906 Halifax; 1923 and 1958 British Columbia Municipal Superannuation Act, province-wide[2]

Notes: 1 Declared unconstitutional.
2 Individual municipalities had introduced occupational pension plans prior to this in various locations throughout Canada as early as the early 1920s.

Sources: Robert Myers, *Social Security* (Bryn Mawr: McCahn Foundation, 1975), chapters 2 and 3; William C. Greenough and Francis P. King, *Pension Plans and Public Policy* (New York: Columbia University Press, 1976), chapters 2, 4 and 5; Hewitt Associates "Employee Retirement Systems: How it all Began," *Pension World* 12 (July 1976): William Robinson, ed., *Social Security* (London: Fabian Society, 1943), chapter 10; Gerald Rhodes, *Public Sector Pensions* (Toronto: University of Toronto Press, 1965), chapter 1; G. D. Gilling-Smith, *The Complete Guide to Pensions and Super-annuation* (Harmondsworth: Penguin Books, 1967), chapters 1–3 and 22; Canada Department of Labour, *Labour Gazette*, various issues; Laurence E. Coward, *Mercer Handbook of Canadian Pension and Welfare Plans* (Don Mills: CCH, 1977), chapters 18 and 19 and Desmond Morton and Margaret E. McCallum, "Superannuation to Indexation: Employment Pensions in the Public and Private Sector in Canada, 1870–1970," in *Task Force on Inflation Protection for Employment Pension Plans*, Research Studies, vol. 1 (Toronto: Queen's Printer for Ontario, 1988), pp. 1–41.

intensive firms or industries, part-time and mobile employees, women, non-unionized employees and non-earners. In general, occupational pension plan coverage corresponds to the configuration of the labour force in primary and secondary labour markets.

An historical overview of occupational pension plans indicates the limited extent to which the private pension system has been an effective means of ensuring retirement income for the labour force. Employer-based pensions in Britain, Canada and the United States were first introduced by the railroads, banks, insurance companies, and public utilities, and only later in the capital-intensive oligopolistic manufacturing sector. A similar evolutionary pattern emerges in all three countries.[5] (See Table 4.1.) The early origins of pension plans correspond to the development of the modern capitalist state (central and sub-central) and the transformation to industrial capitalism with its large scale units of production, economies of scale, capital intensive investment and oligopolistic market structure.

The extent of occupational pension plan coverage in Canada can be constructed and traced from various sources.[6] Studies undertaken by the National Employment Commission (1937), a Queen's University Industrial Relations Survey (1938) and the first Dominion Bureau of Statistics survey of pension and welfare plans in industry (1947) all provide an insight into its evolution and growth. (See Table 4.2.)

There were few occupational pension plans in Canada at the turn of the century. Canadian developments were influenced by British

TABLE 4.2

INDUSTRIAL PENSION PLANS BY YEAR ESTABLISHED,
ALL INDUSTRIES, CANADA, 1900–1947

DATE ESTABLISHED	NO. OF PLANS	% OF PLANS
Before 1900	7	0.2
1900–1909	59	1.7
1910–1919	172	4.8
1920–1929	369	10.4
1930–1939	465	13.1
1940–1947	2,340	66.0
Not Stated	133	3.8
Total	3,545	100.0

Source: Retabulated and calculated from the Dominion Bureau of Statistics, *Survey of Welfare Plans in Industry 1947* (Ottawa; Queen's Printer, May 1950), Table 13, p. 29.

example in the public sector and American events in the private sector.[7] American corporate "welfare capitalism" as a managerialist ideology and strategy in the oligopolistic sectors of the economy in the late 1800s and early 1900s included the unilateral introduction of non-contributory, employer-sponsored and controlled pension plans. In Canada the number of occupational pension plans in the private sector did not begin to increase until the 1910–1919 period, coinciding with early American corporate penetration of the Canadian market.[8] According to the Queen's University study, Canada pension developments "were either the result of the direct extensions to Canadian subsidiaries, or of the indirect influence of United States plans in the same industries."[9]

The prolonged business boom of the 1920s witnessed the expansion of "welfare capitalism" and the "pension movement." Between 1910 and 1929 the number of employer-sponsored pension plans in Canada more than doubled. Examples of American firms which introduced occupational pension plans into their Canadian operations included International Harvester (1908), Swift & Co. (1915), Bell Telephone (1919), Imperial Oil (1925) and Goodyear Tire and Rubber Company (1929). During the 1920s such plans became a permanent feature of liberal corporate industrial relations policy in North America.[10] They became a means of promoting labour market stability, improving efficiency, strengthing loyalty to the firm and undermining unions, and so they fulfilled an important "role as an ideological and economic control mechanism within the labour market."[11]

It was World War II which signalled the expansion of the private pension system. This growth is explained by three factors. First, during the war employee benefits, including pensions and vacations, were exempt from wage controls in Canada, Britain and the U.S. In all three countries government encouraged employers and unions to introduce pension plans in lieu of direct monetary compensation on the grounds that they were non-inflationary. Second, income tax act regulations were clarified or amended so that occupational pension costs could be deducted as legitimate business expenses by corporations, thereby encouraging their introduction. Third, in the immediate postwar period, unions seriously negotiated the introduction of pension plans for the first time. Nearly two-thirds of all occupational pension plans in Canada were implemented between 1940 and 1947. Examples of those introduced in this period include Weston's (1946), Great Lakes Paper (1947),

Dominion Bridge (1947), Eaton's (1948), Coca Cola (1949), General Motors and Ford (1950). World War II and the immediate postwar period thus mark a watershed in the introduction of private pension plans and the expansion of coverage.

Private Pension Plan Coverage. To assess the private pension system as a source of retirement income requires that pension plan membership, rather than the number of plans, be determined. To facilitate this analysis and place it in perspective, an historical time-series of employer-sponsored pension plan coverage in Canada and the United States has been constructed and related to the total and non-agricultural labour force. For Britain, where background information is more complete, the data has been adapted to place it on a comparable basis. Summary Table 4.3 presents a transnational comparison for Canada, Britain and the U.S. from 1929 to 1985. Since these historical time-series are constructed from disparate sources, they should be interpreted with some caution. But the evidence strongly suggests the employer-based pension system in these countries has proved to be only a limited vehicle for the delivery of retirement income for the majority of the labour force. While there are some national differences, the general pattern of coverage is similar. The broad contours are outlined here.

Before World War II less than 15 per cent of the total labour force in these countries was covered by an employer-sponsored pension plan, and they were highly concentrated in a number of capital intensive industries such as public utilities, railroads and heavy industry. One study in the late 1930s concluded that "industrial retirement plans will probably never be extended to the majority of employees," and "they cannot be regarded as an alternative to an inclusive state-operated plan."[12]

These time-series data confirm that the most dramatic increase in coverage occurred in the post-World War II period. Between 1947 and 1960 private pension plan participation nearly doubled in Canada and the United States, and tripled in the U.K., but employer-sponsored plans covered only in the order of one-third of the total labour force. The increase was most marked in the private sector in the U.S. and Britain, while public sector coverage surged in Canada.

Between 1960 and 1970 there were modest advances in pension coverage in the U.S. and Canada. Britain experienced a period of rapid expansion between 1956 and 1967 when the number of employees in schemes increased from eight to twelve million. Coverage in the United States and Canada was boosted by the dramatic

TABLE 4.3

SUMMARY COMPARISON[1] OF
EMPLOYER-SPONSORED OCCUPATIONAL PENSION PLAN COVERAGE
AS A PERCENTAGE OF TOTAL AND NON-AGRICULTURAL LABOUR FORCE,
CANADA, U.S. AND U.K., SELECTED YEARS, 1929-1985

	EMPLOYEES COVERED BY OCCUPATIONAL PENSION PLANS AS A % OF TOTAL LABOUR FORCE			EMPLOYEES COVERED BY OCCUPATIONAL PENSION PLANS AS A % OF NON-AGRICULTURAL LABOUR FORCE		
YEAR	Canada	U.S.	U.K.	Canada	U.S.	U.K.
1929	—	9.7	—	—	12.9	—
1936	—	—	12.9	—	—	14.1
1938	7.6	11.3	—	16.3	17.9	—
1947	16.8	19.4	—	21.7	23.8	—
1950	—	21.6	—	—	26.3	—
1953	—	—	28.9	—	—	30.1
1955	—	30.3	—	—	36.7	—
1956	—	—	36.0	—	—	37.2
1960	28.1	36.5	—	31.6	43.6	—
1963	—	—	47.0	—	—	48.5
1965	33.8	40.5	—	35.9	46.9	—
1967	—	—	51.3	—	—	52.4
1970	33.7	41.9	—	35.9	48.1	—
1971	—	—	47.8	—	—	48.7
1975	—	45.4	44.0	—	—	44.7
1976	36.8	—	—	41.9	53.6	—
1979	—	45.7	44.7	—	51.0	45.4
1980	39.8	—	—	44.6	—	—
1982	38.9	—	—	40.9	—	—
1983	—	43.7	41.7	—	45.1	42.4
1984	36.8	—	—	38.7	—	—
1985	—	41.8	—	—	42.9	—

Note: 1 See Appendices C 1-3.

Sources: Retabulated from Appendices C 1-3.

increase in public sector unionization. From the end of World War II to 1970 total coverage doubled in absolute terms. Nevertheless, it represented only 34 per cent of the total labour force in Canada, 42 per cent in the U.S., and 48 per cent in Britain.

During the 1970s, the rate of growth in plan coverage declined in all these countries, which suggests that the upper limit under a voluntary employer-based system may have been reached. The U.S. President's Commission on Pension Policy noted that "the low rate of increase since 1969 raises doubts as to whether there will be substantial voluntary gains in the future."[13] In Canada between 1978 and 1984 private pension plan coverage in absolute terms remained virtually static and has actually declined as a proportion of the labour force since 1980.[14] A similar situation has emerged in the United States.

The case of Britain is interesting, if not unique. Employer-sponsored pension coverage peaked in 1967 and has declined in absolute terms since that time. Total occupational pension scheme enrolment decreased by 19 per cent, while in the private sector it declined by 28 per cent between 1967 and 1983.

Currently less than half of the total labour force in these advanced capitalist countries is covered by an employer-sponsored occupational pension plan. Private pension industry representatives and some government agencies, such as Statistics Canada, have argued that the definition of the labour force used in such a measurement should be adjusted to reflect the extent of coverage more accurately. Rather than use the broader total or non-agricultural labour force definition to measure it, they contend that it would be more appropriate to utilize the narrower, full-time employed paid worker statistical base, which would exclude the unemployed, the self-employed, part-time employees, and non-paid family workers; as well, those under 25 and over 65 would be excluded from this calculation.[15] This would result in statistically increasing occupational pension plan coverage in Canada from 37 to 55 per cent of the labour force in 1984. What is to happen to the remaining 45 per cent of this more narrowly defined target group is not explained.

Such methodological rationalizations are dubious, and a number of criticisms can be levelled against such an approach. In the first place the need for income is universal for everyone reaching "normal" retirement age. Therefore, the appropriate target group for the provision of retirement income is the entire retired population, not just a particular stratum of it. Second, using the category of "paid workers" in the labour force and relating it to pension coverage is a tautological formulation because it serves to reinforce the notion that plan participation should be selective rather than universal. Third, redefining the labour force concept and measuring successively smaller target groups merely defines away the problem of limited pension plan coverage. While there are valid reasons why labour economists and statisticians use different labour force definitions, it is questionable whether such an exercise has any particular relevance for social policy in this instance.

While there has been moderate absolute and relative growth in occupational pension plan coverage in the postwar period, the primary determinants of this growth have been the overall increase in the labour force, the expansion of the public sector, increased unionization and the contraction of the agricultural sector. The central issue remains: namely, the majority of the labour force, particularly in the private sector, is not covered by an employer-sponsored pension plan.

Concentration of Pension Plan Coverage. Occupational pension plan coverage is highly concentrated, both in the private and public sectors, and it is closely related to the size of enterprise. This concentration is related to the organization of capital and the labour process in large-scale establishments in the private sector and bureaucracies in the state sector, and it mirrors the more general tendency under advanced capitalism towards the centralization and concentration of capital in the private sector and the expansion of the bureaucratic state.

Pension plan coverage has always been highly concentrated. In the United States during the first quarter of the century, half of all workers covered by an occupational pension plan were employed by thirteen corporations; 40 per cent were employed by the railroads and one-third came under the pension plans of four major corporations: U.S. Steel, American Telephone and Telegraph and the Pennsylvania and New York railroads.[16] In Canada in 1938, 17 industrial pension plans accounted for 63 per cent of the total.[17] Until World War II nearly one-third of all pension plan members were employed by the two railroads.[18] In the late 1940s, 5 per cent of all industrial plans (excluding railroads) accounted for 61 per cent of total pension coverage.[19] In the postwar period employer-sponsored coverage has become even more concentrated. In 1960 in the Canadian case, 1.4 per cent of all pension plans accounted for nearly 70 per cent of all plan members. By 1980 the same proportion of plans accounted for nearly 75 per cent of all members.[20] While the number of large plans increased from 129 in 1960 to 277 in 1980, this was primarily a result of the introduction of multi-employer pension plans in the public and private sectors.

Public sector pension plan membership is more concentrated than in the private sector. In 1980 in Canada the fifteen largest public employee pension plans accounted for nearly 75 per cent of all members in comparison to the thirty largest private sector plans, which represented only 33 per cent of all plan members. This is because "the public sector consists of some of the largest plans in the country notably those for federal employees . . . crown corporations and provincial employees"[21] and large multi-employer public employee plans.

A corollary is that there is a direct relationship between membership in an occupational pension plan and the size of enterprise, which explains the concentration of coverage. In the United States the proportion of workers included ranged from 34 per cent for those in establishments with fewer than one hundred workers to 81 per cent for firms with five hundred or more. Only 33 per cent of all employees in Britain in companies with fewer than one hundred workers were covered by a pension scheme compared to 78 per cent of all employees in firms with a labour force of one thousand or more. A similar pattern exists in Canada.[22]

Pension Plan Coverage by Sector and Industry. Total occupational pension plan coverage as a proportion of labour force, previously indicated in Table 4.3, is misleading because such aggregate statistics disguise its uneven distribution. The statistics must be analysed by sector and industry in order to assess more completely the limited nature of employer-based pension plan coverage.

While less than half of the total labour force is covered by an occupational pension plan, there is a significant difference by sector of the economy. A comparison of occupational pension plan coverage in the public and private sectors is outlined in Table 4.4. Pension

TABLE 4.4

COMPARISON OF OCCUPATIONAL PENSION PLAN COVERAGE AS A PERCENTAGE OF
PAID LABOUR FORCE, BY SECTOR,[1]
CANADA, U.S. AND U.K., 1983–1984

COUNTRY	PUBLIC SECTOR	PRIVATE SECTOR	TOTAL PAID LABOUR FORCE
Canada[2]	97.8	33.0	47.0
U.S.[3]	82.8	49.3	55.2
U.K.[3]	77.9	40.6	52.6

Notes: 1 Including armed forces.
    2 1984.
    3 1983.

Sources: Statistics Canada, *Pension Plans in Canada, 1984* (Ottawa: Minister of Supply and Services, 1986), p. 15; Government Actuary, *Occupational Pension Schemes 1983 — Seventh Survey* (London: HMSO, 1986), Table 2, p. 7. U.S. data is derived from the *Statistical Abstract of the United States 1988* (Washington, D.C.: GPO, 1987), Series 567, p. 344.

plan coverage is two to three times greater in the public sector than in the private sector. For private sector employees, occupational pension plan coverage is especially limited.

The use of global pension plan coverage statistics obscures the limited extent of occupational pension plan coverage, particularly in the private sector. The high level of public sector pension plan coverage inflates the average total coverage figures reported, thus making the situation appear more respectable.

Employer-based coverage also varies widely by industry within the private sector. In general, it tends to be relatively high in capital intensive, high-wage, unionized, oligopolistic industries such as mining, petro-chemicals and manufacturing. Conversely, it is low in poorly paid, non-unionized, labour intensive industries character- ized by either a competitive product market or a high proportion of women workers as in community, business and personal services. This uneven distribution by industry is presented in Table 4.5. A similar variation in pension scheme membership by industry is found in the U.S. and Britain.[23] Significantly, coverage under an occupational pension plan is a necessary, but not sufficient, condi- tion to ensure receipt of retirement income from an employer- sponsored pension plan.

TABLE 4.5

PROPORTION OF PAID WORKERS
IN THE LABOUR FORCE COVERED BY PENSION PLANS,
BY INDUSTRY, CANADA, 1978

INDUSTRY	PERCENTAGE OF PAID WORKERS COVERED BY PENSION PLANS
Public Administration	98.0
Mines, Quarries, Oil Wells	67.6
Transportation and Communication	50.5
Manufacturing	50.2
Construction	47.9
Finance, Insurance and Estate	37.0
Community, Businesses and Personal Service	24.5
Trade	15.8
Agriculture	0.7

Source: Statistics Canada, Pension Plans in Canada, 1978 (Ottawa: Minister of Industry, Trade and Commerce, 1979), Text Table IV, p. 18. This is the last year pension plan coverage by industrial classification was published.

INADEQUATE VESTING STANDARDS

The interaction between occupational pension plan coverage, labour market mobility, vesting (preservation) standards and portability (transferability) arrangements determines whether employees will actually receive an employer-based pension. A fundamental distinction must be made between membership in a plan and *actual* receipt of pension benefits at retirement. The divergence between the two represents lost retirement income (technically referred to as "lapse" or "slippage") to members of the private pension system.

Vesting is defined by Canadian authorities as "the employee's right to all or part of the employer contributions paid on his behalf, on termination of employment before retirement, usually in the form of a deferred pension payable at normal retirement age."[24] Britain's Government Actuary defines preservation (vesting) simply as "a pension the right to which is preserved until retirement age is reached although the member has left employment in respect of which the pension is payable."[25] Vesting is contingent upon an employee satisfying an age and/or service requirement and usually takes three forms: immediate full, deferred full or deferred graduated vesting.

The close relationship between vesting standards and portability arrangements is made clear in a standard text which notes that there has been

> criticism in some quarters over the lack of "portability" or, more accurately, the lack of pension "preservation" for terminating employees. The problem was that employees who changed jobs usually lost their pensions because of inadequate vesting provisions. . . . This . . . meant that [occupational] pension plans were much less effective than they appeared to be, for many employees who had been in several company pension plans received, in fact, little or nothing.[26]

Unless the vesting requirements are satisfied, a person will not be entitled to a deferred pension if he changes employment prior to retirement. Rigorous vesting standards and the portability of pension entitlements between employers are necessary to ensure actual receipt of pension benefits.

Barriers to Adequate Vesting. Inadequate vesting standards in the private pension system are explained by a number of factors. Labour market mobility and length of employment with the same employer are the crucial determinants with respect to acquiring a right to a non-forfeitable or deferred vested pension at retirement. High labour market mobility has resulted in many employees losing pension benefits. According to a background study prepared for the Federal Task Force on Retirement Income Policy, most Canadians will change jobs on average six times during their life;[27] furthermore, mobility rates have increased in recent years.[28] Interestingly, an Economic Council of Canada study found that labour market mobility for those over age 45 was not appreciably different than for those age 25 or over.[29] The fragmentation of the labour market, coupled with this mobility, mitigated against most people ever satisfying the vesting requirements for pension benefits. A considerable body of literature confirms that receipt of a pension is directly related to length of employment with the same employer.[30] The Economic Council of Canada concluded that "the longer the vesting period, the more likely a worker will end up with benefits far below the maximum available to employees who do not change jobs."[31]

The legal basis for vesting or preservation of pension benefits is the deferred wage doctrine.[32] One pension authority has acknowledged that

the concept that pensions should be a form of deferred pay has generally prevailed over the idea that they should be a bonus or gratuity for service. The concept of pensions as deferred pay calls for early vesting, if not immediate vesting.[33]

Until recently, minimum legislative standards recognized neither the reality of high labour market mobility nor the need for early vesting. In Canada the most common legislative standard for many years was known as the "45 and 10" rule,[34] which stipulated that a person must satisfy both an age *and* a service requirement to be entitled to a vested deferred pension at retirement. Under the statutory "45 and 10" rule, a person must have attained age 45 and have worked for the same employer for at least ten years to qualify for a deferred benefit. Recent legislative reforms in respect of vesting requirements in Canada are discussed in a later section. In Britain the preservation rule provided for by legislation is age 26 and five years' service; more recently, the white paper on reform of social security proposed vesting after two years' service. In the United States three alternative vesting schedules are permitted.[35]

The economic and actuarial considerations underlying a defined benefit pension plan are of some significance since this is the most common type of pension scheme. The lack of rigorous vesting standards has had the effect of lowering the total cost of the pension scheme to the plan sponsor while providing the same level of benefits to those plan members who remain. The result is that employees who sever their employment relationship before vesting (early leavers) subsidize the pensions of those who remain and so reduce an employer's pension costs. Employee turnover, which generates this subsidy (referred to as the "fall-in"), is used as an actuarial assumption in the calculation to arrive at the cost of a defined benefit pension plan. It may be true, as Bernstein argues, that "the losses of the many provide the funds with which the payoff is made to the lucky few—just as at any honest race track."[36] However, as a matter of public poliicy we are entitled to ask what the odds are of being a winner. Inadequate vesting requirements have forced those covered by the employer-based private pension system to gamble on receiving their retirement income. It might be suggested that economic security in old age is far too important to be left to chance, especially if the race is fixed.

Another economic function performed by inadequate vesting standards is to compensate a firm for employee mobility. Such an analysis can be placed within the framework of human capital theory associated with the work of Becker, Mincer and Oi.[37] If an employee terminates his employment prior to being vested, the employer contribution on his behalf is returned to the firm or credited to the pension fund against future employer contributions, which lowers the total cost of the pension scheme to the sponsor. In theory, it would also allow higher benefits to be paid at a fixed cost to those who remain. This, however, is not standard practice. In a highly mobile capitalist labour market, poor vesting requirements in occupational pension plans have served as a form of insurance against the loss incurred by a firm for recruiting and training an employee who terminates.

In addition to economic purposes, inadequate vesting provisions have also served a social control and labour discipline function. According to Kincaid, the employer "sees pension rights as a useful adjunct to discipline."[38] Restrictions on pension rights and other social security programmes (i.e., social welfare) serve a social control function either for the individual employer or for the state on his behalf by limiting eligibility for benefits. Historically, the receipt of an employer-sponsored pension has not been a contractual right established through the employment relationship. A pension was paid at an employer's discretion to an employee for "good and faithful service." Early industrial pension plans were, according to Lubove, "first and foremost a technique of labour control. This helps to explain the indifference . . . to vesting employees with legal rights."[39] During the famous 1919 Winnipeg general strike, for example, federal Minister of Labour Gideon Robertson issued the following threat to postal workers:

> Unless they returned to work . . . signed agreements never to support a sympathetic strike and severed their relations with the Winnipeg Trades and Labour Council, they would be discharged at once with the loss of pension rights.[40]

In Britain a director of Pilkington's candidly commented that the

> supplementary [pension] fund controlled and contributed to by the company . . . was useful in the 1926 general strike. Benefits were automatically forfeited but men were reinstated with one shilling per week less pension rights.[41]

Situations such as these prompted Brandeis to condemn occupational pension plans as a "form of strike insurance," which robs the worker of "his remaining industrial liberty."[42] The lack of adequate vesting provisions has therefore served a variety of economic, ideological and social control functions.

Legislative Background. Legislation establishing an employee's legal right on termination to a non-forfeitable deferred pension at retirement has only recently been introduced in Canada, Britain and the United States. Vested deferred pensions based on an age and/or service requirement which protect an employee's accrued pension were not a legislative requirement in Canada until the passage of the Ontario Pension Benefits Act 1965, which introduced the "45 and 10" rule. Other jurisdictions subsequently followed suit.[43] Pension reform initiatives in recent years have resulted in a number of different vesting standards being adopted by the various jurisdictions. In the United Kingdom it was not until the Social Security Act

1973 that preserved (deferred) pensions for "early leavers" were guaranteed in law; the U.S. Employee Retirement Income Security Act 1974 for the first time introduced statutory vesting provision in the private sector. The right of a plan member to an irrevocable pension on termination of employment, based on employer and employee contributions (in the case of a contributory plan), is thus relatively recent. There are no legislative requirements, however, concerning the portability or transferability of pension entitlements between employers.

A comparison of occupational pension plans in the U.S., U.K. and Canada without vesting provisions for the period between 1938 and 1984 is outlined in Table 4.6. A number of considerations may be noted. Prior to the introduction of regulatory legislation in these countries, between *30* and *90* per cent of all pension plans had *no provision* whatsoever for vested deferred pensions. This effectively meant that any employee terminating employment prior to retirement would lose his pension entitlement. The data suggest as well that there has been a considerable difference in the evolution of vesting standards in the U.S. and U.K., in one instance, and Canada in another. The subsequent introduction of statutory vesting standards in the mid-1960s and 1970s has resulted in considerable improvement in vesting requirements in occupational pension plans. Gauging the adequacy of vesting provisions in terms of pension *plans*, however, is misleading since the relevant criterion is the proportion of *employees* who have satisfied these requirements. The most recent information indicates that even after legislative intervention in the U.S. (1974) and U.K. (1973), 42 and 25 per cent of pension plan members respectively were still not vested, particularly in the private sector.

The implications of inadequate vesting standards, particularly in the case of the U.K. and the U.S., will not become evident until some 30 to 50 years in the future when benefits from occupational pension schemes fail to materialize because employees never qualified for pension entitlements. This consideration is especially relevant for the U.K. and U.S., where as late as the early 1970s, 66 to 90 per cent of all pension plans did not have any vesting requirements. The data suggest that the biggest "pension losers" will be the large baby-boom generation, who will suffer a loss of retirement income from the private pension system. A corollary is that this cohort of future elderly will have to rely on tax-based state retirement income programmes, thus exacerbating the fiscal cost associated with an

TABLE 4.6

LONGITUDINAL COMPARISON OF THE PERCENTAGE OF OCCUPATIONAL PENSION PLANS WITHOUT PROVISION FOR A VESTED DEFERRED PENSION, U.S., U.K. AND CANADA, SELECTED YEARS, 1938–1984

COUNTRY	1938	1954	1960	1964	1965	1967	1969	1970	1971	1972	1973	1974	1975	1978	1979	1980	1983	1984
U.S.	—	—	—	—	—	30	40[1]	—	89	66[6]	*	*	—	—	52[7]	—	42	—
U.K.	18[3]	—	31[4]	84	3[5]	—	—	—	—	—	—	—	13[2]	—	25[8]	—	—[9]	—
Canada	73[3]	—	—	—	—	—	—	0.5[6]	—	—	—	0.4[6]	—	0.2[6]	—	0.4[6]	—	0.4[6]

Notes:

* Regulatory pension legislation enacted.
1 Full vesting with 10 to 15 years service.
2 Full vesting at age 26 and 5 years service.
3 Full vesting with 15 years to 20 years service.
4 Full vesting with 20 years service.
5 Full vesting at age 45 and 10 years service.
6 Full vesting with 10 years service.
7 Plan participants in the private sector.
8 Plan participants not receiving either transfer payments or a preserved benefit.
9 Indeterminate.

Source: For the United States, Walter W. Kolodrubetz, "Characteristics of Workers with Pension Coverage on the Longest Job," U.S. Department of Health, Education, and Welfare, Social Security Administration, *Reaching Retirement Age* (Washington D.C.: GPO, 1976), note 1, p. 162; Donald M. Landay and Harry E. Davis, "Growth and Vesting Changes in Private Pension Plans," U.S. Department of Labor, Bureau of Labor Statistics, *Monthly Labor Review*, Reprint No. 2571, May 1968, Table 3, p. 32; Walter W. Kolodrubetz and Donald M. Landay, "Coverage and Vesting of Full Time Employees under Private Retirement Plans," *Social Security Bulletin* 36 (November 1973), p. 20; and Gayle Thompson Rodgers, "Vesting of Private Pension Benefits and Change From 1972," *Social Security Bulletin*, 44 (July 1981), Table 2, p. 19. For Britain, Michael Pilch and Victor Wood, *New Trends in Pensions* (London: Hutchinson, 1964), p. 65; Government Actuary, *Occupational Pension Schemes* (London: HMSO, various years). For Canada, Queen's University, Industrial Relations Section, School of Commerce and Administration, *Industrial Retirement Plans in Canada* (Kingston, Ont.: Queen's University, 1938), pp. 67–69; "Vesting Provisions in Canadian Industrial Pension Plans," *Labour Gazette* (January 1955), Table 1, p. 31; Dominion Bureau of Statistics, *Pension Plans Non-Financial Statistics 1960* (Ottawa: Queen's Printer, 1962), Tables 17 and 18; and Statistics Canada, *Pension Plans in Canada* (Ottawa: Minister of Supply and Services, various years).

aging population. Even in an ideal world with immediate vesting, however, there would be a loss of retirement income to occupational pension plan members because of limited portability (transferability) arrangements and the inadequacy of deferred vested pensions.

Deferred Vested Pensions. Improvements in vesting standards are only a partial solution to the problem of the preservation of pension entitlements because the value of a deferred vested pension depends upon three factors: the preserved value of the deferred benefit from the time of termination of employment to receipt of the benefit, length of service to accrue pension credits, and final salary or earnings at the time of retirement. The interaction of these factors, concurrent with inadequate portability arrangements, limits the viability of deferred (preserved) pensions as a source of retirement income.

In the first instance, especially in the case of Canada and the U.S., the value of pensions paid by occupational pension plans at the time of termination are not upgraded or revalued in accordance with either the price or earnings index during the deferral period. An individual who severs his employment has the value of his deferred pension eroded over the long term, both in absolute and relative terms, as a result of increases in inflation and the gross national product. In Britain, preserved benefits in schemes which have "contracted-out" of the state pension plan must be revalued up to the guaranteed minimum pension (GMP) (up to 3 per cent a year) to allow for increased average earnings. Such a revaluation is not required of schemes which remain "contracted-in" to the state earnings-related plan or benefits that are in excess of the GMP for plans which "contract-out." Therefore, a mobile worker, if covered by a "contracted-out" occupational pension plan and successfully vested, could in theory receive a number of deferred partial pensions, all of which would be eroded by inflation (if it exceeded the increase in the GMP) over the pre-retirement period.

Second, even if there were rigorous statutory vesting standards, without the full portability (transferability) of pension entitlements, the sum of two deferred vested pensions for a person is not the same as that which would have been generated with the same years of service had that person remained with the same employer until retirement age. In pension arithmetic, the whole is not equal to the sum of the parts because a deferred vested pension, under a defined benefit pension plan, is calculated on the basis of the number of years of service times the salary of the person at the time of *termina-*

tion, rather than on the salary at retirement. The employee thus forgoes any increase in salary between termination and retirement, and the salary base upon which the pension is calculated is reduced.

The illustration presented in Table 4.7 demonstrates the limitations associated with deferred vested pensions under current private pension system arrangements. As a result of the interrelationship between the length of service to accrue pension benefits and the lower salary on termination when vested, two people with the same total pensionable service and salary would have a difference of 20 per cent in their pension benefit at the time of retirement. According to a 1981 U.K. Occupational Pensions Board study, "early leavers" who change jobs receive a pension which is 40 to 60 per cent less, depending upon the assumptions used, than a "stayer," even if the total years of pensionable employment are the same.[44] For "early leavers" the problem is compounded by the erosion of the vested pension over the deferral period as a result of inflation.

Receipt of Occupational Pension Benefits. What is of significance from a social policy perspective in terms of assessing the private pension system is the level and distribution of actual pension benefits received by plan members. Determining the "take-up" rate—that is, the proportion of actual pension benefit recipients to occupational pension plan members—is one way to evaluate the social utility of the private pension plan system as a delivery mechanism for retirement income. The best available evidence suggests that there is a low "take-up" rate and a high level of "leakage." As a result, a high proportion of those covered by an occupational pension plan never receive a pension. This is directly attributable to the current poor vesting requirements and limited portability arrangements associated with the employer-based private pension system.

Studies for the United States, Britain, and Canada between 1944 and 1977 have established that only 10 to 54 per cent of those covered by an occupational pension plan ever received a retirement benefit.[45] To date, remedial legislative intervention would appear to have had only a modest effect. After the passage of the Employee Retirement Income Security Act 1974, the U.S. Bureau of Labor Statistics and the Pension Rights Center estimated that only 33 to 45 per cent of all occupational pension plan members would ever receive a retirement benefit. Only 48 per cent of all full-time employees in private sector pension plans in the U.S. had acquired vested

TABLE 4.7

COMPARISON OF PENSION BENEFIT RECEIVED BY
AN EARLY LEAVER AND STAYER UNDER A DEFINED BENEFIT PENSION PLAN[1]
PROVIDING A DEFERRED VESTED BENEFIT, CANADA, 1985

Employment Pattern	Unit Credit (Accrual Rate/Yr.)		Years of Service		Salary		Pension Benefit
Worker A Individual remains in service of same employer	2%	×	35 years	×	$39,373[2]	=	$27,561
Worker B Individual changes employment at age 45	2%	×	15 years	×	$21,800[3]	=	$ 6,540[4, 5]
	2%	×	20 years	×	$39,373[2]		+ $15,749
						Total	$22,289

Notes: 1 In a defined benefit pension plan the benefit is equal to the accrual rate × years of service × salary.
  Assumptions: Entrance age 30 and works for 35 years.
    Salary at age 45 is the 1985 average industrial wage of $21,800.
    Salary at age 65 is $39,373.
    Salary increase assumption of 3 per cent a year.
2 Final salary at time of retirement.
3 Salary at time of termination with deferred vested pension.
4 Deferred benefit not revalued or increased to either the price or earnings index.
5 Vested assuming the "45 and 10" rule.

pension rights as of 1979; by 1983 this had increased to only 51 per cent of persons covered.[46] In Britain, Altmann's quantitative study, based on Family Expenditure Survey (FES) data, determined that in the period between 1970 and 1975 the mean probability of receipt of an occupational pension plan benefit for men aged 65 and over was only 54 per cent.[47] In Canada, a 1973 study undertaken by the Régie des Rentes du Quebec (Quebec Pension Board) found that only 3.1 per cent of all private pension plan "leavers" would have satisfied the statutory "45 and 10" vesting rule. A 1977 Health and Welfare Canada survey determined that only 53 per cent of male and 28 per cent of female pension plan members ever actually received a retirement benefit. All of these studies indicated a strong positive relationship between length of employment with the same employer and actual receipt of pension benefits at retirement.

The proportion of those over retirement age who have actually received a pension from the private system, given current arrangements, is limited. Inadequate employer-based pension plan coverage, coupled with unsatisfactory vesting requirements, explain the low proportion of retirement income received by the elderly from the private pension system. The data reported in Table 4.8 indicate that in Canada in 1983 only 40 per cent of the elderly were in receipt of

TABLE 4.8

PRIVATE PENSION PLAN RECIPIENTS[1]
AS A PERCENTAGE OF ELDERLY,[2]
CANADA, SELECTED YEARS, 1969–1983

YEAR	PRIVATE PENSION PLAN RECIPIENTS	NO. AGE 65 AND OVER ('000s)[3]	PRIVATE PENSION PLAN RECIPIENTS AS A % OF ELDERLY
1969	392,525	1,671	23.5
1972	552,504	1,801	30.7
1975	699,717	1,972	35.5
1978	813,922	2,143	37.9
1981	901,985	2,361	38.2
1983	1,007,018	2,496	40.3

Notes: 1 Total of all pension benefits (retirement, disability and survivors) paid, including full and partial retirement benefits.
2 Those over age 65.
3 Extrapolated between census years.

Sources: Statistics Canada, Pension Plans in Canada (Ottawa: Minister of Supply and Services, various years) for the number of occupational pension plan recipients related to Statistics Canada population figures for those age 65 and over.

occupational pension plan benefits. The increase in the proportion of those in receipt of pension benefits between 1969 and 1983 reflects the growth of the employer-sponsored pension plan coverage in the preceding thirty-five-year period and does not necessarily imply that there has been an improvement in the "take-up" rate for benefits.

The levelling off of occupational pension plan membership in recent years would suggest that the proportion of elderly in receipt of occupational pension plan retirement benefits may not significantly increase in the future. This likelihood is confirmed by a Department of National Health and Welfare study which concluded that "There are serious gaps in pension protection among Canadians, the most notable of which occur among employees in the private sector."[48] According to the same study, occupational pension plan coverage is particularly low for those in the 25 to 44 age group—that is, the baby boom generation—employed in the private sector. Furthermore, according to another survey, 50 to 70 per cent of those earning below the average industrial wage in 1986 did not participate in an employer-sponsored pension plan.[49] Moreover, individual Registered Retirement Savings Plans have failed to fill the gap in private pension coverage because only 15 per cent of tax filers and 20 per cent of the labour force were enrolled in RRSPs as of 1983. The continuing low level of occupational pension plan coverage will limit the proportion of the elderly that will receive income from the private pension system in the future.

There are also strong reasons to believe that occupational pension plan recipients as a proportion of the elderly are statistically over-reported. First, the number of pensions paid, as reported by Statistics Canada, includes *all* pension benefits—retirement, disability and survivors.[50] Recent survey data for the U.S. and the U.K. indicate, however, that only 38 and 51 per cent respectively of the current elderly are in receipt of full *or* partial *retirement* benefits from the private pension system.[51] Second, current vesting provisions coupled with high labour market mobility result in a large number of small *partial* deferred pensions being paid out, rather than robust full pensions.[52] The data with respect to the number of pension benefit recipients in Canada do not differentiate between *full* and *partial* pensions paid out or received. A pension plan beneficiary may therefore be in receipt of a number of small partial deferred pensions from different sources. The total number of pension recipients may be further statistically overstated as a result of the high number of small pensions paid out.

LIMITED PORTABILITY ARRANGEMENTS

Vesting and portability of pension entitlements are integrally related. The vesting problem is in the final analysis a portability or transferability problem. Portability is another form of vesting since it ensures the necessary *continuity of service* required to qualify for a deferred vested pension upon retirement. According to the Federal Task Force on Retirement Income Policy, as little as 49 per cent of a person's working years would count towards pensionable service given current labour market mobility and the former "45 and 10" vesting rule in most jurisdictions.[53] One technical study based on computer simulations concluded that "vesting, which takes the form of a deferred pension, is much less effective . . . than is full portability, which allows pension credits to be transferred from one private plan to another."[54]

If a person changes employment several times before retirement and is unable to make transfers of either pension contributions or benefits when vested, he will be forced to collect benefits from several different pension plans, which explains the large number of partial rather than full pensions generated by the private pension system. More importantly, prior to the recent pension reform package, without transferability a person might not have remained on one job long enough to satisfy the vesting requirements and benefit from the contributions made on his behalf by the employer. Indeed, it is entirely possible, given labour market mobility, that a person could have been covered by a pension plan on every job and never had the continuity of service necessary to satisfy the vesting requirements.[55] And even if he should satisfy the vesting requirements for a deferred pension on successive jobs, however, the retirement income accruing from different private pension plans would not be as great as that generated from one occupational pension plan, as previously indicated, and it would be eroded by inflation over the deferral period until retirement age.

Portability allows the transfer of either pension contributions or benefits under a defined benefit plan from the pension fund of one employer to the fund of another in respect of an employee whose employment is terminated with the first and who finds employment with the second. This is transferability in a literal sense. While transferability arrangements are relatively common in the public and para-public sectors in Britain, Canada and the U.S., portability between pension plans in the private sector is quite rare. This is because, while portability in theory can be arranged between different employer-sponsored pension plans, there are numerous technical difficulties arising from the valuation of contributions or benefits, differing benefit formulas, contribution levels, actuarial assumptions and funding ratios between "importing" and "exporting" pension plans. Resolving the portability problem would require either a central pension agency under public or private sector control to facilitate transferability or improved vesting standards coupled with the indexation (preservation) of deferred pensions. Remedial action to ameliorate these problems would not in itself, however, be sufficient to provide economic security for the elderly because the income generated from the private pension system continues to be eroded by inflation in the retirement period.

THE EROSION OF RETIREMENT INCOME

Inflation hurts those on fixed incomes such as pensioners, who are caught in a fixed income-price spiral squeeze. Retirement income must be increased to offset inflation in order to maintain its real value. Such arrangements under state and occupational pension plans are referred to as "indexation," "escalation" or "inflation-proofing." The lack of inflation-proofing for employer-based occupational pension plans, particularly in the private sector, has become all the more apparent because of the prolonged period of inflation that characterized advanced capitalist economies in North America and Western Europe throughout the 1970s and early 1980s.

In Canada between 1971 and 1981 the average annual inflation rate was 7.8 per cent, ranging from a low of 2.9 per cent in 1971 to a high of 12.5 per cent in 1981.[56] The United States and Britain experienced similar, and often higher, levels of inflation. Such a long-term inflationary climate had serious ramifications on the operation and solvency of occupational pension plans as well as on the economic position of the elderly.

The high inflation rate during that decade seriously eroded the value of occupational pension plan benefits, both those in pay and deferred (vested) pensions. At an average inflation rate of nearly 8 per cent a year over that period, the average retired person saw the purchasing power of his or her occupational pension eroded by 65 to 75 per cent respectively during the retirement period.[57] By way of example, the average annual private pension paid in Canada in 1970 was $1,734. By 1981 it was worth only $732 or 42 per cent of its original value. For a young person with a deferred vested pension payable at age 65, its value at retirement would be virtually nothing. Inflation has similarly resulted in a deterioration of the economic position of those covered by occupational pension schemes in Britain.[58] In economic and human terms it is the elderly who are the most vulnerable to inflation. Its effects compound their economic immiseration and social marginalization.

In the late 1950s industrial nations began to adjust social security retirement programmes by indexing benefit levels to changes in price or wage movements.[59] Doing so raised the issues of which index was the most appropriate for inflation-proofing pensions or whether a special Pensioner's Index should be constructed to reflect the unique expenditure patterns of the elderly.

In Canada, for example, it has been argued that the "Consumer Price Index is not the right measure for indexing pensions" because "the basket of goods and services on which the C.P.I. is based does not represent typical expenditures of [those] over 65."[60] Private pension industry representatives in Canada have promoted the construction of a special pensioner's index in an attempt to justify the partial rather than the full indexation of retirement benefits.[61] Presently, only the Federal Republic of Germany and Britain have a special consumer price index for retired persons. In Britain, however, this index is not used to adjust state social security benefits for inflation. Neither the Canadian nor U.S. governments have published an official Pensioner's Index. The evidence for the U.K. between 1962 and 1968 indicates that the Pensioner's Index rose nearly four percentage points more than did the general price index;[62] between 1970 and and 1980, however, there was less than one percentage point difference.[63] In the United States studies indicate that between 1970 and 1977 " 'prices' for the aged increased 3% to 4% faster than the CPI"[64] because inflation had a disproportionate effect on those items which are weighted heavily in the elderly's budget.

The elderly spend considerably more on basic necessities such as food, fuel and housing than do general households and marginally more on services. The impact of these different expenditure patterns is dependent on both the rate of price increase and the absolute price level. In recent years the major expenditure components of pensioner household budgets have experienced above average price increases. The elderly's expenditure patterns, based on U.S. and British data, differ considerably from those of the general population. It does not follow, however, that their financial needs are any less as is asserted by some representatives of the private pension industry.[65]

Generally, expenditure patterns reflect the allocation of income within a given finite budget. The elderly cannot negotiate wage increases; they cannot raise the prices of their goods and services. Their main alternative is to cut costs, that is, to reduce their standard of living. The constraints faced by the elderly result in substitutions within their budgets from non-essentials to basics, using margarine instead of butter or spending on fuel and housing instead of durable goods and amenities. Inflation reinforces this substitution effect because it is precisely those heavily weighted basic components of the elderly's budget that experienced the most rapid rate of price increase. The indexation of state and occupational pension plan benefits is necessary, therefore, to maintain the elderly's standard of living in an inflationary climate or to ameliorate the cumulative effect of inflation in the retirement period.

Indexation of Occupational Pension Plans. The private pension system provides only limited protection against inflation. As is reported in Table 4.9, 62 to 94 per cent of private sector pension plan members in Britain, Canada and the U.S. have no automatic indexation of post-retirement pension benefits. Most occupational pension plan members have no automatic escalation feature to cover the full increase in the consumer price index. The lack of formal indexation provisions, particularly in the private sector, reflects the reluctance of employers to assume an open-ended financial commitment to protect their former employees from inflation.

The automatic indexation of post-retirement pension benefits is far more common in the public sector. In Canada 66 per cent of public employee pension plan members are covered by full or partial indexing, compared with only 6 per cent of private sector plan members.[66] While only 7 per cent of U.S. private sector pension plans had automatic cost of living adjustments, the federal civil service and half of all state and local retirement systems index post-retirement benefits.[67] Pensions in Britain were adjusted for inflation as early as 1803. The indexing was subsequently formalized in the Pensions

TABLE 4.9

INDEXED PRIVATE SECTOR
PENSION PLANS BY MEMBERS COVERED,
CANADA, U.K. AND U.S., 1983–1986

AUTOMATIC INDEXATION PROVISION	% OF MEMBERS COVERED		
	Canada	U.K.	U.S.
Full Indexing to Consumer Price Index	0.3	22.8	n.a.
Partial Indexing	6.0	15.6	35.0
No Indexing	93.7	61.7	65.0

Sources: Statistics Canada, *Pension Plans in Canada, 1984* (Ottawa: Minister of Supply and Services, 1986), Text Table W, p. 52. For the U.K., derived from the Government Actuary, *Occupational Pension Schemes, 1983 — Seventh Survey* (London: HMSO, 1986), Table 9.1, p. 58, related to Table 3.2, p. 14. For the U.S., incomplete information is available from the U.S. Department of Labor, Bureau of Labor Statistics, *Employee Benefits in Medium and Large Firms, 1986* (June, 1987), Table 67, p. 72.

(Increase) Act 1920, which covered the entire public sector with the exception of nationalized industry.[68] Based on the most complete information available, 85 per cent of public sector pension plan members have automatic indexation arrangements compared to 25 per cent in the private sector.[69]

An uniquely Britain approach to inflation-proofing pension benefits was introduced under the Social Security Pensions Act 1975. Where an employer-based occupational pension scheme "contracts out" of the state earnings-related pension system, the government assumes the open-ended commitment to index (preserve) deferred and retirement pensions. Under the 1975 legislation, the state social security system assumed the cost of indexing the guaranteed minimum pension (GMP) for "contracted-out" plans, up to the level of the earnings-related state plan. Any benefit in excess of the GMP is not indexed.[70] What this means is that private corporations have externalized the cost of indexation to the state, thereby creating a socialized cost of production borne by those who have remained in the earnings-related state plan and tax-paying workers not covered by an occupational pension scheme. The state inflation-proofing "contracted-out" schemes have resulted in a considerable tax loss to the central government.

The private sector in these countries has chosen to rely on discretionary periodic increases to retirement benefits as a way in which to limit the open-ended liability and cost associated with inflation-proofing. While the number of private sector occupational pension plans making periodic adjustments for inflation has increased in recent years, in most instances these adjustments have only offset a portion of the increase in the cost of living. In Canada and Britain, for example, two-thirds of all private sector plans have made ad hoc payments covering at least 50 per cent of the increase in inflation, as compared with only 30 per cent of plans in the U.S.[71] Periodic adjustments, as distinct from automatic indexation, provide only a limited and partially effective mechanism to protect the elderly's standard of living because they are discretionary. Corporations make such payments from current operating expenditures, thus avoiding a permanent financial commitment. Periodic adjustments are a known cost while automatic indexation represents an open-ended liability inasmuch as the actual rate of inflation is only known with certainty after the fact.

The private pension system's limited inflation-proofing stands in marked contrast to that provided for under most state social security retirement arrangements. By 1975 a total of thirty-three countries had some form of benefit escalation, most using the price index, some the general wage index and others the minimum wage.[72] Basic pension benefits provided by the state retirement system in Canada, Britain and the United States are all currently indexed to the Consumer (or Retail) Price Index (C/RPI).

Indexation to the Consumer Price Index or Retail Price Index maintains the absolute purchasing power of state retirement benefits, and the elderly's standard of living, but it does not allow older people to share in any increase in national wealth. Therefore, the relative value of these benefits is not protected and the elderly's standard of living declines in relation to that of the employed labour force. Indexation to the CPI maintains absolute purchasing power, but escalation to the average industrial wage (AIW) is necessary in order to maintain the elderly's relative economic position compared with that of the active labour force. Politically, indexing social security retirement benefits to increases in wage levels has the effect of linking the elderly's fortunes to those of the actively employed labour force. This tends to prevent the exacerbation of sectional interests between the actively employed and pensioners. ·

The International Labour Organization in assessing the indexation features of state social security retirement programmes noted that

market economy countries have found that the impact of inflation and . . . remedies can differ between . . . pension systems
operating under state social security programmes and usually
financed on a pay-as-you-go basis and . . . occupational pensions . . . [which] commonly are funded schemes, so that they
are vulnerable to a rate of inflation higher than the yield from
investments.[73]

This has meant that state retirement income systems have been
used for the difficult parts of social security programming such as
income adequacy and inflation-proofing, while the private pension
system has played a residual role.

The international social security crisis in advanced capitalist
countries is a reflection of the deeper underlying economic crisis
which has generated a similar neo-conservative monetarist
response in terms of "crisis management." In Canada and Britain
there has been a similar reaction by government to singling out the
indexation features of state and public employee pension plans as a
major issue to be dealt with as a result of the prolonged international recession.

The indexation of public employee pension arrangements has
provoked a vitriolic attack by the corporate sector and the private
pension industry in Canada and Britain. In Canada, as a result of
pressure from the pension industry and its lobby group, the
National Citizens' Coalition, the federal Liberal government was
forced in 1978 to commission an independent review of the indexed
federal civil service pension plan. Some four years later a major
reduction in the plan's indexation feature was implemented. A similar review was carried out in 1980 by Britain's Conservative government. Despite these severe political pressures, however, public
employee pension plans are still indexed in most industrialized
countries. The indexation of state social security retirement benefits has come under similar pressure. In Canada the federal Liberal
government in 1982 temporarily limited the inflation-proofing of
the flat-rate old age security pension (OAS), and Britain's Conservative government implemented a lower indexation formula for state
retirement benefits. The Reagan administration in the U.S. threatened at various times to reduce or eliminate the indexation feature
of social security retirement benefits.

The private pension industry was forced to strike out against the example of state and public sector pension plan indexation because it served as a "demonstration effect" for private sector workers, as well as raising the expectations of pensioners. In addition, the lack of private sector indexation forced a more general critical evaluation of employer-sponsored occupational pensions. The private pension industry in these countries proceeded by deliberately cultivating the politics of envy between private and public sector workers. It did so in the hope of exacerbating sectional differences and creating a public backlash or "taxpayers' revolt."

Micro vs. Macro Cost of Indexation. Indexation of retirement benefits is a fundamental issue of public policy. Central to this debate are the cost estimates associated with it. There is a very real difference between the ways in which actuaries and economists conceptualize the cost of employer-sponsored pension indexation. Some actuarial consultants have suggested that the inflation-proofing has "staggering" cost implications,[74] increasing the cost of the scheme by as much as 8 per cent for every 1 per cent of additional pension income.[75] Economists tend to view pension indexation as having a neutral cost impact. These alternative cost estimates are a result of different types of analyses. Actuaries use a micro-economic analysis to arrive at their estimates, while economists bring a macro-economic perspective to the subject.

Actuaries who represent the interests of their corporate clients must of necessity be interested in the economic position of the firm. There are, from an actuary's point of view, especially in the private sector, essentially two considerations. First, what, if any, liabilities will accrue to the pension plan and the individual firm as a result of indexation? This is a crucial concern because in an inflationary environment, where the real rate of return on investment to the pension fund is less than the inflation rate, in the case of a defined benefit plan the plan sponsor is required to make up the shortfall with additional contributions to guarantee its solvency. Second, from a micro-economic perspective, what are the effects of indexation costs on the firm's cash flow and profit position? The short-term profit horizon of an individual company is of paramount concern. It is the cash outlay today, rather than its relationship to macro-economic indicators in the future, which will affect its immediate profit position. It may be argued, however, that under conditions of monopoly capitalism associated with the giant corporation as described by Baran and Sweezy,[76] where the large firm is stable over the long run as a result of oligopolistic market conditions and "profit-targeting," that the cost associated with indexation would be incorporated into targeted profit levels. Profit margins would then be adjusted accordingly to absorb the cost of pension indexation over the long term.

Economists in general bring a macro-economic perspective to the issue. The cost associated with the indexation of pension benefits is affected at the macro-economic level over the long term by increases in inflation, productivity and economic growth. The indexation of pension benefits at the macro-economic level involves a change in the allocation of resources rather than an increased allocation as such. The Economic Council of Canada summarized the major flaw of actuarial cost estimates for pension indexation by stating that

> some of the doom-and-gloom predictions about the repercussions of indexation derive from a failure to make proper comparisons; they project pensions in inflated (future) dollars while projecting GNP in terms of today's prices.
>
> Preserving the real purchasing power of retirement pensions . . . will not "bankrupt" the Canadian economy. No more real resources are required for price-indexed pensions in an inflationary environment than for unindexed pensions in a non-inflationary environment.[77]

Based on this macro-economic approach, some economists have estimated that over the next fifty years only an additional 0.5 per cent of gross national product would be required to provide for the full indexation of all pension benefits.[78]

In the real world, however, the macro- and micro-economic levels are interrelated and cannot be isolated from one another because

> the indexation of pension benefits does present problems for . . . firms; inflation pushes up benefit liabilities and pushes down the value of pension fund investment.
>
> Industry looks at it from the viewpoint of individual pension plan sponsors, who fear that pension costs may . . . adversely affect their competitive position.[79]

These different cost estimates offer a classic example of what Baran meant when he identified capitalism's primary contradiction as being between "micro-sense and macro-madness."[80] The operation of capitalist economies is interpenetrated by and interdependent on corporate behaviour. Conversely, corporate behaviour is bounded by the operation and imperatives of a capitalist economy. As a result there are structural limitations preventing an individual private sector firm from inflation-proofing retirement benefits.

Limits to Indexation. The micro-economics of the firm are related to the macro-economic structure of capitalism through financial markets, which impose the ultimate external constraint on an individual corporation's ability to inflation-proof pension benefits. The ability of private sector pension plans to provide inflation-proofing is related to the *real* rate of return that can be earned by private pension funds. This exogenous constraint imposed by the broader macro-economy poses three portfolio management alternatives for the individual plan sponsor with respect to indexing benefits. They can be summarized as follows:

1. If the rate of return on investment adequately reflects the rate of inflation, private pension plans can afford to pay indexed pension benefits.
2. To the extent that the rate of return only partially reflects the rate of inflation, the pension fund can only afford to index pensions partially.
3. Where the rate of return on investment is zero or less than the rate of inflation, the pension fund cannot afford the indexation of pensions.

It is the real rate of return (the nominal rate of return adjusted for inflation) to the pension fund which serves as the primary structural limitation to the indexation of private pension benefits. Pension fund investment performance over the past two decades has been inauspicious at best. In Canada between 1961 and 1975 the real average annual rate of return on investment for all trusteed (non-insured) occupational pension plans was 0.7 per cent;[81] in the late 1970s, during a period of high inflation, pension funds were earning a real rate of return of −2.9 per cent.[82] British pension fund investment performance has fared little better. Between 1965 and 1975 the real annual rate of return averaged 0.6 per cent.[83] A 1980 survey bluntly stated that "there seems little doubt that practically every pension fund is now operating on a negative rate of return, and has been doing so for some years."[84] Pension fund investment performance in these countries did not significantly improve until the mid-1980s. For defined benefit pension plans in an inflationary environment, poor investment performance during the 1970s resulted in shortfalls (unfunded liabilities and experience deficiencies) requiring additional cash-flow contributions by corporate plan sponsors. Money purchase (defined contribution) pension plans have not performed much better. The collapse of the equity market in the early 1970s meant that stocks were no longer the hedge against inflation they were once touted to be. Where the real rate of return has been equal to or below the inflation rate simultaneously means that the cost of pension arrangements has increased for corporate plan sponsors and that their ability to inflation-proof benefits for pensioners has been limited.

In order for occupational pension plans to insulate the real value of their members' benefits and remain actuarially sound would require that they have "access to an asset whose real return is unaffected by inflation."[85] Such an asset does not exist. The inability of the private pension system to protect the absolute and relative standard of living of pensioners is systemically limited and unsolvable as long as the indexation of post-retirement income remains tied to the real rate of return on investment instead of wage or price movements.

THE GREAT PENSION DEBATE: REFORM INITIATIVES

Pension reform consumed the political passions and technical expertise of policy-makers in Canada for over a decade. It was symbolically launched when the Ontario Royal Commission on the Status of Pensions was formed in April 1977 and quietly came to an end in 1987 when a "package" of remedial measures was enacted. This reform "package" included legislative amendments to occupational pension plans in various jurisdictions as well as changes to the Canada Pension Plan (CPP) (and the QPP in Quebec).

This was the first comprehensive review and reform of retirement income arrangements in Canada since the introduction of the Ontario Pension Benefits Act 1965 and the Canada/Quebec Pensions Plans (C/QPPs) in 1966. The limitations of the private pension system and the underdevelopment of the state (or public) pension system (C/QPP, OAS and GIS) were the subject of a prolonged, animated and polarized public policy review.

From the beginning the Great Pension Debate resulted in the polarization of policy options—namely, reform of the private pension system or expansion of the public system—that is, the Canada/Quebec Pension Plans. The policy options advocated by the major actors generally corresponded to their class interests, although the situation was often complicated by competing vested interest group politics. Organized labour, social policy groups and women's organizations generally advocated expansion of the public pension system, while the private pension industry and the corporate sector promoted reform of the employer-based occupational pension system. The following section briefly reviews and assesses the recently concluded round of pension reform initiatives in Canada as they affect retirement income arrangements for the current and future elderly.

Reform initiatives regarding retirement income arrangements included a remedial package for both the public and private pension systems. In this regard the Pension Benefits Standards Act was amended effective 1 January 1987 for occupational pension plans in the federal jurisdiction. A number of provinces, including Ontario, Manitoba, Saskatchewan and Alberta, have introduced similar, though not identical, amendments to their private pension plan legislation. The major programme features and provisions affected by the remedial legislation in the federal jurisdiction are summarized in Table 4.10

TABLE 4.10
PRIVATE PENSION SYSTEM REFORM INITIATIVES

PROGRAMME FEATURE	REFORM MEASURE
Coverage	Voluntary occupational pension plan coverage to continue; no mandatory private coverage. However, full-time employees must be allowed to join the occupational pension plan after two years. Part-time employees with earnings at least equal to 35 per cent of the CPP's Year's Maximum Pensionable Earnings are eligible after two years.
Vesting and Portability	Pension entitlements are vested after two years of membership in the pension plan. Employees who terminate with a vested benefit have the following options: 1. leave their money in the plan and receive a deferred benefit at retirement; or 2. transfer the lump sum of their benefits to a new employer's pension plan if this is permitted; or 3. transfer the lump sum value of their benefits to a locked-in RRSP; or 4. buy an annuity that is payable at the time of termination or at retirement age.

Inflation-Proofing	There is no compulsory indexing of retirement benefits to either the price or earnings index to protect pensioners from inflation. The notable exception is the Friedland Task Force on Inflation Protection for Employment Pension Plans in Ontario, which recommended indexation equal to the increase in the Consumer Price Index (CPI) minus one percentage point for deferred pensions and retirement benefits.
Survivor Benefits	Mandatory survivor benefits must be paid so that a surviving spouse will receive at least 60 per cent of the retirement benefit. These benefits may not be terminated as a result of remarriage.
Unisex Tables	Employee contributions and benefits must not differ based on sex.
Splitting of Pension Credits	Pension benefits subject to splitting on marriage breakdown; both common law and legal marriages recognized.
Annual Statement and Plan Text	Annual statement must be provided to plan members; in addition, employees may review pension plan information.
Pension Advisory Committee	A pension advisory committee must be created, with at least one member on it, when the majority of plan members request one.

Amendments to the Canada Pension Plan (CPP), effective 1 January 1987, were an integral part of the reform "package" and complemented the remedial measures undertaken for the private pension system. Reforms to the public pension system are outlined in Table 4.11.

TABLE 4.11

PUBLIC PENSION SYSTEM REFORM INITIATIVES

PROGRAMME FEATURE	REFORM MEASURE
Income Replacement Rate	No increase in the current income replacement rate for the C/QPP; and no increase in the OAS/GIS.

Contribution Level

The combined contribution rate for employers and employees will be increased by 0.2 per cent for the next five years. In addition, increases of 0.15 per cent per year have been scheduled for the succeeding 20 years through 2011. The schedule for the period from 1992 to 2011 can be amended by regularly scheduled federal/provincial meetings. No contribution schedule was introduced for the period after 2011 when the baby boom retires.

Retirement Age

Retirement benefits can begin at any age between 60 and 70. Benefits that begin between age 60 and 65 will be reduced by 0.5 per cent per month prior to a person's 65th birthday. Benefits that begin after a person's 65th birthday will be increased by 0.5 per cent per month.

Sharing of Benefits

When the younger spouse in a legal or common-law marriage has reached age 60 and both have applied for the benefits earned during the marriage, the benefits are shared equally between them.

Splitting of
    Pension Credits

Pension credits earned during marriage will continue to be split between former marriage partners based on a series of administrative guidelines.

Survivor Benefits

Survivors over 65 will now receive 60 per cent of a deceased spouse's retirement benefit even if the survivor is also entitled to a retirement benefit. The combined benefits must not exceed the maximum retirement benefit payable at 65 when the plan member becomes eligible for the second of the two types of benefits. Survivor benefits will now continue to be paid even if the survivor remarries. More recently, however, the federal government issued a discussion paper on CPP survivor benefits in September 1987, which would, if implemented in the future, alter the structure and level of survivor benefits.

Disability Benefits

The flat-rate portion of disability benefits is increased from $91 to $233 (in 1986 dollars). The rules have been changed so that the minimum requirement of having contributed for at least five years has been reduced to two years in the last three. CPP disability benefits also include 75 per cent of the retirement benefit a person would have received had they turned 65 when they became disabled.

ASSESSMENT OF PENSION REFORM

The decade-long pension reform process resulted in many needed and overdue improvements. It is necessary, however, to evaluate these initiatives to determine whether they satisfactorily resolve the critical problems associated with the operation of the public and private pension systems and make them effective in terms of generating retirement income for the current and future elderly.

In order to assess pension reform a comparison of major programme features of the public and private systems is presented in Table 4.12. The assessment is summarized in Table 4.13. Based on this analysis, the public pension system—that is, the Canada/Quebec Pension Plans (C/QPPs)—is rated positively with respect to four evaluation criteria and negatively in one category. The C/QPPs are assessed positively in terms of coverage, vesting, portability and inflation-proofing and negatively in terms of the income replacement rate. The private pension system *after reform* is assessed as being neutral in terms of one evaluation criterion (portability), negative in the four other (income replacement rate, coverage, vesting and inflation-proofing) and positive in none.

With respect to the private pension system, the low level of coverage through employer-sponsored occupational pension plans and the lack of mandatory inflation-proofing of retirement benefits and deferred pensions continue to be major problems. The low level of voluntary occupational pension plan coverage will limit the proportion of the labour force that will receive retirement income from the private pension system in the future. Middle-income earners in particular will experience a significant shortfall in terms of maintaining their pre-retirement income.

In terms of inflation protection, the Friedland Task Force report in Ontario (1988) recommended the *partial* indexation of retirement

TABLE 4.12

COMPARISON OF MAJOR PUBLIC AND PRIVATE
PENSION SYSTEM PROGRAMME FEATURES

EVALUATION CRITERIA	PRIVATE PENSION SYSTEM[1]		CANADA/QUEBEC PENSION PLANS
	BEFORE REFORM	AFTER REFORM[2]	
Coverage	Voluntary and highly selective. Only 37 per cent of total labour force covered		Universal for all wage and salary earners
Vesting	10 years	2 years – federal 2 years – Ontario 5 years – Alta. & Man.[3] Factor 45 – Sask.	Immediate
Portability	Limited	Four options: • deferred pension • transfer value of benefit to new pension plan • transfer value to locked in RRSP • buy annuity	Full portability
Inflation-Proofing	67% of all plan members have no indexing	Only Ontario will require partial indexation of deferred and retirement pensions	Full inflation-proofing to Consumer Price Index
Income Replacement Rate	For three-quarters of unit benefit plan members, pension credit of 2% or more for each year of service to a maximum of 70% of salary, integrated with the C/QPP		25% of career average adjusted earnings up to the average industrial wage

Notes: 1 Based on an analysis of modal provisions for a defined benefit pension plan. This type of plan covers 93 per cent of all occupational pension plan members in Canada.
2 Based on amendments to the federal Pension Benefits Standards Act, except where otherwise noted.
3 Vesting after two years effective 1990.

Source: Statistics Canada, *Pension Plans in Canada 1984* (Ottawa: Minister of Supply and Services Canada, 1986), and relevant legislation.

benefits only for *future* retirees; however, this accounts for less than 40 per cent of all occupational pension plan members in Canada and has not yet been formally enacted.[86] Pension benefits in other jurisdictions would not be increased for inflation in the retirement period. Furthermore, the formula for the partial indexation of benefits would allow, depending on the length of the deferral period and the inflation rate, a reduction in the value of deferred vested pensions by as much as 50 per cent.[87] Pension plans in other jurisdictions would not be required to revalue vested deferred pensions at all, which would negatively affect the vesting and portability of occupational pension plan benefits, despite recent legislative intervention, and the amount of retirement income ultimately generated.

TABLE 4.13

ASSESSMENT OF PUBLIC AND PRIVATE PENSION SYSTEM REFORM
BY EVALUATION CRITERIA

	ASSESSMENT[1]	
EVALUATION CRITERIA	Private Pension System[2]	Public Pension System[2]
Coverage	−	+
Vesting	− [3]	+
Portability	0 [4]	+
Inflation-Proofing	− [5]	+
Income Replacement Rate	−	−

Notes: 1 Comparative ranking where + indicates a superior assessment, 0 a neutral rating and − an inferior evaluation.
2 After pension reform.
3 Provision will generate a large number of partial deferred pensions which will not necessarily be revalued (indexed) over the deferral period.
4 The four options will generate a large number of partial vested deferred pensions. The cumulative amount of the pensions generated, if transferred, will depend on investment performance and annuity rates. Risk-taking has been externalized from the plan sponsor to the former member.
5 Partial indexation only in Ontario, which accounted for less than 40 per cent of all private pension plan members as of 1984.

The primary limitation of the public pension system—the Canada/Quebec Pension Plans—continues to be the low income replacement rate for middle-income earners. This inadequate replacement rate compounds the low level of voluntary employer-sponsored pension plan coverage (RPP) and registered retirement savings plan (RRSP) enrolment through the private retirement system. During the course of the pension reform debate there were numerous proposals to expand the public and/or private pension systems to generate a combined income replacement rate in the order of 70 per cent of pre-retirement earnings for middle-income earners.

The public policy review of retirement income arrangements in Canada and the remedial reform "package," however, failed to expand either the private or the public pension system. As a result of conflicting views and pressures concerning the extent and nature of pension reform based on the opposing class interests of the major actors, the critical issues of coverage, inflation-proofing and an adequate income replacement rate were left unresolved. Throughout the reform process, the private pension industry adopted a minimal accommodation strategy in order to allow the employer-sponsored system time to mature in anticipation of the baby boom's retirement. In the final analysis, however, as this assessment indicates, pension reform in Canada was a failure.

The inability to consummate pension reform was a result of the political and structural limits imposed on the welfare state by the dominant class interests.[88] The conservative interregnum in Britain, the United States and Canada during the 1980s has generated a similar response with respect to pensions policy. Conservative governments in these countries have pursued a policy characterized by the privatization of retirement income arrangements, limiting the role of the state pension system and fiscal restraint.

In the United States the Reagan administration undertook a prolonged and bitter congressional struggle to "rescue" the social security system from its chronic deficit position.[89] The result was a controversial measure raising the retirement age from 65 to 67, rather than reducing benefits, although the financial outcome is the same. Remedial legislation regarding private pensions has generally centred on the wind-up or termination provisions of such plans (note Appendix A).

In Britain, the Thatcher government's public policy review culminated in the Social Security Act 1986, which reduced the benefit formula under the state earnings-related pension (rather than eliminating SERP as had originally been recommended in the 1985 green paper). "Contracting-out" from the state pension system by occupational pension plans was continued. Further privatization of retirement income arrangements was fostered by introducing personal pensions (PPs) for the first time. These personal savings vehicles were modelled on Individual Retirement Accounts (IRAs) in the U.S. and Registered Retirement Savings Plans (RRSPs) in Canada. However, individuals with personal pensions in Britain are now permitted to "contract-out" from both their employer's occupational pension plan and from the earnings-related state pension. The earlier 1985 white paper on social security also recommended improving vesting (preservation) for occupational pension plan members after two years of service.

Both Liberal and Conservative governments in Canada rejected an expansion of the public pension system and, instead, opted for incremental, and basically ineffective, reform of the private pension system. The Conservative government of Brian Mulroney has pursued the privatization of retirement income arrangements by substantially increasing the contribution limits for individuals to fiscally regressive RRSPs, which cover only 15 per cent of all tax filers. Compounding this situation was the unwillingness of progressive social policy groups and organized labour (CLC) to politicize the pension issue and engage in extraparliamentary action. Within this political and policy context, serious pension reform was ultimately doomed. As a consequence, the most important limitations of the private pension system remain and will negatively affect the economic position of the current and future elderly.

Pension reform, however, is politically popular, and it has had the effect of raising the elderly's expectations. According to a Gallup Poll survey in January 1984, 43 per cent of Canadians favoured adequate retirement income provided through government pensions, while 37 per cent favoured private pensions and 18 per cent supported individual efforts. Support for government pensions was highest among the young (18 to 29), the relatively old (50 +), women (48 per cent) and middle-income earners (42 per cent).[90] A more recent Decima poll (Fall 1986) indicated that 37 per cent favoured providing adequate retirement through the government (federal and provincial), 31 per cent favoured individual responsibility and 29 per cent held the view that employers are responsible for adequate retirement income arrangements.[91] For the elderly, pension reform will be a protracted struggle.

THE PRIVATE PENSION SYSTEM'S LIMITATIONS: IMPLICATIONS

The universal limitations of the employer-based private pension system in Canada, Britain and the United States are limited coverage, inadequate vesting (preservation) standards, restricted portability (transferability) arrangements, and the lack of inflation-proofing for deferred and retirement pensions. These limitations are mutually interactive and explain the low proportion of income derived by the current elderly from the private pension system. This in turn necessitates the elderly's reliance upon the state pension system and tax-based "safety net" programmes sponsored by government. The inadequacies of the occupational pension system will have important repercussions for the future elderly.

The problems associated with the operation of the private pension system are central to the political economy of pensions. Based on the preceding analysis a number of implications can be identified. First, the limitations of occupational pension plans explain the low proportion of income received by the current elderly from the private pension system. A corollary is that the deficiencies of the private pension system, in conjunction with the underdevelopment of the state retirement income system, have resulted in the immiseration and marginalization of the elderly.

Second, the limitations of employer-sponsored pension plans will have a major impact upon the large "baby boom" cohort of future elderly. To the extent that existent private pension arrangements are incapable of generating adequate retirement income, despite recent reform initiatives, it will mean that the future elderly will have to rely on the state pension system. The limitations of employer-based pension plans will not become apparent for another thirty to fifty years until a new and larger generation of poor elderly is created by the aging of the population. Because of demographic aging, reliance upon the state retirement system may produce intergenerational and intersectoral fiscal tensions.

A third, and important, implication is that as a result of these universal limitations, the private pension system is not an efficient and cost-effective delivery system for retirement income. Pension reform is incomplete and has not improved this situation. The disadvantages of the private pension system must be compared with the advantages of the public pension system. In Canada, Britain and the United States the state retirement income system's programme features include universal coverage for all wage and salary earners, immediate vesting, total portability of pension credits and the full indexation of benefits to the consumer price index.

Fourth, under normal circumstances it requires thirty to forty years for a pension system to mature; therefore, reform of both the public *and* the private systems is required in the near term so it can be synchronized with the retirement of the baby boom generation.

The failure of the recently concluded round of pension reform will result in limiting the range of viable policy options in the long run. Reform of the private and/or state pension systems will impose additional costs upon the corporate sector and the active labour force. The cost of pension reform, given existing socio-economic arrangements, may be expected to generate sectoral and sectional strains between and among the various pension actors—the elderly, the state, the corporate sector and the unionized labour force—as each pursues its structurally determined interests.

Fifth and last, the limitations of the private pension system have generated the politics of pension reform and evoked a highly polarized public policy debate. Pension reform in the short term has been a failure, which ensures that pensions and the elderly will continue to be a long-term issue of public policy. Unless it is resolved, the pension issue will become more politically volatile as the structural pressures increase and converge in the future in these countries. Pension reform will ultimately, however, depend on realpolitik and political mobilization.

The elements of the political economy of pensions identified and analysed thus far have included the immiseration of the elderly, the economics of an aging population, and the limitations of the private pension system. The universal limitations of employer-sponsored occupational pension plans affect the entire labour force. The specific limitations of the private pension system under conditions of collective bargaining, however, are of special importance and concern because of the impact on cost, power and equity issues which affect the stability of the industrial relations system.

5

The Limitations of the Private Pension System under Conditions of Collective Bargaining

Social security is not . . . marginal to the main interests of the union . . . but is one of their most important fields of action.

Tony Lynes

In addition to the universal limitations of the private pension system, there are others which are specifically related to conditions of collective bargaining. The relationship between the industrial relations system and the political economy of pensions is analysed here. The central theme developed is that the problems associated with the private pension system in Britain, Canada and the United States will serve to heighten tensions in an already strained industrial relations system. The pension issue will have a destabilizing influence upon collective bargaining arrangements in the future because it has an impact upon the basic issues of cost, power and equity.

The factors which affect the structure and undermine the stability of the industrial relations system are identified as follows: first, increasing total pension costs, especially those associated with the occupational pension system; second, a set of power-related issues, particularly the absence of a bargaining agent's legal right to negotiate pensions and bargain post-retirement benefits; third, an equity issue arising from the lack of a mandatory benefit adjudication (grievance and arbitration) procedure to resolve disputes between pension plan members or beneficiaries and trustees; and fourth, the co-management of pensions as a catalyst or "flash point" within the industrial relations system because issues related to control over pension capital, cost and equity converge into a "critical mass" in terms of power relationships under conditions of collective bargaining.

HISTORICAL BACKGROUND

"The fringe benefit movement [was] basically a management movement," according to Allen, and "unions took what they could get and made the best of it."[1] Prior to World War II the form and limits of welfare benefits were decided upon by management without negotiation or consultation with trade unions. Consequently, unions in North America, for ideological and organizational reasons, had a strong antipathy towards employer-sponsored welfare benefits and occupational pension plans. Between 1870 and 1920, business unionism in North America established its hegemony, with the resultant bureaucratization of the labour movement. The ascendancy of industrial unionism in the 1940s witnessed the rise of labour leaders as the "new men of power."[2] The expansion of the modern union as a welfare institution in the post-war period was a manifestation of this "social unionism" and increased the internal rationalization and specialization of union functions in response to a more complex bargaining environment.[3]

From an historical perspective the introduction of employer-sponsored welfare benefits served a series of interrelated ideological, organizational and labour market functions for the corporate sector. While there was no single cause for the introduction of employee benefits, certain common lines of development can be traced. Welfare benefits served multiple purposes, including attracting a labour supply and reducing turnover, serving as an investent in human capital by improving morale, increasing productivity and efficiency by rationalizing the human element in the work process, promoting loyalty to the firm, preventing or forestalling unionization, preventing government intervention with respect to compulsory social insurance, maximizing the tax position of certain benefits by increasing non-taxable compensation to employees, minimizing the cost per unit of benefit through group arrangements, thereby compensating for imperfect individual knowledge of insurance markets, and creating a favourable corporate public relations image.

Pensions assisted in promoting these corporate objectives. Occupational pension plans were specifically introduced to remove elderly persons, who were generally viewed as "inefficient," from the production processes of modern industry and to eliminate patronage in the civil service; to open channels of promotion for younger employees; and to compensate employers for recruitment and training costs should a worker terminate. Pensions also served as a social control function by making receipt of retirement benefits contingent upon "good and faithful service." Historically, employers have attempted to maximize their control over welfare plans by making such payments discretionary. Conversely, workers and unions have attempted to minimize management control, viewing such benefits as being earned.

Employee benefits came to the fore as a subject of collective bargaining after World War II for a number of reasons. First, during the war the "fringe benefit movement" was part of the wage control programme in Britain, Canada and the U.S. Employers were allowed, and encouraged, to substitute benefit programmes such as paid vacations and occupational pensions for direct monetary compensation. Second, welfare benefits were made income tax deductible as a legitimate business expense, which served as an inducement to introduce employee benefit plans. Third, the 1949 U.S. National Labour Relations Board *Inland Steel* ruling subsequently deemed welfare and pension plans to be wages and therefore an appropriate and mandatory subject for collective bargaining.[4] This established a demonstration effect for Canadian employers, who were often unionized by American-based "international" unions. Fourth, in the immediate postwar rounds of negotiations in the U.S., labour unions for the first time spearheaded a drive to negotiate health, welfare and retirement programmes. Unions such as the United Mine Workers of America (UMWA), the United Auto Workers (UAW) and the United Steel Workers of America (USWA) became innovators in the field. Union-negotiated benefit programmes and occupational pension plans became new and important issues for collective bargaining. "The pressure for extending the range of subjects dealt with by collective agreements" in the postwar period, according to Flanders, came "almost exclusively from the trade unions."[5] Such benefit or welfare plans have generally evolved, according to Barbarino and Allen, in three phases: recognition of need and introduction of a programme; improved benefit levels; and a broadening of coverage and eligibility.

The expansion of the employee benefit package in the postwar period has significant implications for social policy and labour organizations. In the first instance, the development of the negotiated benefit package has created a dual allocative mechanism for the provision of income security against universal and employment-related risks. An underdeveloped "distanced" social security system exists for the majority of wage and salary earners at the state level, while a "non-distanced" mechanism — the negotiated employee benefit package — has evolved for unionized workers, particularly in the oligopolistic sectors, at the plant or industry level.[6] The modern union as a welfare institution therefore engages in a "micro-social function"[7] as an organization on behalf of its membership at the shop floor level through collective bargaining, while the labour confederation or national union serves a "macro-social function" at the state level on behalf of all workers based on its lobbying and political activities.[8]

The "non-distanced" welfare benefit package introduced and expanded through collective bargaining at the plant or industry level is a response to the inadequacies of the "distanced" social security system at the state level. Trade unions under capitalism in general "have largely achieved at the level of the firm . . . for their own members social policies they have failed to achieve for all workers through political struggle at the level of the state."[9] As one pragmatic American trade unionist put it, "Unions decided that they would attempt through bargaining to win for their members what they were unable to convince government to provide for all its citizens."[10] Under conditions of collective bargaining, particularly in North America, employee benefit plans now constitute a "system of private social security"[11] or a "corporate social security system,"[12] which is either a substitute for or a supplement to the state social security system. From a social policy perspective, however, the distributional impact of the dual public-private social security system generates and reinforces sectional interests between the unionized and non-unionized labour force as a result of the uneven allocation and level of benefits.

Workers have developed a collective "security" or "protectivism" response, to use Barbash's formulation, as a reaction to the modern corporation's "cost discipline" and profit maximization behaviour.[13] For labour organizations this "security" response has included the regulation of conditions of employment such as wages, as well as income maintenance protection against the universal and employment-related risks of sickness, disability, maternity, unemployment, death and old age. Modern unions with their organizational imperatives act as a welfare institution[14] to satisfy their membership's need for economic security. By maximizing this social security function, unions are in opposition to the cost minimization/profit maximization behaviour of the corporate sector. The expansion of employee benefit programmes has thus broadened the scope of collective bargaining in the postwar period. Unions in the future will be forced to engage in intensified distributive and intra-organizational bargaining[15] with respect to pension related issues.

The term "fringe benefit," broadly defined, now includes negotiated as well as voluntary benefit programmes to which an employer contributes on behalf of an employee; in addition, the cost of any legally required payment made by an employer is also included as a fringe benefit cost. This term, implying a gratuity based on "good and faithful service," has now been replaced by the more modern expressions "supplementary wage provision," "related wage practices," "social charges," "welfare plans" or "employee benefit plans," suggesting an earned benefit based on the deferred wage doctrine. The terms "employee benefit," "benefit" or "welfare" plans are used here. The more contemporary terms signify that benefit plans are no longer "fringe" but now are central to the collective bargaining process in terms of complexity, cost and importance.

In recent years under conditions of collective bargaining, as a result of the expansion of the employee benefit package and the associated cost, many sophisticated employers have adopted a total compensation approach to the negotiation of labour costs. Now "the pattern of package deals are based on the total value of labour remuneration, wages and fringes having become interchangeable costs."[16] As a result of this approach, where total compensation is equal to employee benefits plus wages, unions have been able to exert a positive influence on the level (amount) and distribution (mix) of compensation between salary and employee benefits and within the benefit package. Employee benefit and occupational pension plans under conditions of collective bargaining are now incorporated into a firm's wage and salary structure and its long-run profit perspective.

THE COST OF EMPLOYEE BENEFITS

The cost associated with employee benefit programmes has increased dramatically in the past thirty-five years under conditions of collective bargaining. A number of significant characteristics and relationships associated with employee benefits can be summarized as follows.[17] The incidence and cost of employee benefit plans is higher in capital intensive, oligopolistic sectors of the economy than in the labour intensive, competitive sector; the cost and frequency of welfare benefits are related to firm size and are positively related to wage and salary levels; there is a direct correlation between the profitability of an industry and its expenditure on employee benefits; the higher the profit per employee, the higher the benefit expenditure per employee; the ratio of employee benefits to total compensation is greater in unionized firms than in nonunionized firms; the stronger a union, the greater the expenditure by a firm on benefits; the skilled-nonskilled total compensation differential exceeds the skilled-nonskilled wage differential; and the decertification of unions (in the U.S.) is inversely related to the ratio of employee benefits to compensation in unionized firms. The evidence regarding the level and distribution of employee benefits generally confirms the dual labour market theory which postulates that there is a "primary" labour market comprised of highly paid, unionized workers in capital intensive, oligopolistic industries and a "secondary" labour market characterized by low paid, nonunionized workers in labour intensive, competitive sectors.

In order to determine the dramatic acceleration of welfare benefit plan costs as a percentage of employer's gross payroll in Canada, Britain and the U.S. an historical time-series has been constructed for the period between 1953 and 1986. This information is presented in Table 5.1. The data for the United States and Canada are fully comparable, covering employees in all industries. In Britain, however, where "the cost of benefits to employers . . . are hard to assess, since most firms do not . . . cost their benefit schemes,"[18] the time-series was constructed from disparate sources for the manufacturing sector (manual and clerical). Therefore, the comparative trends outlined here must be viewed as only an approximation.

TABLE 5.1

EMPLOYEE BENEFIT PROGRAMMES AS A PERCENTAGE OF GROSS PAYROLL, CANADA, U.S. AND U.K., SELECTED YEARS, 1953–1986

YEAR	CANADA	U.S.[2]	U.K.
1953	15.1[1]	21.6(E)	10.0[3]
1957	16.4	23.4	—
1959	22.2	24.5	14.4[4]
1961	24.3	25.8	—
1963	26.2	26.8	—
1965	25.2	27.0	—
1967	27.8	29.9	13.6[5]
1969	29.1	30.8	—
1971	29.0	32.8	21.1
1973	28.1	34.8	23.7[5,6]
1975–76	31.1	37.4	26.4[5,6]
1977–78	32.4	40.5	25.4[5,6]
1979–80	33.1	36.6	28.5[5,6,7]
1982	32.7	36.7	28.0[5,6]
1984	32.5	36.6	n.a.
1986	36.3	38.3	n.a.
PERCENTAGE INCREASE 1953–86	140.4	77.3	180.0

Notes: 1 Between 1953–54 and 1969–70 includes the Old Age Security Tax (OAST), which was eliminated in 1971 and put on a general revenue basis.
2 The data in this time series between 1957 and 1977 is based on an ongoing sub-sample of 159 large firms from the U.S. Chamber of Commerce's survey of 158 companies. Because of sample bias a somewhat higher figure is reported here than is the case with the other information in the survey.
3 1955 for five SIC manufacturing industries.
4 For manual workers only.
5 For all manufacturing industries.
6 Average for manual and non-manual employees combined for production and construction.
7 For 1981.

Sources: Stevenson, Kellogg, Ernst and Whinney, Employee Benefit Costs in Canada (Toronto: Thorne Stevenson and Kellogg, various years); Chamber of Commerce of the United States, Employee Benefits 1978 (Washington, D.C.: Chamber of Commerce, 1978) Table 19, p. 27, and the U.S. Chamber of Commerce, Employee Benefits 1986 (Washington, D.C.: Chamber of Commerce, 1987), p. 5. For Britain this time-series was constructed from the Ministry of Labour *Gazette*, August 1957, pp. 277–80; G. L. Reid and James Bates, "The Cost of Fringe Benefits for Manual Workers in British Industry," *British Journal of Industrial Relations* 1, no. 3 (1963), Table 7, p. 5; R. I. Hawkesworth, "Fringe Benefits in British Industry," *British Journal of Industrial Relations* 15, no. 3 (1977), Table 1, p. 397; Jane Moonman, *The Effectiveness of Fringe Benefits in Industry* (Epping Essex: Gower Press, 1973): Lord Diamond, *Royal Commission on the Distribution of Income and Wealth*, Report no. 8, Fifth Report on the Standing Reference (London: HMSO, October 1979), Figure 9.2, p. 131; The Royal Commission on the Distribution of Income and Wealth, *An A to Z of Income and Wealth* (London: HMSO, 1980), Table L, p. 16; "Labour Costs in 1975," Department of Employment *Gazette*, September 1977, Table 6, pp. 9–10, and p. 8; and *Employment Gazette*, July 1985, Table 1, pp. 281–82.

In the United States, Canada and Britain the cost associated with employee benefit plans increased from an average of nearly 20 per cent of gross payroll in 1953 to nearly 33 per cent in 1982. In general, well over one-third of gross payroll expenditure is now spent on employee benefits, and the proportion is expected to increase well into the 1980s.[19] Between 1953 and 1986 the expenditure on benefits as a proportion of gross payroll increased by 77 per cent in the U.S., 140 per cent in Canada, and 180 per cent in Britain (1982). According to one Statistics Canada survey, total expenditure for welfare and benefit plans by unionized firms was 94 per cent greater than for non-union employers.[20] This significant expenditure reflects both a broadening and a deepening of the employee benefit package, particularly under conditions of collective bargaining. Today employee benefit plans are no longer "fringe"; they are big money. For labour unions the expansion of their "micro-social" welfare function has generated tensions within the framework of distributive and intra-organizational bargaining, which is central to the labour-management power relationship in capitalist societies.

Distributive Bargaining and Benefit Costs. Benefit costs have increased at a considerably faster rate than wages. In Canada between 1960 and 1986, for example, employee benefit costs increased at a rate which was nearly 1.5 times greater than the increase in the average industrial wage (AIW). A similar pattern has emerged in other industrialized countries. It not unreasonable to expect that management will resist any future expansion of employee benefit costs in order to contain total labour costs, particularly in periods of slow economic growth.

Increasing benefit costs affect the level and distribution of total compensation between salary and benefits. While welfare benefits mean that the value of the total compensation package is increased, it often comes at the expense of a corresponding reduction in direct monetary income because of the trade-off between wages and benefits. The expansion of the employee benefit package has the effect of relatively reducing the current consumption (take-home pay) of workers, regardless of whether these are contributory or non-contributory programmes. Consequently, there is still pressure on wages from workers, despite the utility of benefit plans and the increased value of the compensation package. This trade-off is exacerbated in periods of inflation and slow economic growth. There is the prospect of continued pressure from workers and unions for an expansion of the employee benefit package *and* wage increases. In the future the welfare maximization behaviour of unions will increasingly conflict with the cost minimization imperative of the corporate sector, which will sharpen the tensions already inherent in distributive bargaining.

Intra-Organizational Bargaining and Benefit Costs. The increasing strain on labour-management relations is compounded by the modern union's intra-organizational (internal) bargaining and its own organizational imperatives. Internal bargaining refers to the reconciliation of diverse sectional interests, or competing claims, within the labour force represented by the union: skilled and less skilled, married and single, men and women, young and old, employed and retired, and so forth. As a welfare institution, the union must engage in intra-organizational bargaining regarding the cost of employee benefit plans as it affects two crucial issues: first, the level and distribution of total compensation *between* salary and benefit plans; and second, the mix of programmes *within* the employee benefit package. These issues have different effects upon the various segments of a union's diversified membership.

The union as an organization mediates the conflicting sectional claims of its membership through internal bargaining. Distributionally, for example, young workers have a propensity to place greater emphasis on direct monetary compensation, while older workers place a priority on deferred compensation such as improved pensions. Women also tend to assign a priority to wage increases rather than to employee benefits. Married men generally favour a balance between direct and indirect compensation. The mix within the benefit package is also subject to competing claims. For example, young married workers in North America (and now in

Britain) are usually interested in life, health and disability insurance, whereas older workers are concerned about pensions; older workers, women and single men place a low priority on dental plans, while married men approve of their implementation. It falls to the union to resolve these internal distributional issues.

The final consideration bringing unions into conflict with the cost minimization behaviour of the private sector with respect to the pension issue are the institutional imperatives of unions as organizations. These include organizational survival, growth, sovereignty, job regulation, prestige, and maximization of membership, average wage rates, the wage bill, employment and their membership's social welfare. The expansion of employee benefits, including occupational pension plans, under conditions of collective bargaining in the postwar period has served to promote, either directly or indirectly, a number of these purposes.

Nineteenth-century unions in Britain and the United States realized that friendly benefits and union-sponsored welfare programmes served the purpose of stabilizing the labour organization by attracting and holding members by promoting a sense of loyalty to the union. The negotiation of welfare and pension plans by industrial unions in North America after World War II served a similar purpose. Innovative welfare programmes served to enhance the prestige of industrial unions with the public. Benefit plans advanced the welfare of the membership and were identified with the union. The negotiation of costly and complex welfare and pension plans furthered the union's organizational imperative for institutional survival and growth. The negotiation of these programmes symbolized the reluctant acceptance by management of the permanence of the union and a commitment to a long-term collective bargaining relationship. In a hostile environment this provided unions with institutional security.

Collectively bargained health and welfare plans have also served as an impetus for organizational bureaucratization and the specialization of internal union functions. A number of major American unions — for example, the United Mine Workers, United Auto Workers, United Steel Workers and the Teamsters — established social security or welfare departments and have employed the necessary technical staff. In Britain in the early 1970s, with the renewed interest in occupational pension schemes, the Transport and General Workers' Union and the General and Municipal Workers' Union pursued a similar course. In addition, negotiated or union-sponsored welfare plans have enhanced the power and prestige of union leaders. The technicalities of employee benefit and pension plan arrangements have forced them "to acquire specialized knowledge and skills" with the result that their "power has been increased by the greater complexity of [the] problems which have to be resolved in determining union policy."[21] The union leader claims credit for "delivering the goods" to "his" members.

In the most fundamental sense, under conditions of collective bargaining, unions have acquired a vested interest in the maintenance and expansion of negotiated welfare and pension arrangements. This emphasis is suggested by the significantly increased proportion of gross payroll devoted to employee benefits and the greater cost associated with such arrangements in the postwar period. The modern union's organizational imperatives, coupled with its benefit maximization approach to distributive bargaining, conflict with the cost minimization behaviour of the corporate sector. The collective bargaining relationship as it relates to pension arrangements will become more strained as the underlying cost pressures increase.

THE COST OF PENSIONS

Pension arrangements generally represent the most important non-wage expenditure within the total compensation package and are the largest monetary item within the employee benefit package. The costs associated with employer-sponsored pension plans have increased considerably in the past thirty years and have exceeded the growth of wages. The total cost of pension arrangements and those associated with occupational pension plans under conditions of collective bargaining are significantly greater than for non-union firms.

A number of factors, including inflation, poor investment performance, actuarial deficiencies and unfunded liabilities, the aging of the labour force, slower labour force growth and the cost of pension reform will all contribute to escalating the cost per unit of pension benefit and increasing the cost of employer-sponsored occupational pension plans. In addition, the cost of state pension arrangements over the long term will also rise as a result of population aging and improved benefit levels, requiring greater corporate and individual contributions to maintain the solvency of the plans. Such increases will result in higher labour costs for employers and a reduction in employee's current consumption, with corresponding pressure on wages by workers to maintain their standard of living.

Because of the strong correlation between unionization and occupational pension plan coverage, with unionized workers being the largest and most concentrated group covered by the private pension system, unions may be in a position to resist higher contributions and a reduction in their members' standard of living. Similarly, it may be expected that the corporate sector will resist increased pension costs in order to protect profit margins. A potential exists that unions will be brought into conflict with the corporate sector, the state, and possibly their own members over this issue. In the long run the conflict may have a destabilizing impact on collective bargaining relationships and the industrial relations system.

Table 5.2 outlines total pension costs as a proportion of gross payroll and in relation to total employee benefit costs.[22] Employer contributions to the state and occupational pension plans when considered as separate items within the total compensation package lag behind expenditures on vacations in Canada and Britain and rank first in the United States. However, when *total* pension costs (public plus private plans) are treated as one component, they generally assume the pre-eminent position as the leading non-wage gross payroll expenditure and the largest component within the employee benefit package. Total pension costs as a percentage of gross payroll were 5.4 per cent in Canada, 12.8 per cent in the U.S. and nearly 13 per cent in Britain. Total pension costs therefore represented 15 per cent of all employee benefit costs in Canada, 33 per cent in the U.S., and 45 per cent in Britain.

Total pension costs, as these data suggest, are an important component within the total compensation package and have a significant impact on an employer's gross payroll expenditure. This is particularly the case in Britain and the United States. The relatively modest order of magnitude in Canada is attributable to the inordinately low level of contributions to the state pension plan by international standards. Any increase in either state or occupational pension plan contributions will result in greater total pension costs. Total pension costs in excess of wage growth will, in turn, result in the expansion of the employee benefit package in relation to total compensation or gross payroll. Supplementary labour costs (employee benefits including pensions) will therefore grow relative to direct monetary compensation, posing the issue of distributive bargaining between labour and management and intra-

TABLE 5.2

TOTAL EMPLOYER PENSION COSTS AS A PERCENTAGE OF GROSS PAYROLL AND IN RELATION TO TOTAL EMPLOYEE BENEFIT COSTS,
U.K., U.S. AND CANADA, 1983–1986

COUNTRY	EMPLOYER PENSION COSTS AS A % OF GROSS PAYROLL			EMPLOYEE BENEFITS AS A % OF GROSS PAYROLL	PENSION COSTS AS A % OF EMPLOYEE BENEFIT COSTS
	Occupational +	State =	Total		
U.K.[1]	5.0	7.5[3]	12.5	27.9	44.8
U.S.[2]	6.7	6.1	12.8	38.3	33.4
Canada[3]	4.1	1.3	5.4	36.3	14.9

Notes: 1 1983.
2 1986.
3 National Insurance, inclusive of all programmes.

Sources: Department of Employment, *Employment Gazette* (July 1985), Table 1, p. 282, and the Government Actuary,
Occupational Pension Schemes 1983 (London: HMSO, 1986), p. 35; U.S. Chamber of Commerce, *Employee Benefits
1986* (Washington, D.C.: Chamber of Commerce, 1987), Table 6, p. 13; Stevenson, Kellogg, Ernst and Whinney,
Employee Benefit Plans in Canada 1986 (Toronto: Stevenson, Kellogg, Ernst and Whinney, 1987), Table 8, p. 22.

organizational bargaining among sectional interests within the union.

The cost of the employer-based occupational pension system is the primary component of total pension costs. The information in Table 5.2 indicates it represents 40 per cent of the total in the U.K., 52 per cent in the U.S., and 76 per cent in Canada. Employer-sponsored occupational pension plan costs as a percentage of gross payroll and annual expenditure per employee are outlined in Table 5.3 for Canada where complete information is available. Between 1953 and 1986 the annual per capita expenditure by employers for occupational pension plans increased by 872 per cent or over 25 per cent a year. Occupational pension plan costs have substantially exceeded wage growth.

TABLE 5.3

EMPLOYER OCCUPATIONAL PENSION PLAN COSTS,[1] CANADA, 1953–1986

| | ANNUAL COST | |
YEAR	% of Gross Payroll	$ Per Employee
1953	4.0	$ 137
1957	3.9	167
1959	3.6	182
1961	4.3	216
1963	4.4	230
1965	3.6	191
1967	3.2	210
1969	3.3	242
1971	3.8	332
1973	3.8	392
1975/76	4.2	552
1977/78	4.6	750
1979/80	5.2	974
1982	4.9	1,137
1984	4.1	1,204
1986	4.1	1,332

Note: 1 Employer contributions including payments towards unfunded liabilities and experience deficiencies where applicable.

Source: Information supplied courtesy of Stevenson, Kellogg, Ernst and Whinney, *Employee Benefit Costs in Canada* (Toronto: Stevenson, Kellogg, Ernst and Whinney, various years).

In Canada a number of important payroll relationships were established within the total compensation package: namely, that the growth in annual per capita occupational pension plan costs has exceeded the increase in wages and total compensation; however, the rate of growth for total employee benefit package expenditures, and for benefits net of pensions, has been greater than the increase in occupational pension plan costs. The broadening and deepening of total employee benefit expenditures relative to pensions explains the deceptively moderate increase in occupational pension plan cost as a percentage of gross payroll, despite the substantial increase in per capita costs. There are good reasons to believe, however, that total pension costs will increase in the future.

The Escalation of Future Pension Costs. There are a number of converging factors which will result in the escalation of occupational pension plan costs. They are identified as follows: first, the impact of financial markets on the operation of the pensions system; second, the cost associated with improved pension benefits; third, the impact of population aging on pension expenditures; and fourth, the cost of pension reform. Each of these considerations is briefly reviewed.

First, inflation over the past decade has had an adverse impact on the operation of the private pension system and will affect future pension costs. An inflation rate in excess of conservative actuarial salary and rate of return assumptions plays havoc with pension plan funding and stable contribution rates. In Canada, for example, per capita expenditure on occupational pension plans by employers nearly tripled between 1971 and 1980; between 1980 and 1986 they increased by 36 per cent (Table 5.3). In Britain, company outlay on contributory pension schemes recorded similar advances.[23] Inflation increases the salary base upon which retirement benefits are calculated. This impact is particularly severe in the case of final average earnings pension plans, resulting in what has been termed the "linebacker" or "three martini effect," necessitating increased company contributions.

Poor pension fund investment performance has required additional contributions by corporate plan sponsors to cover shortfalls. The real average annual rate of return on investment for trusteed pension plans in Canada averaged 0.7 per cent between 1961 and 1975 and was running at −2.9 per cent in the late 1970s during a period of high inflation.[24] In Britain the average annual real rate of return on pension funds in the period between 1965 and 1975 was 0.6 per cent.[25] Pension fund investment performance generally lags the stock market. Inflation made a significant positive rate of return on investment to pension plans more difficult to achieve.

As a result of the combination of rising salaries, poor investment performance, the divergence between conservative actuarial assumptions and actual experience and improved benefits, there has been a dramatic increase in actuarial and experience deficiencies for many occupational pension plans. This has resulted in many employer-sponsored plans having liabilities which exceed the assets to pay for accrued pension benefits, especially in the United States and to a lesser extent in Canada. Substantial additional contributions have been required from corporate plan sponsors to cover the shortfall and maintain the solvency of the pension scheme. Actuarial deficiencies and unfunded liabilities are amortized—that is, carried forward and written off over fifteen years in Canada and usually forty years in the U.S. — and hence by definition are a long-term problem. For private sector plan sponsors actuarial deficiencies and unfunded liabilities are of particular importance because they adversely affect a corporation's cash flow position and serve as a drag on future profits.

In Canada this situation, while not as severe as that experienced in the United States, is nevertheless of considerable concern. In the late 1970s nearly 70 per cent of all major corporate pension plans were in a deficit position. "The rate of change in the dollar magnitude of unfunded past service liabilities and experience deficiencies," according to the Financial Executives Institute of Canada, "continues to grow at an alarming pace."[26] Between 1969 and 1983 unfunded liabilities and experience deficiencies in the private sector increased by nearly 415 per cent and accounted for nearly 20 per cent of occupational pension plan contributions.[27] In 1980, as a result of inflation, total actuarial liabilities represented 38 per cent of shareholders equity and were 34 per cent of three-year average pre-tax income.[28] In recent years the absolute magnitudes of unfunded liabilities and actuarial deficiencies have been kept in check in relation to accounting ratios only as a result of an increase in the equity and earnings base of corporations.[29]

In the United States in an inflationary climate, the unfunded liabilities of employer-sponsored occupational pension plans reached alarming proportions. Unfunded pension liabilities for 10 of the top 100 U.S. corporations listed in the Fortune 500 in the late 1970s were equivalent to one-quarter to one-third of the net worth of

the company and in some cases even more.[30] For 7 of those companies, unfunded pension liabilities exceeded the value of the company's stock. A subsequent survey of 1,644 large U.S. industrial and
service companies in the early 1980s, again, confirmed these findings.[31] For major corporations such as Westinghouse, LTV, Western
Union, Bethlehem Steel, International Harvester, GM, Uniroyal and
Chrysler unfunded pension liabilities ranged from 35 to 278 per
cent of net worth. Among large U.S. corporations, contributions
were equivalent to 20 per cent of pre-tax earnings in the mid-
1970s—double the amount of a decade earlier—and "that proportion," according to business sources, "is bound to increase
further."[32] These pension plans are now unfunded liabilities with a
company. These liabilities and actuarial deficiencies have to be built
into the long-term debt structure of a corporation, thus requiring
increased contributions in the future. Higher costs, however, will
exert downward pressure on wages and profits, unless the compensation package is squeezed elsewhere. This poses structural
contradictions within the framework of distributive and intra-
organizational bargaining.

Since the early 1980s, however, a number of factors have contributed to a positive cash flow position for employer-sponsored occupational pensions, resulting in considerable plan surpluses. On the
revenue side, high interest rates on bonds acquired during the inflationary period are now maturing and generating high levels of
investment earnings. With the decline of interest rates in the mid-
1980s, equity values rose accordingly, further increasing pension
plan income. Concurrently, on the benefit side, lower wage
increases in recent years have had the effect of reducing pension
fund liabilities. The relative stability of wage movements throughout the 1980s has limited the amounts which have to be paid out in
pension benefits. Consequently, many occupational pension plans
generated surpluses between 1979 and 1984 as a result of this rapidly rising investment income, which recorded annual increases of
between 10 and 29 per cent in the same period and which grew from
37 to 58 per cent of total income, replacing employer contributions
as the largest source of revenue. Within this context many plan
sponsors have attempted to secure a "contribution holiday."

This situation is the opposite of that experienced by occupational
pension plans during the past decade. According to surveys by the
Ontario Pension Commission, 66 per cent of plans were in a deficit
position and 34 per cent had a surplus in 1984. By late 1988, 62 per

cent of plans had a surplus and 38 per cent a deficit (unfunded liability). Since 1984, however, investment earnings as a proportion of total pension income have declined. Pension fund surpluses are essentially a form of "windfall" earnings and may be viewed as a short-term abnormality which will be substantially reduced or eliminated when maturing assets are reinvested in lower-yielding investments reflecting a decreased inflation rate. As the influential actuarial consulting firm of William A. Mercer put it, "The decade of ever-growing pension surpluses is almost certainly ending."

The second factor generating pressure for increased pension costs in the postwar period is the considerable improvement in the level and types of benefits provided for by employer-sponsored occupational pension plans. The inclusion of past service credits, improved early retirement provisions such as "30 and out," the upgrading from a career to a final average earnings retirement benefit formula and ad hoc post-retirement inflation-proofing are examples of costly pension plan improvements. In Canada employer contributions to occupational pensions for current service benefits increased by 570 per cent between 1969 and 1983, reflecting rising wage rates, improved benefits and more rigorous funding requirements.[33] In Britain, "more than half of those schemes which increased ordinary contributions" in the mid-1970s "did so because of an increase in benefit levels" while nearly "40% of schemes which paid special contributions did so as a provision for pension increases."[34]

The third reason underlying the long-run pressure for increased occupational pension plan costs is population aging. The aging of the labour force is a concomitant of an aging population, with a rising median age as discussed in Chapter 3. A corollary to the general aging of the labour force is the reduced proportion of young and the increased proportion of elderly. Labour force growth in Canada will decline from the 3.1 per cent a year experienced in the period between 1966 and 1979 to 0.5 per cent per annum by 2011.[35] By definition, a consequence of an aging labour force and a declining rate of labour force growth will be an increasing cost per unit of pension benefit. This will generate increased occupational pension plan costs as a result of the larger proportion of older workers in the labour force. The generally increasing cost per unit of pension benefit, while varying by industry and employer, is a long-term structural pressure increasing the level of occupational pension plan contributions required of employers and employees.

The aging of the labour force, and union members more generally, may augur a shift in bargaining priorities. It is well established that interest in pensions and retirement-related matters increases significantly after age 45. In some occupational jurisdictions this shift in priorities may in fact already be occurring. The new emphasis on improved pension arrangements by the increasing proportion of older union members will, on the one hand, conflict with the importance placed on direct monetary compensation by young workers and, on the other, force older workers to confront the "trade-off," between direct and deferred compensation. It is problematic whether older workers will be prepared to "trade" money today for pensions tomorrow. To fulfil its social security function and organizational imperatives the union may be forced into a conflict with one or the other generational factions of its membership.

The fourth and final factor is the cost of pension reform. It will almost inevitably impose higher contribution levels on employers and employees, resulting in reduced profit margins for corporations and a reduction in current consumption for workers. When the Employee Retirement Income Security Act 1974 was enacted in the United States, for example, it increased employer-sponsored pension plan costs by an estimated 5 to 10 per cent.[36] The 1983 Parliamentary Task Force on Pension Reform in Canada estimated the cost of its private pension reform "package" to be in the order of an additional 1.5 to 2 per cent of payroll.[37] These cost estimates, however, did not take into account increased Canada/Quebec Pension Plan contributions for current and/or improved benefits.

Compounding the increasing cost of the occupational pension plans is the cost of reforming the state pension system. The total long-run contribution rate for the Canada/Quebec Pension Plans, shared equally between employers and employees, for *current*— that is, existing— benefits will increase from 3.6 per cent in 1986 to 7.6 per cent in 2011, or by 111 per cent over the next quarter-century. However, the contribution rate required to support the baby boom generation when it retires after 2011 has not been announced. If the income replacement rate for the C/QPP were increased in the future from the present 25 to 50 per cent in order to conform to international standards, it would require a total (full-cost) contribution rate of roughly 16 per cent, or nearly 300 per cent above the level in 1988. While the method used to phase-in the higher rates may somewhat moderate the cost impact, it nevertheless remains true that employers and workers in Canada will be faced with increasing contributions to the state pension system over the next forty years. Contributions to the U.S. social security retirement system, shared equally between employers and employees, have risen continuously over the past thirty years from a total of 3 per cent in 1960 to 15.3 per cent in 1990. Significantly, the National Commission on Social Security conveniently avoided making a recommendation regarding the required level of social security contributions in the period after 1990 or when the baby boom generation retires.[38] It is not unreasonable to surmise, however, that the rapidly rising proportion of elderly in the population, compounded by the pay-as-you-go (PAYGO) financing, will necessitate a considerably increased level of contributions in the future. Similar pressures may affect the U.K. earnings-related retirement system.

Pension costs under conditions of collective bargaining, however, assume a particular significance because of their magnitude; they are significantly greater than for non-unionized employers. In Canada the expenditure on welfare and health plans, total pension costs, and occupational pensions is nearly 94, 115 and 179 per cent greater respectively for unionized firms than for non-union firms as is reported in Table 5.4. These data indicate that unions have been successful in advancing the social welfare and retirement income needs of their members compared with other sections of the labour force.

Under conditions of collective bargaining the relative rank order of pension costs and their absolute magnitude is of critical importance, and they will be of prime concern within the distributive collective bargaining framework between labour and management. This pre-eminence will be magnified in the future as pension costs increase as was previously determined. As one business representative stated, "pension costs are simply part of the total cost of doing business."[39] Managers will probably attempt to cut or restrain other components within the total compensation package. It has been established, however, that once introduced, employee benefit costs are more rigid than wages as part of the compensation structure,[40] which poses a direct "trade-off," or conflict, between monetary and non-monetary items. Management's cost minimization behaviour is then in direct opposition to the union's organizational imperative and the maximization of its social welfare function. Pension costs under conditions of collective bargaining may therefore become one of the most contentious issues in the future because they will accentuate the structural contradictions inherent in the industrial relations system.

TABLE 5.4

COMPARISON OF TOTAL EMPLOYEE COMPENSATION,
EXPENDITURE FOR WELFARE AND HEALTH PLANS AND PENSION COSTS
FOR UNION AND NON-UNION WAGE-EARNERS, CANADA, 1978

PAY ITEM	EMPLOYERS WITH AT LEAST 100 EMPLOYEES		DIFFERENTIAL OF UNION OVER NON-UNION EMPLOYEES
	Union	Non-Union	
Total Employee Compensation	$16,977	$12,323	37.8%
Expenditure for Welfare and Health Plans[1]	1,742	898	93.9
Total Pensions	815	380	114.5
Occupational	650	233	178.9
State	165	147	12.2
Life & Health Insurance	364	152	139.5
Workers' Compensation	298	165	80.6
Unemployment Insurance	216	187	15.5
Other	49	15	226.7

Note: 1 Statistics Canada classifies vacation pay, paid holidays and sick leave as "Expenditures for paid absence," which are not included here.

Source: Retabulated and calculated from Statistics Canada, *Employee Compensation in Canada, All Industries, 1978* (Ottawa: Minister of Supply and Services, 1980), Text Table X, p. 27. This is the only comparative survey of the subject undertaken by Statistics Canada.

Because union members are the largest and most concentrated group covered by the private pension system, increasing occupational pension plan costs which reduce their standard of living are likely to be of particular relevance to them. In Canada 81 per cent of all trade union members are covered by an employer-sponsored occupational pension plan, compared with 78 per cent in the U.S. and 52 per cent in Britain. Trade union members therefore represent on average nearly 50 per cent of *all* occupational pension plan members in these countries. These data are outlined in Table 5.5. In general, there is a strong positive correlation between the level of unionization (unionization ratio) and occupational pension plan coverage, particularly at the industry level. Table 5.6 presents a transnational comparison of the relationship between unionization and occupational pension plan coverage based on standard statistical tests. For Canada and Britain there is a significant correlation coefficient (r), indicating a strong statistical association, and robust coefficients of determination, suggesting a firm causal relationship. In the United States, however, there is only a modest statistical correlation and a weak causal relationship.

TABLE 5.5

PROPORTION OF TRADE UNION MEMBERS COVERED BY AN OCCUPATIONAL PENSION PLAN AND
AS A PERCENTAGE OF ALL PRIVATE PENSION PLAN MEMBERS,
CANADA, U.S. AND U.K., 1979–1981

COUNTRY	UNION MEMBERS			TOTAL PENSION PLAN MEMBERS	UNION MEMBERS COVERED BY AN EMPLOYER-BASED PENSION AS A % OF ALL PRIVATE PENSION PLAN MEMBERS
	Covered by Pension Plan	Total	% Covered by Pension Plan		
Canada[1]	2,013,868	2,492,719	80.8[5, 6]	4,475,429	44.9
U.S.[2]	12,036,000	15,430,769	78.0	29,867,500	40.9
U.K.[3]	7,000,000[4]	13,498,000	51.9	11,800,000	59.3

Notes: 1 1982;
2 1980;
3 1979;
4 Estimated by Social Insurance and Industrial Welfare Department, Trades Union Congress. Correspondence with author 11 January 1983;
5 Bargaining units with 200 or more employees;
6 A subsequent Statistics Canada, Labour Force Survey in 1984 indicated that 77 per cent of trade union members participated in a pension plan.

Sources: For Canada, information supplied to the author based on a special computer run by the Collective Bargaining Section, Labour Canada, 18 November 1982, and Statistics Canada, *Pension Plans in Canada, 1980* (Ottawa: Minister of Supply and Services, 1982), Text Table II, p. 13. For the U.S., Daniel J. Beller, "Patterns of Worker Coverage by Private Pension Plans," U.S. Bureau of Census and Department of Labour, August 1980, Table 1, p. 10 and Table 4, p. 16. British data based on information supplied to the author by the TUC, Social Insurance and Industrial Welfare Department, 11 January 1983, and the Government Actuary, *Occupational Pension Schemes, 1979—Sixth Review* (London: HMSO, 1981), Table 2.1, p. 5.

TABLE 5.6

RELATIONSHIP BETWEEN OCCUPATIONAL PENSION PLAN COVERAGE[1] AND
LEVEL OF UNIONIZATION.[2] BY SELECTED INDUSTRIES.
CANADA. U.S. AND U.K.. VARIOUS YEARS

INDUSTRIAL GROUP[3]	CANADA		U.S.		U.K.	
	Private Pension Coverage[4]	% Unionized[5]	Private Pension Coverage[6]	% Unionized[4]	Private Pension Coverage[7]	% Unionized[8]
Public Administration	98.0	67.4	82[9]	23.2[9]	69.6	83.1
Construction	47.9	52.1	37	62.1	26.3	27.2
Transportation, Communications & Utilities	50.5	50.0	66	33.9	61.5	83.1[10]
Manufacturing	50.2	43.5	66	38.7	44.6	62.2
Mines, Quarries & Oil Wells	67.6	39.7	70	44.7	77.2	96.2
Service Industries	24.5	22.6	30	11.7	28.1	n.a.
Trade	15.8	8.5	29	8.5	28.1	11.4
Finance and Insurance	37.0	2.7	50	1.0	60.6	44.8
Agriculture	0.7	0.3	13	1.2	25.2	22.2
Correlation Coefficient (r)	.9		.4		.9	
Coefficient of Determination (r²)	.7		.2		.8	

Notes: 1 As a percentage of total paid civilian labour force.
2 As a proportion of paid labour force.
3 The industrial categories have been put on as comparable a basis as possible.
4 For 1978.
5 For 1976.
6 For 1979.
7 For 1970.
8 For 1974.
9 Average of state, local and federal government.
10 Transport and telecommunications are included in public administration.

Sources: For Canada, Statistics Canada, *Pension Plans in Canada, 1978* (Ottawa: Minister of Supply and Services, 1979), Text Table IV, p. 18, and Statistics Canada, *Corporations and Labour Unions Returns Act Report for 1976 Part II – Labour Unions* (Ottawa: Statistics Canada, 1978), pp. 72–74. For the U.S., President's Commission on Pension Policy, *Coming of Age: Toward A National Retirement Income Policy* (Washington, D.C.: PCPP, February 1981), Table II, p. 27 and calculated from the U.S. Department of Labor, Bureau of Labor Statistics, *Handbook of Labor Statistics* (Washington, D.C.: GPO, 1980), Table 162, p. 408 and Table 72, p. 151. For Britain, calculated from NES Department of Employment, *Gazette* (August 1971), and Robert Price and George Sayers Bain, "Union Growth Revisited: 1948–1974 in Perspective," *British Journal of Industrial Relations* 14 (November 1976), Tables 2–3, pp. 342–43.

There are a number of political, collective bargaining and institutional implications regarding the relationship between unionized workers' propensity to be covered by an occupational pension plan and the increasing costs associated with the pension system. Politically, trade unionists are one of the primary groups affected by the limitations of the private pension system, and by virtue of their organized and concentrated membership in the private pension system, they are potentially in a position to act as a catalyst for progressive change.

The institutional response by unions and workers may take three possible forms. First, unionized workers are potentially in a position to offer organized resistance to increasing pension costs which affect their standard of living. Second, increasing pension costs have a destabilizing effect upon distributive bargaining between labour and management. Resistance from an organized and concentrated group of pension plan members to rising costs reinforces this instability. Third, increasing pension costs may provoke a combative response from unions and workers.

Members of unions have been known to reject contracts because of the inclusion or exclusion of benefits.[41] In this regard it is interesting to note that in the U.S. in 1949 employee benefits accounted for over 25 per cent of all strike idleness.[42] In North America two important strikes were fought over pensions: the long 1970 United Auto Workers strike against General Motors in the United States to establish the "30 and out" early retirement pension[43] and the bitter 1979 United Steel Workers (Canadian region) strike against the giant Inco Corporation to achieve the same objective. In Britain, during a period of income policies in 1974, employee benefits accounted for nearly 7 per cent of all pay disputes.[44] In the United States in the mid-1970s wages and benefits accounted for nearly one-quarter of all work stoppages. In Canada in 1981 one-quarter of all person-days lost in strikes were the result of benefit and wage disputes, including the 69-day City of Moose Jaw, Saskatchewan, municipal worker strike over pensions.[45] Pension improvements were the major issue during the 110-day lockout of municipal employees in Bathurst, New Brunswick, in 1983–1984. Both the protracted 1987 Canadian Auto Worker strike against Chrysler and the International Association of Machinists' work stoppage in the airline industry successfully achieved indexed pensions. Strikes in France and Sweden were fuelled by the dissatisfaction of young workers with higher pension contributions. Pensions under conditions of collective bargaining, as indicated by these examples, can become a disruptive issue within the industrial relations system.

POWER ISSUES: THE RIGHT TO CONTROL

Collective bargaining is primarily concerned with the distribution of monetary compensation and power between labour and capital, which generates forces for conflict as well as for accommodation. Power cements the industrial relations system and collective bargaining relationships together, and it is the ability or inability of one party to impose its will on the other. Conversely, power is the ability or inability of one party to resist. Under conditions of collective bargaining in a capitalist political economy, power is the ability or "right" of management or labour to control conditions of employment. The power to control manifests itself through concrete bargaining issues.

Power, inequality and ideology, as Hyman and Brough argue, are closely interconnected.[46] The inequality of power between unions and management with respect to occupational pension plans has generated manifest and latent tensions which may further disrupt the industrial relations system in the future. Here three issues are identified and examined as they relate to the private pension system and the collective bargaining power relationship—namely, the limited scope of pension bargaining, the disclosure of pension plan information and the negotiation of post-retirement benefits. They are all associated in one form or another with the ability of the union to carry out its social security function. Power issues in general, including those specifically associated with employer-sponsored occupational pension plans, go to the heart of the modern union's organizational imperatives and the distribution of power within the collective bargaining relationship.

Negotiability and Recognition: The Scope of Bargaining. The right of a union to negotiate pension arrangements as a condition of employment is a fundamental issue related to the recognition of the union in law as a representative of the individual trade union pension plan member. These issues are of particular relevance to the highly legalistic North American industrial relations system.

In the United States failure to negotiate pension arrangements is deemed to be "bad faith bargaining" and an "unfair labor practice" since the ruling of the U.S. National Labor Relations Board in the 1949 *Inland Steel* case, when pensions were considered to be wages and hence an appropriate and *mandatory* subject for collective bargaining. In Canada, however, whether pensions in the private sector are a mandatory subject for negotiations is a grey area of the labour law. There are in Canada no arbitration or court cases ruling that pensions are a mandatory subject for negotiations. The U.S. jurisprudence clearly recognizes the deferred wage doctrine; however, Canadian labour law is silent on the subject.[47] Effectively, therefore, management in the private sector is under no compulsion to negotiate pension arrangements. In the public sector, pensions are often excluded by legislation from the scope of negotiable issues. A consequence is that unions in Canada must rely on their bargaining strength — power — to deal with pension matters. Such an approach results in making the pension issue all that more volatile, particularly with an aging labour force.

A related problem is the latent conflict in Canada between the pension and labour relations legislation. Pension legislation only recognizes the *individual* employee-employer relationship; it does not recognize the *collective* union-employer relationship which exists under the labour law. The failure of the various jurisdictions' Pension Benefits Act with respect to recognizing a bona fide bargaining agent as the legal representative or agent acting on behalf of individual employees stems from the earlier paternalistic attitude when a pension was a "gratuity" and hence a private matter between the individual employee and employer. Under conditions of collective bargaining, however, group rights are generally recognized as superseding individual rights. In law, the union has the legal right to represent individuals in matters pertaining to labour relations such as pensions. It is the union, not the individual, which negotiates pension arrangements. The union, in law, however, also has certain obligations with which it must comply such as the duty of "fair representation" or financial disclosure to individuals concerning health and welfare plans, for example, under section 76(a)(3) of the Ontario Labour Relations Act.

The tension arises inasmuch as the pension legislation circumvents the union, while the union is held accountable to individual members under the labour relations legislation. Thus the union has the responsibility to represent, or act on behalf of, the individual, but it has no independent rights or powers to carry out its duties. This situation has serious implications for individual pension plan members and unions since it has resulted in problems within the collective bargaining relationship related to fiduciary responsibility, disclosure of pension plan information, adjudication of pension benefit disputes, the ability to negotiate for pensioners and the co-management of pensions. The absence of an explicit right by unions to negotiate pension arrangements in Canada and Britain, coupled with the lack of recognition over pension matters, effectively narrows the scope of collective bargaining, resulting in their becoming fundamental power issues.

The Right to Know: Pension Plan Disclosure. The public's "right to know" and "freedom of information" about matters related to the public interest are rapidly becoming accepted principles. The issue of the disclosure of pension plan information to unions and plan members is based on the deferred wage doctrine. If occupational pensions are an earned, vested and deferred benefit, commonly contributory, and often negotiated, it follows that unions and plan members acquire a proprietorial interest in their operation and management. In the United States, legislation since 1958 has required the public disclosure of pension plan information, and in Britain since the late 1970s, voluntary disclosure has resulted in much the same end. The situation in Canada in the past has been considerably different, however, and has often generated tension.

In Canada most occupational pension plan sponsors have refused to disclose information such as actuarial assumptions and valuations, financial status, portfolio composition and investment performance to unions and individual plan members. Until recently there was no legal requirement for them to do so. Most pension plans in Canada have been treated as an unilateral management right, shrouded in secrecy, so neither unions nor employees received information about them. Many employers administer the pension fund, even if it is a contributory plan, in an antiquated paternalistic fashion. According to one survey, for example, in the late 1970s fewer than 20 per cent of all pension plans in Canada provided members with a summary of investments and only 12 per cent of plans supplied information regarding the actuarial position of the plan.[48] Under conditions of collective bargaining, the reality of the situation is that many employers have refused to supply the union with such rudimentary information as the plan text or trust document.

In most jurisdictions in Canada, until recent legislative intervention, pension plan administrators were only required to issue a popularized informational brochure to employees, who were restricted to making extracts of the plan at the offices of the pension authority. Furthermore, an employee was not entitled to a pension statement except on termination of employment or membership in the plan. The legislation in most jurisdictions made no provision for a union representing employees to directly or independently acquire pension plan information, except as "authorized in writing" from a plan member.[49] During the many hearings dealing with pension reform in Canada, one of the most frequently cited frustrations and complaints made by trade union representatives was the lack of disclosure and the inaccessability of information concerning negotiated pension plans, which is a minimum requirement for intelligent and informed collective bargaining. Fortunately, this longstanding problem has been rectified in some jurisdictions by the recent remedial "package" of pension reform measures.[50]

The situation which has evolved in the United States and Britain stands in marked contrast. As early as 1942 the U.S. National Labor Relations Board ruled, and various court decisions upheld, that an employer must furnish the union with all the information necessary for bargaining on pension matters.[51] The Welfare and Pension Plans Disclosure Act 1958 required the public filing of pension plan information. These provisions were subsequently incorporated into and strengthened under the Employee Retirement Income Security Act 1974. In Britain, disclosure of pension scheme information to plan members was a result of early legislative intervention.[52] The Occupational Pensions Board report upon which the Labour government based its 1976 white paper broadened the thrust by recommending that unions receive all pertinent information and complete disclosure of pension scheme activities. "Occupational pension schemes exist for the benefit of their members," the white paper noted, and "members of a scheme ought to be given all the information necessary." Significantly, the legislation would have provided that "independent recognized trade unions with members in a scheme will have the same right to information . . . as the members themselves,"[53] thus avoiding the quandary that existed in Canada. Despite the fact that the legislation was never enacted, it nevertheless had a very real "threat effect." This has resulted in the voluntary disclosure of pension plan information by employers.[54] An official of the Trades Union Congress concluded that the contemplated legislation had "some effect."[55] A representative of the Transport and General Workers Union reported that they generally had "no trouble getting costing and actuarial reviews" and that "investment data is available" as well.[56] The head of the Pensions and Social Services Department of the General and Municipal Workers' Union summed up the situation by saying that there was no longer a "real problem."[57]

The lack of disclosure of pension plan information traditionally has been viewed by organized labour as a limitation of the private pensions system. It was seen as a problem which inhibited unions from effectively doing their job and advancing the social welfare of their membership. As such, it was an institutional challenge. Legislative intervention in these countries — real or threatened — was required to overcome the intransigence of employers in order to neutralize this issue under conditions of collective bargaining.

Post-retirement Adjustments. The rapid inflation of the 1970s eroded the fixed income of retired union members. North American unions are thus caught between the demands of their actively employed members and retired former members as well as being limited with respect to their scope of action by the current interpretation of labour law.

In North America, decisions by the U.S. National Labour Relations Board (1966) and Supreme Court (1971), and the British Columbia Labour Relations Board (1977) in Canada,[58] have ruled that a union can only legally represent and negotiate on behalf of actively employed employees. Because a union has no legal right to represent its former members, the negotiation of post-retirement adjustments has been deemed a *permissive,* rather than a mandatory, subject for collective bargaining. In practice, improved post-retirement benefits can only be negotiated by *mutual* consent of the parties to a collective agreement. Only a few unions such as the UAW (and the CAW in Canada), the USWA and the IWA have been successful in this regard. While bargaining on behalf of retired members is possible under Britain's voluntaristic industrial relations system, the General and Municipal Workers' Union reports "no real progress in concrete terms" because the cost associated with post-retirement improvements "is part of the total package."[59]

This situation creates a dilemma for unions in terms of distributive and intra-organizational bargaining. Pressures force unions to "trade-off" pension gains against more immediate monetary concerns. This exacerbates the not so latent sectional (intra-class) tension between the actively employed and retired members. It is interesting to note in this regard that while the U.S. Supreme Court held that retirees do not share a community of interest with actively employed union members, the B.C. Labour Relations Board arrived at the opposite conclusion. Deeming the negotiation of post-retirement adjustments a permissive subject for collective bargaining compounds this tension because retired members are becoming better organized and more vocal within their unions.

Unions in North America and Britain have attempted to provide for some of the retirement needs of their former members, including low-cost housing, health clinics, senior citizens' homes and retired workers' chapters. In North America the United Auto Workers, the International Ladies Garment Workers' Union and the Canadian Union of Public Employees are examples of unions which have established retired workers' locals. In Britain union practices vary. In the giant Transport and General Workers' Union, former members are organized into a T&G Retired Members' Association. While they have no formal representation on bargaining committees, their views are made known through the association. According to one source the "T&G are very strong on pensioners,"[60] as is Jack Jones, the former head of the TGWU.[61]

As a result of inflation, internal political pressures and their own organizational imperatives, unions are under increasing compulsion to negotiate post-retirement adjustments. Because of legal precedent in North America and the voluntaristic negotiating framework in Britain, however, unions must rely on their bargaining strength to force employers to deal with this issue. An aging labour force, and an uncertain inflationary climate in the future, may propel labour and management towards each other. The power issues associated with pensions under conditions of bargaining are all related to the union's scope of collective bargaining and its ability to effectively control conditions of employment.

EQUITY AND ADMINISTRATIVE JUSTICE

Equity is related to the distribution of power under conditions of collective bargaining. Management's control over occupational pension plans is an equity issue because it affects the administration of the plan. Few occupational pension plans in Canada or Britain have a formal procedure whereby a dispute between a plan member or beneficiary and the plan administrators or trustees for benefit claims can be resolved. Most employer-sponsored plans, even those which are negotiated and contributory, explicitly state that the decisions of management-appointed plan administrators are "final and binding." Simply, most employer-sponsored pension plans do not have an appeals procedure to challenge or redress administrative decisions concerning the determination of retirement, survivors' and disability (invalidity) benefits. An employee, or beneficiary, is thus denied administrative review and natural justice. While an individual may choose civil litigation to resolve a dispute, it is a lengthy and costly process.

The purpose of a grievance and adjudication (arbitration) procedure for pension and other employee benefit plan disputes is the same as for any other matter falling within the scope of a legally binding collective agreement, that is, to interpret and administer the collective agreement. Two distinct approaches to employee benefit plan adjudication have developed. First, the pension plan is "incorporated by reference" into the collective agreement. The normal grievance and arbitration procedure in the contract is then used to resolve any pension plan or employee benefit dispute in precisely the same way as it would be used for any other issue falling within the scope of the collective agreement. This approach has been used in heavy industry in North America. The second method is to establish an adjudication procedure in the pension plan's trust deed. This latter procedure is most commonly used in the United States.

The need for an adjudication procedure to protect the rights and benefits of all pension plan members was recognized and introduced in the U.S. Employee Retirement Income Security Act 1974, which stipulated that all private pensions and welfare plans must establish a procedure to "afford a reasonable opportunity to any participant whose claim for benefits has been denied for a full and fair review . . . of the decision denying this claim." U.S. Department of Labor Regulation 2560.2 implementing section 1133 of ERISA provides that a "claims procedure which is established and maintained pursuant to a collective bargaining agreement and . . . includes provision for binding arbitration of an appeal . . . will be deemed a reasonable claim procedure." For those occupational pension plans in the United States which do not have a formal adjudication procedure, the International Foundation of Employee Benefits and the American Arbitration Association have developed a recommended set of rules and procedures.[62] In Britain, where grievance arbitration is relatively undeveloped compared with the highly legalistic North American industrial relations system, the Trades Union Congress has endorsed pension plan adjudication noting that "problems are bound to arise concerning the . . . [pension] scheme, and a formal procedure must be established to deal with any that cannot be sorted out . . . . The most satisfactory method would be to refer the matter to independent arbitration."[63] While some unions such as the TGWU have used ad hoc pension plan adjudication in the past, this has been the exception.

In order to remain creditable the employer-sponsored private pension system must be perceived by plan members as being equitable and responsive to their needs. The public pension system and other social welfare programmes in most countries have an appeals procedure to challenge and redress administrative decisions. An adjudication or grievance procedure, in one form or another, exists within most collective agreements for other conditions of employment. The administrative inequities of the private pension system, such as the lack of an appeals procedure, are fundamentally related to the inequitable balance of power between labour and management under existing collective bargaining arrangements.

The limitations of the private pension system under conditions of collective bargaining as represented by cost, power and equity issues inject, albeit for different reasons, a destabilizing element into the industrial relations system. Many of the structural pressures underlying these issues will increase in the future. However, they all converge into one potentially explosive issue—the co-management of pensions.

FLASHPOINT: THE CO-MANAGEMENT OF PENSIONS

Co-management of occupational pensions under collective bargaining poses important issues related to the unilateral control of pension arrangements: pension assets, investment strategy, portfolio composition, structures for co-management, the fusion between pension fund and corporate management, the nature of the union social security function and the democratization of the workplace. Within the formal industrial relations system the co-management of pensions contains within it a contradictory potential for either conflict or incorporation.

Co-management of occupational pension plans is fundamentally a power issue since it relates to the enormous concentration of assets under the control of the private pension industry and dominant financial institutions. This subject is dealt with in Chapter 8. The corporate sector will resist any serious co-management of pensions with unions for two reasons. First, co-management represents a general and specific limitation on management's present unilateral right to control both corporate decision-making and occupational pension plans. In effect, co-management of pensions represents a broadening of the scope of collective bargaining and a widening of concurrent powers, resulting in a redistribution of power. Second, co-management of pensions places a limitation on the unilateral right of organized capital to control and direct private investment. Pension funds have a considerable impact on the operation of capital markets, as will be demonstrated in Chapter 7. The co-management of pensions — administrative operation and investment management — is of concern to *all* of organized capital because pension funds are financial intermediaries and institutional investors linking the finance and industrial sectors of the economy. The co-management of pension funds strikes at the heart of capitalism because it calls into question who should control capital and in whose interests investment decisions should be made. This subject is dealt with in Chapters 6 and 9. Therefore, the co-management of pensions affects the *general interests* of all capital, as well as being a *specific issue* under conditions of collective bargaining.

Unilateral Management Control of Pensions. Unions and workers in Canada, Britain and the United States have virtually no involvement with or control over the administration or investment decisions affecting employer-sponsored pension plans. The anatomy of control has been described as follows:

> financial control has been delegated by . . . employers to the banker-trustee [trust companies in Canada], which exercise considerable power in capital markets as a result. The employer controls the . . . operation of the plan . . . in [some] cases in accordance with a basic agreement . . . with a union. The employee himself, without his union, has little or nothing to say about the pension which is financed out of his earnings.[64]

While "the beneficiary of a pension is the true owner of the property," one banker wryly noted, "he can't act as an owner — so he has a lot of people acting on his behalf."[65] The pension beneficiary — plan member — is in the hands of his pension guardians — the employer, plan trustees, the state, and, depending upon circumstance, his union. According to Harbrecht, "beneficiaries are the group who have the least influence upon the formulation of pension trust policy."[66]

For the most part, employers retain ultimate and effective unilateral control over pensions. In Canada in 1988 only 5 per cent of all major collective agreements covering 3 per cent of employees had any arrangement for joint union-management control of the occupational pension plan.[67] Only a few private sector unions, such as the construction trades, have jointly trusteed pension plans. A number of large public sector plans, however, have a joint labour-management pension committee which acts in an advisory or consultative capacity. Section 302 was added to the 1947 U.S. Taft-Hartley Act specifically to prohibit unions from obtaining exclusive power over multi-employer pension plans. According to one U.S. study in the mid-1950s, about four-fifths of all employees were in pension plans where the employer had ultimate control.[68] A U.S. Department of Labor survey in the mid-1970s found that only 9 per cent of all pension plans covering 30 per cent of members in bargaining units of over five hundred employees had joint union-management administration of the pension plan.[69] In Britain there has been a consultative tradition in the public sector based on the Whitley Councils since World War I. It was extended to nationalized industry such as the National Coal Board, British Rail and the British Steel Corporation after World War II. In the mid-1970s only 18 per cent of all pension scheme members in the public sector were in a plan where there was a joint management committee, and a mere 10 per cent were covered by such an arrangement in the private sector.[70] According to the National Association of Pension Funds survey in 1978, only 2 per cent of all pension scheme trustees were nominated by an independent trade union, 12 per cent were elected by plan members, and 74 per cent were nominated by the employer. And in 1983, fewer than 10 per cent of all private sector pension scheme trustees in the U.K. were elected or trade-union nominated.[71] These data clearly indicate that there is little involvement or control by unions of occupational pension plan administration or investment management.

The primary objective of an occupational pension plan should be to ensure that the pension is adequately funded, that workers' equity in the plan is protected and that workers receive the maximum retirement income possible given the prudent management of the fund. Under conditions of collective bargaining the co-management of pensions is a way of ensuring that these conditions are met.

The reasons for co-management of pensions may be summarized as follows.[72] First, the money in pension plans, whether contributory or non-contributory, belongs to workers. It is part of their compensation package within the deferred wage doctrine. The United Auto Workers in the U.S. as early as 1949 and the American Federation of Labor (AFL) in the mid-1950s took the position that there should be equal labour-management representation of trusteed pension plans based on this doctrine.[73] The deferred wage theory involves "the issue of who shall control the operations of the pension program" because "it becomes the legitimate concern of the worker to see that his expectancy is safeguarded and preserved."[74]

A second consideration is that there are reasons to believe that many pension funds administered by employers are not managed in the best interests of employees, but, rather, are an indirect source of profit for the firm, that is, private sector occupational pension plans are managed in accordance with the "profit-centre" theory of management, where each operation of a corporation is required to show a profit. The pension fund is essentially treated as a mutual fund (with a surplus or deficit net asset value) that results in lower pension contributions for the firm if the rate of return is good and higher contributions if performance is poor. In Britain "self-dealing" or "auto-financing," that is, where a pension fund holds a disproportionate volume of the plan sponsors' financial securities, is all too common. Pension funds have been used as well to promote or inhibit corporate acquisitions and take-overs such as the Unilever pension fund's backing of Sprey Investment's diversified activities in the early 1970s or Grumman Aircraft's use of its pension fund to thwart a 1981 take-over bid by LTV. Public sector pension funds are known to be a "dumping ground" for low interest bonds and are characterized by a high debt-low equity asset mix ratio, resulting in a lack of portfolio diversification. In Canada the Toronto Police Benefit Fund and the giant Ontario Municipal Employee Retirement System (OMERS) in the late 1960s were examples of these practices. In addition, public sector pension plans engage in extensive "self-dealing," that is, buying their own government bonds to finance current government expenditures; reciprocal "bond swaps" between state and local retirement systems in the U.S. are a common practice. "Churning" public and private sector pension funds by investment managers, that is, engaging in unnecessary transactions in order to generate brokerage commissions, is also an all too frequent practice.[75]

Third, unless employees are protected by a union in a co-management arrangement there is no assurance that their pension rights and entitlements will be safeguarded. Co-management establishes a system of checks and balances within the pension programme. The union can then act in a "watch dog" capacity with respect to pension plan administration regarding such equity issues as disclosure and adjudication, as previously examined. In addition, the union can oversee and influence such cost-related issues as investment management and performance measurement, commissions, actuarial assumptions and funding levels. It is known, for example, that a one percentage point difference in the rate of return on investment can result in a 15 to 20 per cent difference in employer contributions or retirement benefits to employees. The co-management of pensions has positive features, as McNulty has concluded, with respect to the security of pension benefits.[76]

The fourth reason for co-management is that it serves a democratizing and educational function. Co-management represents the extension of political democracy to the work place. Like collective bargaining more generally, co-management restricts the scope and exercise of unilateral management rights. The educational process would be enhanced if workers could turn to union representatives among themselves who were knowledgeable and involved with the administration and planning of occupational pension arrangements and were familiar with its technical aspects.

The State and Co-Management of Pensions. In recent years in Britain and Canada the co-management of occupational pensions has also been advanced as part of a broader industrial relations strategy. The initial impetus in Britain came from the Social Security Pensions Act 1975, which required management to "consult" with unions in respect to pension schemes "contracting-out" from the state plan. Subsequently, the Labour government in 1976 issued its white paper on *Occupational Pension Schemes — The Role of Members in the Running of Schemes,* which recommended the co-management of pensions in the private sector through legislated, compulsory union-management committees with equal representation from both parties.[77] The white paper took the position that "workers want to play their part, in accordance with modern ideas of industrial democracy" and that because pensions represent the 'deferred pay of the workers concerned,' occupational pension schemes should not "exclude independent trade unions from the administration of the scheme."[78] The legislation subsequently died.

In Canada there have been two federal government initiatives, or "trial balloons," regarding co-management of pension funds. The first occasion was in 1973 when the Minister of Urban Affairs urged unions to press for a stronger voice in pension fund investment policies to channel money into housing.[79] Subsequently, the federal Minister of Labour in a June 1977 speech to the International Pension Conference advocated the joint trusteeship of occupational pension plans, saying that "there has been quite a lot of interest in the idea of joint participation by labour and management in corporate decision-making . . . . Along these lines we are looking at the case for joint employer-employee trusteeship of private pension plans."[80]

The motivation and ideological legitimization advanced by government in Britain and Canada for the co-management of pensions, however, was quite different. The Labour government couched its advocacy in the Fabian tradition stating that "the proposals . . . are to be seen . . . in the context of the government's wider commitment to . . . extending employee participation."[81] In Canada, co-management of pensions was viewed as a pragmatic "crisis management" technique and as part of integrative bargaining which "should be promoted as a way of reducing confrontation over pension issues at the bargaining table."[82]

Corporate Sector and Co-Management of Pensions. The corporate sectors in Britain and Canada have responded similarly to government initiatives and pressures from organized labour regarding the co-management of pensions. In Britain the Labour government's white paper came under vigorous attack from the private pension industry and business community. The National Association of Pension Funds (NAPF), representing major corporate pension plans, stated that "many funds are angry at the prospect of trade union officials . . . having a major say in the investment of funds, while non-union members of the scheme would have no representation."[83] Speaking on behalf of the private sector the Confederation of British Industry (CBI) predicted grave and dire consequences because "moves to give trade unions control of pension funds are as dangerous to Britain as schemes to nationalize banks and insurance companies . . . *the pension fund proposals . . . give unions power to dominate the financial scene.*"[84] Both the NAPF and CBI countered with proposals for employee, rather than union, participation on pension boards based on a voluntaristic (non-statutory) approach. Canadian employers have been receptive to the idea of the co-management of pensions. According to one survey, 75 per cent of management representatives indicated that corporate pension plans should be jointly managed, compared with only 20 per cent who felt that the plan should be unilaterally controlled. Significantly, however, 71 per cent of corporate spokesmen indicated that there should be "employee representatives apart from unions," while only 19 per cent approved of employee representation through unions.[85]

Two central concerns are evidenced by the corporate sector regarding the co-management of pensions. First, there is recognition of the size and importance of private pension funds and the implications of union involvement. While management is ready to "compromise" on pension plan *administration,* it is not prepared in general to entertain union involvement with respect to pension fund *investment management.* The right to control and direct investment decisions over pension capital is viewed as an absolute unilateral management right. Second, management is prepared to accept employee representation only to the extent that it is not backed by the institutional power of an independent trade union. The private sector's approach to co-management of pensions is essentially integrative or incorporationist in nature, that is, allowing unions to have participation but no power.

Unions and Co-Management of Pensions. Labour centrals or confederations in Britain, Canada and the United States and their largest affiliates have promoted the co-management of pensions with increasing aggressiveness in recent years. Labour's advocacy of an independent trade union role, including equal representation and power-sharing, in all matters related to pension plan management — administrative *and* investment — will collide with management's integrative approach and transform co-management of pensions into a power issue under conditions of collective bargaining.

The policy of the British Trades Union Congress is that "the scheme should be run jointly by the employers and the employees through their trade unions . . . so that . . . union representatives can prevent action being taken against the interests of the members."[86] Major TUC affiliates such as the Transport and General Workers' Union, the General and Municipal Workers' Union, the Association of Scientific, Technical and Management Staffs and the Association of Professional, Executive, Clerical and Computer Staffs are all increasingly turning their attention to the real sources of power within the pension machinery—namely, the trustee and investment committees. They contemptuously dismiss any interest in advisory committees, which are described as "toothless wonders."[87] The GMWU has the most aggressive and articulate pension policy, which states that "we must . . . establish pensions as an area of collective bargaining" and must "work towards an adequate number of employee representatives on pension fund management boards." The GMWU "will not countenance any attempt to limit the activities of member trustees to a secondary role" and demands that "occupational pension schemes should be jointly managed."[88] The TGWU and GMWU have scored breakthroughs in their bargaining relationship with Ford, ICL, Thorne, ICI and Pilkington's on this issue.

The Canadian Labour Congress (CLC) advocated employee participation in the administration of occupational pension plans as early as 1975 and pressed this position before the Ontario Royal Commission on the Status of Pensions (1977). This position was reaffirmed in modified form at its 1978 convention.[89] The Canadian Union of Public Employees (CUPE), the largest union in the country, passed a 1977 convention resolution advocating "a program to challenge the assumed right of the employer to unilaterally administer the pension funds derived from employee . . . contributions."[90] Resolutions were again passed at its 1983 and 1985 conventions on the subject. The United Steel Workers (Canadian region) in 1979 endorsed "the joint administration of pension plans, including the investment of pension funds."[91] The recently concluded public policy review of retirement income arrangements in Canada dealt with this issue in a very cursory fashion. Three jurisdictions have subsequently enacted legislation which allows plan members a permissive right to establish an advisory committee to "monitor the administration of the pension plan."[92] In the U.S., the American Federation of Labor-Congress of Industrial Organizations (AFL-CIO), the UAW, the USWA, and the IAM have all endorsed alternative social investment strategies.[93] The co-management of pensions is now on the collective bargaining agenda in Britain, Canada and the United States.

The contradictory forces associated with the co-management of pensions may result in either conflict or incorporation. A parallel can be drawn between wage determination under collective bargaining and the co-management of pensions because

> employers see it as their right to control wages of all kinds. Unions are allowed to negotiate levels but they cannot

control wage[s]. . . . Employees therefore have as little right
to control investment of the superannuation fund as they
have to control other terms and conditions.[94]

The co-management of pensions therefore constitutes a general
challenge to management's rights.

Management will resist the demand for the co-management of
pensions, but the underlying economic logic is such that unions
may be driven to pursue it as a political demand and strategy, particularly in the private sector. Unions may be forced to challenge management's right to manage and invest pension capital in order to
ensure the security of pension benefits because the payment of
occupational pension plan benefits in the final analysis is linked to
the financial position and solvency of the corporation. As the president of the Institute of Actuaries (Britain) observed, "what is crucial
is the ability of the employer to fulfill his obligations and to increase
his contributions whenever necessary. Solvency is therefore . . .
inextricably bound up with the resources of the employer."[95] This
concern is of particular relevance to the majority of unions in these
countries which have defined benefit pension plans. In periods of
high inflation, negative real rates of return on pension fund investment, increasing unfunded pension liabilities, unemployment and
corporate mergers, if there is an investment shortfall in a defined
benefit plan, the employer is required to make additional contributions to maintain the solvency of the pension plan. This suggests
that workers and unions must not only be interested in pension
fund management and investment performance, but, as well, they
must be concerned with the general management of the firm or
industry to ensure that they are financially viable in order to maintain the solvency of the occupational pension plan. For unions, the
issue of pension fund management may become integrated and
fused with concerns related to the broader management of the corporation. Thus the co-management of pensions as a narrow collective bargaining issue may be transformed into a broader demand for
industrial democracy and worker control.

The demand by unions for the co-management of pensions is
progressive at this historical juncture, according to Ward, because
"pensions have been treated paternalistically and controlled exclusively by managements. Member participation is an actual extension of power, and it cannot be argued that it is an illusion."[96] The
co-management of pensions identifies many fundamental power

and economic relationships and challenges important vested interests as well. For these reasons, it is a volatile issue under conditions
of collective bargaining.

ASSESSMENT OF PENSION REFORM ON COLLECTIVE BARGAINING

The evaluation of pension reform presented in Chapter 4 indicated
that it was a failure with respect to ameliorating the universal limitations of the private pension system. An assessment of reform as it
affects the specific limitations of employer-sponsored pension plans
under conditions of collective bargaining is reported in Table 5.7.

TABLE 5.7
ASSESSMENT OF PENSION REFORM ON OCCUPATIONAL PENSION PLANS
UNDER CONDITIONS OF COLLECTIVE BARGAINING

PENSION PROBLEM	ASSESSMENT OF REFORM MEASURE[1]
Cost of Benefits	–
Scope of Pension Bargaining	–
Disclosure of Plan Information	+
Negotiation of Post-Retirement Benefits	–
Adjudication of Pension Disputes	–
Co-management of Pensions	–

Note: 1 Comparative ranking where + indicates a superior assessment,
0 a neutral rating and – an inferior evaluation or no action.

This analysis evaluates the impact of pension reform on negotiated occupational pension plan arrangements as being negative in
five categories and positive in only one. In this regard, the policy
review limited itself to only three areas of related concern — the cost
of pension benefits, disclosure of plan information and, cursorily,
the co-management of pensions. Positive action was taken with
respect to providing pension plan members, beneficiaries and their
"authorized agents," such as trade unions, with additional information; however, only three jurisdictions have enacted permissive legislation regarding discretionary advisory committees for pension
plans.

Other relevant pension issues were not identified or were ignored,
and no further remedial action was taken. Pension reform thus
failed to address and resolve the many specific limitations of the

private pension system under conditions of collective bargaining. Therefore, the underlying pressures for conflict remain.

THE PRIVATE PENSION SYSTEM'S LIMITATIONS UNDER
CONDITIONS OF COLLECTIVE BARGAINING: IMPLICATIONS

The issues of cost, power, equity and co-management as limitations of the private pension system under conditions of collective bargaining have far-reaching implications over the long term for the stability of collective bargaining relationships and the industrial relations system in Canada, Britain and the U.S. The industrial relations system is linked to the political economy of pensions through the negotiation of pension arrangements by unions. The specific limitations of the private pension system under conditions of collective bargaining affect the interests of an organized and concentrated section of the labour force.

In these countries the cost of employee benefits and occupational pension plans have increased significantly in the postwar period and have exceeded the growth in wages. Employee benefit costs now represent on average one-third of gross payroll. Total pension costs for the private and public pension systems are generally the single largest and most costly employer expenditure within the total compensation package. Under conditions of collective bargaining, expenditures on employee benefits and occupational pensions are significantly greater than for non-unionized firms. There are many reasons which suggest that employers and workers will be faced by increasing total pension contributions and costs in the future.

Increasing pension costs conflict with corporate profit maximization behaviour and reduce current consumption (take-home pay) for workers. Rising pension costs generate downward pressure on both profit margins and real wages. To the extent that unions attempt to maximize their social welfare function by "shifting-back" the increased cost of pensions to corporations so as to protect the standard of living of their membership, this will conflict with management's cost discipline imperative. Management's total compensation approach to collective bargaining imposes resource allocation decisions upon the union, in particular the level and distribution of compensation between salary and employee benefits, including occupational pensions, and the distribution of welfare programme costs within the employee benefit package. For the union, increasing total pension costs exacerbate the "trade-off" between direct (monetary) and indirect (deferred) compensation, since an increase in one results in a corresponding reduction in the other within a total compensation costing framework.

There are implications as well for the union as an institution and for intra-organizational bargaining. The union must reconcile the different generational priorities of its members: direct monetary compensation for today's young workers and deferred compensation in the form of pension improvements for the increasing proportion of older workers. While the aging of the labour force may result in a shift in bargaining priorities, thus decreasing this internal union tension, there is no indication that the unionized labour force will be prepared to reduce its current consumption and standard of living for deferred compensation in the future. The aging labour force with its increased concern for retirement income may demand both increased wages *and* improved pensions. As a result, unions as welfare institutions with their own organizational imperatives may come into conflict with the corporate sector over the level and distribution of total compensation, with the state over rising public pension plan contributions, and possibly with their own membership as union leaders attempt "to protect the members from themselves."

Power and ideology are interrelated in the industrial relations system. The unilateral control of occupational pension plans by employers is a reflection of the imbalance in the distribution of power between labour and management under conditions of collective bargaining in capitalist countries. Various issues limit the scope of collective bargaining, reduce the effectiveness of the union as a social welfare institution, and challenge the organizational imperatives and power of the union. These problems will become more evident, and potentially disruptive, as the pension issue becomes more central to collective bargaining in the future with the aging of the labour force.

The co-management of pensions may become the flashpoint for the private pension system under conditions of collective bargaining because issues related to power, control, cost and equity converge. Co-management of pensions as a bargaining issue identifies and has an impact upon a number of crucial power and economic relationships in a capitalist political economy. The pursuit of this issue by unions will inevitably bring them into conflict with the industrial and finance sectors as their vested interests are challenged. In turn, guarding the security of pension benefits may force unions to become more interested in corporate management in general. The co-management of pensions as a narrow collective bargaining issue may therefore evolve into a broader political demand and strategy for industrial democracy.

Each of the specific limitations of the private pension system examined under conditions of collective bargaining has its own logic, or dynamic, which introduces an element of instability into the industrial relations system as a result of its impact on distributive bargaining between labour and capital and intra-organizational bargaining within the modern union. In general, the underlying structural pressures associated with most of these issues will intensify in the future. The separate pension issues identified here are interactive. When combined, they may constitute a volatile "critical mass" of issues triggering a chain reaction, further heightening tensions in an already strained industrial relations system in advanced capitalist countries.

The limitations of the private pension system and the corresponding underdevelopment of the state pension system resulting in the impoverishment and marginalization of the elderly are ultimately related to a series of economic and power relationships based on the organization and imperatives of a capitalist economy. Under conditions of advanced capitalism, the private pension system's capital accumulation function has been transformed from a latent to a manifest function in order to generate macro-economic investment, supply investment capital to the corporate sector, and provide social capital for the welfare state to meet their respective finance requirements. The limitations of the private pension system in the final analysis are related to the role performed by pensions funds as institutional investors in the capital market, the power of occupational pension funds, and the pension system's relationship to the corporate sector in advanced capitalist economies. These subjects are examined in the forthcoming chapters.

6

The Pension System
and
Capital Accumulation

It is always the direct relation of the owners of the means of production to the direct producers which reveals the . . . hidden foundation of the entire social structure. . . . The form of this relation . . . corresponds to a definite stage in the development of labor and its social productivity. This does not prevent the same economic basis from showing infinite variations and gradations in its appearance even though its principal conditions are . . . the same.

Karl Marx

"Some institutions shape modern society," Mills observed, "others adapt to it."[1] In the postwar era institutional investors have increasingly influenced the course of economic events. Pension funds and other institutional investors now occupy the "commanding heights" of the economy. In the future they will have an even more pronounced impact upon economic affairs. The economic function, structure and power associated with the private pension system under advanced capitalism are central to the political economy of pensions. These subjects are examined in Chapters 6 to 9. Because capital is the heart of capitalism, the private pension system is now integral to the functioning of that economic system and must be critically analysed.

The central purpose of this chapter is to identify and investigate the private and public pension system's capital accumulation function under conditions of advanced capitalism. This is the pension system's functional locus of power. This chapter traces the stream of personal and gross savings channelled through the pension system into gross and net investment for the economy. Under advanced capitalism there has been an institutionalization and socialization of retirement savings through the pension system, broadly defined, to supply the investment requirements of the macro-economy.

A related topic is the transformation of the private pension system's role in the capital accumulation process from a latent to a manifest function in order to channel investment capital to the private sector and social capital to the capitalist welfare state. The private pension system's capital accumulation function is important not only for the pension industry, but for all of organized capital because the pension system's impact on saving, investment and capital accumulation affects the broad *general* interests of both financial and industrial capital. As a result of the symbiotic relationship between the private pension system and the corporate sector, the nature and mode of pension reform is of considerable significance because it affects an important source of investment capital for the private sector. The increased appropriation of the discretionary savings of workers by the private pension industry as a source of investment capital for the corporate sector has been a protracted historical process.

HISTORICAL BACKGROUND: LATENT TO MANIFEST
CAPITAL ACCUMULATION FUNCTION

The transformation of the private pension system's capital accumulation function from a latent to a manifest, or explicit, function under conditions of advanced capitalism mirrors the evolution of capitalist economies and the changing requirements of the corporate sector. The private pension industry in Britain, Canada and the United States has exhibited a continuous and pronounced hostility to the expansion of the state social security system. The reasons for this antipathy, however, have changed as the relationship between the pension system and the capital accumulation process has become more explicit.

In Britain between 1910 and 1911 the Combine, an association of life insurance companies led by the gigantic Prudential Life, mounted a concerted campaign against the health sections of the National Insurance Act 1911. According to Yeo, "it was up to then the most aggressive parliamentary lobby mounted by capital."[2] The commercial insurance lobby's "enemy was not the state, but the originally designated operators of the national insurance plan, the British friendly societies. At that time it was private, not government, competition they sought to destroy."[3] The earlier proposed state-run contributory pension was opposed, as well, by the provident and friendly societies because it was viewed as a competitor for the savings of the working class.[4] In general, "despite earlier labour sentiment on the subject, private insurance outside the state system was left untrammeled."[5]

In the United States at the beginning of the century "a large number of private vested interests," such as Fredrick Hoffman of the U.S. Prudential Life Insurance Company, viewed government sponsored social insurance arrangements "as a threat to their survival." Many industrial employers argued that a government pension programme would restrict the role of the private pension system.[6] Suggestions that the United States emulate a number of Western European countries and enact old-age assistance legislation met with considerable opposition. The U.S. Congress rejected bills introduced in 1909, 1911 and 1913. During the 1920s "the main reason for the failure" of the social insurance movement "was the effective opposition inspired by business organizations" such as the Chamber of Commerce and the National Association of Manufacturers at the state level.[7]

Public pensions in Canada, according to Bryden, "were unmistakably stamped with the market ethos" as a result of the influence of the private pension industry. Opposition to the introduction of an universal state retirement pension in Canada at the turn of the century resulted in the voluntary Annuity Act 1908 because the insurance industry "viewed government competition with disfavour."[8] The introduction of the means-tested, flat-rate Old Age Pensions Act was delayed until 1927, and it was not made universal until 1952. Neither the 1951 Old Age Security Act nor the Old Age Assistance Act "was intended as a complete pension, but instead formed . . . a subsistence supplement."[9] The private pension industry opposed the introduction of the earnings-related Canada/Quebec Pension Plans (C/QPPs) and tried "to block public invasion of the contributory field" because of "the threat . . . which . . . was posed for the . . . sale of annuities and private pension plans."[10]

The economic insecurity experienced by Canada's elderly is a result of the universal limitations of the private pension system and the underdevelopment of the public pension system. The reason for the limited role of the state pension system in Canada was made clear by the former federal Minister of Health and Welfare, Monique Bégin, when she candidly stated that "the Canada Pension Plan was designed in the 60's . . . for the *very purpose of leaving the private sector the scope that it needed.*[11] The private pension industry has been allowed to operate by the welfare state so that it could retain its market share and protect its profits. The underdevelopment of the public pension system ensures the continued existence of the private pension industry, reflecting the capitalist state's ideological bias,[12] and the fundamental structural or systemic imperatives of a capitalist economy for saving, investment and capital accumulation.

THE PENSION SYSTEM'S CAPITAL ACCUMULATION
FUNCTION: OVERVIEW

The role of the institutional investor in the United States and Britain has received considerable attention and study, but little is known about the functioning and behaviour of institutional investors in Canada and their impact on the economy. The immense economic power concentrated in these institutions ultimately resides in their role as financial intermediaries and their ability to meet the investment requirements of the macro-economy and the private profit-making corporate sector.

The role of institutional investors and pension funds, as part of the finance sector, and their control over savings and the direction of investment are of considerable importance for public policy as it relates to the operation and reform of the retirement income system. The Government of Saskatchewan in its 1981 brief to the National Pensions Conference noted, for example, that pension

> funds are now sufficiently large to raise concerns regarding their impact on the efficient functioning of capital markets, and their effects on economic growth and development.
>
> Moreover, pension fund assets are largely controlled by relatively few actors—a small number of large, independent pension plans, the major trust companies, and the main insurance companies. This concentration of control, with its overlap to other major institutional investors—trust and insurance companies—reinforces concerns regarding the public policy implications of the growing power of Canada pension funds.[13]

The economic power of pension funds and the private pension system is substantial and is certain to increase in the future.

The private pension system fulfils a role, not only in the provision of retirement income, but also as a critical source of investment to augment private sector capital accumulation. Institutional investors and pension funds have assumed their pre-eminent position and economic power because they have acquired "the organized concentration of control over the 'economic surplus.'"[14] According to Clement:

> control over decisions about reallocating these funds gives those in command great power. By mobilizing the capital of others, *the financial elite is the central node intermediating between accumulation and investment.* It does not use its own capital; on the contrary, its specialty is gathering together the reserves of [workers] through such devices as pension funds, savings accounts, life insurance policies and other devices to centralize the control of reserve capital. This is the enormous power concentrated at the top of these institutions in the hands of the economic elite.[15]

The reserve capital channelled through financial intermediaries and institutional investors is of increasing importance to the corporate sector. In Britain, according to the Radcliffe Report, insurance companies and pension funds now "constitute by far the largest single source of new capital."[16] The role played by pension funds in supplying the finance requirements of the private sector is increasingly perceived and recognized by the business community. According to one major Canadian trust company, for example, "pension assets are an integral part of our socio-economic system and contribute substantially to . . . capital formation."[17]

The increasing economic power of pension funds is based on their pivotal role as financial intermediaries and institutional investors with significant control over the economic surplus and reserve capital. Private pension funds therefore serve a crucial role in the circulation and reproduction model associated with a capitalist economy: saving, investment, capital accumulation and profits.

THE SAVINGS FUNCTION

Institutional investors, and pension funds as a "region" within the finance sector, are mobilizers of capital, linking savers and investors in the economy. Banks, trust companies, life insurance companies and pension funds as financial intermediaries and institutional investors accumulate the savings of ordinary citizens into vast pools of money which are channelled as investment to the industrial and finance sectors of the economy.

The economic and social implications of the private and state pension systems are of major consequence with respect to savings behaviour, investment, economic growth, the functioning of financial institutions, and the operation of capital markets. The private pension system has become "one of the principal means for channelling peoples' savings into industrial and commercial investment . . . and . . . into securities to help finance public expenditure."[18] Saving and investment through the pension system, broadly defined, become capital in the course of the macro-economic circulation and reproduction process. For workers, however, occupational pensions constitute no more than a form of forced savings, or at best a "deferred wage," because these funds are never used as their capital.[19]

The economic power of pension funds is based on their control over savings or reserve capital. To establish the growing importance of the private pension system in supplying the investment and finance requirements of the private and public sectors, it is necessary to determine the sources, magnitude and extent of control over the savings available for investment purposes.

In Canada between 1963–1967 and 1978–1982 personal saving as a proportion of gross saving increased significantly, while corporate saving declined (Table 6.1). Corporate saving (retained earnings plus depreciation allowances) peaked in the mid-1970s and has steadily declined since that time. Concurrently, there has been a long-run decline in corporate liquidity, which has forced corporations to seek external sources of financing by the sale of stock (new or primary market equity issues), long-term debt (bonds and mortgages) and short-term debt instruments (bank loans, commercial paper and so on). This combination of events has placed the corporate sector under increasing strain in order to satisfy its finance requirements. On this subject the Economic Council of Canada was to state that

> since 1960, there has been a rise in the importance of savings by the personal and unincorporated business sector and a concomitant decline in the relative importance of corporate savings. The corporate sector has . . . been the largest user of funds and has consistently relied on the savings of the other

sectors, notably on personal savings, in the form of bonds, insurance and pension plans, and personal holdings of money. With rising inflation and the consequent drain on corporate liquidity, the magnitude of these borrowings has grown.

Personal saving provided through institutional channels has increasingly been substituted for the relative decline in corporate saving for investment purposes. "Private pension plans," according to the Economic Council of Canada, "will remain an important source of savings as the number of contributors grow and as more employees put larger amounts of current income aside."[20] The magnitude of and control over personal saving by institutional investors and pension funds is therefore of considerable economic and social significance.

TABLE 6.1

COMPOSITION OF GROSS SAVING BY SOURCE, CANADA,
FIVE-YEAR AVERAGES, 1963–1967 AND 1978–1982

SOURCES OF GROSS SAVING	% OF TOTAL SAVING		PERCENTAGE CHANGE
	1963–1967	1978–1982	
Personal	31.3	54.4	+73.8
Corporate	38.4	34.3	–10.7
Government	15.9	–4.2	–126.4
Foreign	5.6	5.0	–7.1
Other[1]	8.8	10.3	+17.0

Note: 1 Including non-financial government enterprises, social security funds and miscellaneous.

Source: Department of Finance Canada, Corporate Finance Division.

To determine the extent of the private pension system's control over the increasing proportion of personal saving, it is necessary to establish the relationship between net pension saving (contributions plus investment income minus benefits and administrative costs) and total personal saving, and net pension saving and gross saving in the economy. The savings of the many in the personal sector become investment for the private sector. Financial intermediaries and institutional investors, such as pension funds, link the personal to the corporate sector in terms of saving and investment behaviour. Table 6.2 reports net private, public and total (private plus public) pension fund saving as a proportion of total personal

TABLE 6.2

NET PRIVATE AND PUBLIC PENSION FUND SAVING[1]
AS A PERCENTAGE OF TOTAL PERSONAL SAVING,
U.K., CANADA AND U.S., 1960–1980

YEAR	NET PRIVATE[2] PENSION SAVING AS A % OF TOTAL PERSONAL SAVING			NET PUBLIC PENSION SAVING AS A % OF TOTAL PERSONAL SAVING			TOTAL NET PENSION FUND SAVING AS A % OF TOTAL PERSONAL SAVING		
	U.K.	Canada	U.S.	U.K.[3]	Canada[4]	U.S.[5]	U.K.	Canada	U.S.
1960	41.7	29.3	30.5	5.5	–	3.6	47.2	29.3	34.1
1965	36.8	n.a.	27.9	10.2	–	-0.3	47.0	n.a.	27.6
1970	32.1	33.3	21.2	10.7	33.3	5.2	42.8	66.6	26.4
1971	43.4	n.a.	28.5	16.9	28.9	3.3	60.3	n.a.	31.8
1972	34.7	n.a.	37.3	11.5	27.5	5.1	46.2	n.a.	42.4
1973	31.5	31.3	22.0	10.9	23.9	2.8	42.4	55.2	24.8
1974	34.9	33.8	16.1	12.3	22.1	3.1	44.2	55.9	19.2
1975	39.1	26.0	16.8	15.2	13.8	0.7	54.3	39.8	17.5
1976[6]	44.0	30.6	25.5	16.5	16.4	-0.5	60.5	47.0	24.9
1977	45.4	35.3	32.4	14.0	16.6	-1.8	59.4	51.9	30.6
1978	37.6	38.8	35.4	16.3	15.6	-3.8	53.9	54.4	31.6
1979	40.3	42.7	34.8	9.4	16.3	-0.9	49.7	59.0	33.9
1980	37.0(E)	46.2	33.4	8.6	15.4	0.2	45.5(E)	61.6	33.6

Notes: 1 Net pension fund saving is equal to contributions plus investment income minus benefits and administrative costs. Administrative costs are of a second order magnitude and have been omitted from the calculations.

2 For the U.K., includes non-insured, insured and general revenue financed occupational pension plans. For Canada and the U.S. only trusteed (non-insured) pension plans are included.

3 National Insurance Fund contributory retirement benefits. Excludes pay-as-you-go (PAYGO) plans such as the Central government and para-public sector plans.

4 Canada and Quebec Pension Plans beginning in 1966. Excludes general revenue pay-as-you-go (PAYGO) federal and provincial civil service pension plans.

5 OASI retirement benefits. Excludes general revenue pay-as-you-go (PAYGO) federal and state retirement systems.

6 After 1975 neither the U.S. Securities and Exchange Commission. *Statistical Bulletin* nor the Board of Governors, Federal Reserve System. *Annual Statistical Digest* provides data on private non-insured pension fund receipts and disbursements to calculate pension saving. The figures used here for the period between 1976 and 1980 are based on a trend analysis from 1960, and may in fact understate the case, thus downwardly biasing the saving ratios.

Sources: Calculated from the Central Statistical Office. *Annual Abstract of Statistics, 1982* (London: HMSO, 1982). Table 3.11, pp. 62–63 and Table 14.7, p. 350: Central Statistical Office. *National Income and Expenditure* (London: HMSO, various years); Central Statistical Office. *Financial Statistics* (London: HMSO, various years); G. Francis Green. *The Increase in Aggregate U.K. Pension Savings*. Kingston Polytechnic. Discussion Paper in Political Economy No. 28, 1980, revised Table 1, p. 3; Statistics Canada. *Trusteed Pension Plans Financial Statistics, 1980* (Ottawa: Minister of Supply and Services, 1982). Text Table IV, p. 12; Health and Welfare Canada. *Canada Pension Plan Annual Report* (Ottawa: Health and Welfare, various years); Régie des Rentes. *Quebec Pension Plan Annual Report* (Quebec City: n.p. various years); Statistics Canada. *Canadian Statistical Review* (Ottawa: Minister of Supply and Services, various years); and the U.S. Department of Commerce. *Statistical Abstract of the United States* (Washington, D.C.: GPO, various years), Series 534, 547, 700 and 718. Note Appendix D.

saving for Canada, Britain and the United States between 1960 and 1980. This indicator establishes the proportion of total personal saving controlled by pension funds. The method used here is the "identified savings" approach, rather than the "residual" approach.[21] Pension saving is treated as "contractual" (or compulsory) rather than as "discretionary" savings. For this reason, it was deemed more appropriate to relate net pension saving to total personal saving rather than to personal disposable income. In this regard, the following may be noted with respect to net pension saving as a component of total personal saving.

First, net pension saving under the domination of the private pension system is a significant component of total personal saving. In these countries net pension saving in 1980 accounted for nearly one-third to one-half of total personal saving. Between 1960 and 1980, in the case of Canada, net private pension saving increased from nearly 30 to 46 per cent of total personal saving or by some 53 per cent. This increase is generally consistent with expanded occupational pension plan coverage and greater employer and employee contributions during this period. In Britain, the fluctuating level of net private pension saving is most likely explained in terms of the absolute decline and subsequent stagnation in occupational pension scheme membership after 1967. In the United States, the increasing ratio of net pension saving to total personal saving was a result of sharply rising pension saving relative to a low personal saving rate. The variation in the order of magnitude between countries, particularly in recent years, is largely explained by the difference in the personal saving rate in each of them. In the late 1970s, the personal saving rate was in the order of 15 per cent in the U.K., 10 per cent in Canada, and 5 per cent in the U.S.[22]

Second, net pension saving from the public pension system constitutes a moderate proportion of total personal saving. In Canada, after the Canada/Quebec Pension Plans were introduced in 1966, net public pension saving modulated between 22 to 33 per cent of total personal saving. After 1975, however, it declined, and it has remained within a stable range. Public pension saving in Canada is now in the order of 15 per cent of total personal saving. The relative decline is explained on the basis of the inordinately low (and constant) level of C/QPP contributions since the inception of the plans. Thus, as total personal saving has increased, net public pension saving has relatively declined. This will marginally increase after 1987, reflecting the recently implemented increase in the contribution rate. Net pension saving from the public pension system increased by a factor of three between 1960 and 1977, from 5.5 to 16.5 per cent of total personal saving, largely as the result of increasing total National Insurance Fund contributions over this period. The Social Security Pensions Act 1975, with its provisions for the "contracting-out" of the state earnings-related pension plan by approved occupational pension schemes, came into operation in April 1978, and it probably explains the sharp decline in net public pension saving from 16 to 9 per cent of total personal saving recorded after 1978. Third, total (private and public) net pension saving represents an important component of total personal saving. In Canada 62 per cent of total personal saving is a result of net public and private pension saving; in Britain 46 per cent of personal saving is derived from total pension saving and in the U.S. 34 per cent of personal saving flows from the pension system.

The trends outlined here are generally compatible with those found by Green for Britain and Samur, Jarvis and McCracken for Canada[23] with respect to contractual saving (mortgage repayments plus the savings portion of trusteed pension plans and life insurance) and private pension saving as a proportion of disposable personal income. In Britain contractual saving increased from 4.3 to 6.4 per cent of personal disposable income between 1960 and 1978.[24] In Canada, contractual saving increased from 4.2 to 4.8 per cent of personal disposable income between 1966 and 1977. Private pension saving dominates contractual saving, accounting for 60 per cent of the total. Trusteed pension fund saving rose from 2 to 3 per cent of personal disposable income and is now the second largest component of the personal savings rate.[25]

It is generally accepted that power follows money. Control over and direction of the reserve capital in pension funds therefore concentrates enormous economic power in the hands of financial intermediaries and institutional investors, and in particular, private pension funds. It is therefore necessary to determine the level of net pension saving as a proportion of gross saving in order to ascertain the pension system's impact on investment for the economy.

In the classical, neo-classical and Marxian economic models, savings is equal to investment (S = I) at the macro-economic level. Pension funds and other financial intermediaries organize and channel savings to the corporate sector for profitable investment. Table 6.3 presents net private, public and total (public and private) pension saving as a proportion of gross saving for Canada, Britain and the

U.S. between 1960 and 1980. Net pension saving as a proportion of gross saving is an indicator of the magnitude and importance of the pension system in supplying saving for investment.

The following may be noted. First, net pension saving as a proportion of gross saving flowing from the private pension system in Britain and Canada is a notable and growing component of gross saving. In 1980 net private pension saving accounted for 24 per cent of gross saving in the U.K. and nearly 18 per cent in Canada. Estimated net pension saving in the U.S. as a proportion of gross saving, however, was considerably lower. In Canada, if net pension saving from unfunded general revenue government employee pension plans were included, net private pension saving as a proportion of gross saving would be in the order of 20 per cent.[26] Between 1960 and 1980 net private pension saving as a percentage of gross saving increased in the U.K. by 91 per cent and in Canada by 67 per cent.

The advanced funding of occupational pension plans, resulting in the accumulation of a fund, is the mechanism through which private pension saving is organized and subsequently invested. The level of net private pension saving as a percentage of gross saving is a function of both the relationship between private pension contributions and benefit payout (numerator) and the level of gross savings (denominator). The increase in net private pension saving in Canada and the U.K. as a proportion of gross saving is generally explained in terms of greater pension contribution inflow in relation to benefit payout and gross saving. Increased net private pension saving in Canada as a proportion of gross saving is attributable to expanded occupational pension plan coverage and higher absolute employee and employer contribution levels. In Britain, despite the absolute decline in occupational pension scheme members after 1967, there was an increase in contributions per member as a result of inflated salary levels and the preservation (vesting) provisions under the 1975 legislation requiring higher employer and employee contributions.[27]

Second, net pension saving from the public (state) pension system, while considerably less than that flowing from the private pension system, nevertheless represents a modest proportion of gross saving. Net savings accumulated through the public pension system, however, do not necessarily generate investment to augment capital stock since they are often used to finance current government expenditures. In 1980, net public pension saving in both the U.K. and Canada was in the order of 5 per cent. In Canada, after the

TABLE 6.3

NET PRIVATE AND PUBLIC PENSION FUND SAVING
AS A PERCENTAGE OF GROSS SAVING.[1]
U.K., CANADA AND U.S., 1960–1980

YEAR	NET PRIVATE[2] PENSION SAVING AS A % OF GROSS SAVING			NET PUBLIC PENSION SAVING AS A % OF GROSS SAVING			TOTAL NET PENSION FUND SAVING AS A % OF GROSS SAVING		
	U.K.	Canada	U.S.	U.K.[3]	Canada[4]	U.S.[5]	U.K.	Canada	U.S.
1960	10.2	8.1(E)	7.4	1.4	–	0.9	11.6	9.0	8.3
1965	10.5	n.a.	7.8	2.9	–	-0.1	13.4	n.a.	7.7
1970	8.1	7.0	7.9	2.9	7.0	1.9	11.0	14.0	9.8
1971	10.2	n.a.	9.5	3.9	6.3	1.1	14.1	n.a.	10.6
1972	11.2	n.a.	10.6	3.7	5.9	1.4	14.9	n.a.	12.0
1973	10.5	7.3	7.4	3.7	5.6	0.9	14.2	12.9	8.3
1974	12.6	7.3	6.0	4.4	4.8	1.1	17.0	12.1	7.1
1975	16.1	7.9	7.2	6.3	4.2	0.3	22.4	12.1	7.5
1976[6]	15.4	8.9	8.1	5.8	4.8	-0.2	21.2	13.7	7.9
1977	14.8	10.2	7.9	4.6	4.8	-0.4	19.4	15.0	7.5
1978	15.2	11.3	7.6	6.6	4.8	-0.8	21.8	16.1	6.8
1979	14.3	11.7	7.3	4.0	4.5	-0.2	21.3	16.2	7.1
1980	19.5(E)	13.5	8.5	4.6	4.5	0.1	24.1(E)	18.0	8.5

Note: 1 The sources of gross savings are defined as the sum of persons and unincorporated business (personal saving) plus corporate and government business enterprises (undistributed profits, government business enterprises, capital assistance and inventory valuation adjustment) plus government and non-residents plus capital consumption allowances. See Table 6.2 for footnotes.

Sources: See Table 6.2 and Appendix D.

introduction of the Canada/Quebec Pension Plans in 1966, net public pension saving levelled off. The modest level of net public pension saving in Canada, despite the low level of contributions, is explained in terms of increasing C/QPP coverage and contributions as the result of an expanding labour force and the Quebec Pension Plan being partially funded. These factors have generated a modest reserve fund. In Britain, the level of net saving attributable to the National Insurance Fund's retirement pension is a result of the maturity of the system and a much higher level of contributions. In the U.S. the social security retirement system has been in a dissaving position in recent years owing to its chronic deficit position, resulting in a drag on net pension saving.

Third, total (private and public) net pension saving in the U.K. and Canada has doubled between 1960 and 1980 and now accounts for 24 per cent of gross saving in the U.K. and 18 per cent in Canada. Nearly one-fifth of all gross investment in these countries is therefore supplied through the pension system broadly defined. In Canada, if a broader definition of retirement savings were used which included all public and private occupational pension plans as well as individual retirement savings vehicles such as RRSPs, in the period between 1972 and 1976, for example, where data is readily available, "23 per cent of the capital stock — factories, homes, schools, roads . . . put in place . . . was financed by [retirement] savings."[28] This information confirms that savings undertaken for retirement purposes, and channelled through the pension system, play an important, if not vital, role in the provision of investment for capitalist economies.

THE INVESTMENT FUNCTION

Pension funds and other institutional investors in Canada, Britain and the U.K. in the postwar period have assumed an increasingly important role in supplying capital resources. According to the Toronto Stock Exchange, institutional investors and pension funds "have vitally influenced macro-economic performance."[29] "Private sector pension plans," the Trust Companies Association of Canada asserts, "are a major savings vehicle . . . and thus a major source for financing . . . capital requirements."[30] And prominent investment managers in the U.K. maintain that private pension funds "increase the flow of money available for capital investment in the most productive and profitable enterprises and thus encourage economic growth."[31] In advanced capitalist economies the needs of the private sector require an increased interpenetration and interdependence of capital. The modern institutional investor and the private pension system have assumed the function of socializing investment by being a conduit for savings, thereby accelerating the socialization of the capitalist mode of production.

To assess the economic power of the private pension system and its impact on the economy and capital markets requires that pension saving be related to the current and projected investment requirements of the corporate sector. In order to establish the significance of net saving flowing from the private pension system for investment in and by the corporate sector and the economy, two indicators have been constructed. The first, outlined in Table 6.4, reports net private pension saving as a percentage of gross fixed domestic business investment. That is, pension saving is related to the replacement of and addition to capital stock. The second and more significant indicator, reported in Table 6.5, relates net private pension saving to net private domestic investment (capital formation); that is, depreciation (capital consumption allowances) on a replacement cost basis (in current dollars) is deducted from gross private domestic capital formation to arrive at the net (that is, new) addition to capital stock.

As Table 6.4 shows, net private pension saving as a proportion of gross private domestic investment has continuously increased over the past twenty years, particularly in the U.K. and Canada. Specifically, net pension saving from the private pension system now represents 26 per cent of gross domestic investment in Britain, 16 per cent in Canada, and 8 per cent in the U.S. In Britain and Canada between 1960 and 1980, net private pension saving as a proportion of gross private investment has doubled. Any diminution of private pension saving would force the business sector to secure alternative sources of funding, such as increased foreign investment, to meet their finance requirements. Capital would become more expensive and corporations would have to either slow their rate of expansion or use capital resources more efficiently.

The full impact of private pension saving for business investment becomes even more evident when it is related to net private domestic investment as presented in Table 6.5. Net private domestic investment is equal to gross private domestic investment minus capital consumption (depreciation) allowances. Gross domestic private investment is thus adjusted for that portion of capital stock

TABLE 6.4

NET PRIVATE PENSION SAVING
AS A PERCENTAGE OF GROSS PRIVATE DOMESTIC INVESTMENT.
CANADA, U.K. AND U.S. SELECTED YEARS, 1960–1980

YEAR	NET PRIVATE PENSION SAVING[1] (BILLION NATIONAL CURRENCY UNITS)			GROSS PRIVATE DOMESTIC INVESTMENT[2] (BILLION NATIONAL CURRENCY UNITS)			NET PRIVATE PENSION SAVING AS A % OF GROSS PRIVATE DOMESTIC INVESTMENT		
	Canada	U.K.	U.S.	Canada	U.K.	U.S.	Canada	U.K.	U.S.
1960	0.4	0.5	6.0	6.5	3.7	75.9	6.8	13.5	7.9
1965	n.a.	0.7	9.4	10.3	5.5	113.5	n.a.	12.7	8.3
1970	1.3	1.1	11.8	14.3	7.0	148.8	9.1	15.7	7.9
1975	3.2	3.6	15.8	37.7	15.4	219.6	8.5	23.4	7.2
1980	9.0	9.4[3]	33.4[4]	57.4	34.6	437.0	15.7	27.2	7.6

Notes: 1 Net pension saving is equal to contributions plus investment income minus benefits and administrative costs.
Administrative costs are of a second order magnitude and have been omitted from the calculations.
2 Including residential and non-residential construction and machinery and equipment expenditures by the private
sector including government enterprises (excluding government departments) plus capital consumption allowances.
3 In 1979 the net growth in funds was £8.1 billion. This was extrapolated on the basis of the long term growth rate.
4 Estimated on the basis of trend analysis.

Sources: Calculated from Appendices D and E and Statistics Canada. "Capital and Repair Expenditures," CANSIM Series and
information supplied by Statistics Canada, Construction Division; Central Statistical Office, Annual Abstract of
Statistics (London: HMSO, various years); Central Statistical Office, National Income and Expenditure (London: HMSO,
various years), and the U.S. Department of Commerce, Statistical Abstract of the U.S., 1982–83 (Washington, D.C.: GPO,
1982), Series 690, p. 419 and Series 905, p. 539. Revised data for the period after 1965 from the U.S. Department of
Commerce, Statistical Abstract of the United States 1988 (Washington, D.C.: GPO, 1987), Series 851, p. 508.

replaced and financed by capital consumption (depreciation) allowances (Table 6.4). Net private pension saving as a percentage of net private domestic investment therefore represents that proportion of new business investment financed through the private pension system.

Net private pension saving as a proportion of net investment is dramatically greater than as a component of gross investment. As reported in Table 6.5, private pension saving is equivalent to 90 per cent of net private domestic business investment in the U.K., 27 per cent in the Canada, and 25 per cent in the U.S. This means that on average in the order of 50 per cent of all new business investment in these countries is financed by the increasing level of personal savings channelled through the private pension system.

The proportion of net business investment financed by the private pension system basically doubled in the U.S. and Canada and tripled in Britain between 1960 and 1980. In the U.S., net pension saving increased from 20 to 25 per cent of net private investment. However, net private pension saving in Canada rose from 16 to 27 per cent of net private investment, while in Britain it soared from 30 to 90 per cent of net domestic business capital formation. The difference between Canada and the U.S. in one instance, and the case of Britain in another, merits some elaboration, particularly the extraordinary situation found in the U.K.

The increase in private pension saving as a proportion of net private investment may be attributed to two factors. First, the significant increase in net pension saving is a result of accelerating contribution inflow relative to net private investment. Pension saving in all of these countries increased at a faster rate than net private investment, resulting in a higher ratio of pension saving to net investment. Furthermore, while net private investment in Canada between 1960 and 1980 increased by a factor of twelve, in the U.S. in the same period net investment increased by a factor of thirteen; however, between 1965 and 1975 it remained virtually constant. Thus, in the U.S., the modest increase in the proportion of business investment financed by net private pension saving was the result of increased pension saving relative to a decline in net investment.

Second, and perhaps more important, particularly in the case of Britain and the U.S., are those causal and arithmetic relationships which determine the level of net private investment. Net private investment is defined as gross private investment minus capital consumption (depreciation) allowances. In Britain between 1960

TABLE 6.5

NET PRIVATE PENSION SAVING
AS A PERCENTAGE OF NET PRIVATE DOMESTIC INVESTMENT[1]
CANADA, U.K. AND U.S., SELECTED YEARS, 1960–1980

YEAR	NET PRIVATE PENSION SAVING (BILLION NATIONAL CURRENCY UNITS)			NET PRIVATE DOMESTIC INVESTMENT (BILLION NATIONAL CURRENCY UNITS)			NET PRIVATE PENSION SAVING AS A % OF NET PRIVATE DOMESTIC INVESTMENT		
	Canada	U.K.	U.S.	Canada	U.K.	U.S.	Canada	U.K.	U.S.
1960	0.4	0.5	6.0	2.7	1.7	9.6	16.3	29.4	20.2
1965	n.a.	0.7	9.4	5.4	2.5	57.5	n.a.	28.0	16.4
1970	1.3	1.1	11.8	7.8	3.2	60.0	16.7	34.4	19.7
1975	3.2	3.6	15.8	20.9	5.7	57.8	15.3	63.2	27.3
1980	9.0	9.4(E)	33.4[2]	33.2	10.5	133.1	27.1	89.5	25.1

Notes: 1 Net private domestic investment is equal to gross private domestic capital formation minus capital consumption (depreciation) allowances in current dollars, on a replacement cost basis, for the private business sector and public corporations. For footnotes, see Table 6.4.
2 Estimated on the basis of trend analysis.

Sources: See Table 6.4. Revised data for the U.S. in the period after 1965 from the U.S. Department of Commerce, *Statistical Abstract of the United States 1988* (Washington, D.C.: GPO, 1987). Series 851, p. 508.

and 1980, depreciation allowances increased from 54 to 71 per cent of gross private investment; in the U.S. over the same period they increased from 61 to 74 per cent. In Canada, however, capital consumption allowances declined from 59 to 42 per cent between 1960 and 1980. As depreciation allowances increase, there is a corresponding reduction in net private investment. Therefore, the unusually high level of net private investment generated by the private pension system in Britain was attributable to the sharp increase in private pension saving relative to the amount of net private investment; this was compounded by the increasing level of capital consumption allowances over that period which affected the level of net private investment.

While varying between countries, the magnitude of net private business investment financed through the private pension system suggests that it is an universal characteristic of these advanced capitalist economies and that it is critical to the investment and capital accumulation requirements of the private sector. The institutional strength associated with the private pension system and the political influence of the private pension industry are ultimately related to the enormous pool of savings and assets under its control. Its strength is structurally determined because the private pension system is a financial intermediary and institutional investor, which promotes and serves the *general* interests of *all* organized capital by satisfying current and future investment requirements.

Private pension saving is perceived by the corporate sector as a vital source of investment capital in the medium and long term. It is therefore necessary to determine its importance for future private sector investment requirements. The perception of this situation within the business community has important implications for public policy with respect to pension reform.

Future investment requirements can be projected on the basis of econometric models and forecasts. In turn, estimated private pension saving, based on demographic assumptions, can be related to these requirements. Such an exercise, however, is fraught with difficulty and must be viewed with considerable caution, particularly since macro-econometric forecasts in recent years have been notoriously inaccurate and have fallen into disrepute. Econometric models are constructed on the basis of certain assumptions about economic relationships and behaviour as well as the external environment. Projected investment requirements are based on assumptions about savings behaviour, particularly the proportion flowing from the personal and corporate sectors. Furthermore, the external environment over the past decade has been extremely dynamic. Sharply rising and falling energy prices and inflation rates, monetary devaluations and a protracted international recession with accompanying high unemployment have all characterized the international economy in recent years. In the case of Canada, which is used here for the purpose of illustration, the now defunct National Energy Program and massive investment in energy-related megaprojects were anticipated to account for 25 to 40 per cent of all investment over the next twenty years. With the advent of the 1981–1982 world oil glut and the pervasive nature of the international recession, projected investment requirements were revised downwards. Some have argued however, that these capital requirements have only been postponed. For all of these reasons long-run capital investment projections must be used and interpreted with care.

Table 6.6 relates estimated net private pension plan saving to near-, medium- and long-term capital investment projections for Canada. Based on this information, private pension saving in the near term (1976 to 1985) will approximate 12 per cent of gross investment. As was indicated in Table 6.4, however, net private pension saving has already exceeded these projections, increasing from 9 to 16 per cent of gross investment between 1975 and 1980. If private pension saving is of significance in the short term at the macro-economic level, it may be even more so in terms of corporate financing and the impact upon capital markets. According to a study by the economic consulting firm of Wood Gundy Limited, in Canada between 1981 and 1985, 70 to 80 per cent of all new capital required by industry and raised through bond and stock issues is expected to be furnished by private pension funds.[32] Similarly, in the United States, according to New York Stock Exchange estimates, $800 billion or nearly 27 per cent of the $3 trillion needed for new capital expenditures between 1975 and 1985 will have to be raised externally by corporations. Private pension funds are expected to be a major source of this corporate financing.

The medium- and long-term projections are of considerable interest. In Canada, over the medium term between 1981 and 1990, private pension saving is projected to be in the order of 11 per cent of gross private investment, and in the long term between 1990 and 2000, 9 per cent. While this is a modest decline relative to current trends, private pension saving would represent, other factors being constant, in the order of 20 per cent of net private investment over

TABLE 6.6

ALTERNATE PROJECTIONS OF ESTIMATED TRUSTEED PENSION PLAN SAVING[1]
AS A PERCENTAGE OF FORECAST GROSS PRIVATE INVESTMENT REQUIREMENTS.[2] CUMULATIVE CURRENT BILLION $.
CANADA, 1976–2000

FORECAST ORGANIZATION	1976–1985		1981–1990		1991–2000		ESTIMATED TRUSTEED PENSION PLAN SAVING AS A % OF FORECAST GROSS INVESTMENT REQUIREMENTS		
	Trusteed Pension Plan Saving	Capital Requirements	Trusteed Pension Plan Saving	Capital Requirements	Trusteed Pension Plan Saving	Capital Requirements	1976–1985	1981–1990	1991–2000
Economic Council of Canada									
Scenario I[3]	$79.9[5]	$612.0	$129.7	—	$338.5	—	13.1	—	—
Scenario II[4]	79.9[5]	784.0	129.7	—	338.5	—	10.1	—	—
Investment Dealers Association	—	—	129.7	$1,318	338.5	$4,197	—	9.8	8.1
Royal Bank of Canada	—	—	129.7	1,271	338.5	n.a.	10.2	n.a.	—
Data Resources of Canada	—	—	129.7	1,118	338.5	—	—	11.6	n.a.
Informetrica	—	—	129.7	1,155	338.5	3,454	—	12.2	9.8

Notes: 1 Projected trusteed pension plan saving on a cumulative basis, based on information from the Economic Council of Canada using the low demographic growth rate assumption. Saving as a flow has been derived from the stock of pension fund assets.
2 Cumulative forecast for gross private investment including residential and non-residential construction, repair and machinery expenditures. Projections by economic forecasting organizations.
3 Assuming moderate external growth and energy prices.
4 Assuming favourable external environment and high energy prices.
5 Actual cumulative trusteed pension plan saving between 1976 and 1980 plus estimated saving between 1981 and 1985.

Sources: Economic Council of Canada, *Twelfth Annual Review: Options for Growth* (Ottawa: Information Canada, 1975), Table B-1, p. 136 and Table B-3, p. 138 and additional information. Andrew G. Kniewasser, president, Investment Dealers Association of Canada, "Address to the 1981 Annual Conference Atlantic Provinces Economic Council," Saint John, New Brunswick, 29 September 1981. Table, p. 2; Edward P. Neufeld, senior vice-president and chief executive officer, Royal Bank of Canada, "Who Will Finance Canada's Economic Growth in the 1980s?" address to the Young President's Organization, Vancouver, 2 October 1981, Table 3, p. 20. Data Resources of Canada, *Canadian Review* (Fall 1982) and Informetrica Ltd., Post-Workshop 1-82 Forecast, 4 July 1982.

the medium term and 16 per cent in the long term. However, should the Canadian economy turn around and begin to recover with an accompanying diminution of inflation and the personal savings rate and a corresponding increase in investment requirements, private pension saving would play an increasingly important role in financing capital investment in the medium and long term for the private sector.

Personal saving flowing through the private pension system for investment in and by the corporate sector is now, and will continue to be, a major source of economic power. The importance of the pension system for financing the future investment requirements of the business community has resulted in a fundamental transformation of the corporate sector's attitude towards the operation of the private pension system under advanced capitalism.

THE PENSION SYSTEM AND PRIVATE SECTOR INVESTMENT REQUIREMENTS

What is recent, and highly significant, is the change in attitude within and perception by the corporate sector towards the use of private pension fund capital for the explicit purpose of financing their future capital requirements. This change in outlook is the fundamental explanation for the private pension system's saving and investment role being transformed from a latent to a manifest function. In terms of the broad economic interests of the business community, the primary purpose of the private pension system is no longer the provision of retirement income, but rather the channelling of investment capital to the corporate sector. In this regard a consultant to the Business Committee on Pension Policy stated that, "the private sector pension system is tremendously important to the national economy. It is not just a means of disbursing retirement income. It is also a primary source of long-term capital" because "it offers the most rapidly growing pool of private capital in the country."[33]

The primary function of the private pension system is now to augment and promote capital accumulation in the private sector. A brief review of the financial and trade literature clearly identifies the change in perception and emerging consensus within the business community about the main purpose of the private pension system under advanced capitalism. The corporate sector now has few reservations about suggesting that the occupational pension fund assets of workers be used to finance the investment requirements of the private sector. Pension fund investment is now viewed as being vital for economic growth and the very survival of capitalism.

The corporate sectors in Canada, Britain and the U.S. have similar perceptions of the role now performed by the private pension system. The chairman of one of the largest and most influential U.S. pension funds explained the decline in economic growth on the basis of the "inadequate provision of capital" and observed that "private pensions are a powerful source of capital for use in expanding the country's plant [and] equipment,"[34] while a leading U.S. pension industry trade journal carried a feature article significantly entitled "Funds' growth rate staggering; could be a major asset pool."[35] In Canada the president of a major life insurance company suggested that reform of the private pension system must recognize "the need of the economy for capital."[36] And a vice-president of a large Canadian corporation was of the view that "the capital needs of the country over the next several decades will require high and sustained levels of pension investment."[37]

The need for capital investment in the long term is viewed as being so acute among certain segments of the corporate community that some private sector representatives have suggested that the U.S. social security retirement system be fully funded in order to promote capital formation.[38] In Canada, spokesmen for the Government of Ontario in 1977 stated that "Ontario has suggested that we seriously consider fully funding the CPP [Canada Pension Plan] and investing those funds in the private sector."[39] While Ontario subsequently abandoned that position, many within the corporate sector have not. The senior vice-president of Canada's largest bank, for example, has argued that "there will need to be an increase in the relative size of financing going to business," and pension reform will need to address "the question of [state] pension funds going into private sector investments."[40] Financial commentators readily identified the relationship between pension reform and capital accumulation in that "expansion of the CPP . . . would reduce pension savings invested in the private sector"[41] and would "deprive the private sector of . . . investment capital."[42]

There is complete unanimity between industrial and financial capital with respect to the defence and preservation of the private pension system's now manifest capital accumulation function. At the National Pensions Conference in March 1981 the Canadian Manufacturers' Association argued that expansion of the CPP would deprive private industry of a massive pool of funds needed to raise productivity and create jobs.[43] The Toronto Board of Trade maintained that a large proportion of all new capital needed by industry in Canada and invested through new stock and bond issues would be supplied by private pension funds. They argued that "it is vital that these funds should be maintained and should grow. They cannot be replaced by public pension funds."[44] As these statements suggest, the private pension system is now viewed as critical to capital accumulation in the private sector and vital to the interests of both financial and industrial capital. Access to and control over pension fund capital for investment in the private sector to promote capital accumulation, therefore, is the fundamental reason for the corporate sector's unalterable opposition to the expansion of the public pension system and its staunch defence of the private pension industry.

THE PENSION SYSTEM'S CAPITAL ACCUMULATION FUNCTION: IMPLICATIONS

The pension system under advanced capitalism has assumed a structurally strategic and pivotal macro-economic function. The institutional strength and power of the private pension industry in the final analysis is directly related to its functional control over savings and the direction of investment. Saving and investment channelled through the private pension system have been transformed from a latent to a manifest function to augment capital accumulation in the private profit-making sector of the economy. This function is now central to the operation of the private pension system under advanced capitalism.

The importance of pension saving to finance the future investment requirements of the economy and corporate sector has resulted in a major transformation of the business community's attitude towards the operation of the private pension system. It is now explicitly viewed as a mechanism to finance, and a source of investment capital for, the corporate sector. This function is the systemic reason for the corporate sector's opposition to an expansion of the public pension system.

A number of broad macro- and micro-economic and political implications regarding the pension system's capital accumulation function can be identified. First, at a macro-economic level, the pension system's control over saving and investment results in it occupying a pivotal position at the "commanding heights" of advanced capitalist economies, where control over and direction of investment is *the* fundamental source of economic power. The pension system, as a financial intermediary and institutional investor, has thus acquired control over a key economic lever, which places it in a strategic structural position to influence the direction of advanced capitalist economies. Second, the impact of the pension system on macro-economic investment has fundamentally altered the corporate sector's view about the purpose and functioning of the private pension system under modern capitalism. The public policy implications with respect to the mode of pension reform are discussed in Chapter 7.

At a micro-economic level, the saving and investment function associated with the private and public pension systems has similar important implications. First, the transformation of the pension system to an essential source of investment capital has resulted in it having an impact on corporate and public sector finance. The importance of the pension system at a micro-economic level as a source of external financing for the corporate sector and social capital for the welfare state is analysed in the Chapter 7. Second, control over savings and investment is the private pension industry's functional locus of power, resulting in a considerable concentration and centralization of pension fund capital. The institutional organization of pension fund power is examined in Chapter 8. Third, the investment function associated with the private pension system is an integrative mechanism which increasingly facilitates an interpenetration and fusion of industrial and financial capital. This amalgamation is investigated in Chapter 9.

The pension system's capital accumulation function also has political implications. First, in terms of the politics of pension reform, the continued existence and operation of the private pension system and the underlying capital accumulation function performed by it are of critical importance to the general interests of both industrial and financial capital. Subordination of the public pension system effectively ensures private sector control over and direction of the increasing proportion of saving and investment channelled through and generated by the private pension system in the *general* interests of *all* organized capital. Concurrently, the underdevelopment of the public pension system ensures the institutional survival of the private pension industry by protecting its market share and profits.

Functionally, there is a symbiotic relationship, that is, a convergence of interests, between the private sector's need for the increased investment capital cycled through the private pension system and the private pension industry's imperative for institutional survival. An expanded public pension system would deprive the corporate sector of capital investment and would further diminish the already marginal role played by the private pension system in the provision of retirement income for the elderly described in Chapter 2. The private pension industry and corporate sector may be expected to react accordingly to protect their structurally determined vested interest.

Second, depending upon political circumstance, the investment function intrinsic to the pension system can be used as a mechanism to promote progressive alternative economic strategies at the micro-economic level through the occupational pension system and at the macro-economic level through the state pension system. This subject is dealt with in Chapter 10.

The pension system performs a variety of important macro- and micro-economic functions under advanced capitalism. The pension system facilitates capital accumulation by institutionalizing retirement savings and socializing investment. As a consequence, the private pension system is now a major economic actor and increasingly dominates capital markets.

7

The Pension System and the Institutionalization of Capital Markets

The continual re-transformation of surplus-value into capital . . . appears in the . . . increasing magnitude of capital that enters into the process of production.

Karl Marx

The stock exchange . . . as it develops, tends to concentrate all production . . . so that . . . [it] becomes the most prominent representative of capitalist production itself.

Frederick Engels

The post-World War II period has witnessed the institutionalization of capital markets and investment. Financial intermediaries, broadly defined, have increasingly supplanted the saving and investment function performed by individuals. The institutional investor now dominates capital markets in Canada, Britain and the United States and is a modern-day Behemoth.

The private pension system has a significant impact on capital markets, the pattern of investment for the economy, corporate and public finance, and the ownership of corporate securities. The influence of pension funds and institutional investors on capital markets is now generally acknowledged. The London Stock Exchange observed that there is a "growing trend towards the domination of the stock market by the savings institutions."[1] In the United States "most experts in the field foresee further institutionalization of equity markets in the years ahead."[2] And in Canada the Toronto Stock Exchange warned that "the trend towards institutionalization will result in . . . concentration of market power and a generally less efficient allocative mechanism."[3] For example, nearly 50 per cent of the dollar value traded on the Toronto Stock Exchange represented institutional investment in the late 1970s. Trust companies, life insurance companies and pension funds accounted for nearly 60 per cent of all institutional savings. All of this indicates the enormous power of the savings being accumulated and invested by such investors through capital markets as well as the institutionalization of retirement savings as a source of investment.

A number of related subjects are analysed in this chapter. First, the increased institutionalization of capital markets under conditions of advanced capitalism: evidence from the U.S. and U.K. in the postwar period indicates a dramatic and continuous absolute and relative increase in equity and bond holdings by institutional investors, including pension funds, and a corresponding decline by individuals. Private pension funds increasingly dominate capital markets and have an important impact on the direction of capitalist economies. Second, there has been a corresponding institutionalization of investment, which is a concomitant of the control institutional investors now exercise over savings and investment previously analysed in Chapter 6.

Third, the institutionalization of investment through pension funds has affected corporate finance and the locus of control over corporate securities. Pension saving and investment channelled to the private sector has become an important source of external corporate financing. Increased pension fund holdings of corporate securities facilitates the interpenetration and interdependence of financial and industrial capital by vesting pension funds with a proprietorial interest in the management of private sector corporations.

The fourth, and last, topic dealt with is the state as an institutional investor. The expansion of the welfare state's economic activities in the postwar period, including the augmentation of the retirement income system, has resulted in important changes in financial intermediation and the structure of capital markets. To finance its own activities and expenditures the state has become an increasingly important actor in financial markets. The state pension system, particularly in Canada, has become a vital source of public sector finance. The capitalist welfare state and the private sector therefore are competitors in capital markets. As a result, the structurally determined interests of the elderly for income security and the welfare state's finance requirements are in opposition to the private sector's need for investment capital and the private pension industry's institutional survival.

THE INSTITUTIONALIZATION OF CAPITAL MARKETS:
THE ANATOMY OF CONTROL

In a capitalist economy control over and direction of investment is the primary source of economic power. The locus of investment decision-making and corporate ownership in advanced capitalist economies now resides in two centres of power: first, a small socio-economic elite of individuals and families — that is, the ruling class; and second, a relatively few, but powerful, institutional investors such as banks, insurance companies, pension funds and other financial intermediaries.

The rise of the institutional investor in the postwar period represents a new phase in the transition from personal to impersonal capitalist ownership. In the 1930s Berle and Means identified three stages in the control of large corporations: first, majority control by the founders of the corporation; second, minority control by an individual or group; and third, internal or "management" control, with the stock widely dispersed.[4] The significant role now played by institutional investors, and in particular pension funds, in supplying the investment requirements of the corporate sector (and government) and the increasing concentration of corporate shareholdings held by institutions suggest a new, fourth stage in the control of the modern corporation.

Recent trends have witnessed the increasing domination of capital markets by institutional investors as a result of institutional investment in the corporate sector through the securities market. Holdings of corporate equity — that is, stock or share issues — are of particular importance since they confer ownership and voting rights. Institutional investors have therefore become the registered (indirect) owners of corporations, while acting on behalf of the beneficial owners whom they represent, such as occupational pension plan members. Corporate ownership has increasingly shifted from the personal to the institutional sector of the economy.

The locus of corporate control and ownership can be determined from the distribution of corporate securities (stocks and bonds) and government bonds between and among the various sectors of the economy. The work of Moyle, Prais, Errit, Briston and Dobbins, and Minns in the U.K., and the Securities and Exchange Commission, Goldsmith, Tilove and Harbrecht in the U.S.[5] has recorded the increasing proportion of share ownership held by institutional investors and pension funds and the corresponding decline of personal sector holdings. In the case of Canada, where these data have not previously existed, a long-term time-series has been constructed from the national flow accounts in order to ascertain the distribution of stock and bond ownership between individual and institutional investors. It is presented in Table 7.1. A transnational comparison of institutional and individual stock ownership in the U.K., U.S. and Canada is reported in Table 7.2

TABLE 7.1

DISTRIBUTION OF INDIVIDUAL AND INSTITUTIONAL STOCK AND BOND OWNERSHIP BY SECTOR, BOOK VALUE, CANADA, SELECTED YEARS, 1962–1979

FINANCIAL ASSET BY SECTOR	1962	1965	1970	1975	1979
STOCK OWNERSHIP					
Personal Sector[1]	45.7%	46.1%	42.9%	41.4%	44.4%
Institutional Investors[2]	7.9	10.5	13.9	17.5	21.8
Other Private Financial Institutions	5.2	6.7	7.3	8.9	7.5
Trusteed Pension Funds	1.5	2.2	3.8	4.6	4.0
Life Insurance Cos	0.7	0.9	1.6	2.1	1.2
Chartered Banks and Near Banks[3]	0.5	0.7	0.0	1.0	8.5
Public Financial Institutions	0.0	0.0	0.3	0.0	0.6
Monetary Authorities	0.0	0.0	0.0	0.0	0.0
Social Security Funds[4]	0.0	0.0	0.0	0.0	0.0
Non-Financial Private Corps	10.5	10.9	10.4	11.0	11.4
Public Sector	0.2	0.2	0.5	0.6	0.4
Federal Gov't	0.02	0.02	0.1	0.2	0.03
Provincial and Local Gov't	0.03	0.03	0.3	0.3	0.1
Non Financial Gov't Corps	0.1	0.1	0.1	0.1	0.3
Foreign Sector[5]	35.8	32.3	32.3	29.4	21.2
BOND OWNERSHIP					
Personal Sector[1]	33.6	31.9	28.0	26.6	20.8
Institutional Investors[2]	42.3	41.1	44.6	46.1	46.5
Other Private Financial Institutions	3.7	3.4	3.5	3.4	3.9
Trusteed Pension Funds	8.6	9.2	8.6	9.5	11.4
Life Insurance Cos	11.3	10.5	8.1	7.3	6.6
Chartered Banks and Near Banks[3]	12.1	11.7	11.9	9.8	7.7
Public Financial Institutions	0.4	0.4	2.0	2.9	3.2
Monetary Authorities	6.2	5.9	5.3	5.1	5.1
Social Security Funds	0.0	0.0	5.2	8.1	8.6
Non-Financial Private Corps	3.1	3.1	1.1	0.4	0.3
Public Sector	7.4	8.1	9.5	8.7	8.9
Federal Gov't	0.8	0.5	0.8	0.1	0.1
Provincial and Local Gov't	5.9	6.7	7.7	7.9	8.3
Non Financial Gov't Corps	0.7	0.9	1.0	0.7	0.5
Foreign Sector	13.6	15.7	16.9	18.3	22.7

Notes: 1 Including unincorporated businesses and non-profit foundations. The limitations of these data do not allow differentiation between individuals and unincorporated businesses, Sectors I and II of the financial flow accounts. The data for Sectors I and II, individuals and unincorporated businesses, is derived residually. In the case of stock assets (corporation common and preferred shares) the figure is estimated by subtracting the estimated aggregate of all share assets held by all other sectors, including the Foreign Sector, from the estimated aggregate value of all shares outstanding (on the liability side) by all sectors.

2 The financial flow accounts do not break-out equity ownership by sector within the institutional investor category. The "control total" for the value of all shares outstanding is the sum across all sectors of category 3520, stocks liability side, which can then be compared to share assets (category 2520) held by persons and unincorporated businesses (categories I and II). It is not possible to derive a frequency distribution of stock ownership by sector within the institutional investor category because the asset category "corporate claims" (category 2512) includes both short- and long-term loans and advances from affiliated companies plus investment in shares of affiliates and thus is a "dirty" figure. The liability category "corporate claims" (category 3512) includes short- and long-term loans and advances from affiliated companies but does not include issues of shares to affiliates. The total across all sectors for category 2512 (corporate claims, asset side) therefore does not equal the total across all sectors for category 2520 (stocks, liability side) by the amount of shares in affiliates held as assets and "buried" in category 2512 (corporate claims, asset side). In order to estimate stock ownership by sector within the institutional investor category it is necessary to derive stock portion "control figures" for each type of institutional investor. The methodology used here to estimate the stock portion "control figures" for each sector within the institutional investor category is as follows: the ratio of category 3512, Total Corporate Claims, liability side to category 2512. Total Corporate Claims, asset side represents the non-stock proportion. The arithmetic inverse, expressed as a percentage, represents the stock portion "control figure." The stock portion control figures are: 60.1% (1962), 59.7% (1965), 60.1% (1970), 63.5% (1975) and 52.4% (1979). The stock portion "control figure" is related to all sub-categories of institutional investors in category 2512, corporate claims asset side. The stock portion "control figure" related to category 2512, corporate claims asset side, plus category 2520 stocks asset side, is thus the "pure" amount of stock held by each sector within the institutional investor category. Figures are rounded.

3 Near banks, in general, refer to trust companies.

4 In the national flow accounts the assets held in equities by the Quebec Pension Plan are owned and invested by the Caisse de Depôt and are classified under Sector 1X-2, Public Financial Institutions, rather than in Sector XII-2, Social Security Funds.

5 Non-residents holding registered stocks and bonds. Approximately 40 per cent of foreign sector holdings are direct investment by corporations, while an estimated 60 per cent is held as portfolio investment by undisclosed non-residents.

Sources: Derived and calculated from a special request computer print-out based on unpublished national flow accounts data provided by Statistics Canada to the author 5 September 1980. The author wishes to acknowledge his professional debt to Randall Geehan, formerly Chief, National Flows and Accounts Section, Statistics Canada for discussing various methodological considerations. Also Statistics Canada, *Financial Flow Accounts, Fourth Quarter, 1979* (Ottawa and Hull: Minister of Supply and Services, 1980), Tables 4–1 and 4–5, pp. 135–45.

A bi-modal typology emerges from the information presented in Table 7.2, where Britain and the U.S. may be viewed as the ideal type and Canada the anomalous case. In Britain and the U.S. there has been a marked long-run decline in corporate shares held by the personal sector and a corresponding increase in the institutional sector since the early 1960s. Individuals have been net sellers of corporate equity, while institutions have been the major net buyers. In Britain, institutional shareholdings in the past twenty years have increased from 30 to 58 per cent of all outstanding equity, while in the U.S. the proportion of corporate shares owned by institutions has increased from 24 to 35 per cent.

The case of Canada is unique for at least two reasons when it is compared with Britain and the U.S. In the first instance, unlike the U.K. and U.S., shareholdings by the personal sector have only marginally declined, from 46 to 44 per cent between 1962 and 1979. Second, in Canada an inordinately large proportion of corporate shares, nearly 20 per cent, are held through the foreign sector as a result of Canada's dependent "branch-plant" economy where major firms are wholly or partially owned subsidiaries of American transnational corporations. As a result, there is a "thin" capital market, which causes a distortion in the sectoral distribution of corporate share ownership. While institutional shareholdings in Canada are relatively less than in the U.K. and U.S., they are nevertheless substantial, having nearly tripled from 8 to 22 per cent of all outstanding equity between 1962 and 1979. During this period the institutional sector has been a net buyer of corporate shares, while the foreign sector, and to a lesser extent individuals, have been net sellers. By 1979 institutional holdings of corporate equity in Canada were of the same magnitude as those held through the foreign sector (Table 7.1). A further indication of the institutionalization of capital markets in Canada is the fact that 47 per cent of all corporate and government bonds are held by institutional investors, as opposed to only 21 per cent owned through the personal sector (Table 7.1).

Projections of corporate shareholdings by institutional investors, while of course tentative, nevertheless are of considerable interest in assessing their importance in the future. Briston and Dobbins projected that shares held by combined institutions in the U.K. would increase from 70 to 85 per cent of outstanding equity by the year 2000.[6] In the United States, Soldofsky and Drucker have estimated that total institutional shareholdings as a proportion of the market

TABLE 7.2

COMPARISON OF THE DISTRIBUTION OF INDIVIDUAL AND INSTITUTIONAL STOCK OWNERSHIP BY SECTOR, MARKET VALUE.[1]
U.K., U.S. AND CANADA, SELECTED YEARS, 1961–1981

SHAREHOLDINGS BY SECTOR	U.K.		U.S.		CANADA		PERCENTAGE POINT CHANGE		
	1963	1981	1961	1974	1962	1979	U.K.	U.S.	Canada
Personal Sector[2]	56.1%	30.4%	73.0%	60.9%	45.7%	44.4%	-25.7	-12.1	-1.3
Institutional Investors	30.4	57.9	23.8	35.1	7.9	21.8	+27.5	+11.3	+13.9
Pension Funds	6.4	26.7	4.5[6]	12.6[6]	1.5[4]	4.0[4]	+20.3	+8.1	+2.5
Life Insurance Cos	10.0	20.5	2.9[5]	5.5[5]	0.7	1.2	+10.5	+2.6	+0.5
Banks and Near Banks[3]	1.3	0.3	11.0	12.5	0.5[7]	9.1	-1.0	+1.5	+8.6
Other Private Financial Institutions	12.7	10.4	5.4	4.5	5.2	7.5	-2.3	-0.9	+2.3
Non-Financial Private Corps	5.1	5.1	n.a.	n.a.	10.5	11.4	0.0	n.a.	+0.9
Public Sector	1.5	3.0	n.a.	n.a.	0.3[8]	0.4[8]	+1.5	n.a.	+0.1
Foreign Sector	7.0	3.6	3.1	4.1	35.8	21.2	-3.4	+1.0	-14.6

Notes: 1 The U.K. and U.S. are at market value. For Canada equity holdings are at book value. The difference between market and book value of the equity holdings would not affect the internal distribution between sectors.

2 Including unincorporated businesses and non-profit foundations.

3 Near banks refer to trust companies in Canada and trust companies and savings and loans companies in the U.S., including their personal and common trust funds.

4 Trusteed (non-insured) pension plans.

5 Including property and liability insurance companies.

6 Private non-insured pension plans and state and local retirement funds.

7 Including monetary authorities and public financial institutions.

8 Including federal, provincial and local government, as well as non-financial government enterprises and social security funds.

Sources: For Britain. M. J. Erritt and J. C. D. Alexander, "Ownership of Company Shares: A New Survey," *CSO Economic Trends,* No. 287 (September 1977), Table 2, p. 100; Royal Commission on the Distribution of Income and Wealth, Report No. 2. *Income from Companies and Its Distribution,* Cmnd. 6172 (London: HMSO, July 1975), Table 9, p. 17, and The Stock Exchange, *Stock Exchange Survey of Share Ownership, 1983* (London: Stock Exchange, 1983), Table 2.16. For the U.S., Securities and Exchange Commission, *Statistical Bulletin 33* (August 1974), pp. 805–6, and *Statistical Bulletin 34* (May 1975), p. 439, and James Bohan, "A Sector Analysis of Supply and Demand for Equities — 1979," *Market Analysis Report* (New York: Merrill, Lynch, Pierce, Fenner and Smith Inc., November 8, 1979), p. 15. For Canada, Table 7.1.

value of all outstanding stock will increase to 55 and 66 per cent respectively over the same period.[7] Drucker's projections, however, have been challenged by some on methodological grounds as being too extreme.[8] For Canada, extrapolating on the basis of past growth trends would suggest that combined institutional corporate shareholdings will increase from 22 per cent to an estimated 42 per cent by the end of the century.

The past two decades have witnessed a basic transformation in the configuration of capital markets and the locus of corporate securities in the advanced capitalist economies of Britain, the U.S. and Canada as the institutional investor has become a force. The distribution of corporate shareholdings and investment decision-making between and within the personal and institutional sectors and the growing importance of private pension funds are now considered.

Personal Sector. Ownership of corporate equity within the personal sector is limited to and concentrated among a small faction or elite of individuals and families within the ruling class. This issue is of considerable importance since it is this group of shareowners which owns and controls the dominant financial institutions responsible for the operation of the private pension system. "In terms of power over the economy," as Johnson has argued, "the extreme concentration of share ownership in the top 1 per cent of income earners allows almost total control . . . because a high degree of concentration . . . permits easy organization of those shares for [corporate] decision-making purposes."[9] In the U.S. 20 per cent of the adult population owned corporate shares in 1984, compared with 13.4 per cent in Canada as of 1986 and an estimated 3.9 per cent in Britain in 1981.[10] Ownership of equity is highly concentrated, as is receipt of dividend income, among the upper socioeconomic group. In Britain the top 1 per cent of the population owned 54 per cent of all equity, while the top 10 per cent held 90 per cent of all outstanding corporate shares in the late 1970s.[11] Studies of stock ownership in the United States indicate that the top 1 and 10 per cent of families and unattached individuals in 1971 accounted for 51 and 75 per cent respectively of the value of all stockholdings.[12] A similar pattern emerges in Canada where the top 1 per cent of income earnings owned 42 per cent of all shares and the top 10 per cent accounted for 72 per cent of all stock ownership in 1968.[13] According to the 1986 Toronto Stock Exchange survey, the likelihood of share ownership increases with the level of household income. Only 8 per cent of households with an income between

$15,000 and $25,000 were shareholders compared with 27 per cent of households with an income of $50,000 or more. Stock and bond ownership in Canada remained constant between 1954 and 1976 as is reported in Table 7.3. Stock ownership, based on a Toronto Stock Exchange (TSE) survey, however, declined from 8.6 to 7 per cent of the adult population between 1976 and 1983 and then sharply increased during the booming equity market prior to the October 1987 "meltdown" and market shake-out.

TABLE 7.3

DISTRIBUTION OF STOCK AND BOND OWNERSHIP
BY VALUE OF HOLDING, CANADA, 1954 AND 1976

| | PERCENTAGE OF FAMILIES AND INDIVIDUALS OWNING | | | |
| | Stock | | Bonds[1] | |
VALUE OF HOLDING	1954	1976	1954	1976
No Holdings	91.1	91.5	72.8	74.5
Total With Holdings	8.8	8.6	27.2	25.5
Less than $1,000	4.1	3.1	16.3	9.1
$1,000 – $4,999	2.6	2.8	7.4	9.3
$5,000 – $9,999	0.9	1.0	1.8	2.9
$10,000 +	1.2	1.7	1.7	4.2

Note: 1 Including corporate and government issues.

Sources: Retabulated and calculated from the Dominion Bureau of Statistics,
*Incomes, Liquid Assets and Indebtedness of Non-Farm Families in
Canada, 1955* (Ottawa: Queen's Printer, 1958), Table 23, p. 41, and Table
26, p. 42, and Statistics Canada, *Income, Assets and Indebtedness of
Families in Canada 1977* (Ottawa: Minister of Supply Services, 1980),
Table 10, p. 46 and special request for update by author 28 September
1981. These are the most recent issues of these publications available.

The diffusion of corporate share ownership reinforces the power of those individuals and families with large shareholdings. The New York Stock Exchange (NYSE) reported that approximately two-thirds of all shareholdings consisted of less than one hundred shares and that the median holding was much lower.[14] A similar situation can be inferred from Canadian data, reported in Table 7.3 for 1976, which indicate that 36 per cent of all shareholders (3 per cent of the population) owned less than $1,000 in stock compared with 19 per cent of all shareholders (1.7 per cent of the population) who held $10,000 or more. A case in point is Bell Canada, the fourth largest corporation in the country, where 53 per cent of stockholders own one hundred or fewer shares, while 10 per cent of investors hold one thousand or more.[15] Among that minority of the population owning corporate stock, there are many small shareholders and a few large ones. Ownership of corporate equity, however, increasingly resides within the institutional sector and among pension funds.

Institutional Sector. The ascendency of financial intermediaries and institutional investors was discernible as early as 1900. This growth has accelerated and become more pronounced since the end of World War II. In Britain, according to Prais, total institutional holdings of all government and corporate securities (bonds and equity) increased from 74 to 80 per cent between 1957 and 1972.[16] Similarly in Canada, total holdings of all outstanding securities by institutional investors increased from 50 to 68 per cent between 1962 and 1979 (Table 7.1).

By way of comparison, while private institutional investors (broadly defined) in Canada accounted for nearly 22 per cent of all equity ownership in 1979, government (including public financial institutions, public enterprises and social security funds) held less than 1 per cent of all shares. Private financial intermediaries held roughly 47 per cent of all bond issues, whereas government held only 26 per cent (Table 7.1). Given present arrangements the private institutional investor clearly dominates capital markets.

Private pension funds have increasingly become the major actors within the institutional sector, having in general experienced the greatest growth in assets of any major financial institution in the postwar period. Pension funds in Canada, for example, now rank as the largest non-bank financial intermediary in terms of assets. In Britain and the United States, private pension funds are the largest institutional holder of corporate equity, while in Canada they have usually ranked second behind "other private financial institutions" (Table 7.1). Trusteed pension funds in Canada hold the largest portfolio of government and corporate bonds (Table 7.1). Between 1961 and 1977 trusteed and insured pension plans in Canada, for example, accounted for 45 per cent of the total increase in corporate stocks held by financial institutions and for 30 per cent of the increase in bonds.[17]

Private pension funds are now in general the largest purchaser of corporate equity as is indicated in Table 7.4. The acquisition of equity by private pension funds is three to four times greater than for all other institutional investors in Britain and the U.S., while approximating the average for combined institutions in Canada.

TABLE 7.4

COMPARISON OF GROWTH RATE IN THE ACQUISITION OF CORPORATE EQUITY
BY INDIVIDUALS, INSTITUTIONAL INVESTORS AND PENSION FUNDS,
U.K., U.S. AND CANADA, SELECTED YEARS, 1961–1981

| | PERCENTAGE CHANGE | | |
CATEGORY	U.K.	U.S.	Canada
Personal Sector	−45.8	−16.6	−2.9
All Institutional Investors	+90.5	+47.5	+ 175.9
Pension Funds	+ 317.2	+ 180.0	+ 166.7

Source: Calculated from Table 7.2.

The institutionalization of capital markets is signified by such indicators as large block trading and common stock activity rates. Large block trading activity, an indicator of institutional involvement in the equities market, has been increasing for nearly twenty years. In the United States, for example, it has increased from 3.1 per cent of total New York Stock Exchange volume in 1965 to over 50 per cent in 1985 (Table 7.5). This activity means that over half of the total trading on the world's largest stock exchange is now attributable to institutional investors such as pension funds. According to the Toronto Stock Exchange, the volume of public trading which originates solely from pension funds is conservatively estimated to be in the order of 12 to 15 per cent.[18] The increasing volume of large block trading activity originating with institutional investors is also reflected by the increasing average size of equity transactions. According to the London Stock Exchange, the average size of transactions has increased from £1.1 million in 1966 to £4.0 million in 1976.[19] On the NYSE the average number of daily large block transactions increased to nearly 2,500 in 1985.[20]

Common stock activity rates similarly indicate the dominance of institutional investors and pension funds in capital markets. Activity rates measure portfolio turnover, that is, equity purchases plus sales as a percentage of market value expressed as an annual rate. Contrary to the view that "private pension funds have not dominated the stock markets" because "they have traded their stocks

TABLE 7.5

LARGE BLOCK TRADING ON THE NEW YORK STOCK EXCHANGE, 1965–1985

YEAR	LARGE BLOCK TRADING[1] (IN 000 SHARES)	PERCENTAGE OF TOTAL NYSE VOLUME
1965	48,262	3.1
1970	450,908	15.4
1975	778,540	16.6
1980	3,311,132	29.2
1985	14,222,272	51.7

Note: 1 A large block is defined as one consisting of 10,000 or more shares.

Sources: Richard J. Briston and Richard Dobbins, *The Growth and Impact of Institutional Investors*. A Report to the Research Committee of the Institute of Chartered Accountants in England and Wales (London, 1978), Exhibit 72, p. 207; 1980 and 1985 figures from the New York Stock Exchange.

relatively infrequently,"[21] a low activity rate in fact reflects the dominance, stability and long-term investment objectives associated with private pension funds. Institutional holdings of common stocks have a stabilizing effect because "they have long-term investment objectives and are not subject to panic selling in the face of market decline and [are] not harried by short-term fluctuations."[22] In general, there would appear to be an inverse relationship between the investment time horizon and the portfolio activity ratio.

The experience in the United States, for example, indicates that in virtually every year between 1966 and 1974 the activity rate of private pension funds was below that of other institutional investors and the market. Over this time period the activity ratio of private pension funds was on average 30 per cent below the market average.[23] In the U.K., on the other hand, between 1967 and 1975 pension fund portfolio turnover was generally equal to or marginally greater than the market average, but normally below that of other institutions.[24] This situation can be explained by two considerations. First, the abnormally high activity rate among Local Authority (municipal) pension funds, which are notorious for "churning," that is, unnecessary portfolio trading to stimulate brokerage commissions,[25] upwardly biases the average pension activity ratio. Second, beginning in 1975, financial intermediaries including pension funds began a major restructuring of their portfolios, reflecting the deteriorating economic climate, and shifted from long- to short-term investment objectives.[26]

These data generally support the view that under advanced capitalism there has been an institutionalization of capital markets with a corresponding concentration and centralization of corporate shareholdings between and among a small group of individual shareholders and large institutional investors. As a result of the dramatic growth of pension fund assets in the postwar period, their investment behaviour in securities markets is of considerable importance to capitalist economies.

THE INSTITUTIONALIZATION OF INVESTMENT:
PENSION FUNDS AND CAPITAL MARKETS

The institutionalization of investment under advanced capitalism is a concomitant of the domination of capital markets by institutional investors. Pension savings, as previously demonstrated, now represent a major source of investment for the economy (Chapter 6). These savings are accumulated by and channelled through the occupational and state pension systems into investment through securities markets. The impact of pension funds on capital markets therefore has serious and far-ranging implications for the pattern of investment, corporate and public finance, and the nexus of ownership and control within the corporate sector. Increasingly, the corporate sector has been appropriating the occupational pension system as a source of investment capital to satisfy its finance requirements. Similarly, government has increasingly used the state pension system as a source of social capital and general revenue. These considerations are now explored.

Pension Saving and the Pattern of Investment. Table 7.6 outlines the various components of the retirement income system and the distribution of pension savings into various types of investment instruments. The private pension system in Canada represented 81 per cent of total accumulated pension savings, compared to 19 per cent flowing through the public (state) pension system. Of the $137 billion in total accumulated pension savings (assets) in 1981, 62 per cent ($85 billion) was invested through capital markets and the remaining 38 per cent ($52 billion) was channelled into non-marketable government securities. The private pension system includes both private and public sector plans. Private sector occupational pension funds are invested in marketable assets, that is, assets that can be bought and sold in the securities market: stocks, bonds, mortgages, real estate and short-term money instruments. While some public sector occupational pension funds are similarly invested, there are many public employee funds which are wholly or partially invested in non-marketable government securities, that is, assets which were not purchased in financial markets and which were issued to essentially captive public employee pension funds. For example, the assets of the Canada Pension Plan (CPP) are wholly invested in non-marketable provincial and federal securities, at or marginally below market interest rates. In contrast, the assets of the Quebec Pension Plan (QPP) are all invested in marketable securities.

The pattern of investment identified in Table 7.6 has resulted in 60 per cent of the accumulated pension savings of the retirement income system being generated by the public sector (state and public employee plans), while 53 per cent of the assets (marketable and non-marketable government bonds) were used to finance this sector. Conversely, this means that 40 per cent of total pension savings were generated through the private sector, while 47 per cent of the retirement income system's assets were used to finance the private sector.

Long- vs. Short-Term Investment. The retirement income system — state and occupational pension plans — in advanced capitalist economies is an important source of funds to meet the long-term investment requirements of the economy and of the corporate and public sectors. Private pension funds generally adopt a long-term investment horizon in structuring their portfolio asset mix because pension plan commitments (liabilities) tend to be very long-term, with the average employee being perhaps twenty to thirty years away from retirement. Liquidity requirements are virtually non-existent because new contribution inflow is typically many times greater than benefits paid out. Pension funds as financial intermediaries and institutional investors, therefore, are the perfect vehicle to accumulate and invest savings over the long term.

In the United States 63 per cent of all funds raised in the economy between 1960 and 1980 were for long-term investment in physical plant and equipment as well as for mergers and acquisitions. In this same period, occupational pension funds provided over 11 per cent of the net funds supplied in the economy. Private pension funds thus supplied nearly 18 per cent of all long-term investment capital. By 1981 pension funds were the second largest non-banking source of funds in the American economy.[27] Similarly in Canada, between 1970 and 1981, 64 per cent of all non-financial corporation investment was long term, a significant proportion of which was supplied through the private pension system.[28]

TABLE 7.6

PENSION SAVINGS MATRIX. SOURCES AND DISTRIBUTION OF ACCUMULATED RETIREMENT INCOME SAVINGS, $BILLION. CANADA, YEAR-END 1981

| SOURCE OF SAVINGS | TOTAL ACCUMULATED SAVINGS | | CORPORATE | | | | GOVERNMENT BONDS | | | | MORTGAGES AND REAL ESTATE | | OTHER[3] | |
| | | | Stocks | | Bonds | | Marketable | | Non-Marketable | | | | | |
	$	%	$	%	$	%	$	%	$	%	$	%	$	%
1 Public Pension System[1]														
CPP	20	14.6	—	—	—	—	—	—	20	100.0	—	—	—	—
QPP	6	4.4	1	16.7	—	—	5	83.3	—	—	—	—	—	—
Sub-total	26	19.0	1	16.7	—	—	5	19.2	20	76.9	—	—	—	—
2 Private Pension System														
Occupational Pensions	86	62.8	16	18.6	5	5.8	15	17.4	32	37.2	8	9.3	10	11.6
Private Sector[2]	30	21.9	11	36.7	3	10.1	6	20.0	—	—	4	0.1	5	16.7
Public Sector[2]	56	40.9	5	8.9	2	7.7	9	16.1	32	57.1	4	0.1	5	8.9
RRSPs	25	18.3	1	4.0	—	—	1	4.0	—	—	2	0.1	21	84.0
Sub-total	111	81.0	17	15.3	5	4.5	16	14.4	32	28.8	10	9.0	31	27.9
Grand Total	137	100.0	18	13.1	5	3.7	21	15.3	52	37.9	10	7.3	31	22.6

Notes: 1 Excluding the general revenue financed Old Age Security (OAS) pension and the income-tested Guaranteed Income Supplement (GIS).

2 Including trusteed and consolidated revenue (pay-as-you-go) public employee pension plans.

3 Including cash, deposits and money market instruments.

Source: Retabulated and calculated from the Business Committee on Pension Policy, *Capital Markets Study*. Prepared by Pension Finance Associates Ltd. (Toronto: BCPP, September 1983). Table 2.3, p. 13.

The situation in the U.K. stands in contrast to that in the United States and Canada. There, the investment policies of pension funds have affected not only the level, but also the type of capital investment. Pension funds have reinforced the failure of banks and other financial institutions to provide long-term finance.[29] According to one study,

> the financial intermediaries that are responsible for channelling available funds into companies have not been prepared to invest long term in British industry. This has meant that British industry has needed to invest for short-term profits. It has also meant that the cost of capital in the U.K. is higher than . . . in other countries.[30]

As a result, British industry has increasingly been forced to rely on short-term financing. According to the Grylls Report, short-term bank loans accounted for almost half of total corporate financing in the U.K., compared with less than a fifth in Germany and Japan between 1970 and 1978.[31]

Pension funds have followed this general pattern and have increasingly invested short term. The Wilson Committee found that pension funds held shares for twenty-four years on average between 1963 and 1967 and for only six years in the period between 1973 and 1977.[32] A report of the National Association of Pension Funds indicated that pension fund managers now consider a "long-term" investment to be of two to five years' duration.[33] This short-term investment pattern and increased portfolio activity by pension funds, coupled with other economic factors, has further depressed the level of capital investment in Britain.

Pension Fund Investment and Portfolio Composition. Pension funds are invested to maximize the rate of return on investment, subject to an acceptable level of risk. Because employer-based occupational pension plans are deemed in law to be trusts, they are required to act in a "prudent" manner to fulfil their fiduciary responsibility to plan members. Pension contributions plus investment income are used to pay retirement benefits in the case of a defined benefit plan, with the plan sponsor accepting the responsibility for an investment shortfall, or, in the case of a money purchase plan, to purchase an annuity at the employee's retirement.

The increasing flow of pension saving cycled through the private pension system into capital markets takes the form of investment in

various types of assets held by pension funds. The portfolio composition, or asset mix ratio, of a pension fund depends upon a number
of considerations. Those factors include the level of acceptable risk
to maximize the rate of return on investment, portfolio diversification to spread risk-taking, the general economic climate, the business and equity cycles, the real rate of return on and spread between
different asset classes, the external financing requirements of the
corporate sector, government policy affecting the supply of equities
and bonds, general investment strategy, market timing for the
acquisition and sale of securities, institutional fundamentals as
they affect specific securities, statutory regulations concerning
"quality" and "quantity" tests in respect of portfolio composition
and the liquidity requirements of the pension fund to pay benefits.
How is pension saving channelled through the private pension system invested?

Table 7.7 reports the portfolio composition of trusteed pension
plans in Canada, by sector, between 1960 and 1986. A transnational
comparison of occupational pension plan asset mix is outlined in
Table 7.8. A number of trends can be briefly identified.

First, depending upon the business and equity cycles, there has
been a long-term trend for pension funds, particularly those in the
private sector, to invest in corporate stock. In the United States, for
example, from 1960 to the peak of the market in the early 1970s,
total equity holdings of all private and public pension funds (non-
insured and insured) increased from nearly 20 to 40 per cent of
portfolio composition. Similarly in Canada, equity holdings of all
trusteed pension plans (public and private) increased from 7 to over
25 per cent of assets between 1960 and the early 1970s. The collapse of the equity market in North America in the early 1970s was
compounded by stagflation over the next decade and pension funds
divested themselves of common stock and accordingly restructured
their portfolios in response to the economic climate. Between 1975
and 1982, pension fund shareholdings in Canada declined and did
not begin to approach their previous peak until the heady equity
market of the mid-1980s. Since the stock market "melt down" in
late 1987, however, pension funds have probably again reduced
their equity exposure.

Second, private sector pension plans have held more common
stock than have public sector pension plans; that is, they have a
lower debt to equity ratio. For example, U.S. private non-insured
pension funds in the early 1970s held nearly 75 per cent of their

TABLE 7.7

PERCENTAGE DISTRIBUTION OF TRUSTEED PENSION PLAN ASSETS, CANADA. BOOK VALUE, BY SECTOR, 1960–1986

YEAR	BONDS[1]			STOCK[2]			MORTGAGES			OTHER[3]		
	Private	Public	Both	Private	Public	Both	Private	Public	Both	Private	Public	Both
1960	72.7	83.4	77.0	11.1	1.3	7.2	7.8	9.2	8.3	8.4	6.1	7.5
1965	55.4	77.6	64.1	20.8	6.2	15.1	9.1	10.0	9.5	14.6	6.1	11.4
1970	39.4	68.2	52.5	33.9	12.0	24.3	8.2	10.6	9.2	18.5	9.2	14.3
1971	38.7	66.7	51.2	35.9	13.3	25.8	8.4	10.5	9.4	17.0	9.5	13.6
1972	36.1	66.1	49.7	38.3	15.2	27.8	8.5	10.1	9.2	17.1	8.7	13.3
1973	33.1	64.6	47.6	37.5	15.5	27.4	9.4	9.9	9.6	20.1	10.0	15.4
1974	31.7	63.6	46.7	35.6	15.4	26.1	10.5	10.7	10.6	22.2	10.3	16.6
1975	33.0	64.3	47.8	34.4	14.6	25.0	12.5	10.7	11.6	20.1	10.4	15.6
1976	31.8	63.2	46.9	33.7	14.9	24.6	14.7	11.8	13.3	19.8	10.1	15.2
1977	32.7	63.9	48.0	29.3	13.7	21.5	15.4	11.5	13.5	22.6	10.9	17.0
1978	32.4	64.6	48.4	25.9	12.0	18.9	15.6	11.5	13.5	26.1	12.1	19.1
1979	34.4	63.4	49.0	24.5	12.6	18.5	13.9	11.0	12.5	27.2	13.0	20.0
1980	35.4	62.6	49.1	25.6	15.3	20.4	12.2	10.1	11.2	26.8	12.0	19.3
1981	33.8	58.8	46.5	27.5	16.2	21.8	11.1	9.1	10.1	27.6	15.9	21.6
1982	34.3	57.7	46.3	28.2	16.4	22.1	9.8	8.2	9.0	27.7	17.9	22.7
1983	34.5	57.7	46.0	32.9	18.2	25.6	8.2	7.5	7.8	24.5	16.6	20.6
1984	34.4	56.4	45.4	33.0	19.2	26.1	6.5	6.9	6.7	26.1	17.5	21.8
1985	36.4	56.9	46.8	34.1	19.4	26.6	5.2	6.3	5.8	24.3	17.4	20.8
1986	37.9	56.2	47.3	33.4	21.1	27.2	4.5	5.9	5.2	23.9	16.8	20.4

Notes:　1　Government and corporate bonds.
　　　　2　Common and preferred shares.
　　　　3　Including real estate, cash, deposits, money instruments, and pooled funds.

Source:　Calculated from Statistics Canada, *Trusteed Pension Plans Financial Statistics 1980* (Ottawa: Minister of Supply and Services Canada, 1982). Text Table VI, p. 19. Updated from Statistics Canada, *Trusteed Pension Funds Financial Statistics 1986* (Ottawa: Minister of Supply and Services Canada, 1988), Text Table I, p. 28.

TABLE 7.8

COMPARISON OF PERCENTAGE DISTRIBUTION OF ALL
TRUSTEED AND NON-INSURED PENSION PLAN ASSETS,
CANADA, U.S. AND U.K., 1980–1981

COUNTRY	BONDS[1]	STOCK[2]	REAL ESTATE AND MORTGAGES	OTHER[3]
Canada	49.1	20.4	12.3	18.2
U.S.	31.0	61.3	n.a.[4]	7.7
U.K.	23.7	51.7	8.6	16.0

Notes: 1 Corporate and government bonds.
2 Common and preferred shares.
3 Miscellaneous including mutual funds, foreign securities, cash and short-term paper.
4 Included in the category of Other.

Sources: Calculated from Christopher Johnson, "Pensions—A Growth Industry,"
Lloyds Bank Economic Bulletin 19 (July 1980), Chart B, p. 3. Statistics
Canada, Trusteed Pension Plans Financial Statistics 1980 (Ottawa:
Minister of Supply and Services Canada, 1982), Text Table VI, p. 19, and
the Statistical Abstract of the United States, 1982–83 (Washington, D.C.:
GPO, 1982), Series 537, p. 330.

assets in equity, compared with public sector funds which held only 9 per cent of their funds in common stock. While this has fluctuated over time in response to economic conditions, in 1986 private non-insured funds held 53 per cent of their assets in common stock compared with 17 per cent in public pension funds. In Canada, over the long term, private sector pension plans have on average held twice as much equity as have public sector plans (Table 7.7). In the early 1970s, for example, private sector pension plans in Canada held 60 per cent of their assets in equity, compared with 15 per cent by public sector plans. At the peak of the strong stock market in 1987, major private pension funds held 43 per cent of their assets in common shares, compared with 28 per cent by public sector funds.[34] In recent years public sector pension plans have fundamentally altered their investment strategy, however, and they are now investing heavily in equity shares in order to restructure their portfolios to maximize their investment results. Third, in response to the inflationary environment of the mid-1970s, pension funds began to invest more heavily in speculative asset classes such as real estate, mortgages and money market instruments (and works of art in the U.K.) in an attempt to secure a positive rate of return.

A fourth, and increasingly important consideration, particularly in Britain, is the proportion of pension fund investment in foreign securities, resulting in the exportation of investment capital. In Britain in the period prior to the abolition of exchange controls in 1979, pension funds invested 8 per cent of their new cash flow overseas; after abolition, this increased to nearly 25 per cent in 1981.[35] The proportion of U.K. pension fund assets invested overseas increased from 5 to 13 per cent between 1978 and 1981. While this flight of capital has seemingly abated, it effectively undermined the long-term financing of domestic U.K. industry. Similarly, in the United States, there has been an internationalization of pension fund investment to maximize performance at a time when domestic industry needs revitalization. In Canada, nearly 6 per cent of pension assets in 1986 were invested in foreign securities. Federal government guidelines formerly set a 10 per cent limit on the amount which could be invested overseas. As a result of pressure from the private pension industry, however, this restriction was eliminated in the Conservative government's 1985 Budget.

Pension funds are an important link in capital markets between the supply of funds and the demand for investment by the corporate sector and social capital by the public sector. The asset holdings of the private pension system—that is, securities such as stocks and bonds—are a source of funds or cash flow for corporate and public sector finance requirements. The full impact of pension funds on capital markets must therefore be analysed and assessed in terms of their relationship to corporate and public sector finance.

PENSION FUNDS AND THE CORPORATE SECTOR

The impact of the private pension system on capital markets as it relates to the corporate sector has two important dimensions: corporate finance and the ownership of corporate securities. One major study suggested that "the ownership of industrial shares is undergoing a substantial transformation, and one must expect . . . consequences for financing, management and concentration."[36] The private pension system's investment function has facilitated this transformation.

The modern corporation under advanced capitalism satisfies its investment, or finance, requirements through two mechanisms: first, through internal funding or financing, that is, undistributed corporate profits (retained earnings) plus capital consumption (depreciation) allowances; and, second, through external financing, that is, the sale of corporate securities through capital markets in the form of debt and equity issues.

Sources of external funds may be divided into two broad categories: equity and debt. Debt-financing is classified into short- and long-term debt instruments such as short-term paper and (bank) loans in the case of the former, and bonds and debentures in the latter. Bonds represent a long-term debt obligation by which the corporate borrower promises to pay a set rate of interest until the bond matures, at which time the principal must be repaid. Corporate bonds, as a debt instrument, do not confer ownership or voting rights on the holder, but they are a preferred liability or lien against property, plant or equipment of the borrower.

The second form of external funding is equity financing. Equity may be raised in two ways: sale of stock (common and preferred shares) and retention of earnings. In order to raise capital, new equity shares, or "rights" issues, are offered for sale by corporations in what is termed the "primary" market. Already outstanding, or "ordinary," shares are recycled, that is, bought and sold in the "secondary" market, but they do not augment the cash flow or capital requirements of the enterprise since these shares were previously issued. Common stock or equity shares represent the residual ownership of an incorporated enterprise and confer ownership and voting rights upon the shareholder in addition to a proportion of distributed profits in the form of dividends. Equity financing, or share capital, is by definition long-term financing. With corporations reluctant to or constrained from undertaking unlimited borrowing through debt instruments such as bonds, equity financing often becomes necessary to satisfy financial requirements. The level of internal financing by corporations is an alternative to distributing profits and subsequently raising funds by means of equity issues.

The significance and implications of internal financing for corporate behaviour under advanced capitalism have been the subject of considerable controversy, particularly among Marxist scholars,[37] since it affects the "independence" or "autonomy" of the corporate sector in relation to the finance sector and the relative strength and dominance of industrial or financial capital. Some have argued that in the post-World War II period the corporation, and the nature of corporate financing in particular, has undergone a fundamental qualitative transformation. The extraordinary level of internal funding (retained earnings and depreciation allowances) has purportedly severed or reduced corporations' dependence upon the finance sector as a source of external funding and has reduced their need to raise capital through the securities market. In short, according to this theory, modern corporations are now relatively "independent" because a significant portion of their capital and growth comes through self-financing. This in turn signals a new phase in capitalist development. Or does it?

In the flush of post-World War II economic expansion and prosperity, in the twenty-year period from roughly 1950 to 1970, corporations in many advanced capitalist economies experienced an exceptionally high level of internal or self-financing.[38] In the United States, according to Menshikov, internally generated financing averaged 62 per cent between 1956 and 1960 and 51 per cent in the 1961 to 1965 period. Between 1964 and 1968 internal funding by corporations, as determined by Fitch and Oppenheimer, declined from 70 to 57 per cent. For Britain, the rate of internal funding has averaged about 70 per cent. While the rate fell in the 1960s, it subsequently rebounded. Thompson's comparative study indicates that in economies with a high level of internal funding, a higher proportion of external funds come from equity and bonds than from bank loans. Prior to 1970 this was the case for both Britain and the U.S.; since that time, however, the situation in the U.K. has dramatically changed. In countries such as Japan and France, where the rate of internal funding is only 40 to 50 per cent, there is a greater reliance on bank loans for external funds.

In the period between 1950 and 1970, the level of internal corporate funding has varied over time and between countries, which in itself mitigates against constructing a "universal" theory of corporate finance under conditions of monopoly capitalism. The evidence based on this short historical time period suggests that the availability of internally generated funds has been clearly related to the profitability of corporations and the scale of investment on the upside of the postwar business cycle. On the downside, however, when corporations experience cash flow problems, as has been the case since the early 1970s in Canada, Britain and the U.S., corporations are forced to borrow from capital markets, with a corresponding increase in the level of external financing. The level of internal funding, and the corresponding reliance on external financing, is in general related to and a function of the business cycle, corporate liquidity and interest rates. This relationship becomes strikingly apparent in the period after 1970, when on the downside of the business cycle corporations in the United States and Canada experienced an increased reliance upon external sources of funds. Britain, however, is an atypical case as shall be elaborated upon.

Relating the level of internal and external corporate financing to the business cycle indicates that corporations have neither escaped from nor become "independent" of the inherent cyclical nature of capitalism, but rather they are bounded by it. On the downside of the business cycle, therefore, it may be expected that corporations will increasingly rely on external sources of financing, depending on interest rates and the strength of the securities market. Within this context, the growth of the private pension system's cash flow and asset base has served the dual function of generating significant investment at the macro-economic level and has become a source of external financing for corporations.

Table 7.9 outlines on a transnational basis the sources of corporate funds and the change in financial position over the past twenty years. In the United States internal funding has declined from 73 per cent in 1960 to 59 per cent in 1980. Total external financing by corporations has correspondingly increased from 27 to 41 per cent. The increased reliance on external sources of financing by corporations is similarly evidenced in Canada. Between 1963 and 1982 internal funding declined from 56 to 44 per cent, while external financing increased from 44 to 56 per cent.

The capital structure and cash flow position of corporations in North America on the downside of the business cycle since the 1970s is nearly the opposite of that experienced during the expansionary period between 1950 and 1970. Three general trends are noteworthy: first, the generally low proportion of new financing that comes from the sale of equities (3 to 12 per cent), compounded by the economic climate and the collapse of the equity market in the early 1970s; second, the concomitant reliance on long-term debt (10 to 16 per cent), with an associated increase in the debt to equity ratio; and third, the growth and use of short-term debt, particularly bank loans, to offset the rise in interest rates in the bond market. These data seriously challenge the contention that the modern capitalist corporation is "independent" of external sources of funds.

Britain is in the anomalous position of having experienced an accelerated rate of internal funding between 1970 and 1976, which was well above that recorded during the 1950 to 1970 period. Two trends are of particular note. First, the principal source of funds for corporations was undistributed income. However, undistributed income was increasingly used to finance the maintenance of exist-

TABLE 7.9

COMPARISON OF THE SOURCES OF CORPORATE FUNDS.[1]

PERCENTAGE DISTRIBUTION.

CANADA, U.S. AND U.K., SELECTED YEARS

SOURCES OF FUNDS	CANADA[2]			U.S.[2]			U.K.[3]		
	1963–67	1978–82	Average, 1963–1982	1960	1980	Average, 1960–1981	1970	1976	Average, 1970–1976
Internal	56.3	44.4	53.4	72.7	58.6	58.9	66.0	82.4	77.1
External									
Other Liabilities	10.5	15.1	12.4	2.5	9.9	11.1	5.7	2.8	4.3
Debt									
Short-Term[4]	7.4	17.6	11.9	9.5	11.8	11.2	26.3	7.7	13.2
Long-Term[5]	13.8	7.3	10.8	12.5	15.9	16.5	0.0	0.0	1.3
Total Debt	21.2	24.9	22.6	22.0	27.7	27.7	26.3	7.7	14.5
Equity Issues	11.9	15.6	11.6	2.9	3.8	2.4	1.9	7.0	4.1
Total External	43.7	55.6	46.6	27.3	41.4	41.2	33.9	17.6	22.9
Total Sources[6]	100.00	100.00	100.00	100.00	100.00	100.01	100.00	100.00	100.00

Notes: 1 Based on national flow accounts.
2 Non-financial corporations, excluding unincorporated businesses, in Canada. For the U.S., non-farm non-financial corporate businesses.
3 Industrial and commercial companies.
4 Bank loans, commercial paper, acceptances, finance company and government loans.
5 Bonds and mortgages.
6 Figures may not total due to rounding.

Sources: Calculated from Appendix F 1–3.

ing assets through depreciation provisions rather than retained earnings. In turn, real investment was reduced, as is evidenced by the virtual lack of long-term borrowing to finance new investment. The inability of corporations to raise equity and debt capital because of high interest rates generated severe liquidity problems. Second, in response to this situation, corporations borrowed short-term. Between 1970 and 1976, 93 and 45 per cent of total debt and external financing respectively were short term. The high level of internal funding experienced over this period is explained by corporations increasingly financing their operations out of internal reserves as a result of their inability to raise long-term capital in securities markets.

In the case of the U.S. and Canada, there was increased reliance upon external financing by corporations in response to the downturn in the economy during the 1970s. It is in the raising of external debt and equity financing for the corporate sector that the securities market performs one of its principal functions. And it is the private pension system which is now a major source of funds to the capital market and the corporate sector. Pension fund purchases of corporate debt instruments and equity offerings have become a source of external financing for firms.

External Funds: Debt and Equity Financing. Long-term debt instruments or financing on average accounted for 23 per cent of total external financing and 11 per cent of total sources of funds for Canadian non-financial corporations in the period between 1963 and 1982 (Table 7.9). During the past twenty-five years the private pension system has held 15 per cent of its total assets on average in corporate bonds, while 25 to 50 per cent of pension fund assets were invested in government bonds. Equity financing between 1963 and 1982 raised through the securities market by non-financial corporations in Canada accounted for 25 per cent of external financing and 12 per cent of total corporate cash flow (Table 7.9). Pension funds in general have therefore supplied a significant proportion of the total external financing requirements (stocks and bonds) of corporations in the postwar period. As one study concluded, "pension funds are now so important as a source of funds that any marked diminution . . . would have very serious consequences for the future financing patterns and growth . . . of Canadian industry."[39]

In this regard, however, it is necessary to differentiate between pension fund acquisitions of corporate equity and bonds in primary and secondary markets. Acquisition of newly issued corporate equities, that is, "rights" shares in the primary market, by pension funds are a source of external financing or new investment for corporations, as are new corporate bonds. However, the trading and purchase of already existing outstanding corporate securities by pension funds, that is, acquisitions in the secondary market, do not directly increase corporate cash flow or capital formation since they were previously issued.

Whether pension funds purchase equity or bonds in the primary or secondary market is therefore a matter of considerable importance with respect to determining the extent to which the private pension system is a source of external funds for the corporate sector. Incomplete statistical information and the inability to differentiate methodologically between primary and secondary market acquisitions of corporate securities by pension funds, however, render such an evaluation difficult. Therefore, indirect proxies must be used in such a determination.

In Britain the evidence suggests that occupational pension funds have played a limited role in supplying financing for corporations through the primary equity market. Minns, for example, concluded that "institutional shareholders . . . have not been the leading source of new capital for industrial investment."[40] Technical work by Briston, Tomkins and King generally confirms that "institutional shareholders have not figured prominently in new issues of shares to the public,"[41] which they explain in terms of the risk-aversive behaviour of institutional investors. Their empirical evidence for the period between 1957 and 1969 indicates, however, that pension funds did in fact increase their holdings of primary market equity issues, though they were well below the average for combined institutions.[42] According to the National Association of Pension Funds, however, of the £2,317 million raised by "rights" issues between 1974 and 1977, "pension funds in general [played] a major role in underwriting these issues."[43] Stock Exchange data indicates that between 1970 and 1976 new issues on average accounted for 20 per cent of the addition to real fixed assets, 16 per cent by way of equity and 4 per cent by means of loan capital.[44] But the proportion of new equity capital purchased by pension funds is indeterminate.

In the case of Britain, the limited role played by pension funds in supplying funds to corporations through the primary equity market was clearly related to the capital structure of firms with their high level of internal funding and low level of equity financing (Table 7.9). New share issues represented only 1 per cent of the market value of all U.K. quoted equities between 1966 and 1976.[45] Pension funds could not purchase what was not offered, which has effectively restricted U.K. pension funds to trading in the secondary market and has limited their role in supplying new equity financing to the corporate sector.

The case of Canada, where more complete information is available, is of some interest with respect to illustrating the impact of pension fund acquisitions on corporate sector equity financing. On the upside of the business cycle, between 1962 and 1974, Grant's research indicates that total trusteed pension plan purchases, that is, primary *and* secondary market acquisitions, amounted to 175 per cent of the net new supply of corporate equities.[46] These findings suggest that pension funds had an impact on both the primary and secondary markets. This reflects the fact that shareholders in the personal and foreign sectors were selling existing or outstanding shares to pension funds (Table 7.1). This explains the high acquisition rate by pension funds of the net new supply of equities. If current trends continue, according to Grant, pension fund acquisitions of corporate securities in Canada would account for almost three-quarters of the new corporate bonds issued and over 130 per cent of the supply of new equity issues. Pension fund acquisitions of corporate securities generally follow the business cycle; nevertheless they supplied a moderate source of funds to the corporate sector during the recent economic downturn.

While it would be preferable to differentiate between primary and secondary market pension fund acquisitions of securities, the data are not available.[47] Knowledgeable estimates by informed sources familiar with the securities market behaviour of institutional investors in Canada, however, suggest that in recent years pension funds have been responsible for purchasing 40 to 50 per cent of all *new* corporate equity issues and 75 to 80 per cent of net *new* corporate bonds; that is, pension funds have purchased in the order of *half* of the net new supply of corporate shares and approximately *three-quarters* of the net new bonds issued in the *primary market* for the purpose of satisfying the external financing requirements of corporations.[48] The institutionalization of pension investment in capital markets has therefore generated an important source of investment at the macro-economic level and has influenced corporate finance.

Pension Funds and the Locus of Corporate Ownership. The private pension system has, over the course of the past twenty years, altered the configuration of control over investment and the ownership of corporate securities. Ownership of corporate securities, stocks and bonds, has increasingly shifted from individual to institutional investors, including pension funds, as was reported in Tables 7.1 and 7.2. The locus of control has become increasingly concentrated in the private pension system, which now has the largest holdings of corporate securities (stocks and bonds) of any major financial institution in Canada. As indicated in Table 7.10, total pension fund holdings of corporate securities have doubled from nearly 25 per cent in 1964 to 50 per cent in 1985. The sheer magnitude of corporate securities invested in and held by pension funds results in their now being the major actor in capital markets.

TABLE 7.10

HOLDINGS OF CORPORATE SECURITIES[1] BY MAJOR FINANCIAL INSTITUTIONS, CANADA, $MILLION, SELECTED YEARS, 1964–1985

INSTITUTION	1964	1971	1979	1985
Trusteed Pension Plans	1,540	4,488	11,651	37,545
Chartered Banks	491	1,269	7,577	22,900
Life Insurance Companies[2]	2,524	4,560	10,972	20,900
Trust/Mortgage Companies	347	648	2,902	7,895
Mutual Funds	757	1,411	1,149	5,096
Fire/Casualty Insurance	357	1,070	2,961	2,900
Closed-end Funds	414	700	393	747
Finance Companies	74	31	8	63
Total	6,484	14,177	37,613	98,073
TOTAL PENSION FUNDS HOLDINGS:[3]	1,566	5,019	13,967	48,843
% OF TOTAL CORPORATE SECURITIES HELD BY PENSION FUNDS:	24.2%	35.4%	37.1%	49.8%

Notes: 1 Corporate stocks and bonds.
2 Including group annuities and segregated funds.
3 Including trusteed pension plans and segregated funds.

Sources: Calculated from the Bank of Canada, Review (Ottawa: n.p., various years), Report of the Superintendent of Insurance—Life Insurance Companies and Fraternal Societies (Ottawa: Department of Insurance, various years), and Statistics Canada, Trusteed Pension Funds Financial Statistics (Ottawa: Minister of Supply and Services, various years).

The ownership of corporate shares through the pension system is of particular significance because it confers ownership and voting rights upon the shareholder. Assessing the pension system's full impact on capital markets and the corporate sector requires that the total equity base of the retirement income system as a whole be determined and that it be related to stock market activity. Table 7.11 relates the total equity holdings of the retirement income system — public and private — to the value of Canadian stocks listed on the Toronto Stock Exchange (TSE) between 1966 and 1980. This time-series would superficially suggest that the total value of equity owned and controlled through the pension system increased from 4 per cent in 1966 to only 15 per cent in 1980.

This measurement, however, is significantly underestimated by the value of control blocks, which are the inactive or untraded portion of stock retained by a company when issuing new shares. Total equity issued is equal to the control block plus the "stock float," that is, the shares actually traded. In turn, the control block is equal to the total equity issued minus the stock float. "Netting-out" the value of control blocks allows the value of the stock float to be determined. Control blocks effectively reduce the value of outstanding shares available in the securities market, thereby increasing the proportion of the stock float controlled by pension funds. Total equity holdings of the retirement income system as a proportion of the value of Canadian stocks and adjusted for control blocks is reported in Table 7.11 (column 10).

These data indicate that between 1966 and 1980, the total value of pension fund equity holdings as a proportion of Canadian stocks on the TSE, adjusted for control blocks, ranged from 15 to 32 per cent. The pension system in Canada over this period on average held 25 per cent of all outstanding corporate equity adjusted for control blocks. By way of comparison, in the United States in 1981 the pension system held 38 per cent of the value of corporate shares adjusted for control blocks. In Britain it is estimated to be in the order of 42 per cent of the value of corporate shares.[49] While no one investment under Canadian legislation can constitute more than 10 per cent of the total value of an individual pension fund or represent more than 30 per cent of a corporation's shares, the pension system — as a system — has had a clearly demonstrable affect on the institutionalization of capital markets, macro-economic investment, corporate finance, and the locus of control over corporate securities.

There is, however, an increasing structural contradiction between the ability of the pension system to satisfy both the investment requirements of the private sector and the public sector's need for social capital and revenue. A systemic tension exists because the "financing needs of the public sector were smaller than those of the

TABLE 7.11

TOTAL EQUITY BASE OF THE RETIREMENT INCOME SYSTEM IN RELATION TO THE VALUE OF STOCKS LISTED AND ADJUSTED FOR CONTROL BLOCKS ON THE TORONTO STOCK EXCHANGE, MARKET VALUE, $BILLION, CANADA, 1966–1980

| | PRIVATE PENSION SYSTEM | | | PUBLIC PENSION SYSTEM | | | | | VALUE OF TOTAL EQUITY HOLDINGS OF ALL PENSION FUNDS AS A % OF | |
| | (1) | (2) | (3) | (4) | (5) | (6) | (7) | (8) | (9) | (10) |
YEAR	Trusteed Pension Plans[6]	Life Ins. Cos.[1]	RRSPs[2]	Quebec Pension Plan	Caisse de Depôt[3]	Total Pension Fund Equity Holdings	Value of Canadian Stocks Listed[4] on TSE	Value of Canadian Stocks Listed on TSE, Adjusted for Control Blocks[5]	Value of Canadian Stocks on TSE (6/7)	Value of Canadian Stocks on TSE, Adjusted for Control Blocks (6/8)
1966	1.295[6]	0.160	0.035	0.000	0.000	1.49	34.5	10.4	4.3%	14.3%
1970	2.840	0.458	0.096	0.212	0.000	3.61	46.5	23.3	7.8	15.5
1971	3.993[7]	0.694	0.120	0.280	0.014	5.10	50.3	25.2	10.1	20.2
1972	5.146[7]	1.135	0.152	0.352	0.019	6.81	64.5	32.3	10.6	21.1
1973	5.052	1.271	0.200	0.491	0.026	7.04	62.5	31.3	11.3	22.5
1974	3.951	1.074	0.256	0.601	0.054	5.94	44.2	22.1	13.4	26.9
1975	5.009	1.455	0.336	0.638	0.082	7.52	51.6	25.8	14.6	29.2
1976	6.106	1.739	0.424	0.661	0.162	9.10	56.9	28.5	15.9	31.9
1977	6.415	1.805	0.483	0.618	0.223	9.54	62.4	31.2	15.3	30.6
1978	7.923	2.203	0.528	0.612	0.307	11.57	79.4	55.6	14.6	20.8
1979	10.719	2.634	0.565	0.720	0.385	15.02	112.6	78.8	13.4	19.1
1980	15.066	3.583	0.580	0.879	0.617	20.73	139.4	97.6	14.9	21.2

Notes: 1 Segregated funds and general pension contracts for federally chartered companies. Federally chartered companies account for 96 per cent of the equity holdings of life insurance companies.

2 Registered Retirement Savings Plans. Note Appendix G 1–3 for derivation of RRSP assets and the amount invested in equity.

3 Segregated funds and beginning in 1971 portfolios under management.

4 Common and preferred shares.

5 A control block is defined in Section 1 (11) (iii) of the Ontario Securities Act 1978 as "any person, company or combination, holding a sufficient number of any securities of that issuer to affect materially the control of that issuer, but any holding . . . [of] more than 20 per cent of the outstanding voting securities of an issuer shall . . . be deemed to affect materially the control of that issuer." In terms of stock market operation, control blocks (inactive shares of a stock held by an issuer as a result of a long-term investment) are equal to total equity issues minus the active shares of a stock (the stock float). The importance of "netting-out" the value of control blocks is that it allows the value of actively traded stocks to be determined. The estimate for control blocks in the 1960s was 30 per cent, based on the Bank of Nova Scotia, "The Stock Market in Canada," *Monthly Review* (October 1960), p. 1. Control blocks during the 1970s were estimated to be in the order of 50 per cent of the value of stocks listed on the TSE by O. M. Petrovici, TSE Internal Study. As a result of mergers and amalgamations in the late 1970s, control blocks were estimated to be in the order of 70 per cent.

6 1965.

7 Extrapolated.

Sources: Calculated on the basis of data contained in Statistics Canada, *Trusteed Pension Plans Financial Statistics, 1978* (Ottawa: Minister of Supply and Services, 1980), Text Table III, pp. 12–13; life insurance company information supplied to the author 5 January 1982 by the Canadian Life and Health Insurance Association; Caisse de Dépôt et Placement du Quebec, *Annual Report* (Quebec City: Government of Quebec, various years); Toronto Stock Exchange, *TSE Historic Trading Summary* and Supplement (Toronto: TSE, 1974 and 1981). The author would like to acknowledge his debt to Dr. O. M. Petrovici for supplying the methodology to derive the equity holdings for all pension funds as a proportion of the value of Canadian stocks traded on the TSE and estimates for control blocks. Information supplied to the author 20 March, 1982 by Dr. Petrovici based on his Paper No. 2 prepared for the TSE, 1976. Appendix G 1–3 for Registered Retirement Savings Plan (RRSP) assets and equity. Appendix H for the estimated value of control blocks.

private sector" while the pension system "met a larger proportion of . . . public sector needs than. . . those in the private sector."[50] The increasing capital requirements of the corporate sector therefore conflict with government's need for financing and public capital because the pension system is also a source of funds for the capitalist welfare state.

PENSION FUNDS AND THE PUBLIC SECTOR

The retirement income system has served a dual purpose in advanced capitalist societies. Social security programmes for the elderly have in one instance been an important mechanism through which the capitalist welfare state has been able to fulfil its legitimation function, that is, maintain social harmony.[51] However, in the post-World War II period, as evidenced by the case of Canada, the public and private pension systems have also become a major source of revenue and social capital for the welfare state. "It is policy in fact to use the monies" of the state pension system "to finance government."[52] The state, particularly in Canada, has therefore acquired an independent vested interest in the operation of the pension system which is not necessarily the same as the private sector's. The opposing structural imperatives — the state for financing and social capital, and the corporate sector for investment capital — may result in considerable political tension, having serious implications for the economic security of the elderly and pension reform in the future.

The fiscal crisis of the welfare state is but one manifestation of the more generalized crises of modern capitalist economies. This crisis has been defined as the capitalist state

increasing its expenditures on social overhead, complementary investment expenditure, socializing . . . the private costs [and risks] of production and an increasing volume of public investment. The state budget continuously expands owing to the increased degree of economic integration and interdependence. This has led to a . . . situation where government expenditures are beginning to outstrip revenues.[53]

The continuous series of deficit budgets and the ballooning debt at all levels of government in Britain, Canada and the U.S. in recent years is symptomatic of this situation.

Within the context of unique Canadian constitutional and fiscal transfer arrangements, the state retirement income system—the Canada/Quebec Pension Plans—has played an important, but neglected, role in partially alleviating the effects of the fiscal crisis of the state. The private pension system to a lesser extent has performed a similar function.

The private pension system is a source of funds for the state. In Canada, private pension funds have purchased 20 per cent of the value of all net new marketable government bonds placed in Canada between 1970 and 1982 (Table 7.12) and were the largest institutional buyer of them. Private pension fund holdings of government bonds (all levels) have increased from 1 to 4 per cent of total government revenue over that period. More significantly, federal govern-

TABLE 7.12

TRUSTEED PENSION FUND ACQUISITION OF GOVERNMENT BONDS[1] AS A PERCENTAGE
OF NET NEW MARKETABLE GOVERNMENT BONDS PLACED IN CANADA, 1970–1982

YEAR	VALUE OF GOVERNMENT BONDS PURCHASED BY PENSION FUNDS (FLOW IN $MILLION)	VALUE OF NET NEW MARKETABLE GOVERNMENT BONDS PLACED IN CANADA ($MILLION)	VALUE OF BONDS PURCHASED BY PENSION FUNDS AS A % OF NET NEW GOVERNMENT BONDS
1970	256	2,381	10.8
1971	298	1,737	17.2
1972	339	2,009	16.9
1973	413	1,815	27.8
1974	464	3,344	13.9
1975	878	4,614	19.0
1976	1,375	7,270	18.9
1977	1,988	10,437	19.1
1978	2,396	10,805	22.2
1979	3,573	12,948	27.6
1980	3,588	20,072	17.9
1981	2,550	10,053	25.4
1982	4,008	16,994	23.6

1970–1982 Average: 20.0

Note: 1 Including marketable federal, provincial and municipal bonds, exclusive of Canada Savings Bonds (CSBs) and non-marketable provincial government bonds held through the CPP which are not bought by institutions.

Sources: The flow of pension fund investment into government bonds was calculated from Statistics Canada, Trusteed Pension Plans Financial Statistics (Ottawa: Minister of Supply and Services Canada, various years), Text Table V. Net new marketable government bonds, exclusive of CSBs and CPP, calculated from the Bank of Canada, Review, August 1988, Table F5, pp. S86–87.

ment bonds held by private pension funds increased from nearly 2 to 9 per cent of total federal government revenue on a consolidated national income accounts basis, between 1970 and 1981.[54]

In Britain, private pension funds are second only to life insurance companies in terms of institutional holdings of government bonds (gilts). Pension funds held 16 per cent of all British government securities in 1978.[55] Pension funds are now sufficiently powerful that a decision to hold back from investing in these securities can force the government to raise interest rates and modify its economic policy as was demonstrated during the so-called "investment" strike by the business community in Britain in 1977.[56] The private pension system has thus served as a source of funds for government. Over the past twenty years in Canada, however, it has been the state pension system which has played an increasingly important economic role as an institutional investor.

Since the inception of the Canada and Quebec Pension Plans in 1966, the state pension system has been an important actor at the macro-economic level. Net public pension saving has accounted for 4.5 to 7 per cent of gross saving in the economy between 1970 and 1980 (Table 6.3). In turn, net public pension saving through the C/QPPs has on average generated the equivalent of 11 per cent of all net private domestic investment (including public corporations) over this period.[57]

The state pension system is an important source of internal government savings as well. Table 7.13 indicates that social security savings have ranged from 30 to 54 per cent of total government savings. The significance of the savings generated through the C/QPPs at the macro-economic level is that "if social security savings were not available for government financing . . . the total government deficit would have been 50 per cent higher in 1978."[58]

In addition to influencing savings and investment, the state retirement system has helped to moderate the federal government's chronic deficit position. It has directly affected capital markets, public finance and economic development by acting as a financial intermediary and institutional investor, and it is the backbone of provincial government financing. The establishment of the Canada/Quebec Pension Plans, according to a major study, has "resulted in some of the most important changes of the decade in financial intermediation and capital market functions in Canada."[59] The federal government "has become a principal with a force" with the "same goals as other financial institutions,"[60] and the state pension

TABLE 7.13

SOCIAL SECURITY SAVINGS AS A PERCENTAGE OF TOTAL GOVERNMENT SAVINGS,
CANADA, 1968–1978

YEAR	SOCIAL SECURITY SAVINGS[1] ($MILLION)	TOTAL GOVERNMENT[2] SAVINGS ($MILLION)	SOCIAL SECURITY SAVINGS AS A % OF TOTAL GOVERNMENT SAVINGS
1968	1,003	3,030	33.1
1969	1,113	4,183	26.6
1970	1,193	3,327	35.8
1971	1,278	2,510	50.8
1972	1,375	2,570	53.5
1973	1,472	3,832	38.4
1974	1,780	6,122	29.1
1975	2,003	–212	100+
1976	2,183	–43	100+
1977	2,259	–1,703	100+
1978	2,383	–4,325	100+

Notes: 1 Total C/QPP revenues minus total C/QPP expenditures.
2 All levels of government.

Source: Arthur W. Donner and Fred Lazar, "The Impact of Social Security Financing on Capital Markets in the 1980s," Report of the Royal Commission on the Status of Pensions in Ontario, Vol. 9, Background Studies and Papers (Toronto: Queen's Printer, 1980), Table 46, p. 210.

system has become a competitor to the private sector in capital markets.

The Canada/Quebec Pension Plans have provided both a source of operating funds and developmental capital for the federal and provincial governments. Net C/QPP saving (contributions minus benefits) was on average equivalent to 3 per cent of total government revenue at all levels and 6.5 per cent of federal government revenue between 1970 and 1981.[61]

The capital pool accumulated through the Canada/Quebec Pensions Plans is one of the largest in Canada. The surplus in the CPP investment fund — that is, those monies left over on a current basis after benefits have been paid — are loaned to the provinces at a preferential interest rate in proportion to the contributions which have flowed from each province. In Canada there is a close relationship between the state pension system and government expenditure and capital accumulation. Capital is the name of the game. Canada's provinces have recognized this relationship for many years. One provincial official involved in the negotiation of the Canada Pension Plan in 1965 commented that "the main reason for us was the creation of a large fund. It would provide money for development . . . and give us more liberty in money markets. The fund was certainly the main reason for me: it was *the* reason."[62] Accordingly, the CPP investment fund has had a substantial impact on provincial government financing and economic development as has the separately managed Quebec Pension Plan (QPP).

The CPP investment fund has become "the backbone of provincial debt financing."[63] It supplied nearly 38 per cent of all provincial borrowing on average between fiscal 1969–1970 and 1978–1979.[64] Previously the provinces relied heavily on private capital markets. The weight of evidence suggests that the provinces have substituted CPP and QPP loans for other forms of borrowing as a result of lower than market interest rates.[65] As Donner concluded, "The provinces and their agencies have relied heavily on [the] CPP and QPP for direct finance," resulting in higher expenditures and lower taxes for the provinces.[66]

This situation has had a significant impact on provincial government financing. In Ontario, Canada's most populated and most industrialized province, non-public sources of borrowing represented 97 per cent of the province's total borrowing between 1966–1967 and 1977–1979. According to one report, "the Canada Pension Plan has been the largest source of funds, accounting for two-thirds of the accumulated total"[67] of Ontario's borrowing. The cumulative financing available to Ontario from non-public sources such as the CPP has exceeded the province's cumulative cash requirements, which has permitted Ontario to limit its public borrowing. In British Columbia between 1967 and 1980, public borrowing provided about one-third of the capital requirements of provincial crown corporations. Without CPP funds, nearly two-thirds of these capital requirements would have been borrowed in private securities markets. In total, it has been estimated that funds borrowed from the CPP have saved the provinces nearly 3 per cent on provincial debt charges.[68]

Depending upon the province, in the early and mid-1970s borrowing from the CPP fund was a source of cash for current operating expenditures or social investment in infrastructure (public capital). In this regard two distinct patterns emerge. In the Atlantic provinces, borrowing from the CPP fund has been part of general borrowing and has been used for current operating expenditures. In Western Canada — British Columbia, Saskatchewan and, until recently, Manitoba — however, CPP borrowings have been used to finance the investment requirements of crown corporations, whereas in Alberta the funds are used to finance municipalities. In Ontario, 43 per cent of all investment in infrastructure between 1972–1973 and 1976–1977 was financed through the CPP.[69] At the provincial level in Western Canada, the use of CPP funds to finance the capital requirements of the crown sector has clearly affected the pattern of economic development.[70] The investment objectives of the Caisse de Depôt, the investment arm of the Quebec Pension Plan, are explicitly related to provincial economic development.

Another source of non-public borrowing which must be analysed in conjunction with the CPP is provincial borrowing from internal pension funds, that is, public employee pension funds. In the order of 7 to 14 per cent of all provincial bonds and debentures were issued to their own captive public sector employee pension funds between 1969–1970 and 1978–1979. This is government "self-financing" through the pension system. In Ontario, for example, between 1966–1967 and 1977–1978, borrowing from public employee pension plans accounted for nearly 32 per cent of total net non-public borrowing.[71] The occupational pension funds of public employees, like the CPP, have thus provided the provinces with an alternative capital market. In aggregate, Canada Pension Plan and public employee pension fund holdings peaked in fiscal 1973–1974, accounting for 55 per cent of total provincial government bond and debenture issues. While this proportion subsequently declined to 40 per cent by 1978–1979, it nevertheless remains the case that non-public borrowing generally continues to be a major source of provincial funds and is the backbone of their borrowing capacity and debt structure.

This evidence suggests that while the Canada Pension Plan investment fund has been in a surplus position it cushioned the fiscal crisis of the state for Canada's provincial governments by providing them with additional "tax room" and a source of social investment for economic development. One of the driving forces underlying the pension reform debate, however, was the need to refinance the Canada Pension Plan because the surplus situation was rapidly coming to an end and would have triggered a chain-reaction of events. Based on the current level of benefits and the total contribution rate of 3.6 per cent of income to the CPP, cash flow to the provinces from the CPP investment was projected to turn negative in 1992.[72] The provinces would then have had to begin repaying the interest on the outstanding loans.[73] By the year 2011, when members of the baby boom begin to retire, the CPP fund would have gone into a disaccumulation or dissavings position. This would have meant that the provinces would have had to repay the *principal and interest* on their loans so that the CPP fund could honour its commitment to pay benefits. Clearly, this sequence of events would have had serious negative implications for provincial government finance. More to the point, it would have set in motion a "domino effect" having fiscal repercussions for all levels of government.

The contribution rate for the Canada/Quebec Pension Plans was recently increased, however, to pay for current or existent benefits. The total level of contributions to the C/QPPs was incrementally raised from 3.6 per cent in 1986 to 7.6 per cent in 2011. This will, however, only temporarily ameliorate the fiscal dilemma for the provinces, because the C/QPP rates have not yet been set for the period after the year 2011 when the large baby boom generation retires. Simply, this means that the level of contributions to the C/QPP will, again, have to be increased or the provinces will find themselves in a similar predicament in the future. Current arrangements are merely a reprieve. Furthermore, the newly implemented contribution rates only cover current benefits without improving the income replacement rate for the future elderly.

To the extent that contribution rates are increased to pay for improved benefits and depending on the method of funding and the phase-in of the new rates, the cash flow into the CPP investment fund and the size of the fund might double.[74] While such an expansion of the public pension system would improve the economic position of the elderly, and the cash flow position of the provinces, it would come at the expense of the private pension system. This is because a doubling of the income replacement rate under the C/QPP to improve the economic position of the elderly would reduce the savings and investment flowing through and under the control of the private pension system by an estimated $88 billion or some 31 per cent, with a considerable impact on private capital markets. If the public pension system was expanded the "funds . . . made available to governments . . . would have the effect of eliminating the need for provincial borrowing for a long time to come and could have an enormous effect on provincial budgets and financial power."[75] Thus, the structurally determined interests of the elderly for improved retirement income and the financing requirements of the provinces conflict with the private sector's need for capital and the private pension industry's institutional survival.

In the most fundamental sense what is at issue is power, control over capital, and capital accumulation. "Pension policy," one study concluded, is "an issue of power, power to control and allocate the capital generated through the savings put aside by workers for their old age."[76] What public policy and the pension reform debate turns on in Canada is the structure of the capital market and who will control pension savings, investment and capital formation: the private sector, the provinces, or the federal state. Given that there are five major pension actors — the federal government, the provinces, the private sector, the labour movement and the elderly — various scenarios might unfold in the future.

Under conditions of advanced capitalism the public and private pension systems are integrally related to the capital accumulation process and financing arrangements in the private and state sectors. Control of the capital accumulated by pension funds in Canada by the federal or provincial governments is one way in which they will attempt to grapple with their respective fiscal crises. At the same time they can provide a source of developmental capital for the state, should the political will exist. The structurally determined interests of the elderly and the state are, however, opposed to those of the private sector and private pension industry. In the final analysis, it is the impact of the private pension system on capital markets and the fiscal implications underlying the state pension system which will be the driving forces behind pension reform in the long term and the form in which it is realized.

THE INSTITUTIONALIZATION OF CAPITAL MARKETS: IMPLICATIONS

The pension system performs a series of important economic functions in the advanced capitalist economies of Britain, Canada and the United States and now occupies a strategic position. In the postwar period the pension system as a financial intermediary and institutional investor has become a dominant force in capital markets. The institutionalization of retirement savings and investment has affected the operation and configuration of capital markets and the level, type and pattern of investment, with a consequent impact on the macro-economy and corporate and public sector finance.

The central role now performed by the private pension system in generating investment to promote capital accumulation in the private sector and the concomitant impact on financial markets in advanced capitalist economies generate, as demonstrated in the case of Canada, a number of important structural contradictions having serious implications for public policy and the operation of the pension system. The recently concluded pension reform debate in Canada was dominated by a series of policy and political trade-offs. They will affect the realpolitik of pension reform in the future. These structurally determined trade-offs, based on the opposing class interests of the various pension actors, are identified and briefly examined below.

First, there are the opposing interests of the private sector and the elderly. There is a conflict between the capital accumulation requirements of the corporate sector, and the operation of capital markets to satisfy them, and the elderly's imperative for economic security. Pension funds as a source of capital formation are central to this policy debate because the business community fears that an expansion of the public pension system would result in it being deprived of a prime source of investment capital. A related concern is that an expansion of the public pension system would result in government domination of capital markets. Nevertheless, the private pension system, characterized by a series of universal limitations as analysed in Chapter 4, has proven itself to be an inadequate delivery system for retirement income. Pension reform was a failure. The elderly's need for adequate retirement income, described in Chapter 3, therefore requires an expansion of the public pension system. The opposing interests of the private sector and elderly have been clearly identified by the business media. One editorial argued, for example, that "the disposition of pension assets needs just as thorough an airing . . . as does the question of benefits."[77] Therefore, in terms of public policy formulation and the politics of pension reform over the long term, the alternative becomes private sector capital accumulation through the inadequate private pension system or adequate retirement income for the elderly based on an expanded public pension system.

Second, there is a tension in capital markets, particularly in Canada, between the interests of the private sector and the state: an antagonism exists between the corporate sector's requirement for increased investment capital through the private pension system and the federal and provincial governments' requirements for social capital and operating revenue generated through the public pension system. That antagonism manifests itself in terms of corporate resistance to both significantly increased C/QPP contribution levels and an expansion of the public pension system. Expansion of the state pension system (C/QPP) would come at the expense of the private sector by shifting pension savings and investment from the private to the government sector, with a consequent reduction in the control over and amount of capital available for the business community. In the most fundamental political sense, expansion of the state pension system represents the shifting of the saving and investment function from the private to the public sector and a more important role for government in capital markets. This shift will be resisted by the private sector, not only for ideological reasons, but also because of its structural imperative for investment to augment the capital accumulation process. The alternatives are either adequate public pensions and government control over capital formation or inadequate occupational pension plans and private sector control over capital.

From the perspective of political economy, pension reform becomes a battleground over the control and direction of the savings, investment and reserve capital generated from the pension system. Within this context, a political dynamic might develop, especially in Canada, based upon the structurally determined vested interests of the respective pension actors, where there is an alliance between the elderly, organized labour and the state against the corporate sector.

Third, the battle over pension capital will affect the mode of pension reform. In terms of public policy formulation there is a close interrelationship between pension plan coverage and the saving and investment functions performed by the private and public pension systems. The provision of retirement income for the elderly requires that they be covered by some type of pension plan. Social security policy as it has historically evolved has incorporated a tension between compulsory and voluntary coverage. Resolving the coverage problem, however, clearly requires some type of mandatory or compulsory pension arrangement for the labour force. But what type? Within the pension reform debate and from a public policy perspective, the options which have emerged are voluntary coverage—that is, the status quo—or universal coverage through the public pension system or a regime of mandatory coverage through the employer-sponsored private pension system.

Within this context the manifest saving and investment function underlying the operation of the private and public pension systems assumes considerable importance with respect to pension reform and the operation of capital markets. The proposals put forward by the Canadian Life and Health Insurance Association, the Lazar Report's Options II and III, and the Government of Ontario's Royal Commission on the Status of Pensions recommendation for a provincial universal retirement system (PURS) to provide mandatory pension plan coverage through the private pension industry would have had the effect of creating a captive market for pension savings and a private monopoly channelling investment to the private sector. Similar proposals were advanced by the 1981 President's Commission on Pension Policy in the U.S. and the 1985 white paper on the reform of social security in the U.K. The various private pension industry proposals for mandatory private coverage to stave off expansion of the public pension system in Canada would have increased the assets under their control by nearly 25 per cent, from $52 billion to a conservatively estimated $64 billion in 1981.[78] This pool of captive pension savings would, of course, be cycled through capital markets as investment to the private sector to augment capital accumulation and profitable business activity. Conversely, expansion of the public pension system would result in a significant increase in the pool of pension capital available to and under the control of government for investment.

Generating increased investment through either the private or public pension systems for the private sector would increase the already considerable power exercised by the private pension system in capital markets. The battle over the direction of pension reform therefore clearly requires a policy choice between either public or private sector pension reform. The specific modality of reform has serious implications for the locus of control over saving, investment, corporate securities and the operation of capital markets.

Fourth, the type of pension reform — public or private sector — has implications for investment objectives and strategies. The manifest saving and investment functions now incorporated into the operation of the private pension system have resulted in an increasing fusion between and integration of financial and industrial capital as a natural consequence of financial intermediaries and institutional investors, such as pension funds, investing in the corporate sector through the securities market. The private pension system now has the largest institutional holdings of corporate securities, including equity. This power may have political implications for transforming control over the corporate sector and might suggest progressive investment strategies by organized labour based on the occupational pension system at the enterprise or industry level. Alternatively, expansion of the public pension system, particularly in the case of Canada, would generate a surplus (where contributions are greater than benefits) resulting in a substantial investment fund. The existence of such a fund poses the question of the purpose for which it is being accumulated, that is, what are its investment objectives? Depending upon political circumstance, such an investment fund might provide the state with a source of developmental capital to pursue alternative economic strategies under democratic control. Using the public and private pension systems' saving and investment functions to promote progressive economic development strategies and social change in advanced capitalist economies is dealt with in Chapter 10.

Capital is at the heart of the political economy of pensions and pension reform. The manifest functions of the private pension system, the institutionalization of capital markets, and the formal organization of pension fund power are interrelated. These structural relationships are integrally related to a particular mode of production and a specific social formation. The focus must therefore shift from a functional to an institutional analysis of pension fund power.

8

The Structure
of Pension Fund Power

*Expropriation is accomplished by the action of the . . .
laws of capitalism . . . by the centralization of capital.*
                                                    Karl Marx

The elements constituting the political economy of pensions identified and examined in the preceding chapters have established that
the capital accumulation function is now central to the operation of
the private pension system and that it results in the socialization
and institutionalization of retirement savings and capital markets
under conditions of advanced capitalism. The private pension system's economic power comes from its ability to channel investment
capital to and thus augment the capital accumulation process of the
private sector. A symbiotic relationship has developed between the
investment requirements of the macro-economy and corporate sector, supplied through the private pension system, and the private
pension industry's imperative for survival. Correspondingly, the
public pension system is underdeveloped, perpetuating the immiseration and marginalization of the elderly. The economic functions
inherent in the operation of the private pension system are integrally related to and manifest themselves through the institutional
structure, that is, through the organization of pension fund power.
    The purpose of this chapter is to delineate the formal structure of
pension fund power and to identify those "laws of motion" which

result in an increased concentration and centralization of economic power residing in the private pension system under conditions of advanced capitalism. A number of interrelated topics are examined. First, the power associated with the operation of the private pension system is identified as the pool of capital, that is, the asset base under its control. In the postwar period there has been an accelerated growth of private pension fund assets, or reserve capital, with a resulting concentration of economic power. Second, the tendency towards the concentration and centralization of pension fund capital is identified as the primary explanatory factor with respect to the institutional power of the private pension system and is a reflection of these more global tendencies in capitalist economies.

Third, private pension fund assets are controlled by a relatively few dominant financial institutions such as individual trusteed pension plans and trust companies in Canada and banks and life insurance companies in the U.K. and U.S. Fourth, the locus of *control* over pension fund capital resides in the financial sector because pension plan trustees generally delegate investment responsibility to these institutions. The private pension system, as a sphere or "region" within the finance sector, with formal and informal linkages to it, therefore is organically integrated with financial capital.

GROWTH OF PENSION FUND CAPITAL

Funding agencies such as trust companies, banks and life insurance companies, in conjunction with service agencies such as actuarial consultants, plan administrators and investment counsellors, can be described as the private pension industry, constituting the formal institutional structure of pension fund power as it has developed in law and practice. The notion of "formal structure" as used here refers to "that part of . . . a group or organization that is defined explicitly by rules or expectations."[1]

The economic power associated with the private pension industry is explained in terms of its control over the significantly growing pool of pension assets flowing from increased pension saving and investment, the tendency towards the concentration and centralization of pension fund capital among a relatively few economic actors, and the formal and informal linkages to the broader finance sector and industrial capital. The institutional strength of the pension system is related to its now manifest economic function to promote capital accumulation in the private sector.

The growth of pension fund assets, both in absolute and relative terms as a major pool of capital in the post-World War II period in Canada, Britain and the U.S. determines the extent of their economic power. It has significantly exceeded the growth in assets experienced by all financial institutions and non-bank intermediaries in the finance sector. As indicated in Table 8.1 pension fund assets have experienced an annualized compounded growth rate of 13 per cent in the U.S., 15 per cent in Canada and 16 per cent in Britain which contrasts with a growth rate for all financial intermediary assets of 9 per cent in the U.S., 11 per cent in Canada and 18 per cent in Britain. In terms of absolute growth the assets of all financial intermediaries in Canada between 1946 and 1979 increased nearly thirty-three times, while pension fund assets

TABLE 8.1

COMPARISON OF GROWTH RATES OF PENSION FUNDS,
NON-BANK FINANCIAL INTERMEDIARIES AND ALL FINANCIAL INTERMEDIARIES,
CANADA, U.K. AND U.S. IN THE POSTWAR PERIOD

CANADA	$ BILLION		% ANNUALIZED COMPOUNDED RATE OF GROWTH
	1946	1979	
All Financial Intermediaries[1]	11.9	398.8	11.2
Private Non-Bank Intermediaries	4.9	188.6	11.7
Pension Funds[2]	.5	43.3	14.8
U.K.	£ BILLION		
	1963	1981	
All Financial Institutions[1]	30.4	583.7	17.8
Non-Bank Institutions	9.1	252.0	20.3
Pension Funds[3]	5.8	85.0	16.1
U.S.	$ BILLION		
	1950	1980	
All Financial Intermediaries[1]	286.6	3,761.8	8.9
Non-Bank Finance	138.8	2,375.5	9.9
Pension Funds[4]	11.7	484.9	13.2

Notes: 1 Bank plus non-bank financial intermediaries.
2 Trusteed and insured pension plus segregated funds of life companies.
3 Private, public and Local Authority pension funds, and estimated assets of insured pension plans of life companies.
4 Private insured pension funds and state and local government retirement funds.

Sources: Appendix I 1–3.

increased by a factor of ninety-five. In the U.S. their assets increased thirteen times, compared with a forty-one-fold increase in pension fund assets between 1950 and 1980. Projections for the U.S. suggest that total pension fund assets will exceed those of all non-bank savings institutions by 1990.[2]

The significant relative and absolute growth in pension fund capital is attributable to the moderate growth of occupational pension plan coverage (Chapter 4) and the increased proportion of personal saving channelled through and invested by the private pension system (Chapter 6). Between 1960 and 1980 the annualized compounded rate of growth for total private pension assets was nearly 11 per cent in the U.S., 14 per cent in Canada and 18 per cent in Britain. Pension fund assets doubled every six to ten years between 1960 and 1980, depending upon the country, and are now doubling every five years. Pension funds have therefore become the growth centre within the finance sector over the past four decades.

TABLE 8.2

GROWTH OF PENSION FUND ASSETS,
U.K., CANADA AND U.S., 1960–1980

| COUNTRY | BILLION NATIONAL CURRENCY UNITS | | % ANNUALIZED COMPOUNDED RATE OF GROWTH |
	1960	1980	
U.K.[1]	3.3[2]	85.0	17.6
Canada[3]	4.8	65.5	13.9
U.S.[4]	90.8	727.1	10.9

Notes: 1 Non-insured and insured pension schemes. Assets of insured schemes estimated at one-third of the contribution cash-flow of funded schemes.
2 Estimated.
3 Trusteed and insured pension plans plus the segregated funds of life insurance companies.
4 Non-insured and insured pension plans and all government retirement funds.

Sources: CSO, Financial Statistics (London: HMSO, various years); Statistics Canada, Trusteed Pension Plan Financial Statistics (Ottawa: Minister of Supply and Services, various years); Bank of Canada, Statistical Summary (Ottawa: n.p., various years); and the Statistical Abstract of the United States, 1982–83 (Washington, D.C.: GPO, 1982), Series 537, p. 330.

The growth of pension fund assets in the future may be even greater. In the case of Canada, for example, according to projections by the Economic Council of Canada, given current growth rates and depending on demographic assumptions, the assets of trusteed pension plans will increase from 16 per cent of gross national product in 1981 to 50 to 66 per cent of GNP by 2031 (Table 8.3). The private pension system over the next thirty years will therefore be the major repository for the savings of workers and a major source of investment capital for the economy. By any standard, the growth of pension fund capital in recent decades has been impressive, if not startling. It has concurrently altered the configuration of the finance sector and accelerated the concentration of capital among a few major institutions in advanced capitalist economies.

TABLE 8.3

ESTIMATED BOOK VALUE OF
TRUSTEED PENSION PLAN ASSETS
AS A PROPORTION OF GNP, CANADA, 1981–2051

	TRUSTEED PENSION PLAN ASSETS AS A PER CENT OF GNP UNDER VARYING DEMOGRAPHIC GROWTH RATES	
YEAR	Medium	Low
1981	16	16
1991	25	27
2001	35	38
2011	42	50
2021	48	60
2031	50	66
2041	50	66
2051	50	66

Source: Estimated from the Economic Council of Canada, One in Three: Pensions for Canadians to 2030 (Hull: Minister of Supply and Services, 1979), Chart 6–2, p. 54. Figures rounded.

CONCENTRATION OF PENSION FUND CAPITAL:
ACCUMULATION AND POWER

As used by Marx, the term "concentration of capital" refers to the process whereby the quantity of capital controlled by individual capitalists or capitalist corporations (industrial and financial) increases over time. In this sense the concentration of capital is a natural accompaniment of the capital accumulation process.[3]

The configuration of the finance sector in Britain, Canada and the

United States, and the distribution of assets within it, is a product of the particular historical development of each national capitalism— that is, the social formation and the relationship of the finance sector to the industrialization process. In Canada the locus of economic power in the finance sector resides in four private financial intermediaries: chartered banks, trusteed pension funds (individual and corporate), life insurance companies and trust companies. These four institutions accounted for over 75 per cent of the total assets of private financial intermediaries in Canada in 1985 (Table 8.4).

TABLE 8.4

ASSETS OF MAJOR CANADIAN FINANCIAL INTERMEDIARIES,
$BILLION, BOOK VALUE, 1985

| | | % DISTRIBUTION OF ASSETS | |
FINANCIAL INTERMEDIARY	ASSETS ($BILLION)	Total Private Intermediaries	Total Private Non-Bank Intermediaries
Chartered Banks	295.3	40.5	—
Trusteed Pension Funds	108.5 (78.6[2])	14.9 (10.8[2])	24.9 (18.1[2])
Life Insurance Companies[1]	94.3	12.9	21.7
Trust Companies	64.6 (94.5[3])	8.9 (12.9[3])	14.9 (21.8[3])
Local and Central Credit Unions	54.8	7.5	12.6
Mortgage Loan Companies	52.4	7.2	12.1
Property and Casualty Companies	18.3	2.5	4.2
Financial Corporations	16.8	2.3	3.9
Investment Funds[4]	12.8	1.8	2.9
Investment Dealers	12.2	1.7	2.8
Total Assets:			
All Financial Intermediaries	730.0		
Non-Bank Financial Intermediaries	434.7		

Notes: 1 Canadian business only.
2 Excluding assets of corporate trusteed pension funds which are included in the total asset base of trust companies.
3 To place the assets of trust companies on a comparable basis with life insurance companies requires that all assets under their control be included, as in the case of life insurance firms (S&A, segregated funds and life policies). Nearly 28 per cent of all trusteed pension fund assets ($29.9 billion) are controlled by trust companies (as corporate trustees) and are included here. The total asset base of trust companies therefore is now greater than that of life insurance companies.
4 Open- and closed-end investment funds.

Sources: Reports of the Superintendent of Insurance Canada (Hull: Minister of Supply and Services, various years).

Private financial intermediaries in Canada had nearly $730 billion dollars in assets at their disposal, while non-bank financial intermediaries, including pension funds, had assets worth nearly $435 billion under their control in 1985. The assets of trusteed pension plans (private and public sector) represented over $108 billion. To this must be added the $27 billion of assets associated with insured pension plans and the segregated funds of life insurance companies. The assets of the entire private pension system in Canada were therefore in the order of $136 billion or 30 per cent of GNP in 1985. Combined with the public pension system (C/QPP), total pension assets stood at nearly $177 billion, or 38 per cent of the GNP, in 1985.

Private pension funds in Canada, historically dwarfed by the chartered banks and life insurance companies, are now an independent power in financial markets. Today they are the second largest institutional investor, having superseded the assets of life insurance companies for the first time in the early 1970s. They are now the largest private non-bank financial intermediary in Canada, accounting for nearly 25 per cent of all non-bank assets. Historically, "life companies and banks together" were, according to Clement, "the nub not only of Canadian finance but of Canadian capitalism."[4] Private pension funds must now be incorporated into such a formulation.

The growth and concentration of pension fund capital have correspondingly affected the configuration of the finance sector in the U.S., Britain and Canada in the postwar period. The relative and absolute increase in pension fund assets and their concentration into a new growth centre have simultaneously resulted in a redistribution or "re-sectoring" of assets under the control of and the economic power exercised by various financial institutions. This transfiguration of the finance sector is outlined in Table 8.5, which reports pension assets as a proportion of total and non-bank financial intermediary assets.

In the U.S. and Canada, pension fund assets have nearly tripled as a proportion of total and non-bank financial institution assets in the postwar period. In the immediate postwar period pension funds in the U.S. were the fifth largest financial intermediary, and in Britain the third largest. By 1980 pension funds ranked as the third largest institutional investor in the U.S. and were the second largest in the U.K. Pension funds ranked as the fourth largest non-bank financial intermediary in the U.S. and were the second largest in Britain after

TABLE 8.5

PENSION FUND ASSETS AS A PERCENTAGE OF
ALL FINANCIAL INTERMEDIARY AND NON-BANK FINANCIAL INTERMEDIARY ASSETS,
CANADA, U.S. AND U.K., POSTWAR PERIOD

SECTOR	CANADA		U.S.		U.K.	
	1946	1979	1950	1980	1963	1981
All Financial Intermediaries	3.8	10.8	4.1	12.9	19.1	14.6
Non-Bank Intermediaries	9.2	22.9	8.4	20.4	27.2	33.7

Source: Calculated from Appendix I 1–3.

the war. By 1980 pension funds had become the second and first ranked non-bank financial intermediary in the U.S. and Britain respectively.

CENTRALIZATION OF PENSION FUND CAPITAL:
THE MORPHOLOGY OF POWER

The centralization of capital, as distinct from its concentration, refers to the combining or amalgamation of capitals which are already in existence. This "presupposes a change in the distribution of capital" because as "capital grows in one place to a huge mass in a single hand it has in another place been lost by many." The centralization of capital in the finance sector, or the "credit system" to use Marx's term, operates in a different manner than it does in the industrial sphere of production. As Marx used the term, the "credit system" includes not only banks, but the entire financial system of investment houses, security markets, and so on. Under conditions of contemporary capitalism, it is appropriate to include the private pension system as part of the "credit system." The finance sector becomes a "formidable weapon in the competitive struggle"[5] and is able to affect "the amalgamation of . . . capitals which already exist or are in the process of formation."[6] The centralization of capital therefore refers to the general process whereby fewer capitalists or industrial or financial corporations own or control a greater quantity of capital.

The centralization of capital as it relates to the operation of the private pension system is relevant in at least three ways. In the first instance, "the fact that loaned [or invested] capital yields interest whether actually employed as capital or not . . . lends strength to the idea that this form of [money] capital exists independently."[7] That is, the assets and investment activities of financial institutions such as pension funds are an independent sphere of economic power which augments capital accumulation in the industrial sector. Second, centralization reduces competition and creates a tendency towards monopolistic market behaviour. Third, and perhaps most important, it leads to the socialization and rationalization of the labour process within a capitalist political economy.[8]

Pension funds are both an integral part of the finance sector and a separate "region," or industry, within it. The centralization of pension fund capital is an important public policy issue because, according to Titmuss, pension funds are a "force making for greater centralization of [economic] decision-making power" among a relatively few financial institutions which control and direct the pension savings of workers into investment. "It is power concentrated in relatively few hands, working at the apex of a handful of giant bureaucracies . . . and accountable, in practice, to virtually no one."[9]

There is a concentration and centralization of pension capital in a few large pension funds. The comparative data presented in Table 8.6 indicate that the size of pension funds is closely related to the centralization of pension assets. The top ten funds in the U.K., Can-

TABLE 8.6

CENTRALIZATION AND CONCENTRATION
OF PENSION ASSETS IN LARGE PENSION FUNDS,
U.K., CANADA AND U.S., 1978–1983

COUNTRY	% OF TOTAL PENSION FUND ASSETS CONTROLLED BY		
	Top 10 Funds	Top 20 Funds	Top 200 Funds
U.K.[1]	30.8	40.3	55.0
Canada[2]	24.4	33.2	88.9[4]
U.S.[3]	24.1	42.4	75.2

Notes: 1 1978.
2 1980.
3 1983.
4 Largest 397 pension funds with 1,000 or more members.

Sources: Calculated from the National Association of Pension Funds survey and CSO, Financial Statistics (London: HMSO, 1980); "Top 200 Pension Funds/Sponsors," Pensions & Investment Age, 23 January 1984, pp. 16–17; "Canada's Top 20 Pension Funds," Benefits Canada, Vol. 6 (September/October 1982), p. 45 and Statistics Canada. Trusteed Pension Plan Financial Statistics 1980 (Ottawa: Minister of Supply and Services, 1982), Text Table VIII, p. 25.

ada and the U.S. account for 25 to 30 per cent of total pension fund assets, while the twenty largest pension funds represent nearly 40 per cent of the total.

A transnational comparison of the distribution of pension assets by funding agency and sector is presented in Table 8.7. The vast majority of occupational pension plan assets are in trusteed (non-insured) plans administered by bank trust departments in the U.S. and merchant banks in Britain. In Canada, most pension fund assets are administered under individual and corporate trust arrangements.

In Canada the organization of the private pension industry and the locus of control over pension fund capital is concentrated and centralized in three institutions: the individual trusteed (non-insured) pension fund, the corporate trustee, managed by a trust company, and the segregated (pension) funds of life insurance companies. "The trusteed arrangement," according to Statistics Canada, "represents the major repository for pension funds."[10] Within the category of "trusteed" pension plans it is necessary to differentiate between an individual trustee (at least three persons) and corporate trustee arrangements administered under the auspices of a trust company.[11] Table 8.8 indicates that trusteed pension plans (individual and corporate) account for 80 per cent of all pension fund assets (excluding occupational pensions paid from government consolidated revenue). The majority of pension assets in Canada are vested with individual trustees, rather than with trust companies. Specifically, 57 per cent of total pension fund assets were held by individual trustees, 22 per cent by corporate trustees (trust companies) and 20 per cent by insurance companies. Each of these pension fund arrangements in Canada exhibits a significant concentration and centralization of pension capital as a result of their being under the control of a dominant financial institution. These arrangements are examined in greater detail below.

Individual Trusteed Pension Funds. Large individual trusteed pension funds have witnessed a marked increase in the concentration and centralization of pension fund assets under their control. Over the past two decades the average assets of large individual trusteed pension funds in Canada have increased by a factor of seven in current dollars, and fivefold in constant dollars (Table 8.9).

The distribution of pension fund assets clearly indicates the high degree of concentration and centralization of capital held by the largest funds and, in particular, individual trusteed pension funds.

TABLE 8.7

DISTRIBUTION OF PENSION FUND ASSETS BY SECTOR AND FUNDING AGENCY, BILLION NATIONAL CURRENCY UNITS, U.S., CANADA AND U.K., 1960–1980

SECTOR AND FUNDING AGENCY	U.S.		CANADA		U.K.		% DISTRIBUTION OF ASSETS					
							U.S.		CANADA		U.K.	
	1960	1980	1960	1980	1960	1980	1960	1980	1960	1980	1960	1980
Private Funds	57.0	452.6	3.4	39.5	2.4	59.8	62.7	62.2	70.8	60.3	72.7	70.4
Insured	18.9	165.8	1.2[2]	13.8[2]	0.6[4]	30.3[4]	20.8	22.8	25.0	21.1	18.2	35.7
Non-insured (Trusteed)	38.1	286.8	2.2	25.7	1.7	29.5	41.9	39.4	45.8	39.2	51.5	34.7
Public Funds	33.8[1]	274.5[1]	1.4[3]	25.0[3]	0.9[5]	25.2[5]	37.2	37.8	29.2	39.7	27.3	29.6
Total, All Types	90.8	727.1	4.8	65.5	3.3(E)	85.0(E)	100.0	100.0	100.0	100.0	100.0	100.0

Notes: 1 Federal, state and local government retirement funds.
2 Insured plans plus segregated funds of life insurance companies.
3 Trusteed pension plans only, excluding consolidated revenue plans of the federal and provincial governments.
4 Estimated at one-third the contribution cash-flow of non-insured schemes.
5 Local Authority and other public sector plans.

Sources: U.S. Department of Commerce, *Statistical Abstract of the United States, 1982–83* (Washington, D.C.: GPO, 1982), Series 537, p. 330; Statistics Canada, *Trusteed Pension Plans Financial Statistics 1980* (Ottawa: Minister of Supply and Services, 1982), Text Table VI, p. 19; Bank of Canada, *Statistical Summary* (Ottawa: n.p., various dates); and CSO, *Financial Statistics* (London: HMSO, various years).

TABLE 8.8

PENSION FUND ASSETS,

BY FUNDING AGENCY, $MILLION BOOK VALUE, CANADA, 1985

	VALUE OF PENSION FUND ASSETS	
FUNDING AGENCY	$Million	% of Total
Trust Arrangements	108,042	79.6
Corporate Trustee	29,849	22.0
Individual Trustee[1]	77,562	57.2
Other[2]	631	0.4
Insurance Companies	26,946	19.9
Government Annuities	687	0.5
Total[3]	135,675	100.0

Notes: 1 Individual trustees and pension fund societies.
        2 Combination of corporate and individual trustees.
        3 Excluding government consolidated revenue employee pension plans
           financed on a pay-as-you-go basis.

Source: Calculated from Statistics Canada, Trusteed Pension Funds Financial
         Statistics 1986 (Ottawa: Minister of Supply and Services Canada, 1988),
         Table 5, p. 54 and Text Table C, p. 12 and information supplied to author.

The independent economic power residing with these large funds is closely related to and reinforced by the type of pension fund investment management. The management of large or individual trusteed pension funds is generally handled internally, that is, managed in-house under the direct control of the plan sponsor. It is the small- and medium-sized pension funds which are usually managed externally by various financial institutions.

The centralization of pension assets by type of investment management for Canada's largest pension funds is reported in Table 8.10. This information indicates that Canada's ten largest pension funds are wholly or largely managed in-house. Specifically, nearly 85 per cent of the assets of the ten top pension funds in Canada are self-managed, including such major private and public sector corporations as Canadian Pacific Ltd., CN Railways and Ontario Hydro. In Britain, 75 per cent of the total assets of the ten largest pension funds are managed in-house, including British Coal, the Post Office, and ICI (Table 8.11). In the United States in recent years there has been an accelerating trend towards in-house management, particularly among the largest corporate pension funds such as General Electric, DuPont, U.S. Steel and Exxon. The largest self-managed funds are equally distributed between the private and public sectors.

TABLE 8.9

CONCENTRATION AND CENTRALIZATION OF INDIVIDUAL TRUSTEED PENSION FUND ASSETS, $MILLION, CANADA, 1960–1982

YEAR	TOTAL ASSETS	NUMBER OF LARGE PENSION FUNDS[1]	AVERAGE ASSETS PER LARGE PENSION FUND (CURRENT $MILLION)	CONSUMER PRICE INDEX DEFLATOR (1960 = 100)	AVERAGE ASSETS PER LARGE PENSION FUND (CONSTANT $MILLION)	PERCENTAGE CHANGE IN AVERAGE ASSETS PER LARGE PENSION FUND IN CONSTANT DOLLARS
1960	$ 3,153,718	143	$ 22,054	100.0	$ 22,054	—
1970	9,335,862	257	36,326	130.6	25,210	14.3
1982	63,939,658	400	159,849	352.9	119,423	441.5

Notes: 1 A large pension fund is defined as one having 1,000 or more members.

Sources: Calculated from Statistics Canada, *Trusteed Pension Plans Financial Statistics, 1980* (Ottawa: Minister of Supply and Services, 1981), Table VIII, pp. 24–25, and Statistics Canada, *Trusteed Pension Funds Financial Statistics 1986* (Ottawa: Minister of Supply and Services Canada, 1988), Text Table N, pp. 38–39.

TABLE 8.10

LARGEST CANADIAN PENSION FUNDS,
BY TYPE OF INVESTMENT MANAGEMENT, $MILLION, MARKET VALUE, 1987

PENSION FUND	ASSETS ($ MILLION)	TYPE OF FUND MANAGEMENT
Ontario Municipal Employees Retirement System	8,981	86% in-house
Canadian National Railways	6,100	92% in-house
Bell Canada	4,816	100% outside
Hospitals of Ontario Pension Plan	3,900	97% in-house
Canadian Pacific	3,500	In-house
Ontario Hydro	3,302	In-house
B.C. Municipal Superannuation Fund	2,802	In-house
B.C. Public Service Superannuation Fund	2,752	In-house
Hydro Quebec	2,508	85% in-house
Air Canada	2,161	70% in-house

Source: Retabulated from "Canada's Top 40 Pension Funds," *Benefits Canada* 12 (April 1988), pp. 12–14.

TABLE 8.11

LARGEST U.K. PENSION FUNDS,
BY TYPE OF FUND MANAGEMENT, £ MILLION, MARKET VALUE, 1987

PENSION FUND	CAPITAL VALUE (£ M)	TYPE OF FUND MANAGEMENT[1]
British Coal	8,962	In-house
British Telecommunications	8,211	n.a.
Electricity Council	6,236	In-house
British Railways	5,757	25% in-house
Post Office	4,810	75% in-house
Barclays Bank	4,566	External
Universities Superannuation Scheme	3,800	n.a.
British Gas	3,799	In-house
British Steel	3,659	In-house
Imperial Chemical Industries	3,575	In-house

Note: 1 As of 1980. More recent information on the type of fund management was not available from the NAPF.

Source: Information supplied to the author courtesy of the National Association of Pension Funds, 16 August 1988.

The concentration and centralization of pension assets in self-managed funds suggest that the largest funds are managed in accordance with the "profit centre theory" of pension fund management.[12] The pension fund is "one of the most important . . . assets in the company," according to one fund manager, and "should receive the same intensity of consideration that any other aspect of the business should."[13] Large individual trusteed pension plans which are internally managed are under the direct control of the plan sponsor and become an integral part of corporate profit maximization behaviour. This leads to the further centralization of economic decision-making and concentration of power in the corporate sector.

Trust Companies (Corporate Trustees). The idea of the trust was British in origin and was subsequently introduced into the United States and the British Empire, including Canada, in the early nineteenth century. The concept of the corporate trustee as it has evolved, however, is essentially a North American innovation.

The superiority of trust companies over individual trustees or executors is a result of their large volume of business, financial expertise, and their permanent corporate status. According to Neufeld,

> the unique contribution to the [Canadian] financial system of . . . trust companies is their provision of executor, administrator and *trust services.* They are unique among the financial institutions in this respect because banks, life insurance companies and loan companies are *not* permitted to act in a fiduciary capacity. . . . The decisive change occurred when the trust companies were permitted to accept funds. . . . Trust companies borrowing and lending activities [are] little different . . . [from] the savings business of the chartered banks.[14]

The business activities of Canadian trust companies fall into two distinct categories—financial intermediary, or "banking," and fiduciary (custodial) functions. When a trust company is acting in a "banking" capacity, it is a principal in the transaction, such as taking deposits from the public. The fiduciary or trustee functions are unique to trust companies in Canada. In this capacity, trust companies serve as administrators of estates, trusts and agencies. They do not obtain ownership of the assets under their administration but, rather, act with varying degrees of authority as the trustee, or custodian, of the assets. The trust document defines the powers and discretion of the trust manager. "The trust company," according to Baum, "is peculiar to Canada. It functions as a corporate fiduciary, administering trusts of all kinds, including funds for investment," such as pension funds.[15] The custodial function coupled with deposit-taking make Canadian trust companies near-banks.

Funds controlled by trust companies in Canada are divided into three categories: company funds, guaranteed trust accounts, and estate, trust and agency (ETA) accounts. Company ("own") funds or assets are the basic capitalization of the trust company. Monies on deposit are the guaranteed funds and are secured by company funds. All other funds administered by a trust company may be characterized as estate, trust or agency accounts (ETAs). Accordingly, "money managed by a trust company is divided in separate accounts or trusts. Many of these are set for a specific client. For example, the assets of an estate are usually managed as a separate account or trust. Similarly, a large pension fund may be so managed."[16] Small accounts or pension plans are placed in pooled funds, while large ones are separately managed and given special attention. In recent years pension funds have become the most important source of funds to be administered by trust companies.

The institutional arrangements with respect to exercising trust functions is quite different in the United States and Britain. "Canadian tradition [and legislation] is firmly opposed to a bank being in the trust or fiduciary business because of possible conflicts of interest." Trustees hold huge portfolios and "have enormous powers to choose what companies to invest in, how to vote their shares, and whether to help finance companies by loaning money or buying new [stock] issues."[17] If trust companies also did the banking for these same companies, it would give them even more economic power. In Britain and the United States however, the trustee function for pension plans is performed by banks and individual trustees.

To determine the concentration and centralization of trust company assets and the associated economic and social power within the unique structure of the Canadian financial system, it is necessary to ascertain the total assets under their control as distinct from corporate assets ("company funds"). While trust companies argue that the corpus of the trust is not theirs and that they have no proprietary interest in such assets, Baum concluded that

> this rationale complicates measuring the size and power of trust companies. . . . When the strength of a bank, life insurance company, or mutual fund is considered, the deposits on hand, the sum of the policies written, or the net asset value,

rather than capitalization, is the measure of institutional strength. . . . In view of this, discounting the importance of estate, trust and agency funds is improper, for they assume the same importance as bank deposits [or] insurance policies. The [ETA] funds give the corporate fiduciaries considerable investment powers.[18]

Total assets under the control of trust companies, therefore, are the relevant measure of their institutional strength and power.

In Canada the assets administered and managed by trust companies are highly concentrated and centralized among a few firms. The two largest trust companies account for nearly 50 per cent of total assets and the top five companies control nearly 80 per cent of the assets of all trust companies. This is reported in Table 8.12.

Trust companies administering corporate trustee arrangements for pension plans currently represent 22 per cent of the total assets of the private pension system (Table 8.8). Of particular importance to trust companies are their estate, trust and agency (ETA) accounts or funds, which include monies administered under individual and corporate custodial and trustee arrangements, including pension funds. Two trust companies account for 65 per cent of all ETAs, while the top five companies control nearly 85 per cent of total ETA account assets (Table 8.12).

Pension fund assets have become an increasingly important component of ETA accounts and the overall asset structure of trust companies. Table 8.13 indicates that for the four largest trust companies in Canada, pension fund assets represent on average nearly 60 per cent of total ETA accounts. More significantly, pension funds now represent nearly 50 per cent of the total assets controlled by major trust companies, and they are now vital to the economic survival of these major financial institutions.

Life Insurance Segregated Funds. Life insurance companies have historically been Canada's second largest financial institutions after the chartered banks, and they have exerted considerable influence on capital markets.[19] The life insurance industry is characterized by significant market concentration and is dominated by the five largest companies.

The centralization and concentration of pension fund assets evidenced by individual trusteed pension funds and the pension funds managed by trust companies are similarly exhibited by the insured pension plans and segregated funds administered by life insurance

TABLE 8.12

CONCENTRATION AND CENTRALIZATION OF TRUST COMPANY ASSETS, MAJOR COMPANIES ON AN UNCONSOLIDATED BASIS.[1]
BOOK VALUE, $MILLION, CANADA, 1982

COMPANY	COMPANY FUNDS	÷	GUARANTEED TRUST FUNDS	+	ESTATE, TRUST AND AGENCY FUNDS UNDER ADMINISTRATION[2]	=	TOTAL ASSETS CONTROLLED $	%
Royal Trustco	298,748		5,268,048		34,552,109		40,118,905	35.9
Canada Trustco	159,771		3,075,110		10,942,009		14,176,890	12.7
Montreal Trustco	42,564		974,997		11,629,481		12,647,042	11.3
National Trust	129,192		2,662,905		9,885,204		12,677,301	11.4
Canada Permanent	239,739		3,539,927		4,614,892		8,394,558	7.5
Total: 5 major companies:	870,014		15,520,987		71,623,695		88,014,696	78.8
Total: All federally chartered companies:[3]	1,426,617		24,783,918		85,477,599		111,688,134	100.0

Notes: 1 There is a significant difference in the reporting procedures used by the federal Superintendent of Insurance and the respective trust company annual reports. Trust company annual reports are on a consolidated balance sheet basis, whereas the data reported by the Superintendent of Insurance is on an unconsolidated basis and is only for the federal jurisdiction. The information reported by the Superintendent of Insurance is thus an understatement of an estimated 40 per cent of the actual assets under administration by trust companies. Furthermore, this results in a considerable distortion in terms of rank ordering by total assets. These problems become apparent with respect to Royal Trustco (federally chartered), Canada's largest trust company, which does not report the assets of its Quebec operation for Royal Trust (provincially chartered) in the Superintendent's report. The same situation exists in respect of Montreal Trustco, the third largest trust company. Canada Trustco and Canada Permanent, subsidiaries of their respective mortgage holding companies, are reported on an unconsolidated basis as well. In addition, the consolidated annual reports of the trust companies differ widely with respect to their accounting practices, definitions of ETAs, whether ETAs are or are not included in the balance sheet, and aggregate accounting categories which must often be "broken-out" for the purpose of analysis. Therefore, in the interest of accounting consistency and clarity the federal Superintendent of Insurance Report is used here, except for Royal Trust as reported in Table 8.13, despite the fact that it understates total assets under administration by federally chartered trust companies.

2 Estate, trust and agency (ETA) funds refer to those monies under administration by the trust company in its custodial or trustee capacity, including pension fund assets.

3 Thirty-two federally chartered companies and National Trust, which is provincially chartered in Ontario.

Sources: Calculated from the Report of the Superintendent of Insurance for Canada for the year-ended December 31, 1982 Trust and Loan Companies (Hull: Minister of Supply and Services, 1983), p. vi, 17B–23B, 25B–31B, 125B–31B, and 186B–91B.

TABLE 8.13

TRUST COMPANY PENSION ASSETS UNDER ADMINISTRATION IN RELATION TO COMPANY ASSET STRUCTURE.

BOOK VALUE, $MILLION, CANADA, 1982

COMPANY	PENSION FUND ASSETS UNDER ADMINISTRATION[1]	ESTATE, TRUST AND AGENCY FUNDS UNDER ADMINISTRATION[2]	TOTAL ASSETS CONTROLLED[3]	PENSION FUNDS AS A % OF	
				Estate, Trust and Agency Funds under Administration	Total Assets Controlled
Royal Trustco	19,681,513	34,552,109[4]	40,118,905[5]	56.9	49.1
Canada Trustco	6,731,370	10,942,009	14,176,890	61.2	47.5
Montreal Trustco	6,335,150	11,629,481	12,647,042	54.5	50.1
National Trust	6,100,000	9,885,204	12,677,301	61.7	48.1
Canada Permanent	556,000	4,614,892	8,394,558	12.1	6.6

Notes: 1 Assets for federally chartered companies only, except National Trust which is Ontario registered.

2 Estate, trust and agency funds under administration ordinarily include pension fund assets under administration, except for Royal Trustco, as noted in Table 8.12.

3 Company Funds plus guaranteed trust funds plus estate, trust and agency funds under administration (including pension assets), Table 8.12.

4 Royal Trustco reports pension assets and ETAs under administration separately. They have been aggregated here, including $19.7 billion in pension assets, in the interest of reporting consistency.

5 Including company funds plus guaranteed trust funds plus ETAs plus pension fund assets under administration, as cited in notes 2 and 3 above.

Sources: Calculated from the *Report of The Superintendent of Insurance for Canada for the year-ended December 31, 1982.* Trust and Loan Companies (Hull: Minister of Supply and Services, 1983), and Table 8.12. Pension fund assets under administration provided courtesy of the respective trust companies.

companies. Pension plans using this funding medium tend to be the smaller ones and in total account for only 14 per cent of all occupational pension plan members. As a result of competition from trusteed pension arrangements, the pension assets held by the life insurance industry in Canada declined from 46 to 20 per cent of the total between 1962 and 1985.[20]

Insurance companies offer four basic underwriting agencies for the purpose of occupational pension plans: the individual annuity contract, group annuity contracts, deposit administration and segregated funds. Segregated pension funds, that is, monies which are separated from the general fund of life insurance companies, were established after World War II in order to circumvent the statutory restrictions placed on insurance company equity investment in order to make them competitive with trust companies for pension business. They are now the largest funding medium sponsored by life insurance companies with respect to occupational pension plans and account for one-third of all insured pension plan members.[21]

Table 8.14 indicates the concentration and centralization of life insurance company segregated (pension) fund assets. The four largest funds account for nearly 60 per cent of all segregated fund assets, and the top ten funds held nearly 90 per cent of the total.

The information presented here indicates that the private pension system and the component parts of the private pension industry in Canada—individual trusteed pension funds, trust companies (corporate trustees) and life insurance company segregated funds— are characterized by a significant concentration and centralization of pension capital among a few large pension funds and dominant financial institutions. The structure and economic power of the private pension system, as an organic component of the finance sector, is reinforced by and a reflection of the more general propensity towards the centralization and concentration of financial capital.

CONCENTRATION AND CENTRALIZATION OF PENSION AND FINANCIAL CAPITAL

The accelerated tendency towards the concentration and centralization of pension fund capital under the control of dominant financial institutions parallels and corresponds to similar tendencies within the broader industrial and finance sectors of a capitalist

TABLE 8.14

CONCENTRATION AND CENTRALIZATION OF LIFE INSURANCE COMPANY
SEGREGATED (PENSION) FUNDS,
MARKET VALUE, $MILLION, CANADA, 1982

COMPANY	ASSETS OF SEGREGATED (PENSION) FUNDS[1]	% OF TOTAL FUNDS
Sun Life	$1,342,707	18.2
Confederation Life	1,082,199	14.7
Great-West Life	961,050	13.0
Canada Life	779,347	10.6
Manufacturers Life	627,604	8.5
Mutual Life	494,794	6.7
Imperial Life	462,757	6.3
North American Life	346,794	4.7
Excelsior Life	309,936	4.2
Assur.-Vie Desjardins	205,647	2.8
Total: Top 10 Companies	6,612,835	89.7
Total: All Segregated Funds[2]	7,372,538	100.0

Notes: 1 Assets held in Canada.
2 Fifty-seven companies.

Source: Retabulated and calculated from the *Report of the Superintendent of Insurance for Canada, Abstract of Statements of Life Insurance Companies and Fraternal Benefit Societies* (Hull: Minister of Supply and Services, 1983), Table XVI, p. 70 E.

economy (Table 8.15). What is significant is that the distribution of pension fund capital in Canada corresponds to the centralization and concentration of financial capital in general. Within each financial sector the five largest institutions control the mammoth proportion of assets. Each major financial institution, with the notable exception of individually trusteed pension funds, sponsors a funding agency or medium for the administration and management of pension fund assets. For example, while the five largest trust companies control nearly 80 per cent of total assets within that financial sector, they also account for approximately 75 per cent of pension assets under administration, including those managed as corporate trustees. Similarly, the top five insurance companies control nearly 50 per cent of the total assets of the life insurance industry, and their segregated funds account for 65 per cent of the total.

A similar situation prevails in the United States and Britain. In the U.K., for example, merchant banks control two-thirds of contractual savings, such as pension savings, and about twenty nationally based institutions in turn control 70 per cent of this amount.[22] Spe-

TABLE 8.15

SUMMARY TABLE OF CONCENTRATION AND CENTRALIZATION OF
FINANCE SECTOR ASSETS, BY MAJOR FINANCIAL INTERMEDIARY,
CANADA, 1980–1982

FINANCIAL SECTOR AND INSTITUTION	NO. OF TOP RANKING INSTITUTIONS/FUNDS	PERCENTAGE OF TOTAL ASSETS CONTROLLED WITHIN EACH FINANCIAL SECTOR OR BY FUNDING AGENCY
Chartered Banks	5	91
Trust Companies[1]	5	79
Life Insurance Companies[2]	5	48
Pension Funds		
Individual Trustees[3]	10	24
Assets under Administration[4]	5	74
Segregated Funds	5	65

Notes: 1 Including pension assets under administration.
   2 Including segregated funds.
   3 Internally managed pension funds.
   4 Including assets of corporate trustees.

Sources: Calculated from Walter Stewart, *Towers of Gold — Feet of Clay: The Canadian Banks* (Toronto: Totem Books, 1982), Appendix I, Table 1, p. 270; Report of the Superintendent of Insurance for Canada, *Abstract of Statements for Life Insurance and Fraternal Benefit Societies for the year-ended December 31, 1982* (Hull: Minister of Supply and Services, 1983); *Report of the Superintendent of Insurance for Canada for the year-ended December 31, 1982*. Trust and Loan Companies (Hull: Minister of Supply and Services, 1983), and Tables 8.6, 8.10, 8.12, 8.13 and 8.14.

cifically, ten banks and two brokers each control pension assets worth £500 million or more.[23]

These trends have a number of implications. First, because the distribution of pension fund assets by funding agency mirrors the more general tendency towards the centralization and concentration of financial capital and, in turn, corresponds to the organization of the finance sector, pension capital should be viewed as being an integral part of financial capital under conditions of advanced capitalism. Consequently, pension capital and the private pension industry are subordinated to and under the strategic control of related dominant financial institutions. Second, the absolute and relative growth of pension funds assets in the postwar period has increased the concentration of capital and economic power vested in the finance sector, which has clear implications with respect to economic policy. Third, the growth of pension fund assets poses the fundamental issue of ownership of and control over pension capital.

THE CONTROL AND INVESTMENT OF PENSION CAPITAL

Pension funds are the "registered" owners of the assets held on behalf of "beneficial" owners, that is, pension plan members. As such, pension fund trustees have no proprietary interest in the assets of the plan, but rather are responsible for its administration and the "prudent" investment of the fund. In Canada trusteed pension funds are administered by corporate or individual trustees. Traditionally, the trustee assumed all the fiduciary responsibilities, including investment; that is, the trustee was responsible for both the daily administration of the pension plan *and* the investment management of the fund. In recent years, however, these arrangements have undergone a significant change. Many pension plan sponsors, usually to maximize the return on investment and yet to ensure the security of funds, have separated plan administration from fund management.

The fundamental distinction between plan administration and investment management explains why the locus of *control* over pension fund capital generally resides with dominant financial institutions, regardless of the formal ownership of assets, and reinforces the concentration and centralization of capital within the finance sector. The investment management of pension fund assets by major financial institutions further suggests that while the private pension industry is an integral part of the finance sector, it is subordinated to the general interests of financial capital. That is, pension capital is under the broad strategic control of dominant financial institutions and their investment maximization behaviour.

The ultimate criterion with respect to determining whether pension funds exercise ownership or control over the assets held by them turns on who is responsible for the investment of the funds. Individual and corporate trustees may be responsible for both the daily administration of the pension plan *and* the investment management of the fund. Alternatively, trustees may be responsible for the administration of the plan but may choose to delegate, that is, subcontract, the investment management of the pension fund to an outside agency or another financial institution. In the case of individual trusteed pension plans, as a result of their large size and concentration of assets (Table 8.9), plan administration and fund management are both usually retained in-house by the plan sponsor. Increasingly in the case of corporate trustees, however, the trust company is retained by the plan sponsor to act solely in a custodial capacity, that is, to carry out plan administration, while the fiduciary responsibility for the investment of the pension fund is delegated to one or more financial institutions or independent investment managers.

The classification of pension funds by type of funding arrangements therefore does not necessarily indicate where or how the fund is managed in terms of investment decision-making, that is, the institutional focus of control over pension capital. While some employers retain investment managers on staff—that is, in-house—others use the services of external investment counsellors or various other financial institutions to direct the investment of the pension fund. It is therefore necessary to determine and identify the locus of control over pension fund investment management by type of institution and the extent of decision-making which resides with those institutions with respect to investment policy. In the final analysis it is the investment management of pension fund assets which is the crucial determinant with respect to exercising economic power.

Table 8.16 indicates that in Canada, Britain and the U.S. two-thirds of total pension assets are managed externally and one-third internally. The two-thirds externally managed are controlled by dominant financial institutions such as banks, trust companies, life insurance companies, and to a lesser extent investment counsellors. The other third are those of the large individual trusteed pension plans and are usually managed in-house.

The distribution of externally managed pension fund assets by type of investment manager is reported in Table 8.17. Control over pension assets primarily resides with trust companies in Canada and the merchant banks in Britain and to a lesser extent with life insurance companies and investment counsellors. In the case of Canada nearly 60 per cent of externally managed pension fund assets are controlled by ten money managers, including the four top trust companies, three major life insurance companies, and two independent fund managers.[24] In the United States, bank trust departments in conjunction with life insurance companies control 72 per cent of externally managed pension fund assets. The merchant banks in Britain are responsible for the investment management of nearly 50 per cent of externally managed pension funds.

TABLE 8.16

CONTROL OF PENSION ASSETS BY TYPE OF FUND MANAGEMENT,
U.K., U.S. AND CANADA, 1975–1980

| COUNTRY | PERCENTAGE DISTRIBUTION OF ASSETS BY TYPE OF FUND MANAGEMENT | |
	Internally Managed	Externally Managed[1]
U.K.[2]	33	67
U.S.[3]	33	67
Canada[4]	33	67

Note: 1 Distributed among different types of investment managers including trust companies, life insurance companies, investment counsellors, and banks in the U.K. and U.S. Figures rounded.
      2 1975.
      3 1983.
      4 1980. The data for Canada is not totally comparable with the U.K. and the U.S. as a result of incomplete information. In the case of Canada the figures cited represent the internally managed assets of the top 20 funds, rather than as a proportion of all funds, as in the U.S. and U.K.

Sources: For the U.K., Richard Minns, *Pension Funds and British Capitalism* (London: Heinemann, 1980), p. 41; for the U.S., calculated from "The Top 1000 Funds," *Pensions & Investment Age*, Special Profiles Issue, 23 January 1984, p. 32, and for Canada, Table 8.6.

TABLE 8.17

PERCENTAGE DISTRIBUTION OF EXTERNALLY MANAGED
PENSION FUND ASSETS BY TYPE OF INVESTMENT MANAGER,
U.S., U.K. AND CANADA, 1978–1983

TYPE OF INVESTMENT MANAGER	U.S.[1]	U.K.[2]	CANADA[3]
Banks	36.0	49.2	—
Trust Companies	—	—	38.6
Insurance Companies	36.0	33.3	28.8
Investment Counsellors	28.0	15.5	32.6
Other	—	2.0	—
Total	100.0	100.0	100.0

Notes: 1 1983.
      2 1978.
      3 1981.

Sources: For the U.S., *Pensions & Investment Age*, 31 October 1983, graph, p. 47. Canadian data from the "Directory of Pension Fund Investment Services: Top 40 Money Managers," *Benefits Canada* 5 (November/December 1981), p. 24. For Britain, retabulated and calculated from Richard Minns, *Pension Funds and British Capitalism* (London: Heinemann, 1980), Table 1.3, p. 31. Minns in his survey excludes insurance companies which are included here. The distribution of assets has been recalculated for the U.K.

While banking institutions and life insurance companies manage and control nearly three-quarters of total pension assets on average in the U.K., Canada and the U.S., the distribution or "re-sectoring" of pension capital between major financial institutions has undergone considerable change in recent years. In the United States, for example, bank trust department control declined from 75 to 36 per cent of externally managed pension fund assets between the late 1950s and 1981.[25] The share of the market controlled by life insurance companies and independent fund managers has correspondingly increased. A similar pattern has emerged in Canada where there has been a diminution of pension assets under the control of life insurers and an increase in the proportion managed by trust companies and investment counsellors. This "re-sectoring" has resulted in polycentric spheres of control over pension capital and monopolistic competition within the finance sector.

The major financial institutions which manage and control pension fund assets have considerable discretion with regard to investment policy, subject to law and practice. The pension trust agreement establishes the latitude or discretion with which the plan sponsor allows the trustee to carry out investment policy. In most cases plan sponsors

> give the trustee complete discretion in the investment of the fund, while others specify the classes of investment to be purchased and permit the trustee to select specific assets to be bought and sold within the prescribed classes. In extreme cases the trust agreement may stipulate that the trustee shall buy and sell only those investments selected by the employer.[26]

In short, a pension plan sponsor may allow the fund manager "full discretion" or put the manager "under direction." In the United States and Canada 75 to 80 per cent of all pension assets are at the "full discretion" of the investment manager. Pension fund managers in the U.K. have similar latitude.[27]

Thus, pension fund investment managers have significant discretion or control over the funds they manage and how they are invested, which means that the investment of pension funds depends to a considerable extent on the policies and vested interests of the major financial institutions. Obviously there are clear implications with respect to control over saving, direction of investment, economic growth and ownership of corporate securities.

The concentration, centralization and control over pension capital by major financial institutions and the discretion vested with investment managers have resulted in a corresponding tendency with respect to the control over corporate shares, that is, the common stock or equity of companies managed by these same financial institutions through pension funds (Table 7.2). Minns and Coakley's research indicates that in Britain there is a substantial divergence between the ownership and control of company shares by financial institutions. Table 8.18 contrasts the proportion of corporate shares owned and controlled by different sectors. The most significant difference between ownership and control is evidenced by banks. Banks owned less than 1 per cent of all shares, but controlled nearly 18 per cent of corporate equity. Banks, insurance companies and stockbrokers together owned 17 per cent of corporate equity, but in fact controlled 41 per cent of company shares. In Britain, merchant banks were the large institutional controllers, while pension funds were the largest institutional owners. Significantly, while pension funds owned nearly 17 per cent of company shares, in fact, they controlled only 6 per cent as a result of delegating investment management to financial institutions.[28] Coakley and Harris's work generally confirms these trends for 1980.

TABLE 8.18

OWNERSHIP AND CONTROL OF COMPANY SHARES,
U.K., 1975

SECTOR	PERCENTAGE	
	Ownership	Control
Persons	37.5	29.9
Banks	0.7	17.6
Insurance Companies	15.9	17.1
Investment and Unit Trusts	14.1	11.1
Stockbrokers	0.4	6.3
Pension Funds	16.8	5.6
Overseas Sector	5.6	5.6
Public Sector	3.6	3.6
Industrial and Commercial Cos.	3.0	3.0
Non-Profit Organizations	2.3	0.2

Source: Retabulated from Richard Minns, Pension Funds and British Capitalism (London: Heinemann, 1980), Table 1.8, p. 41.

Studies of this important subject do not exist for Canada or the United States; however, similar conclusions can be inferred. In the United States, for example, in the late 1950s only 14 per cent of pension funds held 80 per cent of pension fund equity investment.[29] More recent data indicate that the top ten pension fund money managers in the U.S. in 1982 controlled 45 per cent of fund shares and the top twenty fund managers controlled 76 per cent of total pension fund equity investment.[30] Those money managers include such major financial institutions as J. P. Morgan & Co. Inc., Bankers Trust N.Y. Corp., Mellon National Corp., Prudential Insurance Co., Chemical New York Corp., and Manufacturers Hanover Co.

In conclusion, while pension funds are the formal, or registered, owners of corporate shares, control over these shares, and control over pension capital more generally, resides with and is located in dominant financial institutions as a result of the delegation of investment management to those financial intermediaries. This analysis of the institutional framework surrounding the private pension system suggests that the growth, concentration and centralization of pension capital under the control of financial institutions has resulted in a "large gain in economic power for the financial community"[31] in the postwar period.

THE STRUCTURE OF PENSION FUND POWER: IMPLICATIONS

Pension funds are now one of the largest pools of capital in advanced capitalist economies. Consequently, the private pension system has assumed a strategic position with respect to capital markets and the finance and industrial sectors. This has important public policy and political implications.

A number of broad thematic implications can be drawn with respect to the structure of pension fund power. First, there is a tremendous concentration of private economic power and decision-making vested in the private pension system as a result of the control over and investment of the expanding pool of pension capital. Second, pension capital under contemporary capitalism is organically related to financial capital, and it is a growth centre within the finance sector. The concentration and centralization of pension and financial capital mutually reinforce one another, thereby strengthening the institutional power of the finance sector and the private pension industry, and, in turn, the private sector's control over and direction of pension capital. Third, the role played by the private pension system in terms of organizing and channelling the increasing flow of pension saving and investment places the private pension industry in a pivotal position with respect to the finance sector, capital markets, industrial corporations, and the economy.

Fourth, the concentration and centralization of pension capital under the control of dominant financial institutions result in their having an important vested interest in the continued existence of the private pension system and industry. Within the framework of a capitalist economy, pension capital, as an organic part of financial capital, concurrently serves the specific interests of the financial institutions controlling it and the general interests of the corporate sector and economy with respect to investment and capital accumulation. Fifth, it may be anticipated that as a result of the strategic role played by the private pension system in capitalist economies and the vested interest of the pension industry and financial institutions that they will be the primary political obstacles to the reform of the public and private pension systems over the long term. Sixth, the limitations and inadequacies of occupational pension plans are ultimately based on the institutional strength and economic power of the private pension system, which explains the underdevelopment of the public pension system and the continued impoverishment of the elderly.

The continued existence of the private pension system in the final analysis is related to the systemic imperatives of dominant financial and industrial corporations. Under conditions of modern capitalism the pension system's investment function, intrinsic to its operation and the institutional structure of power, however, has become a mechanism promoting the integration of the finance and industrial sectors into a unified nexus of corporate power.

9

The Pension System
and
Corporate Power

*The [financial] system transforms itself into an
immense social mechanism for the centralization of
capitals.*

Karl Marx

It has been established that the formal structure of pension fund
power is the institutional expression of the concentration and centralization of pension fund capital underlying the operation of the
private pension system. Pension capital is organically related to
financial capital and the organization of the broader finance sector.
The focus of this chapter is the way in which the pension system's
investment function has increasingly facilitated the interpenetration, that is, the integration or fusion of industrial and financial
capital under advanced capitalism. The pension system is linked to
the finance and industrial sectors through a complex series of formal and informal arrangements resulting in a unified nexus of corporate power.

Several related topics are examined. First, the formal linkages
between the private pension system and the broader finance and
industrial sectors are identified and traced in detail through interlocking corporate directorships and direct equity investment resulting in an integrated and interdependent structure of corporate
power, with particular reference to the configuration of control in
Canada. Second, the various ways in which the pension system's

261

investment function acts as an integrative mechanism promoting the fusion of industrial and financial capital are delineated. Pension fund investment through the capital market in the industrial sector is one mechanism by which the consolidation of financial and industrial capital is facilitated and accelerated, with a corresponding series of formal and informal intra- and intersectoral linkages, resulting in a greater concentration and centralization of economic power in the corporate sector.

Third, as a result of this interpenetration, pension funds are changing their traditional role as passive investors and are becoming increasingly more assertive with respect to directly intervening in corporate affairs to protect and maximize their investment. There is a maturing systemic integration and functional convergence between the finance and industrial sectors which has implications with respect to the locus of control over the industrial sector and possible alternative economic strategies. Fourth, a series of mutually reinforcing mechanisms which maintains private sector control over pension capital and the operation of the private pension system is identified and examined. The political behaviour of financial institutions, formal and informal linkages between the corporate, political and bureaucratic elites, and the dominant market ideology all serve to complement the formal economic structure of pension fund power and effectively incorporate it into the broader network of corporate power under advanced capitalism.

THEORETICAL BACKGROUND

To establish the importance of the pension system's investment function as a mechanism which promotes the interdependence of the finance and industrial sectors under advanced capitalism requires conceptual clarity and consistency because many of the terms commonly associated with this relationship have been misinterpreted and obscure the underlying process. The lack of consistency with respect to terminology has often resulted in analytic confusion.

"Finance capital" is the term often used in the Marxist literature to describe the close interrelationship between financial and industrial capital.[1] The term has its origin in the work of Hilferding (1910)[2] and forms the basis of Lenin's analysis (1917) of finance capital and imperialism.[3] Hilferding's formulation specified that "bank capital, i.e., capital in money form, which is actually transformed into

industrial capital . . . [is] 'finance capital.' Finance capital is controlled by banks and employed by industrialists."[4] Building on this
approach, Lenin subsequently argued that a "handful of monopo-
lists subordinate to their will all the operations, both commercial
and industrial," resulting in "the ever growing merger, or . . . coalescence, of bank and industrial capital." Lenin referred to "finance
capital" as "the merging or coalescence of banks with industry
such is . . . finance capital and such is the content of this term." In
this regard Lenin noted that there is a "close connection between
the banks and industry" so that a "union . . . is established between
the banks and the largest industrial and commercial enterprises,
the merging of one with another through the acquisition of shares,
through the appointment of bank directors to . . . [Boards of Direc-
tors] of industrial and commercial enterprises, and vice versa."[5]
Hilferding and Lenin therefore viewed finance capital as the integration or interpenetration, that is, the amalgamation of financial *and*
industrial capital as a result of interlocking directorships *and* direct
equity investment between sectors of the economy. As used here,
"finance capital," by definition, then, is the fusion of financial and
industrial capital.

In recent years, however, some vulgar analyses have confused
this concept of finance capital.[6] The term "finance capital" has been
mechanically equated with "financial oligarchy" by some so that
financial institutions effectively dominate the industrial sector.
This conceptualization lends itself to a conspiracy theory. More
importantly, it is contrary to Hilferding's and Lenin's formulation of
the subject, which clearly stresses that finance capital as the fusion
of financial and industrial capital is a symbiotic, rather than a para-
sitic, process because "only industrial capital . . . contains productive capital, and this creates value and surplus value in which
banking and commercial capital share." Consequently, while banking capital may dominate, "it is at the same time dependent on
industrial capital."[7] Whether financial or industrial capital dominates at a particular time is clearly both historically specific and
related to the economic development of each national capitalist
economy.

Further confusion has resulted because while they rely conceptually on the Hilferding-Lenin formulation, some have used different
terms to describe it. Mandel, for example, characterized "monopoly
capitalism" as that phase where "banking capital increasingly
merges with industrial capital into finance capital" so that "a few

very large financial groups dominate the economy of each capitalist country."[8] Similarly, Aaronovitch has argued that the "fusion of banking and industrial capital means that the spheres . . . have become increasingly integrated . . . by way of . . . coalitions and . . . partly by way of financial organizations entering industry and industrial firms becoming financiers."[9] Aaronovitch makes the interesting and useful analytic distinction between "fusion" as direct equity investment, that is, shareholdings between the finance and industrial sectors, and "linkages" as interlocking directorates. Baran and Sweezy, however, use the term "monopoly capital" to refer to industrial capital's relative "autonomy" or "independence" in relation to the finance sector as a result of the high level of internal funding experienced by corporations.

The position adopted here is that the combination, or consolidation, of financial, industrial and commercial capital is "finance capital." Following Aaronovitch, an analytical distinction is made between fusion as equity investment, that is, shareholdings between the finance and industrial sectors, and linkages, which represent interlocking directorships. Therefore, the nexus of corporate power, incorporating the private pension system, under conditions of advanced capitalism is the fusion of financial institutions and industry "expressed in the system of effective possession, the mode of investment funding, and . . . an extensive network of communication."[10] This formulation captures both the formal and informal elements of corporate power.

PENSION FUNDS AND THE INTERPENETRATION OF CAPITAL

The fusion of financial and industrial capital results in a complex interlocking network and concentration of corporate power and influence in advanced capitalist economies. The main patterns are traced in the case of Canada through direct and indirect interlocking directorships, holding company arrangements and direct portfolio (equity) investment between financial institutions and industrial corporations. What emerges is a pattern of intercorporate ownership, cross-directorships, and intersectoral investment reinforced by a series of common social relations, shared ideology, and formal and informal linkages and mobility between the business, political and bureaucratic elites. This is the nexus of corporate power. And power, as one commentator observed, is what counts . . . power means the ability to get your own way, to shape events.

The pivotal people, [are] the power brokers who carry the proxies for the great law firms and financial institutions. . . . The next group in this category would probably be the invisible men who manage the country's private pension plans.[11]

A complex constellation of power and control is associated with the private pension system. Pension capital, under the domination of financial institutions, is an organic part of financial capital, and it is increasingly integrated with the industrial sector.

Canadian capitalism is characterized by a bifurcated model of economic development. Financial capital historically was and still remains the indigenous bastion of Canadian capitalism. As early as 1911 the Webbs observed the "remarkable development of banking" in Canada.[12] Since the 1920s, however, the industrial sector has been dominated by American transnational corporations, resulting in an externally controlled "branch plant" economy. Only recently has the finance sector become interested in promoting domestic industrial activity.

Historically, there has been a close working relationship between dominant financial institutions within the finance sector in Canada. Of particular importance is the close traditional relationship between banks and trust companies: Royal Trust and the Bank of Montreal, Montreal Trust (now Montreal Trustco) and the Royal Bank, and National Trust and the Canadian Bank of Commerce (now the Canadian Imperial Bank of Commerce). Until recently these linkages were characterized by an extremely high density of formal interlocking directorships.[13] Similarly, in the past there has been a close relationship between life insurance companies, banks and trust companies.

There has been as well a close interrelationship between the finance and industrial sectors in Canada. Numerous studies have demonstrated the central role played by major banks and insurance companies in the concentration of economic power.[14] Porter, for example, shows that directors of the top banks held nearly a quarter of the top industrial directorships and that over half of the top banking directorships were held by directors of major industrial corporations. Insurance company directors held nearly 15 per cent of top industrial directorships, while over half of insurance company directorships were held by industrial directors and almost half by bank directors. Dominant industrial directors held nearly 60 per cent of bank directorships and the same proportion in insurance companies.[14]

The interconnections between the Royal Bank, the Bank of Montreal and the Canadian Imperial Bank of Commerce and the industrial sector are of particular importance. These three banks held two-thirds of all directorships of dominant manufacturing corporations and 60 per cent of Canadian insurance companies in the late 1950s. Life insurance companies, in particular Sun Life, Mutual Life and Confederation Life, represented nearly 60 per cent of directorships in leading industrial corporations held by insurance companies. The largest of these interpenetrating networks, representing the major actors in the finance and industrial sectors, was the group consisting of the Bank of Montreal, Royal Trust, Sun Life, the CPR, and the Steel Company of Canada.[15]

Historically, "the development from personal to impersonal possession is associated with an integration and interdependence between the finance and industrial sectors of the economy." The development from entrepreneurial to finance capital in Britain, Canada and the U.S., however, has occurred at different rates and followed separate routes.[16] What is of significance and interest in recent years in these advanced capitalist economies is the reorganization and rationalization of the finance sector and a change in the modality of interpenetration between financial institutions. As a starting point it is therefore necessary to place those institutions responsible for the control and investment of pension funds within the context of the broader finance sector.

Reorganization and Rationalization of Financial Capital. The finance sector in Canada is in the process of fluid and dynamic change. These changes are taking three forms. First, the finance sector has been undergoing a major reorganization since at least 1980. Specifically, the hard core of formal interlocking directorships between financial institutions has been removed so that traditional relationships are not as close as in the past. Second, the connection between financial institutions is increasingly mediated through holding companies based on the fusion of capital, that is, direct equity participation, rather than through interlocking directorships, resulting in vertical integration within the finance sector and horizontal linkages to the industrial sector. Third, recent years have witnessed the increased integration of financial services, that is, the creation of financial conglomerates or "supermarkets," including pension arrangements. This change will further increase the concentration and centralization of economic power within the finance sector, as well as accelerate the interpenetration and interdependence between the finance and industrial sectors.

Economic power is concentrated among a few dominant institutions within the finance sector (Table 8.4). These same financial intermediaries control the investment of the rapidly growing pool of pension capital (Tables 8.1 and 8.2). This control is secured through formal and informal connections between dominant financial institutions and a series of social relations within the finance sector.

"Within the finance sector," according to Clement, "the banks and insurance companies, along with the trust and mortgage companies . . . have the most extensive interlocks."[17] One of the most important relationships has been between banks and trust companies. Trust companies are the major corporate trustee for pension funds and hold 22 per cent of total pension fund assets. According to the Royal Commission on Banking and Finance, "each of the banks has a close relationship with at least one trust company, some of them loose working relations of long standing and others ownership affiliations."[18] In the past some dominant banks have been major partners in trust companies, having both an equity position and interlocking directorships. Thus, while banks do not have fiduciary powers, according to Neufeld, "they put themselves into a position where they would . . . have an incentive to provide assistance in trust matters to customers by directing [them] to particular trust companies."[19] According to one official government study, "one-half to three-quarters of the trust business of larger corporations went to bank-affiliated trust companies."[20] In this regard, McNulty concluded with respect to the United States that "it does appear that prior connections which the funding agency may have with the client . . . often provide the push which turns . . . pension business to a particular funding agency."[21] The traditional close relationship between banks and trust companies in Canada effectively tightens the control which dominant financial institutions have over pension capital.

Similarly, there have been close ties between banks and insurance companies and, in turn, insurance companies and trust companies. Insurance company segregated funds are the third largest funding medium for pension funds, representing nearly 20 per cent of total pension assets. Granger's study found that in 1979 sixty-three directors of the five largest banks sat on the board of the sixteen largest life insurance companies. For example, Sun Life, the largest insurance company in Canada, had thirteen of its twenty directors sitting on bank boards: four at the Royal Bank, the largest and most influential bank, and three directors on the board of Royal Trust, the major trust company. At that time Sun Life also held large blocks of stock in two major banks. To complete the circuit, eighteen insurance companies had seventy interlocks with twenty trust companies.[22]

Banks also have working relationships with large investment dealers and brokerage firms which trade securities on behalf of and undertake private placements to institutional investors such as pension funds. According to Newman, the Royal Bank in the mid-1970s was closely associated with Wood Gundy, the most powerful investment firm in the country; Dominion Securities reportedly had a link with the Canadian Imperial Bank of Commerce (CIBC), the second largest bank; and A. E. Ames and Co. did most of the floor trading for the Bank of Montreal, the third largest.[23] Since that time, however, there has been a considerable "shakeout" in the securities industry with Dominion Securities merging with Ames and subsequently with Pitfield, MacKay and Ross. Legislative changes in recent years have dramatically altered the relationship between banks and brokerage firms, with most major banks now directly owning an investment dealer. More speculatively, since there are no studies on the subject, the close traditional relationship between banks and trust companies suggests that trust companies, as corporate trustees for pension funds, may direct their trading activity to bank-associated brokerage firms.

Formal interlocking directorships have been the traditional mechanism within the Canadian finance sector to centralize and concentrate economic power, including pension capital, among major financial institutions. They have served as a means to coordinate business activity and to collect and disseminate information. However, over the past twenty years, as a matter of public policy, an attempt has been made to promote "intermodal competition" between financial institutions in Canada.

A number of important legislative changes have been introduced which have substantively altered the character and density of interlocks within the finance sector. Specifically, the Bank Act 1967 forbade formal interlocking directorships between banks and trust companies; concurrently, banks were forced to reduce their equity holdings in trust companies to no more than 10 per cent of out-standing voting stock. In addition, Canadian insurance law was amended to prohibit life insurers from directly owning trust com-panies, mutual funds and investment companies. The use of hold-ing company arrangements, however, allows them to expand into these fields. Significantly, the current legislation still permits inter-locks between banks and insurance companies and between trust companies and life insurers. Furthermore, the legislation allows equity investment of up to 10 per cent of outstanding shares between financial institutions: banks and trust companies in one another, and life insurance and trust companies in banks. Virtually all life insurance companies in Canada are mutualized and do not have outstanding shares. Thus, while formal interlocks between certain financial institutions are now prohibited, direct equity par-ticipation remains.

"Legislative enactment," however, "may not be able to achieve the desired separation" between financial institutions because "banks have too great an interest in trust company operations."[24] The indirect interlock, or the "friend of a friend," for example, is a means to circumvent the Bank Act restriction on bank trust com-pany interlocks. A case in point is when Power Corporation subsidi-ary Laurentide Financial Corporation Ltd. merged with the Provincial Bank in 1979. Paul Desmarais, Chairman and CEO of Power Corporation, and several other of the company's directors were on the board of Montreal Trust Company (now Montreal Trustco), which was 50 per cent owned by Power Corporation. When they had to resign from the newly merged organization, Mr. Desma-rais was quoted as saying, "Maybe we'll ask someone already on the board to look after our interests . . . or we could have someone repre-sent us who wasn't directly related to Power."[25]

There are indications that the character of linkages and fusion within the finance sector in Canada has undergone a fundamental transformation within recent years. The earlier studies of the sub-ject quite correctly emphasized formal interlocking directorships as the co-ordinating mechanism facilitating the centralization and concentration of financial capital. It would appear, however, that direct equity investment and holding company arrangements have increasingly supplanted interlocking directorships as the means of centralizing and concentrating financial capital. Stewart, for ex-ample, reported that major banks had six linkages to the top five life insurance companies in 1980.[26] By 1983, however, an analysis of annual reports indicates that dominant banks had only three links to two of the top life insurers. Similarly, there were only two insurance company interlocks among the top five trust companies.[27] Bank-trust company interlocks are now prohibited by law.

Correspondingly, there has been an increasing reliance upon direct equity investment and holding company arrangements to promote the interpenetration and amalgamation of financial capital in Canada. The shareholdings between major financial institutions, specifically life and trust company investment in banks, is reported in Table 9.1. Table 9.2 outlines significant ownership of trust company shares by life insurance companies and holding companies. In this regard it should be noted that while the Ontario Securities Act designates a shareholding of 20 per cent or more as a "control block" and 10 per cent as an "insider" or "significant" shareholder position, the Bank Act 1980 implicitly deems holdings of one-half of 1 per cent to constitute a significant shareholder position.[28] Trust and life insurance companies as administrators and investment managers for pension funds therefore have an important equity position in the banking sector, further integrating the capital under the control of financial institutions. Moreover, a recent amendment to the Bank Act accelerates the comingling of financial capital by permitting the occupational pension plans of banks to buy shares of other banks. Trust company shares held by other financial institutions similarly integrate financial capital (Table 9.2).

Another significant and emerging trend accelerating the concentration of financial capital is the creation of financial conglomerates or "financial supermarkets"; that is, the creation of formally integrated and rationalized financial services, including credit cards, consumer loans, mortgages, investment services, insurance, annuities and pensions, based on the elimination of traditional barriers between financial institutions. This trend is now clearly evidenced in Britain, Canada and the U.S. In the United States for example, stock brokers such as Merrill Lynch, Bache and Dean Witter are now involved in non-securities businesses such as insurance brokerage. The subsequent purchase of Bache by Prudential Life, American Express Company's merger with Shearson and the expansion of retailers such as Sears Roebuck and J. C. Penney into financial service companies are transforming the character and organization of the finance sector. Similarly, in Canada there has been a "dramatic change in the role of financial institutions," and many "banks, life insurance, and trust companies have become

TABLE 9.1

SHAREHOLDINGS BETWEEN MAJOR FINANCIAL INSTITUTIONS, CANADA, 1983

% OF TOTAL OUTSTANDING SHARES HELD BY

BANKS[1]	LIFE INSURANCE COMPANIES[1]					TRUST COMPANIES[1]					OTHER	
	(1) Sun Life	(2) Manu-facturers Life	(3) Great West	(4) London Life	(5) Canada Life	(1) Royal Trustco	(2) Canada Trustco	(3) Montreal Trustco	(4) Canada Permanent	(5) National Trust	Investors Group	Caisse de Dépot
(1) Royal Bank	1.5	—	—	—	—	—	—	—	—	0.8	—	6.4
(2) Canadian Imperial Bank of Commerce	0.7	—	0.7	—	0.8	1.2	—	—	—	1.6	2.2	4.9
(3) Bank of Montreal	1.3	—	0.5	—	—	2.4	—	—	—	2.3	—	6.5
(4) Bank of Nova Scotia	1.6	—	—	—	—	3.2	—	—	—	2.3	—	6.5
(5) Toronto Dominion	1.2	—	0.6	—	—	—	—	—	—	2.3	—	4.1

Note: 1 Numbers in brackets refer to sectoral ranking based on assets.

Source: Calculated from the "Return of Shareholder Listing" filed with the Inspector-General of Banks, Department of Finance, as of 31 October 1983.

TABLE 9.2

SIGNIFICANT SHARE OWNERSHIP OF TRUST COMPANIES BY FINANCIAL INSTITUTIONS, CANADA, 1983

TRUST COMPANY[1]	MAJOR SHAREHOLDER	CORPORATE AFFILIATION
Royal Trustco	47% Trilon Financial Corp. (holding company)	To Edper Investments (Bronfman family trust) through Brascan
Canada Trustco	23% Manufacturers Life	To Canada Trust Mortgage Company
Montreal Trustco	40% Investors Group; 10% Power Financial	To Power Corporation
Canada Permanent	100% Canada Permanent Mortgage Company	—
National Trust	Widely held	—

Note: 1 Ranked by assets.

Sources: *Financial Post 500* (June 1983); Lawrence Welsh, "Trilon Plans to Intensify Financial Services," *Financial Post*, 12 November 1983. Sonita Horvitch, "Canada Trustco Stays Out of Financial Furor," *Financial Post*, 24 December 1983, and Robert Giddens, "Power Corp. Studying Switch into an Operating Company," *Globe and Mail*, 4 May 1984.

financial conglomerates."[29] The ruling of the Ontario Securities Commission allowing banks to act as stockbrokers (1983), the passage of Bill 75 by the Quebec National Assembly to promote "financial supermarkets" (June 1983), the merger of Dominion Securities-Ames-Pitfield MacKay Ross (1983–1984), the merger of National Trust and Victoria and Grey into the third largest trust company (July 1984), Brascan's creation of a new financial group in addition to Trilon (August 1984), Manulife's acquisition of Dominion Life (early 1985), the merger between Canada Trustco and Canada Permanent (1985) and the acquisition of brokerage firms by banks as a result of amendments to the federal Bank Act (Bill C-56) in 1987 are all indications of the accelerating trend towards the integration, rationalization and consolidation of financial capital.

As the distinction between banks, trust companies, investment dealers, and life insurers has become increasingly blurred, a functionally integrated financial system is now emerging. Holding company arrangements are pivotal to the creation of financial conglomerates and the amalgamation of financial capital in Canada, including pension fund assets. Two cases are of particular interest with respect to the use of holding company arrangements and direct equity investment to create financial conglomerates: Power Corporation and Edper Investments Limited.

Power Corporation, the largest diversified holding company in Canada on a consolidated asset basis, owns and controls Montreal Trustco and Great West Life through its subsidiaries Power Financial and the Investors Group, using a combination of direct equity participation and interlocking directorships. Montreal Trustco and Great-West are the third largest trust company and life insurer respectively. Montreal Trustco has the third largest pool of corporate trusteed pension fund assets under administration, while Great-West manages the assets of the third largest segregated (pension) fund in the insurance industry (Tables 8.13 and 8.14).

The creation by Edper Investments, one of two privately held Bronfman family trusts, of Trilon Financial Corporation through its Brascan subsidiary is an example of the formation of a financial conglomerate using direct equity participation through holding company arrangements. Trilon Financial Corporation was formed in 1982 explicitly to integrate and co-ordinate financial services.[30] Trilon owns London Life, the fourth ranked life insurer, and has a controlling equity position in Royal Trustco, the largest trust company in the country. Royal Trustco controls the largest volume of pension assets under administration of any trust company (Table 8.13). In addition, Trilon has a substantial equity position in the fifth ranked Toronto-Dominion (TD) bank. In turn, the Toronto-Dominion bank pension fund has a 15 per cent interest in Trilon Financial. Reinforcing this control are interlocks from Brascan, owned by Edper Investments and the holding company for Trilon, to Royal Trustco and the TD bank.

The foregoing suggests that the finance sector in Canada is in the process of significant transformation and reorganization. Whatever the final configuration, it is evident that there will be a considerable expansion of the concentration of economic power under its control. The rapidly growing pool of centralized and concentrated pension capital, controlled by a few financial institutions, enhances this power and accelerates the tendency towards the amalgamation of capital within the finance sector. The finance sector, in turn, has become increasingly integrated with industrial capital.

Integration of Financial and Industrial Capital. The amalgamation of financial capital is paralleled by a similar process in the industrial sphere. This accelerates the integration, or "fusion," between the finance and industrial sectors, with the resultant strengthening of capital in general. The close relationship between the finance and industrial sectors in Germany, Japan, France, Britain and the United States is well documented.[31] In the U.K., for example, "the separation of banking and industry," according to Prais, is "being . . . slowly replaced by an association between the new financial institutions and industry . . . bringing the British system closer to that of the Continent."[32]

Studies of the subject with respect to Canada in the early 1960s indicated that top banks held nearly a quarter of the major industrial directorships; conversely, over half of the major banking directorships were held by directors of leading industrial corporations. Insurance company directorships were equally shared by top industrial and bank directors. In turn, top industrial directors held nearly 60 per cent of bank and insurance directorships.[33] Using 1972 data Clement reported a density ratio for interlocks, that is, the proportion of potential to actual interlocks, of 0.62 between finance and manufacturing, and Granger noted that the directors of the Royal Bank and Bank of Montreal sat on 110 of the 250 largest non-financial corporations in Canada in 1979.[34] This "concentration of power in six financial corporations," according to Johnson, "is made even more impressive when one remembers these corporate directors meet together on the boards of directors of their innumerable smaller interests."[35] Thus there are a series of interconnected corporate networks unifying the finance and industrial sectors in Canada into "fused" capital.

Figure 9–1 identifies and reports selected equity linkages and interlocks between and among major corporations in the finance and industrial sectors in Canada in 1983-1984, including those which control pension capital. It presents the various connections within the transfigured finance sector in relation to the manufacturing sector. Equity linkages and interlocks were traced within the finance sector as well as to and from the industrial sector. Only those industrial corporations with equity exposure or which satisfied the significant shareholder citerion are included, thereby omitting many important U.S. subsidiaries and privately held corporations. Interlocks from the finance to the industrial sector were limited to major corporations, or to those which were previously established, because of the plethora of linkages.

Based on this information three centres of power can be identified. First, the dominant characteristic is first tier linkages between the industrial, commercial and financial sectors and among financial institutions where allowed. The Royal Bank, the largest and most powerful financial institution in Canada, for example, has at least forty interlocks to key industrial corporations throughout the economy[36] (these are not reported in Figure 9–1). Sun Life, Canada's major life insurance company, has one director on the Royal Bank's board (compared with four in 1979) and one on Royal Trustco's, the largest trust company. Royal Trustco and Sun Life are the major corporate trustee and segregated fund managers respectively for pension fund assets (Tables 8.13 and 8.14). Olympia and York, the largest commercial real estate developer, has two representatives on Royal Trustco's board of directors. Power Corporation, the largest holding company on a consolidated balance sheet basis with 195 companies under its control, has a 12 per cent equity interest in Canadian Pacific (CP), the largest industrial based conglomerate which controls some 130 corporations. Paul Desmarais, Chairman and CEO of Power Corporation, was elected a director of CP Enterprises in 1984, the second ranked holding company, which was 70 per cent owned by Canadian Pacific Ltd., thus at that time interlocking the first and second ranked holding companies. In turn, Canadian Pacific Ltd. interlocks with Sun Life, thereby connecting the top industrial conglomerate with the major life insurance company. What clearly emerges is a series of horizontal linkages between the dominant economic actors in the finance and industrial sectors of the Canadian economy.

Second, in addition to primary linkages, there are a series of intense subordinate interconnections and groupings within and between the various sectors at different tiers. At the first tier within the finance sector, for example, there was a close working relationship between the two major banks and brokerage firms.[37] Subsequently, beginning in 1987, the main banks acquired investment firms. Specifically, the Royal Bank took over Dominion Securities, the Canadian Imperial Bank of Commerce (CIBC) obtained Wood Gundy, the Bank of Montreal secured Nesbitt Thompson Deacon and the Bank of Nova Scotia procured McLeod Young Weir. Top ranked Royal Trustco has a series of equity links with the Canadian Imperial Bank of Commerce and the Bank of Nova Scotia, the second and fourth ranked banks respectively. The Bank of Nova Scotia is interlocked with Canada Life, and London Life with Royal Trustco. Mutual Life, the sixth ranked insurer, is also interlocked to Royal Trustco. At the second tier, Manufacturer's Life has a 23 per cent (non-voting) interest in Canada Trustco. In addition, Sun Life and Edper Investments (through Brascan) have connections with the fifth ranked Toronto Dominion Bank.

FIGURE 9-1

Selected Interlocks and Equity Linkages between Finance and Industrial Capital, Canada 1983-1984

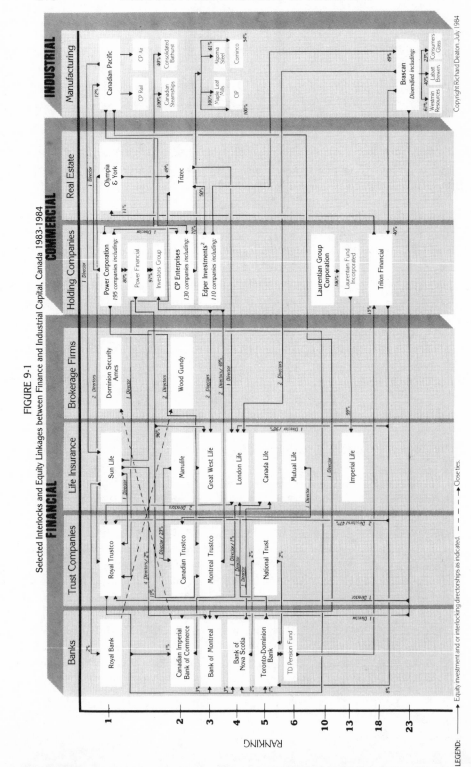

Copyright Richard Deaton, July 1984

LEGEND: Equity investment and/or interlocking directorships as indicated. – – – ➤ Close ties.

Notes: 1 Ranking by sector is on the following basis: within the finance sector, banks and life insurance companies by assets; trust companies by assets under administration; brokerage firms by total capital employed. Corporations in the commercial and industrial sectors ranked on a consolidated asset balance sheet basis from various sources.

2 Ranked on the basis of "insider" information.

Sources: The figures cited reflect a highly fluid business environment. This diagram was constructed from the following sources: *The Financial Post 500* (June 1983); "Canada's Top 500 Companies," *Canadian Business* 56 (July 1983); *Globe and Mail, Report on Business 1000* (June 1984); Lawrence Welsh, "Trilon Plans to Intensify Financial Services Growth," *Globe and Mail,* 18 February 1983; Amy Booth, "Brascan's Strategic Push into Financial Services," *Financial Post,* 12 November 1983; Sonita Horvitch, "Canada Trustco Stays Out of Financial Furor," *Financial Post,* 24 December 1983; "Inside Report on Financial Institutions," *Financial Times,* 12 September 1983; Andrew H. Malcolm, "The Canadian Conglomerates: Monopoly or Oligarchy?" *New York Times,* 23 March 1981; Deborah McGregor, "CP: The Empire Strikes Back," *Financial Times,* 24 October 1983; David Olive, "Canada's Top Private Companies: A Special Report," *Canadian Business,* 56 (November 1983), pp. 33–60, and Robert Giddens, "Power Corp. Studying Switch into an Operating Company," *Globe and Mail,* 4 May 1984. In addition, information and proxy circulars supplied by the Toronto Stock Exchange; *Financial Post, Survey of Industrials;* corporate searches by the federal Superintendent of Insurance and the 1983 annual reports of the top five banks, trust, and life insurance companies.

The sectoral integration between and among dominant financial and industrial corporations is also evidenced by first and third tier linkages. For example, Canadian Pacific, Royal Trustco and Sun Life are all connected with the Bank of Montreal. Trizec Corporation, the second largest commercial realtor, owned jointly by Olympia and York and Edper Investments, is interlocked to Royal Trustco and London Life. The interconnecting chaining of industrial, financial and commercial networks is endless. This evidence indicates that in addition to important horizontal linkages *between* the finance and industrial sectors, there are deep vertical connections *within* the finance sector.

Third, holding company arrangements have increasingly become the interface between the industrial and finance sectors in Canada. Holding companies have effectively served to fuse financial and industrial capital into finance capital. Three constellations, or groupings, are of particular significance. It is useful to differentiate for analytical purposes between what might be termed industrial based conglomerates and commercial based holding companies. An example of the former is Canadian Pacific Ltd. (CP), which owns and controls 130 corporations, including CP Enterprises Ltd. (CPE), which acts as an investment and holding company and, in turn, controls many other firms in key sectors. The holding company CP Enterprises subsequently was merged into the parent CP Ltd. in late 1985, and five of the eighteen CPE directors were moved to the CP Ltd. board, thus effectively retaining a core of interlocks in addition to direct equity control of subsidiary companies. CP Ltd., as previously established, has linkages to and from Sun Life, Power Corporation and the Bank of Montreal. The CP Ltd. pension fund is the fifth largest in Canada (1987).

Edper Investments Limited and Power Corporation are examples of commercial based holding companies which are extensively connected to other sectors. The Edper Investments complex encompasses 110 companies including a controlling interest in the diversified industrial based Brascan holding company and the recently created Trilon Financial Corporation; Trilon is the holding company for Royal Trustco and London Life. In addition, Edper is interlocked to the Bank of Montreal and has a significant equity interest in the Toronto Dominion bank. Power Corporation's control over 195 companies includes Montreal Trustco and Great-West Life; in addition, it formerly owned Imperial Life (until forced to divest in 1977) and the Laurentide Group (now the Laurentian Group). In

1984 the president of Imperial Life, owned by the Laurentian Group, however, was a former senior executive with the Power Corporation.

These three conglomerates—CP, Edper and Power Corporation—therefore own and/or control over 435 corporations throughout the economy and directly or indirectly have under their strategic control some $28 billion or nearly 45 per cent of total pension assets in Canada through dominant interconnected corporations (1980).[38] These data lend support to Porter's claim that the nuclei of economic power in Canada are the large holding and investment companies.[39] Despite the contention that the different funding agencies for pension plans sponsored by financial institutions—trust and life companies—purportedly compete with each other, there are marked "tendencies towards segmentation of the market."[40] Segmented or differentiated markets are a classic characteristic associated with monopolistic competition and oligopolistic market structure.

In general, what appears are horizontal linkages between financial sectors, where permitted, and vertical integration between tiers as a result of direct equity investment through holding companies which interface and horizontally link the finance and industrial sectors. These connections have resulted in the increased amalgamation and growth of capital within and between the financial and industrial spheres. This interdependence through interpenetrating corporate networks has significantly unified and fused capital. It may signify the transition to "spheres of influence" and "interest groups" as the dominant forms of business organization in Canada, as is the case in some other capitalist economies.[41] The increased fusion of financial and industrial capital in Canada is, by any other name, monopoly capitalism. What is new is the role of pension funds as a mechanism to facilitate and promote the interpenetration and interdependence of financial and industrial capital.

PENSION FUNDS AND THE AMALGAMATION OF CAPITALS

The pension system's investment function has become a vital link between the finance and industrial sectors. The socialization of the industrial sector is a consequence of investment by pension funds and other institutional investors in corporate securities and, in particular, in equity shares of major corporations. In Britain, Canada and the U.S., institutional investors in general are now the dominant force in the securities market and have the largest holdings of corporate shares (Tables 7.2 and 7.10). The penetration of the industrial sector by pension funds through the securities market suggests that they might exercise potential control over it. The implications with respect to strategies for social change are dealt with in Chapter 10.

"Through the acquisition of stock in corporations," Harbrecht argued, "financial organizations have begun to gather to themselves the . . . rights of control that have always been attached to shares of stock," placing "institutions in a position of control in the most influential . . . corporations." In the United States in the mid-1950s bank trustee shareholdings of individual corporations through pension funds ranged from 0.5 to 7 per cent of outstanding issues.[42] Institutional share ownership is now considerably greater. Based on 1981 survey data, for example, institutions owned 89 per cent of AMP, 80 per cent of Mattel, 79 per cent of Lockheed, 77 per cent of Motorola, 77 per cent of Nalco Chemical and 71 per cent of Texas Instruments.[43] Consequently, the growth of bank control over companies in the U.S. has increased as a result of their concentrated pension fund shareholdings.[44]

The concentration of corporate shareholdings among institutional investors and pension funds is similarly evidenced in Britain and Canada. In Britain, according to Minns, thirty financial institutions control over 20 per cent of the share capital in thirty-six of the fifty largest corporations, 25 per cent in thirty companies, over 30 per cent in seventeen firms and over 35 per cent in three companies.[45] Recent years have witnessed an increased rate of penetration of large-scale industrial enterprises by the financial institutions responsible for the administration of pension funds. In Canada, some publicly traded companies have 30 to 40 per cent or more of their outstanding common shares held by seven or eight pension funds.[46] Private placements of securities and the "thin" equity market in Canada have compounded this concentration by placing large blocks of shares under institutional control. Significantly, some major corporate pension funds, and in one instance a consortium of funds, have directly bought into energy companies and acquired direct ownership of real estate.[47] Pension funds under the control of dominant financial institutions therefore promote the integration of the industrial, commercial and finance sectors, with a corresponding concentration and centralization of capital. The following identifies and examines some of the specific mechanisms which facilitate this process.

Pension fund investment in the common shares of well established companies with good earnings records and long-time dividend payments, that is, blue chip corporations, promotes intersectoral fusion. This investment behaviour is largely attributable to pension funds being risk-aversive in order to satisfy the obligation of pension trustees to act in a "prudent" manner to protect the interests of plan members. In order to fulfil the fiduciary requirements of law and practice, pension funds must simultaneously maximize investment return and minimize risk through portfolio diversification, and they are restricted to investing in only those securities which meet certain "quality" tests, such as the payment of dividends over a long period of time.

These practices effectively restrict pension fund investment to the shares of dominant, stable, and profitable firms in the oligopolistic sectors of the economy. The concentration of blue-chip shareholdings by pension funds in the limited universe of publicly traded corporate shares satisfying these requirements in turn reinforces the penetration of major industrial corporations by financial institutions and the interdependence between the two sectors.

In the United States the fact that pension fund holdings are generally limited to the top 50 to 100 corporations out of the 1,550 companies listed on the NYSE in 1983 is an indication of this concentrated share ownership.[48] It is popular to refer to the "nifty-fifty," that is, the fifty most commonly held stocks, which include such corporate giants as IBM, Exxon, AT & T, GE, GM, Xerox and so on. In Canada, pension fund shareholdings are generally held in 20 of the 872 listed companies, accounting for nearly 50 per cent of the value of the TSE Composite Index.[49] And in Britain, 68 per cent of pension fund investment is concentrated in the largest companies worth £130 million or more.[50]

The role of the pension system as a source of long-term investment capital and external financing for the corporate sector was examined in Chapter 7. The external financing raised by corporations in securities markets, however, is used not only for the purpose of satisfying corporate investment requirements, but also for "intercorporate investment" and an "increase in financial assets." The pension system's investment function thus accelerates the concentration and centralization of capital by supplying firms with liquidity for inter- and intrasectoral corporate acquisitions, that is, quite literally, the amalgamation of capital units.

The late 1960s and 1970s witnessed an unprecedented number

of mergers among industrial, commercial and financial corporations in North America and Britain. An increasing proportion of corporate funds and external financing is used to promote corporate growth through mergers and take-overs, that is, the centralization or amalgamation of capital, rather than through internal growth. The pension system has directly and indirectly generated a significant proportion of the required cash for these activities.

In the United States the proportion of corporate funds used to finance mergers and take-overs rose from 9 to 20 per cent between 1960 and 1981.[51] A similar trend was evidenced in Canada with respect to intercorporate investment between 1978 and 1981. Significantly, such investment, including resources for mergers and takeovers, was equivalent to 70 per cent of all long-term private nonfinancial business borrowing raised in securities markets in Canada in 1981.[52] In Britain, 10 per cent of external finance, that is, issues of shares and deventures, was explicitly used for acquisitions by industrial and commercial companies between 1949 and 1953, and it subsequently increased to nearly 75 per cent of issue value in the 1969–1973 period.[53] Therefore a significant proportion of external financing, and funds generated through the pension system including primary market acquisitions, promote the amalgamation of capital.

Pension funds, especially in Britain and the United States, have been used with increasing frequency as a weapon in corporate take-overs, as well as a means to enhance the liquidity position of firms. Table 9.3 is a partial survey of reported instances where pension funds have been used either to promote these take-overs or to improve the cash position of firms in Britain, the U.S. and Canada between 1950 and 1982.

TABLE 9.3
USE OF PENSION FUNDS TO PROMOTE
CORPORATE TAKE-OVERS AND LIQUIDITY POSITION,
SELECTED EXAMPLES, U.K., U.S. AND CANADA, 1950–1982

	UNITED KINGDOM	
DATE	Company	Activity
1965–1971	Sprey Investments	Use of Imperial Chemical, Unilever and Barclay pension funds for takeover bids of various companies.
1967	London Co-operative Society	Self-investment—favourable loan from pension fund to LCS.

1973–1974	Slater Walker	Use of Leyland and Standard Triumph pension funds for take-overs, companies then stripped of assets.
1974	Brooke Bond Liebig	Self-investment—favourable terms on loan to Welfare Insurance, formerly a subsidiary of Brooke Bond.
1976	J. Lyons	Self-investment—property subsidiary sold £1.7 m of assets to Lyons Pension Trust to improve liquidity position of parent firm.
1977	J. Sainsbury	Self-investment—company a tenant of its own pension fund, accounting for 25% of fund assets.
1977	Arthur Guiness	Self-investment—pension fund deposited £100,000 at call with company.
1978	Eurotherm International	Self-investment—loan from pension fund to company representing 68% of total fund assets.
1978	Lucas Industries	Self-investment—over 26% of pension fund invested in parent firm, accounting for 13% of total Lucas equity.
1978	McKechnie Brothers	Self-investment—take-over of Frederick W. Evans and investment of 15% of Evans pension fund assets in McKechnie shares.
1978	Ricardo and Company, Engineers	Nearly 25% of pension fund assets invested in parent firm; used as defence against take-over bids.
1980–1981	Over 40 "dawn raids" and "sudden death" take-overs	Including offensive bids for Amalgamated Power Engineering and Eagle Star Insurance; to block bids at Revertex Chemicals and British Sugar.

UNITED STATES		
DATE	Company	Activity
1950 to date	Various state and local gov't retirement systems	Self-investment and bond swaps.
1981	Grumman Aircraft	Use of pension fund assets by Grumman to block take-over bid by LTV.
1982	A&P, J. P. Stevens, Stroh Brewery, Celanese and Reynolds Metal, AMAX and Occidental Petroleum	Over 200 spin off/terminations to acquire excess cash and reduce merger debts.

1982	Bendix Corp.—Martin Marietta Corp.—Allied Corp.	During take-over, Citibank as trustee for Bendix Corp. tendered Bendix shares to Martin Marietta through ESOP.
1982	U.S. Steel—Marathon Oil Co.	Active opposition by pension funds and investment managers to U.S. Steel take-over of Marathon Oil Co.
1982	Tactron Inc.—KDI Corp.	Active use of pension funds in Tactron take-over of KDI.

	CANADA	
DATE	Company	Activity
1964	Canadian Pacific	Acquisition of 18% of Central Del Rio's outstanding shares through CPR pension trust.
1963 to 1980	Ontario Municipal Employees Retirement System	Self-investment—98% of assets in non-marketable bonds of Gov't of Ontario.
Early 1980s	Turbo Resources— Merland Exploration Ltd.	Pension Investment Association of Canada (PIAC) organized opposition to take-over bid.
1980	Royal Trustco	Used company pension fund to buy its own shares to assist in thwarting take-over bid by Campeau Corp.

Sources: For Britain Richard Speigelberg, *The City: Power without Accountability* (London: Blond & Briggs, 1973), pp. 33–68; Richard Minns, *Take Over the City* (London: Pluto Press, 1982), p. 19; Jerry Coakley and Laurence Harris, *The City of Capital* (Oxford: Blackwell, 1983), p. 116; "£20 Billion of Pension Funds In Need of Regulation," *Economist*, 4 November 1978, pp. 109–15. For the U.S., Daniel Jay Baum and Ned B. Stiles, *The Silent Partners: Institutional Investors and Corporate Control* (Syracuse: Syracuse University Press, 1965), pp. 69–80; "Hoot and Holler: LTV Drops Its Grumman Bid," *Fortune*, 14 December 1981, p. 8; Pavan Sahgal, "Who Owns Corporate America?" *Pensions & Investment Age*, 31 October 1983, pp. 66–67; "Companies Strike It Rich by Tapping Excess Pension Funds," *Business Week*, 14 November 1983, p. 28; John Howley, "Occidental's Diversification Strategy," *Economic Notes* 52 (March 1984), p. 11, and Robert Tilove, *Public Employee Pension Funds* (New York: Columbia University Press, 1976). For Canada "C.P.R. And Its Pension Fund," *Labor Facts*, 16 (March 1965), p. 13, and Eric Evans, "Pension Funds Make Corporate Waves," *Financial Post*, 25 June 1983.

Pension funds by tendering their shares have been used as part of a corporate strategy to promote or block take-over bids as well as to generate liquidity through self-investment ("self-dealing") and spinoff/terminations for mergers. In Britain, Sprey Investments' use of the Imperial Chemical, Unilever and Barclay pension funds for offensive take-over bids, the notorious manipulation by Slater

Walker of pension funds for the same purpose, and the recent rash of "dawn raids" and "sudden death" take-overs are but some of the better known examples of how pension funds have been used to promote the amalgamation of capital. In the United States pension fund shares were used, for example, by Martin Marietta in the take-over of the Bendix Corporation and by Tactron Inc. in the take-over of KDI Corporation.

Alternatively, pension funds have been used as part of a defensive strategy to block take-over bids. In Canada, Royal Trustco bought its own shares through the company pension fund to help thwart a take-over bid by the Campeau Corporation in 1980. Similarly in the U.S., Grumman Aircraft tendered its own shares through the company pension fund to block a take-over bid by LTV in 1981. Pension funds actively opposed the take-over bid by U.S. Steel of the Marathon Oil Company a year later. The use of occupational pension funds for corporate take-overs in recent years has become so pronounced that the U.S. Federal Department of Labor "is taking a hard line on corporations using plans in acquiring other companies, or where the fund owns company stock forbidding tendering . . . in hostile take-over bids."[54]

Pension funds have also been used to generate additional internal cash flow for the plan sponsor through self-investment or "self-dealing," that is, where an occupational pension fund has significant shareholdings of the plan sponsor. Sainsbury, Guinness and Lucas Industries in Britain and public employee employee pension funds in North America are prime examples of this questionable practice. Invariably, some of this internally generated self-investment is substituted for the external financing raised in securities markets for intercorporate investment, acquisitions and mergers.

A recent and extremely dubious practice to generate corporate cash flow which indirectly promotes mergers is the "spinoff/termination," or excess asset recapture. A spinoff/termination is the wind-up or cessation of a defined benefit pension plan by a company, which in turn buys annuities to cover pension obligations and claims the excess cash. Alternatively, some large companies set up a new pension plan for active employees while spinning off retirees and excess assets into a separate plan, which is then terminated so that the assets can be recaptured by the corporate sponsor. Past years have witnessed a rash of over one hundred spinoff/terminations in the U.S., including such major firms as A & P, J. P. Stevens, United

Airlines, Texaco, and Celanese and Reynolds Metals. Over $2 billion is estimated to have been recaptured by U.S. corporations through this method.[55] This practice is now emerging in Britain. More recently, corporate plan sponsors in Canada and Britain have used pension fund surpluses to improve their financial position by taking a "contribution holiday." While the primary purpose of a spinoff/ termination or a "contribution holiday" is to enhance the liquidity position of the corporate plan sponsor, the cash recaptured is known to have been used for merger-related activities. Occidental Petroleum, the ninth largest energy-based conglomerate in the U.S., is a well documented case in point. It purchased the Cities Service Company to expand its domestic oil reserves and then terminated Cities' pension plan, which freed $400 million. The excess cash was in turn used by Occidental to reduce the merger debts associated with the take-over.[56] The pension system's investment function under advanced capitalism thus directly and indirectly promotes the integration and amalgamation of industrial and financial capital into an unified nexus of corporate power through various mechanisms.

PENSION FUND INFLUENCE ON CORPORATE AFFAIRS:
FUNCTIONAL CONVERGENCE

The increasing organic unity between the industrial and finance sectors may become even more pronounced and overt in the future as the pension system promotes a functional convergence between these sectors as institutional investors become more directly involved in corporate affairs. As institutional investors, pension funds are increasingly abandoning their traditional role as neutral shareholders and are being compelled to fuse their custodianship role with an active involvement in the management of the corporations in which they invest in order to protect the interests of beneficial owners, that is, the pension plan members whom they represent. This tendency to influence corporate behaviour through their shareholdings is propelled, as shall be outlined, by a basic underlying structural dynamic.

The involvement of financial institutions in industrial corporations, as Hilferding observed as early as 1910, increasingly results in "the banker . . . being transformed into an industrial capitalist."[57] A U.S. Senate committee report in 1955 recognized that "continuation of the rapid increase in stock buying by institutional purchasers may result in financial institutions having a dominant influence over the managerial policies of industrial enterprise."[58] Harbrecht has argued that

> the logic inherent in the objectives of the pension trust . . . has led . . . trustees to invest to an increasing extent in corporate stock to obtain . . . maximum investment yields. . . . The possible control of corporations that may result from this . . . is of great significance for the structure of ownership and control of property.[59]

In brief, there is a considerable *potential* for institutional investors and pension funds to exercise control and influence in key sectors of advanced capitalist economies through their corporate shareholdings.

This underlying logic poses many important and interesting issues with respect to public policy, investment objectives, pension reform, and political strategies regarding the public and private pension systems. In the most fundamental sense, the issue that must be assessed is whether institutional investors, and in particular pension funds, have in fact exercised the power associated with share ownership? Or are we witnessing a transition from silent to actual involvement in and control over corporate affairs? Put another way, are institutional investors transforming their ownership of corporate shareholdings into direct control? Ancillary questions and issues must be addressed as well. For example, have pension funds and institutional investors intervened in the past in corporate affairs? If so, how often, in what ways, and under what circumstances? Is there a discernible trend towards more institutional involvement in corporate decision-making? If so, why?

Pension funds have traditionally adhered to a convention referred to as the "Wall Street rule." That is, pension funds, and other institutional investors, would either abstain from voting their shares or would support the incumbent management in a proxy fight. If institutional investors were, for some reason, displeased with management or its policies they would, in accordance with this convention, "vote" by selling their shares, rather than by actively opposing management policy or attempting to influence it.

There are a number of premises underlying the operation of the Wall Street rule. In the first instance, it is based on the legal requirement of fiduciary responsibility. That is, pension fund investment

managers must act in the best interests of plan members by maximizing investment return subject to reasonable risk. Second, it
follows that institutional shareholdings in industrial corporations
are primarily investments, to be bought and sold solely on the basis
of investment criteria. Third, to the extent that investment criteria
are satisfied and the interests of plan members protected, institutional investors do not involve themselves in corporate affairs.
Should the investment performance of a firm be unsatisfactory or
management policies be deemed contrary to the interests of plan
members as they affect investment criteria, a pension fund trustee
is obliged to divest the shares. Fourth, it is argued, institutional
investors do not, or should not, become involved in corporate affairs
because their area of expertise is investment policy, not corporate
management. For all of these reasons it has been suggested that
institutional investors in the past have played an essentially neutral
or passive role with respect to corporate management and have
limited themselves solely to acting as rational and prudent investors
on behalf of pension plan members.

The Wall Street rule as the dominant view of institutional investor
behaviour has become "conventional wisdom," masking a considerably more complex reality. In recent years dispute has arisen
about whether institutional investors actually wield the power
inherent in their shareholdings, that is, whether they are active-
interventionist or passive non-interventionist investors. Baum and
Stiles, Fitch and Oppenheimer, and Chevalier argue, based on various institutional and structural considerations, that institutional
investors are "locked-in" to their corporate investments and that the
volume of their shareholdings will compel them to abandon their
neutrality. Contrary to this position, Herman, O'Connor, Perry,
Allen and Blumberg argue that intervention by institutional investors is rare. The fact that there is now a vigorous debate in the U.K.,
Canada and the U.S. between "hawk" (interventionist) and "dove"
(non-interventionist) pension fund investment managers about
which role institutional investors should play in itself suggests that
the traditional institutional framework is undergoing a fundamental transformation.

The extent of and details surrounding pension fund, and other
institutional investor, intervention in corporate affairs is rarely a
matter of public record and can only be documented in a fragmen-
tary way. "Intervention by professional investors in the management of . . . companies," Spiegelberg has suggested, "is comparable

to an iceberg. Only a small part of it is visible. . . . If the top of the iceberg has loomed larger, the iceberg . . . must have expanded."[60]

Table 9.4 is a partial survey of recorded interventions by institutional investors in corporate affairs in Britain, the United States and Canada between 1949 and 1982. Three trends are discernible. First, intervention by institutional investors can be detected in one form or another as early as the late 1940s in the U.S. and by the mid-1960s in Britain and Canada. Second, this information suggests that where pension funds and institutional investors have intervened, they have done so with respect to the most fundamental issues related to corporate policy and decision-making — mergers and take-overs, management reorganization, corporate structure, product diversification, payment of dividends, level of retained earnings, corporate capital structure, executive compensation, and institutional representation on the board of directors. Intervention regarding such matters goes to the heart of corporate management. Third, the incidence of institutional intervention in corporate affairs since the early 1980s would appear to have significantly increased. This suggests that there is an underlying dynamic compelling intervention by institutional investors in corporate management in order to defend their investments.

TABLE 9.4

INTERVENTION IN CORPORATE AFFAIRS
BY INSTITUTIONAL INVESTORS,
SELECTED EXAMPLES, U.K., U.S. AND CANADA, 1949–1982

UNITED KINGDOM		
DATE	Company	Activity
1965–1971	Sprey Investments	Use of Imperial Chemical, Unilever and Barclays pension funds for take-over bids of various companies.
Early 1970s	Vickers Engineering	Management reorganization forced by Prudential Life Insurance Co.
Early 1970s	Rank Organization	Institutional opposition successfully blocks entry into brewery business and take-over of Watney Mann.
Early 1970s	Hill Samuel	Institutional opposition prevents merger with Metropolitan Estate and Property Corp.
1973–1974	Slater Walker	Use of Leyland and Standard Triumph pension funds for corporate take-overs.

1980–1981	Over 40 "dawn raids" and "sudden death" take-overs	Including offensive bids for Amalgamated Power Engineering and Eagle Star Insurance; defensive bids at Revertex Chemicals and British Sugar.
1982	Turner and Newell; Rank Organization	Management restructuring forced by Prudential Life Assurance.
1982	F. W. Woolworth (U.K.)	Institutional investors and pension funds sell off real estate and implement management reorganization.

	UNITED STATES	
DATE	Company	Activity
1949	Montgomery Ward	Avery-Wolfson proxy fight.
1954	New York Central Railroad	NY Central in disfavour with institutional investors because it curtailed dividend. Ensuing Young-White controversy.
Mid-1950s	Unidentified	Pressure from life insurance companies on industrial corporations to increase level of retained earnings in order to provide additional security for loans.
Late 1950s	Unidentified	Pressure from institutional investors with respect to bank mergers and capital structure of corporations.
1958	Massachusetts Investors Growth Stock Fund	Voted against management recommendation.
1959	Bethlehem Steel	Successful pressure from institutional investors to reduce level of executive compensation.
1981	Grumman Aircraft	Use of pension fund shares by Grumman to block take-over bid by LTV.
1982	Bendix Corp.–Martin Marietta Corp.–Allied Corp.	During proxy fight Citibank as trustee for Bendix Corp. tendered Bendix shares to Martin Marietta through ESOP.
1982	Trans World Corp.	Active support of management by pension fund managers Morgan Guaranty Trust and Forstmann-Leff during proxy fight.
1982	U.S. Steel–Marathon Oil Co.	Active opposition by pension funds and investment firms to take-over by U.S. Steel.
1982	Tactron Inc.–KDI Corp.	Active involvement by two union pension funds in take-over by Tactron Inc.

| DATE | CANADA | |
	Company	Activity
1980	Domtar Inc. and Gas Metropolitan	The Caisse de Depôt, the investment arm of the Quebec Pension Plan, as a major shareholder has representation on the board of directors.
Early 1980s	Turbo Resources– Merland Explorations Ltd.	Pension Investment Association of Canada (PIAC) organized opposition to take-over bid.
Early 1980s	Hiram Walker Resources Ltd.	PIAC co-ordinated voting against a proxy resolution proposed by management.
Early 1980s	Consolidated-Bathurst	Institutions, including the Dominion Bridge pension fund, go to court to prevent "squeeze-out" of Domglas Inc. minority shareholders.
Early 1980s	Unidentified privately held companies	Various forms of intervention, including corporate restructuring, in which pension funds have a direct interest.

Sources: Table 9.3.

Institutional intervention has and does take a variety of forms. In Britain, Spiegelberg reported how one pension fund manager in the early 1970s "kicked out directors of one company, presented boardroom changes . . . in the case of another, and forced another company to sell off some of its assets," in addition to refraining from putting another firm into liquidation.[61] The view of the Wilson Report was that covert institutional intervention in corporate management was increasing in the U.K.[62] In the United States a Congressional report on commercial bank trust activities concluded that trustee banks influence "the behavior of large segments of . . . U.S. industry."[63] One business source recently noted that "the influence of institutional investors" in 1988 "has never been stronger" and that they have "challenged company officials with record vote levels against them."[64] Fund managers are now saying they want more influence in such key decisions as the election of the directors, anti-takeover measures and the sale of assets.

In Canada a similar trend towards intervention in corporate affairs by pension funds would now seem to be emerging. In testimony to the 1979 Committee on Mutual Funds, for example, one

large fund boldly stated that "we intend to support any move by
another corporation to acquire [XYZ] and thereby recoup part of the
capital loss . . . as a result of management incompetence."[65] According to one authoritative business source, "the attitude of [pension]
funds towards their role as shareholders is changing. There are
strong indicators that a growing number of fund managers are con-
sidering becoming more vocal shareholders" and are already
closely involved in corporate affairs. One Canadian pension fund
manager, for example, indicated that there are instances where a
"company itself, realizing how much money we have invested in [it]
. . . will [voluntarily] take the first step by giving us information" for
investment purposes. The vice-president of Inco Investment Management Services, which manages one of the major industrial pension funds in Canada, while acknowledging that he does not like
crossing the line between investment and corporate manager, has
stated that he will make "suggestions" and "if the company has
good managers, they'll listen."[66] Carmend Normand, former director general of the Caisse de Depôt, the investment arm of the Quebec
Pension Plan (QPP) and a major financial institution in Canada,
argued vigorously *against* the Wall Street rule and for *more* pension
fund intervention, stating that "rather than sell the stock when a
company has a problem, we prefer to try to help to solve it and keep
the investment. In the long run, it's better that way. *You don't need
to control the company, you just need . . . some representation . . .
and express your views.*"[67] The private and public pension systems
in recent years are therefore adopting a more interventionist
approach.

A structural dynamic propels institutional investors and pension
funds towards increased involvement in corporate management,
generating a functional convergence between the finance and
industrial sectors. At a systemic level pension funds occupy a strategic position in advanced capitalist economies. In the case of Canada,
total pension fund shareholdings, adjusted for control blocks,
accounted for an average 25 per cent of all equity between 1966 and
1980 (Table 7.11). In Britain, pension funds hold an estimated 42 per
cent of all outstanding shares, adjusted for control blocks, and in the
United States, in the order of 38 per cent. Based on the legal convention that 20 per cent of shares constitutes a "control" position, it is
evident that the pension system holds a "dominant" position in
relation to the corporate sector. The institutionalization of Canadian capital markets is indicated by a Montreal Stock Exchange

study which found that only 22 of Canada's 400 largest corporations were widely held, compared with 187 companies which involved foreign control blocks and 162 firms which were controlled by domestic residents or legal entities such as pension funds.[68]

Pension funds effectively become "locked-in" to the relatively narrow rage of leading "blue-chip" corporate investments, limiting the extent of portfolio diversification available to them to satisfy their fiduciary responsibility. This concentration and the lack of portfolio diversification, in turn, increasingly generate pressures which force institutional investors to intervene, in various ways, in corporate affairs. Pension funds and the dominant financial institutions which are responsible for the investment management of two-thirds of total pension fund assets (Table 8.16) have effectively acquired a significant proprietary interest in the operation of the corporations in which they have invested. The concentration of corporate shareholdings in pension funds therefore generates a convergence of interest between dominant financial institutions and major industrial corporations. As one pension fund manager put it, the "need for diversification . . . is going to . . . force . . . funds to become more expert in a lot of areas. They will become more critical of how their investments are being operated."[69] Pension funds are increasingly forced to "stand and fight . . . to oppose managements whose actions [are] inimical to shareholder interests" because if "institutional shareholders don't like . . . management, to whom will they . . . sell . . . shares, and at what price?"[70] The institutionalization of capital markets has meant that it is much more difficult for pension funds to unload large blocks of their shares and move their money into other corporate investments.

The logic is such that pension funds are increasingly compelled to intervene in corporate affairs in order to protect and maximize their investment. The poor economic climate in recent years has undoubtedly compounded these underlying structural pressures. As pension funds act "in defense of their investments," they may "take the next step [and] go on the offensive."[71] Traditionally, institutional investors and pension funds have relied upon covert intervention where possible and have only directly intervened in corporate affairs if necessary to maintain "strategic control."[72] The available evidence clearly suggests, however, that pension funds in recent years have exhibited an increased propensity to intervene directly in corporate management with respect to both strategic and operational activities (Table 9.4). The evolution or transformation from passive to active investment management in recent years may therefore be viewed as a "natural result of the increased economic activity of [pension] funds."[73] This increased involvement by pension funds in corporate management may signify a functional convergence between the finance and industrial sectors.

Under advanced capitalism the impact of pension funds on capital markets as they affect large block trading, the price of securities, the external finance requirements of corporations, and the concentration of corporate shareholdings are all factors which generate forces creating a systemic integration and functional convergence between the industrial and finance sectors resulting in a general fusion of capital and may represent a new phase in the evolution of the modern capitalist corporation and the organization of capital. The system of corporate power, including the private pension system, under advanced capitalism is the concrete manifestation of the symbiotic relationship between the finance and industrial sectors.

PRIVATE CONTROL AND THE OPERATION OF THE
PENSION SYSTEM

Private control over pension capital and the operation of the private pension system is maintained by a series of mutually reinforcing socio-economic arrangements. The formal structure of pension fund power and the fusion of financial and industrial capital into an interlocking nexus of corporate power are reinforced by social structure, politics, ideology, and formal and informal linkages between elite groups or factions within the ruling class.[74]

Those who own or control Canada's dominant financial institutions and have strategic control over pension capital as part of the network of corporate power are a small, exclusive, tightly connected group. Only "nine super-rich families or individuals" in Canada hold a "majority, plurality or more than 20 per cent [of shares] . . . or almost half of the value of the [TSE] 300 index" through their direct or indirect corporate and institutional shareholdings (Table 6.9).[75] These include Paul Desmarais of the Power Corporation complex and the Bronfman family constellation. The economic power associated with the private pension system, and the finance sector more generally, resides with that small elite who own or control dominant financial institutions.

In Canada the financial and industrial factions of the ruling class are linked together in a complex pattern of corporate, social and family relationships. In general they share a similar ideology and social background, attend private schools, intermarry, belong to the same clubs, have shared values and attitudes, and travel in the same social circles. Throughout this network, according to Porter, runs a thin, but nevertheless perceptible, thread of kinship,[76] although this is not necessarily critical for its internal cohesion. A case in point is former Prime Minister and Minister of Finance John Turner, who married Geills McCrae Kilgour, daughter of David Kilgour, former president of the Great-West Life Insurance Company. In brief, "being male, attending Upper Canada College, living in Rosedale and having a wealthy father [opens] the doors to the boardroom."[77] A similar pattern emerges in Britain and the U.S. Major financial institutions in the U.K. are "run by people who are part of the power elite . . . with their own educational system, recruitment, traditions, relations and links to government."[78] Research by Whitley and Lisle-Williams indicates that the financial faction in Britain is more socially homogeneous than is the industrial elite.[79] "With increasing economic concentration" in these advanced capitalist economies, "the [social] structure has become increasingly closed."[80] The social cohesiveness resulting from the informal relationships among the corporate elite reinforces the formal structure of economic power because there is, as a senior vice-president of a financial conglomerate noted, an "exchange of knowledge based on personal relationships, not business relationships."[81]

The socio-economic interests of the faction of the ruling class that controls financial institutions and the private pension system is expressed through corporate political behaviour. Financial and industrial corporations are major supporters of mainstream political parties in Canada, Britain and the United States. These parties ordinarily adhere to a capitalist ideology and generally promote economic policies favourable to the corporate community. The interests of the private pension industry are promoted and protected by the political activities of dominant financial institutions which act on behalf of the *general* interests of *all* financial capital.

In Canada, corporations are major financial contributors to the federal Liberal and Conservative parties. Major financial institutions, including trust companies and life insurers which administer and manage pension funds, contributed nearly $1.8 million dollars to the two major parties in the period between 1977 and 1980 (Table 9.5). Banks were the largest contributors, equally endowing the Conservatives and Liberals. Trust companies contributed more to the Conservatives, while life insurance companies favoured the Liberals. No contributions were made to the mildly left of centre New Democratic Party (NDP).

TABLE 9.5

CONTRIBUTIONS BY MAJOR FINANCIAL INSTITUTIONS TO
CANADIAN POLITICAL PARTIES, CUMULATIVE, 1977–1980

	BANKS	
	Liberals	Conservatives
Royal Bank	$150,000	$150,000
Can. Imperial Bank of Commerce	150,375	151,747
Bank of Montreal	151,500	150,000
Bank of Nova Scotia	144,000	140,099
Toronto Dominion	140,000	140,000
Sub-total	$735,875	$731,846

	TRUST COMPANIES	
	Liberals	Conservatives
Royal Trustco[1]	$ 28,685	$ 23,266
Canada Trustco[1]	1,078	16,200
Montreal Trustco[1]	8,925	10,268
Canada Permanent	31,028	800
National Trust	15,056	15,056
Sub-total	$ 84,772	$ 65,590

	LIFE INSURANCE COMPANIES	
	Liberals	Conservatives
Sun Life	$ —	$ —
Manufacturers Life	20,696	19,000
Great-West Life	—	20,476
London Life	27,500	28,295
Canada Life	14,000	14,000
Sub-total	$ 62,196	$ 81,771
GRAND TOTAL	$882,843	$879,207

Note: 1 Name change.

Source: Calculated from the Chief Electoral Officer, *Registered Party Fiscal Period Returns* (Ottawa: n.p., various years.)

What is of interest is that total contributions from the finance sector were nearly evenly distributed between the federal Conservatives and Liberals. While individual corporations may have a political preference, it is clear that the finance sector as a whole feels equally comfortable with either party, since they generally represent and promote the same business interests. A 1983 survey indicates that both industrial and financial corporations "over time, give equally to both major parties."[82] This seeming "neutrality" suggests that in Canada the corporate sector as a whole expects equal consideration and treatment, regardless of which mainstream party is in power.

The political behaviour of British corporations stands in marked contrast to that exhibited in Canada. Corporate donations to political parties in Britain, a far more overtly class conscious and polarized society, are ideologically less oblique. Simply, there is massive political support by the corporate sector for the Conservative Party. Between 54 and 80 per cent of all corporate political donations were directed to the Conservative Party between 1977 and 1983. Nearly 70 per cent of banking, insurance and finance sector political contributions went to the Conservative Party, accounting for 26 to 35 per cent of all corporate donations to that party between 1974 and 1983.[83] These contributions came from such major financial and banking concerns as Consolidated Goldfields, Wills Faber, Hambros, and the Hill Samuel Group. Political contributions from banks and insurance companies, that is, major pension fund managers, are greater than their size on the stock market. In Britain there is no pretence of ideological or political neutrality by the corporate sector and financial institutions in defence of their interests.

"A confraternity of power develops" between the political, bureaucratic and corporate elites, according to Porter, "and this in turn is reinforced by kinship . . . class" and ideology.[84] The interests of financial capital and the private pension industry are strengthened through political and bureaucratic linkages as well as by mobility to and from the private sector and government.

Political representatives in Canada, Britain and the United States at the national level have generally come from high socio-economic backgrounds. Britain is an interesting case in point under the Conservative government. Conservative MPs in 1979 were, not unexpectedly, primarily drawn from the business world: 23 per cent had a management and executive background, while 17 per cent were lawyers. Significantly, another 18 per cent of Tory MPs had occupations broadly associated with the private pension industry: management consultants (5 per cent), merchant bankers (5 per cent), insurance brokers and underwriters (3 per cent), stockbrokers (3 per cent) and accountants (2 per cent).[85] Overall, 339 Conservative MPs held 475 corporate directorships, including 44 who are members of Lloyds, the insurance brokers. In addition, Conservative MPs held 42 consultancies with 29 of the top 300 industrial firms, including 15 consultancies and 8 directorships with life companies, banks and pension funds.[86]

Similar linkages between the private sector and government exist in Canada. For example, when John Turner re-entered public life after a nine-year hiatus to become prime minister (June-September 1984), he held at least ten corporate directorships, including positions with Canadian Pacific Ltd., Crown Life, Credit Foncier and the Canadian Investment Fund Ltd. The new Conservative prime minister, Brian Mulroney (September 1984), in addition to being president and director of the Iron Ore Co. of Canada and the Quebec North Shore and Labrador Railway, sat on at least eight corporate board of directors, including that of the Canadian Imperial Bank of Commerce.[87]

As well as mobility from the private sector to government, there is considerable mobility in Canada from the political elite to financial institutions related to the operation of the private pension industry.[88] At the federal level, for example, when former Liberal Prime Minister Lester Pearson retired, he took a position on the board of directors of Crown Life Insurance Company (1972), as did John Turner after he left Cabinet in February 1976. Louis Raminsky, former head of the Bank of Canada, was listed as a director of Canada Trust (1978).

According to reliable sources, "more than half of Canada's senators [spent] part of their time acting on board of directors" in 1977.[89] For example, Salter Hayden, chairman of the influential Senate Committee on Banking, Trade and Commerce for twenty-seven years, was an honorary director of the Bank of Nova Scotia, while two other senators on the same committee were also directors of trust companies. As well, Senator Hays was on the board of Canada Permanent. Other political-finance industry linkages include Senator Louis Beaubien, who is on the boards of five insurance companies and one trust company, Senator Hartland MacDougall, who was a vice-president and director of the Bank of Montreal, and Senator Paul Desruisseaux, who served as a director of the Royal Bank. An analysis of 1983 trust company annual reports indicates that Senators Riel and Belfour were on Royal Trustco's board, while Senator Lewis was on the board of Canada Permanent.

Linkages and mobility between Canada's provincial governments and the finance sector are similarly impressive. John Robarts, former Conservative premier of Ontario, retired to thirteen seats on various boards of directors, including Power Corporation, Metropolitan Life and the Canadian Imperial Bank of Commerce.[90] Jean Lesage, former Liberal premier of Quebec, became a member of Montreal Trust's board of directors, while E. C. Manning, former premier of Alberta, became a director of the Canadian Imperial Bank of Commerce and Manufacturers Life. Robert Stanfield, former premier of Nova Scotia and Leader of the federal Conservative Party, was listed on the board of Canada Life in 1983. What is of some interest, based on Olsen's data, is that while over half of provincial cabinet ministers had pre-political occupations related to business, only 2 per cent had backgrounds connected with the insurance industry. This compares with Orren's study, which found that nearly 20 per cent of Illinois state representatives and senators between 1961 and 1968 were associated with the insurance business.[91] Political contributions by financial institutions to federal political parties and mobility between the finance sector and the political apparatus reinforce the influence and economic power of the corporate network.

Bureaucratic linkages to and from the finance sector strengthen a private sector orientation towards pensions policy. Porter has argued in this regard that the link which bypasses the political process is more effective for the business community,[92] which suggests that the ideal connection between the private pension industry and the state may be through the bureaucracy at various levels. Government "bureaucrats, like the specialists of the business world," Olsen observed, "seem to share a common ideology concerning their right to rule."[93] Any number of studies have demonstrated the relationship and affinity between the corporate elite and senior bureaucrats as it generally affects government decision-making and the formulation of public policy. Few data, however, exist with specific reference to bureaucratic-pension industry links. Therefore, only selected and isolated examples can be identified and cited.

With respect to Britain, Titmuss argued as early as 1959 that "the great insurance corporations and pensions . . . will recruit to their inter-locking directorates and consultant ranks . . . from the universities [and] the civil service."[94] The private pension industry recruited senior bureaucrats from the Ministries of Pensions and National Insurance as well as from Inland Revenue. One senior government official became the executive chairman of the Society of Pension Consultants, which was formed to present the views of the pension industry to government. This mobility between the state bureaucracy and the private pension industry could only exist if similar views were shared with respect to the operation of the private pension system.

In Canada, at the federal level, three interesting examples may be noted. The former federal Superintendent of Insurance, Richard Humphrys, worked for the Great-West Life Insurance Company in 1939 and went to the Department of Finance (1940) before assuming the Superintendent's position. In addition, he was past president of the Canadian Institute of Actuaries. And in 1988 Michael Cohen, formerly director of the federal pension benefits division, joined the actuarial consulting firm of William M. Mercer Ltd. Beryl Plumptre, who held a number of important appointments in government, was married to a high-ranking member of the Ottawa bureaucratic elite. Mrs. Plumptre is listed as being on the board of directors for Canada Permanent (1979) and Canada Life (1983). At the provincial level the Superintendents of Pensions, that is, those who are responsible for the regulation and monitoring of the private pension industry, generally have a private sector background and orientation. For example, J. M. Crozier, superintendent of pensions for the province of Saskatchewan, told the Canadian Pension Conference, a leading trade association, that "Governments do not wish to take over the private pension plan industry," and the industry should "help the provincial and federal governments find a solution to the pension issue."[95] The linkages and mobility between the financial, political and bureaucratic elites which complement the formal structure of corporate and pension fund power are reinforced by the dominant market ideology.

Ideology plays an important role in the formulation of social security policy and is a boundary affecting the control and operation of the private pension system within the broader framework of a capitalist economy. Ideology at a global level serves to legitimize prevailing social and economic structures and their functioning in order to maintain social cohesiveness and stability.

In a capitalist society the market ethos is the dominant ideology governing socio-economic arrangements. As the dominant value system it is, to use Gramsci's term, an "ethico-cultural hegemony." Hegemony is

a socio-political situation . . . in which the philosophy and practice of a society fuse or are in equilibrium; an order in which a certain way of life and thought is dominant . . . [and] is diffused throughout society in all its institutional [forms] . . . with its . . . taste, morality, customs, religious and political principles, and all social relations. . . . An element of direction and control, not necessarily conscious, is implied.[96]

A society's stability and equilibrium is a reflection of the penetration and internalization of hegemonic social values by classes and individuals.

"The ruling ideas" or ideology "of each age," Marx and Engels suggested, have "been the ideas of its ruling class."[97] The hegemonic market ideology of a capitalist economy includes the notions of private ownership of the means of production, private control and direction of investment, the sanctity of contract, and production for profit, rather than for use. The faction of the ruling class that owns and controls dominant financial institutions, including strategic control over pension capital, shares a similar world view or ideology. They have shared "habits of thought and action, common sets of values [and] beliefs" and "hold assumptions so deeply that they communicate through raised eyebrows and shared silences" because "they think the same way naturally." Those within the "higher circles" have "little need to conspire" and "have few conflicts of interest because their broad interests seldom conflict."[98] The outlook and critical assumptions shared by the corporate elite, according to Alfred Powis, president of Noranda Mines, is "the same attitude toward profit."[99]

The market ethos explicitly and implicitly governs the operation of the private pension system. The private pension industry, controlled by dominant financial institutions, is big business. As one study concluded:

when a bank says that its objective is to maximize the return on investment of its pension funds assets, what it . . . means is to maximize . . . [the] objective of making money for the bank itself. . . . The fact is that the banks are not the instrument for serving the fund. Rather, the [pension] fund is the instrument serving the banks.[100]

In Canada, for example, fees and commissions to the top five trust companies for managing trusteed pension arrangements accounted on average for 35 per cent of pretax income in 1983, ranging from 15 to 64 per cent of net income before taxes, depending upon the company.[101] The private pension industry is a profitable business.

The market ethos as the dominant ideology legitimizes the existence and operation of the private pension system. Central to the contemporary regulatory framework for the private pension industry are the legal concepts of "fiduciary responsibility" and the "prudent man" rule as previously elaborated upon.[102] The purpose of these requirements is to ensure the safety of pension fund assets and plan benefits. As such, the notions of "fiduciary responsibility" and the "prudent man" rule serve critically important ideological and economic functions.

Ideologically these requirements legitimize the impression that pension funds are managed safely in the interests of plan beneficiaries. As one study concluded, however, "Safety is a pseudo policy. Preservation of revenue and profitability are [the] genuine ones. In practice the goal of safety . . . has served as a protection and . . . mystification for the status quo."[103] In reality, then, these notions serve to obscure the limitations of the private pension system described in Chapter 4 and the investment and capital accumulation functions performed under conditions of contemporary capitalism described in Chapter 6.

In terms of economic function these legal conventions regarding the operation of the private pension system serve to maintain the pattern of pension fund investment in major industrial corporations and the corresponding concentration of shareholdings, with the resulting fusion of industrial and financial capital into a unified nexus of corporate power. This has effectively resulted in "legislated capitalism"[104] and has secured private sector control over pension capital. Thus, fiduciary responsibility and the prudent man rule have become a way in which to legitimize ideologically the structure of pension fund power and the operation of the private pension system in the interests of the corporate sector and the financial faction of the ruling class. Politics, ideology, social structure and the various formal and informal linkages between the financial, political and bureaucratic elites all complement and reinforce the formal structure of pension fund power described in Chapter 8 and integrate it into the broader nexus of corporate power under advanced capitalism.

THE PENSION SYSTEM AND CORPORATE POWER: IMPLICATIONS

There are a number of broad social policy and political implications which result from the relationship between the private pension system and the nexus of corporate power. First, the structure of
pension fund power, described in Chapter 8, and its integration into
the corporate network under conditions of advanced capitalism represent a considerable concentration and centralization of private
economic power. The power of the private pension system and
industry, based on its now manifest capital accumulation function,
described in Chapter 6, is grounded in the socio-economic structures of a capitalist political economy. In the final analysis the institutional strength and economic power of the private pension system
rest on the private control and direction of capital and investment in
the interests of the corporate sector. "The organized concentration
of control over the 'economic surplus,'"Titmuss argued, "represents a primary source of power in our society."[105]

By serving the broad interests of organized capital at the macro-
and micro-economic levels, the private pension industry ensures its
own survival because the corporate sector needs the private pension
system to organize and channel investment capital. The inadequacies of the private pension system exist because reform of the
private pension system would result in increased labour costs to the
industrial sector and a relatively less profitable pension industry.
Reform of the private pension industry serves the interests of neither the finance nor industrial sector. Expansion of the public pension system, however, is a direct threat to the existence of the private
pension industry and the level of capital investment flowing to the
corporate sector; it would represent a fundamental challenge to
private sector control over and direction of investment and capital
accumulation.

As a result there has been a dual political response from the
corporate sector with respect to pension reform. In the first
instance, as suggested by Bottomore, "the evident division of the
elite into divergent interest groups at one level does not preclude the
existence at another level of important *common* interests . . . which
tend to produce an uniformity of outlook and action on fundamental issues of social policy."[106] And "it is over the subject of pensions,"
according to Baum, "that disparate interests converge."[107] Because

the private pension system is structurally and ideologically related to investment, capital accumulation and profit levels, it affects the general interests of the corporate sector and the specific interests of the pension industry. If forced by circumstance to choose between either private or public pension reform, the private sector may be expected to make the necessary *minimal* accommodations to keep the private pension system intact in order to forestall expansion of the public pension system.[108] This was confirmed by the assessment of pension reform outlined in Chapter 4.

Second, reform of the pension system is a political issue because if it is to be successful, the institutional power of the private pension industry must be confronted by the main parties of interest—the elderly, workers and unions. To the extent that the private pension industry continues to operate on the basis of market criteria it will remain a "capitalist trap"[109] for the majority of workers and elderly, as is evidenced by the limitations of the private pension system and the low income of the elderly (Chapters 2 and 4). Public policy towards pensions and aging must therefore be actively politicized.

Third, the role of institutional investors in general, and the private pension system in particular, cannot be ignored. Their activities affect everyone and influence the direction of advanced capitalist economies. Leaving that type of economic power in private hands without public control and accountability is the hallmark of what Titmuss called "the irresponsible society."[110] The institutional strength of the pension system and its relationship to the industrial sector are in fact its weaknesses because the investment function intrinsically related to the operation of the occupational and state pension systems renders them vulnerable to alternative economic strategies to promote social change.

The pension system in general has resulted in the socialization of savings and investment. The occupational pension system's investment function has, in turn, facilitated the interpenetration and interdependence of the finance and industrial sectors. Consequently, the private pension system in advanced capitalist economies now occupies a position of potential strategic control over the industrial sector, investment and capital formation as a result of its concentrated corporate shareholdings. There are already indications that pension funds are becoming more assertive in exercising their proprietorial rights through their shareholdings and are increasingly intervening in corporate affairs. At a micro-economic or sectoral level this situation may provide unions with an opportunity to develop various strategies with respect to the co-management of pension funds, industrial democracy, and alternative approaches to the economic reorganization of industry. The investment function associated with the operation of the state retirement income system could similarly be used to satisfy a multiplicity of socio-economic objectives. An expanded state pension system would be able to generate an adequate retirement income for the elderly, and depending upon the level of funding, it could also serve as a countervailing force to the power of private institutional investors by accumulating an investment fund at the macro-economic level for alternative economic strategies.

The investment function underlying the operation of the public and private pension systems is a unique mechanism with which to socialize key sectors of advanced capitalist economies. Keynes clearly foresaw the need for "a somewhat comprehensive socialization of investment"[111] to maintain aggregate demand, employment and economic growth within the existing capitalist framework. Alternatively, as Titmuss suggested, pension funds are "a power, a potential power to affect many important aspects of our economic life" and might be utilized to develop "forms of public ownership, public responsibility, and public accountability."[112] Whether this potential is realized will depend upon the politics of pension reform and the use of pension funds to promote progressive strategies for social change.

10

The Pension System
and
Strategies for Social Change

The masses of capital amalgamated by centralization
. . . become new and powerful levers of social accumula-
tion.

Karl Marx

Marxism is a guide to action not a dogma.

Frederick Engels

This study has suggested that the political economy of pensions
and the interaction of its constituent elements have an internal
dynamic generating a series of structural conflicts or contradictions. Pensions policy affects the vital interests of capital, labour, the
elderly and the state with respect to capital accumulation, the
industrial relations system, private and public sector finance, and
the economic security of workers, and the increasing proportion of
the aged. The pension issue has an impact upon the most fundamental economic and power relationships in capitalist economies,
suggesting that it may be turned into an ideologically defined political issue in the future and may be used as an instrument to promote
progressive strategies for social change.

The purpose of this chapter is to report, analyse and assess
directed or alternative investment strategies based on the operation
of the state and occupational pension systems. An analytic or typological distinction is made between macro-strategies pursued
through the state pension system and micro-strategies based on the
occupational pension system. These strategies are a concomitant of
the operation of the pension system as a result of its important

position in advanced capitalist economies. Investment strategies based on the pension system are progressive at this historical juncture, it is suggested, because they are an attack on organized capital at the macro- and micro-economic levels and challenge private control over the direction of investment and capital formation. The pension system is one means by which to establish public control and accountability over investment, the industrial sector and capital accumulation.

Social change based on the operation of the pension system is, in turn, examined from a Marxist perspective and related to the transition from capitalism to socialism. It is argued that the use of the state and occupational pension systems to advance alternative investment policies is consistent with and corresponds to one model of social transition envisioned by Marx, that is, the "pattern of competing systems" and "encroaching control" based on the socialization of the economic surplus. From a political perspective, alternative investment strategies through the state pension system may identify issues related to state power and public control over investment and economic planning, whereas targeted investment based on the occupational pension system may raise issues related to industrial democracy. Strategies for social change based on the pension system may therefore be incorporated into a broader socialist programme. The politicization of the pension issue and pension reform formulated as a radical demand may ultimately stretch the limits of economism and welfarism, thereby facilitating the transition to socialism.

THE FUNDING DEBATE AND DIRECTED INVESTMENT STRATEGIES

The funding debate and alternative investment policies have been recurring themes in twentieth-century social security history.[1] They assume a contemporary relevance because of the position the pension system now occupies within advanced capitalist economies. The investment function underlying the operation of the pension system affects savings, investment, capital accumulation and the control of corporate shareholdings, which make it possible to use the pension system to promote strategies for social change. An expanded state pension system, with a high level of advanced funding, would serve a multiplicity of purposes by providing adequate retirement income for the future elderly, reducing potential intergenerational and sectoral tensions, serving as a "countervailing" force to the private economic power of institutional investors, and generating an investment fund for capital formation under public control. Depending upon political circumstances, it might result in the socialization of key sectors of advanced market economies in the public interest.

The financing of the state social security retirement system is closely related to such macro-economic considerations as the level of contributions required to support the benefit structure, taxation, the impact on capital markets, ownership of corporate securities, the size of investment fund accumulated and overall investment strategy. It must be emphasized that the method of funding a national retirement income system is a separate and distinct issue from how the investment fund is used. The method of financing is important, however, because it determines the size of the fund being accumulated. The existence of the fund in turn poses the questions of investment strategy and the purposes for which the fund is accumulated. Thus the method of social security financing, fund size and investment objectives are inter-related.

The way in which a national retirement income is financed is related to directed investment strategies because the method of funding will affect the size of the fund accumulated for investment purposes. On this subject the International Labour Organization has stated that the

> allocations to technical reserves and/or contingency funds are . . . [the] difference between receipts and expenditure. If the figures . . . are relatively high this may indicate the degree to which the [state pension] system contributes to national savings and the capital formation of the country—*depending, of course, on how the amounts concerned are utilized, for instance whether they are spent by the State . . . to meet current expenditure or whether they are in fact placed in productive investments in the interest of the national economy.*[2]

Because "funding and investment go hand in hand in pension planning,"[3] the method of funding is an important determinant with respect to generating an investment fund (where contributions exceed benefits) in order to pursue an alternative or directed investment strategy to satisfy socially productive objectives.

The way in which pension plans are funded is related to the

security of benefits, the level and stability of contributions, intergenerational transfers or equity, and the need for capital. Funding methods differ considerably between state and employer-sponsored occupational pension plans. The latter are usually fully funded in advance in order to guarantee the payment of benefits to plan members. Advance funding ensures that if a plan were terminated it would be able to meet its commitment to beneficiaries and plan members for all accrued (earned) benefits. The state pension system, however, does not necessarily have to be funded on the same basis since government, in theory, exists "in perpetuity," and it is the ultimate guarantor of benefits based on its "unlimited" taxing powers. While some have suggested that "trust funds are unnecessary for a government pension plan, and are established on the basis of a false analogy with private plans,"[4] others have argued that "there is an extra element of danger that the generation facing the [pension] bill may—resist paying it" and "future ability to pay is by no means certain or unlimited."[5]

The advantages and disadvantages of funding a national retirement income system are compared in Table 10.1. Despite traditional welfare state adherence to pay-as-you-go (PAYGO) financing where "tomorrow's young will in turn pay for tomorrow's old ,"[6] it is now increasingly recognized that pension promises "cannot absolutely bind successor governments."[7] Thus, a degree of funding may be required to protect state pension entitlements in the future.

Funding of pensions refers to any systematic schedule of contributions based on long-term commitments. There are three alternative methods of funding state pension arrangements, each with its advantages and disadvantages. These funding methods represent a continuum when compared with formal actuarial standards. *Pay-as-you-go* (PAYGO) funding refers to retirement benefits which are financed from current contributions so that over the long run contributions are equal to benefits. This method results in each generation paying for the cohort which precedes it. For a national pension system operated on a PAYGO basis, a contribution rate would be set each year (or for a number of years) based on expected earnings and benefit levels in that year (or those years). Pensions systems financed on a PAYGO basis, while unaffected by inflation, are unfavourably influenced by demographic shifts and recessionary conditions. Most, but not all, welfare state national retirement income systems since World War II have operated on this basis.

TABLE 10.1

THE FUNDING DEBATE

THE CASE AGAINST FUNDING	THE CASE FOR FUNDING
• A national retirement income programme should be considered a transfer between generations, rather than a savings plan. • Intergenerational equity cannot be established simply by funding pension plans, but must be placed within the total legacy passing from one generation to another. • If society wishes to increase saving, considerations of social equity suggest that the basis for deferring consumption should be more selective and progressive than would be appropriate for pension financing. This would depend on the progressivity of the contribution structure. • Although large funds may be accumulated through pension arrangements, saving on such a scale and in such a form may be inappropriate. Restraining consumption at a time when demand is weak may result in diminishing investment and economic growth during a period when there is already capacity underutilization. • A large fund may pose investment problems. A large fund may result in a concentration of financial power under government control that might squeeze out private investment.	• Funding leads to relatively stable contributions since each generation "pays its own way." PAYGO rates, which vary with changes in the proportion of elderly, are likely to be unfair between generations. • Funding would eliminate the regressivity associated with current contribution rates under which high-income earners receive a larger wealth transfer from the next generation of workers than do low-income earners. • Funding ensures that the pension "contract" between the contributor and the government of the day is honoured. There is no guarantee that future governments will honour pension promises made by previous governments unless paid for. A number of Western European countries and the U.S., which are funded on a PAYGO basis, have experienced financial difficulty and have allowed their benefits to be eroded in various ways. • Funding promotes intergenerational equity inasmuch as each generation is required to forgo consumption equivalent to the estimated value of the pensions it has promised itself. From a financial perspective, a separate fund exists to pay benefits, so that future generations will not be required to meet any part of the cost of paying pensions to earlier generations. Economically, the fund helps to ensure that no decline in the rate of saving per worker, and hence in the accumulation of capital stock per worker, occurs because of pension promises. • PAYGO funding, or a low degree of partial funding, encourages demands for increased benefits since it under-values the true cost of pension benefits so they are perceived as "free goods."

- A fund or reserves are not necessary because government exists "in perpetuity" and has infinite resources based on its taxing power.

- Funding provides a source of capital accumulation which could be used to finance industrial revitalization and an industrial strategy.
- An investment fund under public control could serve as a countervailing force to private institutional investors.

Source: Adapted from the Report of the Task Force on Retirement Income Policy, *The Retirement Income System in Canada: Problems and Alternative Policies for Reform* (Hull: Canadian Government Publishing Centre, 1980), pp. 292–93.

Alternatively, national retirement income systems may be advanced or prefunded, that is, each generation pays for the value of its own benefits. Two advanced funding methods exist: full-cost (partial) funding and full-funding. *Full-cost or partial funding* is that contribution rate which generates sufficient contributions and interest during a "typical" person's working years to pay for expected retirement benefits excluding any unfunded liability. The full-cost contribution rate will create a moderate investment fund during the time contribution levels exceed those required for benefit payments. *Full-funding* is that contribution rate which will provide sufficient assets to cover the value of accrued benefits under the plan plus any unfunded liability. Pension systems based on full-funding are immune to demographic shifts because each generation pays for the value of its own benefits, but they are sensitive to inflation. The full-funding contribution rate will generate a significant fund through contributions and interest.

The contribution rate required to support the national pension system is determined by the degree of funding, level of benefits, and the underlying demographics. Each of the methods discussed above entails a progressively higher contribution rate. Under the baby boom demographic scenario, the full-funding contribution rate is usually higher than the full-cost rate because of the need to service any unfunded liability. In the short term the full-cost rate may be higher than the PAYGO rate, *but the PAYGO contribution rate associated with welfare state pension arrangements will exceed the full-cost rate in the long run.* A comparison of PAYGO and full-funding financing methods is outlined in Table 10.2. Figures 10-1 and 10-2 graphically present the short- and long-term cost implications of these funding methods under alternative demographic scenarios.[8]

TABLE 10.2

COMPARISON OF PAYGO AND FULL-FUNDING FINANCING METHODS[1] FOR
THE STATE PENSION SYSTEM UNDER "BABY BOOM" DEMOGRAPHIC SCENARIO

CRITERIA	PAYGO	FULL-FUNDING
Security of Benefits	Note Table 10.1	Note Table 10.1
Level of Cont.		
Short-run	Less than full-funding rate	Greater than PAYGO rate
Long-run	Greater than full-funding rate	Less than PAYGO rate
Stability of Cont.		
Short-run	Increasing over time	Level over time
Long-run	Increasing over time	Level over time
Intergenerational Transfers	Large intergenerational subsidies and transfers	Intergenerational subsidies and transfers minimized or eliminated
Fund Size and Capital Accumulation	No investment fund accumulated since contributions equal benefits over long run	Significant investment fund generated since contributions plus investment earnings exceed benefit payout until maturity
Phase-in of Contributions and Fund Size		
Short Phase-in	Creates a small fund in short-run by that amount in excess of required PAYGO rate; but PAYGO < FF rate	Maximizes fund size in short-run by moving immediately to full-funding rate; because FF > PAYGO rate results in larger fund than in PAYGO case with short phase-in
Long Phase-in	No fund created over long-term because contributions equal benefits (C = B)	Size of fund over long-term reduced, but a large fund still created because FF > PAYGO rate until maturity

Note: 1 The full-cost (partial) funding method would be an intermediate case.

The extent to which the contribution rate is set *above* the PAYGO rate, as well as the speed with which contribution levels are increased, will determine the size of the investment fund. The magnitude of the investment fund is therefore a function of the contribution level which, in turn, is related to the method of funding. The

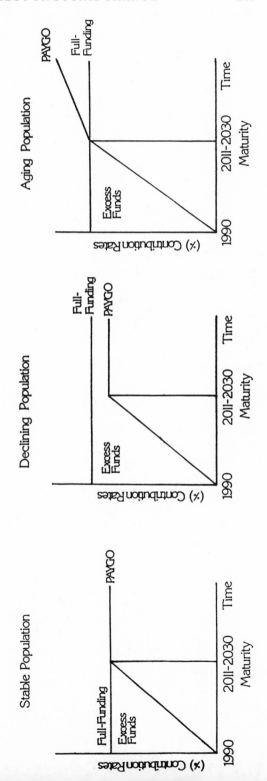

FIGURE 10-1

Comparison Between Short and Long-Term
Full-Funding and Pay-as-you-Go (PAYGO)
Social Security System Contribution Rates
Under Alternative Demographic Scenarios

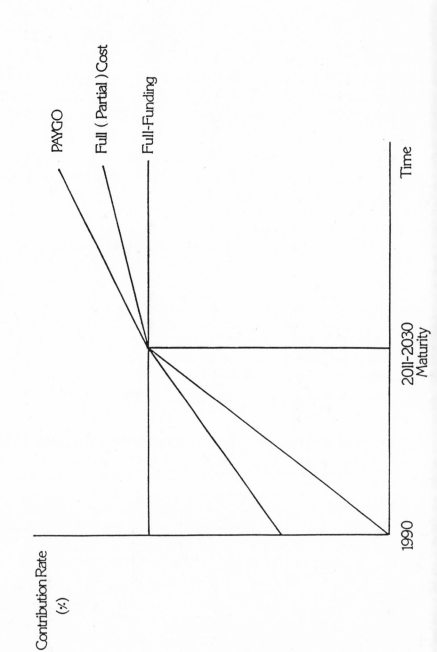

FIGURE 10-2

Comparison of Social Security System Contribution Rates Under
Alternative Funding Methods, Aging Population Scenario

more rapidly the new contribution rates are phased-in to finance improved benefits, the larger the size of the investment fund. A long phase-in period for contributions would minimize the size of an investment fund, whereas a short phase-in would result in a rapid build up of a reserve which could be used for investment purposes. By way of example, a PAYGO system with a long phase-in would result in virtually no investment fund, whereas a full-cost or fully-funded system with a fast phase-in would generate a significant fund until the benefits are paid at maturity. Figure 10-3 graphically reports the relationship between funding method, contribution phase-in and fund size.

The advantages associated with the advanced funding of a national retirement income system, outlined in Tables 10.1 and 10.2, have led some progressive governments to the conclusion that, if

a major confrontation between generations . . . is to be reduced . . . there is an immediate need to set in place mechanisms to ensure that the active work force, and employers on their behalf, save more for their own retirement in order to provide more adequate retirement incomes for themselves in the future. . . . In this way workers will be providing part of the investment capital required, so that . . . they . . . receive a portion of their retirement income by way of an accumulated return on their investment rather than from tax supported programs. . . . This should contain the potential tax burden on future generations.[9]

Some form of advanced funding of the state pension system therefore provides a way in which to improve retirement income for the future elderly, reduce intergenerational tensions, and generate an investment fund under public control. It remains to be determined for what purpose an investment fund accumulated through the state retirement income system might be used in order to promote the public interest and progressive political strategies. In this regard it is useful to differentiate between micro- and macro-directed investment strategies.

MACRO-DIRECTED INVESTMENT STRATEGIES

Directed investment strategies based on the operation of the

FIGURE 10-3

Relationship Between Funding Method, Contribution Phase-In,
and Fund Size, Aging Population Scenario

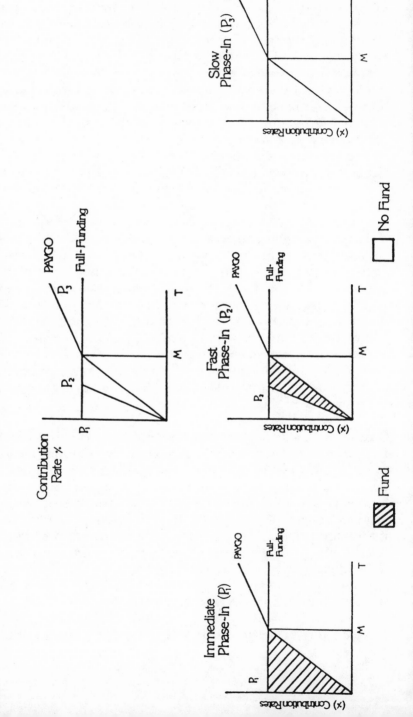

national retirement income system are a mechanism through which to pursue alternate ("directed," "selective," "targeted" or "social") economic goals at a macro-economic level to meet broader social policy objectives. To the extent that any investment fund is accumulated through the public pension system poses the question for what purpose such a fund exists—that is, what are its investment objectives?

National social security arrangements have been described as a "social intervention which was brought into being to perform a specific function in a specific economic and social environment."[10] Accordingly, there "is no single best method of financing since this will depend upon the economic, institutional and cultural context of the social security program," and "no program and financing arrangement [can] be considered permanent since the context is always changing."[11] Economic and institutional changes may, therefore, result in the evolution and modification of social security and pension arrangements from single to *multiple objective* programmes.

This possibility was recognized by the International Labour Organization (ILO) as early as 1939 when it recommended that social security "investments be made with regard to their social and economic utility."[12] In recent years there has been increasing recognition in both industrialized and less developed countries that social security programmes cannot be viewed separately or in isolation from broader economic policies and objectives because income security arrangements not only are an effect of social development, but may also exert an influence on the direction of the economic development process.

Table 10.3 reports existing arrangements and various proposals for macro-economic directed investment strategies based on the state pension system or related modalities. What these different national arrangements have in common is an attempt to promote economic development in the public interest through the social security system and to prepare for the demographic transition. In some countries such as

Sweden, Switzerland, and West Germany—whose [social security] systems are the most developed and mature in the world— [there] was the concern for problems of long-term financing in anticipation of mounting . . . [pension] costs. Two general approaches to the problems were adopted by these countries.

Sweden and Switzerland elected to build up large reserves for future contingencies. Germany, however, retained the pay-as-you-go principle and supplemented it with a limited reserve fund.[13]

TABLE 10.3

MACRO-LEVEL DIRECTED INVESTMENT STRATEGIES, STATE PENSION SYSTEM

COUNTRY	CURRENT ARRANGEMENTS
Sweden	Part of the surplus of the state pension fund is invested in the private sector through three bond funds and one equity fund. The investment objectives for these funds were defined to include housing, municipalities, small business and government. The new equity fund was created to supply risk capital for employment-generating areas of the economy and industrial revitalization. The equity fund now represents nearly 3 per cent of the capital market. The funds have a tripartite administrative structure.
	The passage of the 1983 law for wage-earner funds was designed to transfer profits and company shares to workers and unions. This is a modification of the Meidner proposal, which was endorsed by the Swedish Confederation of Trade Unions (LO) in 1976. The funds' income will be from a new tax on corporate profits and a special payroll tax. There are five regional funds. Each of the funds has a nine-person board. At least five of the members must be employees. The funds are used for loans to start new enterprises or to buy shares in existing companies. Unions are limited to a maximum of 20 per cent of the voting shares. The funds are required to earn at least a 3 per cent return on investment, with the interest going to the national pension fund. The objective is to strengthen employee influence at the workplace through ownership in Swedish corporations. Despite the wage-earner funds' operation at the firm and industry level, it may viewed as a macro-level strategy because of its impact on the ownership and control of industry.
Canada/Quebec	The Quebec Pension Plan (QPP) is separately administered and managed from the Canada Pension Plan (CPP). It is an actively managed fund through its investment arm, the Caisse de Depôt, which is now the fourth largest financial institution in Canada. The investment objectives of the QPP are explicitly related to provincial economic development. The Caisse invests exclusively in Canadian securities; 30 per cent of the QPP fund may be placed in equity investment. The Caisse is a major shareholder in the financial and industrial sectors

having a 4 to 7 per cent equity position in the top 5 banks, a 9 per cent investment in the Royal Trust Company, a 23 per cent equity holding in Domtar Inc., a 27 per cent share of Provigo, and a 56 per cent interest in Gaz Metro. The Caisse has invested in over 100 private placements within the province, some of these being classified as venture financing. The investment pattern of the Caisse is affected by the financing requirements of the province. The real average annual rate of return on investment to the QPP was on average 1.3 percentage points greater than the CPP and was comparable to that earned by private pension funds between 1966 and 1979.

Singapore	In the order of 70 per cent of total housing stock has been built by the government's two housing corporations. This has been accomplished through a reinvestment arrangement between the Central Provident Fund (CPF), the compulsory contributory retirement insurance scheme, and the public housing corporations. Thirty-seven per cent of the country's wage bill is forced saving which is directed towards social investment.
COUNTRY	**GOVERNMENT PROPOSALS**
Province of Saskatchewan (Canada)	A 1982 proposal to establish a "coherent and consistent" investment policy through a Canadian Public Investment Fund (CPIF) to satisfy public investment needs. Joint federal and provincial government participation on an equity basis in "projects of national significance" through the CPIF for energy, transportation, industrial and social projects.
France	A 1982 proposal advanced by France's socialist government to introduce jointly managed funds, similar to the Meidner proposal in Sweden, to promote industrial investment.
	LABOUR PROPOSALS
Canada	The Canadian Union of Public Employees (CUPE), the largest union in the country, endorsed a policy advocating that the Canada Pension Plan (CPP) Investment Fund be used to promote an industrial strategy and repatriate key sectors of the economy from U.S. transnational corporations (1977). The Canadian Labour Congress (CLC), the national labour confederation, endorsed a policy advocating that the CPP Investment Fund maximize its investment performance and be used to promote an industry strategy (1978). The United Steel Workers (Canadian region) endorsed a policy advocating that the CPP Investment Fund be used to promote a "leading edge" resource development strategy, coupled with national economic planning (1979).

U.K.   The Trades Union Congress (TUC), based on a 1979 Con-
                  gress resolution, recommended to the (Wilson) Commit-
                  tee to Review the Functioning of Financial Institutions
                  (1980) the creation of an independent investment fund to
                  promote industrial revitalization by providing new long-
                  term venture capital. This investment fund is based on
                  the operation of the occupational (private) pension sys-
                  tem, with 5 per cent of all new contributions (cash flow)
                  being placed with and invested by the independent fund.
                  The overall direction of the investment fund would be co-
                  ordinated and integrated with the National Investment
                  Board (NIB), and for that reason may be viewed as a
                  macro-strategy.

Sources: For Sweden, Staffon Sonning, "The Employee Fund Issue Moves toward a
          Decision," Current Sweden. No. 309 (October 1983): 1–10 and Claes-
          Goran Kjellander, "Employee Shareholder Funds Introduced," Current
          Sweden, 326 (October 1984): 4–5. An explicit statement regarding the
          operation and investment objectives of the Quebec Pension Plan (QPP)
          through the Caisse de Depôt is outlined in the Quebec Deposit and Invest-
          ment Fund, Annual Report, 1966 and the 1982 Annual Report. For
          Singapore, note "Singapore: A Survey of the Sovereign Municipality," The
          Economist, 29 December 1979, pp. 5–24. The French proposal for wage-
          earner funds is reviewed in "The Employee Funds Debate," European
          Industrial Relations Review 117 (October 1983): 17–18. For labour union
          proposals, note text citations.

The alternative funding methods employed in these countries have
resulted in different investment objectives being pursued. Because
"the significance of . . . an expanded public retirement income system would . . . in part depend on the method of financing . . . as well
as . . . the investment policy,"[14] it is desirable to briefly review the
investment objectives of those pension systems which are of special
relevance to this study.

The case of Sweden is of particular interest because it is one
model of social democratic development which has a reputation for
a comprehensive social security system. The surplus of the state
pension system is invested in three bond funds and one equity fund.
The investment objectives of these funds include housing, municipalities, small business and government. The equity fund was
established to supply risk capital for employment-generating areas
of the economy and industrial revitalization. The Swedish state
social security system therefore has been able to maintain its commitment to provide retirement income and, in addition, has become
a source of capital formation for the private and public sectors.

The passage of the 1983 law establishing wage-earner funds in

Sweden represented a new and ambitious initiative to transfer power to trade unions and expand economic democracy. Because the investment function associated with the operation of employee investment funds is similar to that of other institutional investors, they may be viewed as being in the same category. The proposal for employee investment funds grew out of the deliberations of the Swedish Confederation of Trade Unions (LO) in 1971 and resulted in the Meidner proposal (1975 and 1976) for collective capital formation through wage-earner funds under trade union control.[15]

Employee investment funds were conceived of as a method of accelerating capital accumulation, extending the democratic ownership of industry, redistributing the proportion of capital owned by workers, and expanding employee influence over economic decision-making. These objectives were to be achieved by requiring corporations above a certain size to reissue or direct their equity shares to the firm's wage-earners' fund proportionate to their gross profits. Share issues would be restricted to employee investment funds, which would each year receive an issue of shares without other investors having a similar entitlement. The wage-earners' fund would utilize part of the dividends that accrued from their aggregate holdings to purchase new (rights) issues in order to obtain new investment capital for the firm. This process would allow for the gradual transfer of economic power from private capital to democratically elected collectives, resulting in the socialization of industry over a thirty-year period. Much of this thrust, however, was blunted when the 1983 legislation, contrary to the original proposal, restricted trade union shareholdings to 20 per cent of a company's voting shares, thus limiting the effectiveness of this approach.

From the perspective of progressive politics, because employee investment funds have the effect of transferring "profits to trade union control rather than . . . socialising the capital stock directly . . . they [are] a gradualist strategy that may render them politically feasible in a *non-revolutionary* situation."[16] The advantages of employee investment funds are that they undertake capital accumulation and economic development, while simultaneously initiating industrial democracy by enabling labour to acquire increasing influence through their shareholdings. The investment function inherent to the operation of the state pension system offers a similar potential.

The Canada/Quebec Pension Plans (C/QPPs) are the product of

what has come to be regarded as the "Canadian compromise," which provides the federal state with an important source of political power and legitimacy[17] and the provinces with developmental capital or operating revenues as discussed in Chapter 7. It was a compromise between Ontario, which did not want a public pension system, and Quebec, which wanted a significantly expanded public retirement income system under provincial control. Ontario took the position that government had no role in the management of large pools of capital. Conversely, Quebec, then experiencing the "Quiet Revolution" of the 1960s, advocated a pension system under public control which would generate a large investment fund to promote provincial economic development. At that time, both the federal and Ontario governments wanted the Canada and Quebec Pension Plans on a PAYGO basis; Quebec, however, wanted a plan with a high level of funding since it intended to use the investment fund as a means to promote economic modernization. The separation of the QPP from the CPP was made possible by the "opting-out" provision which allowed Quebec to establish its own plan. Subsequently, the CPP was put on a PAYGO basis (generating a modest surplus until the early 1990s as a result of the underlying demographics), while the QPP was placed on a partially funded basis.

The Caisse de Depôt, the investment arm of the Quebec Pension Plan, was viewed from its inception as an instrument for economic development. The Caisse, Jean Lesage, then premier of Quebec, said when implementing the plan, "is destined to become the most important and powerful financial instrument Quebec has had so far . . . [it] must not be envisaged as an investment fund like others, but as a growth instrument, a more powerful lever than we have possessed," and it must co-ordinate its operations with "the general economic policy of the state."[18] The Caisse de Depôt has been able to satisfy its fiduciary or trustee responsibility successfully by providing pension benefits and, at the same time, it has promoted provincial development. Its 1982 *Annual Report* described this situation by noting that "the investment policy of [the] Caisse hinges on two major elements. First, it is essentially bound by criteria of security and return; secondly, its action is directed towards the support of Quebec economic development. For [the] Caisse these requirements are absolutely compatible."[19] As an actively managed investment fund under public sector control, the Caisse de Depôt has acquired, even by private sector standards, a reputation for aggressive and competent investment management. The real average annual rate of return earned by the Caisse between 1966 and 1979, for example, was 1.3 per cent, compared with 1.4 per cent for all trusteed (private and public sector) pension funds and 0 per cent for the Canada Pension Plan.[20] This suggests that there is no inherent reason why an investment fund accumulated through the public pension system cannot provide retirement benefits, generate social capital and earn a competitive rate of return. And what has been done through the QPP at a provincial level could be undertaken by the CPP at the national level.

The Caisse de Depôt is now one of the largest financial institutions in Canada and is a major actor in capital markets. It invests exclusively in Canadian securities and is permitted to invest up to 30 per cent of its assets in equity, although it has rarely approached this limit. It is a major shareholder in the finance and industrial sectors as is indicated in Table 10.3. The Caisse has conducted itself as an activist shareholder and has insisted on representation on the board of directors of its major corporate investments. Its clout in financial markets is now so considerable that the former federal Liberal government attempted to restrict its investment in the transportation sector in order to prevent a takeover of the Canadian Pacific Railway (Bill S-31).

Building upon the potential associated with the state system's investment function, a number of national labour confederations and their affiliates have recommended pursuing macro-economic directed investment strategies in order to promote progressive social change. In Canada, for example, the Canadian Union of Public Employees recommended in 1977 that the CPP Investment Fund be used to promote industrial strategy and repatriate key sectors of the Canadian economy from American transnational corporations. It proposed that

the public money accumulated through the . . . funded Canada Pension Plan and public employee pension funds, instead of being used to finance the investment requirements of the private corporate sector, should instead be used in the public interest to:
1. Repatriate the Canadian economy by using the Canada Pension Plan and public employee pensions funds as an active investment vehicle to co-ordinate and direct an industrial strategy by . . . buying the outstanding *equity* interest of foreign owned or controlled corporations in Canada.

2. Pursue an industrial strategy at both the federal and provincial levels by using the . . . funded CPP and public employee pension fund assets to invest *directly* in new physical plant and equipment in the manufacturing sector and the petroleum and natural gas sector through federal and provincial crown corporations.
3. In this latter case, a competitive market rate of return should be guaranteed to the CPP and public employees pension plans to preserve the integrity of the fund for member beneficiaries and in order to meet the outstanding fiduciary responsibility.[21]

Towards this end CUPE recommended a targeted investment strategy aimed at the dominant foreign and domestic corporations in key sectors of the economy based on their equity exposure in financial markets.

The Canadian Labour Congress (CLC) subsequently endorsed a policy in 1978 advocating that the CPP investment fund maximize its investment performance and be used to promote an industrial strategy. The United Steel Workers (Canadian region) in 1979 recommended the establishment of an agency such as the Caisse de Dêpot et Placement in Quebec for the CPP which would be "capable of receiving pension fund monies for social impact and economic development" in order to "facilitate the aims of our industrial strategy"[22] by acquiring "substantial equity participation . . . in each of the key sectors."[23]

The Trades Union Congress (TUC) in Britain, on the basis of a 1979 convention resolution,[24] recommended to the Wilson Committee to Review the Functioning of Financial Institutions the creation of an independent fund to promote industrial revitalization.[25] This proposal was based on the operation of the occupational pension system, with 5 per cent of all new contributions (cash flow) being deposited and invested by the fund. The activities of the investment fund would be co-ordinated and integrated with broader macroeconomic planning agencies such as the National Investment Board. The TUC proposal may be placed within the framework of the alternative economic strategy advocated by the left wing of the Labour Party. In Britain, according to Minns,

nationalizing 30 of the major financial institutions would result in the state controlling between 20 to 40 per cent of the shares in nearly three-quarters of the top 50 companies.

The nationalization of financial institutions would provide substantial control over the shares of major companies. The management of these shareholdings could be the responsibility of a planning and investment agency, or . . . the shareholdings could be co-ordinated by a central ministry.[26]

The macro-level investment fund accumulated through the occupational pension system envisioned by the TUC proposal would therefore be used as a means of directly acquiring an equity position in key sectors of the economy to facilitate a fundamental economic transformation. The occupational pension system would thus complement broader macro-economic objectives and policies.

Macro-economic directed investment policies undertaken through the state pension system may promote progressive social change by increasing the social utility and marginal efficiency of capital in the public interest. The various current and proposed directed investment strategies based on the operation of the state pension system, while reflecting specific historical and national conditions, nevertheless have three characteristics in common.

First, most of these arrangements are predicated upon the existing institutional apparatus of the state social security system. Second, this approach to investment objectives effectively transforms the state pension system into a multiple purpose programme. The social security system becomes an instrument at the macro-economic level to affect savings, investment, capital accumulation, the ownership and control of the finance and industrial sectors, economic development and planning in the public interest, as well as to generate retirement income.

Third, the various alternative or macro-strategies related to an actively managed social security investment fund are based on the savings and investment function associated with the operation of institutional investors. That is, the investment function intrinsic to the operation of the pension system may be turned on its head and used against the corporate sector. Since the pension system's investment function provides the link between the finance and industrial sectors of the economy, it follows that it may be used to directly socialize the "commanding heights" of the economy through capital markets. The immense financial resources, that is, the savings of workers, organized and accumulated through a public pension system with a high level of funding, may therefore promote social change and economic accountability in the public interest. Micro-directed investment strategies based on the occupational pension system may serve a similar purpose.

MICRO-DIRECTED INVESTMENT STRATEGIES

The regulatory framework of the employer-sponsored occupational pension system has generally made little attempt to relate investment practices to the social utility of investment objectives. The private pension system, however, can be put under direction to achieve broader socio-economic objectives. Social or selective investment goals pursued through the private pension system would result, as Harbrecht put it, in employees as beneficial owners of pension capital having "some share in the direction and control of . . . pension trusts. . . . A voice in investment policy would allow employees to . . . direct fund investment into channels beneficial to them."[27]

Micro-social investment objectives have been broadly defined to include such goals as community development projects, industrial revitalization and employment generation, retention of capital within a geographic region, restriction of investment in anti-union firms or those who trade with South Africa, and investment in low-cost housing and social services. Directing the considerable assets of the private pension towards socially desirable goals has been referred to as "pension clout," and it may be viewed as a form of shareholder activism. While such projects may result in either a lower rate of return or higher risk for an equivalent return, they use the social utility of investment, rather than conventional market indicators, as the relevant measurement criterion. Social investment objectives based on the occupational pension system are reported in Table 10.4 for various countries.

TABLE 10.4

MICRO-LEVEL DIRECTED INVESTMENT STRATEGIES, OCCUPATIONAL PENSION SYSTEM

COUNTRY	CURRENT ARRANGEMENTS
U.K.	A number of unions, notably the Postal Workers and the National Union of Mine workers, have used their respective occupational pension fund for job creation

purposes. The Postal Workers' fund, the largest non-government fund in Europe, sets aside in the order of 2 per cent for investment in small business. The NUM seeks investment opportunities in mining communities.

U.S. The State of Wisconsin Investment Board (SWIB), the agency responsible for the investment of public employee pension funds, has, since 1921, followed a social or targeted investment policy in an attempt to keep money within the state.

The American Federation of Labour-Congress of Industrial Organization (AFL-CIO), at its 1979 convention, endorsed a "gray belt" strategy for industrial revitalization and social investment through occupational pension plans. The objectives are employment creation, social projects (such as housing), and the advancement of workers' interests through investment activities which might affect corporate policy, such as withholding pension fund investment from anti-union firms or those which invest in South Africa. Not withstanding these objectives, the policy noted that social "investment should not interfere with the primary responsibilities of pension fund trustees" to provide and secure pension benefits.

Major industrial unions, such as the UAW, USW and IAM, have endorsed social investment policies, as have major public employee unions and the construction trades.

Canada The Quebec Federation of Labour (FTQ) in 1983 introduced an employee investment fund, in some ways modelled on the Swedish Meidner proposal in conjunction with the Government of Quebec. The purpose of this "Solidarity Fund" is to promote investment in small-and-medium business (PME) in Quebec to create, maintain and save jobs; in addition, the fund is to be used for venture capital investments. The fund is financed through individual share subscriptions to workers and controlled by the FTQ. It is estimated that the fund will have $200 million of assets within five years.

Denmark The ATP, the mandated occupational pension plan, is used for venture capital to promote industrial development and for home mortgages. It is now permitted to invest up to 20 per cent of its assets in the equity market. The PKA, the occupational pension plan sponsored by the labour confederation, is used for equity investment "to strengthen the economy."

France Through the pay-as-you-go financed occupational pension system negotiated by the labour and employer confederations (the régime complimentaires), and recognized in law, there is a 1 per cent greater than required employer contribution to a "social action fund." This is primarily used for housing and other facilities for the elderly.

Israel   As a result of the labour confederation having direct
                     responsibility for the administration of major occupa-
                     tional pension funds, the funds are used for various social
                     and developmental purposes such as co-ops.

Sources: These data are drawn from the American Federation of Labour-Congress
           of Industrial Organizations, *Investment of Union Pension Funds* (Wash-
           ington, D.C.: AFL-CIO, circa 1980) pp. 53–74; Jeremy Rifkin and Randy
           Barber, *The North Will Rise Again: Pensions, Politics and Power in the
           1980s* (Boston: Beacon Press, 1978), and Donald A. Smart, *Investment
           Targeting: A Wisconsin Case Study* (Madison: Wisconsin Center for
           Public Policy, 1979).

Investment fund managers and labour organizations have traditionally subscribed to the view that "pension funds are designed to
serve but a *single* major purpose: to help meet the need for an
assured income after a person's working life is over."[28] Despite the
recent controversy surrounding social investment, particularly in
the U.S. and to a lesser extent Britain, and its advocacy by some
labour confederations and their affiliates,[29] the use of occupational
pension fund assets for alternative investment strategies is hardly a
new idea.

In the United States, John L. Lewis, former head of the United
Mine Workers, invested millions of dollars from the welfare fund in a
major coal company in the late 1940s. While this did little to maximize investment return to provide adequate pensions, it did subsidize coal exports and buoy employment. Such policies have been
denounced by some as "trade union capitalism,"[30] while others
such as Ted Hill, former chairman of the TUC in Britain, denounced
his colleagues in 1962 for investing in industrial shares and recommended that it "would be wise to leave the Stock Exchange to the
wolves."[31] Nevertheless, as early as 1956 a group of prominent U.S.
labour leaders testified before a Senate subcommittee that unions
were interested in having pension funds invested in projects which
would benefit their members, such as low-cost mortgages and housing. In 1959 the United Auto Workers (UAW) urged the Ford Motor
Company to use their workers' pension funds to invest in housing
and other community projects.[32] By 1979, Lane Kirkland, the new
president of the AFL-CIO, would state that "there are areas of risk
and ambiguity in switching to a consideration of the social over-
tones of investment policy. Whatever we do must conform to the
overriding concern that the investments be safe and that the return

be adequate to satisfy the funds obligations."[33] If the AFL-CIO has its way, however, "money power—that traditional mainstay of the bosses—will be directed away from investments in 'anti-union' corporations . . . into enterprises that . . . [are] friendly to the interests and goals of workers."[34] As Lloyd McBride, the late president of the United Steel Workers (USW), put it, "we can no longer tolerate this situation of using worker-produced capital against ourselves."[35]

Subsequently a number of influential AFL-CIO affiliates including the UAW, the USW, the International Association of Machinists, major public employee unions and the construction trades have all endorsed, with certain important qualifications, a social investment policy for occupational pension funds. A dubious victory was scored by the UAW on the issue with the Chrysler Corporation in the 1979 round of negotiations. As a result of the union foregoing one year's contributions to the pension fund in the order of $200 million, Chrysler agreed to introduce social investment criteria into the management of the fund and, as well, divested the portfolio of five stocks in companies involved in South Africa. Money directed to socially useful investments include low- and-middle income housing, day-care and community projects.

In Britain as early as 1959, Titmuss argued that "there can be little doubt that what is needed is the direction of [the] increasing flow of savings into . . . domestic areas of public squalor."[36] The Labour government's proposals in its 1976 white paper on occupational pension plans would have given workers, through their unions, much greater involvement in pension fund investment management. The government of the day must have realized that with greater union participation, pension fund investment policy would have been influenced by social and political considerations. Renewed interest by British unions in occupational pension plans in the 1970s witnessed a corresponding interest in the direction of pension fund investment. Some major TUC affiliates, the General and Municipal Workers' Union for example, called for a "comprehensive investigation into the question of using [occupational] pension fund resources for social purposes"[37] and related this to the "public ownership of [the] pension and life assurance industry as part of a wider plan for the financial sector of the economy"[38] in order to give "priority to . . . the national industrial strategy." Other unions such as the postal workers and the National Union of Miners have pursued social investment policies such as venture financing and housing. The "route by which [British] trade unions are going to extend their functions . . . in corporate affairs," one commentator suggested, "is through . . . pension funds. . . . Equipped with the Trojan Horses of pension funds, organized labour cannot be kept for long outside the citadels of corporate power."[39]

In summary, micro-directed investment strategies based on the occupational pension system, as a form of shareholder activism, are an attempt to mobilize the pension capital of workers to serve their broad socio-economic interests. Central to such an approach are three characteristics. First, reformulating the investment goals of the private pension system is an attempt to transform it into a multiple objective programme to generate both retirement income and social capital at the enterprise or community level. Second, the social utility of investment is used as the relevant criterion, rather than market indicators. Third, and this perhaps should be emphasized, social investment through the occupational pension system at the plant or sectoral level has absolutely nothing in common with the various theories of "people's capitalism," including Drucker's recent notion of "pension fund socialism."[40] Micro-directed investment strategies, unlike these "theories," are predicated on the economics of collective action in the interest of workers.

ASSESSMENT OF ALTERNATIVES

Directed investment strategies are a means by which to mobilize and channel the enormous resources of the pension system—public and private—towards socially productive and useful purposes in the public interest. From a social policy perspective, macro- and micro-alternative directed investment strategies must first be assessed in terms of their technical feasibility before relating them to broader political strategies for social change. These technical considerations are analysed here.

Investment Objectives. Central to the concept of alternative investment strategies based on the pension system is the ability to channel investment to socially useful or productive areas of economic activity. The targeted investment objectives undertaken through the state and occupational pension systems, as evidenced by current practice and proposals, vary considerably.

Investment objectives based on the state pension system may be formulated to achieve a number of goals at the macro-economic level. These might include investment to promote economic development and diversification, investment in crown corporations, reduction in government non-public borrowing requirements, reduction in government external borrowing requirements, investment in the private sector for take-overs and a control interest in dominant industrial and financial corporations, passive investment recycled through the private sector, venture capital financing, and bail-out operations. Social investment strategies predicated on the occupational pension system, on the other hand, have generally concerned themselves with employment generation, industrial revitalization, and the provision of social services at the plant, sectoral or community level. These ostensible economic goals are commonly formulated in terms of community development models, rather than as national economic objectives or strategies.

At issue is whether specific investment objectives correspond to the means to bring about their realization. This subject is relevant with respect to both macro- and micro-level directed investment strategies. Regarding the state pension system, it has been argued by some government and private sector representatives that it "is designed to provide a source of retirement income" and "if a new goal is added — i.e., the manipulation of the economy through the fund on the basis that more wealth can be created—we encounter a conflict of objectives."[41] Furthermore, if the state system "is to be put on a funded basis, it is important that the investment policy of the fund . . . be free of political interference" because "social objectives should be pursued through political, not fiduciary, means."[42]

Contrary to this view three arguments may be advanced. First, in advanced market economies there is a high level of "unsatisfied demand" (to use the Keynesian term), resulting in public needs and private wants. Diminishing these considerable social and economic disparities and inequities will require more state intervention and economic planning in the public interest. Second, channelling the resources of the state pension system into productive (although not necessarily profitable) investment will generate economic growth and capital accumulation to strengthen the economy in order to support an expanded public pension system. Macro-directed investment policies therefore complement and are entirely compatible with the retirement income objective of the national social security system. Third, assuming that any social institution or policy is free of "political interference," or is "neutral," is itself a political statement. "Neutrality" within this context is merely an ideological cloak for maintaining current social arrangements. The private sector maintains that the public pension system should "be free of political interference" in order to maintain its control over pension capital and the direction of investment.

The investment objectives of a national social security fund are related to the macro-economic levers of power, whereas micro-level strategies are related to the workplace or community. An important issue differentiating the types of directed investment strategies pursued is based on the distinction between productive investment and capital formation (plant and infrastructure) at the macro-economic level and investment in bail-out operations, venture financing, and the provision of social services at the micro-level. There is a thin, but real, line between using occupational pension funds for economic development and for what are, in effect, bail-out operations. Despite the social merits of such undertakings, such as employment protection in the case of a bail-out operation or a high rate of return with venture financing, it may be argued that investment by workers in such endeavours is inappropriate given the high risk of an investment shortfall being inflicted upon the pension fund. To the extent that such investments are deemed desirable at the micro-level, more conventional methods of financing exist to avoid jeopardizing the retirement savings of workers.

Pooling and Risk. The fact that investment objectives are related to a level of acceptable risk is of particular relevance when assessing the propriety of macro- and micro-directed investment strategies based on the pension system. In this regard three fundamental principles associated with the operation of a national social security system are of particular importance: compulsory enrolment, the pooling of risk over the population, and the resulting cross-subsidies between covered groups. Compulsory enrolment spreads the risk over the entire covered population rather than just one segment of it as would be the case with employer-sponsored pension plans.

Micro-level social investment strategies have a number of pernicious distributional effects as a result of voluntary and limited occupational pension plan coverage. First, limited occupational pension plan coverage mitigates against spreading the investment risk based on the pooling principle. Put another way, particular segments of the labour force, that is, those covered by an employer-sponsored plan, would be subjected to higher risk-taking than would be the case if a similar investment strategy were followed through the state social security system. Second, because of limited coverage and pooling, the nature of the risk incurred is different.

Specifically, selective investment strategies based on the occupational pension system result in *individual* plan members becoming risk-takers, whereas there is a *social* risk associated with the operation of the national retirement income system. Third, social investment strategies based on the occupational pension system are an externalized risk and cost of production to individual firms — that is, specific groups of workers effectively subsidize their employer, or government, depending on the type of investment.

Risk-taking associated with social investment strategies, therefore, varies according to the type of institutional arrangement. The nature of risk-taking associated with micro-level investment goals suggests, however, that such an approach may exacerbate sectoral tensions between groups within the labour force, whereas these objectives based on the state pension system would represent a socialized or pooled risk. The level of risk, in turn, is related to the way in which pension assets are invested.

Portfolio Composition. Investment objectives and the corresponding level of risk determine asset mix or portfolio composition. The ability of alternative investment strategies at either the macro- or micro-level to promote the public interest and economic accountability will depend on the type of investment. For directed investment strategies at the macro-level to be successful in terms of affecting economic policy and social change requires that the social security investment fund have a substantial equity portfolio in the private sector so that it can exert control over the "commanding heights" of the economy. Alternatively, such an investment fund might be used for direct investment in the public sector or placed in non-marketable government bonds of crown corporations at a guaranteed or competitive rate of return.

The private sector is aware of this attempt at "socialism through the back door." As one source put it, "the potential effect of such massive government intervention in the market causes shudders" because of "the prospect of ultimate government control of private industry through the CPP."[43] The prospect of cycling the same massive funds from an expanded CPP to the private sector, however, is greeted with jubiliation, as was evidenced by the Government of Ontario's proposal for the full-funding of the CPP.[44] In order to forestall government intervention in the private sector and to remove "political interference," it has been suggested by some business representatives that these monies be invested in debt instruments such as corporate bonds. Thus, workers would effectively underwrite the private sector while being denied the proprietary rights associated with equity ownership. It was for this reason that the Canadian Council on Social Development suggested that "it would be wise to approach with caution the prospect of [increasing] the funds available [to the private pension system] without . . . establishing some controls on their usage in the national interest."[45]

Social investment objectives at a micro-level may take a number of different forms. To the extent that occupational pension funds follow a social investment strategy based on their equity holdings results in their resembling other shareholder activists in attempting to influence corporate behaviour. Whether such a strategy is viable will depend on the amount and concentration of such shareholdings in a pension fund's portfolio. A formal difficulty with respect to an occupational pension fund exerting control over corporate behaviour, however, is that such shareholdings are ordinarily limited to 30 per cent of the value of the fund or 10 per cent of a firm's outstanding shares. This restriction may, depending upon the diffusion of outstanding shares, effectively limit an individual occupational pension fund's ability to pursue an alternative investment strategy or affect corporate behaviour. Whether an alternative investment policy is viable through the occupational pension system without doing injury to the retirement income objective remains to be determined.

Fiduciary Responsibility. The issue of social investment through occupational pension plans is strewn with contradictions and problems which must be confronted. A formal obstacle to unions pursuing a social investment strategy is the fiduciary obligation placed upon pension fund managers and trustees (and union's as trustees), explicitly and implicitly contained in the relevant legislation, requiring them to act "solely in the interest of the participants and beneficiaries" and to act in a "prudent" manner.

While the legal notions of "fiduciary responsibility" and "prudent man" serve as an elaborate ideological artifice to legitimize the operation of the employer-sponsored pension system to maintain private sector control over pension capital, they nevertheless fulfil an important purpose. That purpose is two-fold: first, to guarantee an adequate rate of return, subject to acceptable risk levels, to ensure pension benefits to plan members; and second, especially in the case of a defined benefit pension where the plan sponsor is responsible for any short-fall in investment earnings, to minimize the cost of the programme. The issue in large part turns on what is meant by "prudent" as well as "prudent" for "whom."

Many of the proposals for micro-level alternative investment strategies have suggested that occupational pension plans invest their assets in the plan sponsor or community in order to protect or generate employment; others have advocated investing in low-cost mortgages or housing as well as social services such as day-care or nursing homes. Some advocates have gone so far as to suggest that it is imprudent not to take into account the social consequences of pension fund investment (a "social audit") or to fail to function as an activist shareholder."[46]

While such proposals may improve the social utility of investment by satisfying the needs of the active labour force in the short term, it is highly questionable whether they will preserve the integrity of the pension fund in the long run. Furthermore, the interests of pensioners may be jeopardized by strategies which ignore portfolio diversification or less than arms-length investments or which earn a lower rate of return than might otherwise have been the case, thus endangering accrued pension benefits. It may even be argued that such micro-social investment strategies are counterproductive in terms of advancing the interests of the active labour force. A short-fall in investment earnings, particularly in the case of a defined benefit pension plan, that necessitates additional contributions from the plan sponsor may result in lower wages within a total compensation costing framework. For these reasons social investment strategies through the medium of the employer-sponsored occupational pension system should be approached with considerable caution.

Experience to date suggests that the co-management of pension funds has had little effect on investment practices because of the constraints imposed by fiduciary responsibility. In Britain, the Economist Intelligence Unit, for example, reports that "whenever trade union representatives become [trustees] they are just as keen, if not more so, to act in a capitalist fashion."[47] One study in the United States noted that union trustees "become more concerned with the business aspects of the pension fund than with the economic impact."[48] Another study concluded that

while pension funds can be divested and redirected into firms and projects adhering to community-defined goals, or used to influence the direction of corporate activities through stock-voting rights . . . retirement systems are . . . inextricably tied to the capitalist system. . . . Pension funds are limited to achieving desired social and economic goals only within activities that provide "adequate" investment income.

Thus, occupational "pension funds may simply evolve into new alternative investment opportunities rather than worker control over . . . assets."[49]

The issue of fiduciary responsibility, as that term is ordinarily understood, has little relevance to macro-economic directed strategies because the state is the ultimate guarantor of social security benefits. Government therefore is in a position to provide a guaranteed or competitive rate of return to an actively managed social security investment fund and preserve the security of retirement benefits.

Market Impact and Economic Planning. In order for alternative investment strategies to be effective, they must maximize their impact in capital markets. In the case of macro-investment strategies based on the state pension system, a necessary prerequisite to fulfil this condition is a high level of funding (full-cost or full-funding) as discussed above. Without it, it is impossible to accumulate an investment fund large enough to serve as a countervailing force to private institutional investors in order to pursue alternative investment strategies.

The compulsory enrolment associated with a national social security programme serves as a natural conduit to mobilize savings for investment purposes. Conversely, the voluntary nature of the occupational pension system mitigates against it fulfilling a similar role despite the advanced funding of benefits. This problem might be overcome, depending upon institutional arrangements, as in the case of the Trades Union Congress proposal, which channels a proportion of the contributions of the private pension system to a national investment agency. The considerable centralization and concentration of private pension fund assets under the control of a few dominant financial institutions may effectively serve a similar purpose, should those institutions be put under public control.

The ability to centralize pension fund assets is an important consideration if the pension system — public or private — is to be coordinated and integrated with broader economic planning structures to serve the public interest. National social security systems readily lend themselves to such an arrangement, while the private pension system might be adapted to such a purpose.

Draw Down of Benefits. While the national social security system and occupational pension funds may be utilized as a source of investment and developmental capital, they must continue to fulfil their primary function of providing retirement income. In this regard, it is necessary to identify a potential problem which may result in a conflict if the social investment and retirement income objectives are incorporated into one institutional apparatus. The conflict will not become apparent until the baby boom generation draws down benefits from the pension system at the demographic peak. The dilemma, in brief, is how pension benefits are to be paid from assets which are locked into non-marketable or non-liquid social investments. This issue has been ignored too often. It must be resolved or it must be concluded that social investment through the pension system — public or private — is not compatible with the retirement income objective.

In this regard three distinct cases may be identified: first, where social investment is channelled through the state pension system; second, where social investment is cycled through an occupational pension plan; and third, where occupational pension funds have conventional portfolios. In the case of a national social security system which pursues a directed investment strategy it is likely to take two forms: first, shareholdings in private sector enterprises; and second, direct investment in public sector crown corporations. In either instance, pension benefits could not be paid at the demographic peak unless the assets of the investment fund could be liquified. One hypothetical answer might be to sell back the assets — equity or an entire firm — to the private sector in order to cover obligations. Politically, however, this would result in a situation little different from that which existed prior to a directed investment strategy being implemented. The second, and more viable, course would be to "roll-over" the value of the outstanding pension obligations into marketable or non-marketable government bonds in order to cover the benefits.

The ability of occupational pension funds following a social investment policy to honour pension obligations is considerably more problematic. It would in large part depend upon the amount and type of social investment. The basic problem confronting such a plan is that it may be locked into assets having no market value. Such a situation might arise if a pension fund were to invest too greatly in its parent firm as part of a bail-out operation or in social services such as day-care or nursing homes. To the extent that an occupational pension fund was locked into non-marketable or illiquid assets or earned a reduced rate of return as a result of certain types of investment such as low-cost mortgages or housing, it might be unable to honour its pension commitments. There might be no way in which employer-sponsored pension plans following a social investment policy could extricate themselves from this quandary.

The third situation is the typical advanced funded occupational pension plan with a conventional portfolio. The assets of that portfolio (stocks, bonds and so on) cover the outstanding pension obligations (liabilities). As the baby boom begins to retire around the year 2011, private pension funds will go into a disaccumulation (dissaving) position to cover the draw-down of benefits. Effectively, this means that pension funds as major shareholders of corporate equity will become net sellers of securities. There will in turn be a concomitant impact on capital markets, albeit over a twenty-year period, which may be expected to exert downward pressure on the price of securities as they are divested. Little, if any, attention has been paid to this issue in the technical literature or to its implications for the private pension system's ability to fulfil its commitments. It is necessary for macro- and micro-social investment strategies to be compatible with the retirement income objective of the pension system in order for them to be technically feasible. Other design features affect their political viability.

Contribution Structure and Fiscal Impact. Social investment policies must be distributionally and fiscally equitable for them to be politically acceptable—that is, they must not place an undue burden on those who can least afford it. The Economic Council of Canada has argued, for example, that

> the required increase in the contribution rate [for a fully funded CPP] would fall more heavily on those with lower earnings because it is a payroll tax. To ask this group for increased contributions to improve their pension benefits is one thing; to ask them to bear the brunt of programs to reduce foreign ownership of . . . industry or accelerate economic growth . . . is quite another. . . . We [question] the fairness of achieving this alternative objective through a method that bears most heavily on lower-income groups.[50]

Considerations of fiscal equity might therefore serve as an impediment to implementing macro-social investment policies through the pension system.

From a public policy perspective, however, such a formulation is incomplete and confuses "ends" with "means." The source of this regressivity is the existing contribution structure found in most national social security systems in North America and Western Europe, not macro-alternative investment policies as such. To overcome this technical problem and introduce macro-directed investment policies on a fiscally equitable basis would therefore require the implementation of a progressive contribution structure to nullify any negative effects on low-income earners. A progressive contribution structure, based on the pooling principle underlying a national social security system, would also have the effect of promoting redistributive policies. It would be both horizontally and vertically redistributive by forcing the corporate sector (i.e., employers) and the upper income group to contribute more to the public pension system.

Unintended and anomalous distributional and fiscal inequities might result from the implementation of micro-social investment strategies through the occupational pension system. The current regressive and inequitable distribution of revenue loss and tax expenditure (lost interest to government) associated with the operation of the private pension system involves a considerable fiscal cross-subsidy *from* low- *to* high-income groups. The cost of the private pension system was in the order of £1,400 to £2,900 million in the U.K. (1983), compared with $28.4 billion in the U.S. (1982) and an estimated $6.1 billion in Canada (1980). The current fiscal framework governing the private pension system is extremely regressive, favours upper income earners, and results in those without pension plan coverage supporting those with coverage because of the tax deductibility status of pension contributions. The fiscal subsidization of the private pension system ultimately serves to limit the expansion of the public pension system by depriving it of revenue.

Implementing micro-social investment policies through occupational pension plans would compound this situation in at least two ways. First, as a consequence of the fiscal cross-subsidy, the majority of the labour force without pension coverage would continue underwriting occupational pension plan members through the tax system. While some of the advantages of social investment policies, such as employment generation, would positively affect everyone, other programmes, such as low-cost housing, would only benefit plan members. Second, to the extent that a social investment policy results in an investment shortfall requiring additional employer contributions (as in the case of a defined benefit plan), it would result in this increased business expenditure being written off through the tax system and subsized by all taxpayers while the benefits would be unevenly distributed. *To facilitate the introduction of macro-directed investment strategies through the state pension system on an equitable basis would require a progressive contribution structure.* This is a technical adjustment. Eliminating the fiscal and distributional inequities underlying the operation of the private pension system would require nothing less than a revolution in the income tax system.

The technical assessment of macro- and micro-alternative investment strategies based on the pension system is summarized in Table 10.5. This evaluation suggests that macro-alternative investment strategies through an actively managed social security investment fund are generally more feasible than are micro-social investment policies based on the occupational pension system. Macro-directed investment strategies are assessed as being superior in terms of five evaluation criteria, neutral in one category, and inferior in another. Micro-social investment strategies are assessed as inferior with respect to six evaluation criteria and neutral in one category.

A significant implication of this analysis is that the feasibility of directed social investment strategies based on the operation of the pension system will, in the final analysis, depend upon political, rather than technical, considerations and circumstances. Such strategies must, however, be viewed as being progressive at this time, given the balance of political forces, because they promote the public interest by improving pension arrangements for the increasing proportion of the elderly, limit the economic power of institutional investors, accelerate capital accumulation, and offer the possibility of socializing key sectors of market economies. Alternative directed investment strategies based on the pension system, therefore, are one way in which to expand public control and accountability over economic decision-making in the public interest.

TABLE 10.5

ASSESSMENT OF PENSION SYSTEM
MACRO- AND MICRO-ALTERNATIVE DIRECTED INVESTMENT STRATEGIES
BY EVALUATION CRITERIA

| | ASSESSMENT OF STRATEGIES[1] | |
EVALUATION CRITERIA	Macro Level	Micro Level
Investment Objectives	+	−
Pooling and Risk	+	−
Portfolio Composition	+	−
Fiduciary Responsibility	+	−
Market Impact and Economic Planning[2]	0	0
Draw Down of Benefits	+	−
Contribution Structure[3] and Fiscal Impact	−	−

Notes: 1 Comparative ranking where + indicates a superior assessment, 0 a
neutral position and − an inferior evaluation.
2 Depending upon the level of funding for the national social security
system and institutional arrangements for the occupational pension
system.
3 Assuming no change to current arrangements.

THE POLITICAL ECONOMY OF PENSIONS AND THE COMING PENSION CRISIS

This study has traced the complex series of linkages between the experience of old age, the pension system and broader socio-economic structures in Canada, Britain and the United States. Those interactive elements affecting the formulation and direction of public policy towards pensions and aging over the next three to five decades have been identified and analysed with regard to their possible implications. The coming pension crisis in these advanced capitalist countries is a consequence of the interaction between and among a series of conjunctural factors which converge in the future—the inadequate level of retirement income of the elderly, the increasing proportion of the elderly in the population and the costs associated with an aging population, the universal and specific limitations of the private pension system, the underdevelopment of the public pension system, and the corporate sector's appropriation of pension capital as a source of investment—all of which are based on the conflicting, structurally determined interests of the elderly, labour, capital and the capitalist state. Other analytic approaches to the pension issue emphasize different causes for and solutions to the impending pension crisis,[51] but generally corroborate the central conclusion arrived at here.

The logic associated with the pension issue inevitably leads from the current economic and social position of the elderly, to the inadequacies of the private and public pension systems, to the symbiotic relationship between the pension system and the finance and industrial sectors, to the private control and direction of capital, and to possible consideration of alternative investment strategies based on the pension system. The pension crisis examined in this study is in the final analysis systemic in origin, as are the limits to reform. Reforming the pension system is a potentially volatile political issue because it affects the structurally determined interests of all major groups and institutions in a capitalist political economy: workers, unions, the finance and industrial sectors, the state, and the increasing proportion of the elderly. The factors underlying the pension crisis identified in this study are essentially long-term in nature, but the structural pressures propelling the pension systems in these countries towards a crisis will inevitably intensify. The severity and form in which the pension crisis manifests itself will, however, undoubtedly vary according to specific national conditions.

The protracted struggle for pension reform, and the impending pension crisis, poses a series of interrelated public policy and political issues about control over investment, capital accumulation, the relationship between investment and economic growth, the social utility of investment, distributional and fiscal equity, the role-typing of the elderly, and how we are qualitatively to live the last fifteen to twenty years of our lives. The pension issue links the personal experience of old age with structural issues. For workers and the elderly, the battle for pension reform will not be fought out with the decisiveness of Waterloo or Stalingrad, but, rather, it will be the next Thirty Years' War. As with Marx's analysis of the legislative struggle to reduce the length of the working day,[52] there is much political capital to be gained by mobilizing around the concrete demand for pension reform and relating it to broader issues of political economy.

Because aging and pensions policy is "a topic that has not clearly . . . been politicized"[53] in the past, it is necessary for progressives to turn the pension crisis and reform of the pension system into an ideologically defined issue and draw the linkages between the personal and the broader structures of economic and political power in capitalist societies. The political economy of pensions and the history of aging is that conjuncture where the personal and the structural meet. We all grow old. What is socially determined is individually experienced. How, then, as individuals are we to confront old age? Philosopher and novelist Simone de Beauvoir put it well: "There is only one solution if old age is not to be an absurd parody of our former life, and that is to go on pursuing ends that give our existence a meaning—devotion to individuals, to groups, or to causes, social, political."[54] For old age as part of the human condition to become a meaningful experience for individuals will ultimately require collective action on the pension issue in order to affect power, politics and social change. As Lange suggested, however, for "the economist who is called upon to advise a socialist government . . . there exists only one economic policy which he can commend . . . as likely to lead to success. This is a policy of *revolutionary courage*."[55] Within this context, the relationship between the political economy of pensions and strategies for social change may be related to the transition from capitalism to socialism.

PENSIONS AND THE TRANSITION TO SOCIALISM: A THEORETICAL PERSPECTIVE

"Capital," Marx and Engels argued, "is social power."[56] Pensions are pure money-capital. That "the growth of social capital is effected by the growth of many individual capitals," such as pension funds, means that "the masses of capital amalgamated . . . by centralization . . . become new and powerful levels of social accumulation."[57] For Marx, the financial system in advanced capitalist economies plays an important role in accelerating and facilitating the transition to socialism because of the increasingly social nature of production. Pension funds, because they are part of that system, and given their strategic position within advanced capitalist economies, may potentially "constitute the form of transition to a new mode of production"[58] under contemporary conditions.

Under the specific historical conditions of advanced capitalism, strategies for social change based on the state and occupational pension systems may be incorporated into a broader transitional programme for socialism by fulfilling a number of important economic and political objectives. Directed investment strategies pursued through the national social security system accelerate the accumulation and socialization of capital and identify the issue of state power; alternatively, social investment strategies based on the occupational pension system may raise the issue of workers' control and shop floor democracy. Thus, the concrete struggle for pension reform may result in the politicization of the pension issue and serve as a direct link to broader issues of power and politics. The pension issue therefore becomes a means of stretching the limits of economism and welfarism in advanced capitalist economies. Strategies for social change associated with the operation of the pension system correspond to the Marxist theory of "encroaching control," based on the socialization of capital, and more contemporary theories of radical or militant reformism. Such strategies, as one mode of transition from capitalism to socialism, must therefore be examined in terms of their historical specificity and the relationship between reform and revolution.

Marxist political theory is "for the most part the product of historical episodes and specific circumstances" according to Miliband, and has resulted in "contradictory interpretations — tensions, contradictions, and unresolved problems."[59] In their theoretical and practical work Marx and Engels were aware that political strategies, programmes and tactics had to be adapted to changing circumstances and that "these measures will of course be different in different countries."[60] Subsequently, Lenin argued that it was necessary for socialists to work out an independent application of Marxist theory depending upon concrete historical and national conditions. In an early article he emphasized that

> we do not regard Marx's theory . . . as completed and inviolable; on the contrary . . . it has only laid the . . . foundation. . . . We think that an *independent* elaboration of Marx's theory is especially essential . . . for this . . . theory provides only general *guiding* principles, which, in *particular*, are applied in England differently than in France, in France differently than in Germany, and in Germany differently than in Russia.[61]

Later, in a rarely noted speech to the Fourth Congress of the Communist International in 1922, he acknowledged that "the methods and content of . . . activities" were "too Russian, [and] reflects Russian experience. . . . Foreigners . . . cannot be content with hanging it in a corner like an icon and praying to it. Nothing will be achieved that way."[62] The experience of the Soviet revolution demonstrated, Lenin said, "that things have turned out differently from what Marx and Engels expected."[63] The general conclusion is that "to the extent that historical conditions change, policies correct at one time become incorrect at another. In discussing tactics, the decisive comparison is not with past tactics but with present facts."[64]

To ignore historical specificity is to reject historical materialism and the dialectical relationship between theory and practice. As Engels concluded, "if conditions have changed in the case of war between nations, this is no less true in the case of the class struggle."[65] And if conditions change in terms of the class war, so too must the weapons. Strategies for social change associated with the pension system must therefore be understood within the context of the relationship between reform and revolution because the struggle for social reforms may play an important role in promoting a socialist transformation of society. In this regard it is necessary to differentiate between "reforms" as a means to an end and "reformism" as an end in itself. From an historical perspective "it is clearly the case that the struggle for reforms in a . . . democratic regime was never taken by classical Marxism to be incompatible with the advancement of revolutionary aims and purposes. On the contrary such a struggle is an intrinsic part of the Marxist tradition." "The real issue," Miliband argued, "is the perspective from which reforms are viewed, what they are expected to achieve, and what else than reforms is being pursued."[66] From a Marxist perspective, the issue is not reform *or* revolution but, rather, reform *and* revolution. How particular reforms are formulated will determine their ability to promote socialist policies.

Marx and Engels, and Lenin at a later date, stressed the complexities of the transition from capitalism to socialism. In terms of economic analysis and political strategies, the Marx of Volume 1 of *Capital* is considerably different from the one found in Volume 3; and the Engels who appears in *Anti-During* is different from the one who subsequently emerges in his late correspondence. In these later works the focus and emphasis shifts to problems related to socialist revolution in developed capitalist societies. Marx and Engels had no formal theory of the state and party;[67] similarly, they advanced no coherent theory or blueprint with respect to the transition to socialism in advanced capitalist countries. While their early economic analysis emphasized the "immiseration" or "breakdown theory" based on the inherent contradictions of capitalism, they later seemed to postulate an alternative mode of transition based on the gradual socialization of capital.

It is necessary in this regard to differentiate between the "socialization" of capital as an economic process intrinsic to capitalism and "socialism" as a system of political power based on the interests of the working class. For Marx, the shift from individual to corporate enterprise, with the accompanying integration, concentration, centralization and interdependence of capital, was a concomitant of the increasingly social nature of production—that is, the socialization of productive forces. This process generates new and higher forms of collective economic activity which ultimately result in the "transcendence of the capitalist mode of production within the capitalist mode of production."[68]

In this regard Marx emphasized that "no social order ever disappears before all productive forces . . . have been developed; and new, higher relations of production never appear before the material conditions of their existence have matured in the womb of the old society."[69] "At a certain level of development," however, "a new mode of production grows within and develops out of the old mode of production."[70] Thus, Moore concludes, Marx was suggesting that the "economic transition from capitalism to socialism can start *before* the working class attains state power."[71] Pension funds, which represent a pool of collective labour power, or "living labour" (to use Marx's term), have systemically increased the socialization of savings and investment in advanced market economies. As the fastest growing pool of capital they have become a mechanism for the accumulation of social capital and may therefore accelerate and facilitate the transition to socialist forms of economic organization.

A parallel may be drawn with Marx's concept of the "political economy of labour."[72] In the *Communist Manifesto* it was suggested that "the proletariat will use its political supremacy to wrest, by *degrees*, all *capital* from the bourgeoisie, to *centralize* all instruments of production in the hands of the *state* . . . and to increase the total . . . *productive forces as rapidly as possible*."[73] Marx subsequently elaborated upon this theme in his 1864 Inaugural Address to the First International. For the first time, according to Harrison,

Marx accepted that the proletariat might establish *its own forms of property* and principles of productive organization *within the capitalist mode of production.* . . . Consequently, the working class might . . . seek to secure, extend, fortify and generalize these achievements. Its advance is now measured not merely by the perfection of its party organization, *but by the inroads which it can make on the existing mode of production.*[74]

Such a formulation clearly signals a shift in emphasis with respect to strategies regarding the transition from capitalism to socialism. While Marx was generally pessimistic regarding a peaceful transition to socialism, he nevertheless viewed it as a possibility, at least in some countries, noting that "heed must be paid to the institutions, customs and traditions of various countries, and we do not deny that there are countries, such as America and England . . . [and] Holland, where . . . workers may attain their [socialist] goal by peaceful means."[75] The different strategies or roads leading to socialism will thus depend upon specific historical and national conditions.

"Instead of a single model of the transition from capitalism to socialism," according to Moore, "the tradition of competing systems presents a large family of models."[76] The process of "encroaching control" by workers on the existing capitalist mode of production, as one approach or model of transition to socialism, is a recurrent theme in Marxist political theory including Marx, Bernstein, the Guild Socialists, Lenin, Trotsky and Gramsci. "Integral to any theory of encroaching control is the conception of social revolution as a process rather than as an act," according to Hyman, and "while such theories need not exclude the perspective of a 'classic' revolutionary climax, they emphasis the possibility . . . of inroads *within* capitalism as a basis for [an] eventual transition to socialism."[77] Such a strategy envisions or results in "dual power"[78] or "dual sovereignty"[79]—that is, a shared sphere of economic and political power between labour and capital. Consequently, there may be a transitional period characterized by a "coexistence of different and . . . contradictory forms" of economic organization and a "juxtaposition of collectivist . . . and private property."[80]

Dual sovereignty or power is a characteristic often associated with a pre-revolutionary situation. "While the concept of dual power is customarily used in analysis of the control of the state," it is also of "relevance . . . in the context of the control of production within the factory."[81] Dual power which may evolve out of "encroaching control" has a dialectical character which manifests itself at *both* the state *and* shop floor levels. It is within this framework that macro- and micro-alternative investment policies based on the pension system are of relevance and may be incorporated into broader political strategies for social change. Macro-alternative investment strategies are a "top down" approach at the state level, whereas goals based on micro-social investment are a "bottom up" initiative from the shop floor. As a totality, they constitute a *dual* attack upon capital at different levels of power with respect to the control and direction of investment and in whose interests such decisions are made. Within the historically specific *non-revolutionary* context which currently characterizes modern capitalist countries, alternative social investment policies may become one way in which to promote accelerated capital accumulation and economic development, the gradual socialization of investment and key sectors of advanced market economies, and the democratization of the workplace.

At a macro-economic level, policies based on alternative directed investment correspond to the theories proposed by the Austro-Marxists and Tsuru. The leading economic theorists of Austro-Marxism[82]—Hilferding, Renner and Bauer—suggested that the transition to socialism was possible based on the "socialisation of circulation," that is, the finance sector. "Socialization effected by finance capital," according to Hilderding, "has made it enormously easier to overcome capitalism" because "finance capital has brought the most important branches of production under its control."[83] The socialization of the economy by finance capital has been reinforced by the expanded role of the modern capitalist state. "State penetration of the economy," according to Renner, has increasingly resulted in "direct state management of the economy."[84] Thus, under historically specific political circumstances, the state might play an active and progressive role by placing the "commanding heights" of the economy under public control, provided there is mass mobilization and a political will.

The transition from capitalism to socialism envisioned by the Austro-Marxists would therefore take the form of an

> extension of the welfare functions of the state and of the rational organization of the economy under a regime of public ownership; although the transition . . . still has to be accomplished by a working-class party through political struggles.[85]

Renner believes this process may offer a means to achieve a gradual and peaceful transition to socialism,[86] what Bauer called the "slow revolution."[87] This approach may be viewed as the intellectual progenitor of what has become known as the Swedish theory of "functional socialism,"[88] or the "third way," which proposes that the regulation of an economic institution's functions, rather than formal ownership as such, is the critical determinant with respect to establishing public control and accountability. Regulation of the pension system's investment function and directed investment strategies in the public interest correspond to such a formulation.

While some have criticized the theory of "socialisation of circulation" on the grounds that it emphasizes the sphere of circulation over production in capitalist economies,[89] it may be argued that under conditions of monopoly capitalism, characterized by the fusion of industrial and financial capital and the increasing importance of the finance sector in regulating capitalist economies, this distinction is no longer critical in terms of formulating political strategies. The systemic and functional fusion of financial and industrial capital suggests that regulation of the state pension system's investment function to promote alternative investment policies in the public interest may offer the opportunity, under specific political conditions, of "socialising circulation" and key sectors of the economy from the "top down."

A similar approach was advanced by Tsuru, a Japanese Marxist economist, who argued that in some capitalist countries

> the strategy of the transition into socialism can effectively be developed with focus upon the *form of [economic] surplus*, utilizing all . . . occasions to make the issue clear and weakening the hold which private capital has on the surplus, gradually shifting it into a socially-controlled fund. . . . The transition of capitalism to socialism certainly does not have to involve the sudden and overall shift of ownership from private hands to public. Surplus is a *flow* in contrast to the means of production which is a *stock*. . . . For the purpose of *gradual* transformation of capitalism into socialism it will be strategically easier in many cases to think in terms of the flow and to take measures connected with the form of the flow.[90]

Because the pension system has increasingly organized and socialized the flow of savings and investment at a macro-economic level in modern capitalist economies, it has become a potential instrument for the accumulation and direction of capital under public control at the state level. Macro-alternative investment policies through the state pension system may therefore serve to focus on the *global struggle* over the economic surplus, rather than on isolated local demands based on the occupational pension system.

Keynes argued that only the "state . . . is in a position to calculate

. . . the general social advantage" and that it will be "taking an even greater responsibility for directly organizing investment" because "*investment cannot safely be left in private hands*."[91] To organize investment for the "general social advantage" will require that it be put under public control. And while Engels cautioned that "state ownership of productive forces is not the solution of [class] conflict . . . it provides the formal means, the levers, of that solution."[92] As suggested here, the state pension system may assume the role of a macro-economic lever facilitating progressive social change in a non-revolutionary situation. While the "results of capitalist social-ization are variegated expressions of the historical process from capitalism to socialism," they may also represent "the development of objective and subjective *preconditions* for a revolutionary transi-tion to socialism."[93]

Macro-level alternative investment policies are an important link relating pension reform to broader political struggles. As Bernstein noted, the "task of social democracy is to fight for all reforms in the State which . . . raise the working classes and transform the State in the direction of democracy."[94] Concrete demands for pension reform, including an expansion of the state pension system and macro-directed investment policies in the public interest, serve to establish the relationship between the "struggle against forms of relations of the state" with the "demand that social needs be met."[95] Linking the struggle for pension reform to broader issues of political economy, therefore, has the effect of focusing political attention on the nature of state and class power in modern capitalist societies.

Micro-level social investment policies through the occupational pension system similarly have the potential of identifying impor-tant economic and political issues at the point of production, that is, at the factory level. Such an approach effectively serves to focus on, and call into question, fundamental management prerogatives such as corporate control over investment decision-making, as they affect the solvency of the firm and the security of occupational pen-sion plan benefits. To protect the security of pension benefits, work-ers and unions maybe forced to become directly involved in corporate affairs. Micro-alternative investment goals, intended to serve the interests of workers at the sectoral and community level, despite their technical limitations, may nevertheless become an important political link between the employer-sponsored occupa-tional pension system and the broader struggle for shop floor democracy.

The politicization of the pension issue as a result of the pension crisis may, in turn, transcend the constraints of trade union economism and welfare statism by stretching the limits of reform. "The capitalist system," Miliband has argued, "produces mystification as to the real nature of its 'relations of production.'"[96] Limiting pension reform solely to the issue of benefit adequacy, as important as it may be, perpetuates and reinforces this ideological obscuration because it fails to establish the systemic relationship between the impending pension crisis and the broader structures of political and economic power in advanced capitalist economies. Widening the focus and politics of pension reform to include macro- and micro-alternative investment policies may penetrate this ideological veil and stretch the limits of economism and welfarism by challenging fundamental economic and power relationships.

"The economic struggle," Lenin forcefully argued, "serves as the basis for the . . . development of the class struggle against the whole capitalist system."[97] Reforms which stretch the limits of the capitalist system serve as a means of promoting social change. Pension reform, formulated to include alternative investment policies, therefore becomes a "radical reform"[98] which may be incorporated into a broader strategy promoting "militant reformism."[99] Gorz has suggested that radical reforms are those "which . . . prepare [workers] to assume the leadership of society" and "establish certain limiting mechanisms . . . which restrict or dislocate the power of capital."[100] In a non-revolutionary situation, alternative investment strategies based on the pension system represent such an initiative.[101]

The politicization of the pensions and aging issue as a result of the conflicting structural interests of the pension actors and formulating pension reform policies as a radical demand may, in turn, ultimately reveal the systemic origins of the pension crisis. To recognize the constraints imposed by broader social structures is "to point to the limits of reform . . . and . . . make possible a strategy of change which attacks the mode of production that imposes the constraints."[102] Relating the political economy of pensions to the coming pension crisis and to strategies for social change may therefore promote, and ultimately facilitate, a socialist transformation of society, liberating both workers and the elderly.

Notes

1 Gaston V. Rimlinger, *Welfare Policy and Industrialization in Europe, America and Russia* (New York: Wiley, 1971), and Hugh Heclo, *Modern Social Politics in Britain and Sweden: From Relief to Income Maintenance* (New Haven and London: Yale University Press, 1974).

2 The seminal work on this subject is Thomas S. Kuhn, *The Structure of Scientific Revolutions* (Chicago: Phoenix, 1970).

3 C. Wright Mills, *The Sociological Imagination* (New York: Oxford University Press, 1959), p. 71.

4 Marios Raphael, *Pensions and Public Servants: A Study of the Origins of the British System* (Paris: Mouton, 1964).

5 Kenneth Bryden, *Old Age Pensions and Policy-Making in Canada* (Montreal: McGill-Queen's, 1974), p. 46, and Elizabeth Wallace, "The Origins of the Social Welfare State in Canada, 1867–1900," *Canadian Journal of Economics and Political Science* 16 (August 1950): 390.

6 For a critical interpretation, note Barton J. Bernstein, "The New Deal: The Conservative Achievements of Liberal Reform," in *Towards a New Past: Dissenting Essays in American History*, ed. Barton J. Bernstein (New York: Pantheon, 1968), pp. 263–88.

7 Sir William Beveridge, *Social Insurance and Allied Services*, Cmnd. 6404 (London: HMSO, 1942).

8 Michael Bliss, "Preface" to Leonard Marsh, *Report on Social Security for Canada 1943* (Toronto: University of Toronto Press, 1975), p. xvi.

9 Ibid., p. ix. A neglected but equally important work is Harry M. Cassidy, *Social Security and Reconstruction* (Toronto: Ryerson, 1943).

10 Leonard Marsh, "Introduction" to *Report on Social Security*, p. xxixn. Emphasis added.

11 Tamara K. Hareven, "An Ambiguous Alliance: Some Aspects of American Influences on Canadian Social Welfare," *Histoire sociale/Social History* 3 (April 1969): 82–98.

12 Karl Marx developed and elaborated upon the methodology of political economy in *A Contribution to the Critique of Political Economy* (Moscow: Progress, 1970). Perhaps the best example of the application of political economy as a method of inquiry is Karl Marx, *Pre-Capitalist Economic Formations* (New York: International Publishers, 1964).

13 A recent example is the excellent Canadian work of John F. Myles, *The Aged, the State and the Structure of Inequality*, Departmental Working Paper 79–1, Department of Sociology, Carleton University. Laura Katz Olson, *The Political Economy of Aging: The State, Private Power and Social Welfare* (New York: Columbia University Press, 1982), and Carroll L. Estes, *The Aging Enterprise* (San Francisco: Jossey-Bass, 1981), for the U.S., and in the U.K., Alan Walker, "Towards a Political Economy of Old Age," *Ageing and Society* 1 (1981): 73–94. A critical perspective is also provided by Victor W. Marshall and Joseph A. Tindale, "Notes for a Radical Gerontology," *International Journal of Aging and Human Development* 9 (1978–79): 163–75.

14 For social history in Britain, see Maurice Bruce, *The Coming of the Welfare State* (London: Batsford, 1979), Bentley B. Gilbert, *The Evolution of National Insurance in Great Britain: The Origins of the Welfare State* (London: Michael Joseph, 1966), and *British Social Policy, 1906–1914* (London: Macmillan, 1977), and *The Development of the British Welfare State, 1880–1975* (London: Edward Arnold, 1978); and Pat Thane, ed., *The Origins of British Social Policy* (London: Croom-Helm, 1981). For Canada, the history of pension arrangements is presented in Bryden, *Old Age Pensions;* Dennis Guest, *The Emergence of Social Security in Canada* (Vancouver: University of British Columbia Press, 1980); and Wallace, "Origins of the Social Welfare State." The social history of pensions in the U.S. is outlined in I.M. Rubinow, *Social Insurance: With Special Reference to American Conditions* (New York: Holt, 1913); Arthur J. Altmeyer, *The Formative Years of Social Security* (Madison: University of Wisconsin Press, 1966); Charles McKinley and Robert W. Frase, *Launching Social Security, A Capture-and-Record Account, 1935–1937* (Madison: University of Wisconsin Press, 1970); and Roy Lubove, *The Struggle for Social Security, 1900–1935* (Cambridge, MA: Harvard University Press, 1968). On ideology in the U.S., Harold L. Wilensky, *The Welfare State and Equality: Structural and Ideological Roots of Public Expenditures* (Berkeley: University of California Press, 1975). For Britain, Victor George and Paul Wilding, *Ideology and Social Welfare* (London: Routledge and Kegan Paul, 1976). For social work studies in the U.S., Harold L. Wilensky and Charles N. Lebeaux, *Industrial Society and Social Welfare* (New York: Free Press, 1965). Andrew Armitage, *Social Welfare in Canada: Ideals and Realities* (Toronto: McClelland and Stewart, 1975) is the standard text. Critical perspectives on social work in Britain are found in Paul Corrigan and Peter Leonard. *Social Work Practice under Capitalism: A Marxist Approach* (London: Macmillan, 1978), and Noel Parry, Michael Rustin, and Carole Satyamurti, *Social Work, Welfare and the State* (London: Arnold, 1979). Classic treatises from a social policy perspective are Richard M. Titmuss, *Essays on the Welfare State* (Boston: Beacon, 1969) and *Commitment to Welfare* (London: Allen and Unwin, 2nd ed., 1976). Comprehensive treatments are Victor George, *Social Security and Society* (London: Routledge and Kegan Paul, 1973); and J. C. Kincaid, *Poverty and Equality in Britain: A Study of Social Security and Taxation* (Harmondsworth: Penguin, 1979). More recent analyses from a Marxist perspective are Norman Ginsburg, *Class, Capital and Social Policy* (London: Macmillan, 1979); Ian Gough, *The Political Economy of the Welfare State* (London: Macmillan, 1979); and Eric Shragge, *Pensions Policy in Britain* (London: Routledge and Kegan Paul, 1984).
15 Ginsberg, *Class, Capital and Social Policy*, p. 148n66.
16 Gough, *Welfare State*, p. 182n10. Gough mentions pensions seven times: four times descriptively and three times analytically.
17 George, *Social Security and Society*, p. 1.
18 Cited in Oskar Lange, *On the Economic Theory of Socialism* (New York: McGraw-Hill, 3rd., 1976), p. 132n86.
19 *The Correspondence of Marx and Engels* (New York: International Publishers, 1934), p. 246. Emphasis in original. The issue of resource allocation as it affects social security programming under capitalism and socialism is dealt with in an important article by Ramesh Mishra, "Marx and Welfare," *Sociological Review*, n.s. 23 (May 1975): 287–313. In this regard it is necessary to differentiate between "socialism" as a transitional phase and "pure" communism. During the transitional period of socialism, the allocation and distribution of scarce resources must still be priorized, despite the expansion of the social product. As Lange has pointed out (*Economic Theory*, pp. 93–94, 139–41), as the supply of a commodity or service increases during the socialist transition, the price will correspondingly decline. Under "pure" communism, with the expansion of productive forces, all commodities ultimately become "free goods." In terms of

resource allocation, the analytic confusion between "socialism" and "communism" has resulted in the transitional period being viewed by some as a type of "cornucopia socialism." With respect to social welfare policy, Mishra ("Marx and Welfare," pp. 303–5) identifies a continuum ranging from "pure market distribution" to "pure need distribution," thereby recognizing the requirement to priorize the allocation of scarce resources during the period of transitional socialism.

20 Paul M. Sweezy, *The Theory of Capitalist Development* (New York: Monthly Review Press, 5th ed., 1964), p. 47; for monopoly pricing and its relationship to the labour theory of value, note pp. 54–55.

21 An excellent typological analysis differentiating between the various forms of state functions which is readily applicable to social welfare analysis is Leo Panitch, "The Role and Nature of the Canadian State," in *The Canadian State: Political Economy and Political Power*, ed. Leo Panitch (Toronto: University of Toronto Press, 1977), pp. 3–27. Examples of these two broad tendencies are Ginsberg, *Class, Capital and Social Policy*, and Gough, *Welfare State*.

22 Alvin W. Gouldner, "Politics of the Mind," in *For Sociology: Renewal and Critique in Sociology Today* (Harmondsworth: Penguin, 1975), p. 113.

23 Alvin W. Gouldner, *The Coming Crisis of Western Sociology* (New York: Avon, 1970), p. 12.

24 Peter N. Stearns, *Old Age in European Society* (New York: Holmes and Meier, 1976), p. 8.

25 Mills, *Sociological Imagination*, pp. 10–11.

26 Stearns, *Old Age in European Society*, pp. 23, 18–19.

27 Karl Marx, "The Eighteenth Brumaire of Louis Bonaparte," in *Selected Works*, Karl Marx and Frederick Engels (London: Lawrence and Wishart, 1968), p. 98.

28 Note the 1859 Preface to Marx's *Contribution to the Critique of Political Economy*.

29 Frederick Engels, letter to Joseph Block (21 September 1890), "The Economic Element Not the Only Determining One," in *Reader in Marxist Philosophy*, eds. Howard Selsam and Harry Martel (New York: International Publishers, 1963), pp. 204–5. Referring to the primacy of economics, Engels noted that Marx and he "had to emphasize this main principle and we had not always the time . . . to allow the other elements included in the interaction to come into their rights." Engels dismissed economic determinists by noting that "what these gentlemen all lack is dialectic" (letter to Conrad Schmidt, 27 October 1890). The reciprocal, or dialectical, relationship between culture and structure which makes history a dynamic process as opposed to it being a form of mechanical reductionism is exemplified by the work of E. P. Thompson, *The Making of the English Working Class* (Harmondsworth: Penguin, 1968), and Herbert Gutman, *Work, Culture and Society in Industrializing America: Essays in American Working-Class Social History* (New York: Vintage, 1977).

30 Peter N. Stearns, "Aging in the Working Class: An Exploratory Essay," *Newsletter—European Labour and Working Class History* 8 (November 1975): 20–28.

31 William Graebner, *A History of Retirement* (New Haven: Yale University Press, 1980), p. 282.

32 Note W. Andrew Achenbaum, who states that he has "excluded the ideas of the inarticulate and lower classes and concentrated on . . . a predominantly white middle-to upper-middle-class population" (*Old Age in the New Land* [Baltimore and London: Johns Hopkins University Press, 1978], p. 175). For Canada, neither Terry Copp, *The Anatomy of Poverty: The Condition of the Working Class in Montreal, 1897–1927* (Toronto: McClelland and Stewart, 1974), chapters 2 and 8, nor Michael J. Piva, *The Condition of the Working Class in Toronto, 1900–1921* (Ottawa: University of Ottawa Press, 1979), mentions the elderly. An interesting, but notable, exception is Michael B. Katz, "Social Structure in Hamilton, Ontario," in *Nineteenth-Century Cities—Essays in the New Urban His-*

tory, eds. Stephen Thernstrom and Richard Sennett (New Haven: Yale University Press, 1969), pp. 209–44.

33 Stearns, *Old Age in European Society*, p. 43, and David Hackett Fischer, *Growing Old in America* (Oxford: OUP, expanded ed., 1978), p. 60. Peter Townsend, *The Family Life of Old People* (Harmondsworth: Penguin, 1977) is a study of working class families in east-end London in the mid-1950s which concluded that family obligations towards the elderly were taken more seriously than before. This may be true, but one must differentiate between "obligations" and "respect." Indeed, it may be argued that "obligations" towards the elderly in the modern family generate their own intra-family tensions.

34 Stearns, *Old Age in European Society*, p. 12. Working-class history "from the bottom up" has been penetratingly dealt with by George Rude. *The Crowd in History, 1730–1848* (New York: Wiley, 1964), and Eric Hobsbawn, *Laboring Men* (Garden City, NY: Anchor, 1964), Thompson, *English Working Class;* and Gutman, *Work, Culture and Society*. The notion of various strata of the working class being inarticulate is explored by Jesse Lemisch, "The Radicalism of the Inarticulate: Merchant Seamen in the Politics of Revolutionary America," in *Dissent: Explorations in the History of American Radicalism*, ed. Alfred F. Young (Dekalb: Northern Illinois University Press, 1968). pp. 37–82, and Melvyn Dubofsky, "The Radicalism of the Dispossessed: William Haywood and the IWW," ibid., pp. 175–213.

35 The concept of agism is developed and analysed by Robert N. Butler, *Why Survive? Being Old in America* (New York: Harper and Row, 1975). Gerontophobia, or the fear of aging, is explored in A. Comfort, *Ageing: The Biology of Senescence* (London: Routledge and Kegan Paul, 1964), also Christopher Lasch, *The Culture of Narcissism* (New York: Norton, 1979), who quite correctly differentiates between medical and social theories of aging.

36 Erdman B. Palmore and Kenneth Manton, "Ageism Compared to Racism and Sexism," *Journal of Gerontology* 28 (1973): 367 and Table 6.

37 Early studies identifying the negative social attitudes towards the elderly and aging include Jacob Tuckman and Irving Lorge, "The Best Years of Life: A Study in Ranking," *Journal of Psychology* 34 (1952): 137–49; Raphael Ginzburg, "The Negative Attitude toward the Elderly," *Geriatrics* 7 (1952): 297–302; Jacob Tuckman and Irving Lorge, "Attitudes toward Old People," *Journal of Social Psychology* 37 (1953): 249–60; Nathan Kogan, "Attitudes toward Old People: The Development of a Scale and an Examination of Correlates," *Journal of Abnormal and Social Psychology* 62 (1961): 44–54, and Arnold M. Rose, "The Subculture of Aging: A Topic for Sociological Research," *Gerontologist* 2 (1962): 123–27.

38 The National Council of Aging, *The Myth and Reality of Aging in America*, prepared by Louis Harris and Associates (Washington, D.C.: NCOA, 4th ed., 1977) is the most comprehensive and current survey of attitudes towards the elderly.

39 On the cult of youth pervading Western society, note Donald O. Cowgill, "The Aging of Population and Societies," *Annals of the American Academy of Political and Social Science* 415 (1974): 15–16, and Lasch, *Culture of Narcissism*, chapter 9. David Gutman, "The Premature Gerontocracy: Themes of Aging and Death in Youth Culture," in *Death in the American Experience*, ed. Arien Mack (New York: Schocken Books, 1974), pp. 50–82, and Vivian M. Rakoff, "Psychiatric Aspects of Death in America," ibid., pp. 149–61 also deal with the subject.

40 Graebner, *History of Retirement*, pp. 215, 214.

41 Simone de Beauvoir, *Old Age* (Harmondsworth: Penguin, 1978), pp. 16–17. For a review of the literature on the relationship between aging and class, see Gordon E. Streib, "Social Stratification and Aging," in *Handbook of Aging and Social Sciences*, eds. Robert Binstock and Ethel Shanas (London: Van Nostrand Reinhold, 1976), pp. 160–85.

42 On the difference between a stratum and social class, note T. B. Bottomore, *Classes in Modern Society* (London: Allen and Unwin, 1967), chapter 2.

43 The National Council on Aging, *Myth and Reality of Aging*, p.129.

44 On old age and the elderly as a social problem, note David Hobman, *The Social Challenges of Ageing* (London: Croom-Helm, 1978), preface, p. 11; Nicholas Bosanquet, *A Future for Old Age* (London: Maurice Temple Smith, 1978), pp. 1–2; Peter N. Stearns, "Future Shock: The Old Folks' Version," *Perspective on Aging* (November/December 1979), pp. 11–15, and Achenbaum, *Old Age in the New Land*, pp. 157–64.

45 de Beauvoir, *Old Age*, p. 250.

46 Karl Marx, *Capital: Volume One* (London: Lawrence and Wishart, 1954), pp. 589, 601–3, analyses three forms of the industrial reserve army. He defined the stagnant reserve army, or "Lazarus stratum," as including orphans, paupers, the disabled and the elderly. Marxist labour economists who use a primary and secondary labour market framework are R. C. Edwards, M. Reich, and D. M. Gordon, *Labour Market Segmentation* (London: Heath, 1975); Andrew L. Friedman, *Industry and Labour: Class Struggle and Work and Monopoly Capitalism* (London: Macmillan, 1977), and Michael Joseph Piore, "Notes for a Theory of Labor Market Stratification," Working Papers for a New Society, no. 95 (1972).

47 Social security expenditures are analysed as a form of variable capital by James O'Connor, *The Fiscal Crisis of the State* (New York: St. Martin's, 1973), pp. 137–45. The notion of the "social wage" occupies an ill-defined, confusing and often contradictory position in Marxist theory. On the differentation between collective and individual goods, note Lange, *Economic Theory of Socialism*, pp. 90–91. Ernest Mandel, *Marxist Economic Theory*, vol. 2 (New York: Monthly Review Press, 1970), p. 665n, defines the "social wage" as being "distinguished by being an allocation in *kind*;" also pp. 656–65. Sweezy, *Theory of Capitalist Development*, pp. 232–33, refers to social security expenditures as merely being "state transfers" because they "have no connection with the sale of commodities or rendering services to the state . . . social security and relief payments, subsidies." Ginsburg, *Class, Capital and Social Policy*, pp. 25–27, while discussing the "social wage" never defines it. Gough, *Welfare State*, defines the "social wage" as being "welfare benefits in *cash and in kind* back to the employed and non-employed population," p. 108. He further notes that "there are many problems in deciding where any individual service should be placed," p. 160. P. Nitkin, *Fundamentals of Political Economy: Popular Course* (Moscow: Progress, 2nd rev. ed., 1966) defines the "social wage" as payments in *cash or in kind* paid for "out of the public consumption funds" including "housing, communal services . . . children's institutions, free education, organization of recreation and medical services, buildings for cultural purposes, *pensions*, etc.," p. 297; also S. Lukianenko, "Financing and Administration of Social Security in Socialist Countries," *International Social Security Review* 31 (1978): 419–38. Marxist theorists are to be faulted because they have not studied the literature (even that which is in translation) of socialist social security practitioners and administrators who deal extensively with the issue of the "social wage." An interesting attempt to define and compare the "social wage" in the United States and the Soviet Union is "Workers' Incomes in the Soviet Union," *Monthly Review* (1953): 234–42; also Bernice Q. Madison, *Social Welfare in the Soviet Union* (Stanford: Stanford University Press, 1968), especially chapters 4 and 11, and Robert J. Osborn, *Soviet Social Policies: Welfare, Equality and Community* (Homewood, IL: Dorsey, 1970), pp. 31–53.

48 Bosanquet, *Future for Old Age*, p. 2.

49 de Beauvoir, *Old Age*, p. 27.

50 Ibid., p. 604.

NOTES TO CHAPTER TWO

1 Karl Marx, "The Eighteenth Brumaire of Louis Bonaparte," *Collected Works*, vol.2 (Moscow: Progress, 1979), p. 103.
2 Peter N. Stearns, *Old Age in European Society* (New York: Holmes and Meier, 1976), p. 7.
3 Ibid., pp. 18–19.
4 Karl Marx, *Capital: Volume One* (London: Lawrence and Wishart, 1954), pp. 589, 601–3.
5 Stearns, *Old Age in European Society*, p. 21.
6 On the lack of an idyllic past for the aged in pre-industrial society, note Peter Laslett, "The History of Ageing and the Aged," in *An Ageing Population*, eds. Vida Carver and Penny Liddiard (Kent: Hodder and Stoughton, 1978), 6–13; Stearns, *Old Age in European Society*, pp. 18–19 and W. Andrew Achenbaum, *Old Age in the New Land* (Baltimore and London: Johns Hopkins University Press, 1978), p. 27, and Simone de Beauvoir, *Old Age* (Harmondsworth: Penguin, 1978), chapters 2 and 3.
7 Frederick Engels, letter from Engels to Conrad Schmidt, 5 August 1890, *Selected Correspondence*, Karl Marx and Frederick Engels (New York: International Publishers, 1934), p. 473.
8 Donald O. Cowgill, "The Aging of Populations and Societies," *Annals of the American Academy of Political and Social Science 415*(Spring 1974)): 10.
9 Laslett, "History of Aging and the Aged," p. 7. An example of the British literature is Nicholas Bosanquet, *A Future for Old Age* (London: Maurice Temple Smith, 1978), who states that "New initiatives can build on past achievement, which has been considerable," p. 2. A summary of the debate is contained in W. Andrew Achenbaum and Peter N. Stearns, "Old Age and Modernization," *Gerontologist* 18 (June 1978): 307–13.
10 Achenbaum, *Old Age in the New Land*, p. 143.
11 Paul Corrigan and Peter Leonard, *Social Work Practice under Capitalism: A Marxist Approach* (London: Macmillan, 1978).
12 Judith Fingard, "The Winter's Tale: The Seasonal Contours of Pre-industrial Poverty in British North America, 1813–1860," Canadian Historical Association, *Historical Papers* (1974): 66.
13 *Royal Commission on the Relations of Capital and Labour, 1889, Report, Minutes of Evidence—Ontario* (Ottawa: Queen's Printer and Controller of Stationery, 1889), p. 806.
14 Michael B. Katz, "Social Structure in Hamilton, Ontario," in *Nineteenth-Century Cities—Essays in the New Urban History*, eds. Stephen Thernstrom and Richard Sennett (New Haven: Yale University Press, 1969), Table 8, p. 222, and Table 6A, p. 220.
15 *Royal Commission on the Relations of Capital and Labour*, p. 807.
16 Cited in Hugh Heclo, *Modern Social Politics in Britain and Sweden: From Relief to Income Maintenance* (New Haven and London: Yale University Press, 1974), p. 162.
17 Doreen Collins, "The Introduction of Old Age Pensions in Great Britain," *Historical Journal* 8 (1965): 255, 247n5.
18 Pat Thane, "Non-Contributory Versus Insurance Pensions 1878–1908," in *The Origins of British Social Policy*, ed. Pat Thane (London: Croom-Helm, 1981), p.96.
19 Cited in Kenneth Bryden, *Old Age Pensions and Policy-Making in Canada* (Montreal: McGill-Queen's University Press, 1974), p. 42.
20 Ibid., pp. 42–43.
21 John G. Turnbull, *The Changing Faces of Economic Insecurity* (Minneapolis: University of Minnesota Press, 1966), Table 20, p. 51, cites the decent elderly couple budget (family budget) in 1910 as being $600 a year. This was related to

the median income for a male head 55 years of age and over in 1939 which was $1,243 a year and adjusted for inflation to put income on a 1910 basis. Between 1913 and 1939 inflation increased by 30 per cent. Therfore, the median income of a person age 55 and over in 1910–13 was $1,243 minus 30 per cent or $871 per year. Therefore, proportionately 35 per cent of those over the age of 55 were below the $600 a year family budget. However, this does not take into account that income decreases with age and therefore is probably an understatement. Based on time-series in the U.S. Department of Commerce, Bureau of Census, *Historical Statistics of the United States, Colonial Times to 1957* (Washington, D.C.: GPO, 1957), Series G 147–168, p. 167, and Series E113–139, p. 126.

22 Achenbaum, *Old Age in the New Land*, p. 122.
23 Robert W. Kelso, *Poverty* (New York: Longmans, 1929), p. 156.
24 Economic Council of Canada, *Fifth Annual Review: The Challenge of Growth and Change* (Ottawa: Queen's Printer, 1968), p. 104.
25 Terry Copp, *The Anatomy of Poverty: The Condition of the Working Class in Montreal: 1897–1929* (Toronto: McClelland and Stewart, 1974), pp. 36–38.
26 Michael J. Piva, *The Condition of the Working Class in Toronto 1900–1921* (Ottawa: University of Ottawa Press, 1979), pp. 38–51.
27 B. S. Rowntree, *Poverty and Progress: A Second Social Survey of York* (London: Longmans, 1941), p. 39.
28 J. Stevenson, *Social Conditions in Britain between the Wars* (Harmondsworth: Penguin, 1977), p. 108.
29 L. M. Grayson and Michael Bliss, eds., *The Wretched of Canada: Letters to R. B. Bennett 1930–1935* (Toronto: University of Toronto Press, 1973), introduction, p. xxiv.
30 Ibid., pp. ix-x.
31 Ibid., pp. 155, 171, 60. Letters from Alma Ward, Calgary, 18 June 1935, Mr. and Mrs. Jonathan A. Stewart, Magdalen Islands, Quebec, 19 July 1935, and Mrs. Clara Leibert, McVittie,Saskatchewan, 22 November 1933.
32 de Beauvoir, *Old Age*, p. 8.
33 B. S. Rowntree and G. R. Lavers, *Poverty and the Welfare State* (London: Longmans, 1951), p. 35.
34 Richard M. Titmuss, "Pension Systems and Population Change," in *Essays on the Welfare State* (Boston: Beacon, 1969), p. 74.
35 Economic Council of Canada, *Fifth Annual Review*, p. 120.
36 Jenny R. Podoluk, *Incomes of Canadians*, 1961 Census Monograph (Ottawa: Queen's Printer, 1968), Tables 9.4 and 9.5, p. 219.
37 The 1960 data is cited in K. Coates and R. Silburn, *Poverty: The Forgotten Englishman* (Harmondsworth: Penguin, 1970)p. 23, and Peter Townsend, *Poverty in the United Kingdom: A Survey of Household Resources and Standards of Living* (Harmondsworth: Penguin, 1979), Table 26.2, pp. 900–901.
38 Cited in Michael Harrington, *The Other America: Poverty in the United States* (New York: Penguin, 1966), p. 103.
39 The term is Michael Harrington's.
40 Senate Special Committee on Aging, *Final Report of the Special Committee of the Senate on Aging* (Ottawa: Queen's Printer, 1966), p. 9.
41 Statistics Canada, *Statistics on Low Income in Canada 1969* (Ottawa: Queen's Printer, 1969), Text Table 2, p. 16.
42 Sir William Beveridge, *Social Insurance and Allied Services*, Cmnd. 6404 (London: HMSO, 1947), appendix F, para. 16.
43 Ibid., p. 170.
44 Cited in J. C. Kincaid, *Poverty and Equality in Britain: A Study of Social Security and Taxation* (Harmondsworth: Penguin, 1979), pp. 50–53.
45 Leonard Marsh, *Report on Social Security for Canada 1943* (Toronto: University of Toronto Press, 1975), pp. 174–75.

46 Senate Special Committee on Aging, *Final Report*, p. viii.
47 Cited in Laurence E. Coward, *Pensions in Canada* (Don Mills: CCH, 1964), p. 18.
48 Marc Lalonde, Minister of Health and Welfare Canada, "Notes for an Address by the Honourable Marc Lalonde to the Canadian Pension Conference," Toronto, 26 November 1973, p. 2.
49 Bentley B. Gilbert, "The Decay of Nineteenth-Century Povident Institutions and the Coming of Old Age Pensions in Great Britain," *Economic History Review*, 2nd ser., 17 (1963): 552.
50 Geoffrey Crossick, *An Artisan Elite in Victorian Society* (London: Croom-Helm, 1978), p. 198.
51 *Royal Commission on the Relations of Capital and Labour*, p. 807.
52 Stephen Thernstrom, *Poverty and Progress: Social Mobility in a Nineteenth-Century City* (Cambridge, MA: Harvard University Press, 1968), chapter 5.
53 Bryden, *Old Age Pensions*, p. 24.
54 Elizabeth Wallace, "Old Age Security in Canada: Changing Attitudes," *Canadian Journal of Economics and Political Science* 18 (1952): p. 127.
55 Cited in Joan C. Brown, *How Much Choice? Retirement Policies in Canada* (Ottawa: Canadian Council on Social Development, 1975), p. 111.
56 Government of Canada, *Working Paper on Social Security in Canada* (Orange Paper) (April 1973), p. 4.
57 D. S. Juneja, "Private Pension Plans, Getting Better All the Time," *Financial Post*, 30 August 1975.
58 Juanita Kreps, *Lifetime Allocation of Work and Income* (Durham, NC: Duke University Press, 1971), p. 116. For savings patterns in Canada, note Statistics Canada, *Family Expenditure in Canada, Selected Cities, 1984* (Ottawa: Minister of Supply and Services, 1986), Table 2, p. 29.
59 Note, for example, Noel A. Hall, *Report of the Industrial Inquiry Commission into Canadian Railway Pension Plans (Benefits, Financing and Administration)* (Vancouver: Labour Canada, September 1976), p. 116.
60 James. H. Schultz, "The Economic Impact of an Aging Population," *Gerontology* 13 (1973): 115.
61 Hall, *Canadian Railway Pension Plans*, p. 109.
62 Robert Tilove, *Public Employee Pension Funds* (New York: A Twentieth Century Fund Report, Columbia University Press, 1976), p. 81.
63 Roy Chittick, *Pension Adequacy*, a summary of a workshop presentation made at the Canadian Pension Conference Annual Meeting, Toronto, 30 April and 1 May 1979 (Toronto: TA Associates, 1979), p. 1.
64 Economic Council of Canada, *Fifth Annual Review*, p. 127.
65 Statistics Canada, *Income Distribution by Size in Canada 1986* (Ottawa: Minister of Supply and Services Canada, 1987), pp. 34–35.
66 The most important quantified technical work is Philip Cutright, "Political Structure, Economic Development and National Social Security Programs," *American Journal of Sociology* 70 (1965): 537–50; Frederic L. Pryor, *Public Expenditures in Communist and Capitalist Nations* (Nobleton, Ontario: Irwin-Dorsey, 1968), chapter 4, and Harold L. Wilensky, *The Welfare State and Equality: Structural and Ideological Roots of Public Expenditures* (Berkeley: University of California Press, 1975), pp. 9–49.
67 Pryor, *Public Expenditures*, p. 132; also the International Labour Organization, *The Cost of Social Security, Ninth International Inquiry, 1972–1973* (Geneva: ILO, 1979), pp. 70–80, and the Organization for Economic Co-operation and Development, *Old Age Pension Schemes* (Paris: OECD, 1977), Table 5, p. 41. The rank order of social security expenditures, in descending order, are: old age pensions, sickness insurance, family allowances, disability insurance, occupational injuries and unemployment insurance.
68 Pryor, *Public Expenditures*, and Wilensky, *Welfare State and Equality*.
69 Leif Haanes-Olsen, "Earnings-Replacement Rate of Old-Age Benefits, 1965–75, Selected Countries," *Social Security Bulletin* 41 (January 1978): 4.

70 International Labour Organization, "Convention 128—Convention Concerning Invalidity, Old Age and Survivor's Benefits, Adopted by the Conference at its Fifty-First Session, Geneva, 29 June 1967."

71 Organization for Economic Co-operation and Development, *Public Expenditure on Income Maintenance Programmes,* (Paris: OECD, 1976), p. 2.

72 Colin Lindsay and Shelley Donald, "Income of Canada's Seniors," *Canadian Social Trends* 10 (Autumn 1988): 20, and Hans Messinger et al., *The Poverty Gap in Canada.* A paper presented to the Economic Council of Canada Seminar, 26 November 1987. Note also Health and Welfare Canada, *Incomes of Elderly Canadians in 1975* with respect to rising median incomes and the National Council of Welfare, *Sixty-five and Older* (Ottawa: NCOW, 1984).

73 *The Retirement Income System in Canada: Problems and Alternative Policies for Reform. A Summary of the Report of the Task Force on Retirement Income Policy 1979* (Hull: Canadian Government Publishing Centre, 1980), pp. 27–30.

74 Ibid., p. 30. Emphasis added.

75 Data Development, Policy, Liaison and Development, Income Security Programs Branch, Health and Welfare Canada, *Survey of Old Age Security and Canada Pension Plan Retirement Benefit Recipients July 1981* (n.p.: Minister of Health and Welfare, November 1983), Questions 4 and 17, and Policy, Communications and Information, Health and Welfare Canada, *1986 Old Age Security and Canada Pension Plan Beneficiary Survey* (forthcoming), Question 8.

76 "The *Maclean's*/Decima Poll," *Maclean's,* 7 January 1985, and special cross-tabulations provided to the author courtesy of *Maclean's,* Table 21, p. 21, Table 27, p. 33 and Table 7, p. 7.

77 National Council of Welfare, *Sixty-five and Older,* p. 24. See also pp. 1, 25–26, 29–30, 34–35.

78 Ibid., p. 36.

79 Messinger et al., *The Poverty Gap in Canada,* pp. 8, 15.

80 Note, for example, Robert Clark, Juanita Kreps, and Joseph Spengler, "Economics of Aging," *Journal of Economic Literature* 16 (1987): 919–62, James H. Schultz, "Income Distribution and the Aging," in *Handbook of Aging and the Social Sciences,* eds. Robert H. Binstock and Ethel Shanas (London: Van Nostrand Reinhold, 1976), pp. 561–91, and Elizabeth L. Meier and Cynthia C. Dittmar, *Income of the Retired: Levels and Sources,* a working paper prepared for the President's Commission on Pension Policy (Washington, D.C.: PCPP, 1980), and the earlier work of Harrington, *Other America.* More recently note the work of Susan Grad, "Incomes of the Aged and Nonaged, 1950–82," *Social Security Bulletin* 47 (June 1984): 3–17; Martynas A. Ycas and Susan Grad, "Income of Retirement-Aged Persons in the United States," *Social Security Bulletin* 50 (July 1987): 5–14, and Daniel B. Radner, "Money Incomes of Aged and Nonaged Family Units, 1967–84," *Social Security Bulletin* 50 (August 1987): 9–28.

81 Grad, "Incomes of the Aged and Nonaged," p. 19.

82 Radner, "Money Incomes," p. 9.

83 Note Achenbaum, *Old Age in the New Land,* p. 150, and Schultz, "Income Distribution," pp. 566–69, in the U.S. and the National Council of Welfare in Canada, *Sixty-five and Older,* for examples of this uncritical acceptance of the declining incidence of poverty among the elderly. The decline in the incidence of poverty among the elderly, measured on the basis of the "official" poverty line, is traced in the U.S. Department of Commerce, *Statistical Abstract of the United States 1988,* Series 716, p. 435.

84 U.S. Department of Commerce, *Statistical Abstract of the United States 1988,* p. 406.

85 Meier and Dittmar, *Income of the Retired,* pp. 2–3, 78.

86 The BLS intermediate budget in 1978 was $7,846 for an elderly couple and $5,884 for an aged individual. This was inflation-adusted by 68.1 per cent (from

195.4 to 328.4 points on the basis of the All Items Consumer Price Index) for the period between 1978 and 1986.

87 The derivation of the total proportion of elderly persons living in poverty in the U.S., based on the BLS intermediate budget in 1986 is as follows:

Elderly Category	1986 BLS Intermediate Budget	No. of Persons	No. Below BLS Budget	% Below BLS Budget
Unattached Individuals 65 +	$ 9,892	8,317,000	5,313,000	63.9%
Couples Head 65 +	$13,189	18,889,000	4,364,000	23.1%
Total, Non-institutionalized Elderly		27,206,000	9,677,000	35.6%

Therefore, nearly 36 per cent of all elderly persons—approximately ten million people—in the United States were below the BLS intermediate budget in 1986. Information calculated and supplied courtesy of the U.S. Bureau of Census, Age and Sex Stastics Branch, 8 July 1988.

88 Patricia Hewitt, *Age Concern on Pensioner Incomes* (Surrey: Age Concern England, 1974), p. 12.

89 Townsend, *Poverty in the United Kingdom,* Table 26.1, p. 897, and Table 26.2, pp. 901–2.

90 Calculated from 1983 U.K. Department of Health and Social Security data cited in J. Bradshaw, "Poverty in the United Kingdom: A Challenge for Policy and Politics," in *The Future of Social Welfare Systems in Canada and the United Kingdom,* ed. Shirley B. Seward (Halifax: Institute for Research on Public Policy, 1987), Table 2, p. 102.

91 Kincaid, *Poverty and Equality,* p. 370; Bosanquet, *Future for Old Age,* p. 48; "Living Below Their Means—Supplementary Benefits," *Labour Research* 67 (February 1978): 42–44; "Supplementary Benefits Reviewed," *Labour Research* 67 (November 1978): 236–37, and "Poor Law: Modern Style," *Labour Research* 69 (January 1980): 18–19.

92 Townsend, *Poverty in the United Kingdom,* p. 822.

93 Bradshaw, "Poverty in the United Kingdom," p. 103.

94 For Canada, unpublished information from Statistics Canada, Census Family Public Use Tape, SCF 1987, based on 1987 data; data for aged couples in the U.S. is calculated from Linda Draza Maxfield and Virginia P. Reno, "Distribution of Income Sources of Recent Retirees: Findings from the New Beneficiary Survey," *Social Security Bulletin* 48 (January 1985), Table 4, p. 11, and information for the U.K. is derived from Andrew Dawson and Graham Evans, "Pensioners' Incomes and Expenditure 1970–85," *Employment Gazette* (May 1987), Table 5, p. 247.

95 On this subject, note Charles A. Barnell, "Why Are Canadians Saving So Much?" *Canadian Business Review* (Summer 1978): 5–8.

96 Statistics Canada, Census Family Public Use Tape, SCF 1987.

97 Maxfield and Reno, "Distribution of Income," Table 5, p. 12.

98 Cited in Meier and Dittmar, *Income of the Retired,* p. 70.

99 In the U.K., 49 per cent of the elderly receive no occupational pension plan income (1985), 60 per cent receive no employer-sponsored pension benefit in Canada (1983), and 62 per cent of the aged in the U.S. (1984) were without any payments from the private pension system. For the U.K., Dawson and Evans, "Pensioners' Incomes and Expenditures," p. 246, and for the U.S., Ycas and Grad, "Income of Retirement-Aged Persons," Table 1, p. 6. For Canada, the number of private pension plan beneficiaries cited in Statistics Canada, *Pension Plans in Canada 1984* (Ottawa: Minister of Supply and Services, 1986), Table 31, p. 94, has been related to the 2.5 million persons aged 65 and over.

100 For Canada, Statistics Canada, *Pension Plans;* the U.S. Department of Health and Human Services, *Income of the Population 55 and Over, 1984* (Washington, D.C.: Government Printing Office, 1984), Table 37, p. 73, and the Government Actuary, *Occupational Pension Schemes, 1983—Seventh Survey* (London: HMSO, 1986), p. 14. Converted at the 1983 annual average exchange rate of £1 = C$1.87.

101 Daniel Jay Baum, *The Final Plateau* (Toronto: Burns and MacEachern, reprinted, 1976), chapter 2, and Bosanquet, *Future for Old Age*, p. 2.

102 Bosanquet, *Future for Old Age*, p. 2.

103 Corrigan and Leonard, *Social Work Practice*, p. 56.

104 George S. Talley and Richard Burkhauser, "Federal Economic Policy toward the Elderly," in *Social Policy, Social Ethics and the Aging Society*, eds. Bernice L. Neugarten and Robert G. Havighurst (Washington, D.C.: National Science Foundation, 1976). p. 47.

105 Laura Katz Olson, *The Political Economy of Aging: The State, Private Power and Social Welfare* (New York: Columbia University Press, 1982), p. 217.

106 In 1986, Statistics Canada's weighted average low-income cut-off for individuals was $9,635. The combined OAS/GIS rate in 1986 was $7,728. This resulted in a "poverty gap" of $1,907— that is, 19.8 per cent *below* the low-income cut-off for individuals. For couples, the weighted average cut-off was $12,635, while the combined OAS/GIS rate was $12,552 or $83 (0.7 per cent) below the low-income threshold.

107 Senator David Croll, author of the Special Senate Committee on Retirement Age Policies Report, *Retirement without Tears*, quoted in the *Globe and Mail*, 20 December 1979.

108 Leroy O. Stone and Michael J. McLean, *Future Income Prospects for Canada's Senior Citizens* (Montreal: Institute for Research on Public Policy, 1979), p. 14.

109 *Retirement without Tears*, A Report of the Special Senate Committee on Retirement Age Policies (Hull: Canadian Government Publishing Centre, 1979), p. 7.

NOTES TO CHAPTER THREE

1 The relationship between demography and class analysis is identified in Karl Marx, *A Contribution to the Critique of Political Economy* (Moscow: Progress, 1970), appendix, "The Method of Political Economy," p. 205. The impact of demography on economics was analysed by Marx in terms of the effect of "surplus population" on the creation of the industrial reserve army and its relationship to the declining rate of profit (Karl Marx, *Capital*, vol. 1 [New York: Modern Library, reprint of the 1906 Kerr edition], chapter 25, and vol. 3 [Moscow: Progress, 1970], chapter 14, p. 236). An important article attempting to reestablish the relationship between demography and the "material base" of society is John F. Myles, "The Aged and the Welfare State: An Essay in Political Demography," paper presented to the International Sociological Association, Research Committee on Aging, Paris, 8–9 July 1981. More recently, Wally Secombe, "Marxism and Demography," *New Left Review* 137 (January-February 1983): 22–47.

2 Paul Sweezy, *The Theory of Capitalist Development* (New York: Monthly Review Press, 1964), p. 224.

3 Standard background sources include David Hobman, ed., *The Social Challenge of Ageing* (London: Croom-Helm, 1978); Vita Carver and Penny Liddiard, eds., *An Ageing Population* (Suffolk: Hodder and Stoughton, 1978); Victor W. Marshall, ed., *Aging in Canada* (Don Mills: Fitzhenry and Whiteside, 1980); and Lewis Auerbach and Andrea Gerber, *Implications of the Changing Age Structure of the Canadian Population,* a study on population and technology prepared for the Science Council of Canada (Ottawa: Supply and Services Canada, 1976). Important articles include James H. Schulz, "The Economic Impact of

an Aging Population," *Journal of Gerontology* 13 (1975): 111–17; Donald O. Cowgill, "The Aging of Populations and Societies," *Annals of the American Academy of Political and Social Science* 415 (1974): 1–18; Robert Havighurst, "Aging in Western Society," in *Challenge of Ageing*, ed. Hobman, pp. 15–44; and Jon Hendricks and C. Davis Hendricks, "Ageing in Advanced Industrialized Societies," in *Ageing Population*, eds. Carver and Liddiard, pp. 28–34.

4   Harold L. Wilensky, *The Welfare State and Equality: Structural and Ideological Roots of Public Expenditures* (Berkeley and Los Angeles: University of California Press, 1975), p. 47.

5   P. Paillat, "Europe is Aging: Causes, Aspects and Repercussions of Demographic Aging," *International Social Security Review* 29, no. 2 (1976): 2.

6   Harry Weitz, *The Foreign Experience with Income Maintenance for the Elderly*, a study prepared for the Economic Council of Canada (Hull: Canadian Government Publishing Centre, 1979), Table 2-1, p. 6.

7   On the difference between the North American and Western European "baby booms," note John Kettle, *The Big Generation* (Toronto: McClelland and Stewart, 1980); C. D. Howe Research Institute, *Anticipating the Unexpected: Policy Review and Outlook, 1979* (Montreal: C. D. Howe Research Institute, 1979), pp. 130–35; and David K. Foot, *Canada's Population Outlook: Demographic Futures and Economic Challenges* (Ottawa: Canadian Institute for Economic Policy, 1982), Figure 1-1, p. 17.

8   There are two schools of thought concerning the direction of future fertility rates. The dominant school, led by Charles Westoff of Princeton's Center for Population Research, argues that the downward fertility trend is essentially irreversible. Historically, the trend in fertility has been declining for over two hundred years in North America. Today twenty-six of thirty-three developed countries have fertility rates below the replacement rate. The opposing position is advanced by Richard Easterlin of the University of Pennsylvania, who argues that the recent decrease in fertility is typical of the fertility of large cohorts and that in the future, with smaller cohorts, the fertility rate should increase. This latter approach is basically grounded in the theory of the labour market. When the labour market situation is favourable, people get married and have children; when the job situation deteriorates, marriage and children are postponed. Proponents of this theory hypothesize that the birth rate will begin increasing in the 1980s as the cohorts of the "baby bust" mature. It might be noted that the logic of this argument, namely, that fertility is related to the business cycle, does not seem to have halted the long-term decline in fertility. However, even accepting this formulation *prima facie* would suggest that the prolonged period of "stagflation" of the 1970s (and continuing into the 1980s) would further reinforce and depress fertility rates. Preliminary data for Canada based on the 1981 Census confirm the continuing downward trend in fertility. Note, for example, Dorothy Lipovenko, "Baby-boom Fertility Rates Plummeting," *Globe and Mail*, 20 December 1984, which reports, based on a 1984 Statistics Canada study, that the fertility rate in Canada is now the lowest since the 1930s. The elderly are now forecast to constitute 25 to 27 per cent of the population after 2011.

9   Telephone conversation between Treasury-Secretary Henry Morgenthau, Jr., and Harry Hopkins, cited in William Graebner, *A History of Retirement* (New Haven: Yale University Press, 1980), p. 256.

10 Richard M. Titmuss, "Pension Systems and Population Change," *Essays on the Welfare State* (Boston: Beacon, 1969), p. 57. In fairness to Beveridge, he used secondary source material provided in the white paper on the current trend of population in Great Britain, *Social Insurance and Allied Services*, Cmnd. 6404 (London: HMSO, 1942), Table XI, p. 91.

11 Leonard Marsh, *Report on Social Security for Canada 1943* (Toronto: University of Toronto Press, reprinted, 1975), p. 155.

12 President's Commission on Pension Policy, *Coming of Age: Toward a National Retirement Income Policy* (Washington, D.C.: PCPP, April 1981), p. 7, and Bar-

bara Boyle Torrey, *Demographic Shifts and Projections: The Implications for Pension Systems*, a Working Paper prepared for the President's Commission on Pension Policy (Washington, D. C.: PCPP, April 1979).

13 The most important studies regarding this issue are the Economic Council of Canada, *One in Three: Pensions for Canadians to 2030* (Hull: Canadian Government Publishing Centre, 1979), chapter 3, and Frank T. Denton, Christine H. Feaver, and Byron G. Spencer, *Population and Labour Force Projections to 2051*. A study prepared for the Economic Council of Canada (Hull: Canadian Government Publishing Centre, 1980), and Foot, *Canada's Population Outlook*. For Britain, note for example, Sir Ferguson Anderson, 'Aging Population "May Cause Social Disaster,'" *The Times*, 26 November 1976. Demographics played an important role in the recent Fowler Green Paper on *The Reform of Social Security*, 3 vols., Cmnd. 9517, 9518, 9519 (London: HMSO, June 1985).

14 Weitz, *Foreign Experience with Income Maintenance*, p. 5.

15 Statistics Canada, *Population Projections for Canada, Provinces and Territories, 1984–2006* (Ottawa: Minister of Supply and Services, 1985), Projections 3 and 4, pp. 340–41, and Projections 1 and 2, pp. 338–39.

16 Economic Council of Canada, *One in Three*, p. 24.

17 This draws on the Government of Canada, *Fact Book on Aging in Canada* (Ottawa: Minister of Supply and Services, 1983), pp. 14, 20.

18 Foot, *Canada's Population Outlook*, p. 135. Also Leroy O. Stone and Michael J. Maclean, *Future Income Prospects for Canada's Senior Citizens* (Montreal: Institute for Research on Public Policy), pp. 86–92. L. O. Stone and S. Fletcher, *A Profile of Canada's Older Population* (Montreal: Institute on Public Policy, 1980), p. 92, also argue that between 2021 and 2041 the pressure will intensify.

19 For this kind of formal economic analysis, note Brian J. Powell and James K. Martin, "Economic Implications of an Aging Society in Canada," Survey Research and Special Projects Directorate, Policy Research and Strategic Planning Branch, Health and Welfare Canada, a paper prepared for the National Symposium on Aging, Ottawa, 25–27 October, 1978, p. 9. Also M. Penning and P. Krishnan, *The Social Implications of the Canadian Population: Some Strategies and Solutions*, Discussion Paper No. 22, Department of Sociology, University of Alberta, November 1980, and Foot, *Canada's Population Outlook*, p. 215.

20 On this issue, note James O'Connor, *The Fiscal Crisis of the State* (New York: St. Martin's Press, 1973), chapter 3.

21 Foot, *Canada's Population Outlook*, p. 218.

22 Havighurst, "Aging in Western Society," pp. 33, 37.

23 C. D. Howe Research Institute, *Anticipating the Unexpected*, Table 16, p.133.

24 Ibid, p. 135.

25 Ibid., Table 16, p. 133, and "Population," *CSO Social Trends 10 1980 Edition* (London: HMSO, 1980), Chart 1.5, p. 66.

26 "Population." No population projections are available after the year 2010.

27 Ibid. Population projections based on varying fertility assumptions contained in Table 1.2, p. 64.

28 Organization for Economic Co-operation and Development, *The 1980 Tax/Benefit Position of a Typical Worker in OECD Member Countries* (Paris: OECD, 1980), Chart 1, p. 26, and Chart 3, p. 28.

29 D. C. L. Wroe, "The Elderly," *CSO Social Trends No. 4* (London: HMSO, 1973), p. 23.

30 A Report of the Special Senate Committee on Retirement Age Policies, *Retirement without Tears* (Hull: Canadian Government Publishing Centre, 1979), p. 51. This view is also put forward by Leroy O. Stone, "Population Aging and Dependency Ratios in Canada," submission to the Senate Committee on Retirement Age Policies, Ottawa, 30 November 1978. Dr. Stone is Chief Demographer for Statistics Canada. Other scholarly efforts which have arrived at similar conclusions are Neil B. Ridler, "Will Canada Be Able to Support Its Elderly?" in *The Aged in Society*, Social Science Monograph Series, vol. 3 (Saint John:

University of New Brunswick at Saint John, Spring 1979), pp. 6–16, and Frank T. Denton and Byron G. Spencer, "Some Economic and Demographic Implications of Future Population Change," *Journal of Canadian Studies* 14 (Spring 1979): 81–93. A recent study is Ivan P. Fellegi, "Can We Afford an Aging Society?" *Canadian Economic Observer* (October 1988): 4.1–4.34. This article has come under some criticism for its underlying assumptions.

31 For Canada, Linda McDonald, "Changing Population and the Impact on Government Age-Specific Expenditures," unpublished study prepared for the Federal Treasury Board Secretariat, Ottawa, 1977. Comparable findings for the U.S., are contained in R. Clark and J. Spengler, "Changing Demography and Dependency Costs: The Implications of New Dependency Ratios and Their Composition," in *Aging and Income: Programs and Prospects for the Elderly*, ed. Barbara Herzog (New York: Human Science Press, 1978), pp. 55–89. Data for Britain can be deduced from Wroe, "The Elderly," pp. 23–33. Wroe notes that in 1971–72, "when the elderly comprised 16 per cent of the total population, the proportion of public expenditure on social security, health and welfare absorbed by the elderly was 48 per cent," p. 32. This would mean that by 2020, when the elderly are nearly 19 per cent of the population (under the low fertility assumption), that they would absorb 57 per cent of all social security, health and welfare expenditures.

32 This analysis relies heavily upon Foot, *Canada's Population Outlook*, pp. 132–42.

33 Economic Council of Canada, *One in Three*, p. 28. Stone and Maclean, *Future Income Prospects*, p. 89, arrive at similar figures.

34 Economic Council of Canada, *One in Three*, p. 32.

35 Examples of analyses using this unwarranted assumption are the Senate Committee, *Retirement without Tears;* Ridler, "Will Canada Be Able"; and Denton and Spencer, "Economic and Demographic Implications."

36 Denton and Spencer, "Economic and Demographic Implications" Table 13, p. 92. Based on Experiment 1, current demographic trends, total net expenditure taking into account the shift in dependency categories, would increase by 88 per cent of the total output by 2031. The breakdown for the key expenditure categories are: state pensions + 125 per cent, healthcare + 13 per cent, and education – 50 per cent. The increase in health care costs seems inordinately low when compared to other estimates; it also assumes that fixed overhead costs in the education sector can be transferred or liquidated.

37 L. A. Lefebvre, Z. Zigismond, and M. S. Devereaux, *A Prognosis for Hospitals: The Effects of Population Change on the Need for Hospital Space, 1967–2031* (Ottawa: Statistics Canada, Minister of Supply and Services, November 1979), p. 13.

38 Department of Health and Social Security, Welsh Office, *A Happier Old Age: A Discussion Document on Elderly People in Our Society* (London: HMSO, 1970), p. 10.

39 Cited in Laura Katz Olson, *The Political Economy of Pensions: The State, Private Power, and Social Welfare* (New York: Columbia University Press, 1982), pp. 6–9.

40 For the United States these studies include the National Council on Aging, *The Myth and Reality of Aging in America,* prepared by Louis Harris and Associates (Washington, D.C.: NCOA, 1975); Johnson and Higgins, *American Attitudes towards Pensions and Retirement,* prepared by Louis Harris (New York, February, 1979); Employee Benefit Research Institute, *Survey of the Aged,* prepared by Louis Harris (Washington, D.C.: EBRI, November 1981); the National Commission on Social Security, *Summary of Nationwide Survey of Attitudes toward Social Security,* a report prepared for the National Commission on Social Security by Peter D. Hart Research Associates (Washington, D.C.: NCSS, 1981); "Baby Boomers Push for Power," *Business Week*, 2 July 1984, pp. 52–59; and the American Council of Life Insurance Health Insurance Association of America, *The Baby Boom Generation* (Washington, D.C., 1983).

For Canada, "A Survey on the Awareness and Attitudes of Ontario Residents towards Retirement Programs and Particularly Pension Plans," Report of the Royal Commission on the Status of Pensions, vol. 8, *Background Studies and Papers* (Toronto: Queen's Printer, 1980), pp. 19–95; Saskatchewan Department of Labour, Pensions Branch, *The Saskatchewan Retirement Income Issues Survey* (Regina: Saskatchewan Labour, November 1981); Health and Welfare Canada, *Results of a National Health and Welfare Telephone Survey on Pension Issues*, prepared by Program, Evaluation and Liaison Security Programs (Ottawa: Health and Welfare, November 1981); Saskatchewan Department of Social Services, Planning and Evaluation, *Home Care Survey* (Regina: Department of Social Services, 1981); Canadian Pension Conference, *A Report on the CPC Opinion Survey—Retirement System Changes* (Toronto: CPC, 1982); Canadian Gallup Poll Limited, National Omnibus—Newspaper—5–7 January 1984, as reported in the *Ottawa Citizen*, 27 February 1984, and special cross-tablulations requested by the author; "The *Maclean's*/Decima Poll," *Maclean's*, 7 January 1985, pp. 10–43, and special cross-tabulations requested by the author; also the *Decima Quarterly Research Report* (Fall 1986), Tables 210 and 211, pp. 220–21.

For Britain, Age Concern England, *Public Opinion on Pensions* (Surrey: Age Concern, 1974), and Age Concern England, *The Attitudes of the Retired and the Elderly* (Surrey: Age Concern, 1975).

41 For the U.S., the Employee Benefit Research Institute, *Survey*, Table, pp. 2–3, and Johnson and Higgins, *American Attitudes*, p. iv. For Canada, the Ontario Royal Commission on the Status of Pensions, *Report*, vol. 8, Table 14, p. 39; Saskatchewan Department of Labour, *Retirement Income*, pp. S-19 and 345; Saskatchewan Department of Social Services, *Home Care*, question no. 115; and Health and Welfare Canada, *Pension Issues*, pp. 13–14, and the "*Maclean's*/Decima Poll," special print-out, pp. 21, 41.

42 Health and Welfare Canada, "Old Age Security and Canada Pension Plan Benefit Recipients Survey, 1979" (forthcoming), Question 37.

43 For Canada, Saskatchewan Department of Labour, *Retirement Income*, pp. S-2, 35, 37. For the U.S., Employee Benefit Research Institute, *Survey*, pp. 4–5.

44 For a psycho-sociological interpretation, note Caroline Bird, *The Invisible Scar* (New York: Pocket Books, 1967).

45 For the U.S., National Council on Aging, *Myth and Reality*, Table 225, and Johnson and Higgins, *American Attitudes*, p. iv. For Canada, Saskatchewan Department of Labour, *Retirement Income*, pp. S-2, 33.

46 For Canada, Health and Welfare Canada, *Pension Issues*, pp. 7, 13–14, 18; and Saskatchewan Department of Labour, *Retirement Income*, p. 51. For Britain, Age Concern England, *Public Opinion*.

47 For Canada, the Ontario Royal Commission on the Status of Pensions, *Report*, Table 27, pp. 46. In the U.S., Johson and Higgins, *American Attitudes*, p. vi.

48 The Employee Benefit Research Institute, *Survey*, pp. 6 and 14 and Table, p. 32.

49 Age Concern England, *Public Opinion*, p. 8 and Table 3, p. 9.

50 The Ontario Royal Commission on the Status of Pensions, *Report*, Table 15, p. 40, and the Saskatchewan Department of Labour, *Retirement Income*, pp. 158, 169 and 170.

51 A confidential Goldfarb survey commissioned by the Secretary of State Canada, cited in Dave Todd, "Canada's Youth: Defeated Hopes, Passion for Security," *Ottawa Citizen*, 11 July 1984, and "A Tale of Two Generations" (Editorial), *Ottawa Citizen*, 12 July 1984.

52 "The *Maclean's*/Decima Poll," p. 37, and special computer print-out, p. 27.

53 The literature on this subject includes Vern L. Bengston and Neal E. Cutler, "Generations and Intergenerational Relations: Perspectives on Age Groups and Social Change," in *Handbook of Aging and the Social Sciences*, eds. Robert H. Binstock and Ethel Shanas (Toronto: Van Nostrand Reinhold, 1976), pp. 130–

59; Robert B. Hudson and Robert H. Binstock, "Political Systems and Aging," and Gordon F. Streib, "Social Stratification and Aging," both in *Handbook of Aging*, eds. Binstock and Shanas; popularized pieces include Bryant Robey and Mary John, "The Political Fortune: The Demographics of Politics," *American Demographics* (October 1980): 15–20; and Val Ross, "The Coming Old-Age Crisis," *Maclean's*, 17 January 1983 pp. 24–29. Also Kingsley Davis and Pietronella van der Oever, "Age Relations and Public Policy in Advanced Industrial Societies," *Population and Development Review* 7 (March 1981): 1–18.

54 Georg Simmel, *Conflict* (Glenco: Free Press, 1955).

55 The classic formulation is S. N. Eisenstadt, *From Generation to Generation: Age Groups and Social Structure* (New York: Free Press, 1956), esp. chapter 6. Other work on the subject includes Leonard D. Cain, Jr., "Age Status and Generational Phenomena: The New Old People in Contemporary America," *Gerontologist* 7 (June 1967): 83–92. An interesting summary from a social policy perspective is J. K. Martin, "Social Policy Concerns Related to Retirement: The Implications for Research," presentation to the Research Symposium on Canada's Age Structure: Implications for the Future, Simon Fraser University, 20 August 1981.

56 For the United States prior to 1900, note Peter N. Stearns, *Old Age in European Society* (New York: Holmes and Meier, 1976), p. 35, and W. Andrew Achenbaum, *Old Age in the New Land* (Baltimore and London: Johns Hopkins University Press, 1978), pp. 117–20, for the period between 1914 and 1930. On the role of the pensioners' organizations in Canada, note Kenneth Bryden, *Old Age Pensions and Policy-Making in Canada* (Montreal: McGill-Queen's University Press, 1974), pp. 183, 194–200.

57 Jackson K. Putnam, *Old-Age Politics in California* (Stanford: Stanford University Press, 1970), chapters 3–4, and Abraham Holtzman, *The Townsend Movement: A Political Study* (New York: Bookman Associates, 1963).

58 Achenbaum, *Old Age in the New Land*, p. 132.

59 Noreen Branson and Margot Heinemann, *Britain in the Nineteen Thirties* (Frogmore: Panther Books, 1973), p. 248.

60 Bryden, *Old Age Pensions*.

61 Richard B. Calhoun, *In Search of the New Old: Redefining Old Age in America, 1945–1970* (New York: Elsevier North Holland, 1978), p. 3.

62 For recent developments in the U.S., note Ruth H. Jacobs, "Portrait of a Phenomeon—The Gray Panthers: Do They Have a Long-Run Future?" in *Public Policies for an Aging Population*, eds. Elizabeth W. Markson and Gretchen R. Batra (Toronto: Heath, 1980), pp. 93–103, and William W. Lammers, *Public Policy and the Aging* (Washington, D.C.: QC Press, 1983), pp. 58–67. In the United States in 1984 the four largest organizations of the elderly represented 20 million people: the American Association of Retired Persons, 15 million; the National Council of Senior Citizens, 4 million; the National Alliance of Senior Citizens, 770,000, and the National Association of Older Americans, 225,000 people. In Canada the four largest pensioners' organizations represent approximately 765,000 people: National Pensioners and Senior Citizens Federation, 500,000; The Quebec Federation of Elderly, 200,000; Canadian Council of Retirees, 35,000, and Canadian Pensioners Concerned, 30,000 people. In Britain the major organization, the National Federation of Old Age Pensions Association, represents 1 million people or about 11 per cent of the elderly.

63 William G. Davis, Premier of Ontario, "Notes for An Address to the Joint Meeting of Toronto Society of Financial Analysts and Toronto Association of Business Economists," Toronto, 22 April 1982, p. 13.

64 An example of the uncritical acceptance of the "aging-conservatism" thesis is the Ontario Economic Council, *The Ontario Economy to 1987* (Toronto: Queen's Printer, 1977), p. 25.

65 For a refutation of the "aging-conservatism" thesis, note Norval D. Glenn,

"Aging and Conservatism," *Annals of the American Society of Political and Social Science* 415 (September 1974): 176–87; John Creighton Campbell and John Strate, "Are Old People Conservative?" *Gerontologist* 21 (1981): 580–91; Elizabeth B. Douglas, William P. Cleveland, and George L. Maddox, "Political Attitudes, Age and Aging: A Cohort Analysis of Archival Data," *Journal of Gerontology* 29 (1974): 666–75; and Robert E. Garland, "The Politics of Aging," in *The Aged in Society*, Social Science Monograph Series, vol. 3 (Saint John, N.B.: University of New Brunswick at Saint John, Spring 1979), pp. 25–39. Robert H. Binstock, "Aging and the Future of American Politics," *Annals of the American Academy of Political and Social Science* 415 (September 1974): 199–212, deals with related issues, although his conclusions would seem to contradict his own evidence and arguments.

66 Campbell and Strate, "Are Old People Conservative?" pp. 590–91.
67 Douglas, Cleveland, and Maddox, "Political Attitudes."
68 For example, Martin Harrop, "The Changing British Electorate," *Political Quarterly* (1982): 385–402.
69 American Council of Life Insurance Health Insurance Association of America, *Baby Boom Generation*, p. 3.

NOTES TO CHAPTER FOUR

1 The major reports of government in the public policy review of the retirement income system in Canada and making recommendations for reform were the Comité D'Etude sur le Financement du Régime de Rentes du Québec et sur les Régimes supplementaires de Rentes (Confirentes +), *La Securité Financière des Personnes Agrées au Quebec* (Quebec City: Editeur Official du Quebec, 1977); Economic Council of Canada, *One in Three: Pensions for Canadians to 2030* (Ottawa: Canadian Government Publishing Centre, 1979); *Retirement without Tears*, The Report of the Special Senate Committee on Retirement Age Policies (Ottawa: Canadian Government Publishing Centre, 1979); Task Force on Retirement Income Policy, *The Retirement Income System in Canada: Problems and Alternative Policies for Reform*, 2 vols. (Ottawa: Canadian Government Publishing Centre, 1980); *Report of the Royal Commission on the Status of Pensions in Ontario*, 10 vols. (Toronto: Government of Ontario, 1981); the Government of Saskatchewan, Saskatchewan Labour, *Brief To the National Pensions Conference: Reform of Canada's Retirement Income System—A Saskatchewan View* (Regina: Pensions Branch, Saskatchewan Labour, 1981); Ontario Select Committee on Pensions, *Final Report* (Toronto: Government of Ontario, Queen's Printer, April 1982); the Province of British Columbia, *Developing a Pension Policy for the Future: A Discussion Paper* (Victoria: Information Services, June 1982); Government of Canada, *Better Pensions for Canadians* (Ottawa: Minister of Supply and Services Canada, 1982); Special Committee on Pension Reform, *Report of the Parliamentary Task Force on Pension Reform* (Ottawa: Canadian Government Publishing Centre, 1983); Government of Ontario, *Ontario Proposals for Pension Reform: Adapting to Social and Economic Transformation* (Toronto: Queen's Printer, 1984); Canada, Minister of Finance, *Action Plan for Pension Reform—Building Better Pensions for Canadians*, February 1984 Budget; Canada, Minister of Finance, *Building Better Pensions for Canadians—Improved Tax Assistance for Retirement Savings*, February 1984 Budget; Canada, Minister of Finance, *Securing Economic Renewal—Budget Papers*, May 1985 Budget, and Québec, Ministre des Affaires sociales et Ministre de la Main d'oeuvre et de la Sécurité du revenu, *Agir maintenant pour demain—Une politique québécoise de sécurité du revenu à la retraite* (Québec: Direction générale des publications gouvernementales, 1985).

2 Health and Welfare Canada, Policy Research and Strategic Planning Branch,

The Incomes of Elderly Canadians in 1975, Social Security Research Report No. 06 (Ottawa: Minister of National Health and Welfare, February 1979), pp. 37–38.

3 Monique Bégin, Minister of Health and Welfare Canada, "Notes for an Address by the Honourable Monique Bégin to the Association of Canadian Pension Management," Toronto, 17 September 1980, pp. 2 and 5. Emphasis added.

4 On this point note the interesting, but somewhat arcane work by Hugh Mosley, *Public and Private Social Welfare Systems: A Working Paper on the Underdevelopment of State Social Welfare Institutions in the United States*, Publication series of International Institute for Comparative Social Research (Berlin: December 1978). Other Marxist labour economists using a primary and secondary labour market framework are R. C. Edwards, M. Reich, and D. M. Gordon, *Labour Market Segmentation* (London: Heath, 1975); Andrew L. Friedman, *Industry and Labour: Class Struggles and Work and Monopoly Capitalism* (London: Macmillan, 1977); and Michael Joseph Piore, "Notes for a Theory of Labour Market Stratification," *Working Papers for a New Society*, no. 95(1972).

5 On the early history of occupational pension plan arrangements in the United States, note William C. Greenough and Francis P. King, *Pension Plans and Public Policy* (New York: Columbia University Press, 1976), chapters 2, 4 and 5. For Britain, early employer-based pension plans are described in Gerald Rhodes, *Public Sector Pensions* (Toronto: University of Toronto Press, 1965), chapter 1.

6 The early studies from which the extent of occupational pension plan coverage in Canada can be reconstructed are the National Employment Commission survey, April 1937, reproduced in Leonard Marsh, *Report on Social Security for Canada 1943* (Toronto: University of Toronto Press, 1975), appendix V, pp. 301–3; Queen's University, Industrial Relations Section, School of Commerce and Administration, *Industrial Retirement Plans in Canada* (Kingston, Ont.: Queen's University, 1938); and the Dominion Bureau of Statistics, *Survey of Welfare Plans in Industry 1947* (Ottawa: Queen's Printer, May 1950).

7 For the impact of British civil service pension arrangements on early Canadian public sector pension plans, note Marios Raphael, *Pensions and Public Servants: A Study of the Origins of the British System* (Paris: Mouton, 1964), and Rhodes, *Public Sector Pensions*. American private sector pension plan influence on Canadian developments is traced in Luther Connant, *A Critical Analysis of Industrial Pension Systems* (New York: Macmillan, 1922), and M. W. Latimer, *Industrial Pension Systems in the United States and Canada*, 2 vols. (New York: Industrial Relations Counselors Inc., 1932).

8 On this subject, note Stephen Scheinberg, "Invitation to Empire: Tariffs and American Economic Expansion in Canada," *Business History Review* 47 (1973): 218–38, and Wallace Clement, *The Canadian Corporate Elite: An Analysis of Economic Power* (Toronto: McClelland and Stewart, 1975), pp. 110–12, who identifies a permanent American corporate presence in Canada in the mid-1920s.

9 Queen's University, *Survey of Welfare Plans*, p. 16.

10 For welfare capitalism as an ideology, see Stephen J. Scheinberg, "Progressivism in Industry: The Welfare Movement in the American Factory, *Annual Report*, Canadian Historical Association (1967): 184–97. As part of a union substitution policy, see David Brody, "The Rise and Decline of Welfare Capitalism," in *Workers in Industrial America: Essays on the Twentieth Century* (New York: Oxford University Press, 1980), pp. 48–81.

11 Francis Green, "Occupational Pension Schemes in British Capitalism," *Cambridge Journal of Economics* (September 1982): 268.

12 Queen's University, *Industrial Retirement Plans*, pp. 304–5.

13 President's Commission on Pension Policy, *Coming of Age: Toward a National Income Policy* (Washington, D.C.: PCPP, February 1981), p. 12.

14 Statistics Canada, *Pension Plans in Canada, 1980* (Ottawa: Minister of Supply and Services Canada, 1982), p. 15, and *Pension Plans in Canada, 1984* (Ottawa: Minister of Supply and Services 1986), Text Table D, p. 13.

15 This methodological approach was first suggested in an unprecedented gesture to the private pension industry by Harry Weitz, Chief, Pension Section, Statistics Canada, "Private Pension Plan Coverage," address to the Canadian Pension Conference, Ottawa, 21 October, 1976. This first became official in Statistics Canada, *Pension Plans in Canada, 1976* (Ottawa: Minister of Industry, Trade and Commerce, 1978), p. 15, and later in Statistics Canada, *Pension Plans in Canada, 1980*, pp. 14–16.

16 Greenough and King, *Pension Plans*, chapter 1.

17 Queen's University, *Industrial Retirement Plans*, p. 17.

18 Louis Ascah, *Government and Private Pensions in Canada* (Ph.D. dissertation, Department of Economics, McGill University, March 1979), Table F-4, p. 173.

19 Dominion Bureau of Statistics, *Survey of Welfare Plans*, Table 4.

20 Statistics Canada, *Pension Plans in Canada, 1980*, Table 1, p. 61.

21 Statistics Canada, *Pension Plans in Canada, 1976*, p. 16.

22 For the U.S., Daniel J. Beller, "Coverage Patterns of Full-time Employees under Private Retirement Plans," *Social Security Bulletin* 44 (July 1981): 6; For Britain, Government Actuary, *Occupational Pension Schemes, 1975—Seventh Survey* (London: HMSO, 1983), Table 2, 5, p. 9, and for Canada, Statistics Canada, *Pension Plans in Canada, 1980*, Table 1, p. 61.

23 Note, for example, the President's Commission on Pension Policy, *Coming of Age*, Table 11, p. 27, and for Britain, Department of Employment *Gazette*, August 1971.

24 Statistics Canada, *Pension Plans in Canada 1974* (Ottawa: Queen's Printer, 1972), p. 129.

25 Government Actuary, *Occupational Pension Schemes 1975—Fifth Survey*, appendix A5, p. 107.

26 Laurence E. Coward, *Mercer Handbook of Canadian Pension and Welfare Plans* (Don Mills: CCH Canadian, 1977), pp. 241–42.

27 R. Prefontaine and Y. Balcer, *Job Mobility and Its Implications for the Employer-Sponsored Pension System in Canada*, a study undertaken for the Task Force on Retirement Income Policy, Department of Finance, Ottawa, September 1977(mimeo).

28 R. Préfontaine and Y. Balcer, "Interaction of Labour Mobility Rates and Vesting Rates on Years of Pensionable Service," *The Retirement Income System in Canada: Problems and Alternative Policies for Reform*, vol.2, appendix 8, pp. 8, 5.

29 Economic Council of Canada, *People and Jobs: A Study of the Canadian Labour Market* (Ottawa: ECC, 1976), p. 11.

30 Note, for example, Lenore Bixby and Virginia Reno, "Second Pensions among Newly Entitled Workers: Survey of New Beneficiaries," *Social Security Bulletin* 34 (November 1971): 5; Walter W. Kolodrubetz and Donald M. Landay, "Coverage and Vesting of Full-Time Employees under Private Retirement Plans," *Social Security Bulletin* 36 (November 1973); 20–36; Walter W. Kolodrubetz, "Characteristics of Workers with Pension Coverage on the Longest Job," *Reaching Retirement Age*, U.S. Department of Health, Education, and Welfare, Social Security Administration (Washington, D.C.: GPO, 1976), p. 162; and Health and Welfare Canada, *Survey on Retirement in Canada—Retirement in Canada*, vol. 2 (Ottawa: Minister of National Health and Welfare, 1977), Table 1-10.

31 Economic Council of Canada, *One in Three* p. 73.

32 For the legal basis of vesting and the deferred wage doctrine, see Dan M. McGill, *Fulfilling Pension Expectations* (Homewood, IL: Irwin, 1962), chapters 4–6; R. W. McInnes, *Welfare Legislation and Benefit Plans in Canada* (Toronto: Law Society of Upper Canada, 1974), pp. 57–66, and Donna Allen, *Fringe Benefits: Wages or Social Obligations*, (Ithaca: Cornell University Press, 1969), chapters 1 and 2.

33 Coward, *Mercer Handbook*, p. 242.
34 Until the recently concluded pension reform package was implemented, the minimum legislative norm for vesting standards in Canada for those provinces having pension benefits legislation, except two, was age 45 *and* 10 years' service. That is, an employee must satisfy both the age *and* service requirement in order to have an irrevocable right to the employer's contribution for the pension entitlement. The two exceptions were: Manitoba with vesting (employer contributions) with 2 years' service (effective 1990) and lock-in (employee's contribution) at age 45 and 10 years' service; Saskatchewan amended its Pension Benefits Act, effective 1 July, 1981, to provide an improved vesting requirement based on a factor 45 formula, that is, vesting and lock-in occur when a person's age and service *total* 45. Despite the fact that the minimum legislative norm for vesting was 45 and 10, in fact, the prevailing vesting standard was 10 years' service. Note Statistics Canada, *Pension Plans in Canada, 1984* (Ottawa: Minister of Supply and Services, 1986), Text Table T, p. 46.
35 For Britain note the Labour Research Department, *Guide to Company Pension Schemes and The Social Security Pensions Act 1975* (London: LRD Publications, 1977), pp. 25–26. For the U.S., Bankers Trust, *The Pension Reform Act (An Explanation)* (Englewood Cliffs, NJ: Prentice-Hall, 1974), pp. 145–47.
36 Testimony to the U.S. Senate Subcommittee on Labour, cited in Ralph Nader and Kate Blackwell, *You and Your Pension* (New York: Grossman, 1973), p. 11.
37 On this subject, G. S. Becker, "Investment in Human Capital: A Theoretical Analysis," *Journal of Political Economy*, 70, supplement (October 1962): 9–49; Jacob Mincer, "On-the-Job Training: Costs, Returns, and Some Implications," ibid., pp. 50–73; and Walter Y. Oi, "Labour as a Quasi-Fixed Factor," ibid., (December 1962): 538–55.
38 J. C. Kincaid, *Poverty and Equality in Britain: A Study of Social Security and Taxation* (Harmondsworth: Penguin, rev. ed., 1975), p. 132.
39 Roy Lubove, *The Struggle for Social Security, 1900–1935* (Cambridge, MA: Harvard University Press, 1968), p. 129.
40 K. McNaught and David J. Bercuson, *The Winnipeg General Strike: 1919* (Don Mills: Longman Canada, 1974), p. 66. The threatened loss of pension benefits during an industrial dispute remains a contemporary issue in the Canadian industrial relations system. This is because most pension plans stipulated and interpreted the "45 and 10" vesting rule as meaning 10 years of *consecutive* service. A strike would break this continuity of service. On this subject, note "Management Right: Most Strikers Lose Benefits," *Financial Times*, 7 July, 1975.
41 Quoted in Green, "Occupational Pension Schemes," p. 271.
42 Quoted in Lubove, *Struggle for Social Security*, p. 119.
43 Six jurisdictions have introduced Pension Benefits Acts since 1965, including Ontario, Quebec, Manitoba, Alberta, Saskatchewan and the federal government. New Brunswick, Newfoundland and British Columbia have contemplated implementing legislation. Presently 85 per cent of all pension plan members are covered by a Pension Benefits Act.
44 Occupational Pensions Board, *Improved Protection for the Occupational Pension Rights and Expectations of Early Leavers*, Cmnd. 8271 (London: HMSO, June 1981), pp. 25–28. Also on this issue, Roger Hardman, "Pensions-Scandal of the Golden Handcuffs," *Sunday Times*, 17 May 1981; Roger Hardman, "Pensions-Part 2: Cost of Cutting the Golden Handcuffs," *Sunday Times*, 24 May, 1981; and John Whitmore, "How Employees Lose Out When They Change Jobs," *The Times*, 23 April 1982.
45 Those U.S. studies prior to 1974 dealing with vesting and the "take-up" rate include an early study in the mid-1940s by Dan M. McGill, *Pensions: Problems and Trends* (Homewood, IL: Huebner Foundation for Insurance Education, University of Pennsylvania, 1955), pp. 33–34, and p. 40; Kolodrubetz, "Characteris-

tics of Workers"; *Private Welfare and Pension Plan Legislation,* Hearings, General Subcommittee on Labor, Committee on Education and Labor, U.S. House of Representatives, 92d Congress, 1st and 2nd sessions (Washington, D.C.: GPO,1970), p. 262; Kolodrubetz and Landay, "Coverage and Vesting"; and Nader and Blackwell, *You and Your Pension,* p. 5. In the post-ERISA period (1974), note the studies by the Pension Rights Center and Bureau of Labor Statistics cited in Jeremy Rifkin and Randy Barber, *The North Will Rise Again: Pensions, Politics and Power in the 1980s* (Boston: Beacon, 1978), p. 259n5; and Gayle Thompson Rogers, "Vesting of Private Pension Benefits in 1979 and Change from 1972," *Social Security Bulletin* 44 (July 1981): 12—29. For Canada, note Régie des Rentes, *Les Régimes de Rétraite au Québec,* no. 3 (December 1976): 29–37; Health and Welfare Canada, *Survey on Retirement in Canada—Retirement in Canada,* vol. 2 (Ottawa: Minister of National Health and Welfare, 1979), Table 110, and "A Survey of the Awareness and Attitudes of Ontario Residents towards Retirement Programs and Particularly Pension Plans Survey," prepared by Southam Marketing Research Services, *Report of the Royal Commission on the Status of Pensions in Ontario,* vol. 3, *Background Studies and Papers* (Toronto: Queen's Printer, 1980), pp. 36, 72. For Britain, Rosalind M. Altmann, "An Analysis of Occupational Pensions in Great Britain," *Applied Economics* 14 (1982): 53–77.

46 Rogers, "Vesting," p. 15, and derived from the *Statistical Abstract of the United States 1988* (Washington, D.C.: GPO, 1987), Table 567, p. 344.

47 Altmann, "Occupational Pensions," Table 3, p. 562.

48 Department of National Health and Welfare, Planning, Evaluation and Liaison Division, Income Security Programs, *Pension Plan Coverage by Level of Earnings and Age 1978 and 1979* (n.p.: Minister of National Health and Welfare, June 1982), p. 12.

49 Decima Research, *Decima Quarterly Report* (Fall 1986): 222.

50 Statistics Canada, *Pension Plans in Canada 1976,* p. 57, and subsequent editions.

51 For the U.S., Martynes A. Ycas and Susan Grad, "Income of Retirement-Aged Persons in the United States," *Social Security Bulletin* 50 (July 1987), Table 1, p. 6, and in the U.K., Andrew Dawson and Graham Evans, "Pensioners' Incomes and Expenditure 1970–85," *Employment Gazette* (May 1987): 246.

52 Unfortunately, there are no empirical studies indicating the proportion and distribution of partial versus full retirement pensions paid. The logic of the situation suggests, however, that the number of partial pensions paid is considerable as a result of high labour market mobility and the long service requirement for vesting. In the U.K., this is recognized by the Government Actuary, *Occupational Pension Schemes 1983—Seventh Survey* (London: HMSO, 1976), pp. 14, 73.

53 Préfontaine and Balcer, "Interation of Labour Mobility Rates and Vesting Rates," p. 6.

54 Frank T. Denton, Melvin L. Kliman, and Byron G. Spencer, *Pensions and the Economic Security of the Elderly* (Montreal: C. D. Howe Institute, 1981), p. 65.

55 The Economic Council of Canada, *People and Jobs,* determined that the people will change jobs on average 6 times during their working life. The "Survey of Awareness on Attitudes of Ontario Residents towards Retirement Programs," prepared for the Ontario Royal Commission on the Status of Pensions, found that people will change jobs 6.6 times over their life. Assuming entry into the labour force is age 20 will result in a person staying on a job, on average, 6.8 to 7.5 years (65–20 = 45/6 = 7.5 years and 65-20 = 45/6.6 = 6.8 years). Thus, a person would have to be able to transfer pension entitlements between at least two jobs (2 x 6.8 = 13.6 years or 2 x 7.5 = 15 years) in order to satisfy the "45 and 10" vesting rule.

56 Calculated from Statistics Canada, *Consumer Price Index* (Monthly publication 62-001).

57 J. E. Pesando and S. A. Rea, Jr., *Public and Private Pensions in Canada: An Economic Analysis* (Toronto: Ontario Economic Council), Table 7, p. 50.

58 Peter Townsend, "Social Policy in Conditions of Scarcity," *New Society,* 10 May 1979, p. 320.

59 Martin B. Tracy, "Maintaining Value of Social Security Benefits during Inflation: Foreign Experience," *Social Security Bulletin* 99 (November 1976): 33.

60 William M. Mercer Limited, *Brief to Royal Commission on the Status of Pensions in Ontario* (Toronto: Mercer, February 1978), p. 3.

61 Ibid. The most vigorous case put forward for limited indexation by a private pension industry spokesperson is Geoffrey N. Calvert, *Pensions and Survival: The Coming Crisis of Money and Retirement* (Toronto: A Financial Post Book, Maclean-Hunter, 1977), pp. 69–74.

62 Cited in Kincaid, *Poverty and Equality,* pp. 156–57.

63 Lois S. Copeland, "Consumer Price Indexes for the Elderly: British Experience," *Social Security Bulletin* 45 (January 1982): 21.

64 As reported in "Special Report: Inflation, Fixed Incomes — The Inflationary Squeeze on the Over-65s," *Business Week,* 22 May 1978, p. 43.

65 Calvert, *Pensions and Survival.*

66 Statistics Canada, *Pension Plans in Canada, 1984* (Ottawa: Minister of Supply and Services, 1986), Text Table W, p. 52.

67 Cited in *Pensions & Investments,* 9 April 1979, p. 32, and Robert Tilove, *Public Employee Pension Funds* (New York: A Twentieth Century Fund Report, Columbia University Press, 1976), Table 2.14, p. 44.

68 Raphael, *Pensions and Public Servants,* p. 82, and Income Data Services, *Public Sector Pensions,* Study 188 (London: IDS, February 1979), pp. 24–25.

69 Calculated from the Government Actuary, *Occupational Pension Schemes, 1979 — Sixth Survey* (London: HMSO, 1981), Table 10.1, p. 56.

70 Labour Research Department, *Guide to Company Pension Schemes,* pp. 10, 23.

71 For Canada, federal Treasury Board, *Report on Certain Aspects of the Public Service Employee Pension Program,* prepared by Tomensen—Alexander Ltd. (Ottawa: Minister of Supply and Services, 1978), p. 131. For Britain, the Government Actuary, *Sixth Survey,* Table 10.2, p. 57, and the National Association of Pension Funds, *Survey of Occupational Pension Schemes—1978* (Croydon: NAFP, 1979), Table 44, p. 25. For the U.S., Greenwich Research Associates, *Large Corporate Pension Funds 1980: Report to Participants* (Greenwich, CN: Greenwich Research Associates, 1980), p. 77.

72 Tracy, "Maintaining Value," Table 1, p. 38. Also the European Economic Communities, *Comparative Tables of the Social Security Systems in the Member States of the European Communities* (Brussels: ECC, 8th ed., July 1974), Table V11-3.

73 International Labour Organization, *Pensions and Inflation* (Geneva: ILO, 1977), p. vi.

74 William M. Mercer Ltd., *Brief,* quoted in the *Globe and Mail,* 25 April 1975.

75 Labour Research Department, *Guide to Company Pension Schemes,* p. 22.

76 The classic Marxist analysis of modern corporation behaviour under advanced capitalism is Paul A. Baran and Paul M. Sweezy, *Monopoly Capital* (New York: Monthly Review Press, 1966), esp. chapter 2.

77 Economic Council of Canada, *One in Three,* pp. 83, 86.

78 L. W. C. S. Barnes, R. B. Crozier, and G. T. Jackson, *Submission to the Pension Policy Review Task Force Examining the Adequacy of Pension Arrangements in Canada,* (Ottawa 28 April 1977).

79 Economic Council of Canada, *One in Three,* pp. 86, 82.

80 The reader is referred to Paul A. Baran, "Marxism and Psychoanalysis," in *The Longer View,* ed. John O'Neil (New York and London: Monthly Review Press, 1969), p. 101. For a formal economic treatment, note Baran's "Economics of Two Worlds" in the same volume.

81 Calculated from Statistics Canada, *Trusteed Pension Plans Financial Statistics* (Ottawa and Hull: Minister of Trade and Commerce, various years). Computed as an internal rate of return.

82 Economic Council of Canada, *One in Three*, Table 8.1, p. 81.

83 E. A. Johnson, "The Effects of Inflation and Currency Instability on Pension Schemes in the United Kingdom," in *Pensions and Inflation*, International Labour Organization (Geneva: ILO, 1977), pp. 104–5.

84 Income Data Services, *Guide to Pension Schemes* (London: IDS, 1980), p. 83.

85 James E. Pesando, *The Impact of Inflation on Financial Markets in Canada* (Montreal: C. D. Howe Research Institute, February 1977), p. 69.

86 Note, for example, "Indexed Pensions—A Major New Invervention," *Mercer Bulletin* 38 (February 1988). The recommendations of the Friedland report were to be enacted in September 1988.

87 The following example will illustrate the point. Worker A earns a vested deferred benefit of $12,000 a year at age 45. Over the deferral period of 20 years (to age 65) there is an inflation rate of 4 per cent per annum. Assuming that the deferred pension is fully indexed, it would generate a benefit of $26,294 a year at retirement ($12,000 x 20 years x 4% compounded = $26,294). Worker B, using the Friedland recommendation for revaluating deferred benefits on the basis of 75 per cent of the consumer price index (CPI) minus 1 percentage point, over a 20-year deferral period and assuming a 4 per cent inflation rate, would receive a deferred annual pension at age 65 of $17,831 ($12,000 x 20 x 2% compounded [4% x .75 –1%]). Worker C, on the other hand, with a $12,000 a year deferred pension which is not revalued over the 20-year period with a 4 per cent inflation rate, would have his deferred pension at retirement age reduced by 80 per cent and worth only $2,400 per annum.

88 A detailed political analysis and institutional history of pension reform between 1977 and 1987 has not yet been written and awaits future scholarly examination. The classic history of pension reform up to 1966 is Kenneth Bryden, *Old Age Pensions and Policy-Making in Canada* (Montreal: McGill-Queen's University Press, 1974). An early and incomplete historical treatment of this round of pension reform is Laurence E. Coward and Nicholas J. M. Simmons, "The Influence of Government on Pension Planning in Canada—A Study of Recent History and Trends," *Employee Benefits Journal* 4 (Fall 1979): 2–7, 23.

89 A detailed analysis is Paul Light, *Artful Work: The Politics of Social Security Reform* (New York: Random House, 1985).

90 Canadian Gallup Poll, National Omnibus—Newspaper—5–7 January 1984, Nos. 481–82, "Pension Plans—Ensuring Adequate Income upon Retirement," and special cross-tabulations provided to the author.

91 Decima Research, *Decima Quarterly Report* (Fall 1986), Table 213, p. 223.

NOTES TO CHAPTER FIVE

1 Donna Allen, *Fringe Benefits: Wages or Social Obligations?* (Ithaca: Cornell University Press, 1969), pp. 241, 256.

2 The classic treatment of this subject is C. Wright Mills, *The New Men of Power* (New York: Augustus M. Kelley, 1971).

3 Jack Barbash, "Rationalization in American Unions," in *Essays in Industrial Relations Theory*, ed. Gerald G. Somers (Ames: Iowa State University Press, 1969), pp. 147–62, and Arnold S. Tannenbaum, "Unions," in *Handbook of Organizations*, ed. James G. March (Chicago: Rand McNally, 1964), pp. 710–63.

4 *Inland Steel Co. v. NLRB*, 170 F.2d 247 (7th Cir. 1948) cert. denied, 336 U.S. 960 (1949).

5 Allan Flanders, *Trade Unions* (London: Hutchison University Library, 4th ed. 1963), p. 80.

6 Hugh Mosley, *Public and Private Social Welfare Systems: A Working Paper on*

the Underdevelopment of State Social Welfare Institutions in the United States, Publication series of the International Institute for Comparative Social Research (Berlin, December 1978).

7 Mark van de Vall, *Labor Organizations: A Macro- and Micro-Sociological Analysis on a Comparative Basis* (London: Cambridge University Press, 1970), chapter 2.

8 Note David Kwavnick, "Labour's Lobby in Ottawa: How the Canadian Labour Congress Influences Government Policy," *Labour Gazette* 73 (July 1973): 13–20.

9 Mosley, *Social Welfare Systems,* p. 21.

10 Peter Henle, Assistant Director of Research, AFL-CIO, quoted in Allen, *Fringe Benefits,* p. 255.

11 Joseph W. Garbarino, *Health Plans and Collective Bargaining* (Berkeley and Los Angeles: University of California Press, 1960), p. 4.

12 The term comes from Harland Fox, "The Corporate Social Security System and Workmen's Compensation," *Conference Board Record* (February 1964): 2–16.

13 Jack Barbash, *The Elements of Industrial Relations,* mimeo (Madison: University of Wisconsin, Department of Economics, 1971), pp. 4–5, and chapters 2 and 3. The organizational imperatives of labour unions are dealt with in chapter 5, and Jack Barbash, "Rationalization in American Unions." An excellent review article dealing with unions as formal and informal organizations is Tannenbaum, "Unions."

14 On unions as a welfare institution and their social security function, note Jack Barbash, *The Practice of Unionism* (New York: Harper, 1956), pp. 300–304; Jack Barbash, "The Unions and Negotiated Health and Welfare Plans," in *New Dimensions in Collective Bargaining,* eds. Harold W. Davey, Howard S. Kalternborn, and Stanley H. Rutenberg (New York: Harper, 1959), pp. 91–117; Jack Barbash, "The Structure and Evolution of Union Interests in Pensions," Reprint Series No. 90, University of Wisconsin, Industrial Relations Research Institute, Madison, 1967; Garbarino, *Health Plans;* and Raymond Munts, *Bargaining for Health: Labor Unions, Health Insurance, and Medical Care* (Madison: University of Wisconsin Press, 1967).

15 This functionalist typology is based on Robert B. McKersie and Richard E. Walton, *A Behavioral Theory of Labor Negotiations* (New York: McGraw-Hill, 1965).

16 Alex Rubner, *Fringe Benefits: The Golden Chains* (London: Putnam, 1962), p. 136.

17 This summary is based on the following studies. For the United States, Mark R. Green, *The Role of Benefit Structures in Manufacturing Industry* (Eugene: University of Oregon Press, 1964); Richard A. Lester, "Benefits as a Preferred Form of Compensation," *Southern Economic Journal* 33 (April 1967): 485–95; T. J. Gordon and R. E. LeBleu, "Employee Benefits 1970–1985," *Harvard Business Review* (Jan.–Feb. 1970): 93–107; Walter W. Kolodrubetz, "Two Decades of Employee Benefit Plans, 1950–1970: A Review, "*Social Security Bulletin* 35 (April 1972): 23–34; Bevars Marby, "The Economics of Fringe Benefits," *Industrial Relations* 12 (February 1973): 95–106; Bradley R. Schiller and Randall D. Weiss, "The Impact of Private Pensions on Firm Attachment," *Review of Economics and Statistics* 61 (August 1979): 369–80; Francis M. Wistert, *Fringe Benefits* (New York: Reinhold, 1959); and Allen, *Fringe Benefits.* The standard source of data for compensation costs is the U.S. Chamber of Commerce, *Employee Benefits,* published annually. Background studies and surveys for Canada include Robert Swidinsky, "The Economics of Employee Benefits," *Industrial Relations Industrielles* 26 (1972): 915. Harish C. Jain and Edward P. Janzen, "Employee Pay and Benefit Preferences," *Industrial Relations Industrielles* 29 (1974): 99–110; Statistics Canada, *Employee Compensation in Canada, All Industries, 1978* (Ottawa: Minister of Supply and Services, 1980); and

Thorne, Stevenson and Kellogg, *Employee Benefit Costs in Canada,* various years. For Britain, material includes Rubner, *Fringe Benefits;* G. L. Reid and James Bates, "The Cost of Fringe Benefits for Manual Workers in British Industry," *British Journal of Industrial Relations* 1 (1963): 348–69. The classic Glasgow studies are reported in *Fringe Benefits, Labour Costs and Social Security,* eds. G. L. Reid and D. J. Robertson (London: Allen and Unwin, 1965); A. F. Young and J. M. Smith, "Fringe Benefits—A Local Survey," *British Journal of Industrial Relations* 5 (1967): 63–73. Jane Moonman, *The Effectiveness of Fringe Benefits in Industry* (Epping Essex: Gower, 1973); R. I. Hawkesworth, "Fringe Benefits in British Industry," *British Journal of Industrial Relations* 15 (1977): 396–402; Incomes Data Services, *Staff Benefits,* Study 176 (London: IDS, August, 1978); and Incomes Data Services, *Salary Surveys 1979,* Study 209 (London: IDS, January 1980); and "Earnings and Top Pay in 1979," *Labour Research* 69 (January 1980): 6–7. The standard source of compensation information is "Labour Costs," Department of Employment, *Gazette,* various years.

18 Lord Diamond, *Royal Commission on The Distribution of Income and Wealth.* Fifth Report (London: HMSO, October 1979), p. 130.

19 Gordon and LeBleu, "Employee Benefits."

20 Statistics Canada, *Employee Compensation in Canada, All Industries, 1978,* Text Table X, p. 27. For firms with one hundred or more employees.

21 Flanders, *Trade Unions,* p. 52.

22 For the U.S., note the Chamber of Commerce, *Employee Benefits,* Table 6, p. 11; for Britain, the Department of Employment, *Gazette,* Table 6, pp. 9–10. Canadian data are found in Thorne, Stevenson and Kellogg, *Employee Benefit Costs in Canada, 1982* (Toronto: Thorne, Stevenson and Kellogg, 1982), Tables 8 and 9, pp. 22, 24. The data were supplied to the author courtesy of Thorne, Stevenson and Kellogg. It should be noted that for Canada in 1979–80 total pension costs were the largest single payroll expenditure. In 1986, total pension costs were marginally behind vacations (6.2%). This minor difference does not seem sufficient to negate the general proposition, especially given the long-term trends.

23 National Association of Pension Funds, *Survey of Occupational Pension Schemes—1978* (Croydon: NAPF, 1979), Table 20, p. 11.

24 Calculated from Statistics Canada, *Trusteed Pension Plans Financial Statistics* (Ottawa and Hull: Minister of Trade and Commerce, various years). Computed on the basis of an internal rate of return. Also the Economic Council of Canada, *One in Three: Pensions for Canadians to the Year 2030* (Ottawa: Canadian Government Publishing Centre, 1979), Table 8.1, p. 81.

25 E. A. Johnson, "The Effects of Inflation and Currency Instability on Pension Schemes in the United Kingdom," in *Pensions and Inflation,* International Labour Organization (Geneva: ILO, 1977), pp. 104–5.

26 Financial Executives Institute of Canada, *Report on Survey of Pension Plans in Canada* (n.p.: FEI, March 1978), p. 1, and the Pension Commission of Ontario, *Preliminary Report on the Funded Status of Certain Pension Plans Registered with the Pension Commission of Ontario* (Toronto: PCO, April 1975).

27 Calculated from Statistics Canada, *Pension Plans in Canada, 1980,* Text Table XXV.

28 Financial Executives Institute of Canada, *Report on Survey of Pension Plans in Canada* (n.p.: FEI, November 1981), p. 32.

29 Ibid., p. 33.

30 Edmund Faltermayer, "A Steep Climb up Pension Mountain," *Fortune,* January 1975, pp. 75–81, 157–58, 162–65; also A. F. Ehrbar, "Those Pension Plans Are Even Weaker Than You Think," *Fortune,* November 1977, pp. 104–8, 110, 112, 114. On-going surveys of this situation include "The 'Hidden' Corporate Debt," *Business Week,* 24 August, 1974, pp. 46–47; "When Pension Liabilities Dampen Profits," *Business Week,* 16 June 1975, 80–81; "Unfunded Pension Liabilities: A Growing Worry for Companies," *Business Week,* 18 July 1977, pp.

86–88; "Unfunded Pension Liabilities: A Continuing Burden," *Business Week*, 14 August 1978, pp. 60–63; and "Pension Liabilities: Improvement Is Illusory," *Business Week*, 14 September, 1981, pp. 114–15, 118.

31 "Unfunded Pension Liabilities," p. 86.

32 Faltermayer, "Steep Climb," p. 78.

33 Calculated from Statistics Canada, *Pension Plans in Canada, 1980* (Ottawa: Minister of Supply and Services Canada, 1982), Text Table XXV, pp. 59–60.

34 National Association of Pension Funds, *Survey*, Table 20.

35 David K. Foot, *Canada's Population Outlook: Demographic Future and Economic Challenges* (Toronto: Canadian Institute for Economic Policy, 1982), pp. 204, 196, and Table 6–11, p. 199.

36 Faltermayer, "Steep Climb," p. 81.

37 Special Committee on Pension Reform, *Report of the Parliamentary Task Force on Pension Reform* (Ottawa: Canadian Government Publishing Centre, 1983), Table 11.1, p. 85.

38 National Commission on Social Security, *Social Security in America's Future*, Final Report (Washington, D.C.: NCOSS, 1981),Table 4-1, p. 78.

39 Statement by James M. Black, executive vice-president of the American Association of Institutional Management, April 1967, quoted in Allen, *Fringe Benefits*, p. 259.

40 On this point note Rubner, *Fringe Benefits*.

41 Wistert, *Fringe Benefits*, pp. 4–5.

42 Lester, "Benefits," p. 489.

43 For a fascinating account of the bargaining relationship between the UAW and GM, and in particular the 1970 strike, note William Serrin, *The Company and the Union* (New York: Vintage Books, 1974), esp. chapter 8 on the pension issue.

44 Hawkesworth, "Fringe Benefits," table, p. 402.

45 U.S. Department of Labor, Bureau of Labor Statistics, *Analysis of Work Stoppages, 1975*, Table 11, p. 23, and information supplied to the author by Labour Canada, 25 March, 1983.

46 Richard Hyman and Ian Brough, *Social Values and Industrial Relations: A Study of Fairness and Inequality* (Oxford: Blackwell, 1975).

47 On this issue note R. W. McInnes, *Welfare Legislation and Benefit Plans in Canada* (Toronto: Law Society of Upper Canada, 1974), pp. 62–67. In Canada the deferred wage doctrine is now recognized in tort law, but not in labour relations law.

48 Financial Executives Institute of Canada, *Report* (1978), Table 22, p. 50.

49 Section 23(c) of the Ontario *Pension Benefits Act*, R.S.O., 1983.

50 Remedial legislation was enacted under the federal Pension Benefits Standards Act, 1987, section 28(1)(c) and the Ontario Pension Benefits Act, 1986, section 30(1)(e). Manitoba and Quebec had previously provided legislative relief.

51 On this issue note Jacobs Manufacturing Co., 94 N.L.R.B. 124(1951); enforcement granted, 196 F.2d. 680 (2d Cir. 1952); *Aluminum Ore* v. *NLRB*, 131 F.2d 485 (7th Cir. 1942); Phelps Dodge Copper Products Corp., 101 N.L.R.B. 360 (1952); Reed and Prince Manufacturing Co., 96 N.L.R.B. 850 (1951).

52 Legislative intervention regarding pension scheme information and disclosure includes the Trustee Act 1925, the Contracts of Employment Act 1972, and the Employment Protection Act 1975.

53 Occupational Pensions Board, *Report of the Occupational Pensions Board on the Questions of Solvency, Disclosure of the Information and Member Participation in Occupational Pension Schemes*, Cmnd. 5904 (London: HMSO, 1975), pp. 34, 2, 6.

54 Government Actuary, *Occupational Pension Schemes 1975—Fifth Survey* (London: HMSO, 1978), Table 14.1 p. 76.

55 Interview with Bryne Davies, Assistant Director of Social Insurance and Industrial Welfare, Trades Union Congress, Congress House, London, 23 January

1980. The issue has again been raised; note, for example, the *TUC Occupational Pensions Bulletin,* 10 November 1982, p. 15.

56 Interview with James Moher, Pensions Officer, Transport and General Workers' Union, Transport House, London, 22 January 1980.

57 Interview with Myles White, Head of Pensions and Social Services Department, General and Municipal Workers' Union, Thorne House, Surrey, 23 January 1980.

58 For the U.S., note *Allied Chemical and Alkali Workers* v. *The Pittsburg Plate Glass Company* 78 LRRM 2974. The legal history surrounding this case is recounted in Henry Graham and Brian Becker, "The Pittsburgh Plate Glass Case, Collective Bargaining and Retirement Benefits," *Industrial Gerontology* 2 (Fall 1975): pp. 281–88. The Weiler ruling of the British Columbia Labour Relations Board in the *Canadian Paper Workers Union* v. *The Pulp and Paper Industrial Relations Bureau* (1977) is reported in "B.C. Union Wins Right to Bargain for Its Retirees," CCH, *Canadian Industrial Relations and Personnel Developments,* p.807.

59 Interview with Myles White, Head of Pensions and Social Services Department, General and Municipal Workers' Union.

60 Interview with James Moher, Pensions Officer, Transport and General Workers' Union.

61 Note Jack Jones, *The Case for Pensioners,* a T.G.W.U. pamphlet (London: Pension Campaign Centre, 1978).

62 American Arbitration Association, *Employee Benefit Plan Claims Arbitration Rules* (New York: AAA, 1977).

63 Trades Union Congress, *Occupational Pension Schemes—A TUC Guide* (London: TUC, 1976), p. 74.

64 Paul P. Harbrecht, *Pension Funds and Economic Power* (New York: Twentieth Century Fund, 1959), p. 236.

65 Quoted in Jeremy Rifkin and Randy Barber, *The North Will Rise Again: Pensions, Politics and Power in the 1980s* (Boston: Beacon, 1978), p. 259n11.

66 Harbrecht, *Pension Funds,* p. 119.

67 Special request computer print-out supplied to the author by Labour Canada, "Provisions in Major Collective Agreements in Bargaining Units over 500 Employees," 7 March 1988.

68 New York State Banking Department, *Pension and Other Employee Welfare Funds 1955* cited in Harbrecht, *Pension Funds,* Table 29, pp. 221–22.

69 Figures derived from Harry E. Davis, "Multiemployer Pension Plan Provisions in 1973," *Monthly Labor Review* 97 (October 1974): 10–16.

70 Government Actuary, *Occupational Pension Schemes 1975,* Table 14.2, p. 77.

71 National Association of Pension Funds, *Survey,* Table 56, p. 30, and the Government Actuary, *Occupational Pension Schemes 1983* (London: HMSO, 1986), Table 12.2., p. 78. A recent review and analysis of member participation in pension scheme management is Tom Schuller, *Age, Capital and Democracy* (Aldershot: Gower, 1986).

72 This summary is based on the classic article by Ed Finn, "The Case for Co-Management of Employee Pension Funds," *Labour Gazette* 6 (June 1973): 356–65.

73 American Federation of Labor, *Pension Plans under Collective Bargaining—A Reference Guide for Trade Unions* (Washington, D.C.: AFL, 1954), pp. 2–3.

74 Harbrecht, *Pension Funds,* p. 75.

75 On the subject of pension fund abuses, note James E. McNulty,Jr., *Decision and Influence Processes in Private Pension Plans* (Homewood, IL: Irwin, 1961), pp. 114–15; Robert Tilove, *Public Employee Pension Funds* (New York: Columbia University Press, A Twentieth Century Fund Report, 1976), p. 215; "Pension Funds as Profit Centers," *Pension and Welfare News* 10 (June 1974): 36–38; Edwards S. Herman, *Conflicts of Interest: Commercial Bank Trust Departments* (New York: Twentieth Century Fund, 1975): Louis M. Kohlmeiner, *Con-*

flicts of Interests: State and Local Pension Fund Asset Management (New York: Twentieth Century Fund, 1976); "Warning: A Hyper-Active Bank Can Damage Your Pension," *Economist,* 2 February 1980, pp. 83–84; and Finn, "Case for Co-management."

76 McNulty, *Decision and Influence Processes,* p. 38.
77 *Occupational pension Schemes—The Role of Members in the Running of Schemes,* Cmnd. 6514 (London: HMSO, 1976), pp. 8–9. Also the Occupational Pensions Board, *Report of the Occupational Pensions Board on the Questions of Solvency, Disclosure of Information and Member Participation in Occupational Pension Schemes,* Cmnd. 5904 (London: HMSO, 1975).
78 *Occupational Pension Schemes,* pp. 1, 7, 8.
79 "Labour Pension Push Begins to Roll," *Financial Times,* 2 April 1973.
80 John Munro, Minister of Labour, "Pensions for Canadian Workers," address to the International Pension Conference, 15 June 1977.
81 *Occupational Pension Schemes,* pp. 8–9.
82 John Munro, "Pensions."
83 Quoted in the *Financial Times,* 28 June 1976.
84 Quoted in the *Daily Telegraph,* 29 September 1976. Emphasis added.
85 "Management Willing to Compromise on Pension Plans," *Financial Times,* 4 February 1973.
86 Trades Union Congress, *Occupational Pension Schemes,* p. 86.
87 Interview with James Moher, Pensions Officer, Transport and General Workers' Union.
88 General and Municipal Workers' Union, *The GMWU Policy on Pensions* (Surrey: GMWU, May 1973), pp. 10–11, and the General and Municipal Workers' Union, *Pensions in the 1980's—Program for Action,* Annual Congress, 20–24 May 1979, Torquay (Surrey: GMWU, April 1979), pp. 5, 7.
89 Canadian Labour Congress, *Policy Paper on the Regulation of Private Pension Plans* (Ottawa: CLC, 1975), and the Canadian Labour Congress, *Submission to the Royal Commission on the Status of Pensions in Ontario* (Ottawa: CLC, March 23, 1978), Appendix A, p. 2.
90 Canadian Union of Public Employees, Convention Resolution No. 46, Quebec City, 1977.
91 United Steel Workers of America (Canadian Region), *Policy Statement: Pensions,* Canadian Policy Conference, Fall 1979, (Toronto: USW, 1979), p. 5.
92 Manitoba, Ontario and the federal jurisdictions permit this discretionary arrangement. Note Michael R. Ternosky, "The Pension Committee Conundrum," *Benefits Canada* 12 (April 1988): 7–10.
93 American Federation of Labor and Congress of Industrial Organizations, *Investment of Union Pension Funds* (Washington, D.C.: AFL-CIO, circa 1980), and the American Federation of Labor and Congress of Industrial Organizations, *Pensions: A Study of Benefit Fund Investment Policies* (Washington, D.C.: IUD, AFL-CIO, May 1980); and A. H. Raskin, "Pension Funds Could Be the Unions' Secret Weapon," *Fortune,* 31 December 1979, pp. 64–67.
94 "Pension Funds: What Are They, Who Controls Them?" *Labour Research* 67 (October 1978): 215.
95 Frank Mitchell Redington, "Presidential Address," *Journal of the Institute of Actuaries* (1959): 6.
96 Sue Ward, *Controlling Pension Schemes* (London: Workers' Educational Association, 1978), p. 16.

NOTES TO CHAPTER SIX

1 C. Wright Mills, *The Power Elite* (London: Oxford University Press, 1959), p. 6.
2 Stephen Yeo, "Working-Class Association, Private Capital, Welfare and the State in the Late Nineteenth and Twentieth Centuries," in *Social Work, Welfare and*

the State, eds. Noel Parry, Michael Rustin, and Carole Satyamurti (Beverly Hills: Sage, 1979), p. 59.

3 Bentley B. Gilbert, "The British National Insurance Act of 1911 and the Commercial Insurance Lobby," *Journal of British Studies* 4 (1965): 126–48.

4 On this subject, note Bentley B. Gilbert, "The Decay of Nineteenth-Century Provident Institutions and the Coming of Old Age Pensions in Great Britain," *Economic History Review,* 2nd ser., 17 (1965): 551–63, and James H. Treble, "The Attitudes of Friendly Societies towards the Movement in Great Britain for State Pensions, 1878–1908," *International Review of Social History* 15 (1970): 266–99.

5 Arthur Marwick, "The Labour Party and the Welfare State in Britain, 1900–1948," *American Historical Review* 73 (1967): 401.

6 Roy Lubove, *The Struggle for Social Security, 1900–1935* (Cambridge, MA: Harvard University Press, 1968), p. 9.

7 Lubove, *Social Security,* pp. 140, 139.

8 Kenneth Bryden, *Old Age Pensions and Policy-Making in Canada* (Montreal: McGill-Queen's University Press, 1974),p. 1.

9 Daniel J. Baum, *The Investment Function of Canadian Financial Institutions* (New York, Washington and London: Praeger, 1973), p. 136.

10 Bryden, *Old Age Pensions,* pp. 188, 191.

11 Monique Bégin, Minister of Health and Welfare Canada, "Notes for an Address by the Honourable Monique Bégin to the Association of Canadian Pension Management," Toronto, 17 September 1980, p. 7. Emphasis added.

12 On the capitalist state's ideological bias to support and protect private sector activities, note Ian Gough, *The Political Economy of the Welfare State* (London: Macmillan,1979), chapters 1, 3, 7; Ralph Miliband, *The State in Capitalist Society* (London: Weidenfeld and Nicolson, 1972), chapters 2–4; Nicos Poulantzas, *Political Power and Social Classes,* trans. Timmy O'Hagan (London: New Left Books, 1973), chapters 2 and 3; James O'Connor, *The Fiscal Crisis of the State* (New York: St. Martin's, 1973), chapter 3; Suzanne de Brunhoff, *The State, Capital and Economic Policy,* trans. Mike Sonenscher (London: Pluto Press, 1978), chapters 3–5; Ernest Mandel, *Late Capitalism,* trans. Joris De Bras (London: New Left Books, 1975), esp. chapter 15; and Leo Panitch, ed., *The Canadian State: Political Economy and Political Power* (Toronto: University of Toronto Press, 1977), chapters 1, 3, 7 and 8.

13 Government of Saskatchewan, Saskatchewan Labour, *Brief to the National Pensions Conference. Reform of Canada's Retirement Income System—A Saskatchewan View* (Regina: Pensions Branch, Saskatchewan Labour, March 1981), p. 6.

14 Richard M. Titmuss, "The Irresponsible Society," *Essays on the Welfare State* (Boston: Beacon, 1969), p. 243.

15 Wallace Clement, *The Canadian Corporate Elite: An Analysis of Economic Power* (Toronto: McClelland and Stewart, 1975), p. 159. Emphasis added.

16 Lord Radcliffe, Chairman, *Committee on the Working of the Monetary System Report.* Cmnd. 827 (London: HMSO, 1959), p. 290.

17 Canada Trust, *Canada Trustco Annual Report 1977* (n.p.: Canada Trust, 1977), p. 11.

18 Labour Research Department, *Guide to Company Pension Schemes and the Social Security Pensions Act 1975* (London: LRD, 1977), p. 28.

19 Francis Green, "Occupational Pension Schemes in British Capitalism," *Cambridge Journal of Economics* 6 (September 1982): 281.

20 Economic Council of Canada, *Fourteenth Annual Review: Into the 1980s* (Ottawa: Minister of Supply and Services, 1977), p. 46. Also note "The Long-Run Decline in Liquidity," *Monthly Review* 22 (September 1970): 1–17. Between 1946 and 1969, for example, the corporate liquidity ration in the U.S. declined from 73.4 to 19.3 per cent. Sources of external financing for U.S. corporations in

relation to corporate capital requirements are dealt with in "Capital Shortage: Fact and Fancy," *Monthly Review* 27 (April 1976): 1–19.

21 On the distinction between the "identified" and "residual" saving approach, note J. C. Odling-Smee, "Personal Savings Revisited: More Statistics, Fewer Facts," *Oxford Bulletin of Economics and Statistics* 35 (February 1973): 21–29. Personal savings vehicles for retirement income such as RRSPs and IRAs are excluded.

22 Note the Central Statistical Office, *Annual Abstract of Statistics, 1982 Edition* (London: HMSO, 1982), Table 14.3, p. 347n3; Charles A. Barrett, "Why Are Canadians Saving So Much?" *Canadian Business Review* (Summer 1978): 5–8, and C. E. Samur, W. D. Jarvis, and M. C. McCracken, *Analysis of the Recent Behaviour of the Personal Savings Rate* (Ottawa: Informetrica, March 1979).

23 G. Francis Green, *The Increase in Aggregate U.K. Pension Savings*, Kingston Polytechnic, Discussion Paper in Political Economy No. 28 (Surrey on Thames: Kingston Polytechnic, 1980); Samur, Jarvis, McCracken, *Personal Savings Rate.*

24 Green, *U.K. Pension Savings*, Figure 2, p. 10.

25 Samur, Jarvis, McCracken, *Personal Savings Rate*, Table 4, p. 31, Graph no. 4, p. 32, and Appendix II, p. 13.

26 Economic Council of Canada, *One in Three: Pensions for Canadians to the Year 2030* (Hull: Canadian Government Publishing Centre, 1979), Table 5–1, p. 44.

27 Green, *U.K. Pension Savings*, pp. 6–7.

28 *The Retirement Income System in Canada: Problems and Alternative Policies for Reform*, A Summary of the Report of the Task Force on Retirement Income Policy, 1979 (Hull: Supply and Services Canada, 1979), Table 7, p. 21.

29 Toronto Stock Exchange, *Submission to the Royal Commission on the Status of Pensions in Ontario* (Toronto: TSE, January 1978), p. 40.

30 Trust Companies Association of Canada, *Submission to the Royal Commission on the Status of Pensions in Ontario* (Toronto: TCAC, May 1978), p. III-4.

31 Roger Kitson and Michael Pilch, *Pension Funds and the Economy* (n.p.: Lowndes Lambert Group, 1977), p. 47.

32 J. Grant, *The Role of Private Pension Plans in the Financing of the Corporate Sector of the Canadian Economy* (Toronto: Wood Gundy, March 1976), Table IX, p. 11.

33 D. Don Ezra, *The Struggle for Pension Fund Wealth* (Toronto: Pagurian, 1983), pp. 15, 27. Mr. Ezra was consultant to and co-author of the Business Committee on Pension Policy, *Capital Markets Study* (n.p.: Pension Finance Associates, August 1983).

34 "Editorially Speaking—Pension Promises Depend on Growth," *Pensions & Investments, 18 June 1979, p. 8.

35 Paul N. Wilson, "Funds' Growth Rate Staggering: Could Soon Be Major Asset Pool," *Pensions & Investments*, 26 February 1979, pp. 41–42.

36 John H. Panabaker, "Remarks by John H. Panabaker, President and Chief Executive Officer, Mutual Life of Canada to the National Pensions Conference," 31 March 1981, Ottawa, p. 10. Also note Andrew G. Knieswasser, "Opportunity From East to West," address by Andrew G. Knieswasser, President, Investment Dealers Association of Canada to the 1981 Annual Conference, Atlantic Provinces Economic Council, Saint John, New Brunswick, 29 September 1981, p. 8.

37 H. E. C. Stoneham, "Pension Money Is Vital to Future Capital Needs," *Financial Post*, 11 April 1981.

38 Note, for example, Geoffrey N. Calvert, "Found Money: Let's Start *Funding* Social Security," *Pension World* 12 (February 1976): 20–27, 54.

39 Tristam S. Lett, "Savings or Consumption? The Role of the Public Pension Plan in the National Economy," address to the Association of Canadian Pension Management, Toronto, September 1977. Darcy McKeough, Treasurer for the

Province of Ontario, was similarly quoted by the Ontario Economic Council, *The Ontario Economy to 1987* (Toronto: Queen's Printer, 1977), p. 28.

40 Edward P. Neufeld, "Who Will Finance Canada's Economic Growth in the 1980s?" Address to the Young Presidents' Organization, Third Canadian Conference, Vancouver, 2 October 1981, pp. 5, 10.

41 Ronald Anderson, "Private Sector Pension Funds Crucial to Financing Growth," *Globe and Mail,* 8 November 1983.

42 Clayton Sinclair, "Private Pension Industry Seeks Escape from Crisis in the '80s," *Ottawa Citizen,* 2 April 1981.

43 "CMA Wants Pension Reform Focused on Private Sector," *Globe and Mail,* 23 May 1981.

44 Board of Trade of Metropolitan Toronto, *Pension Policy in Canada,* submission to National Pensions Conference (Toronto: BTMT, 1981), p. 5.

NOTES TO CHAPTER SEVEN

1 "Written Evidence by the Stock Exchange," *Committee to Review the Functioning of Financial Institutions* (Wilson Committee), vol. 4 (London: HMSO, March 1979), p. 37.

2 Edward Malca, *Pension Funds and Other Institutional Investors* (Lexington, MA: Lexington Books, 1975), p. 11.

3 Toronto Stock Exchange, *Submission to the Royal Commission on the Status of Pensions in Ontario* (Toronto: TSE, January 1978), p. 75.

4 A. A. Berle, Jr., and G. C. Means, *The Modern Corporation and Private Property* (New York: Macmillan, 1932).

5 J. Moyle, *The Pattern of Ordinary Share Ownership, 1957–1971,* Department of Applied Economics, Occasional Paper 31 (Cambridge: Cambridge University Press, 1971); M. J. Erritt, J. C. D. Alexander, and A. J. Watson, *The Ownership of Company Shares: A Survey for 1975* (London: HMSO, 1977); Richard J. Briston and Richard Dobbins, *The Growth and Impact of Institutional Investors,* a Report of the Research Committee of the Institute of Chartered Accountants in England and Wales (London: Institute of Chartered Accountants in England and Wales, 1978), and Richard Minns, *Pension Funds and British Capitalism* (London: Heinemann Educational, 1980). The Securities and Exchange Commission, *Institutional Investor Study Report of The Securities And Exchange Commission,* 2 vols. and Summary. 92d Congress, 1st Session (Washington, D.C.: GPO, 1971); Raymond W. Goldsmith, *Institutional Investors and Corporate Stock—A Background Study* (New York and London: National Bureau of Economic Research, 1973); Robert Tilove, *Pension Funds and Economic Freedom* (New York: Fund for the Republic, 1959); and Paul Harbrecht, S.J., *Pension Funds and Economic Power* (New York: Twentieth Century Fund, 1959).

6 Briston and Dobbins, *Institutional Investors,* Exhibit 49, p. 180.

7 Robert M. Soldofsky, "Institutional Holdings of Common Stock 1900–2000," *Michigan Business Studies* 18 (1971): 209, and Peter Drucker, *The Unseen Revolution: How Pension Fund Socialism Came to America* (New York: Harper and Row, 1976), p. 2.

8 Richard Deaton and Robert Deaton, "An Honest Valuation of Drucker's Pension Fund 'Socialism,'" *Pensions & Investments,* 21 June 1976, pp. 15–16.

9 Leo Johnson, "The Development of Class in Canada in the Twentieth Century," *Capitalism and the National Question,* ed. Gary Teeple (Toronto: University of Toronto Press, 1972), p. 157.

10 These figures have been derived by relating common stock ownership to adult population based on information supplied by the New York, Toronto and London Stock Exchanges. For the U.S., *Statistical Abstract of the United States 1986* (Washington, D.C.: GPO, 1987), Series 728, Table 441, and for Canada, Toronto Stock Exchange, *Canadian Shareowners: Their Profile and Attitudes*

(Toronto: TSE, 1986), pp. 7–8. British data courtesy of the London Stock Exchange.

11 "The Unequal Society," *Labour Research* 68 (October 1979): Table D, p. 215. An in-depth comparative study, with particular reference to the distribution of wealth in Britain is H. F. Lydall and D. G. Tipping, "The Distribution of Personal Wealth in Britain," in *Wealth, Income and Inequality*, ed. A. B. Atkinson (Harmondsworth: Penguin Education, 1973), pp. 243–67. The distribution of wealth in Canada and various measurement considerations are dealt with by J. B. Davies, "On the Size and Distribution of Wealth in Canada," *Review of Income and Wealth* 25 (September 1979): 237–59.

12 Victor Perlo, "People's Capitalism and Stock Ownership," *American Economic Review* 48 (June 1958): 333–47, traces stock ownership in the U.S. between 1922 and 1956; Marshall E. Blume, Jean Crockett, and Irwin Friend, "Stock-ownership in the United States: Characteristics and Trends," *Survey of Current Business* 54 (November 1974): Table 4, p. 27 is an excellent review article. The early classic work, now dated, is Robert J. Lampman, *The Share of Top Wealth-Holders in National Wealth* (Princeton: Princeton University Press, 1962).

13 Derived from the Department of National Revenue, *Incomes of Canadians, 1970* (Ottawa: DNR, 1972), Table 2.

14 Cited in Harbrecht, *Pension Funds*, p. 16.

15 Greg Barr, "Ma Bell Kicks Up Her Heels," *Financial Times*, 5 December 1983.

16 S. J. Prais, *The Evolution of Giant Firms in Britain: A Study of Growth of Concentration in Manufacturing in Britain 1909–70* (Cambridge: Cambridge University Press, 1976), Table 5.7, p. 118.

17 Economic Council of Canada, *One in Three: Pensions for Canadians to the Year 2030* (Hull: Canadian Government Publishing Centre 1979), p. 54.

18 Toronto Stock Exchange, *Status of Pensions*, p. 76.

19 Briston and Dobbins, *Institutional Investors*, Exhibit 64, p. 200.

20 Pavan Sahgal, "Who Owns Corporate America?" *Pensions & Investment Age*, 31 October 1983, p. 24.

21 William C. Greenough and Francis P. King, *Pension Plans and Public Policy* (New York: Columbia University Press, 1976), p. 140.

22 Dorsey Richardson, Chairman of the Executive Committee of the National Association of Investment Companies quoted in Harbrecht, *Pension Funds*, pp. 30–31 and "Institutions Stabilize Market," *Pensions & Investments*, 3 December 1979, p. 8.

23 Calculated from Securities and Exchange Commission data cited in Greenough and King, *Pension Plans*, Table 6.5, p. 142.

24 Briston and Dobbins, *Institutional Investors*, Exhibit 55, p. 193.

25 "Warning: A Hyper-Active Bank Can Damage Your Pension," *Economist*, 2 February 1980, pp. 83–84.

26 On this subject note the 1974 and 1975 one-day transaction studies by the Stock Exchange (London).

27 Calculated from the U.S. Department of Commerce, *Statistical Abstract of the United States, 1982–83* (Washington, D.C.: GPO, 1982), Series 818, p. 508.

28 Calculated from the Bank of Canada, *Review* (Ottawa: n.p., various years).

29 Trades Union Congress, *Report on Pension Fund Investment and Trusteeship*, TUC Conference (London: TUC, 11 November 1982), p. 7.

30 *Finance in Europe* (London: Institute of Chartered Accountants, 1975).

31 *Grylls Report on Bank Lending*, November 1981 cited in the Trades Union Congress, *Report*.

32 Trades Union Congress, *Report*, p. 8.

33 Ibid.

34 Business Committee on Pension Policy, *Capital Markets Study*, prepared for Business Committee on Pension Policy by Pension Finance Associates (Toronto: PFA, September 1983), Figure 3.3, p. 25, and "Canada's Top 40 Pension Funds," *Benefits Canada* 12 (April 1988), graph, p. 14.

35 Richard Minns. *Take Over the City: The Case for Public Ownership of Financial Institutions* (London: Pluto Press, 1982), p. 15.

36 Prais, *Giant Firms*, p. 120.

37 The alternative positions in this debate are outlined as follows. V. Perlo, *The Empire of High Finance* (New York: International Publishers, 1957), argues the thesis of "financial domination" over industrial capital in the U.S. The classic work postulating the independence of the modern corporation under conditions of advanced American capitalism is P. A. Baran and P. M. Sweezy, *Monopoly Capital* (New York: Monthly Review Press, 1966). Sweezy engaged in an acidic polemic with Fitch and Oppenheimer including P. M. Sweezy, "The Resurgence of Financial Control: Fact or Fancy," *Monthly Review* 23 (1971). Barratt Brown, "The Limits of the Welfare State," in *Can Workers Run Industry?* ed. K. Coates (London: Sphere, 1968), and R. Williams et al., *May Day Manifesto* (Harmondsworth: Penguin, 1968) provide empirical evidence for the U.K. S. Menshikov, *Millionaires and Managers* (Moscow: Progress, 1969), takes a position similar to Perlo. J. M. Chevalier, *La Structure financiére de l'industrie américaine* (Paris: Cujas, 1970) is a useful study. The standard rejoinder to Sweezy is R. Fitch and M. Oppenheimer, "Who Rules the Corporations?" Parts I–III, *Socialist Revolution*, vols. 4–6 (1970). R. Fitch, "Reply to James O'Connor," *Socialist Revolution* 7 (1971), and "Sweezy and Corporate Fetishism," *Socialist Revolution* 12 (1972); also James O'Connor, "Who Rules the Corporations? The Ruling Class," *Socialist Revolution* 7 (1971). An interesting study is G. Thompson, "The Relationship between the Financial and Industrial Sector of the United Kingdom Economy," *Economy and Society* 6 (1977): 235–83.

38 This summary is based on the excellent review of the literature contained in John Scott, *Corporations, Classes and Capitalism* (London: Hutchinson, 1979), pp. 95–97.

39 J. Grant, *The Role of Private Pension Plans in the Financing of the Corporate Sector of the Canadian Economy* (Toronto: Wood Gundy, March 1976), p. 1.

40 Minns, *Take Over the City*, p. 18.

41 Briston and Dobbins, *Institutional Investors*, p. 40.

42 Ibid.

43 National Association of Pension Funds, "Written Evidence by the National Association of Pension Funds," *Committee to Review the Functioning of Financial Institutions* (Wilson Committee), vol.3 (London: HMSO, November 1977), p. 137.

44 London Stock Exchange, "Evidence," p. 15.

45 Briston and Dobbins, *Institutional Investors*, Exhibit 68, p. 203.

46 Grant, *Private Pension Plans*, p. 11, and Table XIII, Case I.

47 Based on information supplied to the author by the Corporate Finance Division, federal Department of Finance Canada, which is now in the process of undertaking a major study of this important subject.

48 These estimates were supplied to the author by the Head of Institutional Services for a major Canadian underwriting and brokerage firm, 20 January 1984. Subsequently, these estimates were independently confirmed by the Heads of Institutional (Stock and Bond) Services for another dominant brokerage firm on 5 October 1988. Both of these firms are recognized as being the leading investment dealers in Canada.

49 For the United States, calculated from the *Statistical Abstract of the United States*, Series 859, p. 519, and Series 537, p. 330. Estimate for the U.K. derived from Table 7.2, based on the arbitrary assumption of a 50 per cent control block.

50 *The Retirement Income System In Canada: Problems and Alternative Policies for Reform*, Summary of the Report of the Task Force on Retirement Income Policy, 1979 (Hull: Supply and Services Canada, 1979), p. 23.

51 On this point note Clause Offe, "Advanced Capitalism and the Welfare State," *Politics and Society* 2 (Summer 1972): 479–88.

52 Daniel J. Baum, *The Investment Function of Canadian Financial Institutions* (New York, Washington and London: Praeger, 1973), p. 154.

53 Richard Deaton, "The Fiscal Crisis of the State in Canada," in *The Political Economy of the State*, ed. Dimitrios I. Roussopoulos (Montreal: Black Rose, 1973), pp. 37–38. The seminal work is James O'Connor, *The Fiscal Crisis of the State* (New York: St. Martin's Press, 1973). For Britain, Ian Gough, *The Political Economy of the Welfare State* (London: Macmillan, 1979), chapters 5–7.

54 Calculated from the Department of Finance, *Economic Review April 1982* (Ottawa: Canadian Government Publishing Centre, 1982), Table 49, p. 176.

55 Christopher Johnson, "Pensions—A Growth Industry," *Lloyds Bank Economic Bulletin* 19 (July 1980): Chart B, p. 3.

56 Trades Union Congress, *Report*, p. 6.

57 Calculated from Table 6.5 and Appendix D.

58 Arthur W. Donner, *Financing the Future: Canada's Capital Markets in the Eighties* (Toronto: Canadian Institute for Economic Policy, 1982), p. 121.

59 David Shaw and Ross T. Archibald, *The Management of Change in the Canadian Securities Industry*, vol.6 (Toronto: Toronto Stock Exchange, 1976), p. 19.

60 Baum, *Investment Function*, p. 150.

61 Calculated from the Department of Finance, *Economic Review*, Table 50, p. 177, Table 51, p. 178 and Table 49, p. 176.

62 Quoted in Richard Simeon, *Federal-Provincial Diplomacy: The Making of Recent Policy in Canada* (Toronto: University of Toronto Press, 1972), p. 176. Emphasis in original. On the central role of the CPP investment fund as a source of provincial financing in the negotiation of the C/QPP, also note Peter Desbarats, *The State of Quebec* (Toronto: McClelland and Stewart, 1965), pp. 128–32; Peter Newman, *The Distemper of Our Times: Canadian Politics in Transition, 1963–68* (Toronto: McClelland and Stewart, 1968), chapter 22, and the late Judy LaMarsh, Minister of Health and Welfare Canada, responsible for introducing the CPP, *Memoirs of a Bird in a Gilded Cage* (Toronto: McClelland and Stewart, 1969), pp. 58–59, 78–82. From an historiographic perspective, while many of the details surrounding the negotiation of the CPP remain obscure, the centrality and importance of the CPP investment fund is well established.

63 The Advisory Committee of the Canada Pension Plan, *The Rate of Return on the Investment Fund of the Canada Pension Plan* (Ottawa: Health and Welfare Canada, June 1975), p. 7.

64 Kevin Collins, "The Canada Pension Plan as a Source of Provincial Capital Funds," in *How Much Choice? Retirement Policies in Canada* (Ottawa: Canadian Council on Social Development, 1975), Table 4, p. 255; Advisory Council of the Canada Pension Plan, *Rate of Return*, p. 7; and Statistics Canada, *Provincial Government Finance: Assets, Liabilities, Sources and Uses of Funds* (Ottawa: Minister of Supply and Services, various years).

65 K. Horner and M. Gupta, "Implications of the Expansion of Public Pension Plans for Investment in Canada," unpublished (Ottawa: Department of National Health and Welfare, 1974).

66 Donner, *Financing the Future*, p. 130; also E. Bower Carty, "The Impact on Provincial Treasuries and on Capital Markets for Provincial, Municipal and Corporate Securities of Investing CPP Funds through Financial Markets," *Retirement Income System*, vol.2, Appendix 17, pp. 17-1–17-8. For an opposing view based on dubious simplifying assumptions, note Keith Patterson, *The Effect of Provincial Borrowings from Universal Pension Plans on Provincial and Municipal Government Finance*, Discussion Paper No. 192, prepared for the Economic Council of Canada (Ottawa: ECC, March 1981). And Horner and Gupta, "Implications".

67 Government of Ontario, *Ontario Budget 1978* (Toronto: Queen's Printer, 1978), p. 6.

68 D. K. Foot, *Provincial Public Finance in Ontario: An Empirical Analysis of the Last Twenty-Five Years* (Toronto: Ontario Economic Council, 1977), p. 173.

69 Based on the Advisory Committee of the Canada Pension Plan, *Rate of Return,* and updated from various government sources.

70 On the important role of provincial crown corporations in economic development in Western Canada, particularly Saskatchewan and Alberta, note John Richards and Larry Pratt, *Prairie Capitalism: Power and Influence in the New West* (Toronto: McClelland and Stewart, 1979).

71 Calculated from Statistics Canada, *Provincial Government Finance,* and the Government of Ontario, *Ontario Budget 1978,* Table 3, p. 7.

72 Based on Fund A projections for the CPP contained in Health and Welfare Canada, *Canada Pension Plan—Report for the year ending March 31, 1979* (Ottawa: Health and Welfare Canada, 1980), p. 27.

73 Five out of the ten provinces in Canada have established sinking funds to repay their loans to the CPP investment fund. Ontario, the province which has largest cumulative debt to the CPP investment fund, and has benefited the most, does not have a repayment schedule or a sinking fund to repay its debt. Ontario has a veto over changes to the CPP.

74 Until 1987 total contributions to the Canada Pension Plan were 3.6 per cent of earnings up to the yearly maximum pensionable earnings (ympe). The value of CPP benefits, on an actuarial basis, greatly exceed the contributions which pay for them. The real value of CPP benefits on what is technically called a full-cost basis (excluding liabilities), as distinct from the fully-funded contribution rate (full-cost rate plus liabilities) for total contributions, is in the order of 8 to 10 per cent. CPP contributions are thus undervalued by nearly 100 to 250 per cent. The contribution rate of 3.6 per cent generated an investment fund of $16 billion as of 1979. If the various reform proposals to increase the CPP benefit formula from 25 to 50 per cent career average adjusted earnings were implemented, it would mean that total contributions would have to increase to 16 per cent (full-cost rate), and the CPP investment fund would double in size from $16 to $32 billion. In Western Europe, the average total contribution to social security retirement systems is nearly 20 per cent; in the U.S. the total contribution rate for social security benefits was 15.02 per cent in 1988. The Canada Pension Plan contribution rate is very low when compared with other industrialized countries.

75 Business Committee on Pension Policy, *Capital Markets Study,* p. 50.

76 John Myles, "The Aged, the State and the Structure of Inequality," Departmental Working Paper 79–1, Department of Sociology, Carleton University, January 1979, pp. 24–26.

77 "Private Pension Plans Should Get Priority," *Financial Post,* 18 October 1981.

78 Business Committee on Pension Policy, *Capital Markets Study,* p. 43.

NOTES TO CHAPTER EIGHT

1 G. A. Theodorson and A. C. Theodorson, *Modern Dictionary of Sociology* (New York: Apollo, 1969).

2 *Pensions & Investment Age,* 31 October 1983, p. 63.

3 Paul M. Sweezy, *The Theory of Capitalist Development* (New York: Monthly Review Press, 1964), p. 254.

4 Wallace Clement, *The Canadian Corporate Elite: An Analysis of Economic Power* (Toronto: McClelland and Stewart, 1975), p. 135.

5 Karl Marx quoted in Sweezy, *Capitalist Development,* p. 255.

6 Karl Marx quoted ibid., p. 256.

7 Karl Marx quoted in Richard Minns, *Pension Funds and British Capitalism* (London: Heinemann, 1980), p. 15.

8 Sweezy, *Capitalist Development,* pp. 256–57.

9 Richard M. Titmuss, "The Irresponsible Society," *Essays on the Welfare State* (Boston: Beacon, 1969), p. 237.

10 Statistics Canada, *Trusteed Pension Plans Financial Statistics 1978* (Ottawa: Minister of Supply and Services, 1980), p. 25.

11 Statistics Canada, *Trusteed Pension Plans Financial Statistics 1980* (Ottawa: Minister of Supply and Services, 1982), p. 26. An individual trustee is defined as three persons in Department of National Revenue Bulletin 72-13R7, section 6(e).

12 On this subject, note "Pension Funds as Profit Centres," *Pension and Welfare News* 10 (June 1974): 36–40, 57.

13 "Why Pension Funds Are Quitting the Institutions," *Business Week,* 15 May 1978, pp. 105–6.

14 E. P. Neufeld, *The Financial System of Canada: Its Growth and Development* (Toronto: Macmillan, 1972), pp. 290–91.

15 Daniel J. Baum, *The Investment Function of Canadian Financial Institutions* (New York: Praeger, 1973), p. 69.

16 *Report of the Canadian Committee on Mutual Funds and Investment Contracts: A Provincial and Federal Study* (Ottawa: Queen's Printer, 1969), p. 35.

17 Alix Granger, *Don't Bank on It* (Toronto and New York: Doubleday, 1981), p. 29.

18 Baum, *Investment Function,* p. 77.

19 An historical analysis of the impact of life insurance companies on capital markets is contained in Ian M. Drummond, "Canadian Life Insurance Companies and the Capital Market, 1890–1914," *Canadian Journal of Economics and Political Science* 28 (May 1962): 204–24; W. C. Hood and O. W. Main, "The Role of the Canadian Life Insurance Companies in the Post-War Capital Market," *Canadian Journal of Economics and Political Science* 22 (November 1956): 468–80; and Randall Geehan, "The Life Insurance Industry in Canada, 1961 to 1979," *Canadian Statistical Review* 56 (July 1981): vi-x. For Britain, note J. C. Dodds, *The Investment Behaviour of British Life Insurance Companies* (London: Croom-Helm, 1979), and "The Strength of the Insurance Companies," *Labour Research* 69 (May 1980): 108–9.

20 Derived from Statistics Canada, *Trusteed Pension Plan Financial Statistics* (Ottawa: Minister of Supply and Services, various years) and Statistics Canada, *Trusteed Pension Funds Financial Statistics 1986* (Ottawa: Minister of Supply and Services, 1988), Text Table A, p. 11.

21 For a general discussion of funding agencies, note Statistics Canada, *Pension Plans in Canada 1980* (Ottawa: Minister of Supply and Services, 1982), Text Table IX, p. 24.

22 Trades Union Congress, *Report on Pension Fund Investment and Trusteeship,* TUC Conference (London: TUC, 11 November 1982), p. 8.

23 Minns, *Pension Funds,* Table 1.6, pp. 38–40.

24 Calculated from the "Directory of Pension Fund Investment Services: Top 40 Money Managers," *Benefits Canada* 5 (November/December 1981): 24.

25 Paul Harbrecht, S.J., *Pension Funds and Economic Power* (New York: Twentieth Century Fund, 1959), pp. 225–27, and *Pensions & Investment Age,* 31 October 1983, graph, p. 47. For Canadian trust companies, note "Trust Firms Face Major Shift in Lending," *Globe and Mail,* 12 November 1982. The redistribution or "re-sectoring" of financial institution assets in Canada is examined in "Growth and Change in the Financial System—Some Evidence from The National Balance Sheet Accounts, 1961–1984," *Canadian Statistical Review* 60, no. 10(1985), pp. vii–xv.

26 Statistics Canada, *Trusteed Pension Plans Financial Statistics 1981* (Ottawa: Minister of Supply and Services, 1983), pp. xxvi, xxviii.

27 For the U.S., *Pensions & Investments,* 31 March 1980, p. 1; for Canada, Statistics Canada, *Trusteed Pension Plans Financial Statistics 1981,* Text Table X, p. xxix, and for Britain, *Pension Funds,* p. 30.

28 Minns, *Pension Funds*, p. 41.
29 Harbrecht, *Pension Funds*, p. 224. Also Jerry Coakley and Laurence Harris, *The City of Capital* (Oxford: Blackwell, 1983), Table 5.6, p. 111, who follow Minns's methodology.
30 Calculated from Pavan Sahgal, "Who Owns Corporate America?" *Pensions & Investment Age*, 31 October 1983, table, p. 26, and related to the asset mix derived from Kimberly Blanton, "Profiles: The Top 200," *Pensions & Investment Age*, 23 January 1984, graphs, p. 13.
31 Harbrecht, *Pension Funds*, p. 284.

NOTES TO CHAPTER NINE

1 An excellent review of the literature on the differing concepts of finance capital is contained in John Scott, *Corporations, Classes and Capitalism* (London: Hutchinson, 1979), pp. 75–76, and Richard Minns, *Pension Funds and British Capitalism*(London: Heinemann Educational, 1980),pp. 13–16.
2 R. Hilferding, *Finance Capital*, ed. Tom Bottomore (London: Routledge and Kegan Paul, 1985).
3 V. I. Lenin, *Imperialism, The Highest Stage of Capitalism* (Moscow: Foreign Language Publishing House, n.d.).
4 R. Hilferding quoted in Lenin, *Imperialism*, p. 75.
5 Lenin, *Imperialism*, pp. 54, 69, 76, 64, 65.
6 For example S. Aaronovitch, *Monopoly: A Study of British Monopoly Capitalism* (London: Lawrence and Wishart, 1955), and V. Perlo, *The Empire of High Finance* (New York: International Publishers, 1957). Lenin, unfortunately, added some confusion to the definition of finance capital by remarking that "the supremacy of finance capital . . . means the *predominance* . . . of the financial oligarchy" (*Imperialism*, p. 98). Emphasis added.
7 Minns, *Pension Funds*, p. 14.
8 Ernest Mandel, *Late Capitalism* (London: Verso, 1978), p. 594.
9 S. Aaronovitch, *The Ruling Class* (London: Lawrence and Wishart, 1961), pp. 37–38.
10 Scott, *Corporations*, p. 104.
11 Peter C. Newman, *The Canadian Establishment*, vol.1 (Toronto: McClelland and Stewart-Bantam, rev. ed., 1979), p. 221. On the role of pension fund managers, note Margaret Wente, "The Fund Managers," *Canadian Business* (March 1980): 34–39.
12 George Feaver, "The Webbs in Canada: Fabian Pilgrims on the Canadian Frontier," *Canadian Historical Review* 58 (September 1977): 266. On the early history of the finance sector, note Wallace Clement, *The Canadian Corporate Elite: An Analysis of Economic Power* (Toronto: McClelland and Stewart, 1975), p. 134.
13 On this issue, note Leo Johnson, "The Development of Class in Canada in the Twentieth Century," in *Capitalism and the National Question in Canada*, ed. Gary Teeple (Toronto: University of Toronto Press, 1972), p. 154, and Clement, *Canadian Corporate Elite*, pp. 161–62.
14 In particular, note John Porter, *The Vertical Mosaic* (Toronto: University of Toronto Press, 1965), chapter 8, Johnson, "Development of Class," pp. 154–55 and Clement, *Canadian Corporate Elite*, pp. 132–39 and 156–58.
15 Johnson, "Development of Class," pp. 154–55.
16 Scott, *Corporations*, pp. 94, 91, 95.
17 Clement, *Canadian Corporate Elite*, p. 162.
18 Royal Commission on Banking and Finance (1964), cited in Daniel J. Baum, *The Investment Function of Canadian Financial Institutions* (New York: Praeger, 1973), p. 195.

19 E. P. Neufeld, *The Financial System of Canada: Its Growth and Development* (Toronto: Macmillan, 1972), p. 130.
20 Royal Commission on Banking and Finance cited in Baum, *Investment Function*, p. 196.
21 Paul McNulty, *Decision and Influence Processes in Private Pension Plans* (Homewood, IL: Irwin, 1961), p. 77.
22 Alix Granger, *Don't Bank on It* (New York and Toronto: Doubleday 1981), pp. 35, 41–42.
23 Newman, *Canadian Establishment*, p. 119n.
24 Ibid., p. 63.
25 Quoted in the *Globe and Mail*, 5 May 1979, and cited in Granger, *Don't Bank on It*, p. 44.
26 Calculated from Walter Stewart, *Towers of Gold—Feet of Clay: The Canadian Banks* (Toronto: Totem, 1983), Appendix 1–6, pp. 274–76.
27 This is based on an analysis by the author of 1983 annual reports for the top 5 banks, life insurance companies, and trust companies in Canada.
28 The Ontario Securities Act 1978, Section I(ii)(iii) and the Bank Act 1980, Sections 77 and 229.
29 Baum, *Investment Function*, p. x.
30 Note Lawrence Welsh, "Trilon Plans to Intensify Financial Services Growth," *Globe and Mail*, 18 February 1983, and Amy Booth, "Brascan's Strategic Push into Financial Services," *Financial Post*, 12 November, 1983.
31 An in-depth transnational historical study is Rondo Cameron, ed., *Banking in the Early Stages of Industrialization* (New York: Oxford University Press, 1967). Scott, *Corporations*, pp. 91–94, contains an excellent review of the literature. For the U.S., D. Kotz, *Bank Control of Large Corporations in the United States* (London: University of California Press, 1978), and for the U.K., "The Strength of the Insurance Companies," *Labour Research*, 69 (May 1980): p. 108–9.
32 S. J. Prais, *The Evolution of Giant Firms in Britain: A Study of the Growth of Concentration in Manufacturing in Britain 1909–70* (Cambridge: CUP, 1976), p. 114.
33 Porter, *Vertical Mosaic*, chapter 8.
34 Clement, *Canadian Corporate Elite*, pp. 161–62; Granger, *Don't Bank on It*, p. 35.
35 Johnson, "Development of Class," p. 155.
36 Derived from Stewart, *Towers of Gold*, Appendix 1–6–7, pp. 274–77.
37 Newman, *Canadian Establishment*, p. 119n.
38 Based on 1980 data this is arrived at as follows:

Conglomerate	Pension Assets ($ Billion)
Edper Investments	
Royal Trustco (trusteed)	$19.7
Power Corporation	
Montreal Trustco (trusteed)	6.4
Great-West Life (segregated)	0.4
Canadian Pacific	
In-house managed fund	1.4
Total	$27.9 billion

Total pension fund assets (trusteed and insured) were $64.9 billion as of 1980.
39 Porter, *Vertical Mosaic*, pp. 255–63.
40 McNulty, *Decision and Influence Processes*, p. 78.
41 Scott, *Corporations*, pp. 94–95.
42 Paul P. Harbrecht, S.J., *Pension Funds and Economic Power* (New York: Twentieth Century Fund, 1959), pp. 4, 29, 198–99.

43 Pavan Sahgal, "Who Owns Corporate America?" *Pensions & Investment Age,*
    31 October 1983, pp. 24, 25.
44 Kotz, *Bank Control.*
45 Richard Minns, *Take-Over the City: The Case for Public Ownership of Finan-
    cial Institutions* (London: Pluto Press, 1982), pp. 69–70.
46 Eric Evans, "Pension Funds Make Corporate Waves," *Financial Post,* 25 June
    1983.
47 Note, for example, Wente, "Fund Managers," pp. 34, 94: "Pension Fund Money
    Begins to Find Its Way into Real Estate," *Globe and Mail,* 20 April 1981, and
    "How Pension Money May Get to Oil Search," *Financial Post,* 12 December
    1981.
48 Note Edward Malca, *Pension Funds and Other Institutional Investors* (Lexing-
    ton, MA: Lexington Books, 1975), pp. 2–7; William C. Greenough and Francis P.
    King, *Pension Plans and Public Policy* (New York: Columbia University Press,
    1976), p. 146; and "P & I Index Top 100 Stocks," *Pensions & Investments,* 7
    January, 1980, p. 2.
49 Wood Gundy, *Evaluation of Investment Performance Report, December 31,
    1979* (Toronto: Wood Gundy, 1979), p. MA-3.
50 Minns, *Pension Funds,* pp. 46–47.
51 Calculated from the U.S. Department of Commerce, *Statistical Abstract of
    the United States, 1982–83* (Washington, D.C.: GPO, 1982), Series No. 916,
    p. 544.
52 Department of Finance Canada, *Economic Review April 1982* (Ottawa: Cana-
    dian Government Publishing Centre, 1982), Table 4.6, p. 44, and related to Table
    3.4, p. 25.
53 Calculated from Prais, *Giant Firms,* Table 5.9, p. 129.
54 Joel Chernoff, "Rulings Conflict on Asset Use in Take Overs," *Pensions & Invest-
    ment Age,* 5 March 1984, p. 1.
55 Calculated from "Companies Strike It Rich by Tapping Excess Pension Funds,"
    Business Week, 14 November 1983.
56 John Howley, "Occidental's Diversification Strategy," *Economic Notes,* 52
    (March 1984): 10–11, and "Reagan's Pension Funds," *Economic Notes,* 52 (June
    1984): 10.
57 R. Hilferding quoted in Lenin, *Imperialism,* p. 75.
58 Quoted in Harbrecht, *Pension Funds,* p. 31.
59 Ibid., p. 110.
60 Richard Spiegelberg, *The City: Power without Accountability* (London: Blond
    & Briggs, 1973), p. 59.
61 Ibid., p. 58.
62 *The (Wilson) Committee on the Functioning of Financial Institutions* (London:
    HMSO, 1977), p. 26.
63 U.S. Congress, House, Subcommittee on Domestic Finance of the Commitee on
    Banking and Currency, *Staff Report on Commercial Banks and Their Trust
    Activities: Emerging Influence on the American Economy* (Washington, D.C.:
    GPO, 1968), p. 913.
64 Quoted in Anise Wallace, "U.S. Firms Facing New Activism by Fund, Bond
    Managers," *Globe and Mail,* 9 July 1988.
65 Cited in Baum, *Investment Function,* p. 222n172.
66 Evans, "Pension Funds."
67 Quoted in ibid. Emphasis added.
68 Montreal Stock Exchange study (1982) cited in the Business Committee on
    Pension Policy, *Capital Markets Study,* prepared by Pension Finance Associ-
    ates (Toronto: BCPP, September 1983), p. 66.
69 Quoted in Evans, "Pension Funds."
70 "A Move to Make Institutions Start Using Their Stockholder Clout," *Business
    Week,* 6 August 1984, p. 70.

71 Quoted in Evans, "Pension Funds."
72 On the concept of "strategic control," note Scott, *Corporations*, chapter 4, and esp. pp. 100–104.
73 Quoted in Evans, "Pension Funds."
74 On the subject of factions within the ruling class, note Karl Marx and Frederick Engels, *The German Ideology* (New York: International Publishers, 1967), pp. 48–49.
75 Dan Westell, "Big Chunk of Business in Hands of a Few," *Globe and Mail*, 25 August 1984, and Diane Francis, "Is Canada Heading for New Feudalism? The Canadian Dynasties," *Toronto Star*, 25 September 1984.
76 Porter, *Vertical Mosaic*, pp. 524–28.
77 Granger, *Don't Bank on It*, p. 39.
78 Minns, *Take Over the City*, p. 65. For the U.S., note G. William Domhoff, *The Higher Circles: The Governing Class in America* (New York: Random House, 1970).
79 Richard Whitley, "Commonalities and Connections among Directors of Large Financial Institutions," *Sociological Review* 21 (November 1973): 613–32, and Richard Whitley, "The City and Industry: The Directors of Large Companies, Their Characteristics and Connections," in *Elites and Power in British Society*, eds. Philip Stanworth and Anthony Giddens (Cambridge: Cambridge University Press, 1974), pp. 65–80; also Michael Lisle-Williams, "Continuities in the English Financial Elite 1850–1980," paper presented to the conference on Capital, Ideology and Politics, University of Sheffield, January 1981.
80 Clement, *Canadian Corporate Elite*, p. 464.
81 Interview by the author 23 May 1984 with the Vice-President of Communications for a major Canadian financial conglomerate who requested anonymity.
82 Barry Estabrook, "Business Backs off from Political Role, but Activists Defend Involvement, "*Financial Times*, 20 August 1984.
83 Extensive information on political contributions by U.K. corporations is contained in "Tory Funds: Political Donations in Election Year," *Labour Research*, 73 (August 1984): 204–7; "Tory Funding Crisis," *Labour Research*, 72 (September 1983): 225–27; "Political Donations in 1978," *Labour Research* 68 (November 1979): 234–36; and "Big Business and Politics: Political Donations In 1977," *Labour Research*, 67 (September 1978): 190–93.
84 Porter, *Vertical Mosaic*, p. 541. On the bureaucratic elite in Canada, see Dennis Olsen, *The State Elite* (Toronto: McClelland and Stewart, 1980).
85 "Background of Labour and Tory MPs," *Labour Research* 68 (July 1979): pp. 156–58, and "Background of Tory Candidates," *Labour Research* 68 (May 1979): 98–99.
86 "MPs Interests: Capital vs Labour," *Labour Research* 73 (June 1984): 150–52.
87 Richard Deaton, "Election '84: It's No Contest," *The Facts* 6 (August-September 1984): 7.
88 This section draws on the personal correspondence between the author and Dennis Olsen, Associate Professor of Sociology, Carleton University, 4 February 1980 and relies on unpublished information not appearing in Olsen, *State Elite*.
89 *Globe and Mail*, 25 July 1977 cited by Granger, *Don't Bank on It*, p. 42.
90 Kieran Simpson, ed., *Canadian Who's Who 1982* (Toronto: University of Toronto Press, 1982), p. 897.
91 Karen Orren, *Corporate Power and Social Change: The Politics of the Life Insurance Industry* (Baltimore: Johns Hopkins University Press, 1974), pp. 49–51.
92 Porter, *Vertical Mosaic*, chapter 14.
93 Olsen, *State Elite*, p. 80.
94 Richard M. Titmuss, "The Irresponsible Society," in *Essays on the Welfare State* (Boston: Beacon Press, 1969), p. 233.
95 Quoted in "'Common Front': Industry Committee Urged to Help Government Solve Pension Problems," Canadian Pension Conference, *Newsletter*, vol. 2 (July 1979), p. 3.

96 Gwyn A. Williams, "The Concept of 'Egemonia' in the Thought of Antonio Gramsci: Some Notes on Interpretation," *Journal of the History of Ideas* 21 (October–December 1960): 587; also on this subject, Eugene D. Genovese, "On Antonio Gramsci," *Studies on the Left* 7 (March–April 1967): 83–107.

97 Karl Marx and Frederick Engels, *Communist Manifesto* (New York: Washington Square Press, 2nd ed. 1964), p. 91.

98 Newman, *Canadian Establishment*, pp. 465, 299, 464.

99 Ibid., p. 209.

100 Jeremy Rifkin and Randy Barber, *The North Will Rise Again: Pensions, Politics and Power in the 1980s* (Boston: Beacon, 1978), p. 117, and Edward Herman, *Conflicts of Interest: Commercial Bank Trust Departments* (New York: Twentieth Century Fund, 1975), p. 16.

101 Calculated from the Financial Statements and Statement of Earnings contained in the 1983 annual reports of Canada's top five trust companies.

102 These legal requirements are found in the U.K. Trustee Act 1925 and the Trustee Investment Act 1961, and the Employee Retirement Income Security Act 1974 in the U.S., and they are implicit in the various Pension Benefit Acts in Canada and have now been made explicit in the Ontario Pension Benefit Act, RSO 1986, section 23.

103 Orren, *Corporate Power*, p. 69.

104 Rifkin and Barber, *North Will Rise Again*, pp. 253–54 n11.

105 Titmuss, "Irresponsible Society," p. 243.

106 T. B. Bottomore, *Classes in Modern Society* (London: Allen and Unwin, 1967), p. 57. Also Karl Marx and Frederick Engels, *German Ideology*.

107 Baum, *Investment Function*, p. 125.

108 The minimal accommodation strategy used by capital to protect its interests is examined by Fred Block, "The Ruling Class Does Not Rule: Notes on the Marxist Theory of the State," *Socialist Revolution* 33 (1977): 6–28.

109 Bob Dumbleton and Bob Shutt, "Pensions: The Capitalist Trap," *New Society* 7 September 1979, pp. 334–37.

110 Titmuss, "Irresponsible Society," pp. 215–44.

111 John Maynard Keynes, *The General Theory of Employment Interest and Money* (London: Macmillan, 1967), p. 378; also pp. 164, 320.

112 Titmuss, "Irresponsible Society," pp. 238, 243.

NOTES TO CHAPTER TEN

1 The type of funding or financing of state pension arrangements and alternative directed investment strategies are both issues which have arisen periodically throughout the twentieth century. With respect to the funding debate, this issue arose in Britain in 1910 when Lloyd George was evolving the national health insurance scheme. While his officials favoured advanced funding, Lloyd George had strong objections to the state accumulating a fund. The advocates of pre-funding prevailed, and for the next few decades state health insurance was funded. On the subject of capitalizing the state pension system in Britain, note W. J. Braithwaite, *Lloyd George's Ambulance Wagon: The Memoirs of W. J. Braithwaite* (London: Methuen, 1957), pp. 27–29, 45–46, 88–90. A similar debate arose with respect to the financing of the U.K. central government superannuation scheme. Note Marios Raphael, *Pensions and Public Servants: A Study of the Origins of the British System* (Paris: Mouton, 1964), p. 154.

An active debate on social security funding took place within the French labour movement between 1911 and the early 1930s according to Peter N. Stearns, *Old Age in European Society* (New York: Holmes and Meier, 1976), pp. 48–50, 61. When the social security retirement system was introduced in the U.S. in 1935 the initial plans for a large old-age insurance trust fund were scrapped on the basis of Keyesian economic principles, according to W. Andrew

Achenbaum, *Old Age in the New Land* (Baltimore and London: Johns Hopkins University Press, 1978), p. 137. The issue has never seriously been raised again in the U.S.

In Britain, the 1942 Beveridge Report, the foundation of the welfare state, favoured the advanced funding of state retirement pensions on a "full-cost" basis. While the actual implementation of Beveridge's recommendations effectively abandoned pre-funding, it was not until 1959 that the advanced funding of state retirement pensions in Britain was formally relinquished. Note W. Beveridge, *Social Insurance and Allied Services*, Cmnd. 6404 (London: HMSO, 1942), Appendix A, esp. pp. 177–82, and Income Data Services, *Public Sector Pensions*, Study 188 (London: IDS, February 1979), p. 3. The issue was subsequently raised by Richard Crossman, Minister of State for Social Services, and architect of the Labour government's earnings-related state pension plan (1969), who advocated some type of advanced funding. Note Richard Crossman, *The Diaries of a Cabinet Minister, Volume Three, Secretary of State for Social Services, 1968–70* (London: Hamish Hamilton, 1977), pp. 153–54 176.

The creation of an investment fund was central to the implementation of the Canada/Quebec Pension Plans. Note for example, Richard Simeon, *Federal-Provincial Diplomacy: The making of Recent Policy in Canada* (Toronto: University of Toronto Press, 1972), chapter 3

Alternative directed investment strategies, based on the investment function of financial intermediaries, have been actively debated as well, particularly in the U.S. The original impetus for directed investment laws came from the Populist movement in the 1890s. According to Kimball, "from a surprisingly early date insurance was regarded . . . as a business affected with a public interest," and "there were indications that the law might treat insurance as a full-fledged public utility." During the New Deal, the Fletcher Bill (1933) authorized the Reconstruction Finance Corporation to purchase the preferred stock of insurance companies and raised "the unnerving possibility that the federal government might control life insurance assets by becoming a major stockholder." According to Orren, between 1965 and 1972, at least thirteen American states proposed directed investment laws and "often only narrowly missed passage." On these subjects, note Spencer L. Kimball, *Insurance and Public Policy* (Madison: University of Wisconsin Press, 1960), pp. 304–8, and Karen Orren, *Corporate Power and Social Change: The Politics of the Life Insurance Industry* (Baltimore: Johns Hopkins University Press, 1974), esp. chapters 2, 3, and 7.

2 International Labour Office, *The Cost of Social Security, Ninth International Inquiry, 1972–1974* (Geneva: ILO, 1979), p. 7. Emphasis added. Also on this subject, S. Boye, "The Cost of Social Security, 1960–71: Some National Economic Aspects," *International Labour Review* 115 (1977): 305–25.

3 *Report of the Royal Commission on the Status of Pensions in Ontario, Summary Report: A Plan for the Future* (Toronto: Queen's Printer, 1980), p. 61.

4 A. Asimakopulos and J. C. Weldon, "On the Theory of Government Pension Plans," *Canadian Journal of Economics* 1 (1968): 700.

5 Robert Tilove, *Public Employee Pension Funds* (New York: A Twentieth Century Fund Report, Columbia University Press, 1976), p. 137.

6 International Labour Office, *Into the Twenty-first Century: The Development of Social Security* (Geneva: ILO, 1984), p. 86.

7 Asimakopulos and Weldon, "Government Pension Plans," p. 705. A more recent and forceful statement, significantly altering his earlier position, and knowledging the limitations of welfare state PAYGO financing of pension arrangements, is A. Asimakopulos, "Comments on Pensions," in *Pensions: Public Solutions vs. Private Interest*, Proceedings of the Canadian Centre for Policy Alternatives (Ottawa: CCPA, 1982), p. 118–25.

8 The funding issue and the level of required contributions must be related to demographic scenarios. Three general demographic cases can be identified: stable population state, zero population growth (ZPG), that is, a declining popu-

lation, and the baby boom scenario. In the case of a stable population state, in the short run, the full-funding rate is greater than the PAYGO rate. In the long run the full-funding rate is equal to the PAYGO rate. With zero population growth (ZPG), as is now the case in many European countries, the full-funding rate is greater than the PAYGO rate in both the short and long terms. Under the baby boom scenario, the PAYGO contribution rate is lower than the full-funding rate in the short term; however, in the long term the PAYGO rate is higher than the full-funding contribution rate because of population aging and continues to increase after maturity as the unfunded liability is carried forward.

9 Government of Saskatchewan, Saskatchewan Labour, *Reform of Canada's Retirement Income System—A Saskatchewan View*, Brief to the National Pensions Conference (Regina: Saskatchewan Labour, March 1981), p. 6.

10 Eveline M. Burns, "Social Insurance in Evolution," *American Economic Review* 34, Supplement, part 2 (March 1944): 199.

11 E. M. Murphy, "Methods of Financing Social Security: An Introductory Analysis," paper presented to the International Social Security Association, Research Conference, Ottawa, 28–30 May 1979, pp. 21–22.

12 International Labour Organization, *L'investissement, aspects des institutions d'assurances sociales* (Geneva: ILO, 1939). An extensive technical literature exists on the relationship between social security systems and economic development in industralized and underdeveloped countries. The general literature on the subject includes Philip Cutright, "Political Structure, Economic Development and National Social Security Programs," *American Journal of Sociology* 70 (1965): 537–50; Paul Fischer, "Social Security and Development Planning: Some Issues," *Social Security Bulletin* 30 (1967), 13–25; and V. George, *Social Security and Society* (London: Routledge & Kegan Paul, 1973), pp. 15, 18–19.

The literature as it pertains to underdeveloped or less developed countries (LDCs) includes E. M. Kassalow, ed. *The Role of Social Security in Economic Development*. Research Report 27 (Washington, D.C.: GPO, 1968); the International Labour Organization, *Social Security and National Development* (Geneva: ILO, 1978); Elliott Sclar, "Aging and Economic Development," in *Public Policies for an Aging Population*, eds. Elizabeth W. Markson and Gretchen R. Batra (Toronto: Heath, 1980), pp. 29–38; Christine Cockburn, "The Role of Social Security Development," *International Social Security Review* 33 (1980): 337–58; Mohammed Gourja, "The Contribution of Social Security to Development Objectives: The Role of Income Support Measures," *International Social Security Review*, 34 (1981), pp. 131–50; "Round Table Meeting on 'The Role of Social Security in Development,' " ibid., pp. 112–21.

The impact of income maintenance programs on various aspects of economic policy in advanced market economies is dealt with by Bruno Stein, *Work and Welfare in Britain and the USA* (New York: Wiley, 1976), and Orley Ashenfelter and James Blum, eds., *Evaluating The Labor-Market Effects of Social Programs* (Princeton: Industrial Relations, Department of Economics, Princeton University, 1976).

13 Harry Weitz, *The Foreign Experience with Income Maintenance for the Elderly*, a Background Study prepared for the Economic Council of Canada (Ottawa: ECC, 1979), p. 19.

14 A. Kirstina Liljefors, "Canada's Retirement Income System and Recent Economic Developments: A Discussion Paper," *Pensions and Inflation: An International Discussion*, International Labour Office (Geneva: ILO, 1977), p. 127.

15 The seminal work on this subject is Rudolf Meidner, *Employee Investment Funds: An Approach to Collective Capital Formation* (London: Allen and Unwin, 1978).

16 Brian Burkitt, *Radical Polical Economy: An Introduction to the Alternative Economics* (Frome: Wheatsheaf Books, 1984), pp. 180, 182, 184n14. Emphasis added.

17 D. V. Smiley, *Canada in Question: Federalism in the Seventies* (Toronto: McGraw-Hill Ryerson, 2nd ed., 1976), chapters 1 and 4–5, and Keith G. Banting, *The Welfare State and Canadian Federalism* (Kingston: McGill-Queen's University Press, 1982), chapters 4–7.

18 Quoted in Joan Fraser, "Quebec May Interfere in Pension Fund Operations," *Financial Times*, 25 July 1977.

19 *1982 Annual Report of the Caisse de Depôt et Placement* (Montreal, 1982), p. 19.

20 The rate of return for the Caisse de Depôt was calculated from the Caisse de Depôt et Placement du Québec, *Annual Report* (Montreal, various years) on the basis of the long-term weighted average yield for equities, bonds and other instruments for the General Fund (QPP). The rate of return for all trusteed (private and public sector) pension plans was calculated on the basis of an internal rate of return from Statistics Canada, *Trusteed Pension Plans Financial Statistics* (Ottawa and Hull: Minister of Trade and Commerce, various years), Tables I and II, pp. 7, 9. For the CPP, the dollar weighted average bond yield on old money since the inception of the plan was calculated from the *CPP Annual Reports* (n.p.: National Health and Welfare, various years). All figures are inflation adjusted. Also note "Quebec Fares Better Than Ottawa in Handling Pension Fund: Parizeau," *Montreal Gazette*, 14 December 1982. As a result of the Caisse's policies it has earned an estimated $1.5 billion more in investment income than the CPP between 1966 and 1981.

21 Canadian Union of Public Employees, *Brief to the Royal Commission on the Status of Pensions in Ontario* (Ottawa: CUPE, December 1977), p. 101.

22 United Steel Workers of America (Canadian region), "Discussion Paper: Pensions," Canadian Policy Conference, Fall 1979 (Toronto: USW, 1979), pp. 5, 3.

23 United Steel Workers of America (Canadian region), "Policy Statement: The Economy," ibid., p. 3.

24 Trades Union Congress, "Pension Funds" (Resolution No. 20), 1979 Congress.

25 Trades Union Congress, *The Role of the Financial institutions*, TUC Evidence to the Committee to Review the Functioning of Financing Institutions (London: TUC, July 1979). A summary is contained in Richard Minns, *Take Over the City: The Case For Public Ownership of Financial Institutions* (London: Pluto Press, 1982), pp. 50–53.

26 Minns, *Take Over the City*, p. 74.

27 Paul P. Harbrecht, S.J., *Pension Funds and Economic Power* (New York: Twentieth Century Fund, 1959), p. 270.

28 American Federation of Labour, *Pension Plans under Collective Bargaining— A Reference Guide for Trade Unions* (Washington, D.C.: AFL, December 1954), p. 4. Emphasis added.

29 The key trade union studies on social investment are the American Federation of Labor and Congress of Industrial Organizations, *Investment of Union Pension Funds* (Washington, D.C.: AFL-CIO, circa 1980), and their *Pensions: A Study of Benefit Fund Investment Policies* (Washington, D.C.: IUD, AFL-CIO, May 1980).

30 For a critique of "trade union capitalism" in the United States during the 1920s and 1930s, note William Z. Foster, *American Trade Unionism: Principles, Organization, Strategy, Tactics* (New York: International Publishers, 1970), pp. 91–111.

31 Quoted in Alex Rubner, *Fringe Benefits: The Golden Chains* (London: Putnam, 1962), p. 151.

32 Harbrecht, *Pension Funds*, pp. 97–98.

33 A. H. Raskin "Pension Funds Could Be the Unions' Secret Weapon," *Fortune*, 31 December 1979, p. 65.

34 Ibid., p. 64.

35 Ibid., p. 66.

36 Richard M. Titmuss, "The Irresponsible Society," in *Essays on the Welfare State* (Boston: Beacon, 1969), p. 240.

37 General and Municipal Workers' Union, *Pensions in the 1980's—A Programme for Action*. Annual Congress, 20–24 May 1979, Torquay (Surrey: GMWU, April 1979), p. 7.

38 General and Municipal Workers' Union, *The GMWU Policy on Pensions—Up to 1978 and Beyond*, Annual Congress 6–10 June 1976, Bournemouth (Surrey: GMWU, May 1976), p. 18.

39 John Hughes, Principal of Ruskin College, Oxford, in his 1977 Stockton Lectures, quoted in Harry Lucas and Sue Ward, *Studies for Trade Unionists: Pensions Bargaining* (London: Workers' Educational Association, June 1977), pp. 18–19.

40 On the various theories of "people's capitalism," note Harry W. Laidler and Norman Thomas, eds, *New Tactics in Social Conflict* (New York: Vanguard, 1926), and J. M. Budish, *People's Capitalism: Stock Ownership and Production* (New York: International Publishers, 1958). Peter Drucker, *The Unseen Revolution: How Pension Fund Socialism Came to America* (New York: Harper and Row, 1976), despite its provocative title and the barrage of publicity, is nothing more than a sophisticated and updated variation of "people's capitalism." For a technical critique of Drucker, note Richard Deaton and Robert Deaton, "An Honest Valuation of Drucker's Pension Fund 'Socialism,' " *Pensions & Investments*, 21 June 1976, p. 15–16; also James Henry, "How Pension Fund Socialism Didn't Come to America," *Working Papers for a New Society* (Winter 1977): 78–87.

41 *Report of the Royal Commission on the Status of Pensions in Ontario*, vol.5, *Ontario and the Canada Pension Plan*, p. 95.

42 Business Committee on Pension Policy, *Capital Markets Study*, prepared for Business Committee on Pension Policy by Pension Finance Associates (Toronto: PFA, September 1983), p. 70.

43 "Funding the Canada Pension Plan," *Mercer Actuarial Bulletin* 28 (March 1978): 2.

44 Tristam S. Lett, "Savings or Consumption? The Role of the Public Pension Plan in the National Economy," address to the Association of Canadian Pension Management, Toronto, 1977.

45 Canadian Council on Social Development, *How Much Choice? Retirement Policies in Canada* (Ottawa: CCSD, 1975), p. 102.

46 Robert Monks, "Funds Can't Hide Any Longer from Activist Shareholder Role," *Pensions & Investments Age*, 28 May 1984, p. 46.

47 Quoted in Bob Dumbleton and John Shutt, "Pensions: The Capitalist Trap," *New Society*, 7 September 1979, p. 335. Hugh Jenkins, investment manager for the miners' pension fund (NUM), was similarly quoted as stating that, "in 26 years of equal participation it had no marked effect at all" on investment practices.

48 Jeremy Rifkin and Randy Barber, *The North Will Rise Again: Pensions, Politics and Power in the 1980s* (Boston: Beacon Press, 1978), p. 254n1.

49 Laura Katz Olson, "Pension Power and the Public Sector," in *Crisis In The Public Sector*, Reader by the Economics Education Project of the Union for Radical Political Economics (New York: Monthly Review Press, 1981), p. 109.

50 Economic Council of Canada, *One in Three: Pensions for Canadians to 2030* (Hull: Canadian Government Publishing Centre, 1979), pp. 52, 62.

51 The impending pension crisis has been analysed from a number of interdisciplinary and mainstream political perspectives. The general case is made by Paul Fischer, "The Social Security Crisis: An International Dilemma," *International Social Security Review* 31 (1978): 383–96; Kingsley Davis and Pietronella van den Oever, "Age Relations and Public Policy in Advanced Industrial Societies,"

Population and Development Review 7, no. 1 (1981): 1–18; and Robert B. Hudson and Robert H. Binstock, "Political Systems and Aging," in *Handbook of Aging and the Social Sciences*, eds. Robert H. Binstock and Ethel Shanas (New York: Van Nostrand Reinhold, 1976), pp. 369–400.

　　The pension crisis in the U.S. has been investigated at length including James H. Schultz, "The Economic Impact of an Aging Population," *Journal of Gerontology* 13 (Spring 1973): 111–17; Carl V. Patton, "The Politics of Social Security," in *The Crisis in Social Security*, ed. Michael J. Boskin (San Francisco: Institute for Contemporary Studies, 1977), pp. 147–72; Martha Derthick, *Policy Making for Social Security* (Washington, D.C.: Brookings Institution, 1979), chapter 19; Bruno Stein, *Social Security and Pensions in Transition: Understanding the American Retirement System* (New York: Free Press, 1980), chapter 1. Popularized treatments are "The Crisis in Social Security," *Newsweek*, 1 June 1981, pp. 24–37 and "Social Security: What Can the Nations Afford?" *Time*, 24 May 1982, pp. 12–23. For Canada, note Val Ross, "The Coming Old-Age Crisis," *Maclean's*, 17 January 1983, pp. 24–29.

52　Karl Marx, *Capital*, vol. 1, chapter 10.

53　Stearns, *Old Age in European Society*, p. 9.

54　Simone de Beauvoir, *Old Age* (Harmondsworth: Penguin, 1978), p. 601.

55　Oskar Lange, *On the Economic Theory of Socialism* (New York: McGraw Hill Paperback, 3rd ed., 1966), p. 129. Emphasis in original.

56　Karl Marx and Frederick Engels, *The Communist Manifesto* (New York: Washington Square Press, 1964), p. 83.

57　Karl Marx, *Capital*, vol.1 (New York: Modern Library, reprint of the 1906 Kerr and Co. ed.), pp. 685, 689.

58　Karl Marx, *Capital*, vol. 3 (Moscow: Progress, reprinted, 1978), p. 441.

59　Ralph Miliband, *Marxism and Politics* (Oxford: Oxford University Press, 1977), pp. 1, 5–6.

60　Marx and Engels, *Communist Manifesto*, p. 93. The issue of historical specificity was also dealt with by Frederick Engels, *Anti-During* (Moscow: Progress, 1977), Part 3.

61　V. I. Lenin, "Our Programme," *Selected Works* (London: Lawrence and Wishart, 1968), p. 34. Emphasis in original. This was written in 1919, but was not published until 1925.

62　V. I. Lenin, "Five Years of the Russian Revolution and the Prospects of the World Revolution", report delivered at the Fourth Congress of the Communist International, 13 November 1922, *Selected Works*, vol. 3 (Moscow: Foreign Languages Publishing House, 1961), pp. 779–80.

63　V. I. Lenin, "Third All-Russian Congress of Soviets of Workers', Soldiers' and Peasant Deputies," *Collected Works*, vol. 26 (Moscow: Progress, 1975), p. 472.

64　Stanley Moore, *Three Tactics: The Background in Marx* (New York: Monthly Review Press, 1963), p. 12.

65　Frederick Engels, 1895 introduction to Karl Marx, *The Class Struggles In France* (Moscow: Progress, 1972), p. 22.

66　Miliband, *Marxism*, pp. 160, 40. The classic formulation regarding this issue is Rosa Luxemburg, "Social Reform or Revolution," *Selected Political Writings of Rosa Luxemburg*, ed. Dick Howard (New York and London: Monthly Review Press, 1971), pp. 52–134.

67　Note, for example, Hal Draper, "The Death of the State in Marx and Engels," *The Socialist Register 1970*, eds. Ralph Miliband and John Saville (London: Merlin Press, 1970), pp. 281–307; Ralph Miliband, "Marx and the State," *The Socialist Register 1965*, eds. Ralph Miliband and John Saville (London: Merlin Press, 1965), pp. 278–96; and Ralph Miliband, "Lenin's The State and Revolution," in *The Socialist Register 1970*, pp. 309–19.

68　Marx, *Capital*, vol. 3, p. 438.

69　Karl Marx, *A Contribution to the Critique of Political Economy* (Moscow: Progress, 1970), p. 21.

70 Marx, *Capital*, vol. 3, p. 438.

71 Moore, *Three Tactics*, p. 82. Emphasis added.

72 This is discussed by Richard Hyman, *Marxism and the Sociology of Trade Unionism* (London: Pluto Press, 1971), pp. 47–49.

73 Marx and Engels, *Communist Manifesto*, p. 93. Emphasis added.

74 Royden Harrison, "The British Labour Movement and The International in 1864," *The Socialist Register 1964*, eds. Ralph Miliband and John Saville (London: Merlin Press, 1971), p. 305.

75 Quoted in Miliband, *Marxism*, p. 79. The shift in emphasis became most apparent in Engels's 1895 introduction to Karl Marx, *The Class Struggles in France*, pp. 5–26. As Miliband has demonstrated, this was not a result of the editing undertaken by Kautsky, as some have argued, but was contained in the original text. Miliband has gone to some lengths to demonstrate that a defensive-offensive "reformist" strategy is viable (pp. 178–90).

76 Moore, *Three Tactics*, p. 66, and Miliband, *Marxism*, pp. 94–96.

77 Hyman, *Trade Unionism*, p. 47. Emphasis in original.

78 Lenin, "The Tasks of the Proletariat," and Leon Trotsky, *The History of the Russian Revolution* (New York: Doubleday Anchor Books, 1959), chapter 11.

79 Crane Briton, *The Anatomy of Revolution* (New York: Vintage Books, rev. ed., 1965), pp. 132–37, 148–50.

80 Jean Jaurès, *The Question of Method*, quoted in Moore, *Three Tactics*, p. 66. In the Althusserian schema, this "overlap" of the different levels of the global structure, including the mode of production, is referred to as "regions."

81 Hyman, *Trade Unionism*, p. 48.

82 The theoretical work of the Austro-Marxists has generally been ignored. Their rich intellectual tradition has, fortunately, recently been rediscovered by Tom Bottomore and Patrick Goode, eds. *Austro-Marxism*, introduction by Tom Bottomore (Oxford: Oxford University Press, 1978). The introduction by Bottomore, esp. pp. 22–28, analyses the economic theories of Hilferding, Renner and Bauer. This compendium contains translations of their key theoretical works. Note, for example, Karl Renner, "Problems des Marxismus" (1916), pp. 91–101, and excerpts from *Wandlungen Der Modernen Gesellschaft* (New York: Arno, 1975). Significantly, no reference is made to Renner's *Die Wirtschaft als Gesamtprozess und Die Sozialisierung* (Berlin: Dietz, 1924). Also note Otto Bauer, *Der Weg Zum Sozialismus* (1919), pp. 146–51. The transition to socialism is also explored by Rudolf Hilferding, *Finance Capital*, edited with an introduction by Tom Bottomore (London: Routledge and Kegan Paul, 1985), pp. 367–70, and the article "Die Problem der Zeit," *Die Gesellschaft* 1 (1924). A recent psycho-history of the Austro-Marxist school is Mark E. Blum, *The Austro-Marxists, 1890–1918* (Louisville: University of Kentucky Press, 1985). A brief critical assessment of the Austro-Marxists, and of Renner in particular, is contained in V. Afanasyev, *Bourgeois Economic Thought 1930s–70s*. Translated by James Riordan (Moscow: Progress, 1983), pp. 358–59.

83 Hilferding, *Finance Capital*, p. 367.

84 Renner, "Problems of Marxism," pp. 95–96.

85 Bottomore and Goode, eds. *Austro-Marxism*, p. 26.

86 Renner, *Wandlungen der Modernen Gesellschaft*.

87 Bauer, *Der Weg Zum Sozialismus*.

88 The leading Swedish theoretican of "functional socialism" was Osten Unden, a professor of law. Note Gunnar Adler-Karlsson, *Functional Socialism: A Swedish Theory for Democratic Socialization* (Stockholm: Bokforlaget Prisma, 1967), reprinted as *Reclaiming the Canadian Economy: A Swedish Approach through Functional Socialism* (Toronto: Anansi, 1970). Karl Renner's earlier *The Institutions of Private Property*, translated by Agnes Schwarzschild (London and Boston: Routledge and Kegan Paul, reprinted, 1976), first published in 1904, may be viewed as the origin of this functionalist legal theory which differentiates between the rights and functions associated with ownership.

89 Note Afanasyev, *Bourgeois Economic Thought*, p. 359.
90 Shigeto Tsuru, "Has Capitalism Changed?" in *Has Capitalism Changed*, ed. Shigeto Tsuru (Tokyo: Iwanami Shoten, 1961), pp. 64–65. Emphasis added.
91 John Maynard Kenyes, *The General Theory of Employment Interest and Money* (London: Macmillan, 1967), pp. 164, 320. Emphasis added.
92 Frederick Engels, *Socialism: Utopian and Scientific* (New York: International Publishers, 1935), pp. 67–68, 58n.
93 Afanasyev, *Bourgeois Economic Thought*, p. 37. Emphasis added. Lenin also viewed the state-monopoly stage of development as "a complete material preparation for socialism." Note V. I. Lenin, *Collected Works*, vol. 25 (Moscow: Progress, 1975), p. 359.
94 Eduard Bernstein, *Evolutionary Socialism*, translated by Edith C. Harvey (New York: Schocken, 1975), p. xxviii.
95 Eric Shragge, *Pensions Policy in Britain* (London: Routledge and Kegan Paul, 1984), p. 161.
96 Miliband, *Marxism*, p. 46.
97 V. I. Lenin, quoted in Perry Anderson, "The Limits and Possibilities of Trade Union Action," in *The Incompatibles: Trade Union Militancy and the Consensus*, eds. Robin Blackburn and Alexander Cockburn (Harmondsworth: Penguin, 1967), p. 271.
98 Andre Gorz, "Reforms and the Struggle for Socialism," in *The Capitalist System*, eds. Richard C. Edwards, Michael Reich, and Thomas E. Weisskopf (Englewood Cliffs, NJ: Prentice-Hall, 1978), pp. 529–30.
99 V. L. Allen, *Militant Trade Unionism* (London: Merlin Press, 1966), chapters 6 and 7.
100 Gorz, "Struggle for Socialism," pp. 529–30.
101 Burkitt, *Radical Political Economy*, pp. 180–81, and B. Burkitt, "Post-Keynesian Distribution Theory and Employee Investment Funds," *Economics Studies Quarterly* 34 (1983): 124–32.
102 Miliband, *Marxism*, p. 73.

APPENDIX A

COMPARATIVE CHRONOLOGY OF RETIREMENT INCOME ARRANGEMENTS AND REFORM INITIATIVES.
U.K., CANADA AND U.S.

This chronology is intended to provide the reader with an overview of the historical development of retirement income legislation and programs. The chronology outlines both national and transnational frameworks to which major events and dates can be related.

DATE	UNITED KINGDOM	CANADA	UNITED STATES
1601	Poor Law Act Relief of destitution requiring parishes to provide from local taxation for the needy, homeless, and the sick.		
1699	Newcastle Keelman First known union making provision for widows, children and the aged.		
1818			War Veterans Pensions established.
1829	Metropolitan (London) Police First formal municipal pension scheme.		
1834	Central Government Superannuation Act.	Pre-1900 Limited municipal social welfare programming. Responsibility limited to the poor and indigent, including the elderly, sick and young on a needs basis.	Pre-1900 Limited municipal social services on a needs basis to indigent groups.
1842	Gas and Light Coke Co. First manufacturing pension scheme.		

APPENDIX A (Cont'd)

DATE	UNITED KINGDOM	CANADA	UNITED STATES
1850	Amalgamated Society of Engineers, a British Union, provides retirement benefits in Canada.		
1857			New York City Police First municipal pension plan.
1860		Bank of Montreal Pension plan introduced.	
1870		Government of Canada Federal Superannuation Act.	
1874		Grand Trunk Railway First private sector pension plan.	
1875			American Express Company First employer-sponsored pension plan.
1876		Province of Quebec Superannuation Aid Fund, first provincial pension plan for civil servants.	
1880		Quebec Teachers First pension plan on province-wide basis.	
1888		City of Hamilton, Ontario First known municipality to pay pensions.	

APPENDIX A (Cont'd)

DATE	UNITED KINGDOM	CANADA	UNITED STATES
1900		International Typographical Union First union to pay retirement benefits on a continuous basis.	Patternmakers Union First union-sponsored pension plan to make periodic payments.
1901			Carnegie Steel Company First manufacturing pension plan.
1903		Canadian Pacific Railway Introduces pension plan.	
1908	Old Age Pensions Act Conditional, non-contributory old age pension of up to 5 shillings per week for those over 70.	Government Annuities Act Providing for the voluntary purchase of annuities by individuals from the federal government. International Harvester and N.S. Colliery First manufacturing pension plans.	
1911			State of Massachusetts First state-wide pension plan for employees.
1918	Income Tax Act Income tax deductibility status for employer contributions to occupational pension schemes.	Pension Act and Soldiers Settlements Act Payments to veterans who by age or incapacity were unable to earn an income or had insufficient means.	

APPENDIX A (Cont'd)

DATE	UNITED KINGDOM	CANADA	UNITED STATES
1919		Income War Tax Act Income tax deductibility status for employer contributions to private pension plans.	Federal Civil Service Retirement System Established for employees.
1920		Returned Soldiers Insurance An act which provided for veterans to purchase private retirement annuities.	
1925	The Widows, Orphans' and Old Age Contributory Pensions Act 1925 The legislation was co-ordinated with the health insurance legislation to provide a comprehensive programme of social security. The contributory, means-tested, flat-rate pension was payable at age 65 and survivor pensions for legal dependents. At age 70 these benefits were replaced by those under the 1908 Act.		
1926			Revenue Act and Internal Revenue Code Income tax deductibility status for employer contributions to private pensions plans.

APPENDIX A (Cont'd)

DATE	UNITED KINGDOM	CANADA	UNITED STATES
1927		Old Age Pensions Act The first federal-provincial cost-shared programme. A flat-rate pension paid to those over age 70 on the basis of a means test. Income War Tax Act Income tax deductibility status for pension contributions by employees.	
1930		War Veteran Allowances Similar to 1927 Old Age Pension Act, except earlier retirement.	
1935			Social Security Act (SSA) First national old age insurance (OAI) programme providing for earnings-related pension benefits for retired workers 65 or over. Railroad Retirement Act Consolidation of bankrupt railroad pension plans.
1939			Amendments to SSA Benefits added for survivors and dependents (OASI).

APPENDIX A (Cont'd)

DATE	UNITED KINGDOM	CANADA	UNITED STATES
1942	Beveridge Report on Social Insurance and the Allied Services. Comprehensive programme for the creation of the welfare state. Recommended the development of social insurance services to include provision against want due to sickness, disability and old age. Based on the contributory principle and a minimum standard. Officially accepted as government policy after W.W. II.		Internal Revenue Act Tax treatment for employer-sponsored pension plans clarified.
1943		The Marsh Report on Social Security for Canada, 1943 House of Commons Advisory Committee on Post-War Reconstruction. A comprehensive set of income security proposals to establish minimum standards. Never officially accepted as government policy.	The Burns Report on Security, Work and Relief Policies, emphasizing a full employment policy and long-range planning for public aid. Never accepted as government policy.

APPENDIX A (Cont'd)

DATE	UNITED KINGDOM	CANADA	UNITED STATES
1946	The National Insurance Act 1946 Effective 1948, implementing the Beveridge Report recommend-ations. Enacted to "establish an extended system of national insurance providing pecuniary payments by way of unemployment benefits, sickness benefit, maternity benefit, retirement pension, widows' benefit, guardian's allowance and death grant . . . [and] to provide for the making of payments towards the cost of a national health service."	Income Tax Act Explicit recognition of tax deductibility status for employer and employee contributions to occupational pension plans.	
1947			Taft-Hartley Act Section 302 requiring joint administration of union-sponsored pension plans.
1951		Old Age Security Act Universal, flat-rate old age pension for those age 70 and over. Old Age Assistance Act Means-tested, flat-rate pension for those age 65–70, similar to the 1927 Act.	

APPENDIX A (Cont'd)

DATE	UNITED KINGDOM	CANADA	UNITED STATES
1952	Income Tax Act (Old Code) Income tax deductibility status for pension contributions by employees.		
1956			Amendments to SSA Coverage and benefits expanded; early retirement for women; disability benefits added (OASDI).
1957		Registered Retirement Savings Plan (RRSP) Introduction of individual retirement saving vehicle with tax deductibility status.	
1958		Province of British Columbia introduces province-wide Municipal Superannuation Act.	Pension and Welfare Plans Disclosure Act Provisions of negotiated health and welfare programmes to be made public.
1959	National Insurance Act 1959 (the Boyd-Carpenter Plan) Earnings-related graduated scheme to supplement the flat-rate pension. Effective April 1961; terminated April 1975.		

APPENDIX A (Cont'd)

DATE	UNITED KINGDOM	CANADA	UNITED STATES
1965		Ontario Pension Benefits Act First legislation establishing uniform regulatory standards for vesting, funding, investment and disclosure for occupational pension plans. Eight other jurisdictions follow suit.	Older Americans Act Health Insurance for those 65 and over added to the social security programme (OASDHI). Report of the President's Committee on Corporate Pension Funds and Other Private Retirement and Welfare Programs.
		Canada/Quebec Pension Plan Acts (C/QPP) National earnings-related social insurance plan providing retirement, survivors and disability benefits. The QPP is a separate, but parallel, plan providing similar benefits.	
1966		Canada Assistance Plan Provided for the consolidation of previous federal-provincial cost-shared programmes, including old age assistance.	
1967		Guaranteed Income Supplement (GIS) Federally sponsored income-tested programme to guarantee a minimum income to the elderly in conjunction with the Old Age Security pension.	

APPENDIX A (Cont'd)

DATE	UNITED KINGDOM	CANADA	UNITED STATES
1969	National Superannuation and Social Insurance Bill, 1969 The Crossman Plan based on the Labour government's 1969 white paper, National Superannuation and Social Insurance: Proposals for Earnings-Related Social Security. An earnings-related pension merged with the flat-rate benefit. Progressive contribution structure and redistributive benefit structure. Provided for the "contracting-out" of private schemes from the state plan. Rejected by the Conservative Government in 1970.		
1973	Social Security Act 1973 (the Joseph Plan) Based on the Conservative Government's 1971 white paper, Strategy for Pensions: The Future Development of state and occupational Provisions. Flat-rate scheme supplemented by "recognized" occupational pension schemes. In addition, a "money purchase" state reserve scheme for those not in "recognized" schemes. Occupational Pensions Board created		

APPENDIX A (Cont'd)

DATE	UNITED KINGDOM	CANADA	UNITED STATES
	under the Act to monitor and regulate private schemes. Established the principle of a "partnership" between state and occupational pension plans. Most proposals abandoned by the Labour government in 1974.		Employee Retirement Income Security Act 1974 Introduces major reforms. First national uniform legislation for private sector pension plans establishing minimum standards for vesting, funding, investment and disclosure.
1974			Supplementary Security Income Act (SSI) Needs-tested programme for the aged, disabled and blind. Consolidated previous federal and state programmes.
			Individual Retirement Account (IRA) Introduction of individual retirement saving instrument with tax deductibility status.

APPENDIX A (Cont'd)

DATE	UNITED KINGDOM	CANADA	UNITED STATES
1975	Social Security Pension Act 1975 (the Castle Plan) Based on the Labour government's 1974 white paper, Better Pensions Fully Protected Against Inflation: Proposals for a New Pension Scheme. A major consolidating Act. Introduces a two-tier retirement pension plan and specifies the terms on which an occupational pension scheme may "contract-out" from the state plan. The state plan consists of the basic flat-rate pension and an earnings-related component. The state reserve scheme under the Joseph Plan was rejected, while the Occupational Pensions Board was retained. Effective April, 1978. Report of the Occupational Pensions Board on Solvency, Disclosure and Member Participation.	Spousal Allowance Income-tested supplement to the spouse of an OAS recipient between ages 60 and 65.	Age Discrimination Act of 1975 Abolition of mandatory retirement between age 65–70 in the federal jurisdiction and private sector.

APPENDIX A (Cont'd)

DATE	UNITED KINGDOM	CANADA	UNITED STATES
1976	Labour government's white paper on the Role of Members in the Running of Schemes.		
1977		Province of Quebec Cofirentes Report on Pension Reform	
1979		Report of the Senate Committee on Retirement Age Policies Economic Council of Canada report, *One in Three*	
1980	Social Security Act 1980	Report of the Federal Task Force on Retirement Income Policies	
1981	Report of the Occupational Pensions Board on Early Leavers and subsequent Fowler Inquiry by the Conservative government.	Province of Saskatchewan Brief to the National Pensions Conference Royal Commission on the Status of Pensions in Ontario	Internal Revenue Act Income tax deductibility status for voluntary employee contributions to occupational pension plans. Report of the President's Commission on Pension Policy

APPENDIX A (Cont'd)

DATE	UNITED KINGDOM	CANADA	UNITED STATES
1982		Final Report of the Ontario Select Committee on Pensions	
		Canadian Association of Pension Supervisory Authorities Report on Pension Reform	
		Province of British Columbia Discussion Paper on Pension Policy for the Future	
		Federal Government's Green (Options) Paper on Better Pensions for Canadians	
1983		Report of the Parliamentary Task Force on Pension Reform	Report of the National Commission on Social Security Reform
		Report of the Business Committee on Pension Policy	Social Security rescue amendments, PL 98-21 raising retirement age and contributions.
1984	Health and Social Security Act 1984	Liberal Government Budget, including private pension reform proposals.	Multi-Employer Pension Plan Amendment Act
		Ontario Proposals for Pension Reform	Retirement Equity Act
		Conservative government Throne Speech	
		Flexible retirement introduced into Quebec Pension Plan.	

APPENDIX A (Cont'd)

DATE	UNITED KINGDOM	CANADA	UNITED STATES
1985	Conservative government's Green and White Papers on Reform of Social Security to reduce state earnings-related benefits and introduce personal pensions (PPs). 1985 Social Security Act to protect rights of early leavers.	Conservative government's Budget Speech, May 1985, including the recommendations for Improved Pensions for Canadians, based on individual retirement income vehicles (RRSPs) and no expansion of the public pension system. Quebec government's Orange Paper	
1986	Social Security Act 1986	Conservative government's Budget Speech Abolition of mandatory retirement at Federal level.	Single Employer Pension Plan Amendments Act Tax Reform Act
1987		Remedial package of reforms to occupational pensions in Federal Pension Benefits Standards Act and Ontario Pension Benefits Act, eff. 1987. Amendments to Canada Pension Plan Consultation Paper on CPP Survivor Benefits	Pension Protection Act Omnibus Budget Reconciliation Act Consolidated Omnibus Budget Reconciliation Act
1988		Saving for Retirement, March 1988, new regulations for increased RRSP contribution limits.	

Sources: For Britain, Henry Pelling, *A History of British Trade Unionism* (Harmondsworth: Penguin, 1965), chapter 2; Maurice Bruce, *The Coming of the Welfare State* (London: Batsford, 1979); Harry Lucas, *Pensions and Industrial Relations* (Oxford: Pergamon, 1977), chapter 1; and William C. Greenough and Francis P. King, *Pension Plans and Public Policy* (New York: Columbia University Press, 1976), chapter 10. Background material for Canada includes H. A. Logan, *Trade Unions in Canada* (Toronto: Macmillan, 1948), Kenneth Bryden, *Old Age Pensions and Policy-Making in Canada* (Montreal and London: McGill-Queen's University Press, 1974); Andrew Armitage, *Social Welfare in Canada: Ideals and Realities* (Toronto: McClelland and Stewart, 1975); Dennis Guest, *The Emergence of Social Security in Canada* (Vancouver: University of British Columbia Press, 1980); and Desmond Morton and Margaret E. McCallum, "Superannuation to Indexation: Employment Pensions in the Public and Private Sector in Canada, 1870–1970," *Task Force on Inflation Protection for Employment Pension Plans, Research Studies*, vol. 1 (Toronto: Queen's Printer, 1988), pp. 1–41. For the United States, Philip Taft, *Organized Labor in American History* (New York: Harper and Row, 1964); Hewitt Associates, "Employee Retirement Systems: How It All Began," *Pension World* 12 (July 1976): 6–10; Greenough and King, *Pension Plans*, chapters 2–3, and Paul Light, *Artful Work: The Politics of Social Security Reform* (New York: Random House, 1985). Recent information supplied by Health and Welfare Canada, the U.S. Social Security Administration and the British High Commission (Ottawa).

APPENDIX B

OVERVIEW OF STATE AND OCCUPATION PENSION PLAN
PROGRAMME FEATURES, U.K. CANADA. AND U.S.

STATE PENSION SYSTEMS

PROGRAMME FEATURE	UNITED KINGDOM[1]	CANADA[2]	UNITED STATES[3]
History and Legislation	Conditional, non-contributory pension introduced 1908. Subsequently the contributory, flat-rate 1925 Old-Age and Survivors' Pensions Act. The present system, introducing an earnings-related component, established under the Social Security Pensions Act 1975 became effective April 1978 and was amended as a result of 1985 white paper.	Means-tested old age assistance act passed in 1927. Universal, flat-rate Old Age Security (OAS) Act implemented in 1951. Contributory, earnings-related Canada Pension Plan (CPP), and a parallel Quebec Pension (QPP), introduced in 1966. In 1967, the income-tested Guaranteed Income Supplement (GIS) was est; 1975 income-tested spousal allowance added.	Social Security Act 1935 est. first national contributory, earnings-related pension plan (OAI). Survivors' and dependents added 1939 (OASI); 1956 disability added, as well as expanded coverage and benefits; early retirement for women (OASDI). Early retirement at 62 for men introduced in 1961. Health insurance for the aged added (OASDHI) in 1965. Needs-tested Supplementary Security Income Act (SSI) implemented 1974. Most recent amendments to SSA in 1983 raising retirement age.
Administration	Department of Health and Social Security administers pensions through regional and local offices. Income-tested allowances are awarded by the Supplementary Benefits	1. OAS, CPP, and GIS are decentralized in administration through the National Department of Health and Welfare's district and local offices.	Department of Health and Human Services for general supervision. Social Security Administration, in department, responsible for administration of programme through

STATE PENSION SYSTEMS (Cont'd)

PROGRAMME FEATURE	UNITED KINGDOM[1]	CANADA[2]	UNITED STATES[3]
Administration (Cont'd)	Commission in the Department. The Inland Revenue Department collects earnings-related contributions.	2. CPP benefits paid by National Health and Welfare. Revenue Canada collects contributions for earnings-related CPP. 3. The Province of Quebec administers its own earnings-related pension plan (QPP) through the Quebec Department of Revenue and the Quebec Pension Board.	regional centres, district and branch offices. Treasury Department, collection of contributions through the Internal Revenue Service, payment of benefits and management of funds.
Fund Size and Investment	Accumulated National Insurance Fund (all benefits) as of 1979–80 £4.8 billion. Invested in British government securities.	Accumulated C/QPP funds at C$29.9 billion (April 1981). Under the CPP, "excess funds" are made available to the provinces (excluding Quebec) based on a formula of the ratio of provincial to total contributions. The interest rate on CPP borrowings to the provinces is set equal to the 20-yr. rate on Gov't of Canada bonds. The QPP, however, is a separate actively managed fund with a diversified portfolio which can place up to 30% of assets in equities.	Total assets of OASI Trust Fund at US$22.8 billion (1980). Invested in U.S. government securities.

STATE PENSION SYSTEMS (Cont'd)

PROGRAMME FEATURE	UNITED KINGDOM[1]	CANADA[2]	UNITED STATES[3]
Financing and Contributions	1. Pay-as-you-go (PAYGO) financing with a reserve. 2. For occupational schemes that remain "contracted-in" to the earnings-related state plan total contributions of 17.95%: employee 7.75% of income between lower and upper earnings band and 10.2% of payroll by employer (April 1981). 3. For private schemes which "contract-out" from stage plan contributions are the same for the basic component, but for earnings-related plan: employee 5.25% of income and 5.7% of payroll by employer. 4. General revenue covers 18% of cost; in addition, 3.5% payroll levy paid by employer for social security.	1. Universal, first-rate OAS financed from general revenue. 2. CPP financed on a pay-as-you-go (PAYGO) basis; QPP is partially funded. 3. Total 1988 contributions of 4.0% of pensionable earnings between yearly basic exemption (YBE) and yearly maximum pensionable earnings (YMPE), shared equally between employee and employer. 4. Guaranteed Income Supplement (GIS) financed from general revenue.	1. Social security retirement system financed on a pay-as-you-go (PAYGO) basis with a reserve. 2. Total contribution 15.02% (1988) of pensionable earnings between minimum primary insurance amount (PIA) and annual maximum taxable earnings (AMW), shared between employee and employer. 3. Supplementary Security Income (SSI) financed from general revenue.

STATE PENSION SYSTEMS (Cont'd)

PROGRAMME FEATURE	UNITED KINGDOM[1]	CANADA[2]	UNITED STATES[3]
Tax Position	Contributions to National Insurance are not tax deductible. Pension income taxed as earned income at retirement.	Contributions to Canada/Quebec Pension Plans are tax deductible. Pension income at retirement in excess of $1,000 is fully taxable.	Contributions to social security retirement system are tax deductible. Retirement benefits are non-taxable.
Tax (Revenue) Loss to Government	None	C$540 million tax expenditure for C/QPP, plus an additional $300 million in personal exemptions and deductions for elderly (1980).	US$10 billion tax expenditure for social security benefits, plus an additional $3 billion in personal exemptions and tax credits for the elderly (1982).
Coverage	1. Basic universal, flat-rate component covers all residents. 2. Earnings-related, contributory component is mandatory for all wage-earners, except as noted below. 3. Approved occupational pension schemes may "contract-out" of the state earnings-related component. Over 87% of private scheme members have "contracted-out." Individuals	1. Universal, non-contributory flat-rate Old Age Security (OAS) pension covers all persons with minimum 10 yrs. residency. 2. Contributory, earnings-related Canada/Quebec Pension Plans (C/QPP) compulsory for all wage earners. Covers 94% of labour force. 3. No "contracting-out" from public pension system allowed.	1. Earnings-related, contributory social security retirement system covers 90% of paid labour force. 2. Certain categories of public employees such as federal, state and municipal employees are permitted to "contract-out" from the social security retirement. 3. Supplementary Security Income (SSI) for those below minimum income threshold and previously covered by social security.

STATE PENSION SYSTEMS (Cont'd)

PROGRAMME FEATURE	UNITED KINGDOM[1]	CANADA[2]	UNITED STATES[3]
Coverage (Cont'd)	may now substitute personal pensions. 4. Supplementary benefits for those below a minimum income standard.	4. Guaranteed Income Supplement (GIS) payment for those below a minimum, basic income.	
Type of Benefits	Retirement, survivors', disability, death, medical, sickness, maternity, unemployment and work injury benefits.	Retirement, survivors', disability and death benefits.	Old-age, survivors', disability, death, unemployment benefits, and hospital and supplementary medical insurance for those over age 65.
Benefit Formulas and Income Replacement Rates	1. Retirement Eff. 1986—One-earner couple at Average Nat'l Earnings (ANE) with 10 yrs.' service Earnings-related component = 1¼ PAYE × 10 yrs. = 12½%. No phase-in to full benefit level.	1. Retirement Eff. 1981—One-earner couple at Yearly Maximum Pensionable Earnings (YMPE) with 10 yrs.' service. Earnings-related plan: 25% of career average adjusted earnings over 47 yrs.—15% of low income years up to the YMPE. Ten-yr. phase-in to maximum benefits.	1. Retirement. Eff. 1987—One-earner couple retiring in 1977 at Annual Maximum Taxable Earnings (AMW) with 40 quarters' coverage. Earnings-related benefit formula, excluding 5 lowest years earnings. Special minimum benefit for low-income earners with service in excess of 10 yrs. Dependent care drop-out provision.

STATE PENSION SYSTEMS (Cont'd)

PROGRAMME FEATURE	UNITED KINGDOM[1]	CANADA[2]	UNITED STATES[3]
Benefit Formulas and Income Replacement Rates (Cont'd)	Replacement Rates Basic Component: 21.3% of ANE Earnings-related: 10.2% of ANE Total: 31.5% of ANE Eff. 1998 at maturity Earnings-related component: 25% of career average adjusted earnings over highest 20 yrs. up to PAYE minus dependent care drop-out provision. Scaled down from 25% to 20% after 2010. Replacement Rates Basic Component: 34.1% of ANE Earnings-related: 20.4% of ANE Total: 54.5% of ANE 2. Survivors' 100% of the accrued (pre-retirement) or paid retirement pension (post-retirement) + a flat-rate orphans' benefit.	Replacement Rates OAS: 27.6% of AIW (2 @ 13.8%) C/QPP: 25.0% of AIW Total: 52.6% of AIW 2. Survivors' 60% of deceased contributor's pension at age 65 (post-retirement); prior to age 65 flat-rate benefit + 37.5% of insured's pension (pre-retirement) + orphan's benefit. Pending 1987 Discussion.	Replacement Rates. Primary Earner: 43% of AIW Dependents' Allowance: 21% of AIW (50% of primary earner) Total: 64% of AIW 2. Survivors' 100% of deceased insured worker's pension at age 65 (post-retirement); reduced pre-retirement benefit + orphan's benefit of 75% of deceased's pension/child. Special dependent pension.

STATE PENSION SYSTEMS (Cont'd)

PROGRAMME FEATURE	UNITED KINGDOM[1]	CANADA[2]	UNITED STATES[3]
Benefit Formulas and Income Replacement Rates (Cont'd)	3. Disability Flat-rate benefit according to age at incapacity. After April 1979 an earnings-related component. In addition, a non-contributory invalidity pension + dependents allowances. 4. Death Lump sum benefit.	3. Disability Flat-rate benefit + 75% of retirement pension + child supplement, where applicable. For total and permanent disability. 4. Death Lump sum benefit up to 10% of earnings ceiling.	3. Disability Earnings-related pension + dependents' allowance of 50% of worker's pension (reduced below age 65) to spouse and each child. For incapacity for substantial gainful activity. 4. Death Lump sum payment.
Retirement Age and Retirement/ Earnings Test	Normal retirement is age 65 for men and 60 for women. Retirement test to age 70 for men and 65 for women. Pension reduced for earnings in excess of designated amount. No early retirement.	Normal retirement is age 65; early retirement at age 60 or benefits can be deferred until age 70. Retirement not necessary. Under the GIS benefits reduced $1 for every $2 of income from any source other than OAS.	Normal retirement age increased to 67 (1983), benefits can be deferred until age 72. Between age 65 and 70 benefits reduced by $1 for every $2 earned above $5,500 (1981). Provision for early retirement at age 62 with a reduced benefit.
Indexation	Pensions adjusted annually according to the Retail Price Index.	Adjusted to Consumer Price Index on an annual basis for the earnings-related pension (C/QPP) and quarterly for the universal pension (OAS).	Adjusted to Consumer Price Index.
Vesting (Preservation)	Immediate and full	Immediate and full	Immediate and full
Portability (Trans- ferability)	Full national portability	Full national portability	Full national portability

Notes: 1 As per the Social Security Pensions Act 1975 and the 1985 White Paper on the Reform of Social Security.
2 As of 1981 and amendments to the Canada/Quebec Pension Plans effective 1 January 1987.
3 Based on the 1981 amendments and the subsequent 1983 social security rescue amendments, PL 98-21.

EMPLOYER-SPONSORED OCCUPATIONAL PENSION PLANS

PROGRAMME FEATURE	UNITED KINGDOM	CANADA	UNITED STATES
Legislation	The Social Security Pensions Act 1975 est. national regulatory framework and minimum standards for occupational pension schemes. Must be "recognized" by Inland Revenue Department for income tax exemption status. Occupational schemes may "contract-out" of state plan; individuals may contract-out to personal pensions.	Ontario Pension Benefits Act 1965 est. regulatory framework and minimum standards for registered pension plans (RPPs) regarding vesting, funding, investment and disclosure. Eight other jurisdictions have similar legislation. Must be provincially "registered" plan in order to qualify for federal Income Tax Act exemption status.	The Employee Retirement Income Security Act 1974 est. national regulatory framework and minimum standards for private sector plans regarding vesting, funding, investment and disclosure. No uniform public sector legislation. Must be a "qualified" plan for Internal Revenue Code tax exemption status.
Administration	Merchant banks or individual corporate trustees administer non-insured or self-invested plans; insurance companies administer insured plans of small companies.	Trust companies or individual trustees administer trusteed (non-insured) or self-invested plans; insurance companies administer the insured plans of small companies as well as segregated funds.	Bank trust departments or individual corporate trustees administer non-insured or self-invested plans; insurance companies administer the insured plans of small companies.
Fund Size	£140 billion market value for non-insured and insured pension fund assets in 1983.	C$126 billion market value for trusteed (non-insured) pension fund assets in 1986.	US$826 billion market value for non-insured funds in 1986.

EMPLOYER-SPONSORED OCCUPATIONAL PENSION PLANS

PROGRAMME FEATURE	UNITED KINGDOM	CANADA	UNITED STATES
Contributions and Funding	81% of all plans are contributory with the employee paying contributions of 5% to 6% of salary and employer paying 75% of total cost. Plans which "contract-out" from the state scheme must be funded.	56% of all plans are contributory with the employee paying contributions of 7% to 10% of salary and employer paying 66% of total cost, or 7% of payroll. Plans covered by pension legislation must be advanced funded; amortization of experience deficiencies and unfunded liabilities within 15 yrs.	79% of all plans are non-contributory with the employer paying 72% of total cost, or 9% of total payroll. Legislation provides for three alternative advanced funding and amortization schedules.
Tax Position	Tax deductibility status for employer and employee contributions. Pension income taxed as earned income at retirement.	Tax deductibility status for employer and employee contributions. Pension income in excess of $1,000 is taxed as earned income at retirement.	Tax deductibility status for employer and voluntary employee contributions. Pension income taxed as earned income at retirement.
Tax (Revenue) Loss to Government	Total revenue loss, including "contracting-out," est. at £1,200–2,900 million in 1983–84.	Total tax expenditure loss for registered pension plans (RPP) and retirement savings plans (RRSP) est. at C$6.1 billion in 1980.	Est. total tax expenditure for qualified pension plans and individual retirement accounts (IRA) US$28.4 billion in 1982.
Coverage	42% of the total labour force covered by an approved occupational pension scheme. Voluntary pension scheme sponsorship. Nearly 90% of plan members are	37% of the total labour force covered by a registered pension plan. Voluntary pension plan sponsorship. No "contracting-out" from the public plan permitted.	42% of the total labour force covered by a qualified pension plan. Voluntary pension plan sponsorship. No "contracting-out" from state social security retirement system permitted.

EMPLOYER-SPONSORED OCCUPATIONAL PENSION PLANS

PROGRAMME FEATURE	UNITED KINGDOM	CANADA	UNITED STATES
Coverage (Cont'd)	"contracted-out" from the state pension plan; 100% in public sector and 78% in private sector.		with the exception of Federal, state and municipal employees.

Types of Benefits	1. Retirement benefits
	
	2. Death benefits
	  (i) Pre-retirement
	  (ii) Post-retirement
	
	3. Ill-health retirement
		1. Retirement benefits
		
		2. Death benefits
		  (i) Pre-retirement
		  (ii) Post-retirement
		
		3. Disability pension
			1. Retirement benefits
			
			2. Death benefits
			  (i) Pre-retirement
			  (ii) Post-retirement
			
			3. Disability pension

Benefit Formulas and Income Replacement Rates	1. Retirement: Over 90% of scheme members covered by a defined benefit final average earnings plan calculated at 1.6%/yr. of service × salary to a maximum of 66% of salary with 40 years' service. 2. Death benefit: 86% of scheme members covered by lump sum payment of 2–4 × salary on death before retirement; 97% of members have provision for a post-retirement widow's pension.	1. Retirement: 77% of plan members covered by a defined (unit) benefit plan calculated at 2%/yr. of service × salary to a maximum of 70% of salary with 35 years' service. 2. Survivors' benefits: 51% of plan members covered by a survivor's benefit on death before retirement; 45% of members have no post-retirement survivor's benefit.	1. Retirement: Over 70% of plan members covered by a defined benefit terminal earnings formula. 2. Survivor benefits: Joint and survivor's option must be offered, with some limitations, by plans registered under ERISA.

EMPLOYER-SPONSORED OCCUPATIONAL PENSION PLANS

PROGRAMME FEATURE	UNITED KINGDOM	CANADA	UNITED STATES
Benefit Formulas and Income Replacement Rates (Cont'd)	3. Ill-health retirement: 67% of members covered by a provision which pays a benefit in excess of the accrued pension.	3. Disability pension: 55% of plan members covered for a full accrued pension to date of disability without a reduction in benefit.	3. Disability pension: 77% of plan members covered by some form of disability benefits.
Retirement Age	Normal retirement age is 65 for males and 60 for females.	Normal retirement is age 65.	Normal retirement is age 65.
Indexation	66% of scheme members in private sector have no provision for post-retirement benefit adjustment to offset inflation; public sector plans are nearly all inflation-proofed. Currently two-thirds of plan sponsors have periodic adjustments covering at least half the inflation rate. Deferred (preserved) benefits must be revalued for schemes which are "contracted-out."	95% of plans have no formal indexation; 65% of members in public sector and 6% of members in private sector have escalation. In recent years half of all major plans have made periodic adjustments to offset a portion of the increase in the cost of living. No requirement to revalue deferred benefits. Ontario Friedland Report (1988) recommended partial indexation for future retirees.	Major private sector plans have made periodic adjustments to offset inflation. Public sector plans such as the Federal civil service and half of the state and local retirement systems have automatic escalation of retirement benefits. No requirement to revalue deferred benefits.
Vesting (Preservation)	Legislative minimum standard is age 26 and 5 years' service. Nearly 37% of scheme members covered by a preservation standard which exceeds the	Legislative minimum standard in most jurisdictions was age 45 and 10 years' service. Majority of plans exceed minimum standard with a 10-year	Legislation in private sector sets three alternative vesting requirements. Nearly 75% of private sector and 93% of public sector pension plans have a

EMPLOYER-SPONSORED OCCUPATIONAL PENSION PLANS

PROGRAMME FEATURE	UNITED KINGDOM	CANADA	UNITED STATES
Vesting (Preservation) (Cont'd)	minimum. White paper (1985) recommended vesting after 2 years' service.	service requirement and no age requirement. Pension reform package (1987) introduced vesting after 2 years of service in most jurisdictions.	10-year service requirement for vesting most common provision.
Portability (Transferability)	Less than 40% of all early leavers are eligible for a transfer payment. Transferability primarily found in public sector.	Portability fairly common among and between public sector plans. Limited portability between private sector plans with exception of multi-employer plans.	Central portability networks cover only 2% of all private pension plan members; 19% of participating employers and 8% of non-participating employers.
Other Retirement Income Savings Vehicles	—Personal Pensions (PP) —Deferred Profit-Sharing Pension Plans —Individual annuities and whole life insurance —Personal savings	—Individual Registered Retirement Savings Plan (RRSP) —Group RRSPs —Deferred Profit-Sharing Pension Plans (DPSPP) —Individual annuities and whole life insurance —Personal savings	—Individual Retirement Account (IRA) —Group IRA —Deferred Profit-Sharing Pension Plans —Individual annuities and whole life insurance —Personal savings

Sources: William M. Mercer International, *International Benefit Guidelines 1981* (New York: Mercer, March 1981); International Benefits Information Service, *Special Notes* (Chicago: Charles D. Spencer & Associates, October 1981); U.S. Department of Health and Human Services, Social Security Administration, *Social Security Programs throughout the World 1981* (Washington, D.C.: GPO, July 1982); Barbara Boyle Torrey and Carole J. Thompson, *An International Comparison of Pension Systems,* a Working Paper prepared for the President's Commission on Pension Policy (Washington, D.C.: PCPP, March 1980); Government Actuary, *Occupational Pension Schemes, 1979—Sixth Survey* (London: HMSO, 1981); Labour Research Department, *Guide to Company Pension Schemes and The Social Security Pensions Act 1975* (London: LRD, 1977); Hart D. Clark, "A Comparison of The Retirement Income Systems of Canada and Other Countries," *The Retirement Income System in Canada: Problems and Alternative Policies for Reform,* vol. 2 – Appendices, Task Force on Retirement Income Policy (Ottawa: Canadian Government Publishing Centre, 1979); Statistics Canada, *Pension Plans in Canada, 1980* (Ottawa: Minister of Supply and Services, 1982); Statistics Canada, *Trusteed Pension Plans Financial Statistics* (Ottawa: Minister of Supply and Services, 1982); CCH Canadian Limited, *Your Canada Pension Plan, 1982* (Don Mills: CCH Canadian, 1981); Greenwich Research Associates, *Large Corporate Pension Funds 1980 Report to Participants* (Greenwich, CN: Greenwich Research Associates, 1980); Daniel J. Beller, *Preliminary Estimates of Participant and Financial Characteristics of Private Pension Plans, 1977.* U.S. Department of Labor, Labor-Management Services Administration (Washington, D.C.: n.p., 1981); U.S. Department of Commerce, *Statistical Abstract of the United States, 1981* (Washington, D.C.: GPO, 1982), series 534, p. 328, and CCH, 1983 *Social Security Benefits Including Medicare, January 1, 1983* (Chicago: CCH, 1982). Recent programme information supplied by Health and Welfare Canada, the U.S. Social Security Administration and the British High Commission (Ottawa), as well as data from the Government Actuary, *Occupational Pension Schemes 1983—Seventh Survey* (London: HMSO, 1986); Statistics Canada, *Pension Plans in Canada 1984* (Ottawa: Minister of Supply and Services Canada, 1986); and the U.S. Department of Labor, *Employee Benefits in Medium and Large Firms, 1985* (Washington, D.C.: Bureau of Labor Statistics, 1986).

APPENDIX C-1

EMPLOYEES COVERED BY PRIVATE PENSION PLANS IN RELATION TO THE TOTAL AND NON-AGRICULTURAL LABOUR FORCE. CANADA, 1938–1984

YEAR	PRIVATE PENSION PLAN COVERAGE (MILLION)			LABOUR FORCE (MILLION)		EMPLOYEES COVERED BY PRIVATE PENSION PLANS AS A % OF	
	Private Sector	Public Sector	Total	Total	Non-Ag.	Total Labour Force	Non-Ag. Labour Force
1938	0.265[1]	0.078[2]	0.343	4.5	2.1	7.6%	16.3%
1947	0.652[3]	0.170[4]	0.823	4.9	3.8	16.8	21.7
1960	0.998[5]	0.816[5]	1.8	6.4	5.7	28.1	31.6
1965	1.3[5]	1.1[5]	2.4	7.1	6.5	33.8	35.9
1970	1.5	1.3	2.8	8.4	7.9	33.3	35.4
1976	2.2	1.8	3.9	10.6	9.3	36.8	41.9
1980	2.5	1.9	4.5	11.3	10.1	39.8	44.6
1982	2.7	2.0	4.7	11.9	11.4	38.9	40.9
1984	2.5	2.0	4.6	12.4	11.8	36.8[6]	38.7

Notes:

1 Industrial Relations Section, Queen's University.

2 Total public sector employment was 126.470 derived from aggregating the three levels of government, teachers and the armed forces, excluding the para-public sector, and assuming a level of pension plan coverage of 66 per cent applied as a weighted average.

3 Dominion Bureau of Statistics, *Survey of Pension and Welfare Plans, 1947* and includes the 180.794 railway employees excluded from the DBS survey.

4 Total public sector employment was 394.497 derived from aggregating the three levels of government, teachers and the armed forces but excluding the para-public sector. 1946 data was used for provincial and municipal employment as cited by the Department of National Revenue. Pension plan coverage was assumed to be 75 per cent applied as a weighted average. For 1947, Health and Welfare cites public sector pension coverage as 200,000 to 250,000 including 100,000 for the armed forces. This figure is clearly wrong when cross-referenced with the *Canada Year Book* for 1947 which cites the armed forces at 37,000. The figure of 100,000 more nearly corresponds to the 1942 figure of 107,000 for the armed forces.

5 Public sector pension coverage was extrapolated at 45 per cent of total coverage based on the estimates in Statistics Canada, *Pension Plans in Canada, 1970*. Private sector coverage was calculated as a residual.

6 The result arrived at here is marginally lower than that cited in Statistics Canada, *Pension Plans in Canada 1984* because of a slightly higher 1984 labour force figure used in the denominator.

Sources: Constructed from M. C. Urquhart, ed., *Historical Statistics of Canada* (Toronto: Macmillan, 1965), various series. Dominion Bureau of Statistics and Statistics Canada, *Canadian Statistical Review* (Ottawa: Queen's Printer, various years); Bank of Canada, *Bank of Canada Review* (Ottawa, May 1978), p. 55; Department of National Revenue, *Taxation Statistics 1946* (Ottawa: King's and Queen's Printer, 1946); Dominion Bureau of Statistics and Statistics Canada, *Canada Year Book* (Ottawa: King's and Queen's Printer, various years); Industrial Relations Section, Queen's University, "Industrial Retirement Plans in Canada," Bulletin No. 1, 1938, in Leonard Marsh, *Report on Social Security for Canada 1943* (Toronto: University of Toronto Press, reprinted, 1975), appendix V, pp. 302–3; Dominion Bureau of Statistics, *Survey of Pension and Welfare Plans, 1947 (74-502A)* (Ottawa, May 1950), Table 1, p. 24; Statistics Canada (84–401), *Pension Plans in Canada* (Ottawa: 1970, 1974, 1976, 1980, 1982, and 1984); Health and Welfare Canada, *Retirement Age* (Ottawa: Minister of National Health and Welfare, 14 December 1978), Table V.A.6, p. 114.

APPENDIX C-2

EMPLOYEES COVERED BY PRIVATE PENSION PLANS IN RELATION TO THE TOTAL AND NON-AGRICULTURAL LABOUR FORCE, UNITED STATES, 1929–1985

YEAR	PRIVATE PENSION PLAN COVERAGE (MILLION)			LABOUR FORCE (MILLION)		EMPLOYEES COVERED BY PRIVATE PENSION PLANS AS A % OF	
	Private Sector	Public Sector[1]	Total	Total	Non-Ag.	Total Labour Force	Non-Ag. Labour Force
1929	3.8[2]	1.0[3]	4.8	49.4	37.1	9.7%	12.9%
1938	3.8[4]	2.4[5]	6.2	54.9	34.5	11.3	17.9
1947	8.0	3.8[5]	11.8	60.9	49.5	19.4	23.8
1950	9.8	4.0[5]	13.8	63.9	52.5	21.6	26.3
1955	14.2	6.4	20.6	68.1	56.2	30.3	36.7
1960	18.7	7.6	26.3	72.1	60.3	36.5	43.6
1965	21.8	9.5	31.3	77.2	66.7	40.5	46.9
1970	26.3	9.7	36.0	85.9	74.8	41.9	48.1
1975	30.3	12.7	43.0	94.8	80.3	45.4	53.6
1979	34.8	13.1	47.9	104.9	93.9	45.7	51.0
1983	38.9	10.6	49.5	113.2	109.8	43.7	45.1
1985	40.4	8.5	48.9	117.2	113.9	41.8	42.9

Notes: 1   The public sector was derived by aggregating federal, state and local retirement system coverage, excluding teachers and the para-public sector, from the U.S. Department of Commerce, Statistical Abstract of the United States. This would result in underestimating total coverage in relation to the total labour force.

2   Estimated by M. W. Latimer and cited in William C. Greenough and Francis P. King, Pension Plans and Public Policy (New York: Columbia University Press, 1976), p. 31.

3   Includes federal government employees covered by a pension, but excludes state and local government pension coverage for which data was unavailable. Therefore underestimated.

4   1940.

5   Includes federal government employee pension plan coverage plus 46 per cent of total state and local government employees in the respective year which represents the 1942 ratio of state and local government pension coverage to total state and local government employment.

Sources: Constructed from U.S. Department of Commerce, Bureau of Census, Historical Statistics of the United States: Colonial Times to 1957 (Washington, D.C.: GPO, 1961), various series; U.S. Department of Commerce, Bureau of Census, Statistical Abstract of the United States (Washington, D.C.: GPO, various editions); President's Commission on Pension Policy, Coming of Age: Toward a National Retirement Income Policy (Washington, D.C.: PCPP: February 1981), Table 2, p. 13; International Labour Organization, Year Book of Labour Statistics 1981 (Geneva: ILO, 1981), and information supplied to the author by the U.S. National Social Security Reform Commission, 17 May 1982; and the U.S. Department of Labor, Bureau of Labor Statistics, Employee Benefits In Medium and Large Firms, 1986 (June 1987).

APPENDIX C-3

EMPLOYEES COVERED BY OCCUPATIONAL PENSION SCHEMES IN RELATION TO THE TOTAL AND NON-AGRICULTURAL LABOUR FORCE.
UNITED KINGDOM, 1936–1983

YEAR	OCCUPATIONAL PENSION SCHEME COVERAGE (MILLION)			LABOUR FORCE (MILLION)		EMPLOYEES COVERED BY OCCUPATIONAL PENSION SCHEMES AS A % OF	
	Private Sector	Public Sector	Total	Total	Non-Ag.[1]	Total Labour Force	Non-Ag. Labour Force
1936	1.6	1.0	2.6	20.1[2]	18.5	12.9%	14.1%
1953	3.1	3.1	6.2	21.4	20.6	28.9	30.1
1956	4.3	3.7	8.0	22.2	21.5	36.0	37.2
1963	7.2	3.9	11.1	23.6	22.9	47.0	48.5
1967	8.1	4.1	12.2	23.8	23.3	51.3	52.6
1971	6.8	4.3	11.1	23.2	22.8	47.8	48.7
1975	6.1	5.4	11.4	25.9	25.5	44.0	44.7
1979	6.2	5.6	11.8	26.4	26.0	44.7	45.4
1983	5.8	5.3	11.1	26.6	26.2	41.7	42.4

Notes: 1 The non-agricultural labour force is defined as the total work force minus those employed in agriculture, forestry, hunting and fishing.
2 Interpolated from 1933 and 1938 labour force data.

Sources: Constructed from the Government Actuary, *Occupational Pension Schemes* (London: HMSO, various years); Robert Price and George Sayers Bain, "Union Growth Revisited: 1948–1974 in Perspective," *British Journal of Industrial Relations* 14 (November 1976), Table 1, p. 340; Department of Employment Productivity, *British Labour Statistics Historical Abstract, 1886–1968* (London: HMSO, 1971), Table 118, p. 210, Table 125, pp. 228–29, Table 128, p. 234; Central Statistics Office, *Annual Abstract of Statistics* (London: HMSO, various years) and the International Labour Organization, *Year Book of Labour Statistics 1981* (Geneva: ILO, 1981).

APPENDIX D

NET PRIVATE, PUBLIC AND TOTAL PENSION FUND SAVING IN RELATION TO PERSONAL AND GROSS SAVING.
BILLION NATIONAL CURRENCY UNITS, U.K., CANADA AND U.S., 1960–1980

YEAR	NET PRIVATE PENSION SAVING (BILLION CURRENCY UNITS)			NET PUBLIC PENSION SAVING (BILLION CURRENCY UNITS)			TOTAL NET PENSION SAVING (BILLION CURRENCY UNITS)			TOTAL PERSONAL SAVING (BILLION CURRENCY UNITS)			GROSS SAVING (BILLION CURRENCY UNITS)		
	U.K.	Canada	U.S.	U.K.	Canada	U.S.	U.K.	Canada	U.S.	U.K.	Canada	U.S.	U.K.	Canada	U.S.
1960	.50	.4	6.0	.07	—	+0.7	.57	.4	6.7	1.2	1.5	19.7	4.9	54.0(E)	81.1
1965	.70	n.a.	9.4	.19	—	-0.1	.89	n.a.	9.3	1.9	2.9	33.7	6.7	10.4	120.2
1970	1.06	1.3	11.8	.35	1.3	2.9	1.41	2.6	14.7	3.3	3.9	55.8	12.3	18.5	148.9
1971	1.26	n.a.	16.3	.49	1.3	1.9	1.75	n.a.	18.2	2.9	4.5	57.3	12.4	20.8	171.9
1972	1.56	n.a.	18.4	.52	1.4	2.5	1.08	n.a.	20.9	4.5	5.1	49.4	13.9	23.4	174.2
1973	1.95	2.1	17.4	.68	1.6	2.2	2.63	3.7	19.6	6.2	6.7	79.0	18.6	28.7	235.5
1974	2.58	2.6	13.7	.91	1.7	2.6	3.49	4.3	16.3	7.4	7.7	85.1	20.4	35.8	227.8
1975	3.56	3.2	15.8	1.38	1.7	0.7	4.94	4.9	16.5	9.1	12.3	94.3	22.1	40.1	218.9
1976[1]	4.36	4.1	21.0	1.63	2.2	-0.4	5.99	6.3	20.6	9.9	13.4	82.5	28.3	45.6	257.9
1977	4.72	4.9	24.0	1.46	2.3	-1.3	6.18	7.2	22.7	10.4	13.9	74.1	31.9	48.1	304.0
1978	5.56	6.2	27.0	2.41	2.5	-2.9	7.97	9.7	24.1	14.8	16.0	76.3	36.7	52.4	355.2
1979	8.10	7.6	30.0	1.89	2.9	-0.8	9.99	10.5	29.2	20.1	17.8	86.2	46.8	64.9	411.9
1980	9.40(E)	9.0	34.0	2.19	3.0	0.2	11.59(E)	12.0	34.2	25.4	19.5	101.8	48.2	66.9	400.7

Note: 1 After 1975 neither the U.S. Securities and Exchange Commission, *Statistical Bulletin* nor the Board of Governors, Federal Revenue System, *Annual Statistical Digest* provide data on private non-insured pension fund receipts and disbursements in order to calculate pension savings. The figures used here for the period between 1976 and 1980 are based on a trend analysis from 1960, and may in fact understate the case, particularly in regard to the savings ratios.

Sources: Calculated from the Central Statistical Office, *Annual Abstract of Statistics, 1982* (London: HMSO, 1982), Table 3.11, pp. 62–63 and Table 14.7, p. 350; Central Statistical Office, *National Income and Expenditure* (London: HMSO, various years); Central Statistical Office, *Financial Statistics* (London: HMSO, various years); G. Francis Green, *The Increase in Aggregate U.K. Pension Savings*. Kingston Polytechnic. Discussion Paper in Political Economy No. 28, 1980, revised Table 1, p. 3; Statistics Canada, *Financial Statistics, 1980* (Ottawa: Minister of Supply and Services, 1982), Text Table IV, p. 12; Statistics Canada, *Canadian Statistical Review* (Ottawa: Minister of Supply and Services, various years) and the U.S. Department of Commerce, *Statistical Abstract of the United States* (Washington, D.C.: GPO, various years), Series 534, 547, 700 and 718.

APPENDIX E

NET PRIVATE AND TOTAL PENSION SAVING AS A PERCENTAGE OF GROSS BUSINESS AND TOTAL INVESTMENT. CANADA. 1960–1980

YEAR	NET PRIVATE PENSION SAVING[1] ($BILLION)		CAPITAL AND REPAIR EXPENDITURES ($BILLION)		NET PRIVATE PENSION SAVING AS A % OF INVESTMENT		NET TOTAL PENSION SAVING AS A % OF INVESTMENT	
	Private[2]	Total[3]	Business[4]	Total[5]	Business	Total	Business	Total
1960	$0.4	$0.4	$6.5	$8.4	6.8%	5.4%	6.8%	5.2%
1965	n.a.	n.a.	10.3	12.9	n.a.	n.a.	n.a.	n.a.
1970	1.3	2.6	14.3	17.8	9.1	7.3	18.2	14.6
1971	n.a.	n.a.	15.9	20.2	n.a.	n.a.	n.a.	n.a.
1972	n.a.	n.a.	17.9	22.2	n.a.	n.a.	n.a.	n.a.
1973	2.1	3.7	22.1	26.6	9.5	7.9	16.7	13.9
1974	2.6	4.3	27.3	32.9	9.5	7.9	15.8	13.1
1975	3.2	4.9	37.7	38.2	8.5	8.4	12.9	12.8
1976	4.1	6.3	37.1	43.7	11.1	9.4	16.9	14.4
1977	4.9	7.2	39.6	46.6	10.5	10.5	18.2	15.5
1978	6.2	9.7	42.9	50.4	14.5	12.3	22.6	19.3
1979	7.6	10.5	50.6	58.4	15.0	13.0	20.8	17.8
1980	9.0	12.0	57.4	66.2	15.7	13.6	20.9	18.1

Notes: 1 Net pension saving is equal to contributions plus investment income minus benefits and administrative costs. Administrative costs have not been deducted and are of a second order magnitude.
2 Trusteed and insured pension plans, excluding pay-as-you-go general revenue employee pension plans.
3 Canada/Quebec Pension Plans plus trusteed pension plans.
4 Including capital expenditures on residential and non-residential construction plus machinery and equipment.
5 Government plus business.

Sources: Calculated from Appendix D and Statistics Canada. "Capital and Repair Expenditures," CANSIM Series.

APPENDIX F-1

SOURCES OF FUNDS OF NON-FINANCIAL CORPORATIONS.¹ CANADA, $MILLION, 1963-67 — 1978-82

SOURCES OF FUNDS	1963-67 $	%	1968-72 $	%	1973-77 $	%	1978-82 $	%	AVERAGE. 1963-1982 %
A. Internal	$26,296	56.3	$36,564	58.7	$69,460	54.2	$116,723	44.4	53.4
Net Saving	9,819	21.0	12,089	19.4	23,300	18.2	27,294	10.4	17.3
Depreciation Allowances	16,477	35.3	24,475	39.3	46,160	36.0	89,429	34.0	36.2
B. External	20,389	43.7	25,687	41.3	58,773	45.8	145,936	55.6	46.6
Stocks & Claims	5,531	11.9	6,392	10.3	10,924	8.5	41,035	15.6	11.6
Bonds & Mortgages	6,439	13.8	8,212	13.2	10,798	8.5	19,248	7.3	10.8
Trade Debt	3,794	8.1	4,014	6.4	12,959	10.1	24,302	9.3	8.5
Other Debt	3,475	7.4	5,646	9.1	17,534	13.7	46,192	17.6	11.9
Other Sources	1,130	2.4	1,423	2.3	6,558	5.1	15,159	5.8	3.9
C. Total Sources	46,685	100.0	62,251	100.0	128,233	100.0	262,659	100.0	100.0

Note: 1 Non-financial corporations with assets of $10 million or more, excluding unincorporated businesses.

Source: Calculated from Statistics Canada, *National Flow Accounts* (Ottawa: Minister of Supply and Services, various years), and from information supplied to the author by the Corporate Finance Division, Federal Department of Finance, February 1984.

APPENDIX F-2

SOURCES OF CORPORATE FUNDS, UNITED STATES, $BILLION, SELECTED YEARS, 1960–1980

SOURCES OF FUNDS	1960 $	1960 %	1965 $	1965 %	1970 $	1970 %	1975 $	1975 %	1980 $	1980 %	% AVERAGE 1960–1980
A. Internal Sources	35.4	72.7	58.5	62.6	61.8	57.0	119.7	71.3	196.8	58.6	58.9
B. External Sources											
Other	1.2	2.5	14.8	15.8	5.3	4.9	6.5	3.9	33.2	9.9	11.1
Debt											
Short-Term	4.6	9.5	11.0	11.8	9.0	8.3	−8.0	−4.8	39.7	11.8	11.2
Long-Term	6.1	12.5	9.3	9.9	26.4	24.4	39.8	23.7	53.6	15.9	16.5
Total Debt	10.7	22.0	20.3	21.7	35.4	32.8	31.8	18.9	93.3	27.7	27.7
Equity Issues	1.4	2.9	0.0	0.0	5.7	5.3	9.9	5.9	12.9	3.8	2.4
Total External	13.3	27.3	35.1	37.4	46.4	43.0	48.3	28.7	139.4	41.4	41.2
C. Total Sources	48.7	100.0	93.5	100.0	108.1	100.0	167.9	100.0	336.2	100.1	100.1

Source: Calculated from the U.S. Department of Commerce, *Statistical Abstract of the United States* (Washington, D.C.: GPO, 1982), Series 916, p. 544.

APPENDIX F-3

SOUCES OF CASH FLOW FOR INDUSTRIAL AND COMMERCIAL COMPANIES. U.K., £BILLION, 1970–1976

SOURCES OF CASH FLOW	1970 £	1970 %	1971 £	1971 %	1972 £	1972 %	1973 £	1973 %	1974 £	1974 %	1975 £	1975 %	1976 £	1976 %	% AVERAGE 1970–1976
A. Internal Cash Flow	3.5	66.0	4.3	86.0	5.2	74.3	7.4	69.2	8.6	64.2	9.1	97.9	11.7	82.4	77.1
B. External Cash Flow															
Investment Grants	0.5	9.4	0.6	12.0	0.4	5.7	0.4	3.7	0.4	2.9	0.4	4.3	0.4	2.8	5.8
Other Liabilities	0.3	5.7	0.2	4.0	0.2	2.9	0.8	7.5	0.1	0.7	0.5	5.4	0.6	4.2	4.3
Debt															
Short-Term	0.9	16.9	(0.5)	(10.0)	0.6	8.6	1.9	17.8	4.4	32.8	(1.8)	(19.4)	0.7	4.9	7.4
Long-Term	0.0	0.0	(0.2)	4.0	0.3	4.3	0.1	.9	(0.1)	(0.7)	0.1	1.2	0.0	0.0	1.3
Total Debt	0.9	16.9	(0.3)	(6.0)	0.9	12.9	2.0	18.7	4.3	32.1	(1.7)	(18.3)	0.7	4.9	8.7
Share Issues	0.1	1.9	0.2	4.0	0.3	4.3	0.1	0.9	0.0	0.0	1.0	10.8	0.8	7.0	4.1
Total External	1.8	33.9	0.7	14.0	1.8	25.7	3.3	30.8	4.8	35.8	0.2	2.1	2.5	17.6	22.8
C. Total Cash Flow	5.3	100.0	5.0	100.0	7.0	100.0	10.7	100.0	13.4	100.0	9.3	100.0	14.2	100.0	100.0

Source: Calculated from The London Stock Exchange, *Evidence to the Committee to Review the Functioning of Financial Situations* (London: LSE, July 1977), Table 2, p. 14.

APPENDIX G-1

ESTIMATED REGISTERED RETIREMENT SAVINGS PLAN (RRSP)
ASSETS IN CANADA, 1960–1990

YEAR	ESTIMATED ASSETS ($BILLION)
1960[1]	$ 0.98
1961	0.13
1962	0.16
1963	0.21
1964	0.27
1965	0.34
1966	0.44
1967	0.56
1968	0.72
1969	0.93
1970	1.2
1971	1.5
1972	1.9
1973	2.5
1974	3.2
1975	4.2
1976	5.3
1977	6.9
1978	8.8
1979	11.3
1980	14.5
1981	18.6
1982[2]	20.5
1983	23.3
1984	26.1
1985	28.9
1986	31.7
1987	34.6
1988	37.4
1989	40.2
1990	43.0

Notes: 1 Assets between 1960 and 1982 are estimated using an exponential regression equation based on actual assets between 1977 and 1981 as reported to the author by the Financial Institutions Section, Business Finance Division, Statistics Canada. Earlier work by the Task Force on Retirement Income Policy, *The Retirement Income System in Canada,* vol. 1 (Hull: Canadian Government Publishing Centre, 1979), p. 74, and Harry Weitz, "Contributors and Contributions to Registered Retirement Savings Plans in Ontario," *Report of the Royal Commission on the Status of Pensions in Ontario,* Vol. 8 (Toronto: Queen's Printer, 1981), p. 129, used the "withdrawal rate" method so that gross RRSP contributions minus an arbitrary withdrawal rate assumption were equated to RRSP assets.

2 After 1982 the system is assumed to be at maturity and assets are estimated on the basis of a straight-line fit thereafter.

APPENDIX G-2

COMPARISON OF ACTUAL AND ESTIMATED RRSP ASSETS,
CANADA, 1977–1981

YEAR	$BILLION		% DIFFERENTIAL
	ACTUAL	ESTIMATED[1]	
1977	$ 6.4	$ 6.9	+ 7.8%
1978	9.3	8.8	− 5.4
1979	11.9	11.3	− 5.0
1980	14.5	14.5	0.0
1981	17.9	18.6	+ 3.9

Note: 1 Estimated on the basis of an exponential regression equation as reported
in Appendix G-1.

APPENDIX G-3

ESTIMATED REGISTERED RETIREMENT SAVINGS PLAN ASSETS
INVESTED IN EQUITY, $BILLION,
CANADA, 1960–1980

YEAR	ESTIMATED RRSP ASSETS	×	PERCENTAGE INVESTED IN EQUITY[1]	=	RRSP ASSETS INVESTED IN EQUITY
1960	$ 0.98		8%		$ .078
1961	0.13		8		.610
1962	0.16		8		.013
1963	0.21		8		.017
1964	0.27		8		.022
1965	0.34		8		.027
1966	0.44		8		.035
1967	0.56		8		.045
1968	0.72		8		.058
1969	0.93		8		.074
1970	1.2		8		.096
1971	1.5		8		.120
1972	1.9		8		.152
1973	2.5		8		.200
1974	3.2		8		.256
1975	4.2		8		.336
1976	5.3		8		.424
1977	6.9		7		.483
1978	8.8		6		.528
1979	11.3		5		.565
1980	14.5		4		.580

Note: 1 Between 1960 and 1976 it was assumed that RRSP equity investment was one-third of that for trusteed pension plans. This assumption is based on a study carried out and reported by the Trust Companies Association of Canada, *Submission to the Royal Commission on the Status of Pensions in Ontario* (Toronto, May 1978), Table 6, VIII-24, and studies by Statistics Canada for 1981 and 1982. According to these studies equity investment by RRSPs declined from 7 per cent in 1977 to 2 per cent in 1982. The bulk of funds are invested in mortgages. RRSP assets now represent nearly 40 per cent of total trusteed pension plan assets. Earlier studies erroneously assumed that RRSP asset mix was similar to that for trusteed pension plans.

Sources: For RRSP assets, Appendix G-1, and Statistics Canada, *Trusteed Pension Plans Financial Statistics* (Ottawa: Minister of Supply and Services, various years).

APPENDIX H

VALUE OF STOCK LISTED ON TORONTO STOCK EXCHANGE, ADJUSTED FOR CONTROL BLOCKS, 1966–1980

YEAR	VALUE OF TSE STOCKS ($BILLION)	×	CONTROL BLOCKS (PER CENT)	=	VALUE OF TSE STOCKS, ADJUSTED FOR CONTROL BLOCKS ($BILLION)
1966	$ 35.4		30		$10.4
1970	46.5		50		23.3
1971	50.3		50		25.2
1972	64.5		50		32.3
1973	62.5		50		31.3
1974	44.2		50		22.1
1975	51.6		50		25.8
1976	56.9		50		28.5
1977	62.4		50		31.2
1978	79.4		70		55.6
1979	112.6		70		78.8
1980	139.4		70		97.6

Sources: Calculated from estimates for control blocks from the Bank of Nova Scotia "The Stock Market in Canada: Post War Forces of Supply and Demand," *Monthly Review*, October 1960, p. 1, and estimates by O. M. Petrovici, *Percentage of Pension Plan Stocks (Mkt Value) vs. Canadian QMV Stocks Listed on TSE*. Paper No. 2 prepared for the Toronto Stock Exchange, 1976, pp. 3, 4, 7.

APPENDIX I-1

ASSETS OF FINANCIAL INTERMEDIARIES, CANADA, 1946 AND 1979

	$MILLION	
FINANCIAL INTERMEDIARY	1946	1979
Chartered Banks	6,924	210,200
Private Non-Bank Intermediaries	4,926	188,600
Trusteed Pension Funds	455	43,200 (32,400[1])
Life Insurance Companies	3,066	41,400 [2]
Trust Companies	305	33,400 (44,200[3])
Local and Central Credit Unions	188	32,500
Construction Loan Companies	124	14,100
Mortgage Loan Companies	288	12,300
Property and Casualty Companies	352	10,400
Investment Companies	148	1,300
Total	11,850	398,800

Note: 1 Excluding corporate trusteed pension fund assets under management by trust companies.

2 Canadian business only. Including life insurance and accident and sickness policies ($2.3 billion) plus the segregated (pension) funds ($5.5 billion) of life firms.

3 To place the assets of trust companies on a comparable basis with life companies requires that all assets under their control be included as in the case of life insurance company assets (S&A, segregated funds and life policies). Nearly 25 per cent of all trusteed pension fund assets, or $10.8 billion, are controlled by trust companies and are included here. The total asset base of trust companies is therefore greater than that of life insurance companies.

Sources: Retabulated and calculated from E. P. Neufeld, *The Financial System of Canada: Its Growth and Development* (Toronto: Macmillan, 1972) and updated for 1979 from Statistics Canada, *Financial Institutions, Financial Statistics, Fourth Quarter 1979* (Ottawa: Statistics Canada, 1980).

APPENDIX I-2

ASSETS OF FINANCIAL AND NONFINANCIAL INSTITUTIONS,
U.S., 1950 AND 1980

	$BILLION	
SECTOR	1950	1980
Commercial Banking	147.8	1,386.3
Non-Bank Finance	138.8	2,375.5
Savings and Loan Associations	16.9	629.8
Pension Funds[1]	11.7	484.9
Life Insurance	62.6	469.8
Finance Companies	9.3	198.6
Other Insurance	12.6	180.1
Mutual Savings Banks	22.4	171.5
Money Market Funds	n.a.	74.4
Credit Unions	n.a.	69.2
Investment Companies	3.3	63.7
Security Brokers and Dealers	n.a.	33.5
Total	286.6	3,761.8

Note: 1 Private non-insured and insured pension funds plus government (state and local) retirement funds.

Source: Retabulated and calculated from the U.S. Department of Commerce, *Statistical Abstract of the United States,* 1970 and 1982–83 (Washington, D.C.: GPO, various years), Series 639, p. 437, and Series 813, p. 500.

APPENDIX I-3

ASSETS OF FINANCIAL INSTITUTIONS,
U.K., 1963 AND 1980

	$BILLION	
INSTITUTION	1963	1980
Banks[1]	9.1	331.7
Non-Bank Finance	21.3	252.0
Pension Funds	5.8[2] (4.3[3])	85.0[2] (63.8[3])
Life Companies	7.4[4] (5.9[3])	74.3[4] (53.1[3])
Building Societies	4.0	62.8
Unit and Investment Trusts	3.1	16.1
Other	1.0	13.8
Total	30.4	583.7

Note: 1 Including London clearing banks, Scotland and Northern Ireland banks and other deposit banks.
2 Including private, public and local authority pension funds plus estimated insured pension assets of life companies.
3 Excluding insured pension assets of life companies.
4 Including insured pension assets.

Source: Retabulated and calculated from Central Statistics Office, *Financial Statistics,* 1963 and 1981 (London: HMSO, various years).

Selected Bibliography

GENERAL

Books

Adler-Karlsson, Gunnar. *Functional Socialism: A Swedish Theory for Democratic Socialization.* Stockholm: Bokforlaget Prisma, 1967. Reprinted as *Reclaiming the Canadian Economy: A Swedish Approach through Functional Socialism.* Toronto: Anansi, 1970.

Afanasyev, V. *Bourgeois Economic Thought 1930s–70s.* Trans. James Riordan. Moscow: Progress, 1983.

Allen, V. L. *Militant Trade Unionism.* London: Merlin Press, 1966.

Anderson, Perry. "The Limits and Possibilities of Trade Union Action." In *The Incompatibles: Trade Union Militancy and the Consensus.* Eds. Robin Blackburn and Alexander Cockburn. Harmondsworth: Penguin, 1967, pp. 263–80.

Ashenfelter, Orley, and James Blum, eds. *Evaluating The Labour-Market Effects of Social Programs.* Princeton: Industrial Relations Section, Department of Economics, Princeton University, 1976.

Atkinson, A. B., ed. *Wealth, Income and Inequality.* Harmondsworth: Penguin Education, 1973.

Baran, Paul A., and Paul M. Sweezy. *Monopoly Capital.* New York: Monthly Review Press, 1966.

Bengtson, Vern L., and Neal E. Cutler. "Generations and Intergenerational Relations: Perspectives on Age Groups and Social Change." In *Handbook of Aging and the Social Sciences.* Eds. Robert H. Binstock and Ethel Shanas. Toronto: Van Nostrand Reinhold, 1976, pp. 130–59.

Berle, A. A., Jr., and G. C. Means. *The Modern Corporation and Private Property.* New York: Macmillan, 1932.

Bernstein, Eduard. *Evolutionary Socialism.* Trans. Edith C. Harvey. New York: Schocken Books, 1975.

Bottomore, T. B. *Classes in Modern Society.* London: Allen and Unwin, 1967.

Bottomore, Tom, and Patrick Goode, eds. *Austro-Marxism.* Oxford: Oxford University Press, 1978.

Branch, Ben. *Fundamentals of Investing.* Toronto: Wiley, 1976.

Briggs, A. "The Welfare State in Historical Perspective." In *The Welfare State.* Ed. C. Schottland. London: Harper and Row, 1977, pp. 221–58.

Briton, Crane. *The Anatomy of Revolution.* New York: Vintage Books, 1965.

Burgess, E. W., ed. *Aging in Western Societies.* Chicago: University of Chicago Press, 1960.

Burkitt, Brian. *Radical Political Economy: An Introduction to the Alternative Economics.* Brighton: Wheatsheaf, 1984.

Cameron, Rondo, ed. *Banking in the Early Stages of Industrialization.* New York: Oxford University Press, 1967.

Chamberlin, Edward Hastings. *The Theory of Monopolistic Competition.* 8th edn. Cambridge, MA: Harvard University Press, 1965.

Clark, Robert L., and Joseph J. Spengler. *The Economics of Individual and Population Aging.* Cambridge: Cambridge University Press, 1980.

Comfort, A. *Ageing: The Biology of Senescence.* London: Routledge and Kegan Paul, 1964.

Corrigan, Paul, and Peter Leonard. *Social Work Practice under Capitalism: A Marxist Approach.* London: Macmillan, 1978.

Cowgill, Donald, and Lowell D. Holmes. "Ageing and Modernization." In *An Ageing Population.* Eds. Vita Carver and Penny Liddiard. Suffolk: Hodder and Stoughton, 1978, pp. 14–77.

Day, Lincoln H. "Government Pensions for the Aged in 19 Industrialized Countries: Demonstration of a Method for Cross-National Evaluation." In *Comparative Studies in Sociology.* Ed. Richard F. Tomasson. Greenwich, CN: JAI, 1978. pp. 217–33.

de Beauvoir, Simone. *Old Age.* Harmondsworth: Penguin, 1978.

Draper, Hal. "The Death of the State in Marx and Engels." In *The Socialist Register 1970.* Eds. Ralph Miliband and John Saville. London: Merlin Press, 1970, pp. 281–307.

Edwards, R. C., M. Reich, and D. M. Gordon. *Labour Market Segmentation.* London: Heath, 1975.

Eisenstadt, S. N. *From Generation to Generation: Age Groups and Social Structure.* New York: Free Press, 1956.

Engels, Frederick. *Anti-Duhring.* Moscow: Progress, 1977. First published 1878.

—. Letter to Conrad Schmidt (27 October 1890), "Interaction of Economic Conditions, Institutions, And Ideology." In *Reader in Marxist Philosophy.* Eds. Howard Selsam and Harry Martel. New York: International, 1963, pp. 206–10.

—. Letter to Joseph Block (21 September 1890), "The Economic Element Not the Only Determining One." In *Reader in Marxist Philosophy.* Eds. Howard Selsam and Harry Martel. New York: International, 1963, pp. 204–6.

—. *Socialism: Utopian and Scientific.* New York: International, 1935. First published 1880.

Friedman, Andrew L. *Industry and Labour: Class Struggle and Work and Monopoly Capitalism.* London: Macmillan, 1977.

Gardner, Esmond, ed. *Pension Fund Investment.* Homewood, IL: Irwin, 1969.

George, V. *Social Security and Society.* London: Routledge and Kegan, Paul, 1973.

—, and Paul Wilding. *Ideology and Social Welfare.* London: Routledge and Kegan Paul, 1976.

Goody, Jack. "Aging in Nonindustrial Societies." In *Handbook of Aging and the Social Sciences.* Eds. Robert H. Binstock and Ethel Shanas. New York: Van Nostrand Reinhold, 1976, pp. 117–29.

Gorz, André. "Reforms and the Struggle for Socialism." In *The Capitalist System.* Eds. Richard C. Edwards, Michael Reich, and Thomas E. Weisskopf. Englewood Cliffs, NJ: Prentice-Hall, 1978, pp. 528–32.

Gough, Ian. *The Political Economy of the Welfare State.* London: Macmillan, 1979.

Gouldner, Alvin W. *The Coming Crisis of Western Sociology.* New York: Avon, 1970.

—. "The Politics of Mind." In *For Sociology: Renewal and Critique in Sociology.* Harmondsworth: Penguin, 1975, pp. 82–127.

Gruman, Gerald J. "Cultural Origins of Present-day 'Ageism': The Modernization of the Life Cycle." In *Aging And the Elderly: Humanistic Perspectives in Gerontology.* Eds. Stuart F. Spicker, Kathleen M. Woodward, and David D. Van Tassel. Atlantic Highlands, NJ: Humanities Press, 1978, pp. 359–80.

Gutman, David. "The Premature Gerontocracy: Themes of Aging and Death in the Youth Culture." In *Death in American Experience.* Ed. Arien Mack. New York: Schocken Books, 1974, pp. 50–82.

Hareven, Tamara K. "Family Time and Historical Time." In *The Family.* Eds. Alice S. Rossi, Jerome Kagan, and Tamara K. Hareven. New York: Norton, 1977, pp. 57–70.

Havighurst, Robert. "Ageing in Western Society." In *The Social Challenge of Ageing*. Ed. David Hobman. London: Croom-Helm, 1978, pp. 15–44.

Heclo, Hugh. *Modern Social Politics in Britain and Sweden: From Relief to Income Maintenance*. New Haven and London: Yale University Press, 1974.

Hendricks, Jon, and C. Davis Hendricks. "Ageing in Advanced Industrialized Societies." In *An Ageing Population*. Eds. Vita Carver and Penny Liddiard. Suffolk: Hodder and Stoughton, 1978, pp. 28–34.

Hicks, J.R. *The Theory of Wages*. London: Macmillan, 1966.

Hilferding, Rudolf. *Finance Capital*. Ed. Tom Bottomore. London: Routledge and Kegan Paul, 1985. First published 1910.

Hobman, David, ed. *The Social Challenge of Ageing*. London: Croom-Helm, 1978.

Hudson, Robert B., and Robert H. Binstock. "Political Systems and Aging." In *Handbook of Aging and the Social Sciences*. Eds. Robert H. Binstock and Ethel Shanas. New York: Van Nostrand Reinhold, 1976, pp. 369–400.

Hyman, Richard. *Marxism and the Sociology of Trade Unionism*. London: Pluto Press, 1971.

Hyman, Richard, and Ian Brough. *Social Values and Industrial Relations: A Study of Fairness and Inequality*. Oxford: Blackwell, 1975.

International Benefits Information Service. *Special Notes*. Chicago: Charles D. Spencer & Associates, October 1981.

International Labour Office. *Introduction to Social Security*. Geneva: International Labour Office, 1984.

—. *Financing Social Security: The Options*. Geneva: International Labour Office, 1984.

International Social Security Association. *Methods of Financing Social Security*. Studies and Research Report No. 15. Geneva: International Social Security Association, 1979.

Kassalow, E.M., ed. *The Role of Social Security in Economic Development*. U.S. Department of Health, Education, and Welfare, Research Report No. 27. Washington, D.C.: Government Printing Office, 1968.

Keynes, John Maynard. *The General Theory of Employment Interest and Money*. London: Macmillan, 1967.

Lange, Oskar. *On the Economic Theory of Socialism*. 3rd ed. New York: McGraw Hill, 1966.

Lasch, Christopher. *The Culture of Narcissism*. New York: Norton, 1979.

Laslett, Peter. "The History of Ageing and the Aged." In *An Ageing Population*. Eds. Vita Carver and Penny Liddiard. Suffolk: Hodder and Stoughton, 1978, pp. 6–13.

— ."Societal Development and Aging." In *Handbook of Aging and the Social Sciences*. Eds. Robert H. Binstock and Ethel Shanas. New York: Van Nostrand Reinhold, 1976, pp. 87–116.

Latimer, M. W. *Industrial Pension Systems in the United States and Canada*. 2 vols. New York: Industrial Relations Counselors, 1932.

Lawson, Roger, and Bruce Reed. *Social Security in the European Community*. London: Chatham House, 1975.

Lenin, V. I. "Five Years of the Russian Revolution and the Prospects of the World Revolution." Report Delivered at the Fourth Congress of the Communist International, 13 November 1922. *Selected Works*. 45 vols. Moscow: Foreign Languages Publishing House, 1961, pp. 762–81.

—. *Imperialism, The Highest State of Capitalism*. Moscow: Foreign Languages Publishing House, n.d. First Published 1917.

—. "Our Programme." *Selected Works*. London: Lawrence and Wishart, 1968, pp. 33–36.

Luxemburg, Rosa. "Social Reform or Revolution." In *Selected Political Writings of Rosa Luxemburg*. Ed. Dick Howard. New York: Monthly Review Press, 1971, pp. 52–134.

Mandel, Ernest. *Late Capitalism*. London: Verso, 1978.

Marshall, T. H. "The Welfare State—A Comparative Study." *Sociology at the Cross-roads*. London: Heinemann, 1963, pp. 289–308.

Marx, Karl. *Capital*. Vol.1. New York: Modern Library, n.d. First published 1867.

—. *Capital*. Vol. 3. Moscow: Progress, 1978. First published 1894.

—. *The Class Struggles in France*. Introduction by Frederick Engels. Moscow: Progress, 1972. First published 1895.

—. *A Contribution to the Critique of Political Economy*. Moscow: Progress, 1970. First published 1859.

—. "The Eighteenth Brumaire of Louis Bonaparte." In *Selected Works*. London: Lawrence and Wishart, 1968, pp. 96–166. First published 1852.

—, and Frederick Engels. *The Communist Manifesto*. New York: Washington Square Press, 1964. First published 1848.

—. *The German Ideology*. New York: International Publishers, 1968. First published 1932.

Meak, Ronald L., ed. *Marx and Engels on the Population Bomb*. 2nd ed. Berkeley: Ramparts Press, 1971.

Meidner, Rudolf. *Employee Investment Funds: An Approach to Collective Capital Formation*. London: Allen and Unwin, 1978.

Menshikov, S. *Millionaires and Managers*. Moscow: Progress, 1969.

Mercer, William M., International. *International Benefit Guidelines 1981*. New York: William M. Mercer, March 1981.

Miliband, Ralph. "Lenin's *The State and Revolution*." In *The Socialist Register 1970*. Eds. Ralph Miliband and John Saville. London: Merlin Press, 1970, pp. 309–19.

—. "Marx and The State." In *The Socialist Register 1965*. Eds. Ralph Miliband and John Saville. London: Merlin Press, 1965, pp. 278–296.

—. *Marxism and Politics*. Toronto: Oxford University Press, 1977.

—. *The State in Capitalist Society*. London: Weidenfeld and Nicolson, 1972.

Mills, C. Wright. *The Sociological Imagination*. New York: Oxford University Press, 1959.

Moore, Stanley. *Three Tactics: The Background in Marx*. New York: Monthly Review Press, 1963.

McKersie, Robert B., and Richard E. Walton. *A Behavioral Theory of Labor Negotiations*. New York: McGraw-Hill, 1965.

O'Connor, James. *The Fiscal Crisis of the State*. New York: St. Martin's Press, 1973.

Offe, Claus. "The Theory of the Capitalist State and the Problem of Policy Formation." In *Stress and Contradiction in Modern Capitalism: Public Policy and the Theory of the State*. Eds. Leon N. Lindberg et al. Toronto and London: Heath, 1975, pp. 125–44.

Parry, Noel, Michael Rustin, and Carole Satyamurti. *Social Work, Welfare and the State*. London: Arnold, 1979.

Piven, Frances Fox, and Richard Cloward. *Regulating the Poor*. New York: Pantheon, 1971.

Poulantzas, Nicos. *Political Power and Social Classes*. Trans. Timmy O'Hagan. London: New Left Books, 1973.

Pryor, Frederic L. *Public Expenditures in Communist and Capitalist Nations*. Nobleton, Ont.: Irwin-Dorsey, 1968.

Renner, Karl. *The Institutions of Private Law*. Trans. Agnes Schwarzschild. London and Boston: Routledge and Kegan Paul, 1976. First published 1904.

—. *Wandlugen Der Modernen Gesellschaft*. New York: Arno Press, 1975. (*The Transformation of Modern Society.*) First published 1924.

Rimlinger, Gaston V. *Welfare Policy and Industrialization in Europe, America and Russia*. New York: Wiley, 1971.

Ryan, William. *Blaming the Victim*. Rev. ed. New York: Random House, 1976.

Schulz, James H. et al. *Providing Adequate Retirement Income—Pension Reform in the United States and Abroad.* Hanover, NH: Brandeis University Press, 1974.

Sclar, Elliot. "Aging and Economic Development." In *Public Policies for an Aging Population.* Eds. Elizabeth W. Markson and Gretchen R. Batra. Toronto: Heath, 1980, pp. 29–38.

Scott, John. *Corporations, Classes and Capitalism.* London: Hutchinson, 1979.

Seward, Shirley B., ed. *The Future of Social Welfare Systems in Canada and the United Kingdom.* Halifax: Institute for Research on Public Policy, 1987.

Simmel, Georg. *Conflict.* Glencoe, IL: Free Press, 1955.

Simmons, Leo W. *The Role of the Aged in Primitive Society.* New York: Archon Books, 1970.

Stearns, Peter N. *Old Age in European Society.* New York: Holmes and Meier, 1976.

Stein, Bruno, *Work and Welfare in Britain and the USA.* New York: Wiley, 1976.

Streib, Gordon F. "Social Stratification and Aging." In *Handbook of Aging and the Social Sciences.* Eds. Robert H. Binstock and Ethel Shanas. London: Van Nostrand Reinhold, 1976, pp. 160–88.

Sweezy, Paul M. "Has Capitalism Changed?" In *Has Capitalism Changed?* Ed. Shigeto Tsuru. Tokyo: Iwanami Shoten, 1961, pp. 83–91.

—. *The Theory of Capitalist Development.* New York: Monthly Review Press, 1964.

Tannenbaum, Arnold S. "Unions." In *Handbook of Oranizations.* Ed. James G. March. Chicago: Rand McNally, 1964, pp. 710–63.

Thompson, E. P. "The Peculiarities of the English." In *The Socialist Register 1965.* Eds. Ralph Miliband and John Saville. New York: Monthly Review Press, 1965, pp. 311–62.

Tsuru, Shigeto. "Has Capitalism Changed?" In *Has Capitalism Changed?* Ed. Shigeto Tsuru. Tokyo: Iwanami Shoten Publishers, 1961, pp. 1–66.

van de Vall, Mark. *Labor Organizations: A Macro- and Micro-Sociological Analysis on a Comparative Basis.* London: Cambridge University Press, 1970.

Wander, Hilde. "ZPG Now: The Lessons from Europe." In *The Economic Consequences of Slowing Population Growth.* Eds. Thomas Espenshade and William Serow. New York: Academic Press, 1978, pp. 41–69.

Wedderburn, Dorothy. "Facts and Theories of The Welfare State." In *The Socialist Register 1965.* Eds. Ralph Miliband and John Saville. London: Merlin Press, 1965, pp. 127–145.

Wilensky, Harold L. *The Welfare State and Equality: Structural and Ideological Roots of Public Expenditures.* Berkeley and Los Angeles: University of California Press, 1975.

Wilensky, Harold L., and Charles N. Lebeaux, *Industrial Society and Social Welfare.* New York: Free Press, 1965.

Wilson, T., ed. *Pensions, Inflation and Growth: A Comparative Study of the Elderly in the Welfare State.* London: Heinemann, 1974.

Articles

Achenbaum, W. Andrew, and Peter N. Stearns. "Old Age and Modernization." *Gerontologist* 18 (June 1978): 307–13.

Aldrich, Jonathan. "The Earnings Replacement Rate in 12 Countries, 1969–1980." *Social Security Bulletin* 45 (1982): 3–11.

Asimakopulos, A., and J. C. Weldon. "On Private Plans in the Theory of Pensions." *Canadian Journal of Economics* 3 (1970): 223–37.

—. "On the Theory of Government Pension Plans." *Canadian Journal of Economics,* 2 (1968): 699–717.

Barbash, Jack. "The Elements of Industrial Relations." *British Journal of Industrial Relations* 2 (March 1964): 66–78.

Becker, G. S. "Investment in Human Capital: A Theoretical Analysis." *Journal of Political Economy* 70, Supplement (October 1962): 9–49.

Boye, S. "The Cost of Social Security, 1960–71: Some National Economic Aspects". *International Labour Review* 115 (1977): 305–25.

Burns, Eveline M. "Social Insurance in Evolution." *American Economic Review* 34, Supplement, pt. 2 (March 1944): p 199–211.

Clark, Robert, Juanita Kreps, and Joseph Spengler. "Economics of Aging: A Survey." *Journal of Economic Literature* 16 (1978): 919–62

Cockburn, Christine. "The Role of Social Security in Development." *International Social Security Review* 33 (1980): 337–58.

Cowgill, Donald O. "The Aging of Populations and Societies." *Annals of the American Academy of Political and Social Science* 415 (1974): 1–18

Cutright, Philip. "Political Structure, Economic Development and National Social Security Programs." *American Journal of Sociology* 70 (1965): 537–50.

Davis, Kingsley, and Pietronella van den Oever. "Age Relations and Public Policy in Advanced Industrial Societies." *Population and Development Review* 7 (March 1981), pp. 1–18.

Fisher, Paul. "The Social Security Crisis: An International Dilemma." *International Social Security Review* 31 (1978): 383–96.

—. "Social Security and Development Planning: Some Issues." *Social Security Bulletin* 30 (June 1967): 13–25.

Gold, David A., Clarence Y. H. Lo, and Erik Olin Wright. "Recent Developments in Marxist Theories of the Capitalist State." *Monthly Review* 27 (October and November 1975): 29–43, 36–51.

Gourja, Mohamed. "The Contribution of Social Security to Development Objectives: The Role of Income Support Measures." *International Social Security Review* 34 (1981): 131–50.

Gutchess, Jocelyn F. "Pension Investment: The European Model." *AFL-CIO American Federationist* 87, no 6 (1980): 11–16.

Haanes-Olsen, Leif. "Earnings-Replacement Rate of Old Age Benefits, 1965–75, Selected Countries." *Social Security Bulletin* 44 (1978): 3–14.

Horlick, Max. "The Relationship between Public and Private Pension Schemes: An Introductory Overview." *Social Security Bulletin* 50 (1987): 15–24.

Jessop, Bob. "Recent Theories of the Capitalist State." *Cambridge Journal of Economics* 1 (1977): 353–73.

Lukianenko, S. "Financing and Administration of Social Security in Socialist Countries." *International Social Security Review* 31 (1978): 419–38.

Marshall, Victor W., and Joseph A. Tindale, "Notes for a Radical Gerontology." *International Journal of Aging and Human Development,* 9 (1978–79): 163–75.

Mishra, Ramesh. "Marx and Welfare." *Sociological Review* 23 (1975): 287–313.

Offe, Claus. "Advanced Capitalism and the Welfare State." *Politics and Society* 2 (1972): 479–488.

Paillat, P. "Europe Is Aging: Causes, Aspects and Repercussions of Demographic Aging." *International Social Security Review* 29, no. 2 (1976): 2–12.

Palmore, Erdman B., and Kenneth Manton. "Ageism Compared to Racism and Sexism." *Journal of Gerontology* 28 (1973): 363–69.

"Round Table Meeting on 'The Role of Social Security in Development.' " *International Social Security Review* 34 (1981): 112–21.

Sanderson, George, and Paul Malles. "Profit-Sharing and Employee Investment Funds." *Labour Gazette* (May 1978), pp. 183–88.

Seccombe, Wally. "Marxism and Demography." 137 *New Left Review* (January–February 1983): 22–47.

Stearns, Peter N. "Aging in the Working Class: An Exploratory Essay," *Newsletter—European Labor and Working Class History,* 8 (November 1975): 20–28.

Tracy, Martin B. "Maintaining Value of Social Security Benefits during Inflation: Foreign Experience." *Social Security Bulletin* 39 (November 1976): 33–42.

Williams, Gwyn A. "The Concept of 'Egemonia' in the Thought of Antonio Gramsci: Some Notes on Interpretation." *Journal of the History of Ideas* 21 (1960): 586–99.

Canada

Books

Armitage, Andrew. *Social Welfare in Canada: Ideals and Realities.* Toronto: McClelland and Stewart, 1975.

Babcock, Robert H. *Gompers in Canada: A Study in American Continentalism before the First World War.* Toronto: University of Toronto Press, 1974.

Banting, Keith G. *The Welfare State and Canadian Federalism.* Kingston and Montreal: McGill-Queen's University Press, 1982.

Baum, Daniel Jay. *The Final Plateau.* Toronto: Burns and MacEachern, 1976.

—. *The Investment Function of Canadian Financial Institutions.* New York, Washington and London: Praeger, 1973.

Baum, Daniel, and Ned Stiles. *The Silent Partners: Institutional Investors and Corporate Control.* Syracuse: Syracuse University Press, 1965.

Benson, Winslow. *Business Methods of Canadian Trust Companies.* Rev. ed. Toronto: Ryerson, 1962.

Brown, Joan C. *How Much Choice? Retirement Policies in Canada.* Ottawa: Canadian Council on Social Development, 1975.

Bryden, Kenneth. *Old Age Pensions and Policy-Making in Canada.* Montreal and London: McGill-Queen's University Press, 1974.

Calvert, Geoffrey N. *Pensions and Survival: The Coming Crisis of Money and Retirement.* Toronto: A Financial Post Book, Maclean-Hunter, 1977.

Canadian Centre for Policy Alternatives. *Pensions: Public Solutions vs. Private Interest.* Proceedings of the CCPA Conference on Pensions. Ottawa: CCPA, 1982.

Clement, Wallace. *The Canadian Corporate Elite: An Analysis of Economic Power.* Toronto: McClelland and Stewart, 1975.

Collins, Kevin. "The Canadian Pension Plan as a Source of Provincial Capital Funds." In *How Much Choice? Retirement Policies in Canada.* Ottawa: Canadian Council on Social Development, 1975, appendix, pp. 244–56.

Copp, Terry. *The Anatomy of Poverty: The Condition of the Working Class in Montreal 1897–1929.* Toronto: McClelland and Stewart, 1974.

Deaton, Richard. "The Fiscal Crisis of the State in Canada." In *The Political Economy of the State.* Ed. Dimitrios I. Roussopoulos. Montreal: Black Rose, 1973, pp. 18–58.

—. "The Political Economy of Pensions: The Political and Economic Framework of the Canadian Pension System." *Pensions: Public Solutions vs. Private Interest.* Proceedings of the CCPA Conference on Pensions. Ottawa: CCPA, 1982, pp. 57–106.

Denton, Frank T., Melvin L. Kliman, and Byron G. Spencer. *Pensions and the Economic Security of the Elderly.* Montreal: C. D. Howe Institute, 1981.

Donner, Arthur W. *Financing the Future: Canada's Capital Markets in the Eighties.* Toronto: Lorimer, 1982.

Ezra, D. Don. *The Struggle for Pension Fund Wealth.* Toronto: Pagurian, 1983.

Foot, David K. *Canada's Population Outlook: Demographic Futures and Economic Challenges.* Ottawa: Canadian Institute for Economic Policy, 1982.

Fournier, Pierre. *The Quebec Establishment.* Montreal: Black Rose, 1976.

Garland, Robert E. "The Politics of Aging." In *The Aged in Society.* Social Science Monograph Series, vol. 3. Saint John, N.B.: University of New Brunswick at Saint John, Spring 1979, pp. 25–39.

Goffman, Irving J. "Canadian Social Welfare Policy." In *Contemporary Canada.* Ed. Richard H. Leach. Toronto: University of Toronto Press, 1968, pp. 191–224.

Granatstein, J. L. *Canada's War.* Toronto: Oxford University Press, 1975.

Granger, Alix. *Don't Bank on It.* Toronto and New York: Doubleday, 1981.

Grayson, L. M., and Michael Bliss, eds. *The Wretched of Canada: Letters to R. B. Bennett 1930–1935.* Toronto: University of Toronto Press, 1973.

Guest, Dennis. *The Emergence of Social Security in Canada.* Vancouver: University of British Columbia Press, 1980.

Henripin, Jacques, and Y. Péron. "The Demographic Transition of the Province of Quebec." In *Population and Social Change.* Eds. D. V. Glass and Roger Revelle. London: Arnold, 1972, pp. 213–32.

Herman, Kathleen. "The Emerging Welfare State: Changing Perspectives in Canadian Welfare Policies and Programs." In *Social Space: Canadian Perspectives.* Eds. D. I. Davies and Kathleen Herman: Toronto: New Press, 1971, pp. 131–41.

Johnson, Leo. "The Development of Class in Canada in the Twentieth Century." In *Capitalism and the National Question in Canada.* Ed. Gary Teeple. Toronto: University of Toronto Press, 1972, pp. 142–83.

Kalbach, Warren E. *The Demographic Bases of Canadian Society.* Toronto: McGraw-Hill, 1972.

Katz, Michael B. "Social Structure in Hamilton, Ontario." In *Nineteenth-Century cities—Essays in the New Urban History.* Eds. Stephen Thernstrom and Richard Sennett. New Haven: Yale University Press, 1969, pp. 209–44.

Kettle, John. *The Big Generation.* Toronto: McClelland and Stewart, 1980.

LaMarsh, Judy. *Memoirs of a Bird in a Gilded Cage.* Toronto: McClelland and Stewart, 1969.

Liljefors, A. Kristina. "Canada's Retirement Income System and Recent Economic Developments: A Discussion Paper." In *Pensions and Inflation.* Geneva: International Labour Office, 1977, pp. 119–28.

Logan, H. A. *Trade Unions in Canada.* Toronto: Macmillan, 1948.

Marshall, Victor W., ed. *Aging in Canada.* Don Mills: Fitzhenry and Whiteside, 1980.

McInnes, R. W. *Welfare Legislation and Benefit Plans in Canada.* Toronto: Law Society of Upper Canada, 1974.

McNaught, Kenneth, and David J. Bercuson. *The Winnipeg Strike: 1919.* Don Mills: Longman Canada, 1974.

National Council of Welfare. *Sixty-five and older.* Ottawa: National Council of Welfare, February, 1984.

Neufeld, E. P. *The Financial System of Canada: Its Growth and Development.* Toronto: Macmillan, 1972.

Newman, Peter C. *The Canadian Establishment.* 2 vols. Rev. ed. Toronto: McClelland and Stewart-Bantam, 1979.

Novak, Mark. *Successful Aging: The Myths, Realities and Future of Aging in Canada.* Markham: Penguin, 1985.

Olsen, Dennis. *The State Elite.* Toronto: McClelland and Stewart, 1980.

Penning, M., and P. Krishman. *The Social Implications of the Canadian Population: Some Strategies and Solutions.* University of Alberta, Department of Sociology, Discussion Paper No. 22. Edmonton: November 1980.

Pesando, James E. *The Impact of Inflation on Financial Markets in Canada.* Montreal: C. D. Howe Research Institute, February 1977.

Pesando, J. E., and S. A. Rea, Jr. *Public and Private Pensions in Canada: An Economic Analysis.* Toronto: Ontario Economic Council, 1977.

Piva, Michael J. *The Condition of the Working Class in Toronto—1900–1921.* Ottawa: University of Ottawa Press, 1979.

Porter, John. *The Vertical Mosaic.* Toronto: University of Toronto Press, 1965.

Queen's University, Industrial Relations Section, School of Commerce and Administration. *Industrial Retirement Plans in Canada.* Bulletin No. 1. Kingston, Ont: Queen's University, School of Commerce and Administration, 1938.

Rhodes, Gerald. *Public Sector Pensions.* Toronto: University of Toronto Press, 1965.

Richards, John, and Larry Pratt. *Prarie Capitalism: Power and Influence in the New West.* Toronto: McClelland and Stewart, 1979.

Ridler, Neil B. "Will Canada Be Able to Support Its Elderly?" In *The Aged in Society.*

Social Science Monograph Series, vol. 3. Saint John, N.B.: University of New Brunswick at Saint John, Spring 1979, pp. 6–16.

Samur, G. E., W. D. Jarvis, and M. C. McCracken. *Analysis of The Recent Behaviour of the Personal Savings Rate.* Ottawa: Infometrica, February 1979.

Shaw, David, and Ross T. Archibald. *The Management of Change in the Canadian Securities Industry.* 8 vols. Toronto: Toronto Stock Exchange, 1972.

Simeon, Richard. *Federal-Provincial Diplomacy: The Making of Recent Policy in Canada.* Toronto: University of Toronto Press, 1972.

Smiley, Donald V. *Canada in Question: Federalism in the Seventies.* 2nd ed. Toronto and Montreal: McGraw-Hill Ryerson, 1976.

Splane, Richard B. *Social Welfare in Ontario, 1791–1893: A Study of Public Welfare Administration.* Toronto: University of Toronto Press, 1965.

Stewart, Walter. *Towers of Gold: Feet of Clay—The Canadian Banks.* Toronto: Totem, 1983.

Stone, Leroy O., and Claude Mareau. *Canadian Population Trends and Public Policy through the 1980's.* Montreal: McGill-Queen's University Press, 1978.

Stone, L. O., and S. Fletcher. *A Profile of Canada's Older Population.* Montreal: Institute on Public Policy, 1980.

Toronto Stock Exchange. *Canadian Shareholders: Their Profile and Attitudes.* Toronto: Stock Exchange, 1986.

Urquhart, M. C., and K. A. Buckley, eds. *Historical Statistics of Canada.* Toronto: Macmillan, 1965.

Van Loon, Richard J., and Michael S. Whittington. *The Canadian Political System: Environment, Structure and Process.* 2nd ed. Toronto: McGraw-Hill Ryerson, 1976.

Articles

Ascah, Louis. "Evolution and Assessment of Reform Proposals for Pension Plans." A paper prepared for the Conference of the Canadian Association on Gerontology, Quebec City, 5 November 1986.

—. "Recent Pension Reports in Canada: A Survey." *Canadian Public Policy* 10 (1984): 416–28.

Astimakopulos, A. "Financing Canada's Public Pensions—Who Pays." *Canadian Public Policy* 10 (1984): 156–66.

Barnes, Leslie. "The True Cost of Pension Indexing." *Civil Service Review* 50, no. 3 (1977): 14–18.

Barrett, Charles A. "Why Are Canadians Saving So Much?" *Canadian Business Review* (Summer 1978): 5–8.

"C.P.R. and Its Pension Fund." *Labor Facts* 16 (March 1965): 1, 10–14.

Caron, Robert. "History and Evolution of Private Pension Plans in Canada and Quebec." *Pension Plans in Quebec* 7 (December 1980): xiii–xix.

Coward Laurence E., and J. M. Nicholas Simmons. "The Influence of Government on Pension Planning in Canada—A Study of Recent History and Trends." *Employee Benefits Journal* 4, no. 4 (1979): 2–7, 23.

Davies, J. B. "On the Size of Distribution of Wealth In Canada." *Review of Income and Wealth* 25 (1979): 237–59.

Deaton, Richard. "Election '84: It's No Contest." *The Facts* 6 (August–September 1984): 4–8.

—. *The Economic Position of the Current Elderly: Retirement Income as a Barrier to Independent Living.* A report prepared for the National Advisory Council on Aging. Ottawa: NACA, April 1988.

Denton, Frank T., and Byron G. Spencer. "Some Economic and Demographic Implications of Future Population Change." *Journal of Canadian Studies* 14 (1979): 81–93.

Drummond, Ian M. "Canadian Life Insurance Companies and the Capital Market, 1890–1914." *Canadian Journal of Economics and Political Science* 28 (1962): 204–24.

Feaver, George. "The Webbs in Canada: Fabian Pilgrims on the Canadian Frontier." *Canadian Historical Review* 58 (1977): 263–76.

Fellegi, Ivan P. "Can We Afford an Aging Society?" *Canadian Economic Observer* (October 1988): 4.1–4.34.

Fingard, Judith. "The Winter's Tale: The Seasonal Contours of Pre-industrial Poverty in British North America, 1815–1860." In *Historical Papers*. Canadian Historical Association (1974): 65–94.

Finn, Ed. "The Case for Co-Management of Employee Pension Funds." *Labour Gazette* 6 (1973): 356–65.

—. "Pension Power: Using Pensions to Retire a Union Weakness." *The Facts* 1 (February–March 1979): 147–50.

Gagan, David, and Herbert Mays, "Historical Demography and Canadian Social History: Families and Land in Peel County, Ontario." *Canadian Historical Review* 54 (1973): 27–47.

Geehan, Randall. "The Life Insurance Industry in Canada, 1961 to 1979." *Canadian Statistical Review* 56 (July 1981): vi–x.

"Growth and Change in the Financial System—Some Evidence from the National Balance Sheet Accounts, 1961–1984." *Canadian Statistical Review* 60 (October 1985): pp. vii–xv.

Hareven, Tamara K. "An Ambiguous Alliance: Some Aspects of American Influences on Canadian Social Welfare." *Histoire sociale/Social History* 2 (1969): 82–98.

Hood, W. C., and O. W. Main. "The Role of the Canadian Life Insurance Companies in the Post-War Capital Market." *Canadian Journal of Economics and Political Science* 22 (1956): 468–80.

Irving, Allan. "Canadian Fabians: The Work and Thought of Harry Cassidy and Leonard Marsh, 1930–1945." *Canadian Journal of Social Work Education* 7 (1981): 7–28.

Jain, Harish C., and Edward P. Janzen. "Employee Pay and Benefit Preferences." *Industrial Relations Industrielles* 29 (1974): 99–110.

Katz, Michael B. "The People of a Canadian City: 1851–1852." *Canadian Historical Review* 53 (1972): 402–26.

Kwavnick, David. "Labour's Lobby in Ottawa: How the Canadian Labour Congress Influences Government Policy." *Labour Gazette* 73 (July 1973): 13–20.

Lindsay, Colin, and Shelley Donald. "Income of Canada's Seniors." *Canadian Social Trends* 10 (Autumn 1988): 20–25.

Messinger, Hans, Frank Fedyk and Allen Zeesman. *The Poverty Gap in Canada.* A paper presented to the Economic Council of Canada Seminar, 26 November 1987.

Munro, John. "Pensions for Canadian Workers." *Labour Gazette* 77 (1977): 453–56.

McCrossan, W. Paul. "Pension Reform in Canada." *Employee Benefits Journal* 6, no. 3 (1981): 24–25, 31.

Ross, Val. "The Coming Old-Age Crisis." *Maclean's*, 17 January 1983, pp. 24–29.

Scheinberg, Stephen. "Invitation to Empire: Tariffs and American Expansion in Canada." *Business History Review* 47 (1973): 218–238.

Swindinsky, Robert. "The Economics of Employee Benefits." *Industrial Relations Industrielles* 26(1972): 907–21.

Wallace, Elizabeth. "Old Age Security in Canada: Changing Attitudes." *Canadian Journal of Economics and Political Science* 18 (1952): 125–34.

—. "The Origin of the Social Welfare State in Canada, 1867–1900." *Canadian Journal of Economics and Political Science* 16 (1950): 389–93.

Weitz, H. "Old Age Security in Canada." *Canadian Statistical Review* 42 no. 2 (1967): i–v.

Wente, Margaret. "The Fund Managers." *Canadian Business* (March 1980): 34–39.

—. "The New Power of the Pension Funds." *Canadian Business* (March 1980): 33, 40–41, 88–92, 95–96.

BRITAIN

Books

Aaronovitch, S. *Monopoly: A Study of British Monopoly Capitalism.* London: Lawrence and Wishart, 1955.

—. *The Ruling Class.* London: Lawrence and Wishart, 1961.

Abel-Smith, B., and P. Townsend. *The Poor and the Poorest.* London: Bell, 1965.

Atkinson, A. B. *Poverty in Britain and the Reform of Social Security.* London: Cambridge University Press, 1969.

Blythe, Ronald. *The View in Winter: Reflections on Old Age.* Markham, Ont.: Penguin, 1980.

Booth, Charles. *Old Age Pensions and the Aged Poor: A Proposal.* London: Macmillan, 1899.

—. *A Picture, and the Endowment of Old Age, an Argument.* London: Macmillan, 1892.

Bosanquet, Nicholas. *A Future for Old Age.* London: Maurice Temple Smith, 1978.

—. *New Deal for the Elderly.* London: Fabian Society, July 1975.

Braithwaite, W. J. *Lloyd George's Ambulance Wagon: The Memoirs of W. J. Braithwaite.* London: Metheun, 1957.

Branson, Noreen, and Margret Hinemann. *Britain in the Nineteen Thirties.* Frogmore: Panther Books, 1973.

Briston, Richard J., and Richard Dobbins. *The Growth and Impact of Institutional Investors.* A Report to the Research Committee of the Institute of Chartered Accountants in England and Wales. London: Institute of Chartered Accountants in England and Wales, 1978.

Brown, Michael Barratt. "The Welfare State in Britain." In *The Socialist Register 1971.* Eds. Ralph Miliband and John Saville. London: Merlin Press, 1971, pp. 185–224.

Bruce, Maurice. *The Coming of the Welfare State.* London: Batsford, 1979.

Clegg, H. A. *The Changing System of Industrial Relations in Great Britain.* Oxford: Blackwell, 1979.

—. *Trade Unionism under Collective Bargaining.* Oxford: Blackwell, 1978.

Coakley, Jerry, and Laurence Harris. *The City of Capital.* Oxford: Blackwell, 1983.

Crossick, Geoffrey. *An Artisan Elite in Victorian Society.* London: Croom-Helm, 1978.

Crossman, Richard. *The Diaries of a Cabinet Minister, Volume Three. Secretary of State for Social Services 1968–70.* London: Hamish Hamilton, 1977.

Department of Health and Social Security. *Low Income Families—1983.* n.p.: n.p., July 1986.

Dodds, J. C. *The Investment Behaviour of British Life Insurance Companies.* London: Croom-Helm, 1979.

Ensor, R. C. K. *The Oxford History of England, 14, England 1870–1914.* Toronto: Oxford University Press, 1941.

Ferris, Paul. *The City.* Harmondsworth: Pelican, 1960.

Flanders, Allan. *Trade Unions.* 4th ed. London: Hutchison University Library, 1963.

General and Municipal Workers' Union. *GMWU Guide for Membership Representatives Involved in the Running of Pension Schemes.* Surrey: GMWU, 1978.

Gilbert, Bentley B. *British Social Policy 1914–1939.* London: Batsford, 1973.

—. *Evolution of National Insurance in Great Britain: The Origins of the Welfare State.* London: Michael Joseph, 1966.

Gilling-Smith, G. D. *The Complete Guide to Pensions and Superannuation.* Harmondsworth: Penguin, 1968.

—. *The Manager's Guide to Pensions.* London: Institute of Personnel Management, 1974.

Gosden, P. H. J. H. *The Friendly Societies in England, 1815–1875.*Manchester: Manchester University Press, 1961.

Green, Francis. *The Increase in Aggregate U.K. Pension Savings.* Kingston Polytechnic, School of Economics and Politics, Discussion Paper in Political Economy No. 28. Kingston upon Thames: Kingston Polytechnic, School of Economics and Politics, 1980.

Harrison, Royden. "The British Labour Movement and the International in 1864." In *The Socialist Register 1964.* Eds. Ralph Miliband and John Saville. London: Merlin Press, 1971, pp. 293–308.

Hay, J. R., ed. *The Development of the British Welfare State, 1880–1975.* London: Arnold, 1978.

—. *The Origins of the Liberal Welfare Reforms, 1906–1914.* London: Macmillan, 1977.

Howell, George. *Trade Unions New and Old.* Ed. F. M. Levanthal. 4th ed. n.p.: Redwood Press, 1973. First published 1891.

Hughes, John. *Funds for Investment.* London: Fabian Society, March 1976.

Incomes Data Services Ltd. *Guide to Pension Schemes.* London: IDS, 1980.

—. *Occupational Pensions 1978.* Study 182. London: IDS, November 1978.

—. *Public Sector Pensions.* Study 188. London: IDS, February 1979.

James, Carl. *Occupational Pensions: The Failure of Private Welfare.* Fabian Tract 497. London: Fabian Society, 1984.

Johnston, E. A. "The Effects of Inflation and Currency Instability on Pension Schemes in the United Kingdom." In *Pensions and Inflation.* Geneva: International Labour Office, 1977, pp. 95–106.

Kincaid, J. C. *Poverty and Equality in Britain: A Study of Social Security and Taxation.* Rev. ed. Harmondsworth: Penguin, 1975.

Kitson, Roger, and Michael Pilch. *Pension Funds and The Economy.* n.p.: Lowndes Lambert Group, 1977.

Labour Research Department. *Guide to Company Pension Schemes and the Social Security Pensions Act 1975.* London: LRD Publications, 1977.

Longstreth, Frank. "The City, Industry and the State." In *State and Economy in Contemporary Capitalism.* Ed. Colin Crouch. London: Croom-Helm, 1979, pp. 157–90.

Lucas, Harry. *Pensions and Industrial Relations: A Practical Guide for All Involved in Pensions.* Toronto and Oxford: Pergamon, 1977.

Lucas, Harry, and Sue Ward. *Studies for Trade Unionists: Pensions Bargaining.* London: Workers' Educational Association, June 1977.

Minns, Richard. *Pension Funds and British Capitalism.* London: Heinemann Educational Books, 1980.

—. *Pension Funds and the Ownership of Shares in U.K. Companies.* Research Series 27. London: Centre for Environmental Studies, March 1979.

—. *Take Over the City: The Case for Public Ownership of Financial Institutions.* London: Pluto Press, 1982.

Mitchell, B. R., and P. Deane, eds. *Abstract of British Historical Statistics.* Cambridge: Cambridge University Press, 1968.

Moonman, Jane. *The Effectiveness of Fringe Benefits in Industry.* Epping Essex: Gower, 1973.

Moyle, J. *The Pattern of Ordinary Share Ownership, 1957–1971.* University of Cambridge, Department of Applied Economics, Occasional Paper 31. Cambridge: Cambridge University Press, 1971.

Pelling, Henry. *A History of British Trade Unionism.* Harmondsworth: Penguin, 1965.

Phillipson, Chris. *The Emergence of Retirement.* University of Durham, Department of Sociology, Working Papers in Sociology No. 14. n.p.: University of Durham, c. 1978.

Pilch, Michael, and Victor Wood. *New Trends in Pensions.* London: Hutchinson, 1964.

Prais, S. J. *The Evolution of Giant Firms in Britain: A Study of the Growth of Concentration in Manufacturing in Britain 1909–70*. Cambridge: Cambridge University Press, 1976.

Raphael, Marios. *Pensions and Public Servants: A Study of the Origins of the British System*. Paris: Mouton, 1964.

Raw, Charles. *Slater Walker*. London: André Deutsch, 1977.

Reddin, Mike. "Pensions: Cost and Portability." In *Social Security: The Real Agenda*. Fabian Society Tract No. 498. London: Fabian Society, 1984, pp. 11–14.

—. "Taxation and Pensions." In *Taxation and Social Policy*. Eds. C. Sandford, C. Pond, and R. Walker. London: Heinemann Educational Books, 1980, pp. 114–34.

Reid, G. L., and D. J. Robertson, eds. *Fringe Benefits, Labour Costs and Social Security*. London: Allen and Unwin, 1965.

Rowntree, B. S. *Poverty and Progress: A Second Social Survey of York*. London: Longmans, 1941.

—, and R. G. Lavers, *Poverty and the Welfare State*. London: Longmans, 1951.

Rubner, Alex. *Fringe Benefits: The Golden Chains*. London: Putnam, 1962.

Saville, J. "The Welfare State: An Historical Approach." In *Social Welfare in Modern Britain*. Eds. Eric Butterworth and Robert Holman. Glasgow: Fontana, 1975, pp. 57–70.

Shragge, Eric. *Pensions Policy in Great Britain*. London: Routledge and Kegan Paul, 1984.

Social Security: The Real Agenda. Fabian Society Tract No. 498. London: Fabian Society, 1984.

Speigelberg, R. *The City: Power without Accountability*. London: Blond and Briggs, 1973.

Stansworth, Philip, and Anthony Giddens, eds. *Elites and Power in British Society*. Cambridge: Cambridge University Press, 1974.

Stead, Herbert Francis. *How Old Age Pensions Began to Be*. London: Methuen, 1909.

Stevenson, J. *Social Conditions in Britain between the Wars*. Harmondsworth: Penguin, 1977.

Stone, R., J. Revell, and J. Moyle. *The Owners of Ordinary Quoted Shares*. London: Chapman and Hall, 1966.

Thane, Pat, ed. *The Origins of British Social Policy*. London: Croom-Helm, 1978.

Titmuss, Richard. "British Pension Plans—A Case Study." In *Social Policy*. Eds. Brian Abel-Smith and Kay Titmuss. London: Allen and Unwin, 1974, pp. 102–20.

—. "The Irresponsible Society." In *Essays on the Welfare State*. Boston: Beacon Press, 19969, pp. 215–44.

—. "Pension Systems and Population." In *Essays on the Welfare State*. Boston: Beacon Press, 1969, pp. 56–74.

Townsend, Peter. *The Family Life of Old People*. Harmondsworth: Penguin, 1977.

—. *Poverty in the United Kingdom: A Survey of Household Resources and Standard of Living*. Harmondsworth: Penquin, 1979.

Townsend, Peter, and Dorothy Wedderburn. *The Aged in the Welfare State*. London: Bell, 1965.

Trades Union Congress. *Occupational Pension Schemes—A TUC Guide*. London: Macdermott & Chart, 1976.

Ward, Sue. *Controlling Pension Schemes*. London: Workers' Educational Association, 1978.

—. *Pensions*. London: Pluto Press, 1981.

Webb, Sidney, and Beatrice Webb. *Industrial Democracy*. n.p.: Workers' Eductional Association, 1913.

Whitley, Richard. "The City and Industry: The Directors of Large Companies, Their Characteristics and Connections." In *Elites and Power in British Society*. Eds. Philip Stanworth and Anthony Giddens. Cambridge: Cambridge University Press, 1974, pp. 65–80.

Wrigley, E. A., ed. *An Introduction to English Historical Demography.* London: Weidenfeld and Nicolson, 1966.

Yeo, Stephen. "Working-Class Association, Private Capital, Welfare and the State in the late Nineteenth and Twentieth Centuries." In *Social Work, Welfare and the State.* Eds. Noel Parry, Michael Rustin, and Carole Satyamurti. Beverly Hills: Sage, 1980, pp. 48–71.

Articles

Altmann, Rosalind M. "An Analysis of Occupational Pensions in Great Britain." *Applied Economics* 14 (1982): 553–77.

"Background of Labour and Tory MPs." *Labour Research* 68 (July 1979): 156–58.

"Background of Tory Candidates." *Labour Research* 68 (May 1979): 98–99.

"Big Business and Politics: Political Donations In 1977." *Labour Research* 67 (September 1978): 190–93.

"Britain—A Handsome Package, but What Is Inside?" *Economist,* 8 June 1985, pp. 53–55.

"Britain's Welfare Future—Tinkering with Beveridge." *Economist,* 23 February 1985, pp. 49–52.

Burkitt, Brian. "Post-Keynesian Distribution Theory and Employee Investment Funds." *Economics Studies Quarterly* 34 (1983): 124–32.

Collins, Doreen. "The Introduction of Old Age Pensions in Great Britain." *Historical Journal* 8 (1965): 246–59.

Copeland, Lois S. "Consumer Price Indexes for the Elderly: British Experience." *Social Security Bulletin* 45 (January 1982): pp. 21–25.

Dawson, Andrew, and Graham Evans. "Pensioners' Incomes and Expenditures 1970–85." *Employment Gazette,* May 1987, pp. 243–52.

Dumbleton, Bob, and Bob Shutt. "Pensions: The Capitalist Trap." *New Society,* 7 September 1979, pp. 334–37.

Gilbert, Bentley B. "The British National Insurance Act of 1911 and the Commercial Insurance Lobby." *Journal of British Studies* 4 (1965): 127–48.

—. "The Decay of Nineteenth-Century Provident Institutions and the Coming of Old Age Pensions in Great Britain." *Economic History Review,* 2nd ser., 17 (1965): 551–63.

Green, Francis. "Occupational Pension Schemes in British Capitalism." *Cambridge Journal of Economics* 6 (1982): 267–84.

Hawkesworth, R. I. "Fringe Benefits in British Industry." *British Journal of Industrial Relations* 15 (1977): 396–402.

Hay, Roy. "Employers and Social Policy in Britain: The Evolution of Welfare Legislation, 1905–14." *Social History* 4 (1977): 434–55.

Johnson, Christopher. "Pensions—A Growth Industry." *Lloyds Bank Economic Bulletin* 19 (July 1980): 1–4.

"Living Below Their Means—Supplementary Benefits." *Labour Research* 67 (February 1978): 42–44.

Lydall, H. F., and Tipping, D. G. "The Distribution of Personal Wealth in Britain." In *Wealth, Income and Inequality.* Ed. A. B. Atkinson. Harmondsworth: Penguin Education, 1973, pp. 243–67.

Marwick, Arthur. "The Labour Party and the Welfare State in Britain, 1900–1948." *American Historical Review* 73 (1967): 380–403.

"MPs Interests: Capital vs. Labour." *Labour Research* 73 (June 1984): 150–52.

Murdock, Burt. "The New U.K. Social Security Scheme." *Pension World* 13 (June 1977): 45–46.

Odling-Smee, C. J. "Personal Savings Revisted: More Statistics, Fewer Facts." *Oxford Bulletin of Economics and Statistics* 35 (February 1973): 21–29.

"Pension Funds: What Are They, Who Controls Them?" *Labour Research* 67 (October 1978): 214–16.

"Pension Reforms—Pay More, Get Less." *Labour Research* 74 (July 1985): 178–80.

"Political Donations in 1978." *Labour Research* 68 (November 1979): 234–36.

"Poor to Pay More for the Poorest." *Labour Research* 74 (July 1985): 181–83.

Price, Robert, and George Sayers Bain. "Union Growth Revisted: 1948–1974 in Perspective." *British Journal of Industrial Relations* 14 (1976): 339–55.

"A Private Corporate State." *Economist*, 4 November 1978, pp. 11–15.

Redington, Frank Mitchell. "Address by the President to the Institute of Actuaries." *Journal of the Institute of Actuaries* (1959): 1–13.

Reid, G. L., and James Bates. "The Cost of Fringe Benefits for Manual Workers in British Industry." *British Journal of Industrial Relations*, 1 (1963): 348–69.

Thompson, G. "Relationship between the Financial and Industrial Sector of the United Kingdom Economy." *Economy and Society* 6 (1977): 235–83.

"Tory Funding Crisis." *Labour Research* 72 (September 1983): 225–27.

"Tory Funds: Political Donations in Election Year." *Labour Research* 73 (August 1984): pp. 204–7.

Trades Union Congress. *TUC Occupational Pensions Bulletin*, 10 November 1982.

Treble, James H. "The Attitudes of Friendly Societies towards the Movement in Great Britain for State Pensions, 1878–1908." *International Review of Social History*, 15 (1970): 266–299.

"£20 Billion of Pension Funds in Need of Regulation." *Economist*, 4 November 1978, pp. 109–13.

Walker, Alan. "Towards a Political Economy of Old Age." *Ageing and Society* 1 (March 1981): 73–94.

—. "The Social Creation of Poverty and Dependency in Old Age." *Journal of Social Policy* 9 (1980): 49–75.

Whitely, Richard. "Commonalities and Connections among Directors of Large Financial Institutions." *Sociological Review* 21 (1973): 613–32.

Young, A. F., and J. H. Smith. "Fringe Benefits—A Local Survey." *British Journal of Industrial Relations* 5 (1967): 63–73.

UNITED STATES

Books

Aaron, Benjamin. *Legal Status of Employee Benefit Rights under Private Pension Plans*. Homewood, IL: Irwin, 1961.

Achenbaum, W. Andrew. *Old Age in the New Land*. Baltimore and London: Johns Hopkins University Press, 1978.

Altmeyer, Arthur J. *The Formative Years of Social Security*. Madison: University of Wisconsin Press, 1966.

Allen, Donna. *Fringe Benefits: Wages or Social Obligations?* Ithaca: Cornell University Press, 1969.

American Federation of Labor. *Pension Plans under Collective Bargaining. A Reference Guide for Trade Unions*. Washington, D.C.: AFL, 1954.

American Federation of Labor and Congress of Industrial Organizations. *Investment of Union Pension Funds*. Washington, D.C.: AFL-CIO, c. 1980.

—. *Pensions: A Study of Benefit Fund Investment Policies*. Washington, D.C.: AFL-CIO, Industrial Union Department, 1980.

Bankers Trust. *The Pension Reform Act (an Explanation)*. Englewood Cliffs, NJ: Prentice-Hall, 1974.

Barbash, Jack. *The Practice of Unionism*. New York: Harper, 1956.

—. "Rationalization in the American Union." In *Essays in Industrial Relations Theory*. Ed. Gerald G. Somers. Ames: Iowa State University Press, 1969, pp. 147–62.

—. *The Structure and Evolution of Union Interests in Pensions*. University of Wisconsin, Industrial Relations Research Institute, Reprint Series No. 90. Madison: IRRI, 1967.

—. "The Unions and Negotiated Health and Welfare Plans," In *New Dimensions in Collective Bargaining*. Eds. Harold W. Davey, Howard S. Kaltenborn and Stanley H. Ruttenberg. New York: Harper, 1959, pp. 91–117.

Bird, Caroline. *The Invisible Scar*. New York: Pocket Books, 1967.

Bixby, Lenore E., and Virgina Reno. "Incidence of Second-Pension Rights." In *Reaching Retirement Age*. U.S. Department of Health, Education, and Welfare, Social Security Administration, Office of Research and Statistics, Research Report No. 47. Washington, D.C.: GPO, 1976, pp. 145–49.

Bleakney, Thomas P. *Retirement Systems for Public Employees*. Homewood, IL: Irwin, 1972.

Blodgett, Richard. *Conflicts of Interest: Union Pension Fund Asset Management*. New York: Twentieth Century Fund, 1977.

Boskin, Michael, ed. *The Crisis in Social Security: Problems and Prospects*. San Francisco: Institute for Contemporary Studies, 1977.

Brandes, Stuart D. *American Welfare Capitalism, 1880–1940*. London: University of Chicago Press, 1976.

Brody, David. "The Rise and Decline of Welfare Capitalism." In *Workers in Industrial America: Essays on the Twentieth Century Struggle*. Ed. David Brody. New York: Oxford University Press, 1980, pp. 48–81.

Budish, J. M. *People's Capitalism: Stock Ownership and Production*. New York: International Publishers, 1958.

Butler, Robert N. *Why Survive? Being Old in America*. New York: Harper and Row, 1975.

Calhoun, Richard B. *In Search of the New Old: Redefining Old Age in America, 1945–1970*. New York: Elsevier North Holland, 1978.

Clark, R., and J. S. Spengler. "Changing Demography and Dependency Costs: The Implications of New Dependency Ratios and Their Composition." In *Aging and Income: Programs and Prospects for the Elderly*. Ed. Barbara Herzog. New York: Human Science Press, 1978, pp. 55–89.

Commerce Clearing House. *1983 Social Security Benefits Including Medicare, January 1, 1983*. Chicago: CCH, 1982.

—. *1983, Social Security Explained*. Chicago: CCH, 1984.

Connant, Luther. *A Critical Analysis of Industrial Pension Systems*. New York: Macmillan, 1922.

Cumming, E., and W. E. Henry. *Growing Old*. New York: Basic Books, 1961.

Derthick, Martha. *Policymaking for Social Security*. Washington, D.C.: Brookings Institution, 1979.

Domhoff, William G. *The Higher Circles: The Governing Class in America*. New York: Random House, 1970.

—. *Who Rules America?* Englewood Cliffs, NJ: Prentice-Hall, 1967.

Drucker, Peter. *The Unseen Revolution: How Pension Fund Socialism Came to America*. New York: Harper and Row, 1976.

Fine, Sidney. *Laissez Faire and the General-Welfare State*. Ann Arbor: University of Michigan Press, 1956.

Fischer, David Hackett. *Growing Old in America*. Expanded ed. Oxford: Oxford University Press, 1978.

Fox, Alan. "Income of New Beneficiaries by Age at Entitlement to Benefit." In *Reaching Retirement Age*. U.S. Department of Health, Education, and Welfare, Social Security Administration, Office of Research and Statistics, Research Report No. 47. Washington, D.C.: GPO, 1976, pp. 121–144.

Garbarino, Joseph W. *Health Plans and Collective Bargaining*. Berkeley and Los Angeles: University of California Press, 1960.

Goldsmith, Raymond W. *Institutional Investors and Corporate Stock—A Background Study*. New York and London: National Bureau of Economic Research, 1973.

—. *The Share of Financial Intermediaries in National Wealth and National Assets, 1900–1949*. New York: n.p., 1954.

Graebner, William. *A History of Retirement*. New Haven: Yale University Press, 1980.

Green, Mark R. *The Role of Employee Benefit Structures in Manufacturing Industry*. Eugene: University of Oregon Press, 1964.

Greenough, William C., and Francis P. King. *Pensions Plans and Public Policy*. New York: Columbia University Press, 1976.

Gutman, Herbert. *Work, Culture and Society in Industrializing America: Essays in American Working-Class and Social History*. New York: Vintage Books, 1977.

Harbrecht, Paul, P., S.J. *Pension Funds and Economic Power*. New York: Twentieth Century Fund, 1959.

Harrington, Michael. *The Other America*. New York: Macmillan, 1964.

Herman, Edward S. *Conflicts of Interest: Commercial Bank Trust Departments*. New York: Twentieth Century Fund, 1975.

Holtzman, Abraham. *The Townsend Movement: A Political Study*. New York: Bookman Associates, 1963.

International Foundation of Employee Benefit Plans and the American Arbitration Association. "Employee Benefit Plan Claims Arbitration Rules." In *Two Dispute Resolution Services*. New York: American Arbitration Association, 1977.

Jones, Landon Y. *Great Expectations: America and the Baby Boom Generation*. New York: Ballantine, 1980.

Katz Olson, Laura. "Pension Power and the Public Sector." In *Crisis in the Public Sector*. A Reader by the Economics Education Project of the Union for Radical Political Economics. New York: Monthly Review Press, 1981, pp. 98–111.

—. *The Political Economy of Aging: The State, Private Power and Social Welfare*. New York: Columbia University Press, 1982.

Kelso, Robert W. *Poverty*. New York: Longmans, Green, 1929.

Kennedy, James B. *Beneficiary Features of American Trade Unions*. Studies in Historical and Political Science. Baltimore: Johns Hopkins University Press, 1908.

Kimball, Spencer L. *Insurance and Public Policy*. Madison: University of Wisconsin Press, 1960.

Kohlmeier, Louis M. *Conflicts of Interest: State and Local Pension Fund Asset Management*. New York: Twentieth Century Fund, 1976.

Kolko, Gabriel. *Wealth and Power in America: An Analysis of Social Class and Income Distribution*. New York: Praeger, 1962.

Kolodrubetz, Walter W. "Characteristics of Workers with Pension Coverage on the Longest Job." In *Reaching Retirement Age*. U.S. Department of Health, Education, and Welfare, Social Security Administration, Office of Research and Statistics, Research Report No. 47. Washington, D.C.: GPO, 1976, pp. 151–67.

Kotz, David M. *Bank Control of Large Corporations in the United States*. Berkeley and Los Angeles: University of California Press, 1978.

Kreps, Juanita. *Lifetime Allocation of Work and Income*. Durham, NC: Duke University Press, 1981.

Lamers, William W. *Public Policy and the Aging*. Washington, D.C.: QC Press, 1983.

Lampman, R. "The Share of Top Wealth-Holders in The United States." In *Wealth, Income and Inequality*. Ed. A. B. Atkinson. Harmondsworth: Penguin Education, 1973, pp. 268–94.

Lauriat, Patience, and William Rabin. "Characteristics of New Beneficiaries by Age at Entitlement." In *Reaching Retirement Age*. U.S. Department of Health, Education, and Welfare, Social Security Administration, Office of Research and Statistics, Research Report No. 47. Washington, D.C.: GPO, 1976, pp. 11–29.

Leibig, Michael T. *Social Investments and the Law: The Case for Alternative Investments*. Studies in Pension Fund Investments 3. Washington, D.C.: Conference on Alternative State and Local Policies, August 1980.

Light, Paul. *Artful Work: The Politics of Social Security Reform*. New York: Random House, 1985.

Litvak, Lawrence. *Pension Funds and Economic Renewal*. Washington, D.C.: Council of State Planning Agencies, 1981.

Lubove, Roy. *The Struggle for Social Security, 1900–1935*. Cambridge, MA: Harvard University Press, 1968.

Malca, Edward. *Pension Funds and Other Institutional Investors*. Lexington, MA: Lexington Books, 1975.

Markson, Elizabeth W., and Gretchen R. Batra. *Public Policies for an Aging Population*. Toronto: Heath, 1980.

Massaro, Vincent G. *The Equity Market: Corporate Practices and Issues*. The Conference Board Report No. 764. New York: Conference Board, Inc., 1979.

Mennis, Edmund A., and Chester D. Clark. *Understanding Corporate Pension Plans*. Charlotteville, VA. Financial Analysts Research Foundation, 1983.

Mills, C. Wright. *The New Men of Power: America's Labor Leaders*. New York: August M. Kelley Publishers, 1971.

—. *The Power Elite*. London: Oxford University Press, 1959.

Morgan, J. N. "Measuring the Economic Status of the Aged." In *Wealth, Income and Inequality*. Ed. A. B. Atkinson. Harmondsworth: Penguin Education, 1973, pp. 35–45.

Mosley, Hugh. *Public and Private Social Welfare Systems: A Working Paper on the Underdevelopment of State Social Welfare Institutions in the United States*. Publication Series of the International Institute for Comparative Social Research. Berlin: December 1978.

Munnell, Alicia H. *The Future of Social Security*. Washington, D.C.: Brookings Institution, 1977.

Munts, Raymond. *Bargaining for Health: Labor Unions, Health Insurance, and Medical Care*. Madison: University of Wisconsin Press, 1967.

Myers, Robert J. *Indexation of Pension and Other Benefits*. Homewood, IL: Irwin, 1978.

—. *Social Security*. Homewood, IL: Irwin, 1975.

McGill, Dan M. *Fulfilling Pension Expectations*. Homewood, IL: Irwin, 1962.

—. *Pensions: Problems and Trends*. Homewood, IL: Irwin, 1955.

McKinley, Charles, and Robert W. Frase. *Launching Social Security, A Capture—And—Record Account, 1935–1937*. Madison: University of Wisconsin Press, 1970.

McNulty, James, E., Jr. *Decision and Influence Processes in Private Pension Plans*. Homewood, IL: Irwin, 1961.

Nader, Ralph, and Kate Blackwell. *You and Your Pension*. New York: Grossman, 1973.

Orren, Karen. *Corporate Power and Social Change: The Politics of the Life Insurance Industry*. Baltimore: Johns Hopkins University Press, 1974.

Parker, Richard, and Tamsin Taylor. *Strategic Investment: An Alternative for Public Funds*. Studies in Pension Fund Investments 6. Washington, D.C.: Conference on Alternative State and Local Policies, 1979.

Patton, Carl V. "The Politics of Social Security." In *The Crisis in Social Security: Problems and Prospects*. Ed. Michael J. Boskin. San Francisco: Institute for Contemporary Studies, 1977, pp. 147–72.

Perlo, Victor. *The Empire of High Finance*. New York: International Publishers, 1957.

Putnam, Jackson K. *Old-Age Politics in California*. Stanford: Stanford University Press, 1970.

Rakoff, Vivian M. "Psychiatric Aspects of Death In America." In *Death In American Experience*. Ed. Arien Mack. New York: Schocken, 1974, pp. 149–61.

Rifkin, Jeremy, and Randy Barber. *The North Will Rise Again: Pensions, Politics and Power in the 1980s*. Boston: Beacon Press, 1978.

Rubinow, I. M. *Social Insurance: With Special Reference to American Conditions*. New York: Arno and the New York Times, 1969. First published 1913.

Schultz, James H. *The Economics of Aging*. 2nd ed. Belmont, CA: Wadsworth, 1980.

—. "Income Distribution and the Aging." In *Handbook of Aging and the Social Sciences*. Eds. Robert H. Binstock and Ethel Shanas. London: Van Nostrand Reinhold, 1976, pp. 561–91.

Securities and Exchange Commission. Institutional Investor Study Report of The Securities and Exchange Commission. 2 vols. and Summary. 92nd Congress, 1st session. Washington, D.C.: GPO, 1971.

Serrin, William. *The Company and the Union*. New York: Vintage, Random House, 1974.

Smart, Donald A. *Investment Targeting: A Wisconsin Case Study*. Madison: Wisconsin Center for Public Policy, 1979.

Stein, Bruno. *Social Security and Pensions in Transition: Understanding the American Retirement System*. New York: Free Press, 1980.

Taft, Philip. *Organized Labor in American History*. New York: Harper and Row, 1964.

Talley, George S., and Richard Burkhauser. "Federal Economic Policy toward the Elderly." In *Social Policy, Social Ethics and the Aging Society*. Eds. Bernice L. Neugarten and Robert G. Havighurst. Washington, D.C.: National Science Foundation, 1976, pp. 23–67.

Thernstom, Stephen. *Poverty and Progress: Social Mobility in a Nineteenth-Century City*. Cambridge, MA: Harvard University Press, 1964.

—. "Urbanization, Migration, and Social Mobility in Late Nineteenth Century America." In *Towards a New Past: Dissenting Essays in American History*. Ed. Barton J. Bernstein. New York: Pantheon, 1968, pp. 158–175.

Tilove, Robert. *Pension Funds and Economic Freedom*. New York: The Fund for the Republic, 1959.

—. *Public Employee Pension Funds*. New York: A Twentieth Century Fund Report, Columbia University Press, 1976.

Ture, Norman B. *The Future of Private Pensions Plans*. Washington, D.C.: American Enterprise Institute for Public Policy Research, 1976.

Turnball, John G. *The Changing Faces of Economic Insecurity*. Minneapolis: University of Minnesota Press, 1966.

Van Tine, Warren R. *The Making of the Labor Bureaucrat: Union Leadership in the United States 1870–1920*. Amherst: University of Massachusetts Press, 1973.

Weinstein, James. *The Corporate Ideal in the Liberal State*. Boston: Beacon, 1968.

Wiebe, Robert H. *The Search for Order 1877–1920*. New York: Hill and Wang, 1967.

Wistert, Francis M. *Fringe Benefits*. New York: Reinhold, 1959.

Witte, Edwin E. *The Development of the Social Security Act*. Madison: University of Wisconsin Press, 1963.

Yung–Ping Chen. *Social Security in a Changing Society: An Introduction to Programs, Concepts, and Issues*. Homewood, IL: Irwin, 1980.

Articles

"Baby Boomers Push for Power." *Business Week*, 2 July 1984, pp. 52–59.

Beller, Daniel J. "Coverage Patterns of Full-Time Employees under Retirement Plans." *Social Security Bulletin*. 44 (July 1981): 3–11.

Bixby, Lenore E., and Virginia Reno. "Second Pensions among Newly Entitled Workers: Survey of New Beneficiaries." *Social Security Bulletin* 34 (November 1971): 3–7.

Blume, Marshall E., Jean Crockett, and Irwin Friend. "Stockownership in the United States: Characteristics and Trends." *Survey of Current Business* 54 (November 1974): 16–40.

Bohan, James. "A Sector Analysis of Supply and Demand for Equities—1979." In *Market Analysis Report*. New York: Merrill Lynch, Pierce, Fenner and Smith, 8 November 1979.

Cain, Leonard D., Jr. "Age Status and Generational Phenomena." *Gerontologist* 7 (June 1967): 83–92.

Calvert, Geoffrey N. "Found Money: Let's Start *Funding* Social Security." *Pension World* 12 (February 1976): 20–27, 54.

Campbell, John Creighton, and John Strate. "Are Old People Conservative?" *Gerontologist* 21 (1981): 580–591.

"Capital Shortage: Fact and Fancy." *Monthly Review* 27 (April 1976): 1–19.

"The Crisis in Social Security." *Newsweek,* 1 June 1981, pp. 24–37.

Davis, Harry E. "Multiemployer Pension Plan Provisions in 1973." *Monthly Labor Review* 97 (October 1974): 110–16.

—. "Pension Provisions Affecting the Employment of Older Workers." *Monthly Labor Review* 96 (April 1973): 41–45.

Deaton, Richard, and Robert Deaton. "An Honest Evaluation of Drucker's Pension Fund 'Socialism.' " *Pensions and Investments,* 21 June 1976, pp. 15–16.

"A Debt-Threatened Dream." *Time,* 24 May 1982, pp. 12–23.

Douglas, Elizabeth B., William P. Cleveland, and George L. Maddox. "Political Attitudes, Age and Aging: A Cohort Analysis of Archival Data." *Journal of Gerontology* 29 (1974): 666–675.

Ehrbar, A. F. "Those Pension Plans Are Even Weaker Than You Think." *Fortune,* November 1977, pp. 104–8, 110, 112, 114.

"Employee Pensions in Collective Bargaining." *Yale Law Journal* 59 (1949–50): 678–714.

Faltermayer, Edmund. "A Steeper Climb up the Pension Mountain." *Fortune,* January 1975, pp. 78–81, 157–58, 162–65.

Fox, Harland. "The Corporate Social Security System and Workmen's Compensation." *Conference Board Record* (February 1964): 2–16.

Ginzburg, Raphael. "The Negative Attitude toward the Elderly." *Geriatrics* 7 (1952): 297–302.

Glenn, Norval D. "Aging and Conservatism." *Annals of the American Society of Political and Social Science* 415 (1974): 176–187.

Goldner, William. "Trade Union Structure and Private Pension Plans." *Industrial and Labor Relations Review* 5 (October 1951): 62–72.

Gordon, T. J., and R. E. Le Bleu. "Employee Benefits 1970–1985." *Harvard Business Review* 48 (January-February 1970): 93–107.

Grad, Susan. "Incomes of the Aged and Nonaged, 1950–82." *Social Security Bulletin* 47 (June 1984): 3–17.

—, and Karen Foster. "Income of the Population Aged 55 and Older, 1976." *Social Security Bulletin* 42 (July 1979): pp. 16–32.

Graham, Harry, and Brian Becker. "The Pittsburgh Plate Glass Case, Collective Bargaining and Retirement Benefits." *Industrial Gerontology* 2 (1975): 281–88.

Harris, Louis. "Retirement." *Across the Board* 16 (May 1979): 9–12.

Henry, James. "How Pension Fund Socialism Didn't Come to America." *Working Papers for a New Society* (Winter 1977): 78–87.

Hewitt Associates. "Employee Retirement Systems: How It All Began." *Pensions World* 12 (July 1976): 6–8 and 65.

"How Pension Fund Assets Grew So Quickly." *Business Week,* 21 March 1984, pp. 226–28.

"How They Manage the New Financial Supermarkets." *Business Week,* 20 December 1982, pp. 50–54.

Keyfitz, Nathan. "Why Social Security Is in Trouble." *Public Interest* 46 (Winter 1980): 102–19.

Kirsch, Donald. "How Pension Plans Can Fuel America's Growth." *Pension World* 12 (July 1976): 11–14.

Kogan, Nathan. "Attitudes toward Old People." *Journal of Abnormal and Social Psychology* 62 (1961): 44–54.

Kolodrubetz, Walter W. "Two Decades of Employee Benefit Plans, 1950–70: A Review." *Social Security Review* 35 (April 1972): 23–34.

—, and Donald M. Landay. "Coverage and Vesting of Full Time Employees under Private Retirement Plans." *Social Security Bulletin* 36 (November 1973): 20–36.

Landay, Donald M., and Harry E. Davis. "Growth and Vesting Changes in Private Pension Plans." *Monthly Labor Review* 91 (May 1968): 29–35.

Larson, Reed. "Thirty Years of Research on the Subjective Well-Being of Older Americans." *Journal of Gerontology* 33 (1978): 109–25.

Leotta, Louis. "Abraham Epstein and the Movement for Old Age Security." *Labor History* 16 (1975): 359–66.

Lester, Richard A. "Benefits as a Preferred Form of Compensation." *Southern Economic Journal* 33 (1967): 485–495.

"The Long-run Decline in Liquidity." *Monthly Review* 22 (September 1970): 1–17.

Mabry, Bevars. "The Economics of Fringe Benefits." *Industrial Relations* 12 (February 1973): 95–106.

Maxfield, Linda Drazga, and Virginia P. Reno. "Distribution of Income Sources of Recent Retirees: Findings from the New Beneficiary Survey." *Social Security Bulletin* 48 (January 1985): 7–13.

Mincer, Jacob. "On-the-Job-Training: Costs, Returns, and Some Implications." *Journal of Political Economy,* 70, Supplement (October 1962): 50–73.

"The New Shape of Banking." *Business Week,* 18 June 1984, pp. 104–10.

Nicholas, Walter S. "Fraternal Insurance in the United States: Its Origin, Development, Character and Existing Status." *Annals of the American Academy of Political and Social Science* 70 (March 1917): 109–22.

Norwood, Janet L. "Cost of Living Escalation of Pensions." *Monthly Labor Review* 95 (June 1972): 21–24.

Oi, Walter Y. "Labor As a Quasi-Fixed Factor." *Journal of Political Economy* 65 (1962): 538–555.

"Pension Funds as Profit Centers." *Pension & Welfare News* 10 (June 1974): 36–38.

"Pension Liabilities: Improvement Is Illusory." *Business Week,* 14 September 1981, pp. 114–15, 118.

"The Peril in Financial Services." *Business Week,* 20 August 1984, pp. 52–57.

Perlo, Victor. "'People's Capitalism' and Stock-Ownership." *American Economic Review* 48 (1958): 333–47.

Radner, Daniel B. "Money Incomes of Aged and Nonaged Family Units, 1967–84." *Social Security Bulletin* 50 (August 1987): 9–28.

Raskin, A. H. "Pension Funds Could Be the Unions' Secret Weapon." *Fortune,* 31 December 1979, pp. 64–67.

Robey, Bryant, and Mary John. "The Political Future: The Demographics of Politics." *American Demographics* (October 1980): 15–21.

Rogers, Gayle Thompson. "Vesting of Private Pension Benefits in 1979 and Change from 1972." *Social Security Bulletin* 44 (July 1981): 12–29.

Sahgal, Pavan. "Who Owns Corporate America?" *Pensions & Investment Age,* 31 October 1983, pp. 23–24, 26, 61–68.

Scheinberg, Stephen J. "Progressivism in Industry: The Welfare Movement in the American Factory." Canadian Historical Association. *Annual Report* (1967): 184–97.

Schiller, Bradley R., and Randall D. Weiss. "The Impact of Private Pensions on Firm Attachment." *Review of Economics and Statistics* 56 (1979): 369–80.

Schulz, James H. "The Economic Impact of an Aging Population." *Journal of Gerontology* 13 (Spring 1973): 111–17.

Shapiro, Harvey. "Wall Street's New 'Social Responsibility' Funds." *Saturday Review,* 26 August 1972, pp. 43–45.

Skolnik, Alfred M. "Private Pension Plans, 1950–74." *Social Security Bulletin* 37 (June 1974); pp. 10–25.

—. "Twenty-five Years of Employee Benefits." *Social Security Bulletin* 39 (September 1976): 3–21.

Smart, Donald A. "Investments in the Public Interest." *Pension World* (May 1979): 22–24.

"Social Security: What Can the Nation Afford?" *Time,* 24 May 1982, pp. 12–23.

Soldofsky, Robert M. "Institutional Holdings of Common Stock 1900–2000." *Michigan Business Studies* 8 (1971): 204–15.

Thompson, Lawrence H. "The Social Security Reform Debate." *Journal of Economic Literature* 21 (1983): 1425–67.

Tuckman, Jacob, and Irving Lorge. "Attitudes toward Old People." *Journal of Social Psychology* 37 (1953): 249–60.

—. "The Best Years of Life: A Study in Ranking." *Journal of Psychology* 34 (1952): 137–49.

"Unfunded Pension Liabilities: A Continuing Burden." *Business Week,* 14 August 1978, pp. 60–63.

"Unfunded Pension Liabilities: A Growing Worry for Companies." *Business Week,* 18 July 1977, pp. 86–88.

"Why Pension Funds Are Quitting the Institutions." *Business Week,* 15 May 1978, pp. 105–7.

"Will Money Managers Wreck the Economy?" *Business Week,* 13 August 1984, pp. 86–89, 92–93.

Ycas, Martynas A., and Susan Grad. "Income of Retirement-Aged Persons in the United States." *Social Security Bulletin* 50 (July 1987): 5–14.

Index